MW00337002

THE EUROPEAN UNION SER.__

General Editors: Neill Nugent, William E. Paterson

The European Union series provides an authoritative library on the European Union, ranging from general introductory texts to definitive assessments of key institutions and actors, issues, policies and policy processes, and the role of member states.

Books in the series are written by leading scholars in their fields and reflect the most up-to-date research and debate. Particular attention is paid to accessibility and clear presentation for a wide audience of students, practitioners and interested general readers.

The series editors are **Neill Nugent**, Emeritus Professor of Politics at Manchester Metropolitan University, UK, and **William E. Paterson**, Honorary Professor in German and European Studies, University of Aston. Their co-editor until his death in July 1999, **Vincent Wright**, was a Fellow of Nuffield College, Oxford University.

Feedback on the series and book proposals are always welcome and should be sent to Stephen Wenham, Palgrave, 4 Crinan Street, London N1 9XW, or by e-mail to **s.wenham@palgrave.com**.

General textbooks

Published

Laurie Buonanno and Neill Nugent **Policies and Policy Processes of the European Union**

Desmond Dinan **Encyclopedia of the European Union** [Rights: Europe only]

Desmond Dinan **Europe Recast: A History of the European Union (2nd edn)** [Rights: Europe only]

Desmond Dinan **Ever Closer Union: An Introduction to European Integration (4th edn)** [Rights: Europe only]

Mette Eilstrup Sangiovanni (ed.) **Debates on European Integration: A Reader**

Simon Hix and Bjørn Høyland **The Political System of the European Union (3rd edn)**

Dirk Leuffen, Berthold Rittberger and Frank Schimmelfennig **Differentiated Integration**

Paul Magnette **What is the European Union? Nature and Prospects**

John McCormick **Understanding the European Union: A Concise Introduction (6th edn)**

Brent F. Nelsen and Alexander Stubb **The European Union: Readings on the Theory and Practice of European Integration (4th edn)** [Rights: Europe only]

Neill Nugent (ed.) **European Union Enlargement**

Neill Nugent **The Government and Politics of the European Union (8th edn)**

John Peterson and Elizabeth Bomberg **Decision-Making in the European Union**

Ben Rosamond **Theories of European Integration**

Sabine Saurugger **Theoretical Approaches to European Integration**

Ingeborg Tömmel **The European Union: What it is and How it Works**

Esther Versluis, Mendeltje van Keulen and Paul Stephenson **Analyzing the European Union Policy Process**

Hubert Zimmermann and Andreas Dür (eds) **Key Controversies in European Integration (2nd edn)**

Also planned

The European Union and Global Politics
The Political Economy of European Integration

Visit Palgrave's EU Resource area at www.palgrave.com/politics/eu/

The major institutions and actors

Published

Renaud Dehousse **The European Court of Justice**

Justin Greenwood **Interest Representation in the European Union (3rd edn)**

Fiona Hayes-Renshaw and Helen Wallace **The Council of Ministers (2nd edn)**

Simon Hix and Christopher Lord **Political Parties in the European Union**

David Judge and David Earnshaw **The European Parliament (2nd edn)**

Neill Nugent and Mark Rhinard **The European Commission (2nd edn)**

Sabine Saurugger and Fabien Terpan **The Court of Justice of the European Union and the Politics of Law**

Anne Stevens with Handley Stevens **Brussels Bureaucrats? The Administration of the European Union**

Wolfgang Wessels **The European Council**

Forthcoming

Ariadna Ripoll Servent **The European Parliament**

The main areas of policy

Published

Karen Anderson **Social Policy in the European Union**

Michael Baun and Dan Marek **Cohesion Policy in the European Union**

Michele Chang **Monetary Integration in the European Union**

Michelle Cini and Lee McGowan **Competition Policy in the European Union (2nd edn)**

Wyn Grant **The Common Agricultural Policy**

Martin Holland and Mathew Doidge **Development Policy of the European Union**

Jolyon Howorth **Security and Defence Policy in the European Union (2nd edn)**

Johanna Kantola **Gender and the European Union**

Stephan Keukeleire and Tom Delreux **The Foreign Policy of the European Union (2nd edn)**

Brigid Laffan **The Finances of the European Union**

Malcolm Levitt and Christopher Lord **The Political Economy of Monetary Union**

Janne Haaland Matláry **Energy Policy in the European Union**

John McCormick **Environmental Policy in the European Union**

John Peterson and Margaret Sharp **Technology Policy in the European Union**

Handley Stevens **Transport Policy in the European Union**

Hans Bruyninckx and Tom Delreux **Environmental Policy and Politics in the European Union**

Maren Kreutler, Johannes Pollak and Samuel Schubert **Energy Policy in the European Union**

Forthcoming

Sieglinde Gstöhl and Dirk de Bievre **The Trade Policy of the European Union**

Christian Kaunert and Sarah Leonard **Justice and Home Affairs in the European Union**

Paul Stephenson, Esther Versluis and Mendeltje van Keulen **Implementing and Evaluating Policy in the European Union**

Also planned

Political Union

The member states and the Union

Published

Carlos Closa and Paul Heywood **Spain and the European Union**

Andrew Geddes **Britain and the European Union**

Alain Guyomarch, Howard Machin and Ella Ritchie **France in the European Union**

Brigid Laffan and Jane O'Mahoney **Ireland and the European Union**

Forthcoming

Simon Bulmer and William E. Paterson **Germany and the European Union**

Issues

Published

Senem Aydın-Düzgit and Nathalie Tocci **Turkey and the European Union**

Derek Beach **The Dynamics of European Integration: Why and When EU Institutions Matter**

Christina Boswell and Andrew Geddes **Migration and Mobility in the European Union**

Thomas Christiansen and Christine Reh **Constitutionalizing the European Union**

Desmond Dinan, Neill Nugent and William E. Paterson (eds) **The European Union in Crisis**

Tuomas Forsberg and Hiski Haukkala **The European Union and Russia**

Robert Ladrech **Europeanization and National Politics**

Cécile Leconte **Understanding Euroscepticism**

Steven McGuire and Michael Smith **The European Union and the United States**

Wyn Rees **The US–EU Security Relationship: The Tensions between a European and a Global Agenda**

Magnus Ryner and Alan Cafruny **The European Union and Global Capitalism**

Forthcoming

Thomas Christiansen, Emil Kirchner and Uwe Wissenbach **The European Union and China**

Doug Webber **European Disintegration?**

The European Union in Crisis

Edited by

Desmond Dinan

Neill Nugent

William E. Paterson

 palgrave

First published 2017 by
PALGRAVE

Palgrave in the UK is an imprint of Macmillan Publishers Limited,
registered in England, company number 785998, of 4 Crinan Street,
London, N1 9XW.

Palgrave® and Macmillan® are registered trademarks in the United States,
the United Kingdom, Europe and other countries.

ISBN 978–1–1376–0426–2 hardback
ISBN 978–1–1376–0425–5 paperback

This book is printed on paper suitable for recycling and made from fully
managed and sustained forest sources. Logging, pulping and manufacturing
processes are expected to conform to the environmental regulations of the
country of origin.

A catalogue record for this book is available from the British Library.

A catalog record for this book is available from the Library of Congress.

Printed and bound by CPI Group (UK) Ltd, Croydon, CR0 4YY

Summary of Contents

Contents — vii

List of Boxes, Figures and Tables — xiii

List of Contributors — xiv

Abbreviations and Acronyms — xvi

Preface — xx

1 **A Multi-dimensional Crisis** — 1
Desmond Dinan, Neill Nugent, and William E. Paterson

2 **Crises in EU History** — 16
Desmond Dinan

3 **The Political Economy Context of EU Crises** — 33
Ben Rosamond

4 **Playing for High Stakes: The Eurozone Crisis** — 54
Kenneth Dyson

5 **The UK: Membership in Crisis** — 77
Lee McGowan and David Phinnemore

6 **The European Migration Crisis** — 100
Laurie Buonanno

7 **The Eurozone in Crisis: Core–Periphery Dynamics** — 131
Brigid Laffan

8 **The Aftermath of the Eurozone Crisis: Towards Fiscal Federalism?** — 149
Caroline de la Porte and Elke Heins

9 **The Crisis and the EU's Institutions, Political Actors, and Processes** — 167
Neill Nugent

10 The Legitimacy Challenge 188
Christian Schweiger

11 Germany and the Crisis: Asset or Liability? 212
Simon Bulmer and William E. Paterson

12 Greece: A Crisis in Two-Level Governance 233
Kevin Featherstone and Dimitris Papadimitriou

13 Central and Eastern Europe: The Sacrifices of
Solidarity, the Discomforts of Diversity, and the
Vexations of Vulnerabilities 253
Tim Haughton

14 The European Union, Ukraine, and the Unstable East 269
Wolfgang Seibel

15 The EU's Global Image 294
Amelia Hadfield

16 Theorising Crisis in European Integration 316
Frank Schimmelfennig

17 Can the EU Survive? 336
Douglas Webber

18 Conclusions: Crisis Without End? 360
Desmond Dinan, Neill Nugent, and William E. Paterson

Index 376

Contents

List of Boxes, Figures and Tables   xiii

List of Contributors   xiv

Abbreviations and Acronyms   xvi

Preface
                                                                             xx

1   A Multi-dimensional Crisis   1
      Desmond Dinan, Neill Nugent, and William E. Paterson

      Introduction   1
      The Multi-dimensional Nature of the Crisis   1
      Origins of the Crisis   3
      Implications of the Crisis for the EU System   9
      Supplying Solutions   12
      Conclusions   14
      References   15

2   Crises in EU History   16
      Desmond Dinan

      Introduction   16
      Myth and Reality of the Founding Story   17
      From the European Defence Community to the European
          Economic Community   19
      The Crises of the 1960s   20
      Economic and Financial Crises Before the Single
          European Act   23
      From Maastricht to Lisbon   25
      Many Crises, Few Opportunities   28
      Conclusions   30
      References   31

3   The Political Economy Context of EU Crises   33
      Ben Rosamond

      Introduction   33
      The European Capitalist-Democratic Compact   34
      The Compact Unravelled: Three Dilemmas and
          Three Processes   39

Conclusions	47
References	48

4   Playing for High Stakes: The Eurozone Crisis   54
Kenneth Dyson

Introduction	54
A Multi-dimensional and Mutating Crisis	55
Why the Eurozone Crisis is an Existential Threat	65
Burden-Sharing in Monetary Union: A Historical Perspective on the Eurozone Crisis	69
Conclusions	73
References	75

5   The UK: Membership in Crisis   77
Lee McGowan and David Phinnemore

Introduction	77
Crisis Point	78
Avoiding Crisis through Exceptionalism	80
Heading Towards Crisis: Mounting Pressure for a Referendum on EU Membership	82
Resolving the Crisis: Renegotiation and Referendum	85
Crisis Begetting Crisis and Chaos	90
And for the EU?	94
Conclusions	95
References	96

6   The European Migration Crisis   100
Laurie Buonanno

Introduction	100
Anatomy of the Migration Crisis	101
Asylum Law and Immigration Policy in the EU	110
Member States and the Migration Crisis	111
Implementing the European Commission's Agenda on Migration	117
Conclusions: The Wider Implications of, and the Prospects for, Inward EU Migration	121
References	125

7   The Eurozone in Crisis: Core–Periphery Dynamics   131
Brigid Laffan

Introduction	131
Economic and Monetary Union: A Deliberate Blind Spot	132
What Kind of Crisis?	135

Divergent Economic Fortunes   136
Crisis Politics   139
Conclusions: What Does the Eurozone Crisis Tell Us
   About the EU?   144
References   146

8   **The Aftermath of the Eurozone Crisis: Towards Fiscal
   Federalism?**   **149**
   Caroline de la Porte and Elke Heins

Introduction   149
Governance of EMU and Social Policy before the Eurozone
   Crisis   150
Framework for Analyzing Alterations in EU
   Integration   152
EMU and Social Policy Governance Following
   the Eurozone Crisis   155
Altering the Governance of the European
   Social Dimension   162
Conclusions   163
References   164

9   **The Crisis and the EU's Institutions, Political Actors,
   and Processes**   **167**
   Neill Nugent

Introduction   167
The Crisis, the EU's Institutions, and the Evolving Balance
   Between Supranationalism and Intergovernmentalism   168
The Crisis and the Member States   176
The EU's Continuing Leadership Problem   180
Conclusions   184
References   185

10 **The Legitimacy Challenge**   **188**
   Christian Schweiger

Introduction   188
From *Permissive* to *Constrained Consensus*: The EU's
   Increasingly Contested Legitimacy   189
The European Parliament and the
   Lack of *Social Legitimacy*   191
Crisis Conditions and Germany's Informal EU Presidency   194
Reforming the Governance of the Eurozone and
   'the Suspension of Democracy'   196
Muddling Through the Growing Crisis–Legitimacy Gap?   199

Tackling the Legitimacy Deficit   203
Conclusions   206
References   206

11   Germany and the Crisis: Asset or Liability?   212
Simon Bulmer and William E. Paterson

Introduction   212
Leadership and Domestic Politics   213
The Eurozone Crisis   215
The Ukraine Crisis   220
The Migration Crisis   224
Conclusions   227
References   230

12   Greece: A Crisis in Two-Level Governance   233
Kevin Featherstone and Dimitris Papadimitriou

Introduction   233
Preparing for the Crisis   234
Two-Level Governance: The Challenges of
    Institutional Capacity   239
Bailout Conditionality as a Lever of Domestic Reform   242
Normative Europe: Consequences of the Crisis   246
Conclusions   249
References   250

**13   Central and Eastern Europe: The Sacrifices of
Solidarity, the Discomforts of Diversity, and the
Vexations of Vulnerabilities   253**
Tim Haughton

Introduction   253
Motivations, Expectations, and Realities of Membership   254
The Eurozone: Bailouts and Burdens   257
The Migration Crisis: Numbers and Nationalism   259
On the Edge: Russian Aggression in Ukraine   261
Brexit and Its Consequences   262
Conclusions   264
References   265

14   The European Union, Ukraine, and the Unstable East   269
Wolfgang Seibel

Introduction   269
Writings on the Wall, Misread   270

Run-up to the Crisis 272
The Fate of the Association Agreement 274
Russia's Annexation of Crimea and EU Crisis Management 275
From Minsk I to Minsk II 277
Inherent Asymmetry 280
German Uncertainties 282
Conclusions 286
References 288

15 The EU's Global Image 294
Amelia Hadfield

Introduction 294
EU External Perceptions: Raw Material or Raw Power? 295
Russian Perceptions: Between a Rock and a Hard Place 297
American Debates: Brave Old World 302
Chinese Perceptions: A Bridge Too Far? 307
Conclusions 311
References 312

16 Theorising Crisis in European Integration 316
Frank Schimmelfennig

Introduction 316
Integration Theories and Explanations of Crisis 317
Integration Theories and the Eurozone Crisis 323
Conclusions 333
References 334

17 Can the EU Survive? 336
Douglas Webber

Introduction 336
The Historical Perspective: This Crisis Is Different 337
Can the EU Disintegrate? Theoretical Perspectives 338
European *Dis*integration: Key Determinants 342
Conclusions 354
Acknowledgements 356
References 357

18 Conclusions: Crisis Without End? 360
Desmond Dinan, Neill Nugent, and William E. Paterson

The Unprecedented Nature of the Crisis 360
A Tale of Three Crises 361
The Challenges of Legitimacy 368

Increasing Integration   369
Increasing Differentiation, Leading to Disintegration?   371
Crisis Without End?   373
References   375

Index   376

List of Boxes, Figures and Tables

Boxes

6.1 The EU's legal framework for asylum (1951–2014)   105
6.2 EU's agenda on asylum (2015–16)   118

Figures

3.1 Three ongoing dilemmas of European integration   39
6.1 Asylum applications   106
6.2 Migrant smuggling to and within the EU   108
7.1 Current account imbalances   137
7.2 Long-term interest rate spread   138
7.3 Unemployment in the euro area   139
10.1 The image of the European Union – trend: 2006–16   192
10.2 My voice counts in the EU – trend 2004–16   194
10.3 Evaluation of sectoral reforms   198
10.4 Support for European policies   203

Tables

4.1 The EU and euro area economic and financial crisis:
     key events   58
5.1 Cameron's 'new settlement' demands and key outcomes   86
5.2 EU referendum (23 June 2016) – result   90
8.1 Typology of EU integration of labour market and
     social policy   153
8.2 EU involvement in economic and public policy before and
     after the crisis   156
12.1 Performance against key EMU convergence criteria   235
16.1 Integration theories and explanations of crisis   318
17.1 The decline of the 'pro-European' parties in the
     EU since 2010 (20 selected member states;
     percentages of the vote)   348

List of Contributors

Simon Bulmer, Professor of European Politics, University of Sheffield, UK.

Laurie Buonanno, Professor of Politics, Buffalo State College, USA.

Caroline de la Porte, Professor of European and Comparative Welfare Governance and Policy, Copenhagen Business School, Denmark.

Desmond Dinan, Jean Monnet Professor (*ad personam*), George Mason University, Virginia, USA.

Kenneth Dyson, Professor of Politics, Cardiff University, UK.

Kevin Featherstone, Eleftherios Venizelos Professor of Contemporary Greek Studies and Professor of European Politics, London School of Economics, UK.

Amelia Hadfield, Reader in Politics, Canterbury Christ Church University, UK.

Tim Haughton, Reader in European Politics, University of Birmingham, UK.

Elke Heins, Lecturer in Social Policy, University of Edinburgh, UK.

Brigid Laffan, Director of the Robert Schuman Centre for Advanced Studies and Director of the Global Governance Programme, European University Institute, Italy.

Lee McGowan, Senior Lecturer in Politics, Queens University, Belfast, UK.

Neill Nugent, Emeritus Professor of Politics and Jean Monnet Professor of European Integration, Manchester Metropolitan University, UK.

Dimitris Papadimitriou, Professor of Politics, Manchester University, UK.

William E. Paterson, Honorary Professor of Politics, Aston University, UK.

David Phinnemore, Professor of Politics, Queens University, Belfast, UK.

Ben Rosamond, Professor of Political Science, University of Copenhagen, Denmark.

Christian Schweiger, Senior Lecturer in Government, Durham University, UK.

Wolfgang Seibel, Professor of Politics and Public Administration, University of Konstanz, Germany.

Frank Schimmelfennig, Professor of Politics, ETH Zurich, Switzerland.

Douglas Webber, Professor of Political Science, INSEAD (International Business School), France/Singapore.

Abbreviations and Acronyms

ACP	African, Caribbean, and Pacific countries
ACR	actor-centred institutionalism
AfD	Alternative für Deutschland/Alternative for Germany
AFSJ	area of freedom, security, and justice
ALDE	Group of the Alliance of Liberals and Democrats for Europe
AMR	alert mechanism report
APEC	Asia Pacific Economic Cooperation
ASEAN	Association of South-East Asian Nations
BEPGs	Broad Economic Policy Guidelines
BIS	Bank for International Settlements
Brexit	British exit from the European Union
CAP	Common Agricultural Policy
CCP	Common Commercial Policy
CCT	Common Customs Tariff
CDU/CSU	German Christian Democratic Union/Christian Social Union
CEAS	Common European Asylum System
CEE/CEEC	central and eastern European (country)
CET	Common External Tariff
CFI	Court of First Instance
CFP	Common Fisheries Policy
CFSP	Common Foreign and Security Policy
CGEA	Commissioners' Group on External Action
CIS	Commonwealth of Independent States
CJEU	Court of Justice of the European Union
COPS	Political and Security Committee
CoR	Committee of the Regions
COREPER	Committee of Permanent Representatives
CSDP	Common Security and Defence Policy
CSR	country-specific recommendation
CSU	Christian Social Union
DAAD	German Academic Exchange Service
DBP	draft budgetary plan
DG	Directorate General
EAA	European Agency for Asylum
EASO	European Asylum Support Office

EBCGA	European Border and Coastguard Agency
EBU	European Banking Union
EC	European Community
ECB	European Central Bank
ECHR	European Court of Human Rights
ECJ	European Court of Justice
Ecofin	Council of Economic and Finance Ministers
ECR	European Conservatives and Reformists' Group
ECSC	European Coal and Steel Community
ECU	European currency unit
ED	European Democratic Group
EDA	European Defence Agency
EDC	European Defence Community
EDP	excessive deficit procedure
EEA	European Economic Area
EEAS	European External Action Service
EEC	European Economic Community
EES	European Employment Strategy
EESC	European Economic and Social Committee
EFD	Europe of Freedom and Democracy Group
EFSF	European Financial Stability Facility
EFSI	European Fund for Strategic Investments
EFTA	European Free Trade Association
EIB	European Investment Bank
ELDR	Federation of European Liberal, Democratic and Reform Parties
EMF	European Monetary Fund
EMS	European Monetary System
EMU	Economic and Monetary Union
ENP	European Neighbourhood Policy
EP	European Parliament
EPP	European People's Party
EPU	European Payments Union
ERDF	European Regional Development Fund
ERM	exchange-rate mechanism
ESC	Economic and Social Committee
ESCB	European System of Central Banks
ESDP	European Security and Defence Policy
ESF	European Social Fund
ESFS	European System of Financial Supervisors
ESM	European Stability Mechanism
ESRB	European Systemic Risk Board
EU	European Union

Eurosur	European Border Surveillance System
FCC	Federal Constitutional Court
FDI	foreign direct investment
FRG	Federal Republic of Germany
Frontex	European Agency for the Management of Operational Cooperation at the External Borders of the Member States of the European Union
FRY	Former Republic of Yugoslavia
FTA	Free Trade Area
G8	Group of Eight
G20	Group of Twenty
GAC	General Affairs Council
GAERC	General Affairs and External Relations Council
GATT	General Agreement on Tariffs and Trade
GDP	gross domestic product
GNI	gross national income
GNP	gross national product
Grexit	Greek exit from the eurozone
HRMMU	United Nations Human Rights Mission in Ukraine
IDRs	in-depth reviews
IGC	Intergovernmental Conference
IGO	Intergovernmental Organization
IMF	International Monetary Fund
INGO	international non-governmental organization
JHA	Justice and Home Affairs
MEP	Member of the European Parliament
MFF	multiannual financial framework
MIP	Macroeconomic Imbalance Procedure
MoU	Memorandum of Understanding
MTOs	medium-term budgetary objectives
NAFTA	North Atlantic Free Trade Agreement
NATO	North Atlantic Treaty Organization
NCB	national central bank
NGO	non-governmental organization
NTB	non-tariff barrier
OCA	optimal/optimum currency area
ODIHR	Office for Democratic Institutions and Human Rights
OECD	Organisation for Economic Co-operation and Development
OEEC	Organisation for European Economic Cooperation
OJ	Official Journal of the European Union
OMC	open method of coordination
OMN	Operation Mare Nostrum
OMT	Outright Monetary Transaction

OSCE	Organization for Security and Cooperation in Europe
PCA	Partnership and Cooperation Agreement
PES	Party of European Socialists
PLO	Palestine Liberation Organisation
PP	Partido Popular
PSC	Political and Security Committee
QMV	qualified majority voting
R&TD	Research and Technological Development
RQMV	reverse qualified majority voting
S&D	Group of the Progressive Alliance of Socialists and Democrats
SEA	Single European Act
SEM	Single European Market
SGP	Stability and Growth Pact
SMM	Special Monitoring Mission (in Ukraine)
SPD	Social Democratic Party
SRB	Single Resolution Board
SRF	Single Resolution Fund
SRM	Single Resolution Mechanism
SSM	Single Supervisory Mechanism
TA	technical assistance
TEC	Treaty Establishing the European Community
TEU	Treaty on European Union
TFEU	Treaty on the Functioning of the European Union
TTIP	Transatlantic Trade and Investment Partnership
UK	United Kingdom
UKIP	United Kingdom Independence Party
UN	United Nations
UNHCR	United Nations High Commission for Refugees
USA	United States of America
VAT	value added tax
WGI	Worldwide Governance Index
WTO	World Trade Organization

Preface

The crisis that has confronted the European Union (EU) in recent years has been multi-dimensional in nature, having covered many different aspects of the European integration process and having played out on many levels. The singular noun 'crisis' has, in fact, encompassed several separate, though related, crises that have been multi-faceted in their sources, characteristics, and consequences.

This book identifies and examines the many dimensions of the crisis. It considers the ways in which the EU and its member states have been affected by the crisis and how they have sought to deal with it.

What has made the recent, and still ongoing, crisis different from previous crises has been its scale, depth, breadth, and importance. Such has been the seriousness of the crisis that the very nature and continuing existence of the EU have been brought into question. The crisis has extended beyond the dramatic and headline developments in Greece, the fluctuating fortunes of the eurozone, the challenge of mass migration, and the UK's relationship with the EU. It has cut to the very core of the EU itself. Trust among EU policy actors and between European elites and peoples has eroded; solidarity has frayed; nationalism and populism have surged; confidence in the EU has declined; and power has shifted, both among EU institutions and between EU-level and national-level institutions. In this situation of change and flux, the positions of leading EU states have altered, with Germany arguably becoming too strong, France too weak, and Britain becoming increasingly detached – ultimately to the point of deciding to exit the Union.

The crisis has seen an array of major problems simultaneously, and in many cases unexpectedly, pressing the EU. However, these problems have not been, or have been only partially, resolved, which has further contributed to the crisis. For example, the extent to which the eurozone has an adequate fiscal foundation is still strongly contested. The EU does not yet have a fully developed immigration policy. And an array of 'neighbourhood' foreign policy problems – from the Syrian civil war to the Ukraine conflict – continue to fester.

These and other unresolved issues have resulted in the severity of the crisis being such as to threaten the very existence of the 'European project' – the voluntary sharing of national sovereignty between EU states for the pursuit of mutually beneficial policy objectives. For the first time in the EU's history, the gravity of the crisis has been so great as to raise the spectre of possible disintegration.

A key theme of this book is thus that the crisis has many elements, most of which have raised serious questions and challenges for the EU. A related theme is that not only have the elements of the crisis been many and severe, but they often also have been simultaneous and interdependent, which has made it difficult for the EU to respond to dimensions of the crisis in quick and effective ways.

Another key theme of the book is that some aspects of the crisis are partly self-inflicted, with internal weaknesses having long been recognized but never fully addressed. For example, those elements of the crisis relating to the EU's lack of legitimacy and democracy were known for many years, but were only tackled in somewhat incrementalist and marginal ways. Similarly, those elements of the crisis emanating from original design flaws – most notably the absence of political and fiscal union in the case of the eurozone and the combination of porous external borders and internal freedom of movement in the case of the migration crisis – were largely left aside for many years. Both the eurozone and the migration crises were rooted in classic fair-weather policies, which were found to be wanting in important respects when the weather became less clement and the policies were more severely tested.

The core reason why, before the crisis, known policy weaknesses and inadequacies were left untended was that member states could not agree on how they should be rectified. There were deep divergences on basic preferences. These divergences, which shaped many aspects of the crisis and continue to complicate the search for solutions, also feature prominently as a theme in the book.

* * *

The structure of the book is as follows.

Chapter 1, by the editors, offers reflections on the nature of the crisis and sets the scene for subsequent chapters on specific aspects of the crisis. In particular, the editors develop the idea of dimensions of crisis: internal and external; economic, political, and social; core and periphery; transient and possibly permanent. A key theme of the chapter is that while there have been a number of unprecedented challenges to the EU on the demand side (including a need for improved economic and financial management, for a more effective migration policy, for more political participation, and for clearer and better leadership) there has been an insufficiency of supply-side 'solutions' and a lack of clarity as to who should be providing solutions.

Chapter 2, by Desmond Dinan, puts the crisis in historical context by comparing it with previous crises in the EU's history. In his chapter, Dinan emphasizes the wholly unprecedented nature of the current crisis.

Chapter 3, by Ben Rosamond, is also contextual, placing the crisis in the framework of the EU's political-economic development.

The next three chapters – Chapter 4 on EMU by Kenneth Dyson, Chapter 5 on Brexit by Lee McGowan and David Phinnemore, and Chapter 6 by Laurie Buonanno on migration – examine the three highest profile and most politically charged aspects of the crisis. The eurozone crisis is commonly thought of as marking the beginning of the crisis. The migration crisis is seen as signalling more clearly than any other aspect of the crisis the depth of some of the divisions between member states. And the Brexit crisis, which was triggered by the outcome of the referendum of June 2016 in which UK citizens voted to leave the EU, is viewed as highlighting the EU's weak political foundations and as posing serious questions not just for the future of the UK but also for the EU.

Chapter 7, by Brigid Laffan on conflict and cleavage in the eurozone, and Chapter 8, by Caroline de la Porte and Elke Heins on eurozone social and labour market policy, show some of the disaggregating and dysfunctional implications of the policies pursued in an effort to shore up the eurozone.

In Chapter 9, Neill Nugent demonstrates that the EU's institutional balance and policy processes have experienced a modest shift in an intergovernmental direction during the crisis, but have not undergone the fundamental upheaval that is sometimes suggested as being necessary. In Chapter 10, Christian Schweiger explores the challenge of legitimacy facing an EU apparently in persistent crisis mode.

The next set of chapters examines the positions and stances of key states during the crisis. In Chapter 11, Simon Bulmer and William Paterson ask whether Germany has been an asset or a liability for the EU during the crisis. In Chapter 12, Kevin Featherstone and Dimitris Papadimitriou assess developments in Greece, with reference to its position at the epicentre of the eurozone crisis. In Chapter 13, Tim Haughton provides a panoramic view of the impact of the crisis on the countries of central and eastern Europe.

The next two chapters explore external dimensions of the crisis, with Wolfgang Seibel examining the Ukraine crisis and the EU's deteriorating relations with Russia in Chapter 14, and Amelia Hadfield considering the impact of the crisis on the EU's external image and influence in Chapter 15.

In Chapter 16, Frank Schimmelfennig steps back from the immediacy of particular events and circumstances to consider how integration theory can help to explain the crisis. Douglas Webber, in Chapter 17, also takes a broad perspective, in his case to wonder if a long-term implication of the crisis will be to produce more disaggregation in, or possibly a break-up of, the European project.

In Chapter 18, the editors draw together a number of the main themes that emerge in the book.

* * *

Our thanks go to all of the contributors for producing excellent chapters and to Stephen Wenham of Palgrave for his encouragement and guidance. Many thanks also go to Chloe Osborne and Georgia Walters of Palgrave for providing very helpful production support.

Desmond Dinan
Neill Nugent
William E. Paterson

Chapter 1

A Multi-dimensional Crisis

DESMOND DINAN, NEILL NUGENT, AND
WILLIAM E. PATERSON

Introduction

This chapter provides an overview of the different dimensions of the crisis, sets them in their contexts, outlines their implications for the European Union, and summarizes how the EU has responded so far.

The Multi-dimensional Nature of the Crisis

The 'age of crisis' for the EU began in 2009–10 with the onset of what quickly came to be called the euro or eurozone crisis. This crisis, whose severity has ebbed and flowed over the years that have followed, is the most obvious manifestation of the EU in crisis. It has threatened the very existence of one of the EU's main policy achievements: the single currency – the apotheosis of Economic and Monetary Union (EMU) – which 19 of the EU's 28 member states had adopted as of 2016. At various times during the eurozone crisis, the membership, governing structure, and operating rules of the single currency system have been fundamentally questioned and challenged.

Apart from the eurozone crisis, the most recognizable feature of the EU in crisis has been the migration crisis, which greatly escalated in 2015 when vast numbers of migrants – eventually numbering over 1 million – mostly consisting of asylum-seekers from war-torn Syria, Iraq, and Afghanistan, together with irregular migrants from North Africa, flooded into the EU. This wave became a perfect storm (that is, a situation caused or greatly aggravated by an unanticipated and very rare set of circumstances) in September 2015 when Chancellor Angela Merkel announced that Germany would not limit the number of refugees entering the country, thereby unintentionally encouraging many more arrivals. Migrants benefit from one of the EU's main policy achievements: the free movement of people facilitated by the Schengen system. The migration crisis has put severe strains on free movement within the EU and, indeed, has led to a partial breakdown of Schengen.

1

Another dimension of the crisis pertains to EU governance. The handling of the eurozone and migration crises has demonstrated poor EU leadership, often slow and insufficient decision-making, hardening national positions, uneven burden-sharing, and fraying solidarity among member states. Crucially, in respect of fraying solidarity, there has been a near fracturing of some membership arrangements, notably with Greece's continuing membership of the eurozone being much discussed in EU circles in the summer of 2015 and then the UK, building on an already considerable number of policy 'opt-outs', holding a referendum on membership in June 2016, which resulted in a decision to leave the EU.

These features of EU governance have, in turn, fuelled euroscepticism and put the credibility and democratic legitimacy of the EU system increasingly in question. Originally, public attitudes towards European integration were characterized as constituting a 'permissive consensus' or benign indifference, but that changed in the 1990s as the European Community evolved into the European Union and the impact of EU policies and programmes on the everyday lives of Europeans became more evident and intrusive. Support for European integration gradually declined after the Maastricht Treaty of 1992, which launched EMU and ushered in the EU (Eichenberg and Dalton, 2007). Since the beginning of the crisis this has continued to be the case, with growing doubts about the desirability and effectiveness of EU initiatives and increasing irritation with the cumbersomeness of the EU itself. The apparent hollowing-out of national political institutions and the strengthening of European institutions, which to many people seem remote and technocratic, have exacerbated the EU's inherently weak legitimacy. The EU's democratic credentials have been further undermined as apparently unaccountable, Brussels-based technocrats have been seen to impose, or try to impose, policy solutions that have often been unwanted and/or thought to be inappropriate.

So, too, has the EU's chronic economic underperformance contributed to the crisis. Peace and prosperity are the twin pillars of the EU's existence, but the EU's economic performance has varied greatly over time. The internal market, the core policy field of the EU, has had mixed results. Monetary union, an addendum to the internal market and a highly symbolic undertaking in its own right, was supposed to have facilitated economic convergence among participating countries and stimulated further growth. Yet far from converging, the economies of eurozone countries have diverged and experienced, at best, only modest growth following the introduction of the euro in 1999. Since the outbreak of the crisis, economic performances have become even worse, with most of the economies of eurozone countries having experienced sharp recession. The impact of austerity policies pushed by eurozone creditor states (especially Germany) has intensified economic hardship in debtor states, stoked social tensions, and deepened political divisions. High unemployment, especially among young people, has sapped morale and nurtured a sense of deep despair.

Inevitably, these internal problems have weakened the EU's standing on the world stage. By definition, the migration crisis has had an external dimension, while the eurozone crisis has been closely related to global financial developments. The EU's seeming inability to deal forcefully and effectively with events in Ukraine has constituted a further external dimension of the crisis.

The Ukraine crisis, which erupted in 2014, represents the point at which the aspirations of the EU to extend its influence eastwards collided with Russia's determination to rebuild power and status following the collapse of the Soviet Union. This keenly felt loss impelled President Vladimir Putin to try to regain control of Russia's near abroad and restore Russia's global standing. Putin's pressure on Ukraine to reject a proposed association agreement with the EU in favour of a Russian-led customs union foundered on popular protest in Kiev, which resulted in the ousting of Ukraine's pro-Russian president. This, in turn, triggered violent resistance in eastern Ukraine against the new, pro-Western government, and Russia's annexation of Crimea. Chancellor Merkel took the lead in managing the EU's response, which helped to bring about a fragile peace – the Minsk Accord – and included sanctions against Russia. The conflict is now frozen, but could escalate at any time. Accordingly, the EU faces instability on its eastern border in addition to the instability caused by the migration crisis on its southern border.

There are thus many aspects to the EU crisis. It is truly multi-dimensional in nature, spanning politics and economics, touching on cultural and identity issues, and covering both internal and external affairs.

Origins of the Crisis

General origins

The origins of the EU's crisis are many, various, and often – as the sections below on the EMU, migration, and the Brexit crises show – specific to particular dimensions of the crisis. However, in addition to specific factors, some of which have already been mentioned, three general sources can also be identified.

The first is the weak foundations of aspects of the EU's system of governance and of some of its key policies. The lack of clear, accountable, and treaty-based EU leadership has been an important factor behind the legitimacy/democracy crisis and may even have contributed to what could be called a leadership crisis. Similarly, the weak foundations of two of the EU's core policies – EMU and the Schengen system – have been at the heart of the eurozone and migration crises. The rules of these policies were laid down in relatively good times, when the focus of the EU was on making integrationist advances with great steps forward. Insufficient attention was given to whether the arrangements that were established were sufficiently robust to withstand the pressures of less good and more difficult times.

The second general source of the crisis is that the EU's member states are, in numerous respects, significantly different from one another in terms of national needs and preferences. While it was possible to manage many of these differences in good times, and with fewer member states, it has become much less so in a far larger EU that is being buffeted by severe shocks and policy challenges.

Being part of a highly interconnected global system, the EU is susceptible to what happens elsewhere in the world. As such, external factors constitute the third general source of the crisis. So, for example, it was the sub-prime mortgage crisis and the ensuing recession in the USA that sparked the eurozone crisis. Continuing global financial and economic uncertainty has made it more difficult to stabilize the situation in Europe. It was developments in Iraq, Libya, and Syria that triggered the migration crisis. The global threat of Islamic extremism has reverberated in Europe, most dramatically with the terrorist attacks in France in 2015 and 2016, and Brussels in 2016, and has contributed to the EU crisis in that there have been great uncertainties about how best to deal with this partly internal and partly external security threat. So, too, have Russia's actions in Ukraine added to the crisis. The reasons for the Russian intervention are largely rooted in Russia's view of the world and in domestic Russian politics, but they have presented the EU with a major foreign policy problem.

Particular origins of the three headline crises: eurozone, migration, and Brexit

As noted above, there have been many dimensions of the EU crisis. However, three of these have been of particular importance and have attracted most attention. There are chapters on each of these dimensions – the euro crisis, the migration crisis, and Brexit – later in the book, but given their centrality to the EU crisis an introductory account of their origins is given here.

The eurozone crisis
The proximate cause of the eurozone crisis was, as mentioned above, a development on the other side of the Atlantic. By the late 2000s, the

US financial system was under immense stress, as the bankruptcy in September 2008 of the giant firm Lehman Brothers dramatically demonstrated. The ripple effects were soon felt in the real economy, as output and employment plummeted. Even if the foundations of EMU had been solid, the EU was bound to experience a severe shock from these events in the USA. As it happened, the structural weaknesses of EMU, which hark back to the Maastricht Treaty, accentuated the impact of the shock. Indeed, EMU's foundational flaws arguably portended a crisis in the making.

EMU is a long-standing goal of European integration. It first emerged as a real possibility in the early 1970s, when global exchange rate instability bolstered the desirability of a fixed exchange rate regime, or even a single currency, among European Community countries. The policy debate at that time raised several contentious questions that recurred 20 years later during the Maastricht Treaty negotiations. How much sovereignty would members of a monetary union willingly surrender in order to ensure the success of a supranational currency? What should the criteria be for countries to join? Should economic convergence precede monetary union or would monetary union bring about the necessary degree of convergence?

In the early 1970s, Germany was willing to concede more sovereignty and France less; Germany wanted a high degree of convergence first and France believed that convergence could happen later. In the event, the global economic recession of the 1970s put paid to plans for EMU. When the issue emerged again in the late 1980s, global economic conditions were more benign and the European Community better integrated economically. France and German retained their earlier preferences, but managed to come to an agreement.

Academic economists, especially in the USA, pointed out that the putative EMU-zone did not constitute an optimal currency area. In other words, there would be insufficient fiscal transfers and labour mobility to absorb the impact of asymmetric economic shocks, which would render the currency union unworkable. Ideally, a currency union would include a fiscal union and a banking union as part of an economic union, and a political union as well. Intellectually, the Maastricht negotiators may have understood this point. They certainly understood that such ambitious objectives were politically impossible to achieve. Political union was on the agenda at Maastricht, but only in the form of taking steps to strengthen the legitimacy of the EU, not to engineer a wholesale transfer of national authority to a federal EU. Germany was willing to concede more than France, especially in the run-up to German unification, but Germany could not risk jeopardizing monetary union by getting too far ahead of French preferences on economic and political union. The result was a fudge: EMU was established with a weak 'E' (no banking or fiscal union) and a strong 'M' (a single central bank, single monetary policy, and single currency). A single European government (political union) was nowhere to be seen.

EMU and the eurozone were likely to succeed, given their weak foundations, only as long as the regional and global economy remained reasonably buoyant. The presumption was that monetary union would flourish in a eurozone with an economic growth rate of about 3 per cent, which seemed reasonable by post-war standards. By the mid-2000s, it appeared as if the eurozone was indeed succeeding, with most members having growth rates in the range of 2–4 per cent and some, such as Ireland, having significantly higher rates. However, these healthy figures obscured some disturbing underlying developments, notably growing disequilibria in competitiveness, investment, and exports between financially stronger northern countries and increasingly debt-burdened southern countries. Nonetheless, as long as growth remained high and international borrowing costs low, this did not seem problematical.

However, the shock of the US financial crash caused a sudden drop in capital flows to 'peripheral' eurozone countries, notably Greece, Ireland, Spain, and Portugal. It also exposed the extent of some European banks' reckless lending and some European countries' excessive borrowing. The magnitude of the problem first became apparent in Greece, where a new government revealed, in 2009, that the country was running a deficit of over 12 per cent of GDP, more than four times the permissible deficit for eurozone members. The problem in Ireland was caused not by excessive debt, but by the Irish government's decision to write a blank cheque to rescue the country's failing banks. Spain was also in difficulty because of a banking crisis, and Portugal because of excessive debt.

By 2010, a balance of payments crisis had turned into a public debt crisis, and EMU's inadequate design – notably the lack of a fiscal union and a banking union – resulted in there being no readily accessible solutions to what was becoming a eurozone crisis (Baldwin and Gros, 2015).

The migration crisis
The roots of the migration crisis lie in a mixture of push and pull factors. The push factors are partly accounted for by shortcomings in the EU's external relations. The EU has done little – and perhaps could not have done more – to promote peace and stability in North Africa, to address the turmoil in the Middle East, to prevent the rise of the Islamic State, and to stop the civil war in Syria. All of these developments, and others besides, resulted in attempted mass migration to the EU from Iraq and Syria, and from other war-torn or impoverished countries.

Despite a large amount of money and effort having been spent on a range of elaborate initiatives, the EU was blindsided by the Arab Spring and found that it had little influence in a large, strategically vital, and increasingly unstable part of the world. It would, of course, be absurd to blame the EU for all of the problems of North Africa and the Middle East. But the EU must bear some responsibility for the failure of its diplomacy, which has been backed up with generous economic inducements, to help reduce the factors that push migrants from the Middle East and North Africa towards Europe's shores.

The pull factor for migrants is the lure of living in a peaceful and secure country, with the prospect of employment or, more likely, welfare assistance. Germany and Sweden have been the main destinations of choice. Chancellor Merkel's apparent willingness in the summer of 2015 to allow unlimited numbers of refugees to enter Germany opened the floodgates. Schengen's largely lightly protected external borders made it possible for hundreds of thousands of refugees and other irregular migrants to reach their desired destination.

Merkel's generosity rebounded on her politically in Germany, and exposed the inherent weakness of the Schengen system. Despite years of negotiations, when the numbers of attempted migrants to the EU exploded in 2015, a fully functioning common asylum system had not yet been established. The Dublin Regulation for processing asylum-seekers (which specifies that migrants should be processed in the EU country in which they first arrive) was not effective in dealing with the vast numbers of people attempting to enter the EU, which led to Germany suspending the Regulation, of which it had been a staunch defender, in August 2015. The porousness of the EU's external borders undermined the integrity of the intra-EU free travel area, resulting in several 'temporary' restrictions on free travel being put in place. Like EMU, Schengen had been designed from the perspective of hoping for the best rather than anticipating the worst. When the worst happened, the system was unable to cope.

As with EMU, the influx of migrants has resulted in the EU trying to fix a system (Schengen in this case) while it is in crisis. Like EMU, the Schengen system was not designed for conditions of severe strain. Certainly, there was no systemic anticipation of what would be done if hundreds of thousands of migrants suddenly appeared at Schengen's external borders. To make matters worse, the eurozone crisis has resulted in there being less trust and goodwill among member states to help resolve the migration crisis. Resentment of Germany's preponderance in the EU, and especially of Germany's insistence on austerity, has spilled over into the migration crisis, in which Germany has desperately needed its EU partners to carry out their Schengen obligations and share the burden of refugee settlement.

At the same time, the migration crisis has sown deep divisions between EU member states. This has been especially so with Greece which, having been on the front line of the eurozone crisis, has similarly been on the front line of the migration crisis. The Greek border forms the principal EU external border through which most migrants set out for Germany and other northern states. As countries along the migration route closed their borders in 2015, tens of thousands of migrants became trapped in Greece, sparking a major humanitarian disaster. Given Germany's treatment of Greece during the eurozone crisis, Greece has not been inclined to accommodate Germany during the migration crisis, at least not without the prospect of significant financial assistance and possibly even debt relief.

The Brexit crisis
Whereas the roots of the eurozone and migration crises lay primarily in the inability of EU states to agree on stronger policy foundations, those of Brexit (the term commonly used for the UK exit from the EU) lay firmly in domestic UK politics. Britain had long been the most eurosceptic member state, but the political significance of its euroscepticism was given a much sharper edge when the Prime Minister, David Cameron, promised a referendum on UK membership of the EU if his Conservative Party won an overall majority in Parliament in the 2015 general election. Against most expectations, an overall majority was duly won, which resulted in the referendum having to be held.

Cameron promised the electorate a referendum not because he genuinely wished to consult the British people. Rather, he did so because he was pressurized and saw electoral advantages in being seen to 'let the people decide'. One source of pressure came from a growing body of eurosceptic opinion in his own parliamentary party. Another source was increasing support for the United Kingdom Independence Party (UKIP), which Cameron thought could be diverted by a mainstream party (his own) offering a referendum.

However, it is unwise for governments to hold avoidable referendums unless they can be sure (which they rarely can) that they will receive the answer they want. For, in referendums electorates have a habit of not answering the question they have been asked, but rather of answering the question they wished they had been asked. They have a habit also, in considering how they will vote, of not focusing on the aspects of the question the government wishes to direct them to. Both of these tendencies strongly contributed to 52 per cent of those who voted in June 2016 supporting a British exit. Whereas the government wanted the electorate to concentrate on (the claimed) damaging consequences of an exit vote for the UK economy, many of the electorate chose to give a higher priority to voting on the perceived iniquities of EU migration laws (and the free movement of people principle) and the powers of unaccountable decision-makers 'in Brussels'. 'Let's Take Our Country Back' was an appealing call for many voters.

Implications of the Crisis for the EU System

Greater centralization, but also disaggregation

There is a recurring refrain in EU history that crises are ubiquitous and good for European integration – that at pivotal moments, crises have been catalysts for major breakthroughs and for advancements of the integration process.

The recent and current crises have undoubtedly resulted in some centralizing developments, most notably in respect of EMU where the eurozone's fiscal powers have been strengthened. They have, however, been only slightly strengthened and have not resulted in the (much-needed?) fiscal union – in which there are strong revenue-raising and spending distributional powers at central level – being even remotely on the immediate horizon. Furthermore, because eurozone rules do not apply to non-eurozone countries, such centralizing as there has been only applies to part (albeit the major part) of the EU. In short, the crisis has not had much of a stimulating effect on European integration.

As noted in Chapter 2, the pervasive notion of crisis as opportunity, and a tendency to use the word 'crisis' loosely to label events of varying urgency in EU history, may have blunted EU leaders' appreciation of the seriousness of the crisis, and delayed or undermined their responses to it. Certainly, for the most part, the crisis of recent years has served rather to extend and sharpen European disaggregation and to stiffen differences between EU political actors.

Amidst sharp policy differences about how best to proceed, the eurozone crisis has threatened to unravel monetary union and the migration crisis has threatened to unravel the Schengen free travel area. Monetary union and Schengen are, arguably, the two most iconic and politically important achievements of European integration. The collapse of one or the other, let alone both, would have a devastating effect on the EU. Both policies are linked to the internal market, which might not survive in its present form without monetary union and unimpeded cross-border travel. The blow to the EU's image and international credibility would be incalculable. Even if monetary union, the single market, and Schengen survive the crisis largely intact, the EU has already changed markedly.

Similarly, the outcome of the UK referendum has been devastating for the EU's image and self-esteem. Uncertainty surrounding the precise path to Brexit has greatly exacerbated the sense of crisis in the EU. In the months after the referendum, the remaining 27 EU members were left waiting to hear what terms the UK would be seeking and when exit negotiations would begin. While thorough preparations on these questions were sensible from the UK's perspective, the delay added to the atmosphere of uncertainty in the EU – at a time when it needed to concentrate not only on the implications of Brexit but also on resolving the many other policy challenges and crises facing it.

A related potentially disaggregating and damaging consequence of Brexit is the encouragement it has given to eurosceptics elsewhere in the EU. Some – including in member states where euroscepticism was already strong, such as Italy, Austria, France, Hungary, and Poland – have used it to help marshal support for their own national aspirations of disengaging from the EU. All have been emboldened to use it to try to pressurize national governments either to hold similar referendums or to dilute existing levels of European integration.

Relations between member states

The crisis has strengthened a tendency towards more intergovernmentalism in the conduct of EU affairs at the expense of supranationalism and has elevated separate national interests over shared EU interests. In times of political difficulties and economic strain, governments are less able or inclined to pursue common European rather than individual national preferences, and the two tend to diverge. A widespread political consensus within member states on the value of European integration and the benefits of EU membership has frayed. Nationalist, populist, and anti-EU parties have grown in most countries. For many Europeans, the EU is no longer seen as a solution to a problem or set of problems, but as a problem in itself.

Fault lines between EU member states have thus appeared or reappeared because of the crisis. The distinction between eurozone and non-eurozone members has become acute. Within the eurozone, the distinction between creditor and debtor countries has become politically as well as economically crucial: a distinction that broadly mirrors a core–periphery differentiation within the EU. North–south and east–west fault lines, reflecting deep-seated political, economic, and cultural differences, are more noticeable than ever before.

Among national governments, Germany has become much more influential than previously, but even it has been unable to master the migration crisis. The rise of German hegemony, however uncomfortable for Germany itself, has been a direct consequence of the crisis. At the same time, given its economic weakness, France has barely maintained the fiction of parity in Franco-German relations. The UK's non-participation in monetary union and Schengen, and the result of the Brexit referendum, has accentuated the country's semi-detachment from the EU.

Institutional effects

Institutionally, the severity and suddenness of the crisis have required a response at the highest political level. This has ensured the elevation of the European Council, which officially became an EU institution in December 2009 when the Lisbon Treaty came into effect – coincidentally at the start of the eurozone crisis. European Councils – and on euro-only issues Euro Summits, which bring together the leaders of countries in the eurozone – have met frequently during the crisis in an effort to provide overall political direction and thrash out agreements on specific crisis-related issues.

It is within the European Council that Germany's preponderance has been most noticeable, and where resentment of Germany's role has been most pointed. Traditionally, the leaders of France and Germany dominated meetings of the European Council, but since the onset of the crisis Germany alone has been predominant, though Chancellor Merkel, who has been in office since 2005, prefers to act in concert with others. This does not mean that Merkel always has had things her own way, but Germany's preferences have most often prevailed. However, hegemons are rarely popular and tend to generate countervailing force. Austerity, Germany's preferred remedy for the eurozone crisis, has been hugely disliked in countries that have had to accept the strings attached to the bailouts, and has aroused resentment throughout much of the EU, especially among political parties on the left. The economic and social pain of austerity has gradually eroded the consensus that initially existed in its favour.

The European Commission remains at the institutional heart of the Union and has acquired new powers, notably with regard to fiscal governance, as the crisis has progressed. But the political influence of the Commission, which traditionally has been most clearly expressed through the office of its President, has somewhat receded. Neither José Manuel Barroso, Commission President until November 2014, nor his successor, Jean-Claude Juncker, has been a favoured interlocutor of Merkel, nor a particularly effective actor in the European Council. Whereas the Commission's technical expertise and executive authority have been essential in advancing detailed proposals for combatting the eurozone and migration crises, the Commission has not been a successful trailblazer for major political decisions – such as those concerning the size of and conditions to be attached to bailouts to the heavily indebted countries.

For many years the European Parliament (EP) has been in the ascendant institutionally and its powers were further strengthened by the provisions of the Lisbon Treaty. However, it has exercised only very limited influence in helping to resolve the various dimensions of the EU crisis. Even the novelty of linking the outcome of the 2014 EP elections to the selection of the incoming Commission President did not arouse much public interest. Not only did voter turnout continue its downward trend since the first elections in 1979, but also eurosceptics made large gains. This was symptomatic of growing opposition to austerity and increasing disillusionment with the EU in many member states.

Supplying Solutions

Whereas demand for solutions to crisis-related problems has been considerable, the supply has been conspicuously lacking. Too often, proffered solutions have eventually emerged as watered-down versions of original proposals and as minimalist responses to pressing problems of the day. Take, for example, the eurozone crisis, which the leaders of the main EU institutions (and most outside observers) have thought can only be properly tackled by moving towards 'genuine' EMU (see the two reports by the presidents of the main EU institutions: van Rompuy, 2012; European Commission, 2015). Progress in addressing the eurozone crisis has included the Treaty on Stability, Coordination and Governance (the Fiscal Compact) and related legislation aimed at preventing fiscal profligacy, and the passing of measures to create a (partial) banking union. But there has never been any realistic prospect that the eurozone governments would seriously consider the bigger, and arguably necessary, step of creating a fiscal and political union.

Similarly with the migration crisis, a number of specific measures have been adopted – including a strengthening of the EU's external borders, a reinforcement of naval patrols in the Mediterranean, and financial subsidies to Turkey to reduce the flow of refugees into the EU. But the EU has been largely unable to deal with the 'big picture' issues, especially where they have touched directly on sensitive national interests and cherished national sovereignty. Not surprisingly, the Commission's proposal in 2015 that member states should accept mandatory quotas of migrants made no headway, nor did its protests when several Schengen member states began introducing restrictions on free movement across internal borders.

To some extent, the absence of 'macro' solutions may reflect complacency in the EU about the nature and consequences of crises past. However, even if EU leaders had appreciated at the outset the gravity of the situation, the multi-level character and structure of most EU policies are not conducive to a rapid crisis response. In the case of the eurozone crisis, the European Central Bank (ECB), which initially misread the seriousness of the situation, was able eventually to respond rapidly and forcefully to ease the supply of money and to exercise a leading role in banking reform. But decision-making on fiscal policy, by contrast, remained, and has remained, decentralized within the EU, with responsibilities residing partly at EU level but mainly at national levels. The Eurogroup of finance ministers has met frequently since the onset of the crisis but, given the political salience of the issues being discussed and the existence of many policy differences between the member states, it has often had to defer to national leaders, meeting in the European Council or Euro Summit, for ultimate decision-making.

However, the European Council is not analogous to a cabinet government with a designated chief minister and with the authority to make decisions in a wide array of public policy fields. It is a rather cumbersome body, whose 28 principals (national leaders) are nominally equal. Though the political reality is that some members are more equal than others, the organizational nature of the institution – which almost invariably proceeds only on the basis of consensus – is that its meetings are often indecisive. Of course, EU leaders do not restrict their contacts to meetings of the European Council. They are frequently in touch with each other in all sorts of formal and informal ways. Key players, such as the German Chancellor, the French President, the Eurogroup President, and the ECB President, have kept in close contact since the extent of the crisis became fully apparent. But, even when they have agreed on what needed to be done, they have ultimately required the approval of the entire European Council, which has been by no means automatic. Furthermore, often what EU leaders have been able to agree in the European Council has required approval in national capitals, which has taken time and has not always been without controversy.

Echoing the old adage of crisis as opportunity, some politicians and pundits have called for 'more Europe' – deeper European integration along supranational lines – in response to the crisis. Such calls have an obvious appeal, in that the structural weaknesses of EMU and Schengen could be repaired if the EU was radically redesigned and substantially more sovereignty was transferred to the European level. But the fundamental reason for these structural weaknesses – the unwillingness of national governments to surrender full authority in such sensitive policy areas – has persisted long after EMU and Schengen were first put in place. If anything, the rising tide of euroscepticism has made governments even more wary of transferring additional decision-making responsibility to Brussels. The crisis may have brought about 'a little more Europe', for instance in the area of fiscal governance. But going beyond that and establishing a system of fiscal federalism or a truly common asylum and migration policy with EU-level border enforcement would require a major upheaval in political thinking and ambitions, and also treaty changes. Given the fraught experience of EU treaty change in the 2000s, and growing anti-EU sentiment in the meantime, this is a challenge that few national governments are willing to meet.

There are historical and political limits, therefore, to the potential supply of solutions to the EU crisis. Within those limits, nonetheless, it is hard not to fault the EU for the sluggishness and inadequacy of its responses. Even without the benefit of hindsight, it seems clear that the EU reacted in a piecemeal fashion to the escalating eurozone crisis, and that Merkel's announcement that there would be no limit on the number of refugees allowed into Germany was bound to trigger a flood of new arrivals. In the case of the eurozone crisis, Merkel has been accused of being too cautious; in the case of the refugee crisis, she is seen as having been too rash. Politicians are motivated by a variety of factors, ranging from personal conviction to political opportunism. Decision-making in an age of crisis is especially difficult, not just for Merkel, but for each and every one of the EU's decision-makers, both individually and collectively in EU institutions. Having so many different actors with so many different motives and perspectives involved in crisis resolution, and with resolution processes usually being based on consensus rather than majority voting, EU political decision-making is bound to be complex and protracted. No political system is perfect; by its nature, the EU is less perfect than most.

Conclusions

Economic and political developments within and around Europe remain highly unsettled. The eurozone crisis is quiescent, but hardly resolved. Wars and poverty in the Middle East, North Africa, and beyond continue to propel thousands of desperate migrants towards the EU. Although the outcome of the UK referendum was unequivocal, there is uncertainty about the timing and terms of Britain's departure from the EU. Russia is a revanchist power, eager to exploit weaknesses within the EU and differences among member states for its own advantage. Illiberal regimes in Hungary and Poland, and illiberal movements in other member states, are challenging core EU norms and values. Global economic and financial uncertainty is accentuating Europe's poor economic performance and exacerbating political unease.

It is not unlikely, therefore, that the 'crisis will become the new normal' (Haughton, 2016: 15). Having once been occasional events in EU history, crises may now be a quasi-permanent condition of European integration. The EU may well have entered a new era, clearly distinct from earlier phases of its existence. The domestic political implications of rampant euroscepticism and dissatisfaction with the status quo are already undermining the ability and willingness of national leaders to act decisively on the European stage. Forces that once pushed European countries to share sovereignty in order to resolve collective action problems seem to have given way to forces that are pulling countries apart. The EU is likely to soon lose one of its biggest member states, having already lost many of the intangible elements that define its unique political character. Steady progress over many decades towards deeper political and economic integration has stopped, with the prospect of disintegration suddenly all too real. Such a dramatic change of fortune calls for new thinking about the nature of European integration and the direction of the EU.

References

Baldwin, R. and Gros, D. (2015) 'What Caused the Eurozone Crisis?', *Centre for European Policy Studies (CEPS) Commentary*, 27 November.

Eichenberg, R. and Dalton, R. (2007) 'Post Maastricht Blues: The Transformation of Citizen Support for European Integration, 1973–2004', *Acta Politica*, Vol. 42, No. 2, pp. 128–52.

European Commission (2015) *The Five Presidents' Report: Completing Europe's Economic and Monetary Union*, Brussels: European Commission, 22 June.

Haughton, T. (2016) 'Is Crisis the New Normal? The European Union in 2015.' In N. Copsey and T. Haughton (eds), *The JCMS Annual Review of the European Union in 2015*, 54, pp. 5–7.

Smith, D. (2015) 'Not Just Singing the Blues: Dynamics of the EU Crisis'. In H.-J. Trenz, C. Ruzza, and V. Guraudon (eds), *Europe's Prolonged Crisis: The Making or Unmaking of a Political Union*. London: Palgrave Macmillan, pp. 23–43.

Van Rompuy, H. (2012) *Towards a Genuine Economic and Monetary Union*, Brussels, 5 December.

Chapter 2

Crises in EU History

DESMOND DINAN

Introduction

As noted in Chapter 1, the multi-dimensional crisis facing the EU is unprecedented in seriousness and severity. But crises are nothing new in the trajectory of European integration. Specifically, events to which politicians, officials, journalists, and others have attached the label 'crisis' are almost commonplace for the EU. According to the conventional wisdom, EU history is replete with so-called crises, which have been instrumental in driving the project forward. Indeed, the notion of 'crisis as opportunity' is central to the founding story of the European Coal and Steel Community (ECSC), the European Economic Community (EEC), and the EU itself.

The severity of the current crisis has led to a reappraisal of the role of crises in EU history (Parsons and Matthijs, 2015). This chapter contributes to that reappraisal by reviewing EU history critically, with a view to exploring the relationship between the onset and the impact of supposed crises and the course of European integration. The chapter does not define the concept of EU crisis. Instead, it accepts at face value that a variety of political and economic shocks emanating from inside or outside the EU system constituted crises. Exogenous shocks include global economic and financial jolts; endogenous shocks are rooted in EU politics, policies, and procedures.

The chapter raises a number of questions. How instrumental have these events been in the development of the EU? Why is the idea of crisis as opportunity so deeply woven into the traditional narrative of EU history? Has the EU reacted differently to exogenous and endogenous crises? Is the process of European integration inherently crisis-prone? The answers to these questions are of more than intellectual interest. A widespread belief that crises are not unusual occurrences in EU history, and are perhaps essential for the success of European integration, may have blinded politicians to the seriousness of the euro crisis. A conviction that the EU has always emerged stronger from crises – that crises have propelled integration forward – risks inducing complacency. Many of the statements made by national politicians and EU policy-makers during the current crisis suggest that this has indeed been the case.

The chapter takes a chronological and thematic approach. The first section explores the myth and reality of crisis embedded in the founding story of the European project in the immediate post-World War II period. The second section looks at the role of crises in the failure of the European Defence Community and the success of the European Economic Community in the 1950s. The third section examines the crisis-laden 1960s, a decade that saw the rejection of Britain's application for EEC membership and the outbreak of the empty chair crisis, the most serious constitutional crisis in EU history. The fourth section assesses the impact of economic and financial crises preceding the Single European Act (SEA) of 1986, a precursor of the Maastricht Treaty of 1992. The fifth section looks at the role of crises in the development of European integration from Maastricht to the Lisbon Treaty of 2007, including the rejection of the Constitutional Treaty by French and Dutch voters in 2005. The conclusion ties together a number of key points made throughout the chapter, and relates previous crises to the current one.

Myth and Reality of the Founding Story

The opening sentence of the Schuman Declaration of May 1950, widely seen as having begun the process of European integration, asserted that: 'World peace cannot be safeguarded without the making of creative efforts proportionate to the dangers which threaten it' (Schuman, 1950). The word 'crisis' did not appear in the declaration, but the implication was clear: a radical new direction in Franco-German relations, cemented in a supranational organization to regulate the coal and steel sectors, was essential to safeguard world peace, which was threatened not only by historic Franco-German enmity but also, more immediately, by the Cold War.

The timing and specifics of the declaration were a surprise, but the core concept of Franco-German rapprochement was not (Gillingham, 1991: 137–77; Hitchcock, 1998: 99–132). The declaration represented a novel French approach towards the newly established and economically rising Federal Republic of Germany. By 1950 it was apparent to all but the most recalcitrant of French politicians that the current policy of trying to dominate Germany was no longer feasible. Jean Monnet, the senior French official who designed the Schuman Plan, saw the putative Coal and Steel Community as the best option for France.

Monnet thrived in an atmosphere of crisis. Throughout his long professional life, whether in the family brandy business, in international finance, or in public service on behalf of either the French government or the League of Nations, Monnet had revelled in responding to crises of all kinds. From this experience, Monnet concluded that crises provided opportunities to take bold steps which otherwise might not be possible. It also inculcated in Monnet a tendency to exaggerate the urgency of events in order to facilitate outcomes that he desired (Duchêne, 1994: 27–225).

Monnet's penchant for drama was fully apparent at the time of the Schuman Declaration, notably in the secrecy surrounding the initiative and the way in which Schuman presented the proposal at the last moment to sceptical cabinet colleagues. It suited Monnet to hype the declaration as a major breakthrough at a time of grave danger. The dramatic effect of the declaration, intended to bring about 'the first concrete foundation of a European federation', highlighted the historic importance of Schuman's diplomatic initiative and increased its prospects for success.

The Schuman Declaration may have originated in a crisis, but a crisis that had peaked three years previously. Alan Milward, the foremost historian of European integration, began his ground-breaking book, *The Reconstruction of Western Europe* (1984), with a chapter titled 'The Crisis of 1947'. According to Milward, the decisive crisis was due to the success of post-war reconstruction, not its failure. It occurred because 'for some European countries the deficit in merchandise trade, the gap between imports for domestic consumption and exports of domestically produced goods, which had ... in most cases begun to narrow during the winter of 1946/7, began to widen again in 1947' (Milward, 1984: 20–1).

The unsustainability of growing trade deficits, which the nascent Bretton Woods system, introduced at the end of the war to ensure global economic stability, proved unable to resolve, provided the economic impetus for the Marshall Plan. Implementation of the Marshall Plan, in turn, put intense pressure on France to go along with the USA and the UK and ease the restrictions placed by the wartime allies on Germany's economic revival. The need to resolve the German question became acute in early 1950, as the USA leaned on France to revise its punitive policy towards the Federal Republic. Monnet was the principal interlocutor between Paris and Washington (Gillingham, 1991: 228–33; Hitchcock, 1998: 99–120; Milward, 1984: 380–97). By depicting this development as a crisis, Monnet cast the Schuman Declaration as an opportunistic response to a dire need (Monnet, 1978: 274–306). The idea of crisis as opportunity, in which Monnet deeply believed, seemed entirely vindicated.

From the European Defence Community to the European Economic Community

The outbreak of the Korean War in June 1950, only a month after the Schuman Declaration, occasioned another crisis, which Monnet eagerly exploited in order to move European integration in a new and highly controversial direction. This was the genesis of the European Defence Community (EDC), whose rejection by the French National Assembly in 1954 looms large in the history of European integration. Failure to ratify the EDC treaty is seen as both a great opportunity lost and a residual opportunity gained (Burgess, 2000: 67–71). The opportunity lost was to establish a western European military force under the umbrella of a supranational authority (the European Political Community); the opportunity gained was to overcome the setback of the EDC by returning to the first principles of functional economic integration, resulting in the launch of the EEC.

The emergence of the EEC out of the ashes of the EDC is one of the most persistent myths in the history of European integration, which has strongly bolstered the widespread belief that crises are essential for propelling the process forward. Far from having been an opportunity lost, the demise of the EDC arguably rescued European integration from the political quagmire of an unworkable military commitment. The extent of the controversy in France over ratification of the treaty, which many people at the time compared in its divisiveness to the Dreyfus affair at the turn of the twentieth century, suggests that implementation of the EDC would have been extremely difficult and would likely have poisoned attitudes towards integration in France and beyond for many years to come (Hitchcock, 1998: 169–72). Instead, resolution of the rancorous EDC dispute restricted the field of integration to far less contentious economic issues.

Even before the end of the EDC, ideas were circulating in western Europe for a common market in industrial goods, analogous to the Coal and Steel Community (Gillingham, 2003: 43–52). The momentum to flesh out these ideas came not from a particular crisis or from a prevailing atmosphere of crisis, but from propitious economic circumstances throughout western Europe. France, Germany, and neighbouring countries already had high rates of economic growth, thanks largely to a sizeable increase in international trade since the late 1940s. Further trade liberalization would facilitate more international commerce and greatly benefit all concerned.

The supposed crisis caused by the demise of the EDC may have prompted the French government to explore the possibility of a common market earlier and more openly than it otherwise would have, as a means of demonstrating its continuing commitment to European integration.

Setbacks overseas, including a decisive military defeat in Indochina in May 1954, may also have influenced French thinking about European integration. But the most compelling reasons for France to move away from its traditional policy of protectionism were economic, and were not crisis-related.

The status of the Saar, a French protectorate partitioned from Germany at the end of World War II, was a persistent irritant and a potential cause of crisis in Franco-German relations. To fit the 'crisis as opportunity' narrative of European integration, the launch of the EEC in 1958 might have come about partly or wholly in response to a Saar crisis. However, France and Germany resolved the Saar dispute before completing the negotiations that resulted in the EEC (under the terms of a Franco-German treaty in October 1956, the Saarland joined the Federal Republic in January 1957). Far from a Saar crisis having prompted deeper European integration, it was the prospect of deeper integration that helped bring about a resolution of the Saar dispute (Long, 2015: 208–33).

The crisis precipitated by Egyptian President Abdel Nasser's nationalization of the Suez Canal in July 1956 is sometimes said to have impelled European integration. An Anglo-French military expedition to regain control of the Canal Zone ended disastrously in December 1956. Stung by this reverse, the French Prime Minister Guy Mollet allegedly redoubled his efforts to reach agreement with his European partners on the putative EEC. This explains incongruous references to Nasser as the 'federator of Europe' (Hansen and Jonsson, 2014: 157–9). Nevertheless, a decisive link between the Suez crisis and the formation of the EEC is extremely far-fetched. By the time the crisis ended, negotiations for what became the Rome Treaty were well on their way to a successful conclusion.

The Crises of the 1960s

The 1960s was a paradoxical decade for the EEC. On the one hand, core common policies were put in place, as was a new legal system. On the other hand, the EEC endured a number of endogenous crises, which centred on the vital question of how decisions are taken, specifically having to do with enlargement and everyday policy-making.

British accession

Enlargement arose early on the EEC's agenda, when the UK applied to join in 1961. The crisis came in January 1963, when French President Charles de Gaulle announced his opposition to UK membership and the accession negotiations broke down in Brussels (Bange, 2000; Ludlow,

2006: 11–39). The UK's second application and de Gaulle's second veto, in 1967, sparked another crisis, though less acute than the first (Ludlow, 2006: 125–245).

Although an existing member state had the right to veto the accession of a prospective member state, the high-handed manner of de Gaulle's behaviour in 1963, at a late stage of difficult though constructive negotiations, infuriated the other participants. De Gaulle's ambivalence towards the EEC had already caused friction between France and the Five (the other member states). The possibility of British accession, which the Five supported, alarmed de Gaulle, who feared its possible impact on core Community policies and on his plans for a 'European Europe' independent of the USA (Moravcsik, 1998: 159–238).

Under the circumstances, the failure of the negotiations was not entirely surprising, but the way that de Gaulle put his interests ahead of what the others saw as the common interest of the EEC caused a political shock. Whether it amounted to a crisis is debatable, though commentators and protagonists immediately used that word to describe the fall-out, partly for political reasons. The British even thought that the end of the negotiations could precipitate the end of the EEC, but soon realized that the ties binding the Six together were stronger than they appeared (Bange, 2000: 223).

Britain's second application, submitted in 1967 when de Gaulle was still in power, represented the triumph of hope over experience (Ludlow, 2006: 125–45). The outcome was similar, but expressions of surprise or shock were fewer. The word 'crisis' was again used, but with little real meaning. It was clear to all concerned that Britain's accession to the EEC would have to wait until de Gaulle's departure.

The drama surrounding Britain's applications in 1963 and 1967 suggested that the process of EEC enlargement was crisis-prone, though the idiosyncratic nature of the events – the agency of de Gaulle – demonstrated their unique character. Nor did these so-called crises present much opportunity to deepen European integration. The Five expressed solidarity in the face of de Gaulle's vetoes, but did not take any steps in response to strengthen the EEC.

The empty chair crisis

The empty chair crisis also pitted de Gaulle against the Five, this time over the rules of decision-making in the Council of Ministers (Ludlow, 2006: 71–93; Palayret, Wallace, and Winand, 2006). Though not the proximate cause of de Gaulle's boycott of the Council, which began in July 1965, the extension of majority voting to new policy areas, due to take place in January 1966 under the terms of the Rome Treaty, became the make-or-break issue. De Gaulle insisted that the other governments accept the status quo, whereby decisions in the Council were taken on the basis of unanimity. As an ardent intergovernmentalist, de Gaulle opposed the use of majority voting, a decision-making instrument that epitomized supranationalism.

Whereas de Gaulle had every right to veto EEC enlargement, by attempting to block the transition to majority voting he was challenging both a core value and a legal obligation of EEC membership. Accordingly, the political risks were extremely high. Here was a crisis genuinely worthy of the name. The outcome could have wrecked the Community, or at least changed its character fundamentally.

Yet France needed the Community too much for de Gaulle to risk its destruction. In the face of domestic disquiet and a strong show of unity among the Five, de Gaulle backed down. Nevertheless, he wrung a significant concession from his EEC partners. Under the terms of the ambiguously worded Luxembourg Compromise, a recalcitrant government could delay or possibly prevent recourse to majority voting in the Council by claiming that 'very important interests are at stake' (the text of the Luxembourg Compromise is reproduced in Palayret, Wallace, and Winand, 2006: 325–6). Though the terms of the treaty remained unchanged, the political effect was to give governments the right to insist on unanimity in Council decision-making.

The empty chair crisis has been studied in great detail. There is general agreement that it was indeed grave, though observers dispute the long-term impact of the Luxembourg Compromise. Some say that the Council continued with business as usual; most argue that the threat or use of a national veto stymied decision-making for years to come. None claim that the outcome strengthened the Community due to an opportunistic initiative by advocates of deeper integration.

Luuk van Middelaar, a prominent Dutch political philosopher and historian, nonetheless sees the Luxembourg Compromise in an uncommon light. In his view, the genius of the accord is not only that it provided a clever way out of a political cul-de-sac, thereby allowing 'the Community to continue to exist', but also that it fundamentally transformed the EEC by 'allowing it to operate in a brave new world between the strict interpretation of treaties and the geopolitical world of international relations – the intermediate sphere of the [member states]' (Van Middelaar, 2013: 88, 89). Thus, the Luxembourg Compromise, 'a political accord of historical importance', marked 'a decisive moment of passage for the European order as a whole' (Van Middelaar, 2013: 92, 94).

While not endorsing the view of crisis as opportunity, this novel interpretation highlights the beneficial, though unintended, consequences of the dramatic events of 1965–66. The EEC was indeed a new kind of political entity with a new kind of politics, which were only beginning to take shape in the 1960s. Even before the crisis, the EEC seemed to be moving in the direction that Van Middelaar described. The crisis may have hastened this development, without necessarily having caused it.

Regardless, even Van Middelaar concedes that the impact of the crisis on day-to-day decision-making was far from benign. The shadow of the veto hung over the Council for the next two decades, until eventually displaced by the shadow of the vote in the aftermath of the SEA. Few proponents of crisis as opportunity in the history of European integration cite the events of 1965–66 to bolster their case.

Economic and Financial Crises Before the Single European Act

International exchange rate stability, a hallmark of the post-war period, began to break down in the late 1960s. Fluctuations in the value of national currencies, notably the steep devaluation of the French franc and revaluation of the German mark, inevitably affected intra-EEC trade and played havoc with the Community-wide guaranteed agricultural prices. With the end of the Bretton Woods system in August 1971, currencies began to float freely against each other. This was a powerful incentive for Community leaders to devise a regime for intra-EEC exchange rate stability. The result was the Werner Plan, which called for economic and monetary union (EMU) by 1980. The first stage of the plan sought to reduce exchange rate volatility by means of the 'snake in the tunnel' (Mourlon-Droul, 2012: 12–29).

Yet 'the first twelve months of the Snake's existence [1972–73] were fraught with currency crises' (McNamara, 1998: 107). Economic crisis soon followed, thanks to the Arab oil embargo imposed against Western countries that had supported Israel in the 1973 Yom Kippur War. The 'long 1970s', a decade that stretched into the early 1980s, was one of major economic upheaval in western Europe, with sluggish growth, soaring inflation, and high unemployment, although national experiences varied considerably. The Werner Plan was blown irrevocably off course. Frequent financial and economic shocks generated an atmosphere of chronic crisis among European decision-makers.

The most notable institutional initiative in response to these developments was the launch of the European Council in 1975 (Wessels, 2015). The European Council, which would become a powerful EU institution, began as an informal arrangement for national leaders to meet occasionally in order to direct Community affairs. Born at a time of economic instability, the European Council initially saw itself as a crisis management mechanism. Its original purpose was to hold the Community together, not to provide a means to deepen European integration.

The most striking policy initiative of the late 1970s was in the monetary sphere. It began with a speech by Commission President Roy Jenkins, in October 1977, in support of monetary union, and ended with the launch of the European Monetary System (EMS), in March 1979 (Mourlon-Droul, 2012: 132–260). Jenkins deliberately exploited what he saw as an opportunity to revive both European integration (generally) and the fortunes of the Commission (specifically). The EMS that eventually emerged was less than what Jenkins had hoped for and operated outside the treaty framework, but helped to deepen European integration and contributed to the eventual achievement of EMU.

The most consequential initiative linked to the economic and financial setbacks of the long 1970s came in the form of the single market programme (Cockfield, 1994). National leaders, buoyed by the apparent success of the EMS, weary of persistent economic underperformance, and concerned about western Europe's declining global competitiveness, coalesced in the early 1980s around the idea of deeper market integration. They were driven apart, however, by Prime Minister Margaret Thatcher's insistence on a new deal for Britain's contribution to the Community budget. The 'British budget question', sometimes described as a crisis, preoccupied Community leaders for several years (May, 2013: 69–71). Its resolution by the European Council in June 1984 paved the way for completion of the single market.

Jacques Delors, who became Commission President in 1985, seized upon this opportunity and fashioned a legislative programme to liberalize fully the movement of goods, services, and capital within the Community (Endo, 1999: 129–51). For Delors, the single market programme was a means towards the greater end of EMU and, ideally, political union. Delors was ambitious and opportunistic, though the opportunity that he exploited in 1985 existed because of a decade-long series of economic and financial setbacks, not because of an immediate crisis.

The single market programme formed the centrepiece of the SEA, the first major treaty change since the launch of the EEC (Gillingham, 2003: 228–58). Its impact was immediately apparent. The extension of majority voting to specific single market measures had a knock-on effect on decision-making in other policy areas. Clauses in the SEA covering environmental policy, social policy, and cohesion policy spurred unexpected advances in those fields. The SEA became synonymous with the acceleration of European integration and set the stage for another leap forward within a surprisingly short time. But the single market and the SEA represented an imaginative response to internal and external economic challenges confronting the Community, not to a particular crisis.

From Maastricht to Lisbon

The Maastricht Treaty is seen as the high point of European integration. Whereas the single market was central to the SEA, the more ambitious and glamorous goal of a single currency was central to Maastricht. EMU had been an aspiration of European integration since the beginning and an explicit goal of the EEC since the Werner Plan of the early 1970s. With Maastricht, monetary union finally appeared attainable.

The road to EMU, the Maastricht ratification crisis, and the EMS crisis

The narrative of the Maastricht Treaty does not include a claim of crisis as opportunity (Dyson and Featherstone, 2000). Implementation of the single market programme in the late 1980s took place in benign economic circumstances, which facilitated the move towards monetary union. The fall of the Berlin Wall in November 1989, at a time when planning for EMU was already well under way, was a major geopolitical shock. But it did not cause a crisis for the Community. Nor did German unification, which happened soon afterwards, in October 1990.

The link between German unification and EMU is not that the former made possible the latter, but that the revival of the German question, in the form of concern about the foreign policy orientation of a united Germany, strengthened Chancellor Helmut Kohl's position in the face of domestic unease about EMU. Kohl, who wanted EMU in any case, could now argue that giving up the mark and adopting the single European currency was a price well worth paying to assuage Germany's neighbours. United Germany would remain committed to a uniting Europe, given concrete expression by a common currency (Dyson and Featherstone, 2000: 354–69).

A public backlash against the rapidity and intensity of European integration soon set in. It was evident in Danish voters' rejection of the Maastricht Treaty in June 1992, and French voters' narrow approval of it in September 1992. What immediately became known as the Maastricht ratification crisis risked obstructing the course of European integration. There was no upside to this particular crisis, which ended only when Danish voters approved the treaty, in a second referendum in May 1993, after the other governments had given Denmark sufficient opt-outs from the original treaty to placate public opinion (Laursen, 1994).

The Maastricht crisis contributed to the contemporaneous EMS crisis. A variety of factors, including German unification and uncertainty about ratification of the Maastricht Treaty, suggested that a realignment of intra-EMS exchange rates was imminent. An absence of realignments since 1987 had fostered the impression that the EMS was a quasi-currency union. For some governments 'realignment' had become a dirty word, synonymous with political indecision and economic weakness. Governments whose currencies were weakest within the EMS spent vast amounts of money trying to ward off speculative attacks.

The situation deteriorated in September 1992, in the aftermath of the first Danish referendum and in the run-up to the French referendum, whose outcome was highly uncertain. Some governments pulled out of the exchange-rate mechanism; others devalued their currencies by up to 10 per cent. Only concerted efforts by the French and German governments and central banks prevented a French devaluation, which the EMS might not have survived.

Currency turmoil peaked in the summer of 1993, when a decision by the German central bank not to cut interest rates put other currencies under additional pressure. Following an emergency meeting in August, finance ministers announced the much-anticipated realignment: most currencies in the exchange-rate mechanism would be allowed to float within a new, much broader band. Abandoning the original, narrow band risked undermining the effectiveness of the EMS, but it helped stabilize the system by reducing the incentive for currency speculation (James, 2012: 324–81).

Coming on top of the Maastricht ratification crisis, the EMS crisis caused great unease as the EU came into existence. Regardless, the new EU would have to meet the daunting challenges of enlargement in central and eastern Europe; implementation of EMU; and negotiation and ratification of a series of treaty changes intended to strengthen both its day-to-day operations and its democratic legitimacy. Far from sensing an opportunity to exploit the recent crises, EU leaders were daunted by the challenge of meeting such a formidable set of objectives.

External and internal crises

The violent break-up of Yugoslavia in the 1990s was a crisis for the region and for Europe as a whole. Hostilities broke out during the course of the Maastricht negotiations. Buoyed by their plans for a Common Foreign and Security Policy (CFSP), Community leaders thought that they could broker peace in Yugoslavia. Optimism gave way to deep pessimism as the bloody wars of secession dragged on. Disillusionment with its inability to end the fighting at least pushed the EU to strengthen the CFSP in the Amsterdam Treaty of 1997, and launch the European Security and Defence Policy (ESDP) in 1999. Though still inadequate to meet the military and security challenges facing the EU, these improvements would not have happened without the Yugoslav crisis (Howorth, 2014: 1–24). Here was a rare example of crisis propelling policy change.

Concurrent EU crises were mostly of a political and institutional kind. A political crisis occurred in March 1996 when, in response to the British government's announcement of a link between bovine spongiform encephalopathy (BSE), commonly known as mad cow disease, and its human equivalent, Creutzfeldt–Jakob disease, the EU banned all exports of British beef. Incensed by what he saw as an overreaction by the EU, Prime Minister John Major declared that Britain would obstruct decision-making in Brussels until the ban was lifted. Major got his way at a meeting of the European Council – the 'mad cow summit' – in June 1996 (Van Middelaar, 2013: 106). As crises go, this was a minor affair and had no impact on European integration.

Equally minor was a crisis that erupted in Austria, in February 2000, when the Christian Democratic Party formed a coalition government with the far-right Freedom Party. To signal their displeasure, other governments considered suspending Austria's EU membership rights, under the terms of a provision of the recently concluded Amsterdam Treaty, but opted to impose mild sanctions on a country-by-country basis. They backed down at the end of the year when Austria threatened to hold a referendum on EU participation unless the sanctions were lifted. Aware of the extent of anger in Austria over the sanctions, and fearing that the referendum would embarrass the EU, the other governments relented (Falkner, 2001).

The Austria crisis came soon after a crisis in Brussels involving the resignation of the Commission, in March 1999. Under fire for general financial mismanagement and specific cases of corruption, the Commission resigned rather than being forced out by what would undoubtedly have been a successful vote of censure by the European Parliament (EP). The resignation crisis did not risk political paralysis in Brussels. Business continued as usual, with the old Commission acting in a caretaker capacity until a new Commission took over in November 1999. The real significance of the crisis was that it demonstrated the EP's growing assertiveness and prominence in inter-institutional relations (Judge and Earnshaw, 2002).

More treaty ratification crises

Yet the EP did not reap the reward for its victory that it most craved: a large turnout in the June 1999 elections. Indeed, the continuing decline in voter turnout was symptomatic of public disaffection with the EU, which deepened in the years ahead. Holding referendums on EU issues was particularly risky under these circumstances. Both Denmark and Sweden voted against adopting the euro, in September 2000 and September 2003 respectively (Mendez, Mendez, and Triga, 2014: 26–7). Of greater significance for the EU as a whole, in June 1992 Irish voters rejected the Nice Treaty, which included institutional reforms and arrangements for enlargement. As in the case of Denmark almost a decade earlier, the EU addressed Irish concerns in a way that allowed the government to hold a second referendum, in October 2002, which reversed the original outcome (Tondra, 2005).

The most consequential EU-related referendum results came in mid-2005, when French and Dutch voters rejected the Constitutional Treaty. Whereas the Nice Treaty was narrow in scope, the Constitutional Treaty was a highly ambitious undertaking. As the name implied, the proposed new treaty sought to emphasize the EU's constitutional nature and state-like character. Substantively, the treaty aimed to improve decision-making procedures, bolster key policy fields, strengthen the EU's ability to act internationally, and increase democratic legitimacy. Aware of deep dissatisfaction with the manner and outcome of previous rounds of treaty reform, EU leaders had preceded the Constitutional Treaty with a broadly based Constitutional Convention, held in 2002–03. Even so, the Constitutional Treaty engendered extensive opposition. Though the reasons for the French and Dutch referendum results varied, there was no disguising the fact that the EU was deeply unpopular (Laursen, 2008).

The events of mid-2005 triggered what came to be called the constitutional crisis. Loath to scrap the Constitutional Treaty entirely, EU leaders re-packaged the contents and dropped the more objectionable elements, including the word 'constitutional'. The ensuing Lisbon Treaty was signed in December 2007. In a familiar development, Irish voters rejected the Lisbon Treaty in June 2008, before approving it in a second referendum in October 2009. The French and Dutch governments were careful this time to ratify the treaty without holding referendums (Laursen, 2012).

Failure to salvage anything from the wreckage of the Constitutional Treaty would not have been disastrous for the EU, though the ensuing Lisbon Treaty undoubtedly strengthened the EU institutionally. Understood narrowly, the constitutional crisis simply concerned the fate of the Constitutional Treaty. More broadly, it was symptomatic of profound political problems facing the EU: weak legitimacy, widespread public alienation, and rising euroscepticism. These problems did not necessarily constitute a crisis, but they undermined the EU's ability to act effectively and greatly exacerbated the EU crisis later in the decade (see Chapter 1).

Many Crises, Few Opportunities

Based on the assessment in this chapter, it seems fair to say that the narrative of crisis as opportunity in the history of European integration is vastly overblown. Nor does the process of European integration seem inherently crisis-prone. Like any polity, the EU has faced exogenous and endogenous shocks. Whether such shocks rose to the level of a crisis, in the sense of threatening political or economic stability or policy paralysis, is debatable; whether they were called crises seems entirely arbitrary.

The challenge of post-war reconstruction, set in the context of the worsening Cold War, was demanding and drawn out. A specific economic crisis in 1947 helped bring about the circumstances in 1950 that precipitated the Schuman Plan. Jean Monnet, architect of the Schuman Plan, conjured up a crisis atmosphere in order to improve his chances of success. Monnet's recounting of the founding story of the ECSC, which became the conventional wisdom, stressed the contribution of crises to the development of European integration.

The outbreak of the Korean War in 1950 provided a pretext for Monnet's next integrative initiative – the EDC and later the European Political Community – and helped to reinforce the narrative of crisis as opportunity in EU history. In this case, an exogenous crisis led directly to an ambitious initiative for deeper integration, notwithstanding its unsatisfactory outcome. The collapse of the EDC may actually have averted a crisis for European integration, as implementation of the treaty would likely have proved politically impossible.

The failure of the EDC is generally described as having caused a crisis of European integration, which prompted European leaders to return to first principles and relaunch the process. However, the endogenous crisis of the EDC's collapse, as well as the later exogenous Suez crisis, had little impact on the conclusion of the Rome Treaty and the establishment of the EEC. The exogenous Saar dispute, a major irritant in France–German relations, was resolved bilaterally during the Rome Treaty negotiations.

The endogenous crises of the 1960s were major events in the history of European integration. Yet de Gaulle's veto of UK accession in 1963 and 1967 had no impact on the overall trajectory of the Community, apart from the obvious one of restricting membership to the original six countries. Nor did the empty chair crisis, the most serious constitutional crisis in the history of the EU, provide an opportunity to advance European integration.

The financial and economic crises of the 1970s, exogenous to the EC, were similar to the challenge of post-war reconstruction in that they were multi-faceted and long-lasting. They also called for a concerted European response, which came initially in the form of the EMS and later in the single market programme and the SEA. But these far-reaching initiatives were based not on opportunism, but on the perceived need to meet deep-seated policy challenges confronting western European countries. Nevertheless, the impact of the crises of the 1970s on the development of European integration was unquestionably high.

The various ratification crises of the post-Maastricht period, by definition endogenous to the EU, did not present opportunities to deepen European integration. Other endogenous crises of that era, including the EMS crisis, the 'mad cow' crisis, the Commission resignation crisis, and the Austria crisis, similarly provided little opportunity and had minimal impact on the development of European integration. Only the exogenous Yugoslav crises of the 1990s spurred steps to deepen integration in the policy fields of foreign affairs, security, and defence. Though still inadequate for the challenges that Europe faces, the CFSP and the ESDP would be far less effective had the Yugoslav crisis not happened.

Conclusions

The main theme of this book is that the multi-dimensional crisis confronting the EU since 2009 threatens the future of key policy areas and risks European disintegration. Initially, politicians, officials, journalists, and others attached the label 'crisis' to the explosion of Greek sovereign debt, to the outbreak of hostilities in Ukraine, and to the massive flow of migrants into the EU in the same way that previous generations of politicians, officials, journalists, and others attached the same label to the series of events described in this chapter. As it turned out, developments since 2009 have indeed constituted a crisis by endangering the security and stability of the EU. Yet the term 'crisis' is still used loosely. For instance, another event during the same time, the precipitous collapse of milk prices, was also called a crisis, though its consequences were hardly grave, except for the incomes of dairy farmers (Farm Europe, 2016).

Of the many events in the history of European integration before 2009 that carry the label crisis, only the empty chair crisis comes close in magnitude to the current crisis. De Gaulle's brinkmanship in 1965–66 threatened to bring the fledgling EEC to an inglorious end. The Luxembourg Compromise allowed the EEC to survive, but hardly helped the process of European integration. The lesson of the empty chair crisis is far from reassuring if applied to events in the EU today.

Calls during the post-2009 crisis for 'more Europe' have often invoked EU history to bolster the case for deeper integration. According to this line of argument, just as previous crises have helped to advance European integration, so will the current crisis eventually help to strengthen the EU. This seems like wishful thinking. The eurozone crisis is a serious endogenous crisis, and the history of endogenous crises in the EU suggests that deeper integration is not a probable outcome. The Ukraine and migration crises are serious exogenous crises, which seem to be impeding rather than impelling deeper European integration. Britain's expected departure from the EU is unlikely to spur the remaining member states to deepen European integration. History may well be a guide to the future of the EU, but not in the way that many observers casually interpret the lessons of crises past.

References

Bange, O. (2000) *The EEC Crisis of 1963: Kennedy, Macmillan, de Gaulle and Adenauer in Conflict*. Houndmills, Basingstoke: Macmillan Press.

Burgess, M. (2000) *Federalism and the European Union: The Building of Europe, 1950–2000*. Abingdon: Routledge.

Cockfield, A. (1994) *European Union: Creating the Single Market*. London: Wiley.

Duchêne, F. (1994) *Jean Monnet: The First Statesman of Interdependence*. London: Norton.

Dyson, K. and Featherstone, K. (2000) *The Road to Maastricht: Negotiating Economic and Monetary Union*. Oxford: Oxford University Press.

Endo, K. (1999) *The Presidency of the European Commission Under Jacques Delors: The Politics of Shared Leadership*. Houndmills, Basingstoke: Macmillan Press.

Falkner, G. (2001) 'The EU 14's Sanctions Against Austria: Sense *and* Nonsense', *European Union Studies Association Review*, Vol. 14, No. 1, pp. 14–15.

Farm Europe (2016) 'The Milk Crisis', 23 February, http://www.farm-europe.eu/news/the-milk-crisis-bringing-an-end-to-a-never-ending-crisis/.

Gillingham, J. (1991) *Coal, Steel and the Rebirth of Europe*. Cambridge: Cambridge University Press.

Gillingham, J. (2003) *European Integration, 1950–2003: Superstate or New Market Economy?* Cambridge: Cambridge University Press.

Hansen, P. and Jonsson, S. (2014) *Eurafrica: The Untold History of European Integration and Colonialism*. London: Bloomsbury.

Howorth, J. (2014) *Security and Defence Policy in the European Union*, 2nd edition. Houndmills, Basingstoke: Palgrave Macmillan.

James, H. (2012) *Making the European Monetary Union*. Cambridge, MA: Belknap Press.

Judge, D. and Earnshaw, D. (2002) 'The European Parliament and the Commission Crisis: A New Assertiveness?', *Governance*, Vol. 15, No. 3, pp. 345–74.

Laursen, F., (ed.) (1994) *The Ratification of the Maastricht Treaty: Issues, Debates and Future Implications*. Maastricht: European Institute of Public Policy.

Laursen, F. (ed.) (2008) *The Rise and Fall of the EU's Constitutional Treaty*. Nijhoff: Brill.

Laursen, F. (2012) 'Overview.' In F. Laursen (ed.), *The EU's Lisbon Treaty: Institutional Choices and Implementation*. Farnham: Ashgate, pp. 3–21.

Long, B. (2015) *No Easy Occupation: French Control of the German Saar, 1944–1957.* Rochester, NY: Camden House.

Ludlow, P. N. (2006) *The European Community and the Crises of the 1960s: Negotiating the Gaullist Challenge.* Abingdon: Routledge.

McNamara, K. (1998) *The Currency of Ideas: Monetary Politics in the European Union.* Ithaca, NY: Cornell University Press.

May, A. (2013) *Britain and Europe Since 1945.* Abingdon, Oxon: Routledge.

Mendez, F., Mendez, M., and Triga, V. (2014) *Referendums in the European Union: A Comparative Perspective.* Cambridge: Cambridge University Press.

Milward, A. (1984) *The Reconstruction of Western Europe, 1945–1951.* Berkeley: University of California Press.

Monnet, J. (1978) *Memoirs.* London: Collins.

Moravcsik, A. (1998) *The Choice for Europe: Social Power and State Purpose from Messina to Maastricht.* Ithaca, NY: Cornell University Press.

Mourlon-Droul, E. (2012) *A Europe Made of Money: The Emergence of the European Monetary System.* Ithaca, NY: Cornell University Press.

Palavret, J.-M., Wallace, H., and Winand, P. (eds.) (2006) *Visions, Votes and Vetoes: The Empty Chair Crisis and the Luxembourg Compromise Forty Years On.* Brussels: Peter Lang.

Parsons, C. and Matthijs, M. (2015) 'European Integration Past, Present and Future: Moving Forward Through Crisis?' In M. Matthijs and M. Blyth (eds), *The Future of the Euro.* Oxford: Oxford University Press, pp. 210–32.

Schuman, R. (1950) The Schuman Declaration, 9 May 1950 (http://europa.eu/about-eu/basic-information/symbols/europe-day/schuman-declaration/index_en.htm).

Tondra, B. (2005) 'Ireland: A Tale of Two Referenda.' In F. Laursen (ed.), *The Treaty of Nice: Actor Preferences, Bargaining and Institutional Choice.* Nijhoff: Brill, pp. 179–92.

Van Middelaar, L. (2013) *The Passage to Europe: How a Continent Became a Union.* New Haven, CT: Yale University Press.

Wessels, W. (2015) *The European Council.* London: Palgrave Macmillan.

Chapter 3

The Political Economy Context of EU Crises

BEN ROSAMOND

Introduction

This chapter considers the ways in which the current crises of the EU are nested within a series of broader crisis dynamics that together challenge the standard operating procedures of European capitalist democracies. Of course, it makes little sense to 'factor out' the EU from any analysis of the trajectory of crises in present-day Europe. But equally, it is mistaken to suggest that the EU is straightforwardly the wellspring of all crises currently facing European societies. Rather, this chapter assumes that the relationship between European integration and broader European political development is mutually constitutive, and that this has always been so. The broad argument here is that the EU needs to be understood as the product of a particular moment in the history of European democratic capitalism, and further that the EU's current tribulations can be best understood in relation to the unravelling of the political settlement in which it was born. It goes without saying that 'exogenous shocks' such as the post-2008 global financial crisis and the post-2014 migration/refugee crisis (see Chapters 4 and 6, respectively) place the EU system and its constituent polities under considerable stress and thereby give rise to new and complex forms of political conflict. In the EU's case, this cocktail has generated nothing short of an existential crisis (Zielonka, 2014; see also Chapter 17). The contribution here is to suggest that the particular ways in which those shocks and the resultant politics have developed cannot be understood without a wider appreciation of the changing dynamics of European capitalist democracy.

The argument of this chapter is that the EU is the consequence of a particular 'spatio-temporal fix' in the history of capitalist-democratic development. The EU's institutional genesis in the 1950s and its evolution through subsequent decades coincided with the era in which, for advanced industrial democracies at least, the potentially countervailing logics of allocation through the market and allocation by popular mandate were brought into temporary alignment (Streeck, 2011, 2014). The period since the 1970s has seen a gradual (and recently accelerated) decline of that post-war capitalist-democratic compromise in Europe, a process that has seen by turns 'Europe' posited as first a *solution* to declining growth rates in the face of globalization and latterly as a fundamental *source* of both economic atrophy and democratic emasculation across the member states. This way of thinking about European integration alerts us to the fact that supranational governance and national politics are not polar opposites, but intimately bound up together as components of the political economy of Europe. That they appear in the present as countervailing forces reflects the forms of contestation that have emerged in the aftermath of the global financial crisis and in the context of the refugee crisis.

It cannot be doubted that both of these crises have severely challenged the legitimacy of the EU and posed serious questions about its capacity to deliver solutions to collective action problems. But to talk about dysfunctional supranational institutions in this context is to relay only part of the story. This chapter argues that three key interacting features of the development of Europe's political economy over the past four decades – the decline of high growth rates leading to an era of so-called 'permanent austerity', the dominance of ideas prioritizing a market society over other social preferences, and the decline of political parties – form the backdrop to the EU's current crises. These factors, considered individually and collectively, represent fundamental challenges to the embedded institutional order that temporarily facilitated the consolidation and expansion of capitalist democracy in Europe after World War II. The point is not necessarily that these pressures will precipitate a disintegration of the EU, but rather that they accelerate the corrosion of the broad regime of political economy within which European integration has been embedded.

The European Capitalist-Democratic Compact

The origins of the EU are well known. As the Schuman Declaration of May 1950 made clear, market integration was posited as a solution to the recurring Franco-German security dilemma. A commercial logic of market making was seen as the best means to secure perpetual peace on the troubled continent. At the same time, as the meticulous work of Alan Milward has made clear, supranational institution-building and intensified cooperation served the interests of the governments of the Six. While prevailing economic interests mattered, the key for Milward and his colleagues lay more in a recognition that post-war European governments faced a fundamental existential problem: how to re-establish themselves as autonomous functioning units in the context of post-war recovery and increasing demands from domestic publics. Integration, through the sharing of some sovereign functions, became the means by which the 'European rescue of the nation-state' (Milward, 1992) was accomplished.

While this line of argument has often been enlisted as support for an intergovernmentalist reading of the EU's founding moment of institutional design, it also needs to be placed within the broader context of the reconstruction of democratic capitalism after World War II. The predicament of European state elites in this period was one of ambiguous legitimacy. As Milward and Sørensen note:

> [T]he Great Depression of 1929–32 had shattered the frail political consensus in many [western European states], especially by the fall in agricultural incomes relative to those elsewhere. The claims of ideologies and competing political systems outside their borders on the allegiance of their citizens had in many cases weakened the capacity to rule effectively. Invasion, defeat and occupation left many of their governments eventually clinging in exile to the assertion of a dubious legitimacy. (1993: 5)

Market making through European integration took its particular (and historically peculiar) institutional form, and much has been written about the important path-dependent effects of that original institutional design (Pierson, 1996). The upshot is that European states have been forced to work within an institutional/decision-making template that was designed for geopolitical conditions that have long ceased to be relevant. But this is only part of the story, albeit an important part.

The direct ancestors of the modern EU – the European Coal and Steel Community (ECSC) of 1951 and the European Economic Community (EEC) of 1957 – should be understood within the context of the broader project of reconstruction of capitalist democracies after 1945. Two further developments need to be mentioned. First, the European Recovery Program (Marshall Plan) played, between 1948 and 1952, a vital role in re-establishing the industrial economies of western Europe as open and (crucially) non-communist (Hogan, 1987). Indeed, the Marshall Plan is sometimes seen as critical to the normalization of the 'mixed economy' in the region (De Long and Eichengreen, 1991). Second, the Bretton Woods conference of 1944 established a template for the post-war (non-communist) global economic order that foresaw a managed expansion of international trade liberalization within the context of a fixed exchange rate regime. The preference of its architects to limit the degree of international capital mobility within the new global system is captured by Ruggie's well-known characterization of the Bretton Woods regime as 'embedded liberalism' (Ruggie, 1982). To allow unlimited capital mobility at the same time as fixed exchange rates would have severely limited the scope for domestic policy autonomy among participating countries – the so-called 'impossible trinity' as theorised by later economists (Fleming, 1962; Mundell, 1963). Ruggie's point is that the liberal ambition of the Bretton Woods monetary order was embedded within (indeed subordinated to) domestically negotiated social purposes. In short, there was – for capitalist liberal democracies – a trade-off between an openness to the international economy on the one hand and a capacity to follow domestically oriented policy programmes on the other. The practical upshot, given the dominant tendencies in policy thinking at the time, was the facilitation of variations of the Keynesian Welfare State as the dominant mode of socio-economic management within the capitalist world.

This did not mean that all west European economies were governed identically. Significant differences remained in terms of inter alia industrial and market organization (Coates, 2000; Hall and Soskice, 2001), welfare regimes (Esping-Andersen, 1990), party system types (Lipset and Rokkan, 1967; Sartori, 1976), and models of democracy (Lijphart, 2012). Nevertheless, it is important to think about these sources of variation within the overall patterning described above. In short, the creation of institutionalized European integration starting in the 1950s was undertaken in the context of the globally embedded liberal compromise (Bugaric, 2013). The latter, in turn, reflected and augmented the reconstruction of representative forms of government that were fit for purpose in societies characterized by domestic pluralism on the one hand and a balance of social forces favouring the tempering of market power on the other. In this interpretation, European integration, starting with the creation of the ECSC in 1951, was a local adjunct to the broader embedded liberal settlement. It initiated a set of institutionalized market making solutions to defining the European collective action problem of the time (the Franco-German security dilemma), but did not (in its initiation phase at least) threaten to disturb the capacity of member states to follow domestically appropriate macroeconomic strategies. It is quite possible to argue that the founding Treaties set in motion an isomorphic logic of convergence that came to be realized at a later point in the development of the Communities (resulting, essentially, in the EU becoming an enactment of neoliberalism). Nor should we underestimate the contestations between different models of political economy that informed debates about the design and scope of European integration in the 1950s (Joerges, 2010; Ames, 2004; Rosamond, 2015). The point to make is simply that the initiation of European integration was, at this time, consistent with the post-war capitalist-democratic experiment rather than obviously corrosive of it.

Wolfgang Streeck (2011, 2014) has identified the three decades following World War II as a period in which the fragile articulation of democracy and capitalism was most successfully delivered. Indeed:

Democratic capitalism was fully established only after the Second World War and then only in the 'Western' parts of the world, North America and Western Europe. There it functioned extraordinarily well for the next two decades—so well, in fact, that this period of uninterrupted economic growth still dominates our ideas and expectations of what modern capitalism is, or could and should be. This is in spite of the fact that, in the light of the turbulence that followed, the quarter century immediately after the war should be recognizable as truly exceptional. Indeed, I suggest that it is not the *trente glorieuses* but the series of crises which followed that represents the normal condition of democratic capitalism: a condition ruled by an endemic conflict between capitalist markets and democratic politics, which forcefully reasserted itself when high economic growth came to an end in the 1970s. (Streeck, 2011: 5–6)

Streeck's point is that democracy and capitalism are best seen as two contradictory modes of allocation (the former delivered through the mobilization of collective choices in the polity and the latter supplied through the operation of market forces in the economy). The articulation of democracy to capitalism, while treated in much intellectual and policy discourse as natural, requires either the logic of one to be subordinated to the other or for a compromise between the competing imperatives to be fashioned. The post-war settlement thus described depended, in large part, upon the partial subordination of markets to democracy – or at least to democracy in its national liberal democratic form. This meant not only that national governments could re-emerge as objects of affective loyalty from their citizenries, but also that they were capable of following macroeconomic pathways that emerged from the balance of domestic forces rather than the imperatives of internationally mobile finance capital.

As Streeck makes clear, the accomplishment of this democratic compromise was fleeting and potentially self-contradictory from the start, but it can certainly be read as what Jessop (2000) and others have called a national 'spatio-temporal fix', reflecting a particular balance of social forces, forms of state, dominant ideas, and modes of capital accumulation. The contours of this spatio-temporal fix are quite familiar, involving as they did some combination of a broadly Fordist production regime with national versions of the Keynesian Welfare State. The period between 1950 and 1973 is typically characterized as a 'golden age' of unusually rapid growth in which west European economies saw real gross domestic product (GDP) grow at an average annual rate of some 4.6 per cent (Crafts, 1995: 429) – almost double the average annual rate for the same countries across the full century beginning in 1890. The 'golden age' was a period of 'catch-up' growth, which saw a convergence between the economic performance of west European economies and the USA. The institutional sources of this are well established and much discussed. As Barry Eichengreen puts it, 'Catch-up was facilitated by solidaristic trade unions, cohesive employers' associations, and growth-minded governments working together to mobilize savings, finance investment, and stabilize wages at levels consistent with full employment' (Eichengreen, 2006: 3).

It is worth adding that this governing consensus was facilitated by the broad commitment to the mixed economy that came to be favoured by the dominant political parties of the centre-right and centre-left (Shonfield, 1965; Yergin and Stanislaw, 1998). That such parties dominated the electoral politics of European democracies in the 'golden age' was not simply a matter of ideological convergence. This feature also emerged from both the particular organizational character of these parties, which came to act as crucial mediators between the imperatives of government and the demands of society, and the broader sociological 'stabilization' of west European electorates (Bartolini and Mair, 1990; von Beyme, 1985; Lipset and Rokkan, 1967; Mair, 2013). Moreover, it is often noted that the formal institutions of European integration – from which the modern EU claims direct ancestry – were the creations of politicians from the christian democratic (centre-right) and social democratic (centre-left) party families (Bond, Smith, and Wallace, 1996). Indeed, there is also evidence that intra-European trade liberalization, initiated with the creation of the European Payments Union (an offshoot of the Marshall Plan) in 1950 and facilitated by the creation of both the EEC in 1957 and the European Free Trade Association in 1960, was a major stimulus to European growth during this period (Boltho and Eichengreen, 2008).

In short, the post-war European capitalist-democratic compact was forged within a period of exceptional economic growth. This, in turn, was nurtured through a serendipitous combination of (relative) domestic macroeconomic autonomy on the one hand and a gradual opening of European economies – a process sponsored in part by the emergence of the European Communities – on the other. A broad political consensus for the embedding of markets within broader social purposes was negotiated by strong centrist political parties (acting as intermediaries between society and government) and reflected a wider ideational climate across European societies. This should not be read as an idealization of a particular period in recent European political history, but rather as an illustration of the delicacy, contingency, and temporal specificity of the post-war capitalist-democratic compromise in Europe.

The Compact Unravelled: Three Dilemmas and Three Processes

The remainder of the chapter is dedicated to the claim that the unravelling of the foundations of this spatio-temporal fix is central to understanding the current crisis of the EU. Of course, this does not exclude the EU itself from blame, and a fuller discussion would incorporate the analyses found in other chapters of this book.

European integration emerged from a series of institutional choices that, in turn, reflected security, economic, and policy dilemmas specific to European states and societies in the aftermath of World War II. Those institutional choices and resultant policy trajectories inevitably left a series of unresolved dilemmas that have been ever present in the subsequent history of the EU. These dilemmas include the constant tension between the goal of delivering an EU-wide market order versus the desire to ensure social solidarity; the tension between the development of a legal-constitutional order versus the need to secure appropriate channels for democratic authorization of policy decisions; and the tension between a developing cosmopolitan social order characterized by free movement on the one hand and ongoing national communitarian impulses on the other. The three dilemmas are illustrated in Figure 3.1.

The three dilemmas have not been initiated by the current period of crisis. Rather the current crisis of the EU is better read as a moment in

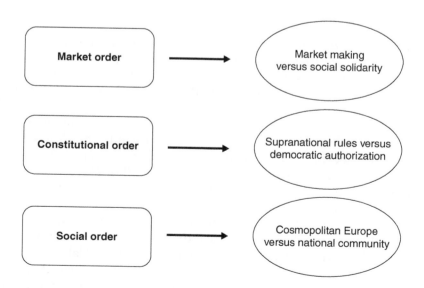

Figure 3.1 *Three ongoing dilemmas of European integration*

which we have seen their radical intensification. So, for example, the first dilemma is most visible in the management of the euro crisis, the treatment of southern debtor states by the Troika (the European Commission, the European Central Bank, and the International Monetary Fund), and the tightening of fiscal rules across the eurozone, while the refugee crisis has most obviously deepened cleavages around the third dilemma. Meanwhile, the various disintegrative impulses within the EU, of which the Brexit referendum of 2016 (see Chapter 5) is perhaps the most spectacular symptom, cut across all three dilemmas.

That the politics of the EU's crisis is predominantly organized through the prism of these ongoing dilemmas is not in dispute. But exogenous shocks, such as the global financial crisis after 2008 and the rapid surge in refugee numbers during 2015, do not in and of themselves explain why, a decade and a half into the twenty-first century, the politics of European integration has come to be organized around the deepening of the three dilemmas. The argument here is that a full understanding of this politics needs to pay heed to three key contextual processes that have contributed to the dissolution of the post-war capitalist-democratic compact in Europe. The three processes are first, the end of growth that has given way to a period of what some scholars have characterized as 'permanent austerity'; second, key ideational shifts that have moved the European governing consensus towards solutions that prioritize the market over other social goals; and third, the decline of political parties as key agents of mediation between government and society.

From growth to permanent austerity

The demise of the 'golden age' of growth in European capitalist democracies is usually associated with the onset of the first oil crisis in 1973. Meanwhile the decision by the Nixon administration in 1971 to end the convertibility of the US dollar to gold effectively brought the Bretton Woods system of fixed exchange rates to an end. The oil shock induced a worldwide recession, in the aftermath of which growth rates in Europe (and across advanced democracies) stabilized at significantly lower rates. The two decades after 1973 saw average annual growth rates in European democracies fall to around 2 per cent (Crafts, 1995). The demise of the Bretton Woods compact was in part a response to the re-emergence of forms of mobile international capital during the 1960s (Garber, 1993), but also ushered in an era from the mid-1970s in which international capital flows were subject to significantly less domestic regulation. This is often taken as the critical juncture from which emerged late-twentieth-century globalization. The Nixon shock is also often associated with the injection of inflationary pressures into Western economies, giving rise to the toxic mix of low growth and inflation commonly known as 'stagflation' (Blinder, 1979). At the same time, unemployment rates in Europe were rising (Blanchard and Wolfers, 2001), driven primarily by the secular decline in manufacturing industry.

What this meant in policy terms from the 1970s was a severe challenge to the embedded liberal compromise. For one thing, the re-emergence of capital mobility in the context of floating exchange rates made it harder for countries to engage in the management of aggregate demand through Keynesian means while supporting programmes of domestic redistribution through the welfare state. Declining growth rates and rising unemployment also meant that government revenues (primarily from direct taxation) contracted. As Pierson (2001a, 2001b) notes, declining GDP growth and post-industrial transition coincided from the 1970s with the maturation of government fiscal commitments, as rising numbers of retirees left the workforce and started drawing on the largesse of the welfare state. Meanwhile, declining birth rates have ever since meant that dependency ratios (the age–population ratio of those not in the labour force to those typically in the labour force) have increased in European democracies. All else being equal, rising dependency ratios put increased fiscal pressure on those in the labour force, who in effect need to finance the welfare needs of those (the young and the old) not in the labour force. Pierson has suggested that these conditions have set in motion an age of permanent austerity in Western democracies. The 'expansionary fiscal regime' of the golden age has given way to an 'austerity fiscal regime' in the present (Pierson, 2001b). In Pierson's discussion, 'austerity' is not used to describe a particular preference for policies that drastically reduce public expenditure (although that is certainly a possibility – see Blyth, 2013). Rather it signals a broader set of imperatives that force governments to think long and hard about the sustainability of the taxation–welfare mix that had served them well from the 1950s through to the 1970s.

Writing several years before the onset of the global financial crisis, Pierson foresaw a particular political dilemma emerging out of the condition of 'austerity': the robust popularity of the welfare state would create electoral dilemmas for any governing parties that sought to address the condition of austerity by scaling back on the types of welfare spending (for example, public pensions) that key median voters had come to expect as an entitlement. Any attempt to solve the problem by raising levels of personal taxation to generate revenues would provoke another form of societal backlash in the form of anti-taxation movements. The overall point is that the spatio-temporal fix of post-war European democratic capitalism was also rooted in a particular kind of legitimacy bargain (with, of course, multiple national variants) whereby the consolidation of the fiscal state was premised on the delivery of a welfare regime that serviced societal demands. It was also a fiscal–welfare bargain that offered a near perfect fit with the nation state (Cameron, 2008), which, as we have seen, was itself able to deliver on this legitimacy bargain in the context of strong growth and increasing volumes of external trade with only modest or highly regulated levels of capital mobility.

The onset of this new age of austerity coincided with the relaunch of European integration and, in particular, the effort from the mid-1980s to accelerate progress towards the goal of a single market. In this light, the ambitions of the Cecchini Report (Cecchini, Catinat, and Jacquemin, 1988) to avoid the costs of 'non-Europe' can be reinterpreted as a collective attempt to offset the effects of 'permanent austerity' by generating dynamic growth and aggregate welfare effects through a radical spurt of cross-border economic integration within the European Communities. In big picture terms, the purposive acceleration of integration represented by both the Single European Act and the Maastricht Treaty set up a European version of the 'trilemma' described by Dani Rodrik (2011). According to Rodrik's trilemma – national sovereignty, international economic integration, and democracy – only two can be enjoyed simultaneously. The forms of political contestation that have grown up around the deepening of economic integration and the parallel emergence of a hybrid multi-level governance regime are well known (Hooghe and Marks, 1999) and inevitably these have helped to shape the particular form taken by the recent crisis politics of the EU. But it is important to remember also the longer-standing domestic politics of permanent austerity that is also constitutive of EU crisis politics in the contemporary period.

If the politics of permanent austerity (as described by Pierson, 2001a and 2001b) gather around the unravelling of domestic tax–welfare compacts, but in the context of an open market EU order beset by exogenous crisis, they accentuate each of the three ongoing dilemmas of European integration. Solidarism takes the form of welfare nationalism, which typically manifests itself in resistance to the civic cosmopolitan aspects of the EU's free movement regime – itself an adjunct of the single market. Thus opposition to intra-EU migrants also becomes a key stress test for the integrity of the single market project itself and support for democracy often becomes a defence of national sovereignty against the encroachment of EU norms, as opposed to a Habermasian attempt to create pan-European sites of constitutionalized democratic governance (see Habermas, 2012). Indeed, research has suggested that support for the core principles of democracy may be one of the public opinion casualties of the global financial crisis (Armingeon and Guthmann, 2014). This is enhanced by what some see as an emergent pan-European cleavage, dividing so-called 'cosmopolitan' and 'backwater' regions within national polities (Jennings and Stoker, 2016), a factor that seems to have played a significant role in the outcome of the Brexit referendum of 2016. So while the rise of nativist political forces across Europe can indeed be read as a societal reaction to the disembedded European market order (Polyakova, 2015), it must also be understood as arising out of the stressed national politics of welfare regimes.

The prioritization of market society

Much ink has been spilled on the concept of neoliberalism, its ubiquity across the capitalist-democratic world, its application to the EU, and its overall utility as an analytical concept. It is commonplace to associate the period since the 1970s with the rise of neoliberal ideas (Harvey, 2007; Peck, 2010). Neoliberalism – the revival and popularization of the notion that the self-regulating market provides the most effective mechanism of resource allocation and the most morally just form of social order – has been regarded as both pervasive and resilient in contemporary Europe (Schmidt and Thatcher, 2013). The standard discussion of neoliberalism tends to focus on its ideational, institutional, and policy aspects. The literature on policy-making after the 'golden age' tends to associate the rise of neoliberalism with a particular diagnosis of the problem of permanent austerity: 'almost everywhere, governments have – albeit in a piecemeal stop-and-go fashion – taken on the task of liberalizing markets' (Schäfer, 2013: 172). Neoliberal restructuring amounts to rather more than the dominance of a series of policy preferences for market solutions. It also involves a fundamental redrawing of the contract between governments and citizens (Forrest and Hirayama, 2015) and the recalibration of the state as an entity tasked with maximizing competitiveness in terms that favour the market over other social goals (Cerny, 1997; Streeck, 2015). The simple point to make here is that the neoliberal turn has seen the dissolution of the form of state – the Keynesian Welfare State – that presided over the post-war European capitalist-democratic compact.

It is also important to note that this transformation in state form associated with neoliberalism was not merely accomplished at the domestic level. The displacement of the Keynesian Welfare State by the 'competition' or 'consolidation' state was also in part a scalar shift, involving a significant degree of internationalization of state functions. Europe, perhaps more than anywhere, was the most explicit site of this changed form of the state and is captured very effectively by Majone's description of the EU as a 'regulatory state' (Majone, 1994). In ideal typical form, the regulatory state's rationale is the supply of a pareto-efficient market order. Moreover, in its supranational form, its legitimacy rests upon the capacity to deliver a functioning market order. This is important because advocates of the supranational regulatory state are also typically sceptical about the utility of democratic contestation for the achievement of efficient markets (see, for example, Majone, 1996).

Indeed, the rise of neoliberalism as the defining common sense of policy-making in advanced capitalist democracies is rooted in a series of intellectual shifts that were being worked through more or less simultaneously with the ending of the 'golden age' of growth in the 1970s. This new thinking presented markets as both technically efficient and normatively appropriate. This advocacy of the market was articulated as a critique of both the expansive tendencies of big government and the allocation of social purposes through democratic means. This work undertaken some four decades ago also laid important foundations for the general drift towards the pursuit of austerity policies in the context of the ongoing euro crisis (Blyth, 2013; Matthijs and Blyth, 2015).

The early 1970s, the time of slowing growth rates and the oil crisis, was a period in which fears for the 'governability' of capitalist democracies were openly canvassed. Samuel Brittan (1975) spoke for many when he identified what he saw as an inherent contradiction of democracy: the incompatibility of the redistributive capacity of government and the sheer scale of the societal demands that were placed upon government. Put more crudely, government overload was being caused by an 'excess' of democracy (Crozier, Huntington, and Watanuki, 1975). The solution to this dilemma (economic crisis meets ungovernability) was not simply posited in terms of the return to self-regulating markets. It was also associated with transferring authority over the market away from majoritarian (i.e. democratic) institutions. The justification for this process, often labelled 'depoliticization' (Burnham, 2014), was developed within the professional economics literature of the time. For example, in developing the 'time inconsistency thesis', Kydland and Prescott (1977) argued that governments manipulate the business cycle to fit the electoral cycle. Policy commitments made at a point in time (T_1) are bound to lack credibility because the routine demands of electoral politics will induce policy changes at T_2. These policy changes, which are seen as both sources of over-expenditure and departures from sound economic reasoning, are explained by the short-term need to secure electoral advantage. Kydland and Prescott insisted that the solution to this problem was the creation of fixed (potentially constitutionalized) macroeconomic rules and/or the delegation of key aspects of macroeconomic policy to new non-majoritarian institutions such as independent central banks.

This line of thinking has been acknowledged as a key influence by European advocates of the supranational regulatory state (Majone, 1996). Writing more than a decade later, and in a paper that has since become a major influence on pro-austerity politicians and policy officials (Blyth, 2013), Alesina and Tabellini (1990) sought to demonstrate that governments normally (indeed rationally) display a deficit bias that follows logically from the imperatives of electoral competition. In the context of monetary integration, this thesis is consistent with the creation of a central bank (the ECB) that behaves not as a monetary sovereign but as the enforcer of tight fiscal rules (Alesina and Grilli, 1994).

In short, the advocacy of market solutions and the subordination of other social purposes to the logic of the self-regulating market were theorised in ways that: (1) contributed to the institutional dismantling of the post-war capitalist-democratic compact in Europe; and (2) ultimately accentuated the first of the three ongoing dilemmas of European integration mentioned above. In Streeck's terms, one of the key achievements of the rise of neoliberal ideas was to challenge the association between markets and democracy that had been so critical to the post-war compact. But this intellectual shift also endorsed one of the inbuilt features of the integration process – the asymmetry between the logic of market making on the one hand and the logic of market correction on the other (Scharpf, 2010). Neoliberals also, by implication, endorsed the EU's democratic deficit as a non-problem shortly before the collapse of the so-called 'permissive consensus' made it a de facto problem (Hooghe and Marks, 2009; see also Hix, 2008). The key point to note once again is that the politics of the present crisis has been played out under the influence of longer-standing features of European political development that, while carrying implications for the EU, are not endogenous to the EU. The general dilemma associated with the separation of markets and democracy has, in the EU's case, become linked to the multi-level character of the EU polity. In the eurozone crisis, the resolute pursuit of a European-level rule-bound monetary order has come into tension with democratic impulses that have only found space for expression at the national level, within the member states.

Political parties and the hollowing of democracy

The post-war capitalist-democratic compact in Europe was, as noted earlier, endorsed and underwritten by political parties of the centre-left and centre-right. These, in turn, were also the architects of European integration in its post-war form. While the two decades following the end of the World War II saw a key organizational transformation of such parties from mass parties (that represented identifiable segments of society) to 'catch-all' parties (that sought to capture the median voter) (Kirchheimer, 1966), their electoral performance remained robust through much of the period of the 'golden age'. The electoral decline of such parties, particularly social democratic parties, has been marked since the 1970s. For example, Philippe Marlière (2010) calculates that northern European social democratic parties have lost roughly 20 per cent of their voters since the 1960s.

The modern social scientific understanding of political parties was forged by scholars working in the period defined by the post-war capitalist-democratic compact. The government of complex industrial democracies was seemingly inconceivable without the strong role played by parties as mediators between the imperatives of government and the demands emerging from society. Parties were not only aggregators of diverse societal interests; they also sought to reconcile contradictions between – for example – inherited constraints on government expenditure and demands for expansive social programmes. In ideal typical terms, parties of this type – because of their central mediating function – were able to reconcile the necessity for efficient and technically competent government with the need for democratic authorization and legitimacy (Mair, 2013; Sartori, 1976; Schattschneider, 1942). This permutation of party functions was, of course, especially well suited to the era of the Keynesian Welfare State and 'embedded liberalism'. Parties were crucial both to the aggregation of societal preferences in ways that allowed clear social purposes to be expressed and to the project of gradual and limited international economic opening.

Peter Mair (2013), writing in the midst of the eurozone crisis, concluded that the age of party government had passed and that the absence of those key mediators between representative and responsible government had serious implications for the viability of democratic politics in Europe. A good deal of Mair's analysis followed through on the implications of his earlier seminal work on the changing organization form of the party – in particular, the rise of the 'cartel party' (Katz and Mair, 1995). According to this argument, the cartel party represents the full transformation of the party into an election-winning machine. Prompted in part by the erosion of their traditional social bases, parties have moved away from the pretence that they could or should be the avatars of particular social groups or classes. Instead parties tend to internalize the guiding rationality of the state. Given the transformations of the state outlined in the previous section, parties become agents for a governing rationale that presumes the technical superiority and normative propriety of market solutions. This is also a recipe for policy convergence among cartel parties. Societal impulses remain, but their expression and aggregation is for the most part no longer the business of centre-right and centre-left parties. The resultant void is often filled by populist movements – of all political complexions.

The rise of populism and nativism as forces within recent European history is beyond the scope of this chapter (see Berezin, 2009, 2013), but, as Douglas Webber shows in Chapter 17, it is clearly a key feature of the contemporary political crisis in Europe. For example, Gifford

(2006) maintains that populist politics undermines the capacity of elites to deliver stable leadership on European integration. If, in turn, the delivery of positive sum EU solutions is a way for elites to insulate their societies from domestic populist impulses, then it follows that governing elites are caught in a vicious circle whereby the problem that is being addressed becomes a significant constraint on solving the problem.

Once again, there is a strong case for looking beyond the EU context when trying to understand the factors that influence the configuration and conduct of crisis politics. Indeed, there is no great evidence of euroscepticism being directly boosted by the global financial crisis (Serricchio, Tsakatika, and Quaglia, 2012). Rather, Serricchio et al's research confirms an earlier finding that the links between economic factors and euroscepticism are relatively weak (Eichenberg and Dalton, 2007). This implies that the rise of euroscepticism is not simply explained by the onset of more precarious economic circumstances. Popular opposition to European integration is associated with economic crisis, but it is hard to sustain the argument that the latter simply causes the former. Recent research suggests that deepening inequality in European societies opens up a cleavage along educational lines, where lower levels of education become a predictor of opposition to the EU (Hakhverdian et al., 2013; Kuhn et al., 2016) – a finding that tallies with studies of European publics that have shown strong positive associations between levels of education and favourable attitudes towards immigration (Hainmueller and Hiscox, 2007). These findings point to significant effects on the politics of European integration, but they leave open the possibility that anti-EU sentiment could be a side effect of a trend associated with the demise of the fragile capitalist-democratic compact.

Conclusions

The EU was built by a generation of post-war centrists at a time when particular party families held sway in most European democracies. As set out by Mair (2013), this was an age of party government that managed to contain the contradictory imperatives of representative and responsible government. Meanwhile the period defined by the end of World War II and the end of the golden age of European growth in the 1970s turns out to have been an exceptional (i.e. not normal) period in the lifetime of capitalist democracies (Streeck, 2014), a period in which the pursuit of economic growth was compatible with both the prioritization of domestic social purpose and modest advances in supranational governance. Put another way, the post-war capitalist-democratic compact allowed for and underwrote a permissive consensus version of European integration.

The broad thrust of the argument presented here has had two components. The first stresses that the politics of crisis is and will continue to be organized around three unresolved dilemmas of European integration. The second part of the argument is that the amplification of these dilemmas can be traced to the consequences of three long-standing and interacting trends within capitalist democracies in Europe: the onset of 'permanent austerity', the normalization of market-based policy solutions, and the hollowing out of democracy via the decline of political parties. Together, these three features conspire to produce something analogous to what Crouch (2004) calls post-democracy – a condition describing the hollowing out of democratic procedures despite their formal survival (see also Bermeo, 2016; Sedelmeier, 2014).

Modern professional social science (including seminal studies of European integration) emerged at the point when the inherently contradictory logics of markets and democracy were in an unusual period of alignment – what has been referred to here as the post-war capitalist-democratic compact. The unravelling of that compact has been going on for at least four decades and raises all manner of legitimacy dilemmas (especially in times of chronic crisis), not just for domestic elites, but also for the broader project of supranational integration.

References

Alesina, A. and Tabellini, G. (1990) 'A Positive Theory of Fiscal Deficits and Government Debt', *Review of Economic Studies*, Vol. 57, No. 3, pp. 403–14.

Alesina, A. and Grilli, V. (1994) 'The European Central Bank: Reshaping Monetary Politics in Europe.' In T. Persson and G. Tabellini (eds), *Monetary and Fiscal Policy*, Vol. 1. Cambridge, MA: MIT Press, pp. 247–78.

Armingeon, K. and Guthmann, K. (2014) 'Democracy in crisis? The declining support for national democracy in European countries, 2007–2011', *European Journal of Political Research*, Vol. 53, No. 3, pp. 423–42.

Bartolini, S. and Mair, P. (1990) *Identity, Competition and Electoral Availability: The Stabilisation of European Electorates 1885–1985*. Cambridge: Cambridge University Press.

Berezin, M. (2009) *Illiberal Politics in Neoliberal Times: Cultures, Security and Politics in a New Europe*. Cambridge: Cambridge University Press.

Berezin, M. (2013) 'The Normalization of the Right in Post-Security Europe.' In A. Schäfer and W. Streeck (eds), *Politics in the Age of Austerity*. Cambridge: Polity Press, pp. 239–61.

Bermeo, N. (2016) 'On Democratic Backsliding', *Journal of Democracy*, Vol. 27, No. 1, pp. 5–19.

Beyme, K. von (1985) *Political Parties in Western Democracies*. Aldershot: Gower.

Blanchard, O. and Wolfers, J. (2001) 'The Role of Shocks and Institutions in the Rise of European Unemployment: The Aggregate Evidence', *The Economic Journal*, Vol. 110, No. 462, pp. 1–33.

Blinder, A. (1979) *Economic Policy and the Great Stagflation*. New York: Academic Press.

Blyth, M. (2013) *Austerity: The History of a Dangerous Idea*. Oxford: Oxford University Press.

Boltho, A. and Eichengreen, B. (2008) 'The economic impact of European integration', Centre for Economic Policy Research Discussion paper, No. 6820.

Bond, M., Smith, J., and Wallace, W. (eds) (1996) *Eminent Europeans: personalities who shaped contemporary Europe*. London: Greycoat Press.

Brittan, S. (1975) 'The Economic Contradictons of Democracy', *British Journal of Political Science*, Vol. 5, No. 2, pp. 129–59.

Bugaric, B. (2013) 'Europe Against the Left? On Legal Limits to Progressive Politics', LSE 'Europe in Question' Discussion Paper Series, LEQS Paper No. 61/2013, http://www.lse.ac.uk/europeanInstitute/LEQS%20Discussion%20Paper%20Series/LEQSPaper61.pdf.

Burnham, P. (2014) 'Depoliticisation: Economic Crisis and Political Management', *Policy and Politics*, Vol. 42, No. 2, pp. 189–206.

Cameron, A. (2008) 'Crisis, What Crisis? Displacing the Spatial Imaginary of the Fiscal State', *Geoforum*, Vol. 39, No. 3, pp. 1145–54.

Cecchini, P., Catinat, M., and Jacquemin, A. (1988) *The European Challenge 1992: The Benefits of a Single Market*. Aldershot: Wildwood House.

Cerny, P. G. (1997) 'Paradoxes of the Competition State: The Dynamics of Political Globalization', *Government and Opposition*, Vol. 32, No. 2, pp. 251–74.

Coates, D. (2000) *Models of Capitalism: Growth and Stagnation in the Modern Era*. Cambridge: Polity Press.

Crafts, N. F. R. (1995) 'The Golden Age of Economic Growth in Eastern Europe, 1950–1973', *Economic History Review*, Vol. 48, No. 3, pp. 429–47.

Crouch, C. (2004) *Post-Democracy*. Cambridge: Polity Press.

Crozier, M., Huntington, S. P., and Watanuki, J. (1975) *The Crisis of Democracy. Report on the Governability of Democracies to the Trilateral Commission*. New York: New York University Press.

De Long, J. B. and Eichengreen, B. (1991) 'The Marshall Plan: History's Most Successful Structural Adjustment Program', NBER Working Paper, No. 3899.

Eichenberg, R. C. and Dalton, R. J. (2007) 'Post-Maastricht Blues: The Transformation of Citizen Support for European Integration, 1973–2004', *Acta Politica*, Vol. 42, No. 2, pp. 128–52.

Eichengreen, B. (2006) *The European Economy Since 1945*. Princeton: Princeton University Press.

Esping-Andersen, G. (1990) *The Three Worlds of Welfare Capitalism*. Princeton: Princeton University Press.

Fleming, J. M. (1962) 'Domestic Financial Policies under Fixed and Floating Exchange Rates', IMF Staff Papers, No. 9, pp. 369–79.

Forrest, R. and Hirayama, Y. (2015) 'The Financialisation of the Social Project: Embedded Liberalism, Neoliberalism and Home Ownership', *Urban Studies*, Vol. 52, No. 2, pp. 233–44.

Froio, C. and Little, C. (2016) 'Responsible Government and Representation during the Eurocrisis.' In F. Müller-Rommel and F. Casal Bértoa (eds), *Party Politics and Democracy in Europe: Essays in Honour of Peter Mair*. Abingdon: Routledge, pp. 242–60.

Garber, P. M. (1993) 'The Collapse of the Bretton Woods Fixed Exchange Rate System.' In M. Bordo and B. Eichengreen (eds), *A Retrospective on the Bretton Woods System: Lessons for International Monetary Reform*. Chicago: University of Chicago Press, pp. 461–94.

Gifford, C. (2006) 'The Rise of Post-Imperial Populism: The Case of Right-Wing Euroscepticism in Britain', *European Journal of Political Research*, Vol. 45, No. 5, pp. 851–69.

Habermas, J. (2012) *The Crisis of the European Union. A Response*. Cambridge: Polity Press.

Hainmueller, J. and Hiscox, M. J. (2007) 'Educated Preferences: Explaining Attitudes Toward Immigration in Europe', *International Organization*, Vol. 61, No. 2, pp. 399–442.

Hakhverdian, A., van Elsas, E., van der Brug, W., and Kuhn, T. (2013) 'Euroscepticism and Education: A Longitudinal Study of 12 EU Member States, 1973–2010', *European Union Politics*, Vol. 14, No. 4, pp. 522–41.

Hall, P. A. and Soskice, D. (eds) (2001) *Varieties of Capitalism. The Institutional Foundations of Comparative Advantage*. Oxford: Oxford University Press

Harvey, D. (2007) *A Brief History of Neoliberalism*. Oxford: Oxford University Press.

Hix, S. (2008) *What's Wrong With the European Union and How to Fix It*. Cambridge: Polity Press.

Hogan, M. J. (1987) *The Marshall Plan: America, Britain and the Reconstruction of Western Europe, 1947–1952*. Cambridge: Cambridge University Press.

Hooghe, L. and Marks, G. (1999) 'The Making of a Polity: The Struggle over European Integration.' In H. Kitschelt, P. Lange, G. Marks, and J. D. Stephens (eds), *Continuity and Change in Contemporary Capitalism*. Cambridge: Cambridge University Press, pp. 70–97.

Hooghe, L. and Marks, G. (2009) 'A Postfunctionalist Theory of European Integration: From Permissive Consensus to Constraining Dissensus', *British Journal of Political Science*, Vol. 39, No. 1, pp. 1–23.

Jennings, W. and Stoker, G. (2016) 'The Bifurcation of Politics: Two Englands', *Political Quarterly*, Published online, 17 March, DOI: 10.1111/1467-923X.12228.

Jessop, B. (2000) 'The Crisis of the National Spatio-Temporal Fix and the Tendential Ecological Dominance of Globalizing Capitalism', *International Journal of Urban and Regional Research*, Vol. 24, No. 2, pp. 323–60.

Joerges, C. (2010) '*Rechtsstaat* and Social Europe: How a Classical Tension Resurfaces in the European Integration Process', *Comparative Sociology*, Vol. 9, No. 1, pp. 65–85.

Katz, R. and Mair, P. (1995) 'Changing Models of Party Organization and Party Democracy: The Emergence of the Cartel Party', *Party Politics*, Vol. 1, No. 1, pp. 5–28.

Kirchheimer, O. (1966) 'The Transformation of Western European Party Systems.' In J. Lapalombara and M. Weiner (eds), *Political Parties and Political Development*. Princeton: Princeton University Press, pp. 177–200.

Kuhn, T., van Elsas, E., Hakhverdian, A., and van der Brug, W. (2016) 'An Ever Wider Gap in an Ever Closer Union: Rising Inequalities and Euroscepticism in 12 West European Democracies, 1975–2009', *Socio-Economic Review*, Vol. 14, No. 1, pp. 27–45.

Kydland, F. and Prescott, E. (1977) 'Rules Rather than Discretion: The Inconsistency of Optimal Plans', *Journal of Political Economy*, Vol. 85, No. 3, pp. 473–92.

Lijphart, A. (2012) *Patterns of Democracy: Government Forms and Performance in Thirty-six Countries,* 2nd edition. New Haven, CT: Yale University Press.

Lipset, S. M. and Rokkan, S. (1967) 'Cleavage Structures, Party Systems and Voter Alignments: An Introduction.' In S. M. Lipset and S. Rokkan (eds), *Party Systems and Voter Alignments*. New York: Free Press, pp. 1–64.

Maes, I. (2004) 'On the Origins of the Franco-German EMU Controversies', *European Journal of Law and Economics*, Vol. 17, No. 1, pp. 21–39.

Mair, P. (2013) *Ruling the Void: The Hollowing of Western Democracy*. London: Verso.

Majone, G. (1994) 'The Rise of the Regulatory State in Europe', *West European Politics*, Vol. 17, No. 3, pp. 77–101.

Majone, G. (1996) 'Temporal Inconsistency and Policy Credibility: Why Democracies Need Non-Majoritarian Institutions', Robert Schuman Centre Working Paper, No. 96/57. Florence: European University Institute.

Marlière, P. (2010) 'The Decline of Europe's Social Democratic Parties', *Open Democracy,* blog post, 16 March, https://www.opendemocracy.net/philippe-marliere/decline-of-europes-social-democratic-parties, date accessed 9 June 2016.

Matthijs, M. and Blyth, M. (eds) (2015) *The Future of the Euro*. Oxford: Oxford University Press.

Milward, A. S. (1992) *The European Rescue of the Nation-State*. London: Routledge.

Milward, A. S. and Sørensen, V. (1993) 'Interdependence or Integration? A National Choice.' In A. S. Milward, F. M. B. Lynch, F. Romero, R. Ranieri, and V. Sørensen, *The Frontier of National Sovereignty: History and Theory 1945–1992*. London: Routledge, pp. 1–32.

Mundell, R. A. (1963) 'Capital Mobility and Stabilization Policy under Fixed and Flexible Exchange Rates', *Canadian Journal of Economic and Political Science*, Vol. 29, No. 4, pp. 475–85.

Peck, J. (2010) *Constructions of Neoliberal Reason*. Oxford: Oxford University Press.

Pierson, P. (1996) 'The Path to European Integration: A Historical Institutionalist Analysis', *Comparative Political Studies*, Vol. 29, No. 2, pp. 123–63.

Pierson, P. (2001a) 'Coping with Permanent Austerity: Welfare State Restructuring in Affluent Democracies.' In P. Pierson (ed.), *The New Politics of the Welfare State*. Oxford: Oxford University Press, pp. 410–56.

Pierson, P. (2001b) 'From Expansion to Austerity: The New Politics of Taxing and Spending.' In M. A. Levin, M. K. Landy, and M. Shapiro (eds), *Seeking the Center: Politics and Policymaking in the New Century*. Washington, DC: Georgetown University Press, pp. 54–80.

Polyakova, A. (2015) *The Dark Side of European Integration: Social Foundations and Cultural Determinants of the Rise of Radical Right Movements in Contemporary Europe*. New York: Ibidem Press/Columbia University Press.

Rodrik, D. (2011) *The Globalization Paradox: Why Global Markets, States and Democracy Can't Coexist*. Oxford: Oxford University Press.

Rosamond, B. (2015) 'Performing Theory/Theorizing Performance in Emergent Supranational Governance: The "Live" Knowledge Archive of European Integration and the Early European Commission', *Journal of European Integration*, Vol. 37, No. 2, pp. 175–191.

Ruggie, J. G. (1982) 'International Regimes, Transactions and Change: Embedded Liberalism in the Postwar Economic Order', *International Organization*, Vol. 36, No. 2, pp. 379–16.

Sartori, G. (1976) *Parties and Party Systems. A Framework for Analysis*, Vol. 1. Cambridge: Cambridge University Press.

Schäfer, A. (2013) 'Liberalization, Inequality and Democracy's Discontent.' In A. Schäfer and W. Streeck (eds), *Politics in the Age of Austerity*. Cambridge: Polity Press, pp. 169–95.

Scharpf, F. (2010) 'The Asymmetry of European Integration, Or Why the EU Cannot Be a "Social Market Economy"', *Socio-Economic Review*, Vol. 8, No. 2, pp. 211–50.

Schattschneider, E. (1942) *Party Government. American Government in Action*. New York: Rinehart & Company.

Schmidt, V. A. and Thatcher, M. (2013) 'Theorizing Ideational Continuity: The Resilience of Neo-Liberal Ideas in Europe.' In V. A. Schmidt and M. Thatcher (eds), *Resilient Liberalism in Europe's Political Economy*. Cambridge: Cambridge University Press, pp. 1–52.

Sedelmeier, U. (2014) 'Anchoring Democracy from Above? The European Union and Democratic Backsliding in Hungary and Romania after Accession', *Journal of Common Market Studies*, Vol. 52, No. 1, pp. 105–21.

Serricchio, F., Tsakatika, M., and Quaglia, L. (2013) 'Euroscepticism and the Global Financial Crisis', *Journal of Common Market Studies*, Vol. 51, No. 1, pp. 51–64.

Shonfield, A. (1965) *Modern Capitalism: The Changing Balance of Public and Private Power*. Oxford: Oxford University Press.

Streeck, W. (2011) 'The Crises of Democratic Capitalism', *New Left Review* 71, September–October, pp. 5–29.

Streeck, W. (2014) *Buying Time: The Delayed Crisis of Democratic Capitalism*. London: Verso.

Streeck, W. (2015) 'The Rise of the European Consolidation State', MPIfG Discussion Paper, No. 15/1, http://www.mpifg.de/pu/mpifg_dp/dp15-1.pdf.

Yergin, D. and Stanislaw, J. (1998) *The Commanding Heights: The Battle Between Government and Marketplace that is Remaking the Modern World.* New York: Simon and Schuster.

Zielonka, J. (2014) *Is the EU Doomed?* Cambridge: Polity Press.

Chapter 4

Playing for High Stakes: The Eurozone Crisis

KENNETH DYSON

Introduction

The EU had invested huge stakes in the creation of monetary union, which was agreed to in the Maastricht Treaty of 1992 and launched with 11 member states in 1999. By 2016 the eurozone area had grown to encompass 19 out of the 28 EU member states, only two of which had negotiated an opt-out, Britain and Denmark. Monetary union was a bold experiment in the absence of a European federal state in which to embed it. It depended on the effectiveness of the new European Central Bank (ECB) in delivering monetary stability and on the member states' loyalty in complying with the rules to support the monetary union. The assumption was that monetary union would act as a catalyst for economic and political union. Clearly in creating monetary union in this way the EU was playing for high stakes. The onset and progression of the eurozone crisis cast serious doubt on the timing of this investment, on the underlying assumption that monetary union would drive economic and political union, and on the will and capability of eurozone states to cede the requisite sovereignty to form an economic and political union. The early signs were not auspicious. In 2003 the German federal government, the chief advocate of tough fiscal rules, had shown a willingness to see the application of these rules suspended (Heipertz and Verdun, 2010). Subsequently, in 2005 two key eurozone member states, France and the Netherlands, had rejected the Constitutional Treaty. With the escalation of the eurozone crisis, fear grew that monetary union could act as a catalyst for EU disunion (Dyson, 2012).

This chapter analyses the multi-dimensional and mutating character of the eurozone crisis. It then examines why it is existentially threatening to the EU. It closes by looking at the problem of burden-sharing in monetary union from an historical perspective. The emphasis is on contextual understanding of the eurozone crisis and on the nature and the degree of risks and uncertainty that it has introduced into the European integration process.

A Multi-dimensional and Mutating Crisis

The eurozone crisis proved difficult to understand for political leaders, policy-makers, and professional analysts alike. It involved a difficult and protracted learning process about the constraints of living in a monetary union, as much for creditor states like Germany as for debtor states like Greece, Ireland, and Portugal. To complicate matters, the eurozone crisis operated on different levels – global, EU, and individual member states – and in different dimensions. It represented a banking and financial crisis, an economic crisis, and a sovereign debt crisis, as well as potentially a security crisis. Moreover, the crisis was by no means a stable construct over time. It mutated in complex ways that complicated attempts to understand its nature, its causes, and appropriate policy prescriptions. The eurozone crisis was deeply and often bitterly contested, above all between creditor states and debtor states (Dyson, 2014). It opened up a new divisiveness, grounded in differences of economic and political interests, of ideologies, and sometimes of personality. Scope emerged for crude political caricature, demonization, and the misuse of historical memory, above all with respect to German power in Europe. The risk was a disorderly process of spillover of member state crises into the eurozone area, mutating, in turn, into a full-blown EU crisis, with defections and disintegration. In this scenario the hopes for a 'new Europe' would lie in ruins.

One issue was what kind of crisis the eurozone faced and whose crisis it was. The crisis was grounded in certain key realities as defined by empirical referents: for instance, GDP figures, unemployment data, liquidity and insolvency measures, and financial data such as fiscal deficits, public debt, and sovereign bond yields. Developments in these figures signalled and triggered crisis. They defined the underlying material reality of the crisis for individual member states, the eurozone area, and the wider EU, as well as whose crisis it was supposed to be. Thus, Germany was not in crisis, other than in 2008–09 in the wake of the collapse of Lehman Brothers, the giant US investment bank, in September 2008, and the subsequent global economic downturn. In contrast, a mix of data suggested that France and Italy were in a long-term crisis. Over time data also seemed to support a picture of the eurozone area itself as in a long-term crisis of economic stagnation, chronically high unemployment rate, and relative global decline.

However, the eurozone crisis was more than just an empirical phenomenon. It was a discursive and typically contested social and political construct, which was mediated through a variety of actors in financial markets, official positions, and the print and electronic media. In particular, media coverage remained dominated by constructions of the crisis through different national prisms rather than focusing on developing a Europe-wide perspective. The figure of the German Chancellor, Angela Merkel, loomed large across European reporting, while the metaphor of war figured more prominently than the metaphors of the eurozone crisis as a 'game' or a 'problem of construction' (Picard, 2015).

The eurozone crisis was, not least, a phenomenon of attribution. Who was responsible for the crisis: reckless bankers, incompetent architects of the eurozone, the EU's undemocratic and leaderless governing structures, individual untrustworthy member states, or particular weak, misguided, and possibly corrupt governing elites? In 2007–08, culminating in the insolvency of Lehman Brothers, the dominant discursive construction was a crisis of Anglo-American financial capitalism, of short-term and reckless speculative financing. The crisis was portrayed as primarily exogenous. The solution was the export of the German model of the social market economy to the global level (see Steinbrück, 2010). For a brief period, the EU believed it could afford to be a teacher rather than a pupil of crisis management and reform. However, by 2010 the Greek crisis had transformed how the crisis was seen. The origins were no longer so readily attributed to Wall Street or the City of London. Initially the inclination was to define it as a domestic Greek crisis, one whose origins lay in the mendacity and duplicity of its governing elites. The eurozone area faced, in the case of Greece, a 'failing' state crisis, a phenomenon that its architects had never envisaged (Dyson, 2014; Dyson and Maes, 2016).

However, from the summer and autumn of 2010 onwards, the crisis was being redefined as a eurozone crisis. As the number of individual member states in urgent need of financial assistance grew, beginning with Ireland, the crisis was increasingly attributed to the design failings of the euro area (on which see Dyson and Maes, 2016). The conflicts were now about the nature of these design failings, who was responsible for them, and what was to be done about them. The eurozone crisis was potentially an international crisis, involving the G20 and the International Monetary Fund (IMF), as well as a crisis of the EU. The fear was no longer of importing crisis into Europe but of Europe exporting its crisis to the rest of the world. This shift left eurozone leaders in a newly embattled position as they were offered advice and implored to act decisively by others, not least the US Secretary of the Treasury, the US President, and the managing director of the IMF, as well as the British Chancellor of the Exchequer and the Polish Foreign Minister.

The eurozone crisis itself took on an increasingly multi-dimensional character. It had started as a banking and financial crisis. In part this aspect of the crisis was exogenous through the engagements of European banks in the US sub-prime mortgage market. In part, it was endogenous through excessive domestic credit expansion to the property and construction sectors, notably in Ireland and Spain, creating a boom/bust cycle. The financial crisis had, in turn, deep effects on member state public finances as banks were rescued from insolvency to cushion domestic economic and political effects, as well as on the macroeconomy as credit dried up and economic confidence dropped. The eurozone area economy became locked into a trajectory of low, sluggish economic growth, large-scale unemployment, and a pervasive climate of economic insecurity. Hence the financial crisis mutated into an economic crisis and a sovereign debt crisis. These three different dimensions of the crisis were interrelated in a potentially vicious chain reaction. Banks in solvency crisis threatened to destabilize public finances through expensive bailouts; economic contraction helped worsen public debt/GDP ratios; and sovereign debt crisis threatened the banks and financial institutions that held their bonds. Banks and sovereigns were locked in a potentially vicious, mutually destructive embrace.

As the multi-dimensionality and self-reinforcing nature of the crisis became increasingly apparent, along with its endogenous character, the scale of the EU and the eurozone reforms deemed necessary grew. Initially reform efforts focused on the G20, the Bank for International Settlements (BIS), and the EU level, particularly banking and finance. At the EU level, the de Larosière Group (2009) brought forward proposals to strengthen macro- and micro-prudential financial supervision. The outcome was the creation of the European Systemic Risk Board (ESRB), located in the ECB, and the European System of Financial Supervisors, comprising three new supervisory authorities. Also at the EU level the Van Rompuy task force on strengthening EU economic governance was the catalyst for proposals to strengthen economic coordination through a new macroeconomic imbalances procedure, a reinforcement of the surveillance, monitoring, and sanction procedures under the Stability and Growth Pact (SGP), and a new 'European Semester' that would produce integrated guidelines for member states (Taskforce to the European Council, 2010). This so-called 'Six-Pack' was soon followed by the 'Two-Pack', designed to achieve a greater advance scrutiny of member state budgets (Hodson, 2011) (See Table 4.1).

However, by 2011–12 there was a growing recognition that reforms at the level of the eurozone area were essential to offer more explicit support to the single currency. One early step was the so-called euro plus pact, a process for coordinating member state structural reforms that was to be monitored by the heads of state or government. This step signalled Merkel's support for the greater use of the intergovernmental Union Method rather than the supranational Community Method in pursuing

Table 4.1   *The EU and euro area economic and financial crisis: key events*

August 2007	ECB begins liquidity operations to support euro area banks
September 2008	Collapse of Lehman Brothers bank
February 2009	Report of the de Larosière Group on financial supervision in the EU
June 2009	European Council agrees to create the European Systemic Risk Board (ESRB) and a European System of Financial Supervisors
December 2009	Greek crisis becomes apparent
March 2010	European Council establishes the Van Rompuy Task Force to strengthen the EU surveillance framework
May 2010	European Council establishes the European Financial Stabilization Mechanism (EFSM) and the European Financial Stability Facility (EFSF): first Greece financial assistance programme
May 2010	ECB launches Securities Markets Programme
October 2010	European Council endorses the Van Rompuy Task Force report
November 2010	Financial assistance programme for Ireland
March 2011	European Council establishes the European Stability Mechanism (ESM) to replace the EFSF
March 2011	European Council adopts the euro plus pact
May 2011	Agreement of Portugal financial assistance programme
October 2011	European Council and Parliament adopt the Six-Pack on strengthening EU economic governance, strengthening the Stability and Growth Pact (SGP) and the new Macroeconomic Imbalance Procedure (MIP)
October 2011	Council agrees to institutionalize the Euro Summits
November 2011	European Commission proposes the Two-Pack to strengthen budgetary surveillance

closer integration. She feared too much authority passing into the hands of the European Commission, which she deemed a lax protector of the rules. The calculation was that German interests could be better safeguarded in the European Council than by relying on the Commission. In

December 2011	ECB announces three-year long-term refinancing operations for euro area banks
December 2011/ January 2012	European Council agrees the Treaty on Stability, Coordination and Governance in the EMU (fiscal compact)
March 2012	Agreement of second Greece financial assistance programme, including haircut on government bonds
May/June 2012	Euro Summit political commitment to go ahead with European banking union; ESM empowered to undertake bank recapitalization
August 2012	ECB president states that the ECB will 'do whatever it takes'
September 2012	ECB announces the technical features of the Outright Monetary Transactions (OMT) programme
December 2012	Euro Summit agrees to establish the Single Supervisory Mechanism (SSM) under the ECB and to go ahead with the Single Resolution Mechanism (SRM), the first two pillars of banking union
December 2012	The final version of the Four Presidents' Report on towards a genuine EMU presented to the European Council
March 2013	Agreement of Cyprus financial assistance programme
December 2013	Ireland exits its financial assistance programme
June 2014	Portugal exits its financial assistance programme
July 2014	Council and Parliament adopt regulation on SRM
October 2014	ECB publishes results of bank stress tests
January 2015	ECB launches quantitative easing (QE)
January 2015	Election of Syriza-led government in Greece
July 2015	Agreement of third Greece financial assistance programme
July 2016	Bank stress tests published

this spirit the Treaty on Stability, Coordination and Governance (Fiscal Compact) of 2012 went further than just tightening up and reinforcing the fiscal rules. It gave a new treaty recognition to formal meetings of the heads of state or government of the member states of the eurozone area, with the institutionalization of Euro Summits. Similarly, the European

Stability Mechanism (ESM) was established as an intergovernmental body, one that ensured a veto position of the German government on any financial aid disbursement to member states in crisis.

The euro plus pact, the Fiscal Compact, the ESM treaty, and the formalization of the Euro Summit represented a new stage of differentiated integration in Europe (Dyson, 2010, 2012). Monetary union in a time of crisis was proving the catalyst for a major redefinition of relationships within the EU. This process of redefinition gained clearest expression in the British government's attempt to renegotiate its membership of the EU in 2015 and the subsequent British referendum in 2016 whose outcome was support for 'Brexit'. One of the central issues in eurozone crisis management and reforms was configuring the relationship between euro 'ins' and 'outs' in such a way that the interests of the 'outs' like Britain would be protected. This demand met up against the interest of the 'ins' in ensuring that the conditions were in place for an effective and sustainable monetary union.

This process of redefining relationships was reinforced from June 2012 as the EU took forward its new commitment to create a banking union. Its central aims were to achieve a better alignment of liability and control in dealing with banks so that investors who lend to a bank should suffer losses in a predictable manner; to break or at least weaken the so-called 'death loop' between banks and sovereigns; and to prevent the spread of panic. Key elements were strengthened European oversight of systemically significant eurozone area banks; provision for a bank resolution mechanism that would include bail-in of bank shareholders and creditors before any commitment of public money; and a common deposit guarantee system. The first of its three pillars took effect in 2014 after the ECB had stress-tested eurozone area banks for their solvency. The ECB became the location for the new Single Supervisory Mechanism, which assumed responsibility for the eurozone's biggest banks. In 2016 the second pillar began operation with the new Single Resolution Board (SRB) as well as a Single Resolution Fund (SRF). Its role was to decide when a bank is failing and how to resolve the problem of when there are more debts than assets. Both the SRB and the SRF were confined to member states of the eurozone area and those other member states that chose to opt in. The SRF built on the EU-wide Bank Recovery and Resolution Directive of 2013.

However, European banking union remained incomplete. The decision-making processes were complex and convoluted, especially with respect to the SRB, and might prove unfit for purpose in a crisis. Fears of pre-commitment to assist and thus encourage imprudent banks remained, notably in Germany. There were also potentially serious political implications if bail-in of bank creditors damaged the savings of small investors. This concern surfaced with respect to troubled

Italian banks in 2016 and posed the risk of a flouting of the resolution rules. Moreover, by 2016 the third pillar of deposit protection had gone no further than a directive to harmonize the national deposit schemes and European Commission proposals that lacked German endorsement. Banking union fell short of adequately addressing the financial-fiscal trilemma, outlined by Maurice Obstfeld (2013). The trilemma stemmed from the problem of reconciling financial integration, financial stability, and fiscal independence. The problem arose when the costs of banking rescues exceeded national fiscal capacity, a risk that Italy faced.

More generally, despite the breadth and the scale of reforms, discourse about the eurozone continued to stress its 'incompleteness' and 'imperfect' nature. This type of discourse was typically associated with a particular form of ideological or theoretical commitment. Thus, seen from a socialist position or from Keynesian theory, the eurozone was deficient as a 'solidarity community'. It failed to provide mutual insurance against asymmetric shocks and thereby spread the burden of adjustment across member states. Or, seen from a strictly liberal ideological position or from ordoliberal theory, the eurozone was fraught with moral hazard, with incentives for irresponsible behaviour and inefficient outcomes. It lacked sufficient authority for eurozone institutions to monitor, intervene, and sanction member state policies. In consequence, liability and control were imperfectly aligned (Dyson, 2014).

However, an evaluation of the eurozone from the perspective of sustaining political consent during 'hard times' was likely to be more forgiving. Seen from this perspective, the problem was essentially the sheer heterogeneity of the structures, interests, and preferences of the member states of the eurozone. Sustaining political consent would have proved easier in a smaller monetary union of member states with more similar economic structures, interests, and policy preferences. The monetary union of 11 member states in 1999 far exceeded what any of its original architects had envisaged and what optimum currency area theory would counsel (for details, see Dyson and Maes, 2016).

The reasons for 11 rather than five or six member states were multiple and essentially political. The French government wished to balance Germany within a monetary union and hence supported early membership for Italy and Spain. The three Benelux states had to be respected as a unity, with Belgium and Luxembourg already in their own monetary union. In turn, bringing in Belgium made it more difficult to exclude Italy as another of the original six founding states. Finally, the negotiation of the SGP in 1996–97 was used to reassure German public opinion that the rules would be clear, firm, and applied. In addition, Chancellor Helmut Kohl put the Bundesbank (German central bank) under considerable political pressure to align itself with the larger foreign policy and security interests of Germany in Europe. By the time of the eurozone area crisis, enlargement to include member states like Greece had made the monetary union even more complex. In this context, the question of eurozone area exit lurked in the background of crisis negotiations, favoured by the German Finance Minister, Wolfgang Schäuble, as early as February 2010 in his proposal for a European Monetary Fund (EMF). It posed an acute dilemma between the threat of exit spreading insecurity and fear and poisoning relations within the EU, and the threat of an excessively heterogeneous monetary union proving economically and ultimately politically unsustainable. The consequence was uncertainty about whether eurozone rules would be adapted to the membership or whether the membership would adjust to the rules.

The eurozone crisis proved so difficult because it was not a self-contained problem. It was nested in even bigger, often intractable issues. Banking and financial crises were a recurrent historical phenomenon and had been made more difficult to manage as freedom of capital movement had encouraged cross-border finance. Moreover, diagnosis of states as facing fiscal crises pre-dated the eurozone area (Dyson, 2014; Streeck, 2013). More generally, problems of economic insecurity, precarious middle-class living standards, undereducated and underskilled employees, and an excluded and aggrieved underclass were endemic across Organisation for Economic Co-operation and Development (OECD) states. The challenges of globalization and technological change were altering their political as well as their economic, social, and cultural fabrics. The effects were manifested in general distrust and disillusionment with governing elites, potential for political radicalization, and short-term populist surges, apparent for instance in the phenomenon of Donald Trump's campaign for the US presidency in 2016. In short, the EU and the eurozone were not alone in facing crises of identity, legitimacy, and leadership. The onset of these crises could be traced back well before the creation of the eurozone area, for instance in disruptive changes within established parties and to party systems.

Nevertheless, the eurozone crisis served to intensify these problems through the eurozone's association with prolonged economic stagnation and intractably high unemployment rates. It had its own problems of identity, legitimacy, and leadership. The problems of leadership need to be set in context. Both the ECB and the European Council/Euro Summit emerged as stronger institutions with the eurozone crisis. The ECB expanded and made an increasingly active use of its non-conventional monetary policy instruments, initially to provide vital liquidity to the euro area banking system and later to head off risks of deflation. It also took on new responsibilities in financial stability and banking union. Initially, Jean-Claude Trichet and his successor as ECB President, Mario Draghi ('Super Mario'), carved out roles as leaders in crisis management and reform. Similarly, the heads of state or government, above all in the newly formalized Euro Summit, became much more actively engaged in eurozone crisis management and reform.

Despite these advances, the leadership problems remained acute. It was clear that the ECB could not alone master a crisis that went beyond banking and finance to include fiscal policies and structural reforms. Draghi reiterated this point and participated actively in the so-called Four Presidents' Report 'Towards a Genuine Economic and Monetary Union', which sketched out a comprehensive road map for banking, fiscal, economic, and political union (Van Rompuy et al., 2012). The ECB risked being dragged outside its treaty remit. The key problem was that the European Council/Euro Summit lacked the capacity to exercise decisive leadership. It hesitated to give full endorsement to either the Four Presidents' Report or to its 2015 refinement, the Five Presidents' Report. Instead, the European Council relied on muddling through with short-term political fixes that brought only temporary respite from crisis. The prolonged Greek crisis was emblematic of a strategy of buying time. By 2015–16 Greece was in its third financial assistance programme and still displaying all the signs of a deeply dysfunctional state.

Paradoxically, the very attempt of the ECB and the European Council to strengthen their leadership role served to increase criticisms of the way in which the eurozone crisis was deepening the legitimacy crisis, defined as the 'democratic deficit' in the EU, and creating a crisis of identity within the EU. The crisis of identity was bound up with the question of 'who belongs' in the euro area. This issue was not simply economic. It was also cultural and political. Old and still politically resonant cultural images of North and South or Mediterranean Europe were brought into play, above all in relation to Greece. Such images took the form of who wished to belong to a 'German Europe' and whose Europe it was. Media coverage helped to reinforce these cultural images and provided little evidence that the eurozone area had encouraged the emergence of a clear and distinct European public sphere (Picard, 2015).

The legitimacy crisis focused on the European Council, the ECB, and the Troika arrangement whereby the European Commission, the ECB, and the IMF oversaw the bailouts (see below). The Troika in particular was seen as representing a form of 'authoritarian managerialism', interfering in the 'constitutional identity' of member states, and hollowing out the democratic process at member state level without building up a democratic framework of legitimacy at the EU/eurozone level (see, for example, Joerges, 2010). The eurozone crisis had not served as a catalyst for a shift to a democratically accountable European economic government. In its absence, the discourse of a crisis of legitimacy seemed destined to endure. In the case of the ECB, monetary financing of member states was judged to deepen this crisis as a gap seemed to open up between the treaty and practice. This sense was sharpened by the ECB's resort to quantitative easing – the purchasing of member state sovereign bonds – which led to criticism, not least from Germany, that the ECB was reducing the incentives for member states to undertake reforms and blurring the line between monetary and fiscal policies.

The lack of eurozone area capacity for self-contained crisis management was exemplified in the Troika arrangement for the financial rescue programmes of member states in crisis. This arrangement was first put in place for the Greek crisis and then extended to Ireland, Portugal, and Cyprus. It involved the IMF, the European Commission, and the ECB in surveillance, monitoring, and review of the implementation of the programme. The Troika arrangement was backed by Merkel for three main reasons. She distrusted the European Commission as too lax in enforcing compliance and wished to rely on the long experience of the IMF in debt sustainability analysis and enforcement. She also saw financial advantage to Germany in involving the IMF as co-financier. And, finally, she calculated that the involvement of the IMF would reassure German public opinion. In fact, the Troika arrangement proved attractive to some other member states for a different reason. They backed the arrangement because they expected the IMF to push the idea of debt restructuring as part of the rescue package. This expectation was fulfilled as IMF staffers began to question the design of the rescue programmes, above all in the Greek case. On this issue the IMF and the German government took opposing positions. Also, in some instances, the Commission officials involved in the Troika took a tougher position than their IMF counterparts.

More fundamentally, the Troika arrangement was the alternative to the German Finance Ministry proposal for an EMF in February 2010. This proposal, backed by Wolfgang Schäuble, sought to use the Greek crisis to establish an independent rescue capacity of the eurozone area. It sought to address the anomaly that under the Lisbon Treaty (and earlier the Maastricht Treaty) the EU had the capacity to aid euro 'outsiders' in crisis but lacked a similar capacity for 'insiders'. This anomaly had been recognized by German officials in managing the earlier Latvian crisis.

The eurozone crisis was also difficult because it was nested in wider problems of EU governance. One problem was the thorny issue of the relationship between euro 'ins' and 'outs'. This problem was manifest at the December 2011 European Council when the British Prime Minister sought – unsuccessfully – to veto the Fiscal Compact unless special safeguards were granted to the UK in financial services. It became even more salient with the creation of banking union and the fear of euro 'outs' like Britain that the eurozone area states could coalesce to push through financial market policies against British interests.

Other problems of EU governance also had the potential to complicate the management of the eurozone crisis. One such problem was the security crisis sparked by Russia's annexation of Crimea and threat to the territorial integrity of Ukraine. At the centre of the EU crisis response were economic sanctions against Russia. Tightening and maintaining these sanctions to enhance their credibility depended on solidarity of the member states. Keeping Greece and Italy on board became a key political consideration. It provided their leaders with an opportunity for political leverage in 2015, influencing not least fear that exit of Greece from the eurozone could provoke an EU sanctions crisis.

Another problem was the EU migration crisis of 2015. This crisis provoked a role reversal in discourse about solidarity through burden-sharing. The huge flow of refugees to Germany generated a German interest in an EU burden-sharing scheme to redistribute refugees. For Germany, the integrity of the Schengen area depended on burden-sharing. The crisis also generated a German reliance on member states such as Greece and Italy to stem the flow of refugees. For Germany, again, the integrity of the Schengen area depended on a secure external EU border. In short, the Crimea/Russia crisis and the migration crisis altered power relationships within the wider EU in ways that had implications for the political dynamics of eurozone crisis management and reform. Germany became a claimant on EU burden-sharing, creating linkage potential in eurozone crisis management.

Why the Eurozone Crisis is an Existential Threat

The eurozone crisis proved existentially threatening to the EU for a number of reasons. In the first place, monetary union was the single most advanced project in European integration. At the Maastricht European Council of December 1991, EMU's political founders, above all Helmut Kohl, had recognized the commitment to monetary union as an historic decision to make European integration irreversible (Dyson and Featherstone, 1999). In a similar spirit, Merkel was to declare during the eurozone crisis that if the euro fails, Europe fails. Politically, the EU had a huge amount invested in the creation of the euro. Its failure would at the very least involve huge reputational costs for the EU.

Second, money is unlike any other good. Among other things, it is a store of value and a common denominator of exchange. Its stability was therefore of primary macroeconomic significance. This factor was to endow the ECB with central strategic significance in the management of the eurozone crisis and was to result in it gaining a prominence that overshadowed the roles of other EU institutions, including the Commission and the European Parliament (EP), in the crisis. Crucially, however, European trade in goods, services, and capital, as well as wages, were governed by contracts, and contracts were denominated in euros. Europe was a complex contractual edifice whose undoing would pose massive technical and logistical problems. To add to existential threat, the creation of the euro had acted as a catalyst for cross-national banking activity. The end of exchange-rate risk and elimination of transaction costs with a single currency had deepened financial integration. The outcome was increased exposure of member states to contagion through financial markets so that the effects of a crisis could spread through the banking systems. Rescuing a eurozone member state in crisis, such as Greece, was more than just an issue of solidarity. It was about putting in place a safety net around one's own banks. Economically, the eurozone – and the wider EU – faced potentially unmanageable risks from a disorderly unravelling of the eurozone area.

Third, the eurozone crisis made visible, and shone a harsh spotlight on, the underlying power relationships in European integration. In the process the idealism that had been associated with the project of monetary union – in Kohl's words, 'never again war in Europe' – lost traction on attitudes to the EU (see Dyson and Quaglia, 2010: 467–9). The classic anchor stone of European integration, the Franco-German relationship, appeared to be an empty shell. It seemed to provide a cover for German leadership in crisis management and reform. A climate of distrust ensued. Eurobarometer polls showed a sharp fall in support for the EU, above all in member states such as Greece and Italy, but also extending to France. Substantively, criticism focused on the economic, social, and political costs of austerity and on the lack of EU solidarity. However, the blame for these failings was attached to Germany. The EU was increasingly pictured as a 'German Europe' and Germany as imposing 'austerity' (e.g. Beck, 2013; Streeck, 2013). The eurozone could be viewed as lacking a benign hegemon, with Germany acting to protect its own interests rather than the general interests of all member states. This picture seemed to find its justification in the delays and evident unwillingness of the German government to act in support of Greece between December 2009 and May 2010; in the Fiscal Compact of 2012, which ensconced in higher law the commitment to a balanced budget over the economic cycle; and in the design and the operation of the financial assistance programmes for eurozone member states in crisis. The Fiscal Compact could be seen as the 'uploading' of Germany's own relatively new constitutional 'debt brake' of 2009 to the eurozone and the export of sustained austerity. It was the price exacted by the German government for the ESM treaty.

Strategically, the eurozone crisis made more visible a sharp creditor–debtor state cleavage which could prove existentially threatening to the European project (Dyson, 2014). On the one hand, the rhetorical take on the eurozone crisis as evidence of a 'German Europe' and 'austerity

Europe' fed the development of new eurosceptic political parties across the EU, as well as strategic reorientation within established parties in a more eurosceptic direction as they sought to contain new electoral threats. This reorientation favoured member state political support for greater flexibility and discretion in economic management, even some support for eurozone exit(s). The French government proved noticeably assertive in seeking out deferment of the obligation to bring down its fiscal deficit below 3 per cent of GDP and reduce the public debt/GDP ratio. For many on the Left, the eurozone area should be about provision of a protective umbrella for expansionary economic policies to combat crises, foster public investment, and support employees. The EU faced a risk that, in the absence of a return to greater economic growth and security, eurosceptic forces would prevail, not least in France and in Italy.

On the other hand, the EU faced the heightened risk that Germans would feel victimized by international criticism and begin to disengage from the European project. German fears centred on four developments. These fears found expression not just among German economists, commentators, and politicians, but also in successive landmark rulings of the Federal Constitutional Court, notably on the Lisbon Treaty, the ESM Treaty, and the Outright Monetary Transactions (OMT) programme of the ECB. First, the eurozone crisis seemed to set in motion a trend towards a 'transfer union', with Germany as the paymaster. German exposure to risk was evident in the scale of official loans and guarantees to the so-called 'programme states' of Cyprus, Greece, Ireland, and Portugal, as well as in the so-called 'Target 2 imbalances' (Sinn, 2012). The pressure to move to a transfer union was further apparent in the political pressures, above all from France, Italy, and the Commission, to introduce eurobonds as a joint liability. Within Germany the Maastricht Treaty was understood to have created an 'economic constitution' for Europe, grounded on the 'no bailout' principle. Fiscal policies remained a member state responsibility for which their governments must be held liable. In practice, therefore, the eurozone was vulnerable to German criticism as being in breach of treaty law and national law. This argument found expression in the preliminary ruling of the Federal Constitutional Court on the OMT programme in 2014.

Second, there was widespread anxiety in Germany about the 'non-conventional' monetary policy measures of the ECB during the crisis. This anxiety was fuelled by the resignation of Jürgen Stark, the German executive board member of the ECB, and by the early departure of Axel Weber as Bundesbank president. Both were very critical of ECB interventions in the sovereign bond markets. These interventions began in May 2010, but gathered a new dimension with the OMT programme of

2012 and the quantitative easing programme from 2015. German fears centred on the risks that the ECB was assuming and on the diminished incentives for member states to reform when protected by the ECB. Above all, the ECB seemed to have shifted away from the Bundesbank model, with its fixation on a narrow mandate of monetary stability, into a wider concern for the financial and macroeconomic stability of the eurozone area. This shift was made apparent by Draghi's statements that the ECB would do 'whatever it takes' to protect the euro – a statement that took ECB officials by surprise and prepared the ground for the OMT programme – and that fiscal policy flexibility could have a positive role to play in supporting economic recovery. The Bundesbank was increasingly isolated within the ECB governing council, not least over quantitative easing.

Third, German fears were fuelled by the lack of compliance with the EU fiscal rules, not least by France – though Germany too had in the past flouted the rules, culminating in the crisis of the SGP in 2003 (when the Commission had sought to take legal action against France and Germany). However, since 2005 the federal government led by Merkel had made fiscal discipline the central reference point of German economic policy. Achieving fiscal balance and reducing public debt had become the measures of German economic virtue. Correspondingly, there was considerable frustration with the failure of others to abide by the fiscal rules, along with deep suspicion of the European Commission as too lenient in granting flexibility to member states like France. In the German view, the precondition for solidarity was 'solidity' in complying with the rules.

Fourth, German fears centred on the weak link between joint liability and control over member state policies. There was a deep distrust of political proposals for closer European integration that advocated the assumption of joint liability, for instance eurobonds, without the willingness – and capability – to transfer sovereignty, for instance in taxation. For this reason, German negotiators linked the ratification of the ESM treaty to the Fiscal Compact. Subsequently, because of the absence of such clear linkage, they were unable to gain sufficient support for their proposal for structural reform contracts with member states. German negotiators noted a general, even declining, willingness of member states to share sovereignty. In the German view, the price of solidarity was shared sovereignty in fiscal policies and in structural reforms. In the absence of credible political support for such a transfer of sovereignty German attention focused on enforcing member state compliance with rules as the test of solidarity. By 2015 there was growing support for establishing an independent expert European fiscal council to strengthen pressure on both the European Commission and the member states.

Burden-Sharing in Monetary Union: A Historical Perspective on the Eurozone Crisis

At the heart of the eurozone crisis was a deeply political and normative question: who should bear the burden of adjustment to asymmetric economic shocks? This question is neither specific to the EU nor new in the history of European integration. It is one of the most difficult problems in political economy and is endemic in all forms of economic and monetary cooperation, integration, and union. It has bedevilled European integration from its inception. Any form of economic and monetary cooperation, integration, or union has to have the political will, as well as the fiscal and financial capacity, to withstand asymmetric shocks to sectors or to its constituent regions if it is to endure. Asymmetric shocks arise either exogenously or endogenously. Exogenous shocks produce asymmetric effects when they occur in a sector that is geographically concentrated, such as finance or tourism. Endogenous shocks are the product of domestic policies, for instance excessive credit expansion to the property sector. The outcome is the differential development of competitiveness, employment, and incomes. Asymmetric shocks represent a sharp and practical test of the meaningfulness and credibility of commitments to solidarity. They expose whether these commitments are matched by shared values, particularly with respect to what constitutes fairness in burden-sharing.

Burden-sharing crises have been a central feature of the European integration process from its outset. An historical examination of the pre-1914 functioning of the gold standard system and of the Great Depression of the 1930s is testament to their politically charged nature and to the endemic tensions and conflicts between creditor and debtor states (Dyson, 2014). Creditor state elites have an interest in reducing their liabilities and in emphasizing the responsibility of debtor states for tackling what they see as domestically originated problems. Debtor state elites have an interest in gaining assistance to ease their adjustment burdens and look to international liquidity provision and policy coordination to ensure symmetric adjustment. Of course, the creditor–debtor state cleavage does not amount to an exhaustive picture of state interests. Nevertheless, it has a powerful influence on how the political dynamics unfold.

The post-war Bretton Woods system, in which the USA was expected to act as the benign hegemon, and the European Payments Union (EPU) provided a foretaste of the complex and difficult political dynamics of burden-sharing. The Bretton Woods system, in which European exchange rates were tied to the US dollar, unravelled by 1971–73 as the tensions and conflicts of creditor–debtor state diplomacy proved too difficult to manage. These tensions and conflicts manifested themselves above all in the Franco-German relationship. Germany was running up huge current account surpluses, while France faced serious problems in financing its deficits. The conflicts reached crisis point in 1968 when the German economics minister robustly rejected the French proposal that Germany should burden-share by revaluing the D-Mark. This rejection prompted the first major public debate in France about the shift of power in Europe from France to Germany. Anxiety about German power became a defining feature of French policy towards European integration decades before the eurozone crisis.

Earlier, the EPU of the 1950s was an attempt to institutionalize burden-sharing in a Europe threatened by crises in financing trade and debt servicing. In this case Belgium was the reluctant creditor state, to be replaced from 1952 by Germany. Though Germany had been the first major recipient of an EPU rescue programme, within three years senior policy-makers in the federal economics ministry were considering a German exit (details in Dyson, forthcoming). They envisaged the creation of a smaller German-led union that would proceed rapidly to liberalization and convertibility. Other states such as France could stay in the EPU and join the new union when they were ready. Such an arrangement would help reduce the costs to Germany of what German policy-makers saw as domestically created crises in states like France and Italy. Reflecting the complexity of German interests in promoting European integration, this proposal did not become official German policy. It found little favour in the Foreign Ministry or the Chancellor's Office. Nevertheless, it highlighted an enduring theme in German economic and financial diplomacy from 1952 onwards.

These difficult burden-sharing issues recurred in the design and the management of the European Monetary System (EMS). Negotiated in 1978 and launched in 1979, it failed to achieve the French negotiating objective of a symmetrically functioning exchange-rate mechanism (ERM) (Ludlow, 1982; Mourlon-Druol, 2012). Though there were support mechanisms, the ERM was constructed around the D-Mark as the anchor currency, not around the European currency unit (ECU). Member states had either to adjust to maintain their exchange-rate commitment (making for a 'hard' ERM) or seek a negotiated realignment within the ERM. The history of the ERM was one of crises and hardening. The ERM crises of 1983 and of 1987 – both centred on the French franc – were turning points. The French government opted for domestic adjustment rather than realignment or exit. The ERM was in this respect new. It meant living within a 'D-Mark zone', a preference for turning to Germany rather than to the IMF in managing exchange-rate crisis. This preference informed French pursuit of European monetary union: taking monetary policy away from Germany to Europe and seeking a more symmetrical regional structure of power. These policy priorities informed how French policy-makers handled the ERM crises of 1992 and 1993. The 'hard franc' became the symbol of French power in Europe and the means to bring (and neutralize) German power within a European framework of monetary union.

However, the design of monetary union in the Maastricht Treaty negotiations did little to alleviate the risk of recurrent crises of burden-sharing (Dyson and Featherstone, 1999: 796–881). Before the eurozone crisis erupted, differences in unit labour costs were already signalling the potential for crisis. ECB President Trichet stressed the risks to the European Council. Member states such as France, Ireland, Italy, and Spain were becoming increasingly less competitive vis-à-vis Germany and the Netherlands. In the case of Ireland and Spain the problem was seriously aggravated by lax domestic credit expansion by the banks to the property sector; and in Greece, by chronic fiscal mismanagement by the state authorities. Yet these macroeconomic imbalances were a secondary rather than primary issue in the design and the functioning of European economic governance. The chief preoccupation was the excessive deficit procedure, regulated by the SGP. Responsibility for addressing macroeconomic imbalances continued to be seen as first and foremost an issue for the member state.

The problem was that monetary union had changed the structure of incentives. The classic Achilles' heel of member state economic policies had been exchange-rate shocks. With monetary union, this vulnerability to crisis was removed, which was a gain. However, in the process member states had lost a key instrument of domestic discipline. It had been replaced by the discipline of sovereign bond yield spreads, above all vis-à-vis German bonds. Unfortunately, as long as capital continued to flow freely to member states with competitiveness problems, this source of discipline remained masked. The turning point was sudden capital withdrawal as investors lost confidence in the solvency of certain banks and in certain member state governments' capacity to service their debts. The subsequent widening of sovereign bond yield spreads reached a point where a crisis of debt sustainability emerged: first in Greece, Ireland, and Portugal; and then, by 2011, more alarmingly, in Italy and Spain; and next in Cyprus.

Monetary union had had a perverse effect on the structure of incentives. The removal of the exchange-rate constraint had induced complacency about the need to take corrective action to address macroeconomic imbalances. Member states such as Greece, Ireland, Portugal, and Spain had pursued indulgent policies with impunity. Monetary union had encouraged a huge flow of capital to these fast-expanding economies. This virtuous circle became suddenly vicious. Faced with crisis, member states found that in a monetary union they lacked the adjustment instrument of nominal currency devaluation. They also lacked an independent monetary policy capacity. Their policy instruments were, in short, reduced to fiscal and structural reform policies.

Faced with crisis, eurozone member states had three strategic options: loyalty, voice, or exit (Hirschman, 1970). They could secure large-scale liquidity support from eurozone institutions, including the ECB, by loyally implementing the programme that was designed by their creditors, in this case the Troika. This option was pursued by the Irish and the Portuguese governments, both of which exited their programmes. Alternatively, they could use various institutional forums, including the euro area, to make the case for alternative measures such as debt restructuring, eurobonds, and public investment programmes. As 'programme states' found that they lacked sufficient credibility to pursue the voice option, this case tended to be made by other sympathetic member state governments such as the French, Italian, and Spanish. The attempt was made to enlist G20 and IMF support to press the case for radical reforms to the euro area and, notably at the European Council in June 2012, to pressurize Merkel. The third option was exit from the eurozone. This option was fraught with radical uncertainty about how, for instance, the banking and credit system would survive, the levels of social distress that would follow, the likely reaction of external creditors, and the period of recovery. Exit also posed huge technical and logistical problems. It was an option that the radical Greek government of Alexis Tsipras eventually chose not to pursue in 2015.

This analysis suggests a paradox: a pre-crisis monetary union that reduced pressures on debtor states to adjust and that supported financially unsustainable policies; followed by the visible reassertion of creditor state power, above all German power in crisis management and reform. However, this analysis needs further qualification. In the Maastricht negotiations, German policy-makers had inserted strict terms on monetary stability and fiscal discipline into the treaty, along with a treaty article that was interpreted as a 'no bailout' rule. It was the classic assertion of creditor state power. It was possible because other member states had a central strategic interest in keeping Germany at the negotiating table on monetary union, above all the independent and prestigious Bundesbank (Dyson and Featherstone, 1999). However, negotiating power was different *within* monetary union (on which see Dyson, 2014). The combination of freedom of capital movement with removal of exchange-rate risk encouraged a rapid integration of financial markets within the eurozone area, far faster than trade integration.

The outcome was increased vulnerability of *all* member states to financial market contagion. Crises in Greece, Ireland, and Spain implicated French, German, and other member state banks. In this new context, rescuing Greece, Ireland, and Spain was a defensive measure for other national banking systems. Against the background of financial market integration and increasing contractual complexity within a monetary union, the credibility of any threat of a German exit was diminished. Germany could be pushed and corralled, by US, G20, and IMF policy-makers, as well as by other eurozone member state governments. Minimizing the risks of contagion became a central shared preoccupation. It did not reduce the German emphasis on member states' prime responsibility for addressing their competitiveness and fiscal problems. It did, however, provide the justification – even if contested in Germany – for establishing the European Financial Stability Facility (EFSF), the permanent ESM, and the structures of banking union, as well as for accepting the OMT and the quantitative easing programmes of the ECB.

Being *in* a monetary union changes the parameters within which the problem of burden-sharing plays out for all the member states and supranational actors involved, for creditor states as well as debtor states (Dyson, 2014). Quite simply, much more is at stake. Burden-sharing in a monetary union is destined to remain an ongoing process of managing different interests and preferences through difficult, contentious, and varying forms of accommodation. It is a political process of trade-offs that is not amenable to definitive resolution in theory, let alone in practice. In the case of the eurozone area it has the potential to lead to recovery, ongoing stagnation, and relative decline, or disintegration.

Conclusions

The comparative and historical examination of financial and economic crises shows that imperfect economic governance is the norm (Dyson, 2013). However, managing such crises in a context of a monetary union without supportive fiscal and political union poses an unusual, if not unique, historical challenge. It places a huge reliance on the quality of the rules and procedures for fiscal, economic, and financial coordination and, not least, on the trustworthiness and the compliance of member state governments. Such reliance is deeply problematic when comparative and historical political economy casts serious doubt on the value of 'one-size-fits-all' rules and sheds insight into the creativity of governments in fiscal gimmickry (Dyson, 2014). Rules breed gaming. The eurozone area's design problems were masked by the fortuitous combination of the euro's launch in a global political economy of good times, the period of the so-called Great Moderation lasting for its first decade.

The eurozone was not designed for bad times. The Maastricht Treaty had incorporated a commitment to irreversibility of monetary union. However, this commitment was limited to launching monetary union by 1 January 1999. It did not extend to the irreversibility of the monetary union *after* its launch (Dyson, 2013). Hence the financial markets had an ongoing incentive to test member state commitment. The outcome was a process of 'muddling through' by both member states and the ECB. This process came to a head in the summer of 2012 when the European Council committed to banking union and Draghi promised to 'do whatever it takes' to protect the euro. However, exit was not precluded, not least because its threat was seen as a discipline on recalcitrant member states like Greece. But keeping exit as a possibility put member states and the ECB under pressure to put in place new mechanisms to prevent contagion within the monetary union. The logic of contagion pointed to full banking union, an extended remit for the ECB in financial stability, and ultimately a European monetary fund. It was a logic that challenged the original Maastricht architecture and many in the German establishment. More controversially still, it meant considering the option of new policy instruments, notably debt restructuring – as pressed by the IMF in relation to Greece – and capital controls to ease the pressures on domestic adjustment.

The underlying problem was that eurozone reforms of this type followed a technocratic trajectory. They helped to create a dangerous gap between elite discourse and bargaining and public engagement. The eurozone became less rather than more transparent. The EP was not a central player in fashioning a European public sphere and lacked visibility in nationally focused media reporting of the crisis. On balance the eurozone area crisis became part of the problems of democratic deficit and identity rather than part of their solution. The twin discourses of technocracy and communitarianism became dissociated. This dissociation was serious because technocratic processes and solutions could in most instances not hope to work unless there was public engagement in helping them to work. European economic governance failed to achieve this synthesis; it lacked public ownership. A key reason was that member state governments remained unwilling to cede or effectively share sovereignty in matters that really mattered for European economic governance.

The outcome was that eurozone member states faced unattractive scenarios: stumbling along from crisis to crisis; retrenchment of membership; and, bleakest of all, disaster. The scenarios were unattractive because of the multiple nature of the risks at a time when more effective European governance was required in an integrating and interdependent economy and in a global economy with new fast-rising powers. The result was a massive overloading of the eurozone area's capacity to act. The risks included bank failure on a scale that overwhelmed national fiscal capacity; state failure, most notably in Greece; decline in legitimacy, common identity, and solidarity; the rise of national populist political forces, especially in France; eurozone exits and their contagious effects; knock-on effects on the migration crisis and on potential crises elsewhere, perhaps sparked by Russian aggression; and German retreat from its hegemonic role. Faced with these risks the eurozone area elite remained committed to the optimistic scenario that member states would in the last analysis loyally comply with what was required to keep the show on the road.

References

Beck, U. (2013) *German Europe*. Cambridge: Polity.

De Larosière Group (2009) *The High Level Group on Financial Supervision in the EU*. Brussels: European Commission.

Dyson, K. (2010) 'Euro Europe: "Fuzzy" Boundaries and "Constrained" Differentiation in Macro-Economic Governance'. In K. Dyson and A. Sepos (eds), *Which Europe? The Politics of Differentiated Integration*. Houndmills: Palgrave Macmillan, pp. 215–34.

Dyson, K. (2012) 'Economic and Monetary Disunion?' In J. Hayward and R. Wurzel (eds), *European Disunion: Between Sovereignty and Solidarity*. Houndmills: Palgrave Macmillan, pp. 181–99.

Dyson, K. (2013) 'Sworn to Grim Necessity? Imperfections of European Economic Governance, Normative Political Theory, and Supreme Emergency', *Journal of European Integration*, Vol. 35, No. 3, pp. 207–22.

Dyson, K. (2014) *States, Debt and Power: 'Saints' and 'Sinners' in European History and Integration*. Oxford: Oxford University Press.

Dyson, K. (forthcoming) *The Ordo-liberal Tradition*.

Dyson, K. and Featherstone, K. (1999) *The Road to Maastricht: Negotiating Economic and Monetary Union*. Oxford: Oxford University Press.

Dyson, K. and Maes, I. (eds) (2016) *Architects of the Euro: Designing Economic and Monetary Union*. Oxford: Oxford University Press.

Dyson, K. and Quaglia, L. (2010) *European Economic Governance and Policies*. Volume 1: *Commentary on Key Historical and Institutional Documents*. Oxford: Oxford University Press.

Heipertz, M. and Verdun, A. (2010) *Ruling Europe: The Politics of the Stability and Growth Pact*. Cambridge: Cambridge University Press.

Hirschman, S. (1970) *Exit, Voice, and Loyalty*. Cambridge, MA: Harvard University Press.

Hodson, D. (2011) *Governing the Euro Area in Good Times and Bad*. Oxford: Oxford University Press.

Joerges, C. (2010) 'Unity in Diversity as Europe's Vocation and Conflicts Law as Europe's Constitutional Form', LEQS Paper, No. 28, London School of Economics, revised version April 2013.

Ludlow, P. (1982) *The Making of the European Monetary System: A Case Study of the Politics of the European Community*. London: Butterworth.

Mourlon-Druol, E. (2012) *A Europe Made of Money: The Emergence of the European Monetary System*. Ithaca, NY: Cornell University Press.

Obstfeld, M. (2013) 'Finance at Centre Stage: Some Lessons of the Euro Crisis', European Economy, Paper No. 493, April. Brussels: European Commission.

Picard, R. (ed.) (2015) *The Euro Crisis in the Media: Journalistic Coverage of Economic Crisis and European Institutions*. London: I.B. Tauris.

Sinn, H.-W. (2012) *Die Target-Falle: Gefahren für unser Geld und unsere Kinder*. München: Carl Hanser.

Steinbrück, P. (2010) *Unterm Strich*. Hamburg: Hoffmann und Campe.

Streeck, W. (2013) *Gekaufte Zeit: Die vertagte Krise des demokratischen Kapitalismus*. Berlin: Suhrkamp.

Task Force to the European Council (2010) *Strengthening Economic Governance in the EU*. Brussels: European Council.

Van Rompuy, H., Barroso, J., Juncker, J.-C., and Draghi, M. (2012) *Towards a Genuine Economic and Monetary Union*. Brussels: European Council.

Chapter 5

The UK: Membership in Crisis

LEE MCGOWAN AND DAVID PHINNEMORE

Introduction

The UK has rarely been a contented member of the EU. Over the last decade an historical wariness towards integration gave way to increasing and vocal euroscepticism and to growing calls for the UK to quit the EU. This led to a crisis in UK membership of the EU, which saw continued membership put into question, culminating in the referendum on 23 June 2016. This resulted in 51.9 per cent of voters opting, on a turnout of 72.2 per cent, to 'leave' the EU. The result was unexpected and the UK government had not prepared for it. The UK thus entered a new stage in the crisis: how to withdraw from the EU. For the EU, the priority became how to prevent others following the UK example.

This chapter explores the nature and implications of the crisis of UK EU membership. It starts by providing an overview of the crisis before illustrating, in the section 'Avoiding Crisis through Exceptionalism', how wariness towards European integration and reservations about its speed and direction have generally been managed by securing various forms of exceptionalism. The UK government may have claimed in its 2016 White Paper on UK membership of the EU that a recently negotiated 'new settlement' provided the UK with a 'special status within the EU' (UK Government, 2016a), but such a special status has long existed. The section 'Heading towards Crisis: Mounting Pressure for a Referendum on EU Membership' explores how a fragile membership moved into a period of profound crisis, triggered in 2013 by a promise from the UK Prime Minister, David Cameron, of an 'in-out' referendum before the end of 2017. It examines shifting domestic political attitudes to membership and the extent to which political leadership gave way to open questioning of whether the UK should leave at a time when the EU, faced with the eurozone crisis, was taking further steps to deepen integration, thus intensifying many of the tensions underpinning UK unease with membership. The section 'Resolving the Crisis: Renegotiation and Referendum' considers how the Cameron government that was returned to power in 2015 both exacerbated the air of crisis surrounding UK–EU relations through its divisions and its handling of relations with the rest of the EU and sought to resolve matters through a renegotiation and demands for greater exceptionalism. The outcome of the EU referendum and the vote for 'Brexit' marks one of the most decisive moments in post-war British history and politics and presents a new phase in the crisis: one that centres on the UK government's endeavours to negotiate its future relationship with the EU. Thus, the section on 'Crisis Begetting Crisis and Chaos' considers the implications of the referendum vote and how withdrawal from the EU could further tensions inside the UK. The final section, 'And For the EU?', examines how the referendum outcome has created a crisis for the EU.

Crisis Point

On 23 June 2016, UK voters were asked whether they wished to 'remain' in or 'leave' the EU. The vote came against a backdrop of increasing euroscepticism within the Conservative Party and unprecedented voter support for the UK Independence Party (UKIP). Together they provided for a particularly tumultuous period in UK political debate on EU membership. Popular scepticism towards European integration has been a feature of UK domestic politics since the early 1990s, but it had essentially been contained within political parties and by successive governments securing a unique accommodation within the EU – through formal opt-outs, grandstanding over 'red lines', vocal assertions of the national interest, cautious engagement, rejections of closer integration, and voluntary abnegation of leadership roles – that had in effect marginalized opposition to continued UK membership. However, during the Cameron governments – first the Conservative–Liberal Democrat coalition (2010–15) and then the Conservative government (2015–present) – the mood of contained awkwardness and scepticism towards the EU was replaced by a sense of crisis as an initial commitment to a referendum on almost any future EU treaty changes (enshrined in the European Union Act 2011) rapidly gave way to a commitment from Cameron in January 2013 – almost 40 years to the day after the UK joined the European Communities in 1973 – that a future Conservative government would hold an 'in-out' referendum on membership of the EU before the end of 2017.

This calculated commitment may have temporarily averted a growing internal crisis within the Conservative Party but it unwittingly paved the way for a much greater political crisis as Cameron struggled to contain hardening euroscepticism within the Conservative Party and his Conservative government and secure a 'new settlement' that would convince voters to support continued membership and not be swayed by the increasingly vocal calls from Conservatives, UKIP and other eurosceptics to leave the EU. With supporters, MPs, and government ministers engaging in an increasingly internecine struggle, the Conservative Party's very foundations and fabric were under threat. The Party was arguably facing its greatest crisis in modern times. Not only did Cameron's gamble for a 'new settlement' and an 'in-out' referendum ultimately turn the Prime Minister into a hostage to fortune, it also threatened a central tenet of UK foreign policy of the previous 40 years: membership of the EU. Against a backdrop of years of persistent sniping at and misrepresentation of the political and functional realities of the EU, Cameron's demands for a vaguely defined 'new settlement' saw him further straining UK relations with EU partners and running the risk of imposing on them, at a time of continued concerns over the eurozone and an intensifying migration crisis, an additional and arguably unnecessary crisis not of their making.

In retrospect, Cameron's approach to the EU issue – from his campaign to lead the Conservative Party in 2005 through the securing of a 'new settlement' for the UK in February 2016 to the referendum defeat in June 2016 – provides an apt case of mismanagement and miscalculation that has not only helped create a crisis but also generated further potential crises for the stability of the EU and the UK. On the former, Cameron's decision to hold a referendum and demand a 'new settlement' could be replicated in other EU member states. The fear of contagion has been palpable, evident in both the uncompromising line taken by the EU institutions and other member states during the 'new settlement' negotiations and in their tough response to the 'leave' vote. On the future of the UK, Cameron's resignation, the absence of any 'Brexit' planning by either the 'leave' campaign or the government, and the regional distribution of the vote, have plunged the UK into serious political and constitutional turmoil. The decision to delay triggering the withdrawal process provided for in Article 50 of the Treaty on the European Union (TEU) and the vacuous 'Brexit means Brexit' mantra of the new Prime Minister, Theresa May, belied the lack of preparedness for the referendum outcome. With 'remain' majorities in Scotland and Northern Ireland, the Conservative government was also quickly faced with the prospect of renewed pressure for Scottish independence and concerns over the future of Northern Ireland and its border with the Republic of Ireland. There was also the question of how to respond to London's overwhelming 'remain' vote and the clear 'leave' majorities in most of the rest of England and Wales. Much of this had been predicted in polls (YouGov, 2016) and informed commentary, but the omens and experts were ignored. The UK was now entering a new period in its crisis of EU membership, one seemingly set to see it leave the EU; but at what cost?

Avoiding Crisis through Exceptionalism

The history of UK membership of the EU is widely recognized as one characterized by profound discomfort with the concept and realities of integration. However, students of European integration also need to acknowledge that political connections with continental Europe have always been limited at least from the sixteenth century until the mid-twentieth century and involvement has only usually occurred when the 'Balance of Power' in Europe has been threatened (Goodlad, 2000; Monger, 1967). Indeed, the UK's geographical 'island' location had prevented from 1066 onwards any serious military incursions, defeat, and subsequent regime change and allowed the English (and then the British state) to evolve gradually. This helped the UK carve out a distinct identity that feeds into domestic assessments of its position in Europe. Stephen George's description of the UK as 'an awkward partner' continues to capture essential features of the seemingly persistent discomfort (Bulmer, George, and Scott, 1992; George, 1990). Stephen Wall's presentation of the UK as 'a Stranger in Europe' (Wall, 2008), a view informed by his practitioner perspective, similarly flags a sense of estrangement and awkwardness. Other analyses promote a sense of persistent wariness. Hugo Young provocatively presented Europe as 'This Blessed Plot' (Young, 1998).

Europe has proven to be a fault line in UK politics and the issue has vexed the Conservative Party in particular since the late 1980s. Indeed, few, if any, historical surveys of the UK's involvement in European integration present a picture other than one of limited enthusiasm for the EU, a generally half-hearted engagement, and an increasingly semi-detached status as a member of the EU. None of this has ever been helped by the fact that the UK joined the then European Communities as a latecomer and once their essential political purpose and sense of direction had been defined. That the political dimension to integration has rarely been embraced and instead generally treated with mistrust has not helped either. Notions of awkwardness, of being uncomfortable with the assumed speed and perceived, if not actual, direction of integration have rarely been absent from either popular analysis or public debate. Evidence of disputes over the EU budget and the decision not to adopt the euro or to become part of Schengen are often cited as illustrative examples of such UK exceptionalism.

Yet such portrayals tend to overlook how much the UK has played a pivotal role in key EU developments. It was a core driver behind the development of the European Regional Development Fund in the 1970s, the single market programme in the 1980s, and a strong advocate of enlargement in the 1990s and 2000s. The UK government has also been an instrumental actor in the Council where, according to Hix (2016), it has generally been on the winning side in terms of majority votes – 87 per cent of the time between 2009 and 2015 – and UK MEPs have played a leading role in the workings of the European Parliament (EP) in the roles of committee chairs and policy rapporteurs. This degree of UK embeddedness in the machinery of EU governance has rarely been recognized among the wider public and large sections of the media. Successive UK governments have done little to explain to voters what treaty revisions entail, how much UK preferences have shaped the current EU, and how much these preferences have been respected. Since the 1980s, the evolution of the European Communities, the establishment of the EU, and the latter's further reform have generally accommodated the misgivings of successive UK governments about further integration. In the original TEU (1992), the UK secured an opt-out from stage III of economic and monetary union and the single currency. It also ensured an existing opt-out from the Community Charter of Fundamental Social Rights for Workers (1988) was carried forward into an opt-out from new social policy activities. In the Treaty of Amsterdam (1997), non-participation in Schengen was respected through a formal opt-out which extended to other aspects of the EU's project to establish an area of freedom, security, and justice (AFSJ). At Amsterdam and subsequently in the Treaty of Nice (2001), UK red lines were generally respected. The accommodation of UK interests was also evident in the Treaty of Lisbon (2007) where limits on the application within the UK of the Charter of Fundamental Rights and an extension of opt-out/opt-in arrangements regarding AFSJ activities were agreed.

The overall effect has been to sustain a sense of historical exceptionalism. Geddes, for example, citing Churchill's view that 'Britain' is 'with but not of Europe', concludes that even after 40 years of membership, other member states arguably still have grounds 'to doubt the extent that Britain is still even "with" Europe' (Geddes, 2013: 260). And Cameron, not just as Prime Minister, did nothing to dispel such doubts. His approach to the EU long reflected the rise of euroscepticism that has taken hold of the Conservative Party. While in opposition he pulled Conservative MEPs out of the European People's Party (EPP) group, thus depriving future Conservative-led governments of valuable pre-European Council intelligence and a chance for informal meetings with fellow centre-right leaders in the EU. Only in the run-up to the 2016 referendum, once he had secured a 'new settlement', was Cameron willing to make a clear case for continued EU membership, a turn of events which caused a degree of frustration and bewilderment domestically and elsewhere in the EU given the criticisms that he and his ministers had previously been levelling against EU institutions and policies.

In making the 'remain' case, Cameron belatedly latched on to the UK's self-evident but long-overlooked 'special status' within the EU and the extent to which its priorities (e.g. regarding competitiveness, administrative and regulatory reform, and a guaranteed voice for national interests) are very much reflected in the long-standing structural and policy priorities of the EU. For despite eurosceptic protestations about the nature and direction of the EU being imposed on the UK by a federalist mindset and an insatiable continental appetite for 'more Europe', the course of EU-based integration has been determined far more by hard-nosed negotiation between states, pragmatic responses to crises, and a logic of incremental change in which successive UK governments have had a prominent voice on the European stage. This same voice was scarcely audible at the national level.

Heading Towards Crisis: Mounting Pressure for a Referendum on EU Membership

The relatively selective approach to European integration pursued by successive UK governments after Maastricht has not been without costs. When viewed over time, with each 'success' questions have arisen not just about the degree of UK engagement but also about the UK's longer-term role as a major EU 'top table' player. Short-term political needs have eclipsed any longer-term strategic planning about the UK's position in the EU. The approach was also short-sighted because securing concessions as a means to appease eurosceptics was never going to work in the longer term as it fed further demands from eurosceptic-minded politicians and fuelled calls for a referendum on further treaty reform.

Such was the dynamic within the Conservative Party while in opposition. Consequently, during the 2010 general election, and very conscious that UKIP had gained 16.5 per cent in the EP elections a year earlier, the party campaigned on a platform of no further extensions to the EU's powers without a referendum and of the repatriation of 'key powers over legal rights, criminal justice and social and employment legislation'. The claim was that the 'steady and unaccountable intrusion of the European Union into almost every aspect of our lives has gone too far' (Conservative Party, 2010: 113–14).

The growing euroscepticism in the Conservative Party was partially curtailed in coalition government with the consistently pro-EU Liberal Democrats. The Coalition sought to balance 'constructive engagement' while 'protecting ... national sovereignty', committing itself to playing a 'leading role' in the EU, but also agreeing that 'no further powers should be transferred to Brussels without a referendum' (UK Government, 2010). The commitment to a leading role proved to be little more than wishful thinking. However, the European Union Act (2011), with its extensive parliamentary oversight of and referendum locks on transfers of power and competence to the EU, was swiftly adopted. Cameron naively hoped that with a referendum on further treaty change on the statute book, the concerns of eurosceptic backbench MPs would diminish. He was mistaken.

In October 2011 backbench Conservative MPs secured a vote on a 'National Referendum on the European Union'; 111 MPs voted in favour. Cameron responded by adopting a more eurosceptic position and at the European Council in December 2011 'vetoed' a proposed EU Treaty on Stability, Coordination and Governance (the Fiscal Compact), only to see 25 other member states proceed with it outside the formal EU framework. While Cameron's eurosceptic grandstanding heartened his backbench MPs, they also demanded more. The government's launch in 2012 of a comprehensive Balance of Competences review – essentially an audit of what the EU does and how EU law affects the UK – was never going to contain hardened eurosceptics, and in June 2013 almost 100 backbench MPs wrote to Cameron to demand the government introduce legislation for a referendum on EU membership during the next parliament. Pressure for an 'in-out' referendum was unprecedented. With the possibility of the UK voting to leave the EU, the English language gained a new word in the summer of 2012: 'Brexit' (The Economist, 2012).

By early October 2012, Cameron had conceded that a referendum on new terms of membership would be the 'cleanest, neatest and simplest' way to gain fresh popular consent for continued UK participation in the EU (The Guardian, 2012a), but it was a strategy laden with risk. Eurosceptic Conservative backbenchers pushed their case harder and forced an extensive debate on whether to repeal the European Communities Act (1972) on 26 October 2012; five days later, 53 Conservative backbench MPs voted against the government on the EU's Multiannual Financial Framework (2014–20). Cameron promptly, and rather unwisely in terms of tactics, conceded that a UK withdrawal from the EU was 'imaginable' (The Guardian, 2012b). He realized he needed to do something and with the EU in the midst of the eurozone crisis, and with further treaty reform in order to safeguard the future of the single currency in his view inevitable, Cameron believed he could use the threat of a UK veto over treaty change to secure the repatriation of unspecified powers as part of renegotiated terms of UK membership.

Cameron delivered his much-awaited 'Europe' speech on 23 January 2013 from the offices of Bloomberg in London. Simply put, if the Conservatives won the 2015 general election, a 'new settlement', based on the outcome of the Balance of Competences Review, governing UK membership of the EU would be negotiated and put to voters in an 'in-out referendum' to be held 'within the first half of the next parliament' and before the end of 2017. Assuming a 'new settlement', Cameron committed to campaign for it 'with all my heart and soul' (Cameron, 2013).

The effect of the Bloomberg speech was twofold. On the one hand, it provided a commitment to and a timeline for an 'in-out' referendum. The forces of hard euroscepticism had achieved a key goal. The possibility of a Brexit vote was now firmly on the agenda and an exit from the EU possible. On the other hand, there was now a need for Cameron and the Conservatives to define what sort of 'new settlement' they wanted. Given the wide range of views among party members, this was a tall order, especially with significant numbers clearly wishing simply to leave the EU. Moreover, there was the question of what could actually be secured from a negotiation with the other member states. Would they in fact be willing to negotiate? Would they stand for treaty reform to safeguard the euro being held to ransom by a UK government seeking to overhaul the terms of its already opt-out laden membership?

Cameron's reasoning was very much predicated on the assumption that his fellow leaders would be minded to reach a new accommodation. The other 27 member state governments had become accustomed to regular UK questioning of European integration. Since they all valued UK membership, Cameron assumed a deal could be struck which would allow him to make the case to the UK electorate for continued EU membership. This strategy was a considerable gamble as much would rest on the willingness of the others to negotiate, the nature of any deal, and Cameron's abilities to pacify his critics and sell any renegotiation package as meaningful to UK voters. From the very start Cameron's strategy was tested. Notably, the promise of a referendum failed to silence many of his eurosceptic backbenchers. Less than four months after the Bloomberg speech, 114 Conservative MPs rebelled against the government by voting to regret the absence from the Queen's Speech of a reference to an 'in-out' referendum. More worryingly for Cameron was the failure of his referendum pledge to diminish UKIP's appeal. Support for UKIP grew stronger and it emerged as the largest UK party in the 2014 EP elections, capturing 27.5 per cent of the vote and returning 23 MEPs.

UKIP's success owed much to its charismatic and media savvy leader, Nigel Farage, its populist agenda which very much focused on eurosceptic and anti-immigrant rhetoric, and its ability to tap into wider public disenchantment with established political parties. UKIP may have failed to make any major breakthrough at the 2015 general election, managing to return just one MP, but its ability to capture 3.8 million votes or 12.6 per cent of the vote and to finish as the second most popular party in 125 constituencies provided clear evidence of considerable eurosceptic sentiment across the country. The Conservatives were the surprising – and surprised – victor, securing enough seats (331) to form the first Conservative-only government since 1997. With victory, however, came the need to secure agreement to a 'new settlement' on UK membership of the EU, deliver on the manifesto commitment to hold an in-out referendum before the end of 2017, and honour the result 'whatever the outcome' (Conservative Party, 2015: 73). Winning the referendum and keeping his party united, when an estimated one-third of the parliamentary party was strongly eurosceptic (Moore, 2015), provided Cameron with major challenges. Divisions ran deep – including in the cabinet. Europe, not for the first time, threatened turmoil at the heart of government. Skilful management and leadership were in order, both at home and on the EU stage.

Resolving the Crisis: Renegotiation and Referendum

During his first period as Prime Minister, Cameron had proved a skilful operator and had successfully pursued and secured at the EU level many of the UK's major interests in terms of promoting competitiveness and opening energy and services markets. The period was also marked by a number of high-profile and controversial moments, particularly regarding the attempted veto of the Fiscal Compact, responses to the management of the eurozone crisis, and Cameron's failed attempt to thwart the selection of Jean-Claude Juncker as Commission President. Embarking on an 'in-out' referendum, however, was new territory and the challenge facing Cameron was now to persuade his fellow EU leaders to support a renegotiation of UK membership.

With the extensive Balance of Competences Review presenting a positive evaluation of UK membership, Cameron was forced to identify issues for the renegotiation. Initial indications were provided in the Bloomberg speech and then in a March 2014 article for the *Sunday Telegraph* where Cameron called for the potential of the single market to be fully realized and the diversity of the member states to be accommodated. He also hinted at repatriating powers, voiced objections to the commitment to 'ever closer union', and suggested a more significant role for national parliaments (Cameron, 2014). All this made for good headlines. Eight months later and in a clear response to UKIP's ever greater emphasis on immigration, demands for curbing migration and restricting migrants' benefits were added to the list.

Having won the 2015 election, a first priority of the new Cameron government was to fulfil its dual commitment to legislate for a referendum and to secure a 'new settlement'. The EU referendum bill was laid before Parliament on 28 May 2015 and a month later, at the European Council on 25–26 June, Cameron explained his plans to fellow EU leaders. Frustratingly for them, as ever, there was no real detail and so it was agreed to 'revert' to the issue in December. In the meantime, officials began to explore technical issues. Cameron and his Chancellor of the Exchequer, George Osborne, set about discussing with EU partners on a one-to-one basis the issues they wanted to see addressed as part of the promised 'new settlement'. Specifics were generally lacking. By October, the European

Council was seeking much greater clarity on the actual focal points for the negotiations. Eventually, on 10 November 2015, Cameron sent a six-page letter to Donald Tusk, President of the European Council, setting out four reform 'baskets' covering economic governance, competitiveness, sovereignty, and migration (Cameron, 2015). Each contained specific demands that essentially echoed earlier pronouncements (see Table 5.1).

Table 5.1   *Cameron's 'new settlement' demands and key outcomes*

		Cameron's demands (November 2015)	European Council outcome (February 2016)
1	Economic governance	• The development of the eurozone must not be allowed to compromise the integrity of the single market or the legitimate interests of non-members of the eurozone • A series of 'legally binding principles' safeguarding the operation of the EU 'for all 28 member states' • A safeguard mechanism to ensure the principles are 'respected and enforced'	• Involvement in closer eurozone integration to be voluntary for non-eurozone member states • Mutual respect between eurozone and non-eurozone member states on the development of the eurozone and of the single market • Mechanism for referral to Council or European Council of 'reasoned opposition' to measures
2	Competitiveness	• An increased commitment to and action on *competitiveness*, so essentially less of a regulatory burden on business and greater efforts to realize the free movement of goods, services, and capital	• Declaration on exploiting fully the potential of the single market and on better and less regulation

According to Tusk there was 'a strong will on the part of all sides to find solutions that respond to the British request while benefiting the European Union as a whole' (European Council, 2015a). His assessment was firm, but cautiously optimistic on reaching agreement on the first, second, and third 'baskets'. As for immigration, there remained 'substantial political differences' to be overcome. The European Council

3	Sovereignty	• A 'formal, legally binding and irreversible' UK opt-out from 'ever closer union' • A veto over unwanted legislative proposals for groups of national parliaments • Confirmation that EU institutions would continue to respect UK opt-out/opt-in arrangements concerning justice and home affairs matters • Commitment to subsidiarity 'fully implemented'	• Agreement that the UK is not committed to further political integration and that references to 'ever closer union' do not apply to the UK • Enhanced powers for national parliaments collectively to block legislative proposals unless concerns are addressed • Declaration on subsidiarity implementation and burden reduction
4	Migration	• A crackdown on the abuse, especially by criminals and fraudsters, of free movement • Four-year qualifying period for EU migrants for in-work benefits or social housing • An end to sending child benefit payments overseas	• Proposed legislation limiting abuse of the right to free movement • Seven-year 'emergency brake' period in which new EU migrants' access to in-work benefits, primarily tax credits and housing benefits, is restricted for the first four years • Child benefit payments overseas to be index-linked to the standard of living in the member state where the child lives

Sources: Cameron (2015), European Council (2016b)

concurred at its December meeting and agreed that 'mutually satisfactory solutions in all the four areas' would be found when they were next scheduled to meet in February 2016 (European Council, 2015b: 7).

The agreement reached by the European Council in February 2016 consisted of a legally binding 'Decision' on 'a new settlement for the UK within the European Union' supplemented by various statements and declarations (European Council, 2016b). These addressed each of Cameron's four 'baskets', but the outcome often differed from what had been originally sought, not least because other member states, led by Germany and its Chancellor, Angela Merkel, pointedly refused to compromise on fundamental principles such as the free movement of workers (see Table 5.1). Most noticeably, no veto was granted to non-eurozone member states over eurozone measures that could affect the operation of the single market; instead a referral mechanism was agreed. Also there would be no four-year ban on EU migrants' entitlement to in-work benefits; rather, access to these benefits would be phased in over four years. Moreover, no informed observer could really claim that the outcome overall represented a major new settlement for the UK. All the same, a number of concessions had been secured. They would apply, albeit assuming a referendum vote to 'remain' in the EU.

The package, hardly transformative, was more a 'collection of modest reforms' (Grant and Springford, 2016), but it did allow Cameron to claim that the deal was a success, protected the economy, safeguarded sterling, and protected UK taxpayers from the costs of the problems in the eurozone. For pro-EU enthusiasts in the UK, Cameron's 'new settlement' could be interpreted as further reinforcing the UK's image as an increasingly semi-detached member of the EU, keen on the single market but suspicious of EU action in other fields, including notably migration and the social dimension. Within a matter of days the UK government published a White Paper on the deal: *The Best of Both Worlds: The United Kingdom's Special Status in a Reformed European Union*. Somewhat disingenuously, Cameron claimed in his foreword that the UK government had 'secured a new settlement to give the United Kingdom special status in the European Union' (UK Government, 2016a: 5). The fact that the special status, secured through opt-outs, already existed was glossed over. Ultimately, however, the deal did allow Cameron to set out his case for remaining in the EU. His argument was that continued membership would make the UK stronger, safer, and better off; as for any decision to leave the EU, this would be 'a great leap into the unknown' (Hansard, 2016).

In making his case to fellow MPs – developed in further statements and speeches in the ensuing weeks – a hitherto unseen side of Cameron was revealed: an apparently enthusiastic if constructively critical and pragmatic supporter of the EU. The contrast with his previous five years as Prime Minister and longer as Conservative leader could hardly have been greater. Prior to the 'new settlement', Cameron's discourse and actions had been characterized by a confusing mix of sniping, disengagement, grandstanding, bluster, and ambiguity. Now he appeared a convert to the cause; a believer in European integration and in the UK's place in Europe; a committed supporter of continued membership.

This was all very well. But he needed to convince an increasingly sceptical public as well as many of his own backbench MPs and grass-roots Conservative Party members. Was his seemingly sudden conversion too late to avert a major economic and political crisis? Certainly Cameron was eager to move quickly and so swiftly announced the referendum for 23 June 2016, a date earlier than originally envisaged and one that would avoid an autumn vote against a backdrop of a possible further intensification of the migration crisis in southern Europe. Attention quickly shifted to campaigning. Unsurprisingly, given its evident feebleness, the fanfare around the 'new settlement' soon faded and attention shifted to the broader issues of the economic, political, and security implications of continued membership and of a 'Brexit'. Indeed, media interest in the details of Cameron's deal quickly dissipated and in less than 24 hours eurosceptics were once again presenting their desire to restore sovereignty to the UK so that Westminster could make its own laws and the UK could take control of its own borders and of immigration and secure better trade deals with the rest of the world. The government quickly responded with detailed reports signalling the shortcomings of different alternatives to membership (UK Government, 2016b) and making it clear how difficult any withdrawal would be (UK Government, 2016c). Crucially, in retrospect, it had very little to say on controlling immigration.

The government's hope of winning support for 'remain' among the public was always going to prove challenging. Many eurosceptics simply dismissed the government's arguments. Fortunately for Cameron, the 'Brexiteers' were divided into a number of rival camps, notably Vote Leave and Leave.EU. Far less comforting was the fact that six leading Conservatives announced their support for Brexit. Among them were two big-hitters: the Justice Secretary, Michael Gove, and the populist Mayor of London, Boris Johnson. Cameron's position secured support time and time again from leading figures from the business and banking sectors and other world leaders, most notably the US President, Barack Obama, but such endorsements had little meaningful effect. The low profile of the Britain Stronger in Europe group was problematic for Cameron's cause as was the lukewarm support coming from the leadership of the Labour Party under Jeremy Corbyn. When the official 'leave' and 'remain' campaign groups were announced in April, opinion polls revealed that voting intentions were equally split between both camps and that the outcome was going to be very close.

Indeed, as voting closed on 23 June many 'leave' campaigners were expecting a defeat, albeit a narrow one. Having seen opinion polls move in their favour in the penultimate week of campaigning, there was a swing back to 'remain' in the final days before the referendum. Yet, as the results were returned in the early hours of 24 June, it soon became clear that the 'leave' campaign had won. Moreover, the UK was divided. While a majority in England, in Wales, and in the UK as a whole opted to leave the EU, majorities to remain were returned in Scotland, Northern Ireland, London, and Gibraltar. When the final result of what was officially an advisory referendum was declared there were 17,410,742 votes to leave and 16,141,241 votes to remain (see Table 5.2). The advice that voters were giving the UK government was that they wished for the UK to leave the EU.

Crisis Begetting Crisis and Chaos

Reaction to the referendum result was a mix of surprise and jubilation for 'leavers' and disbelief and dismay for 'remainers'. Rather than act on the result and trigger Article 50 TEU on withdrawal, as he had indicated he would and many in the EU were expecting and insisting, Cameron announced his resignation as Prime Minister, effectively washing his hands of the referendum outcome. A frenzied and at times farcical Conservative

Table 5.2   *EU referendum (23 June 2016) – result*

	Remain		Leave		Turnout
	Total	%	Total	%	%
England	13,247,674	46.6	15,187,583	53.4	73.0
Northern Ireland	440,707	55.8	349,442	44.2	62.7
Scotland	1,661,191	62.0	1,018,322	38.0	67.2
Wales	772,347	47.5	854,572	52.5	71.7
Gibraltar	19,322	95.9	823	4.1	83.5
Total	16,141,241	48.1	17,410,742	51.9	72.2

Source: Electoral Commission (2016)

Party leadership contest ensued in which Gove crossed his fellow leading 'leave' campaigner, Johnson, only to be forced out of the race, which was quickly won by the former Home Secretary, Theresa May, a nominal yet seemingly lukewarm and low-profile supporter of 'remain'.

Among the new Prime Minister's first tasks was to establish when to trigger Article 50. The decision was to delay until 2017, essentially because the new government desperately needed time to define its position. Not only had the Cameron government studiously avoided undertaking any contingency planning for a 'leave' vote, but the 'leave' campaign, victorious but divided, was simply bereft of any clear and detailed plans of its own. Rather disingenuously it argued that it had merely campaigned for the UK to leave the EU and it was for the government to deliver and plan for the consequences. Notifying the European Council of the UK's intention to leave the EU would trigger Article 50 and start the two-year time frame for withdrawal, but a manifestly unprepared UK government simply could not afford to do this as it scrambled around to determine what sort of post-leave relationship it wanted with the EU. May also had to form a government and appoint a team to deliver on the wishes of the leave voters. Inspired or naive only time will tell, but her choices to lead on 'Brexit' were all prominent but essentially strategy-less 'leave' campaigners: Johnson as Foreign Secretary, David Davis as Secretary of State for Exiting the European Union, and Liam Fox as Secretary of State for International Trade and President of the Board of Trade. None had a developed plan for how 'Brexit' should be managed or what new relationship the UK should seek; Davis and Fox were also saddled with the need to establish new ministries to support their work.

The sense of confusion and chaos merely added to the dismay and frustration of the UK's EU partners. With the referendum over, the EU-27 were keen to move on to withdrawal negotiations, quickly signalling their expectation that the UK would be leaving by gathering without the UK to discuss the future of the EU. Also prominent in their pronouncements was that there would be no 'cherry-picking' as regards the content of any post-Brexit relationship. For example, access to the single market required acceptance of all four freedoms: free movement of goods, services, capital, and importantly, given the prominence of anti-immigration concerns among 'leave' voters, workers. Such statements also acted as timely reminders of the EU's dominant position in the hitherto unused procedure for withdrawal provided for in Article 50, a two-year process only extendable with the unanimous agreement of the other 27 member states and a withdrawal agreement subject to both the agreement of the Council of the EU, acting by a qualified majority, and the consent of the EP. In addition there would need to be negotiations on a new relationship, likely to be some form of association and thus requiring unanimous agreement of EU member states, EP consent, and most probably ratification in each of the member states. Formal negotiations for such an arrangement could only take place once the UK was no longer a member state.

Such negotiations were not the only hurdle facing the UK. 'Brexit' also forces the UK to seek new trading relations with other parts of the world. For the 'leave' campaign this is a major opportunity. Establishing new trade deals, most notably with the USA, Canada, Mexico, Mercosur, India, China, Australia, and New Zealand, offers many opportunities. Moreover, outside the EU businesses would presumably thrive having been freed from 'Brussels' and its associated 'red tape'. However, any new arrangements will take time to negotiate and much will depend on the eagerness and readiness of other states to accommodate the UK. John Major, the former Prime Minister and veteran of the Don Quixote politics of the ratification of the Maastricht Treaty, believed the 'Brexiteers' were building a campaign on fantasy (*Sky News*, 2016) and cast considerable doubt that the UK would be able to strike decent trade deals with the EU. Only time would tell.

Also on May's agenda was what to do with Scotland, Northern Ireland, and Gibraltar, each of which had, as expected, returned majorities in favour of remaining in the EU. Their interests had barely featured in Cameron's decision to hold a referendum, which had been taken to dampen euroscepticism in England. It seems that little attention was given to how this would play out across the UK, even though there were regional voices flagging concerns. These have been borne out by developments since the referendum raising questions about the future political make-up of the UK, which clearly is far from being a united and unitary state. Rather, it is a union of four distinct territories comprising three nations, namely England, Scotland, and Wales, and one region, Northern Ireland, with a variety of layers of regional government across England. Each has been shaped by its own historical legacies and in turn been shaped by language, culture, and religion. Such territorial differentiation (Palmer, 2008) has fuelled demands for greater legislative, judicial, and political autonomy and culminated in the devolution settlements for Scotland, Wales, and Northern Ireland of the late 1990s. Although foreign affairs (including relations with the EU) were deemed a reserved matter for Whitehall, devolving certain policy responsibilities (especially agriculture and fisheries, and the environment) to the devolved administrations ensured interaction and increased relationships with the EU.

Although for the purposes of the referendum outcome the UK was treated as a single constituency, in practice many eyes were on the regional distribution of votes; and rightly so. For as the regional responses to the 'remain' votes in Scotland and Northern Ireland have demonstrated, they have implications for the future of the UK per se as well as its membership of the EU. Both votes have led for calls for the voice of the 'remain' majorities to be respected and for neither Scotland nor Northern Ireland to be forced out of the EU against their wishes and on the back of an essentially English vote. The Scottish First Minister, Nicola Sturgeon, was quick to assert her determination that Scotland should remain in the EU, canvassing support from EU member states and the EU institutions. Equally predictably, the vote in Scotland brought back onto the political agenda the question of Scottish independence, with a third referendum a distinct possibility.

In Northern Ireland, Sinn Féin, immediately after the referendum, called for a 'border poll' on whether there should be a united Ireland. The call was swiftly rejected by the UK government. Instead attention focused on questions around the future of the border with the Republic of Ireland and how its soft, open nature could be safeguarded if the UK were to be outside the EU's customs union and single market. Implementing the 'leave' campaign's calls for strict controls on immigration poses a major problem if the border is not to become an open back door into the UK. The fact that the UK has a land border with the rest of the EU seemed to escape the attention of many 'leave' campaigners. Questions were also raised over the implications of Brexit for the future of the Good Friday Agreement and the peace process more generally, both of which depend, in part at least, on the UK and Ireland being members of the EU.

For Scotland and Northern Ireland – as well as Wales and Gibraltar – the prospect of the UK negotiating its withdrawal from the EU also begs the question whether and how Whitehall and Westminster will ensure their interests are represented and respected. Will the administrations be involved in the negotiations about the new UK relationship with the EU or will the UK government take full responsibility? Will their parliaments and assemblies have a vote on the UK leaving the EU? Will they have a veto? May's claim on a visit to Scotland that she would only trigger Article 50 if there was a shared UK position suggested that Scottish, Welsh, and Northern Irish voices would have to be heard. A further issue to be considered was the implications of withdrawal for the repatriation of the competences from the EU to the UK and which and to what extent they will be devolved down to Edinburgh, Belfast, and Cardiff. After more than 40 years of EU membership, EU law and policy forms a substantive part of governance in the UK's devolved administrations, especially in the areas of agriculture, fisheries, and the environment. EU membership had always impacted unevenly across the UK and this helps explain the different pattern of votes that emerged across the UK. The challenge now facing the devolved administrations is not just about how far their specific policy interests (e.g. regarding renewable energies, agriculture, and freedom of movement), which may not be shared by Westminster, can be protected outside the EU, but how far they have the ability and capacity to handle former EU competences. The outcome of the referendum has real potential to create tensions across the UK and unsettle the constitutional structure of the UK itself.

And for the EU?

It is also a crisis for the EU. Had there been a 'remain' victory, then the hope within the EU would have been that it could now enter a period of relative stability at least as far as the UK's continued membership was concerned. Instead, with the 'leave' victory, the EU is saddled with the question of 'what next' and of negotiating, once Article 50 is triggered, the UK's exit and a new relationship with what is an important partner economically, politically, culturally, and diplomatically. Few continental voices beyond eurosceptic nationalists and some of the most ardent federalists have been heard welcoming the referendum outcome; EU leaders have all generally expressed their regret at the prospect of the UK leaving the EU. This is understandable; a friend and ally is being lost.

Moreover, the UK's decision to exit poses yet another challenge for the EU to navigate, which will absorb human capital and time that the EU would much prefer to direct at other pressing issues, most notably migration and the stability of the eurozone. The impact of an eventual UK withdrawal is not to be underestimated and will be felt on a number of fronts. It will deprive the EU of one of its most powerful, experienced, and resourced diplomatic voices on the world stage; it will leave the EU with just France among the five permanent members of the UN Security Council. This all has implications for the EU delivering on its foreign, security, and trade policy ambitions. While the UK's engagement on such matters has often lacked genuine enthusiasm and been mixed with obstructionist behaviours, there can be little doubt that without the resource and standing that the UK can contribute, the EU's effectiveness in promoting its voice internationally will be constrained, at least in the short term. Then there is also the matter of the EU's military and defence aspirations; it is difficult to see these being advanced without the resource that the UK could have provided, at least notionally, as a member state. Furthermore, the UK's exit will have a bearing on the EU budget; without the UK's annual €7–9 billion net 'contribution', the EU will be forced to scale back and reconsider existing budget lines.

A UK withdrawal on its own is unlikely, however, to lead to a fullblown crisis in the EU's development. Brexit does not mean the end of what is a determinedly resilient political process and project. What concerns EU leaders and officials more is the possibility of contagion and other member states coming under pressure to hold a referendum on continued membership. Eurosceptic forces, forever questioning the legitimacy and remoteness of the EU and, for them, its corrosive impact on sovereignty and national identity, have been quick to call for such a vote, notably in France, Germany, Italy, and the Netherlands. For the moment the calls have fallen on deaf ears. If one is answered, however, and a second member state, especially a large one, leaves, the future of the EU will most certainly be called into question. Until then the position of EU leaders is clear: the EU has to be safeguarded.

Conclusions

The decision in 1961 to seek membership of the European Economic Community (EEC) was a major moment in the post-war history of the UK and was hailed as an opportunity to put the UK at the heart of and steer (west) European political developments. With hindsight, questions might be asked (as they were asked at the time by President Charles de Gaulle) about the UK's readiness for and commitment to European integration. EEC – and later EU – membership proved to be a divisive issue in domestic politics and one that constantly bedevilled, albeit to varying degrees, every administration since the time of UK accession. The issues of contention covered key aspects of integration such as the budget, the free movement of people, the powers of supranational institutions, the euro, energy policy, and social policy. Throughout, the UK's policy towards Europe has been characterized by doubts and crisis: the doubts of whether to join and then to stay; numerous crises inside the EEC/EU; and now, furthered by the 'leave' vote in the referendum on 23 June 2016, a fundamental crisis as the country envisages abandoning membership and securing a new relationship as a non-member state with the EU.

Much has already been debated and written about the UK's engagement with Europe (Simms, 2016). The referendum result marks another landmark in this ongoing relationship and the narrative of crisis. It is not only one that impacts directly on the structure and politics of the UK, but one that represents a major crisis in the history of the EU: the first time a member state has sought to leave. That the crisis involves the UK should cause little surprise given the persistent unease with integration that has characterized UK membership and the increasing levels of euroscepticism that have become a prominent feature of domestic UK politics particularly over the last two decades. More surprising is the fact that the unease should have developed – in part owing to political mismanagement by successive governments and most particularly those of Cameron – into a major crisis. The referendum result was not expected by the establishment. The dominant 'leave' vote in England is best understood as a popular revolt against the economic and political elites in metropolitan areas, against globalization, and against what is for many disgruntlement with the hardships of everyday life. The EU referendum provided an opportunity for many to voice their frustration; and arguments adopted by those wishing to leave the EU that the EU was run by 'faceless bureaucrats', responsible for the rise in immigration and spending vast amounts of national revenues, proved enticing. How far many people realized the full significance of the referendum outcome is open to question.

In retrospect, the EU-27 could have offered more to Cameron on the 'free movement of persons' as part of the 'new settlement' brokered in February 2016. This, however, could have encouraged others, especially in countries where eurosceptic forces have become or are threatening to become significant political forces, to seek similar concessions and thus threatened an unravelling of the integration process. As the UK government follows up on the referendum result and proceeds towards a withdrawal, how the EU responds could become crucial to its own future as well as that of the UK. To concede on core principles would be to risk contagion and to encourage eurosceptic forces to challenge fundamentals. Yet to take a hard and principled stand would significantly limit the options for the UK in establishing a new relationship with the EU. For ardent supporters of 'leave' this may well be welcome; 'leave' will be leave. Yet a minimalist new relationship will only exacerbate tensions within the UK between those parts that voted 'leave' and those, notably Scotland and Northern Ireland, where there were clear votes in favour of 'remain'. Those tensions, so often not fully considered by the UK government, if not addressed could threaten the break-up of the UK. This all assumes that an advisory vote to leave actually translates into the UK leaving the EU. The delay in triggering Article 50, the uncertainties surrounding what the UK wishes from a 'Brexit', and whether a better arrangement outside the EU can be achieved, leads some observers to believe that 'Brexit' may not actually happen. If it does not happen, the domestic political fallout will be considerable. It will also open yet another chapter in the enduring saga of the crisis of UK membership of the EU.

References

Bulmer, S., Goerge, S., and Scott, A. (1992) *The United Kingdom and EC Membership Evaluated.* London: Continuum.

Cameron, D. (2013) *EU Speech at Bloomberg*, London, 23 January, http://www. newstatesman.com/politics/2013/01/david-camerons-speech-eu-full-text, date accessed 24 February 2016. The version of the speech published on the UK government website, http://www.gov.uk/government/speeches/eu-speech-at-bloomberg, date accessed 24 February 2016, is a redacted version that omits references to the time frame for the referendum, it being an 'in-out referendum' and Cameron campaigning with 'all my heart and soul'.

Cameron, D. (2014) 'David Cameron: The EU Is Not Working and We Will Change It', *Sunday Telegraph*, 15 March, http://www.telegraph.co.uk/news/newstopics/eureferendum/10700644/David-Cameron-the-EU-is-not-working-and-we-will-change-it.html, date accessed 13 April 2016.

Cameron, D. (2015) *A New Settlement for the United Kingdom in a Reformed European Union – Letter to Donald Tusk*, London, 10 November, http://www.gov.uk/government/uploads/system/uploads/attachment_data/file/475679/Donald_Tusk_letter.pdf, date accessed 24 February 2016.

Conservative Party (2010) *Invitation to Join the Government of Britain – The Conservative Manifesto*, London, April, http://www.conservatives.com/~/media/files/activist%20centre/press%20and%20policy/manifestos/manifesto2010, date accessed 6 March 2016.

Conservative Party (2015) *Strong Leadership, A Clear Economic Plan, A Brighter More Secure Future*, http://www.conservatives.com/manifesto, date accessed 6 March 2016.

The Economist (2012) 'Britain and the EU: A Brexit looms', 21 June, http://www.economist.com/blogs/bagehot/2012/06/britain-and-eu-0, date accessed 6 March 2016.

Electoral Commission (2016) *EU Referendum Results*, http://www.electoralcommission.org.uk/, date accessed 5 August 2016.

European Council (2015a) *Letter by President Donald Tusk to the European Council on the issue of a UK in/out referendum*, Press release 898/15, Brussels, 7 December, http://www.consilium.europa.eu/en/press/press-releases/2015/12/07-tusk-letter-to-28ms-on-uk/, date accessed 13 April 2016.

European Council (2015b) *European Council meeting (17 and 18 December 2015) – Conclusions*, EUCO 28/15 CO EUR 13 CONCL 5, Brussels, 7 December, http://www.consilium.europa.eu/en/meetings/european-council/2015/12/201512-EUCO-conclusions_pdf, date accessed 13 April 2016.

European Council (2016a) *Draft Decision of the Heads of State or Government, meeting within the European Council, concerning a New Settlement for the United Kingdom within the European Union*, EUCO 4/16, Brussels, 2 February, http://www.consilium.europa.eu/en/european-council/president/pdf/new-settlement/, date accessed 24 February 2016.

European Council (2016b) *European Council meeting (18 and 19 February 2016) – Conclusions*, EUCO 1/16 COEUR 1 CONCL 1, Brussels, 19 February, http://www.consilium.europa.eu/en/meetings/european-council/2016/02/EUCO-Conclusions_pdf/, date accessed 24 February 2016.

Geddes, A. (2013) *Britain and the European Union*. Basingstoke: Palgrave Macmillan.

George, S. (1990) *An Awkward Partner: Britain in the European Community*. Oxford: Oxford University Press.

Goodlad, G. D. (2000) *British Foreign and Imperial Policy, 1865–1919*. London: Routledge.

Grant, C. and Springford, J. (2016) 'Deal Done: Now for the Hard Work', *CER Insight*, 20 February, http://www.cer.org.uk/insights/deal-done-now-hard-work, date accessed 13 April 2016.

The Guardian (2012a) 'David Cameron backs referendum on Europe', 9 October, http://www.theguardian.com/politics/2012/oct/09/david-cameron-backs-referendum-europe, date accessed 17 March 2016.

The Guardian (2012b) 'Cameron: Britain outside the EU is 'imaginable', 18 December.

Hansard (2016), 22 February, Vol. 606, No. 117, col. 25.

Hix, S. (2016) 'Does the UK Have Influence in the EU Legislative Process?', *Political Quarterly*, Vol. 87, No. 3, pp. 200–8.

Monger, G. W. (1963) *The End of Isolation: British Foreign Policy 1900–1907*. London: Nelson.

Moore, L. (2015) 'Euroscepticism in the Conservative Party: The Role of Nationalism and Electoral Pressures', *Brexit blog,* London School of Economics and Political Science, http://blogs.lse.ac.uk/brexitvote/2015/12/31/euroscepticism-in-the-conservative-party-the-role-of-nationalism-and-electoral-pressures/, date accessed 22 March 2016.

Palmer, R. (2008) *Devolution, Asymmetry and Europe: Multi-Level Governance in the United Kingdom*. Brussels: PIE Peter Lang.

Simms, B. (2016) *Britain's Europe: A Thousand Years of Conflict and Cooperation*. London: Allen Lane.

Sky News (2016) 'Brexit Campaign Built On Fantasy, Says Major', 20 March, http://news.sky.com/story/brexit-campaign-built-on-fantasy-says-major-10212812, date accessed 7 December 2016.

UK Government (2010) *The Coalition: our programme for government*, London, May, http://www.gov.uk/government/uploads/system/uploads/attachment_data/file/78977/coalition_programme_for_government.pdf, date accessed 6 March 2016.

UK Government (2012) *Review of the Balance of Competences between the United Kingdom and the European Union*, 12 July, https://www.gov.uk/government/publications/review-of-the-balance-of-competences, date accessed 6 March 2016.

UK Government (2014) *Review of the Balance of Competences – Reports*, http://www.gov.uk/guidance/review-of-the-balance-of-competences, date accessed 6 March 2016.

UK Government (2016a) *The Best of Both Worlds: the United Kingdom's, Special Status in a Reformed European Union*, London, 22 February, http://www.gov.uk/government/publications/the-best-of-both-worlds-the-united-kingdoms-special-status-in-a-reformed-european-union, date accessed 24 February 2016.

UK Government (2016b) *Alternatives to Membership: Possible Models for the United Kingdom outside the European Union*, http:// www.gov.uk/government/publications/alternatives-to-membership-possible-models-for-the-united-kingdom-outside-the-european-union, date accessed 2 March 2016.

UK Government (2016c) *The Process of Withdrawing from the European Union,* http:// www.gov.uk/government/publications/the-process-for-with-drawing-from-the-european-union, date accessed 1 March 2016.

Wall, S. (2008) *A Stranger in Europe: Britain and the EU from Thatcher to Blair.* Oxford: Oxford University Press.

YouGov (2016) 'EU referendum: Provincial England versus London and the Celts', 24 March, https://yougov.co.uk/news/2016/03/24/eu-referendum-provincial-england-versus-london-and/, date accessed 13 May 2016.

Young, H. (1998) *This Blessed Plot: Britain and Europe from Churchill to Blair.* London: Macmillan.

Chapter 6

The European Migration Crisis

LAURIE BUONANNO

Introduction

What is unique about the migration crisis? How is it possible that the waves of asylum-seekers and irregular migrants coming ashore on the eastern Greek isles and Italy's Lampedusa island could threaten to undermine a major accomplishment of the European integration project – the single market, of which the Schengen system of free movement of persons is a key part – and contribute to the UK's decision to leave the EU (anti-immigrant sentiment was a significant influence on 'leave' voters)? Why have the EU and its member states struggled to find 'solutions'? Finally, have such solutions as have been adopted resulted in 'more' or 'less' Europe? These are the broad questions informing this chapter on the European migration crisis.

Two distinct lines of inquiry are followed in the chapter. The first seeks to discover whether the migration crisis arose from a 'perfect storm' of (mainly) unpredictable events. Could a system built for 'normal' times to facilitate the free movement of people, goods, services, and capital be expected to manage such an unprecedented mass migration to Europe? Specifically, was the crisis a 'one-off' event brought about by the confluence of: the (long) civil war in Syria; the inability of Jordan, Lebanon, and Turkey to any longer be able to accommodate hundreds of thousands of Syrians – leaving Europe as the only safe region to which they could flee; the presence of sophisticated European-based criminal networks exploiting middle- and upper-income Syrians able to afford paying exorbitant sums (€5,000–10,000) to be smuggled into Greece or Italy; the failure to form a stable, unity government in Libya (the main transit country for the central Mediterranean route into Europe); opportunistic migration (economic migrants taking advantage of 'wave-throughs' in order to transit to countries where jobs are to be found); and, finally, the austerity policies and rigidities in the national budgets of EU member states, especially Greece?

The second line of inquiry appraises whether the (still very much ongoing) migration crisis could have been, and can be, decoupled from the EU's other crises examined in this book. Could the EU have devised actions so as not to upset the delicate balance between member state sovereignty and the supposedly inexorable logic of centralization associated with quasi-federal systems? In sum, could incremental solutions have been found to manage the migration crisis and restore the Schengen area to 'normalcy'?

The chapter is divided into five sections. The first, 'Anatomy of the Migration Crisis', establishes the magnitude and complexity of the crisis through analysis of irregular migration flows, migratory routes, and asylum applications. The second, 'Asylum Law and Immigration Policy in the EU', explores the extent to which EU asylum and immigration policy had been agreed and implemented before the crisis, by reviewing the Common European Asylum System (CEAS) and its 'recast' regulations and directives. The third, 'Member States and the Migration Crisis', examines gaps in CEAS implementation and actions dealing with irregular migration from the perspective of member state cooperation or lack thereof. The fourth, 'Implementing the European Commission's Agenda on Migration', reviews EU progress towards advancing, agreeing, and implementing new policies aimed at resolving the crisis and considers the viability of the various policy proposals – particularly funding mechanisms requiring joint financing and EU legislation. The fifth and final section, 'The Wider Implications of, and the Prospects for, Inward EU Migration', concludes with some general observations on the migration crisis. It discusses the ways in which the crisis has 'infected' some other EU policies, including policies that are considered 'settled'. It looks at the larger issue that Europeans must ultimately face – namely, Europe's looming demographic crunch and the potential opportunity of establishing a 'rational' system of immigration from war-torn and economically challenged states in the Middle East, Asia, and Africa to replace an ageing European workforce and, ultimately, to preserve the European Social Model. And the section also addresses a key theme of this book: does the European migration crisis corroborate the presumption that crises tend to deepen the European integration project or has it exposed unbridgeable differences among EU member states?

Anatomy of the Migration Crisis

The high volume of migrants seeking entry into Europe

Irregular migration is a ubiquitous concern in advanced industrialized democracies, especially for those countries where a substantial number of migrants have already settled because this in itself acts as a pull factor from the migrants' home countries (mainly owing to chain migration). However, contemporary Europe had never experienced the magnitude of inward migration as it did in 2015–16: there were 1.8 million irregular border crossings into the EU in 2015, an increase of 546 per cent compared with 2014 (Europol, 2016). Member states responded by reinstituting pre-Schengen border checks and talking 'tough' (usually against Brussels or other member states). Yet the migrant numbers showed no sign of abating: 147,000 irregular migrants had entered Greece by the end of March 2016 (Reuters News Service, 2016). At the same time, 53,941 migrants were stranded on their way to northern Europe – 50,308 in Greece alone – when EU member states began to close their borders in February 2016 in response to an anticipated deal of 'one Syrian in and another out' with Turkey (see the section below: 'Implementing the European Commission's Agenda on Migration'). Throughout 2016 the EU's deal with Turkey, which was finalized in July, seemed to be holding, with crossings from Turkey dropping to below 100 a day, compared with 2,000 a day before the agreement was implemented (Timor and Nordland, 2016). However, a failed military coup d'état in Turkey in July increased the (already considerable) strains on Turkey's relations with the West and made the EU–Turkey deal ever more fragile as President Erdogan's government rounded up thousands suspected of being involved in the plot.

Europe had not seen anything quite like the volume of post-2014 asylum-seekers since 1992, when the EU-15 received 672,000 asylum applications from Yugoslavian nationals. Subsequently, asylum applications fell to below 200,000 (2006) before beginning their upward trajectory to the 2015–16 record numbers when, from July 2015 to May 2016, 1 million people applied for asylum in Europe (Connor and Krogstad, 2016; Eurostat, 2016). A significant difference between the migration crisis precipitated by Yugoslavia's civil war and the contemporary crisis was that the EU-15 did not include central and eastern European countries (CEECs), which have not dealt effectively and efficiently with the large numbers of asylum-seekers transiting through to northern Europe from Greece.

If the post-2014 migrants were simply 'economic migrants' whose status could be determined easily, they could be detained and returned without the international protection required by international law. But most of the post-2014 migrants have been 'irregular' and asylum-seeking migrants who have sought international protection (in 2015, 1.3 million, compared with the two previous years of 431,000 (2013) and 627,000 (2014)) (Council of the European Union, 2016a; Eurostat, 2016). This crush of asylum-seeking migrants has required EU member states to have in place, both before and during the asylum-determination process, a large and sophisticated network of border control agents, police, inspection officers, and supporting human services, plus the budgets to support these needs. These, the EU and its member states have not had.

Most of the requests for international protection have been from Syrian asylum-seekers: 125,000 in 2014, and 363,000 – or 29 per cent of total asylum applications – in 2015. Of particular concern to those wanting to provide assistance has been the sheer scale of human suffering: 13.5 million people inside Syria in need of humanitarian assistance; 4.5 million in hard-to-reach besieged areas; 6.5 million internally displaced; and over 4.5 million refugees registered or awaiting registration (primarily in Lebanon, Jordan, Iraq, Egypt, and Turkey) (statistics as of January, 2017) (UNHCR, 2017). The principal relevant intergovernmental organization – the Office of the United Nations High Commissioner for Refugees (UNHCR) – and refugee relief and humanitarian international non-governmental organizations (INGOs) have looked to Europe (and the USA) for help in relocating Syrians. But, meanwhile, hundreds of thousands of Syrians have taken their chances on the high seas rather than wait in limbo in Turkey and the Middle East where they had inadequate accommodations, no schools, limited healthcare, and little to no prospects of earning a living.

Beyond Syria, other third-country asylum-seekers as a percentage of the total have come from Afghanistan (14 per cent), Kosovo and Albania (14 per cent), Iraq (10 per cent), and Pakistan (4 per cent) (Eurostat, 2016). Europol (2016: 5) has also reported significant migratory flows from Senegal, Somalia, Niger, Morocco, and other African countries. Thus, asylum-seekers from beyond the Middle East have also been exerting migratory pressures on the EU and its member states.

Trend analysis

Residents of Calais, Sicily, the Apulian and Calabrian regions of Italy, Spain and Portugal's Atlantic coasts, Malta, Cyprus, and Greece have experienced a migrant crisis for several years. However, the magnitude of the crisis altered substantially in 2015. As former European Council President Herman Van Rompuy has observed:

> We had signals of this problem back in 2013 and 2014. Remember Lampedusa. There was partially an inflow of people fleeing war zones and instability, but probably the majority of them were economic migrants. But still there was a problem. For months we thought we could handle it without the efforts made by the Italians. It was only after a new disaster that we decided to join forces and give Frontex all the means and instruments it needed to save people. That was not our happiest moment. I think we should have decided much earlier to follow up on Mare Nostrum [Italy's short-lived search and rescue operation]. (Vincenti, 2015)

Was the European migrant crisis of 2015–16 predictable and, more to the point, preventable? Evidence that it was to some extent both comes from a number of prior indications and 'warnings'. One was increasing concerns in Mediterranean states about migration, which resulted in Cyprus, Greece, Italy, and Malta forming the Quadro Group in 2008 to pressurize successive Council presidencies to prioritize asylum and migration policy and, in particular, to address solidarity and burden-sharing. Another was events in 2011 when, after the Arab Spring left Tunisia's government in shambles, thousands of Tunisians irregularly migrated to Italy and Malta. Italy responded by issuing thousands of temporary permits to Tunisians to transit to France. Citing the Dublin II Regulation, which in most cases requires migrants to file their asylum applications in the country where they entered the EU (see Box 6.1), France turned these Tunisians back at the border. When Italy complained about the burden on border control operations, Germany's Interior Minister suggested that 'Italy must live up to its responsibilities ... [and] negotiate with Tunisia' (Donadio, 2011a). But Italy's Interior Minister *had* travelled to Tunisia, where he found a government in disarray after the ousting of President Zine el-Abidine Ben Ali in January 2011 and incapable of enforcing and honouring its immigration and repatriation accords with Italy (Donadio, 2011b). Thus, while admittedly on a smaller scale, the pressure on the central Mediterranean irregular migration route in 2011 was arguably the first act of the 2015–16 crisis.

Lending support to the suggestion that 'the EU should have known' is a trend analysis (see Figure 6.1), which suggests a steady increase in asylum applications up to 2013.

But another explanation of the migration crisis – that of a 'perfect storm' – has been advanced as an equally plausible candidate of the migration crisis, and this casts doubts on whether the EU could have predicted or prevented the exponential rise of asylum applications between 2014 and 2015. (See Figure 6.1.) The perfect storm thesis can be supported by two observations. First, the EU could not have been expected to foresee that Syria's civil war would still be raging in 2015 nor that a unity government would not emerge in Libya after the overthrow of Muammar Gaddafi. Second, the EU *had* responded to the pleas of southern Mediterranean states – where 90 per cent of illegal crossings were taking place before 2011 (European Commission, 2011). There *was* a European response to irregular migration with: an increasingly integrated approach to asylum policy through a series of directives and regulations adopted from 2003; the recasting of the CEAS in 2013; and the increased and more systematic patrolling of illegal migration routes, in particular via the European Border and Coast Guard Agency (Frontex), which was established in 2004 and strengthened in 2016, and the European Border Surveillance System (Eurosur), which was created in 2013 with the purpose of furthering information exchange designed to improve the management of Europe's external borders.

Box 6.1   The EU's legal framework for asylum (1951–2014)

International and Regional Treaties and Conventions

The 1950 Convention for the Protection of Human Rights and Fundamental Freedoms (known as the European Convention on Human Rights); the 1951 United Nations Convention Relating to the Status of Refugees; the 1984 United Nations Convention against Torture and Other Cruel, Inhuman or Degrading Treatment or Punishment; and Article 18 of the EU's Charter of Fundamental Rights.

EU Legislation

The Common European Asylum System (CEAS) was established in 2003. It consists of:

Dublin Regulation (604/2013) – Establishes the criteria and mechanisms for determining the member state responsible for examination of an asylum application. Generally, an asylum-seeker must register and go through the asylum process where they entered the EU and remain in that country until a determination has been made (predecessors: Dublin I, 2000; Dublin II 2003).

EURODAC Regulation (603/2013) (recast took effect July 2015) – Fingerprinting to determine in which EU member state an asylum-seeker arrived.

Qualification Directive (2011/95/EU) – Defines 'refugee' and provides for 'subsidiary protection'. Establishes common grounds to grant refugee or subsidiary protection status. (Third-country nationals may also be granted asylum status on humanitarian grounds, but it is not a matter for EU law for this is a national determination as defined in member state legislation.)

Reception Conditions Directive (2013/33/EU) (recast took effect July 2015) – Attempts to standardize rules and cut down on asylum shopping. The rules include such detail as providing access to employment for an asylum-seeker within nine months.

Asylum Procedure Directive (2013/32/EU) (recast took effect July 2015) – Establishes common procedures for granting and withdrawing asylum status.

EU Institutional Support

European Asylum Support Office ((EASO), created in 2011)
European Migration Network ((EMN), created in 2008)

In retrospect, as Van Rompuy rhetorically asked, 'could the EU have done more' to anticipate and prepare for the migration crisis of 2015–16? The answer is 'probably not', because irregular migration had not reached crisis proportions and was still largely confined to and made

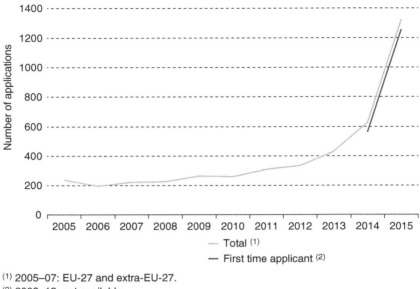

Figure 6.1   *Asylum applications*
Source: Eurostat (2016)

the responsibility of those Mediterranean member states within easy reach of North Africa and the Middle East. The EU had advanced policy activities relating to its external borders, but its approach to irregular migration and asylum-seekers was never intended to be based on 'solidarity' and 'burden-sharing'. Rather, its main goal was sorting out responsibility for determining whether an irregular migrant qualified for international protection.

Area of freedom, security, and justice dimensions

The migration crisis also became a test of the EU's area of freedom, security, and justice (AFSJ) policies because it became increasingly clear that when thousands of asylum-seekers are seeking to illegally enter the EU, national border authorities cannot properly investigate suspicious individuals. At the same time, Europeans were becoming concerned that terrorists and other criminals might be taking advantage of unsecured borders. When police investigations into the Paris and Brussels bombings, which took place in November 2015 and March 2016 respectively, confirmed suspicions that ISIS terrorists were taking advantage of the chaos in Greece's border controls to sneak undetected into Europe, the passport-free Schengen area – thought to have been an established feature of life in the EU – suddenly became highly contested. The large number of irregular migrants arriving in Europe in 2015–16 had now become an internal security problem. So, too, as European and national leaders began to reframe the migration crisis as an internal security issue, the crisis became more difficult to handle on a supranational (EU) basis.

One of the reasons why the EU had established Europol (an AFSJ agency preceded by decades of intra-European police cooperation) in 1998 was to deal with the European-wide criminal and terrorist networks exploiting the removal of internal border controls. Yet keeping Europeans safe is inextricably linked to the EU's complex border control challenges: the EU's member states must monitor a territory that has nearly 1,800 designated external border crossing points, including 665 air borders, 871 sea borders, and 246 land borders (European Commission, 2008). As Figure 6.2 demonstrates, smugglers favour several entry points. When one route closes, another opens. So, for example, the northern, or Arctic, route has caused considerable consternation in Finland, Norway, and Brussels, as the flow through Russia is 'almost entirely dependent' on Russia's Federal Security Service, a situation prompting NATO's Supreme Commander, US General Philip M. Breedlove, to accuse Russia of 'deliberately weaponizing migration in an attempt to overwhelm European structures and break European resolve' (Higgins, 2016).

An estimated 90 per cent of migrants are brought to the EU by criminal networks (Europol, 2016: 4). Europol estimates there are 40,000 smugglers involved, coming mostly from Bulgaria, Hungary, Iraq, Kosovo, Pakistan, Poland, Romania, Serbia, Sweden, Syria, and Turkey. Of those operating within criminal networks, 44 per cent are composed exclusively of non-EU nationals, 30 per cent are composed of EU nationals only, and 26 per cent are composed of both EU and non-EU nationals (Europol, 2016: 7). In addition to human trafficking, criminal networks are also involved in drugs trafficking, document forgery, and property crimes. Thus, existing criminal networks have 'cashed in' on the Syrian crisis. As EU authorities have sought to patrol some areas, route diversification has continued to challenge border management as new centres of smuggling activity have emerged to fill gaps when routes have closed. Europol identified 230 extra- and intra-EU such locations in 2016 where facilitation (for example, document forgery) and migrant smuggling was taking place.

As irregular migrants continued to flow into Europe in 2015–16, Europol (2016: 12) reported 'a significant increase in the number of violent attacks targeting migrants in asylum centres and other accommodation ... [I]n addition to direct assaults on migrants and facilities, many protests and anti-protests were organized by right-wing and left-wing extremist groups, sometimes leading to clashes among protestors.'

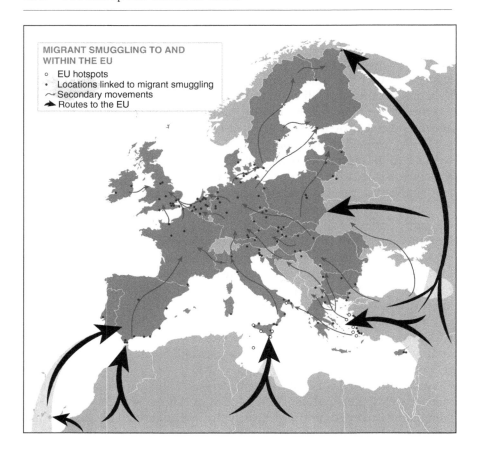

Figure 6.2   *Migrant smuggling to and within the EU*

Eastern Mediterranean – Greece is a crossroads between the EU and the Caucasus, the Middle East, and Turkey.

Central Mediterranean – The Italian island of Lampedusa (at about 113 kilometres from Tunisia) is closer to North Africa than to Italy's mainland, while Adriatic Italy is easily reached by migrants from eastern Europe and the Middle East.

Western Mediterranean – The route to Spain (which at its narrowest distance to the African continent is just 14.5 kilometres) has long been a crossing point into Europe for drugs smugglers and human traffickers, with 'almost every' coastal town having the unmarked graves of bodies washed ashore.

Eastern Entry – 'Via Baltica', that is, entering the EU in one of the member states on the Baltic Sea before travelling to destination countries via Poland.

Northern – Leads migrants through Russia and into the EU through Finland or Norway. This route has been used by an increasing number of migrants since the end of 2015.

Sources: Map from Europol (2016: 6); Higgins (2016); Simons (2004)

Migrants have also been involved in public order disturbances; for example, the former Calais 'Jungle' (the name given to it by its migrant inhabitants) was in the news frequently as migrants clashed with French authorities attempting to clear parts of the camp (Chrisafis, Walker, and Quinn, 2016). Frustrated migrants seeking permission to transit to northern Europe have blocked roads, set themselves on fire, and attempted to tear down border fences (Reuters News Service, 2016).

There are other AFSJ dimensions to the migration crisis that receive less publicity but are no less troubling. For example, a large percentage of asylum-seekers are vulnerable persons. In 2015, 85,482 unaccompanied minors applied for asylum in the EU. In January 2016, 55 per cent of the irregular migrants arriving in the EU were women and minors. A Europol report (2016: 12) concluded that 'the group of people vulnerable for labour or sexual exploitation is increasing' and that unaccompanied minors were disappearing from asylum and reception centres.

Another AFSJ dimension of the European migration crisis revolves around the extremely sensitive issues of citizenship, identity, and inclusion. Hampshire (2013: 9) suggests that the difficulty in agreeing on a migration policy in Europe can be understood as an outcome of the competing values inherent to contemporary liberal statehood: representative democracy (majority opinion tends to support limits on immigration), constitutionalism (fundamental rights and protections of liberties should be afforded to migrants), nationhood (involving 'particularistic ideas of community and belonging'), and capitalism (migrant labour is a necessity in advanced capitalism). Thus, constitutionalism and capitalism favour more liberal migration policy, while representative democracy and nationhood tend towards limiting migration. Hampshire argues that 'the implications of identity-based explanations for anti-immigrant sentiment are particularly problematic for policy-makers. If cultural identity matters more than economic interests, then arguments and evidence about the net socio-economic benefits of immigration are unlikely to make significant inroads into anti-immigration opinion' (Hampshire, 2013: 24). As the Brexit vote demonstrated, and the rhetoric and rise of the far-right in several EU member states suggests, reimagining identity (see Anderson, 1983) to create a 'European identity' is a 'tall order' (Hampshire, 2013: 24). Indeed, 'cultural integration' has become the watchword not just of the European far-right, but also of much of the centre-right as when, for example, in 2011 UK Prime Minister David Cameron declared 'the doctrine of state multiculturalism' had failed (BBC News, 2011).

The cultural integration question has become particularly acute because the vast majority of asylum-seekers to Europe are Muslim. Since the terrorist attacks in the USA on 11 September 2001, cultural and religious frames (see Muddle, 2012: 9–13) have conjoined with a 'security' frame (crime and terrorism) to argue the case for lower immigration levels. However, they have also produced rather bizarre attempts by politicians and street-level bureaucrats (that is, professionals who interact directly with the public and exercise considerable policy discretion) to implement hastily legislated inclusion policies, such as banning the burkini after the 2016 Bastille Day Islamist cargo truck attack at Nice's seaside promenade (Quinn, 2016).

Asylum Law and Immigration Policy in the EU

The EU has had a well-developed 'common' asylum policy (the CEAS) since 2003, which is built on both international treaties and conventions and EU legislation. Asylum in EU member states is based on the principle of non-refoulement (prohibition to be returned) until a proper examination has taken place in the reception state's jurisdiction to determine whether the asylum-seeker meets the conditions for international protection – and can claim 'refugee' status. Economic migrants are not offered asylum and are simply 'irregular' (illegal) immigrants. The EU's legal framework for asylum is summarized in Box 6.1.

The Dublin Regulation is the CEAS's lynchpin, which applies to all EU member states, plus the European Free Trade Association (EFTA) states of Iceland, Norway, Liechtenstein, and Switzerland. The Dublin Convention was negotiated in 1990 as a necessary companion to the Schengen Convention – both of which at the time were extra-EU treaties – to forestall anticipated problems a border-free Europe would bring with respect to asylum-seekers. The main such anticipated problems were: asylum shopping (whereby asylum-seekers submit applications to those member states perceived as more likely to accept them, submit applications to more than one member state, or apply in those member states offering more generous welfare benefits); and 'asylum-seekers in orbit', when no member state accepts responsibility for an application, thereby delaying access to protection. The Dublin system was *never* designed to equalize or share asylum burdens (Fratzke, 2015: 4).

The Dublin system of determining where an asylum application must be lodged depends upon a 'hierarchy of criteria' based on family unity and a valid or recently expired resident document or visa. If none of these criteria apply, asylum-seekers who illegally transited through another member state when entering EU territory are the responsibility of the first member state in which they arrived (Fratzke, 2015: 5). The Dublin II Regulation (2003) brought Dublin under EU governance and established the EURODAC Regulation, requiring all asylum-seekers and irregular migrants to be fingerprinted. EURODAC made it possible to determine where a migrant entered the EU, even if they had lost or destroyed their identification papers. EURODAC is key to Dublin's effectiveness – in 2013, 65 per cent of total outgoing requests were based on EURODAC data (Fratzke, 2015: 6).

Widespread implementation gaps in CEAS legislation have been a persistent concern among the UNHCR, refugee rights groups, the European Commissioner, and several EU member states. The European Court of Human Rights (ECHR), the Court of Justice of the European Union (CJEU), and national courts of the EU member states have made many rulings on application of the CEAS in reaction to asylum-seeker petitions, which in turn have built a substantial body both limiting and interpreting EU legislation.

The AFSJ's Stockholm Programme Action Plan (2010–14) (European Commission, 2010) suggested a new direction for asylum policy, in the form of CEAS recast. This was (like its predecessor) marked by a compromise between a more 'cosmopolitan' (see Miller, 2016) view of immigration (with an emphasis on human rights and solidarity) advocated by the Commission and the European Parliament and, in contrast, a 'harder' view reflecting member state desires to reduce budgetary and political costs. The budgetary costs consisted mainly of asylum determination and social welfare, while the political costs involved public opinion throughout Europe favouring lower migration levels. The Commission had proposed several options ranging from providing joint teams to assist member states with processing to a centralized EU processing mechanism (Guild et al., 2015: ii) – none of which survived into the finally agreed CEAS recast. The reforms included changes to the Dublin system ('Dublin Recast' or 'Dublin III'), which provided more rights for asylum-seekers. However, in a post-CEAS recast study conducted on behalf of the EP's Civil Liberties, Justice and Home Affairs Committee, the authors concluded that the Dublin system has become an instrument of coercion, with massive human costs (Guild et al., 2015).

Member States and the Migration Crisis

The principal factors affecting member state positions on migration include historical experience, a lack of administrative capacity to properly vet asylum-seekers, attitudes about humanitarian obligations, demographic trends, migrant preferences for resettlement, geographic location on the European continent, and public opinion.

Historical experiences

The European experience is one of emigration, especially to the Americas – where in 1900, for example, 86 per cent of the foreign-born population (10 million) of the USA had been born in Europe (Singer, 2013: 81). Southern and eastern European member states, particularly, are nineteenth- and twentieth-century disaporic countries – for example, by 1911, 14 per cent of Italians lived abroad, and in 1920, 9 million of Italy's 26 million lived outside of Italy (Gabaccia, 2000: 177). With the notable (contemporary) exceptions of Belgium, France, the Netherlands, and the UK – which have a history of admitting and integrating third-country nationals from their former colonies – the majority of EU member states are inexperienced in managing multicultural societies and/or integrating new citizens (see Gall, 2016).

In terms of citizenship policies, Howard (2009) argues that two historical factors help to explain more inclusive citizenship policies in some European countries: the experience of being major colonial powers (particularly the UK, Belgium, France, and the Netherlands) and early democratization (with the Netherlands being a middle case due to later democratization). These two historical experiences have supported a more pluralist conception of citizenship (contact with other peoples through colonization) and 'a national identity tied to liberal principles' (Howard, 2009: 447). However, even these four countries are increasingly divided with respect to whether their societies should be more inclusive (emphasizing constitutionalism and economic factors) or closed (emphasizing culture and majoritarianism): the Brexit referendum exposed this cross-cutting split in British society in a spectacular fashion.

Many countries with a recent memory of diaspora have, despite having underdeveloped citizenship policies, welcomed refugees – particularly Greece, Italy, and Portugal. Despite an almost constant battering of their country in the media and by INGOs and European leaders regarding their reception conditions and 'questionable' qualification determinations, Greeks living on the Aegean isles have clothed, fed, and sheltered migrants (without Greek travel papers, migrants cannot rent hotel rooms). This often-overlooked generosity (Huff Post, 2015) is all the more remarkable given the upending of Greece's vital tourist trade – wealthy northern European sunbathers on the beaches of eastern Greek isles, in view of bedraggled asylum-seekers coming ashore in overloaded rubber rafts and dinghies, predictably stopped vacationing in Lesbos and other 'popular' refugee landings (Lucas, 2016). So, too, Sicilians and other southern Italians have been assisting migrants for many years, with Italians often recalling that they also were refugees (and not always welcomed) when earlier generations of Italians landed on New York's

Ellis Island (Tondo, 2016). Portugal, a country which has been particularly welcoming to Syrian refugees (see Ames, 2016), is also diasporic (with one-fifth of Portugal's population living abroad). The Portuguese also have a recent memory of accommodating refugees with, in 1975, 1 million people fleeing to Portugal from countries in Africa as a result of independence revolutions – so that today 10 per cent of Portugal's population is comprised of former colonists of Lusophone Africa.

Lack of administrative capacity

EU member states with little experience of inward migration are characterized by weak institutional structures and resources to vet asylum applications. In southern Europe, which struggled to deal with waves of asylum-seekers long before the 2015–16 migration crisis, the tendency has been to implement 'regularization programmes' to deal with the problem of irregular migrants – so, for example, of 4.7 million applications for regularization in the EU between 1996 and 2007, 3.2 million were granted 'some kind of legal status', with the vast majority of applications in regularization programmes filed in Italy, Greece, and Spain where 'regularization has become a surrogate for legal immigration policy' (Hampshire, 2013: 68–9). Regularization in member state labour markets that have been unable to absorb immigrants (the situation in all three of the aforementioned EU member states) has the effect of these now 'legalized' migrants finding their way to other EU member states. With the vast numbers of asylum-seekers residing in Greece and Italy today, these governments will be tempted to engage in future regularization, which is of obvious concern to other member states who do not want to be responsible for absorbing further migrants into their economies and societies.

Humanitarian obligations

The European Commission, the UNHCR, human rights and refugee INGOs, and national authorities have long accused Greece, Italy, Malta, and Spain of human rights violations in their treatment of asylum-seekers (see, for example, BBC News, 2009; Brunsden, 2008; Crosbie, 2009; Daley, 2012, 2014; Fullerton, 2005) – to which these countries have responded by asking for European solidarity. But humanitarian concerns extend beyond the southern countries. At the height of the 2015–16 migration crisis, refugees reported 'ruthless' Bulgarian border authorities at the Bulgarian–Turkish border (Belgrade Centre for Human Rights, 2015; Lyman, 2015a). Nor have EU candidate states escaped opprobrium, with human rights advocates condemning Macedonian border police for using tear gas and rubber bullets to prevent refugees in the makeshift camp in Idomeni from tearing down the barbed-wired-topped chainlink fence at Macedonia's border with Greece (Alderman, 2016).

So, too, Italy and the UK have notably clashed with respect to assisting asylum-seekers on the high seas. The Italian government launched its search and rescue Operation Mare Nostrum (OMN) after, in October 2014, 366 asylum-seekers drowned when their boat capsized a mile from Italy's Lampedusa island (Scherer and Polleschi, 2014). Italians were horrified, and world opinion seemed to suggest Italians were at fault for not patrolling the seas between Tunisia and Lampedusa. With limited financial assistance from the EU (the Commission provided just €1.8 million from its External Borders Fund), the Italian Navy carried out OMN from October 2013 to October 2014 at a cost of €9 million per month, until a more limited EU mission took over – Frontier's Operation Triton – which focused more on interdiction (operating closer to shore). During OMN, the Italian Navy delivered 150,000 irregular migrants from Africa and the Middle East safely to Europe. Aboard naval ships were representatives of Save the Children to help with information, support, and legal counselling. Refugee agencies praised OMN, but anti-immigrant groups charged that OMN encouraged irregular migration and the UK Government of David Cameron, with Theresa May as his Home Secretary, also added its voice to the opposition (Travis, 2015). The junior Foreign Office minister, Baroness Anelay, stated that 'We do not support planned search and rescue operations in the Mediterranean', opining there was 'an unintended "pull factor", encouraging more migrants to attempt the dangerous sea crossing and thereby leading to more tragic and unnecessary deaths' (Travis, 2014).

Humanitarian issues have thus been a source of contention among the member states during the crisis.

Demographic trends

Demographic factors have also influenced member state positions on the migrant crisis, notably the 'greying' of Europe. The EU population (including the UK) is projected to increase from 507 million in 2013 to 526 million in 2050 and will thereafter decline slowly to 523 million in 2060. The trends suggest that while the EU population, as a whole, will be higher in 2060 as compared with 2013, population decreases are projected for about half of the EU member states (European Commission, 2015a: 1). The EU's Big Four face different demographic scenarios: the populations of the UK, France, and Italy will increase by 25 per cent (80.1 million), 15 per cent (75.6 million), and 10 per cent (66.3 million), respectively, but by 2060 Germany's population is projected to decrease by 12.9 per cent (70.8 million), shifting the Big Four's population ranking such that Germany will be in third place and the UK in first (European Commission, 2015a, 2015c). Furthermore, the old-age dependency ratio (people aged 65 or above relative to those aged 15–64) will be 59 per cent in Germany compared with 43 per cent, 53 per cent, and 43 per cent for the UK, Italy, and France, respectively (European Commission, 2015a, Statistical Annex).

This has led at least one commentator to suggest that these demographic projections account for 'one of the unspoken reasons why Germany is being much more welcoming to asylum-seekers from Syria and elsewhere right now' and why some UK Conservative ministers and business leaders have observed that 'Angela Merkel is creaming off the most economically useful of the asylum-seekers, by taking those that have shown the gumption and initiative to risk life and limb by fleeing to Europe' (Preston, 2015).

Migrants' preferences and immigrants as a percentage of total population

Another factor influencing member state attitudes about migration is migrant resettlement preferences. Generally speaking, migrants arriving in countries such as Slovenia, Hungary, Italy, Malta, Cyprus, and Greece do not wish to settle there permanently. They normally prefer to head north, with Germany being the most favoured destination. This has resulted in migrants often going to great lengths to avoid being fingerprinted in, say, Greece or Italy, so that they are not subject to a Dublin transfer.

There has also been a differential impact of the migration crisis among European member state populations. For example, Sweden, Hungary, and Austria each experienced an increase of at least one percentage point of their foreign-born populations between July 2015 and May 2016, with not always welcome implications for social provisions or budgets. (As a basis for comparison, the immigrant share of the US population increased by about one point over a *decade*, from 13 per cent in 2005 to about 14 per cent in 2015 [Connor and Krogstad, 2016].)

Geographical location

There have been disparate burdens on member states with respect to receiving and processing asylum applications, which inevitably has affected attitudes of governments and peoples to migration policy.

Until 2015, the majority of irregular migrants travelled the central and western Mediterranean routes (by sea) and were thus detained in southern Mediterranean member states, which resulted in these states being responsible for receiving and caring for the vast majority of irregular migrants while they applied for and awaited an asylum determination. However, this situation changed in 2015 with Germany's decision to invoke Dublin's sovereignty clause, which led to member and candidate states 'waving through' refugees travelling from Turkey and Greece, through the Balkan route, into Hungary and neighbouring states (where they were joined by economic migrants from Kosovo).

Seeking a temporary solution to the stream of migrants flowing into Europe, Commission President Jean-Claude Juncker proposed in 2015 a plan to share migrants between EU member states. The UK government opposed scrapping the Dublin system and made it clear that it would not opt into any solidarity/burden-sharing relocation scheme (as with Denmark and Ireland, the UK can opt in or out of many AFSJ actions). The Commission responded with a voluntary relocation plan, but this too was unsuccessful, with the CEECs in particular being uniformly opposed to any burden-sharing plan, although some of their earlier harsh rhetoric softened somewhat (Barigazzi and Cienski, 2015; Lyman, 2015b; Traynor, 2015).

In the end, the Commission's proposed voluntary resettlement plan was an enormous flop with, by January 2016, only 272 refugees having been relocated out of the 160,000 agreed in September 2015 by the Council (European Commission, 2016d). In the meantime, member states continued to press Italy and Greece to accept their Dublin transfer requests; and, while Italy and Greece received 14,000 Dublin transfer requests between January and September of 2015, EU member states accepted only 598 asylum-seekers from Italy and Greece (European Commission, 2016c).

Public opinion

The role of public opinion in reacting to the migration crisis plays out on many levels. One of the levels is increasing anti-immigrant sentiment, which in some member states, including France and the UK, has made it risky for politicians to support a European solution for managing irregular migrant flows (Scherer and Polleschi, 2014). The November 2015 Paris attacks diminished support for asylum-seekers when it was discovered that at least one of the attackers had crossed into Europe illegally through southern Europe (more were discovered after the March 2016 attacks in Brussels). 'Hardliners', such as the Hungarian Prime Minister Viktor Orbán, seized on this to shut down migration to Hungary (Barigazzi, 2015). In Greece, the far-right party, Golden Dawn, began marching in several areas around the country where migrants were encamped or massed (Alderman, 2016).

Another level has been the ability of the far-right to gain seats and/ or pull centrist parties to the right. Member state governments have faced electoral challenges by the far-right capitalizing on nativist sentiments, with far-right parties winning legislative seats in EP, national, and regional elections (Castle, 2010; Germanova, 2016; Karnitschnig, 2016).

And a third level was during the June 2016 UK Brexit referendum, where a desire to decrease the numbers of both intra- and inter-European migrants was a main reason why many voted to leave. The governing Conservative Party seemed to be almost at war with itself, as: a nativist wing of the party advanced the position that immigrants undermine national identity, that inclusion policies had failed, and therefore that migration levels should be decreased; a business wing, by contrast, continued to support their long-held capitalist notion that migration strengthened, and indeed was necessary for, the UK's economy. So, too, the Labour Party was divided on the migration issue, in its case between: the cosmopolitans (who emphasize human rights and are more comfortable with multiculturalism – the so-called 'Third Way' contingent); and the traditional working-class base who believe migrants drive down labour market wages, drive up housing prices in working-class communities, and put enormous pressure on social and health services.

Implementing the European Commission's Agenda on Migration

While struggling with the migration crisis, the EU and its member states have been devising policies and taking decisions both to stem the tide and to accommodate refugees who have made their way to EU member states. Many of these were laid out in 2015 in the Commission's road map 'European Agenda on Migration' (European Commission, 2015b). The proposals and decisions reflect both the intergovernmental and the supranational space which AFSJ currently inhabits. These are summarized in Box 6.2; the following is an explanatory narrative of the most important reforms.

Supranational

At first glance, the Commission's proposals for reform of the CEAS seem to be rather incremental in approach, but taken together they amount to a federalization of European asylum policy. The most supranational of these approaches is the Regulation for a European Border and Coastguard (EBCG). This regulation replaces Frontex (but keeps the name) with the European Border and Coastguard Agency (EBCGA), which includes a 'Return Office' to assist member states in returning illegal migrants to their home countries (European Commission, 2015e).

Box 6.2   EU's agenda on asylum (2015–16)

Regulations and Directives

(Many reforms to the EU's asylum policy were at the proposal stage at the time of this writing. For legislative updates, see European Parliament (2016)).

European Border and Coastguard (EBCG). A regulation creating a new EBCG, which is intended to be a strengthened Frontex, was agreed in September 2016. The EBCG was launched in October 2016 – at the Kapitan Andreevo checkpoint on the Turkey–Bulgaria border, which is one of the world's busiest border crossings).

Dublin IV proposal. This proposal retains the 'Dublin system', but adds a fairness mechanism (proposed May 2016).

Hotspot approach. As of March 2016, six hotspots were operational in Italy and five in Greece, with a total reception capacity of 2,100 and 5,440 respectively (European Commission, 2016e). An EU presence (EASO and EBCG) is maintained at each hotspot, as needed.

Returns. With only 39 per cent of return decisions issued by member states being enforced (European Commission, 2015b: 9), the Commission proposed in 2015 a regulation for a common EU return document (European Commission, 2015d). *The European Travel Document for the Return of Illegally Staying Third-Country Nationals* was approved in October 2016. A 'Return Handbook' with common guidelines, best practices, and recommendations was published in October 2015.

Qualification regulation proposal. This regulation, which was proposed in 2016, aims to replace the existing Qualification Directive and to further harmonize qualification rules.

Asylum procedures regulation proposal. This proposed regulation is intended to replace the Asylum Procedures Directive. Proposed in

→

Most controversial has been the Regulation's provision for the right of the new European Agency for Asylum (EAA) (discussed below) to intervene in a member state's asylum process if a member state does not comply with the EBCGA's vulnerability assessment (Council of the European Union, 2016b).

Under the Asylum Procedures Regulation, the Commission proposed a Safe Country of Origin List. The idea is that asylum applications could be streamlined if member states agree a common list of safe countries (European Parliament, 2015). A safe list, however, is difficult to agree upon. For example, Belgium considers Kosovo safe, but Bulgaria does not; the UK's list includes Ukraine, while most other member states'

→ 2016, it seeks to harmonize asylum procedures and to include a safe
country of origin list.

Reception conditions directive proposal. Some modifications, mainly
designed to improve reception conditions, are included in this
proposal of 2016.

Expanding the Eurodac system. This 2016 proposal extends the
Eurodac system so that it can be used not just for Dublin, but to
facilitate the return of other irregular migrants.

European Agency for Asylum proposal. This was proposed in 2016,
with the aim of upgrading and strengthening the existing European
Asylum Support Office (EASO).

Resettlement Framework. This 2016 proposal establishes a common
set of standard procedures for the selection and treatment of
resettlement candidates: €10,000 from the EU budget for each
person resettled.

Intergovernmental (all the following have been implemented)

- EU–Turkey Joint Action Plan and Turkey Facilitation ('one in one
  out' went into effect in March 2016); Turkey Refugee Facility –
  established in November 2015 at €3 billion, increased to €6 billion
  in March 2016 (will be paid until 2018).
- Trust Fund for Africa – €1.9 billion as of February 2016; financed
  by EU budget and member state contributions.
- EU Regional Trust Fund in response to the Syrian Crisis (established
  2014), also known as the Madad Fund. Total funding: €1 billion
  (by early 2017). Includes funds for Syrians in Lebanon, Turkey,
  Jordan, and Iraq for non-humanitarian aid such as education,
  livelihoods, and health. Financed by the EU budget and member
  state contributions (European Commission, n.d.).

lists do not. So, too, the UK considers many African countries unsafe
for women due to the widespread practice of female genital mutilation
(European Parliament, 2015; Economist Data Team, 2015).

The Commission proposed in May 2016 to preserve the Dublin system (see Box 6.1), but to add to it a 'fairness mechanism' which will
come into effect if 'a country is handling a disproportionate number of
asylum applications' (European Commission, 2016f). If the number of
asylum-seekers in a member state reaches over 150 per cent of a pre-
determined reference number, all further new applicants in that country
will be relocated across the EU until the number of applications is back
below the reference number level. If a member state refuses to take part

in the reallocation, it must make a 'solidarity contribution' of €250,000 for each applicant for whom it would otherwise have been responsible under the fairness mechanism, to the Member State that is reallocated the person instead (European Commission, 2016f).

A European Agency for Asylum (EAA) was proposed in May 2016, with the intention that it should supersede the European Asylum Support Office (EASO) that had been established in 2011. The EAA will operate the Dublin fairness mechanism, work to achieve greater convergence in the assessment of asylum applications, and strengthen cooperation and information exchange regarding European asylum law. In a major shift for European asylum policy, the EAA will be able 'to deploy asylum support to provide operational and technical assistance to those member states subject to exceptionally heavy and urgent demands on its asylum or reception systems' (European Commission, 2016f).

Intergovernmental

The main intergovernmental activities in responding to the migration crisis have been the EU–Turkey Joint Action Plan, the strengthening of agreements with third countries to accept returns, and efforts to reduce migrant smuggling (see Box 6.2).

Unquestionably, the most important initiative in terms of slowing migrant flows to Europe has been the EU–Turkey Joint Action Plan, a 'cash-for-cooperation' arrangement provisionally agreed in October 2015 in which the EU pledged €3 billion to assist Turkey in its efforts of sheltering Syrians 'in exchange' for Turkey increasing the patrolling of its borders so as to prevent asylum-seekers from reaching the eastern Greek isles. Turkey also wrangled an agreement from the European Council to liberalize visas for Turkish citizens travelling in Europe, on which the EU leaders promised to review progress in the spring of 2016 (Barigazzi and Winneker, 2015; European Council, 2015). With spring coming, and expectations of a new flood of migrants setting out from Turkey for Greece, a special summit was convened in March 2016 with Turkey asking to accelerate payment of the €3 billion pledged at the October 2015 European Council summit. In addition, Turkey now wanted an additional €3 billion, concrete action on visa liberalization, and the re-opening of its EU candidacy talks. The resulting agreement centred on a 'wait your turn' scenario for Syrian asylum-seekers of one in and one out, with priority being given to those Syrians who do not try to enter the EU irregularly (European Council, 2016). For every Syrian refugee (who entered irregularly) that Greece sends back to Turkey, the EU accepts and resettles one Syrian registered in Turkey. Any Syrian refugee who arrives irregularly in Greece and who does not apply for asylum there or has their claim rejected, is returned to Turkey.

With the Turkey–EU model in place and refugee attempts to cross into the eastern Mediterranean lower than their record numbers in the fourth quarter of 2015 (Frontex, 2016a), it was expected migration smuggling in 2016 would shift to the Adriatic (Albania) and the central Mediterranean routes, which prompted Italy to negotiate accords with Albania and Montenegro. UNHCR (2016) and Frontex (2016b) data lend weight to this prediction: record numbers of migrants reached Italy in October 2016 and there was an increase in 7 per cent of migrants arriving by sea through the central Mediterranean between January and November 2016 compared with the same time period in 2015.

As part of tackling the problems of the central Mediterranean route, it is expected that the EU will work with North African countries to build reception centres in exchange for humanitarian aid (along the lines of the Turkey facility fund). There are already asylum officers in some African countries and a number of bi-national agreements (such as between Italy and Tunisia), as well as a provision in the EU's Cotonou Agreement (with developing countries) to admit returned migrants (European Commission, 2015b: 7–9; 2016a). However, the EU has considerable difficulty in returning third-county nationals whose asylum applications have been rejected, as was highlighted in late 2016 when it was discovered that both Germany and Italy had unsuccessfully tried to repatriate Anis Amri, the Tunisian who committed the 2016 terrorist Christmas market attack in Berlin. (The Tunisian government had refused to accept Amri due to lack of citizenship papers – which Amri had purposely destroyed in an attempt to pretend he was Egyptian: a common practice among asylum-seekers attempting to fool authorities into thinking they are citizens of countries that qualify for asylum) (Connolly, 2016).

Conclusions: The Wider Implications of, and the Prospects for, Inward EU Migration

A complication in the resolution of the European migration crisis has been the sense of its interconnectedness to simultaneous crises: budgetary (non-enforcement of Dublin III and uneven implementation of asylum directives); social (the three-way culture war of preserving national identity, developing a European identity, and multiculturalism); foreign policy (lack of a coherent European foreign policy in the Middle East and a failed Eastern Partnership/European Neighbourhood Policy); and the EU's leadership deficit. Regarding the latter, failure to resolve the migration crisis threatens to roll back some of the benefits of the EU's major policy accomplishment: the single market, which Schengen's free movement of people facilitates.

So, too, has migration policy exposed deep differences among member states with respect to European solidarity, or as European Council President Donald Tusk put it, a 'test of our Europeanness' (Henley et al., 2016): a test the UK (or, at least, England and Wales) evidently failed when 'leavers' carried the majority in the Brexit referendum. When Herman Van Rompuy, Tusk's predecessor as European Council President, was asked for his opinion about the migration crisis, he replied, 'I believe that the migration crisis is a more difficult one than the eurozone crisis. I wouldn't want to be in Donald Tusk's shoes' – lending credence to the notion that the migration crisis may be the single most important test the EU has faced during the recent years of crises (Cerulus and Kroet, 2016).

Coupled with the related security concerns of open borders (which were much discussed after the Brussels, Paris, and Berlin terrorist attacks), the migration crisis could weaken Schengen to the point where temporary border controls become permanent. Of the 22 EU member states belonging to the Schengen area, several have imposed temporary border checks since the onset of the migration crisis, including Austria, Belgium, Denmark, France, Norway, Sweden, and Germany. Some EU states have even erected fences in Schengen territory, such as along the Austrian–Slovenian frontier (Alderman and Kanter, 2016).

Another damaging consequence of the migration crisis could be its impact on trade and economic growth. France Stratégie (2016), the research arm of the French Prime Minister, has estimated that reinstated border controls would decrease overall trade between Schengen countries by 10–20 per cent and lead to a reduction in Schengen GDP of 0.8 points (€100 billion).

The migrant crisis has also affected elections, with far-right parties taking up nativist themes and winning seats in regional, national, and European legislatures. These parties have campaigned against migrants on the basis of almost every conceivable objection: religion (because migrants are predominantly Muslim, which is fundamentally incompatible with Judeo-Christian traditions); culture (migrants are non-Western and mostly come from pre-industrial societies); security (jihadism among Muslims); budgetary (funds are expended to feed, clothe, house, educate, and integrate migrants); and economic (migrants drive down wages).

In sum, the migrant crisis is widely thought to threaten many of the foundations and bases on which European integration has been built.

* * *

What does the future hold with respect to the migration crisis and what will be the long-term impact of the crisis on EU integration? One answer is that eventually the civil war will end in Syria and, as Chancellor Merkel has suggested, it is likely that about one-half of the Syrian asylum-seekers will return home after the war, just as 70 per cent of Yugoslavia's asylum-seekers returned to their respective states when hostilities ended in the Balkans (Deutsche Welle, 2016).

However, even if political and security turbulence in the neighbourhood diminishes, people will continue to migrate to Europe (see, for example, Friedman, 2016). Europe will continue to be a lure to economic migrants, who tend to be young men (under 45) seeking employment opportunities, in many cases seasonal, whose intention is to send money home (remittances) or return home with their earnings to purchase land, a home, a shop and live permanently in their country of origin. The migrant flow from North Africa will be particularly difficult to control because historically North Africa is part of Europe's economic zone of activity – and people will continue to seek to come to Europe for economic opportunity, just as North Africans have for thousands of years (much as Europeans, too, have migrated to North Africa seeking economic opportunity).

Demographics will be an increasingly significant factor in European debates about both asylum and immigration policy. With the population declining in many EU member states, and the working age to old age ratios becoming unsustainable, the EU will need inward migration flows. The population of the African continent – an area already exerting enormous migrant pressure on Europe – is projected to increase by 103 per cent by 2050. Migrants could be a partial solution to Europe's demographic crisis in some regions or even cities and towns – but the EU and its member states clearly face enormous challenges in integrating migrants, most of whom are Muslims. As Hampshire (2013: 60) has observed, 'with demographic trends as they are, the scale of immigration that would be needed to offset population ageing and maintain dependency ratios is so large as to be politically unviable'. Thus, because of what promises to be a 'permanent crisis', the EU will likely continue to federalize its asylum policy as reviewed in Box 6.2, but will need to go much further in developing what is now an inchoate immigration policy.

As the political philosopher David Miller concludes in his study (2016: 154–7, 161) of the values that should guide the making of immigration policy, 'societies that are already multicultural, and especially those that have adopted multiculturalism as one of their public policies, will approach both the selection of immigrants and integration policy differently from societies that are relatively homogeneous and wish to remain so'. Indeed, there are many reasons why it will be difficult to agree a 'European' immigration policy (even with the British 'out of the way'): the financial burdens of accommodating irregular migrants; public opinion, and particularly the ease with which far-right parties stoke xenophobic fears for electoral gains and the ease with which the centre-right co-opts anti-immigration rhetoric; member state competition to attract highly skilled workers; and member states' historical experience with immigration. Taken together, these factors make it unlikely the EU will develop an immigration policy in the foreseeable future.

As liberal democratic states, however, EU member states must be cognizant of the four values Miller lays out for the making and implementation of immigration policy: 'weak moral cosmopolitanism' (all human beings have moral standing); the right of national self-determination ('citizens in a democracy have the right to decide upon the future direction of their society'); fairness ('a balance has to be struck between the claims that immigrants can rightfully make and the responsibilities they can reasonably be expected to assume'); and social integration (the need for successful states to have a certain degree of coherence). So, despite the unlikelihood of the EU 'federalizing' immigration policy along the lines that the USA did in the late nineteenth century, member states have a responsibility to behave as liberal democratic states in their dealings with migrants – whether individuals arrive as refugees and are invited to stay permanently in an EU member state or as economic migrants. Therefore, the EU institutions, too, have a responsibility to ensure member states live up to the values entailed in and responsibilities required of EU membership.

The migration crisis serves as a stark reminder that if Europeans expect to fully enjoy the economic advantages of the four freedoms, they cannot circumvent the political and security bases upon which they were established. Europe's internal market and Schengen's passport-free travel area are heralded as being among the EU's crowning achievements, but they have been built and have operated while Europe's neighbourhood has been quiet. But geography is destiny. Although globalists have long complained that the Mercator projection's visual legerdemain and other spatial imperialisms (such as the central meridian running through Greenwich) reinforced Europe's centrality in the global landmass, recent events remind us that sometimes all roads do lead to Rome, or in the particular case of the contemporary global migration crisis, to Berlin, London, and Stockholm.

'Modern' European migration history is that of a sending region – Europeans exploring, travelling to, and permanently migrating to the four corners of the world. But this has now changed and migrants (mostly Muslim, from cultures typically more conservative than Europe) are challenging the meaning and practice of national identity at the same time that 'European identity' is challenging national identity from 'above'. Europe's migration crisis has engendered a collective European cognitive dissonance.

The European migration crisis has raised fundamental questions regarding the EU's ability to govern Europe and to protect EU citizens. The EU has responded slowly to the crisis, with a mix of supranational and intergovernmental solutions. Have the solutions adopted by the EU resulted in 'more' or 'less' Europe? This chapter provided an unequivocal answer: 'more' Europe.

References

Alderman, L. (2016) 'Macedonian Police Use Tear Gas to Stop Migrants at Border', *The New York Times*, 10 April, http://www.nytimes.com/2016/04/11/world/europe/macedonia-greece-migrants-refugees.html.

Alderman, L. and Kanter, J. (2016) 'Europe's Border Checks Become Economic Choke Points', *The New York Times*, 1 March, http://www.nytimes.com/2016/03/02/business/international/europes-new-border-controls-exact-a-cost.html?_r=0.

Ames, P. (2016) 'Portugal to Syrians: Come West', *Politico*, 22 March, http://www.politico.eu/article/portugal-to-syrians-come-west-refugee-crisis-portuguese-prime-ministerantonio-costa/.

Anderson, B. (1983) *Imagining Nations*, 2nd edition. New York: Verso.

Barigazzi, J. (2015) 'Divisions Are Getting Deeper', *Politico*, 16 November, http://www.politico.eu/article/refugee-crisis-divisions-deeper-paris-attack-migrants-passport/.

Barigazzi, J. and Cienski, J. (2015) 'Orbán and Juncker to Face Off on Migration', *Politico*, 2 September, http://www.politico.eu/article/orban-crash-juncker-party-asylum-council-september-migration/.

Barigazzi, J. and Winneker, C. (2015) 'EU Leaders Agree New Migration Measures "Cautious Optimism" after a Summit that Produces a Tentative Deal with Turkey', *Politico*, 10 April, http://www.politico.eu/article/eu-strikes-tentative-refugee-deal-turkey-migration-refugees-accession/.

BBC News (2009) 'Italian Migration Policy Draws Fire', *BBC News*, 7 March, http://news.bbc.co.uk/2/hi/europe/7880215.stm.

BBC News (2011) 'State Multiculturalism Has Failed, Says David Cameron', *BBC News*, 5 February, http://www.bbc.com/news/uk-politics-12371994.

Belgrade Centre for Human Rights (2015) *Safe Passage: Testimony of people arriving in Dimitrovgrad, Serbia from Bulgaria 20–22 October 2015*, https://www.dropbox.com/s/8m7oruipue5ck1u/Dimitrovgrad%20Report_final%2011Nov.pdf?dl=0.

Brunsden, J. (2008) 'Greece to Defend its Asylum Procedures', *European Voice*, 17 April, http://www.europeanvoice.com/article/imported/greece-to-defend-its-asylum-procedures/60332.aspx.

Castle, S. (2010) 'Anti-Immigrant Party Rises in Sweden', *The New York Times*, 14 September, http://www.nytimes.com/2010/09/14/world/europe/14iht-sweden.html?partner=rss&emc=rss&pagewanted=print.

Cerulus, L. and Kroet, C. (2016) 'Herman Van Rompuy: "I Wouldn't Want to Be in Tusk's Shoes"', *Politico*, 1 January, http://www.politico.eu/article/catching-up-with-herman-van-rompuy-legacy-european-council-tusk/.

Chrisafis, A., Walker, P. and Quinn, B. (2016) 'Calais "Jungle" Camp: Clashes as Authorities Demolish Homes', *The Guardian,* 1 March, http://www.theguardian.com/world/2016/feb/29/french-authorities-begin-clearance-of-part-of-calais-jungle-camp.

Connolly, K. (2016) 'Anis Amri: From Young Drifter to Europe's Most Wanted Man', *The Guardian,* 23 December, https://www.theguardian.com/world/2016/dec/23/anis-amri-from-young-drifter-to-europes-most-wanted-man.

Connor, P. and Krogstad, J. M. (2016) 'Immigrant Share of Population Jumps in Some European Countries', http://www.pewresearch.org/fact-tank/2016/06/15/immigrant-share-of-population-jumps-in-some-european-countries/.

Council of the European Union (2016a) 'Council Conclusions on Migrant Smuggling' [Press release].

Council of the European Union (2016b) Justice and Home Affairs Council, 10–11 March 2016, http://www.consilium.europa.eu/en/meetings/jha/2016/03/10-11/.

Crosbie, J. (2009) 'Commission Questions Italy's Immigration Policy', *European Voice*, 23 July.

Daley, S. (2012) 'A Tiny Mediterranean Nation, Awash in Immigrants With Nowhere to Go', *The New York Times*, 22 September, http://www.nytimes.com/2012/09/23/world/europe/malta-struggles-under-wave-of-african-migrants.html?pagewanted=all.

Daley, S. (2014) 'As Africans Surge to Europe's Door, Spain Locks Down', *The New York Times*, 27 February, http://www.nytimes.com/2014/02/28/world/europe/africans-battered-and-broke-surge-to-europes-door.html?ref=europe.

Donadio, R. (2011a) 'Italy Lashes Out at European Union Over Immigrants', *The New York Times,* 11 April.

Donadio, R. (2011b) 'Italy Seeks to Use Forces to Halt Illegal Immigrants From Tunisia', *The New York Times,* 14 February.

Deutsche Welle (2016) 'Merkel Expects Most Syrian and Iraqi Refugees to Return Home Once Conflict is Over', 31 January, http://www.dw.com/en/merkel-expects-most-syrian-and-iraqi-refugees-to-return-home-once-conflict-is-over/a-19013957.

Economist Data Team (2015) 'Asylum Applications and Europe's Safe Country Lists', *The Economist*, 8 October.

European Commission (2008) 'New Tools for an Integrated European Border Management Strategy' [Press release], http://europa.eu/rapid/pressReleasesAction.do?reference=MEMO/08/85&format=HTML&aged=1&language=EN&guiLanguage=en.

European Commission (2010) 'Communication from the Commission to the European Parliament, the Council, the European Social and Economic Committee, and the Committee of the Regions: Delivering an Area of Freedom, Security and Justice for Europe's Citizens: Action Plan Implementing the Stockholm Programme', COM (2010) 171 final, http://eurlex.europa.eu/LexUriServ/LexUriServ.do?uri=COM:2010:0171:FIN:EN:PDF.

European Commission (2011) 'EUROSUR: Providing Authorities with Tools Needed to Reinforce Management of External Borders and Fight

Cross-border Crime MEMO/11/896' [Press release], http://europa.eu/rapid/pressReleasesAction.do?reference=MEMO/11/896&type=HTML.

European Commission (2015a) 'The 2015 Ageing Report: Economic and Budgetary Projections for the 28 EU Member States (2013–2060)', http://ec.europa.eu/economy_finance/publications/european_economy/2015/ee3_en.htm.

European Commission (2015b) 'Communication from the Commission to the European Parliament, the Council, the European Economic and Social Committee and the Committee of the Regions: A European Agenda on Migration', COM(2015) 240 final, http://ec.europa.eu/dgs/home-affairs/what-we-do/policies/european-agenda-migration/background-information/docs/communication_on_the_european_agenda_on_migration_en.pdf.

European Commission (2015c) 'Graph of the Week: Ageing Report – Population Projections in EU Member States', 1 July, http://ec.europa.eu/economy_finance/graphs/2015-05-18_ageing_report_en.htm.

European Commission (2015d) 'Proposal for a Regulation of the European Parliament and of the Council on a European Travel Document for the Return of Illegally Staying Third-Country Nationals', COM(2015) 668 final 2015/0306 (COD), http://ec.europa.eu/dgs/home-affairs/what-we-do/policies/securing-eu-borders/legal-documents/docs/european_travel_document_for_the_return_of_illegally_staying_third-country_nationals_en.pdf.

European Commission (2015e) 'Proposal for a Regulation of the European Parliament and of the Council on the European Border and Coast Guard and Repealing Regulation (EC) No 2007/2004, Regulation (EC) No 863/2007 and Council Decision 2005/267/EC', COM(2015) 671 final, http://ec.europa.eu/dgs/home-affairs/what-we-do/policies/securing-eu-borders/legal-documents/docs/regulation_on_the_european_border_and_coast_guard_en.pdf.

European Commission (2016a) 'Communication from the Commission to the European Parliament and the Council, on the State of Play of Implementation of the Priority Actions under the European Agenda on Migration', COM(2016) 85 final, http://ec.europa.eu/dgs/home-affairs/what-we-do/policies/european-agenda-migration/proposal-implementation-package/docs/managing_the_refugee_crisis_state_of_play_20160210_en.pdf.

European Commission (2016b) 'Communication from the Commission to the European Parliament and the Council: Towards a Reform of the Common Asylum System and Enhancing Legal Avenues to Europe', COM(2016), 197 final, http://ec.europa.eu/dgs/home-affairs/what-we-do/policies/european-agenda-migration/proposal-implementation-package/docs/20160406/towards_a_reform_of_the_common_european_asylum_system_and_enhancing_legal_avenues_to_europe_-_20160406_en.pdf.

European Commission (2016c) 'Member States' Support to Emergency Relocation Mechanism', http://ec.europa.eu/dgs/home-affairs/what-we-do/policies/european-agenda-migration/press-material/docs/state_of_play_-_relocation_en.pdf.

European Commission (2016d) 'Refugee Crisis: Commission Reviews 2015 Actions and Sets 2016 Priorities' [Press release], http://europa.eu/rapid/press-release_IP-16-65_en.htm.

European Commission (2016e) 'State of Play Hotspot Capacity', http://
ec.europa.eu/dgs/home-affairs/what-we-do/policies/european-agenda-
migration/press-material/docs/state_of_play_-_hotspots_en.pdf.

European Commission (2016f) 'Towards a Sustainable and Fair Common
European Asylum System', [Press release], http://europa.eu/rapid/press-
release_IP-16-1620_en.htm.

European Commission (n.d.) EU Regional Trust Fund in Response to the Syrian Crisis, http://ec.europa.eu/neighbourhood-enlargement/neighbourhood/
countries/syria/madad_en.

European Council (1999) *Presidency Conclusions*, Tampere European Council, 15 and 16 October, http://www.consilium.europa.eu/en/uedocs/cms_
data/docs/pressdata/en/ec/00200-r1.en9.htm.

European Council (2015) *Conclusions,* 15 October, http://www.consilium.
europa.eu/en/meetings/european-council/2015/10/15-16/.

European Council (2016) Statement of the Heads of State or Government,
07/03/2016 [Press release].

European Parliament (2015) *Safe Countries of Origin: Proposed Common
EU List*. Retrieved from http://www.europarl.europa.eu/EPRS/EPRS-Brief-
ing-569008-Safe-countries-of-origin-FINAL.pdf.

European Parliament (2016) Legislative Train Schedule: Towards a New
Policy on Migration, http://www.europarl.europa.eu/legislative-train/
theme-towards-a-new-policy-on-migration/file-reform-of-the-asylum-proce-
dures-directive.

European Parliament and Council (2013) Regulation (EU) No 1052/2013 of
the European Paliament and of the Council of 22 October 2013 Establishing the European Border Surveillance System (Eurosur).

Europol (2016) *Migrant Smuggling in the EU*, http://www.europol.europa.eu/
content/EMSC_launch.

Eurostat (2016) *Asylum Statistics*, http://ec.europa.eu/eurostat/statistics-
explained/index.php/Asylum_statistics.

France Strategie (2016) Les conséquences économiques d'un abandon
des accords de Schengen, http://www.strategie.gouv.fr/publications/
consequenceseconomiques-dun-abandon-accords-de-schengen?
xtor=xtor%3DEREC-10-%5B20160204-ALERTE038%5D.

Fratzke, S. (2015) *Not Adding Up: The Fading Promise of Europe's Dublin System*, Migration Policy Institute, http://www.migrationpolicy.org/
research/not-adding-fading-promise-europes-dublin-system.

Friedman, T. (2016) 'Out of Africa', *The New York Times*, 13 April.

Frontex (2016a) *FRAN Quarterly*, January–March, http://frontex.europa.eu/
assets/Publications/Risk_Analysis/FRAN_Q1_2016_final.pdf.

Frontex (2016b) 'Record Number of Migrants Reached Italy in October',
11 November, http://frontex.europa.eu/news/record-number-of-migrants-
reached-italy-in-october-sc99xk.

Fullerton, M. (2005) 'Inadmissable in Iberia: The Fate of Asylum Seekers in
Spain and Portugal', *International Journal of Refugee Law*, Vol. 17, No. 4,
pp. 659–87.

Gabaccia, D. R. (2000) *Italy's Many Diasporas: Elites, Exiles and Workers of
the World*. New York: Taylor & Francis Group.

Gall, L. (2016) 'Dispatches: Asylum Seekers Stuck Outside Transit Zones in Hungary', Human Rights Watch, 4 April, https://www.hrw.org/news/2016/04/04/dispatches-asylum-seekers-stuck-outside-transit-zones-hungary.

Germanova, M. (2016) 'Slovakia's Governing Party Loses Majority as Far Right Makes Gains, *The New York Times*, 7 March, http://www.nytimes.com/2016/03/07/world/europe/ruling-party-in-slovakia-loses-majority-in-elections.html.

Guild, E., Costello, C., Garlick, M., Moreno-Lax, V. and Mouzourakis, M. (2015) *New Approaches, Alternative Avenues and Means of Access to Asylum Procedures for Persons Seeking International Protection*. Retrieved from https://www.ceps.eu/publications/new-approaches-alternative-avenues-and-means-access-asylum-procedures-persons-seeking.

Hampshire, J. (2013) *The Politics of Immigration*. Cambridge: Polity Press.

Henley, J., Rankin, J., Smith, H., and Walker, P. (2016) 'Refugee Crisis: European Leaders Demand Support for Greece', *The Guardian*, 1 March, http://www.theguardian.com/world/2016/mar/01/refugee-crisis-european-leaders-demand-urgent-support-for-greece.

Higgins, A. (2016) 'E.U. Suspects Russian Agenda in Migrants' Shifting Arctic Route', *The New York Times*, 2 April, http://www.nytimes.com/2016/04/03/world/europe/for-migrants-into-europe-a-road-less-traveled.html?ribbon-ad-idx=5&rref=world/europe&module=Ribbon&version=context&region=Header&action=click&contentCollection=Europe&pgtype=article.

Howard, M. M. (2009) *The Politics of Citizenship in Europe*. Cambridge: Cambridge University Press.

Huff Post (2015) 'What Island Is This?: Molyvos, Lesvos Island, Greece', *Huff Post*, 15 August, http://testkitchen.huffingtonpost.com/1000-miles/greece/.

Karnitschnig, M. (2016) '5 takeaways from Merkel's Election Drubbing', *Politico*, 13 March, http://www.politico.eu/article/5-takeaways-from-angela-merkels-election-drubbing-german-regional-elections/.

Lucas, A. (2016) 'Lesbos, A Greek Island in Limbo over Tourism, Refugees – and its Future', *The Guardian,* 24 March, https://www.theguardian.com/travel/2016/mar/24/lesbos-greek-island-in-limbo-tourism-refugee-crisis-future.

Lyman, R. (2015a) 'Bulgarian Border Police Accused of Abusing Refugees', *The New York Times*, 24 December, http://www.nytimes.com/2015/12/24/world/europe/bulgarian-border-police-accused-of-abusing-refugees.html.

Lyman, R. (2015b) 'Opposition to Refugee Quotas Softens in Europe's Old Communist Bloc', *The New York Times*, 23 September, http://www.nytimes.com/2015/09/24/world/europe/opposition-to-refugee-quotas-softens-in-europes-old-communist-bloc.html?_r=0.

Miller, D. (2016) *Strangers in our Midst: The Political Philosophy of Immigration*. Cambridge, MA: Harvard University Press.

Muddle, C. (2012) *The Relationship between Immigration and Nativism in Europe and North America*. Washington, DC: Migration Policy Institute.

Preston, R. (2015) 'Why Germany Needs Migrants More than UK', *BBC News*, 7 September, http://www.bbc.com/news/business-34172729.

Quinn, B. (2016) 'French Police Make Woman Remove Clothing on Nice Beach Following Burkini Ban', *The Guardian*, 23 August, https://www.

theguardian.com/world/2016/aug/24/french-police-make-woman-remove-burkini-on-nice-beach.

Rankin, J. (2016) 'EU and Turkey Restart Talks over Migrant Pact', *The Guardian*, 25 August, https://www.theguardian.com/world/2016/aug/25/eu-and-turkey-restart-talks-over-migrant-pact.

Rankin, J. and Shaheen, K. (2016) 'Turkey Reacts Angrily to Symbolic EU Parliament Vote on its Membership', *The Guardian*, 24 November, https://www.theguardian.com/world/2016/nov/24/eu-parliament-votes-freeze-membership-talks-turkey.

Reuters News Service (2016) 'More Aid Agencies Pull Out of Greek Camps, Spurning EU Deal', Reuters, 23 March, http://www.nytimes.com/reuters/2016/03/23/world/europe/23reuters-europe-migrants-greece.html?_r=0.

Scherer, S. and Polleschi, I. (2014) 'Italy in Talks with EU to Share Responsibility for Boat Migrants', Reuters, 8 July, http://www.reuters.com/article/us-eu-italy-migrants-idUSKBN0FD1YL20140708.

Simons, M. (2004) 'Under Pressure, Spain Tries to Close an Open Door', *The New York Times*, 10 October, http://www.nytimes.com/2004/10/10/international/europe/10spain.html.

Singer, A. (2013) 'Contemporary Immigrant Gateways in Historical Perspective', *Daedelus,* Vol. 142, No. 3, pp. 76–91, http://www.brookings.edu/~/media/research/files/articles/2013/09/05-immigrant-gateways-singer/singer-immigration-article-9513.pdf.

Timur, S. and Nordland, R. (2016) 'Erdogan Threatens to Let Migrant Flood Into Europe Resume', *The New York Times*, 25 November, http://www.nytimes.com/2016/11/25/world/europe/turkey-recep-tayyip-erdogan-migrants-european-union.html.

Tondo, L. (2016) 'How One Sicilian Village Learned to Love Migrants', *Time*, 27 January, http://time.com/4186819/sutera-sicily-migrants/.

Travis, A. (2014) 'UK Axes Support for Mediterranean Migrant Rescue Operation', *The Guardian*, 27 October, http://www.theguardian.com/politics/2014/oct/27/uk-mediterranean-migrant-rescue-plan.

Travis, A. (2015) 'Mediterranean Migrant Deaths: UK Sends Just Five Workers to Assist EU', *The Guardian*, 20 April, https://www.theguardian.com/world/2015/apr/20/mediterranean-migrant-deaths-uk-eu-mission.

Traynor, I. (2015) 'Eastern European Leaders Defy EU Effort to Set Refugee Quotas', *The Guardian*, 21 September, http://www.theguardian.com/world/2015/sep/21/eastern-european-leaders-defy-eu-effort-to-set-refugee-quotas.

UNHCR (2016) Weekly Report – 17 November. UNHCR Regional Bureau Europe, http://data.unhcr.org/mediterranean/regional.php#_ga=1.1531008 56.188050932.1480181763.

UNHCR (2017) 'Syrian Regional Refugee Response', 19 January, http://data.unhcr.org/syrianrefugees/regional.php.

Vincenti, D. (2015) 'Van Rompuy: "EU Leaders Only Take Bold Decisions When They Have a Knive Against Their Throats"', Euractiv, 10 September, https://www.euractiv.com/section/david-cameron/interview/van-rompuy-eu-leaders-only-take-bold-decisions-when-they-have-a-knife-against-their-throats/.

Chapter 7

The Eurozone in Crisis: Core–Periphery Dynamics

BRIGID LAFFAN

Introduction

The two interrelated concepts of core and periphery are widely used in historical and social science analysis. The concepts are inherently relational as one implies the presence of the other. Relations between the core and periphery have played a major role in the evolution of economic and political power structures at a global level, within empires, continents, and nation states. Europe's first nation states were moulded by strong cores spreading their writ to surrounding geographical areas. The centre–periphery cleavage was identified by Lipset and Rokkan (1967) as one of the four key cleavages that dominated state formation and the emergence of party systems in Europe. Deutsch and colleagues (1956) identified the 'cores of strength' around which nation states were built (Deutsch et al., 1956). Rokkan and Urwin (1983: 13), in their work on territorial politics in Europe's peripheries, concluded that peripheral regions shared three characteristics, namely they were geographically distant, culturally different, and economically dependent on the core regions.

Scholars of European integration and the actors who forged the early Union were attentive to the challenge of economic divergence in Europe, particularly the Mezzogiorno (the impoverished south of Italy), in the original EU of six member states. That challenge came to the fore as the iterative process of enlargement brought a north-western, Mediterranean and eastern periphery into the Union, beginning with the first enlargement in 1973. In fact, all enlargements, with the exception of the European Free Trade Association (EFTA) enlargement of the mid-1990s, were characterized by new member states whose level of economic development was below that of the core. It was for this reason that the Union developed cohesion policy and a set of related policy instruments.

The objective of this chapter is to analyse the emergence within the eurozone during the financial and economic crisis of divergence between a eurozone core and periphery. The crisis has been experienced in very different ways depending on whether a state is part of the northern core or the periphery. The second objective of the chapter is to explore the political consequences of this for democratic politics in the eurozone and the wider EU. Finally, the chapter assesses why the politics of redistribution are so difficult in the eurozone and the wider Union. The chapter begins with an overview of the eurozone design as fashioned by the Maastricht Treaty.

Economic and Monetary Union: A Deliberate Blind Spot

The achievement of a single currency was for a long time regarded as the 'holy grail' of European integration because of its likely impact on the wider dynamic of integration. It was a symbol of a high level of economic integration that would in its wake necessitate deeper political integration. The 1970 Werner Plan set out to map the various elements that would be essential to a complete economic and monetary union: the minimum that should be carried out (Werner, 1970: 9). It pointed out that differences in economic structure would impact on the achievement of an economic equilibrium within the currency zone and flagged that 'financial measures of compensation' would alleviate the problems and that 'regional and structural policies' would no longer be exclusively within the remit of the member states (Werner, 1970: 11). The 1977 MacDougall Report advocated a much larger EU budget than was the case – a budget of at least 5 per cent of GDP. The 1988 Delors Report on Economic and Monetary Union was explicit in its assertion that the process of integration had been uneven and that '[*greater*]*convergence of economic performance is needed*' (European Union, 1989: 11, italics in the original). In a subsequent part of the report, it was clearly stated that 'if sufficient consideration were not given to regional imbalances, the economic union would be faced with grave economic and political risks' (ibid.: 18). With the absence of the exchange-rate adjustment mechanism, the report was cognizant of the fact that 'wage flexibility and labour mobility are necessary to eliminate differences in competitiveness in different regions and countries of the Community' (ibid.: 19). The Delors Report influenced but did not determine the shape that EMU would take in the Treaty on European Union (TEU), otherwise known as the Maastricht Treaty.

During the TEU treaty negotiations, there was extensive discussion among economists concerning optimal currency areas (OCA) and a broad consensus that the eurozone would not constitute an OCA. Notwithstanding this, there was no agreement in the TEU on policy instruments that might alleviate asymmetric shocks. This was summarized by Tsoukalis in the following terms: 'So the architects of EMU rejected intra budgetary transfers as an automatic adjustment mechanism, while imposing heavy constraints on national federal policy' (Tsoukalis, 2003: 156). The dangers were well signalled: according to Eichengreen, 'By creating a structure that constrains both the monetary and the fiscal independence of EMU member states, the Maastricht Treaty threatens to create an exceedingly rigid and fragile European economy. With the advent of monetary union, the participating states will lose all recourse to independent monetary policies to offset disturbances affecting them asymmetrically' (Eichengreen, 1996: 3). The architects of the TEU introduced the concept of convergence criteria (price stability, interest rate convergence, and budget deficits) which were designed to limit the number of countries that could join the single currency at least in the initial phase. In practice, rather than act as a constraint, the convergence criteria spurred a phase of fiscal consolidation among those member states that wanted to join; this was accompanied by a degree of fudging that meant that the single currency consisted of countries with such diverse economic structures as Germany and Greece. By the mid-1990s, Germany, the most influential country in the design of EMU, began to worry about the fiscal behaviour of the likely members of the currency union, which led in 1997 to a new set of rules – the Stability and Growth Pact (SGP) – focusing on fiscal responsibility. The underlying system of ideas in the Union's EMU was captured by the Commission in its volume *Stable Money–Sound Finances* (European Commission, 1993).

The euro's first decade was, on the face of it, largely trouble-free. The transition went smoothly and Europe's citizens adjusted to the daily reality of a new currency in their pockets. In fact, in early 2008 at the end of the euro's first decade, the tone was celebratory. The Commission's 2008 communication to the other institutions on *EMU@10* included the following paragraph:

> Ten years into its existence, the euro is a resounding success. The single currency has become a symbol of Europe, considered by euro-area citizens to be amongst the most positive results of European integration together with the achievement of free movement within the EU and peace in Europe. One in two people in the euro area asserts that for them, the EU means the single currency. EMU has secured macroeconomic stability and boosted cross-border trade, financial integration and investment. The number of countries that share the euro has increased from the original eleven to fifteen at the beginning of 2008 and is set to increase further. (European Commission, 2008: 3)

The report did, however, identify what were to become the fault lines of the system. First, it acknowledged that the single currency had acted as a powerful spur to financial integration which in reality represented a large flow of capital from high-savings countries to capital-poor countries. The level of financial integration built on massive capital flows would prove to be the Achilles' heel of the system. Second, the report found that 'there have been substantial and lasting differences across countries in terms of inflation and unit labour costs. The tendency for persistent divergences between eurozone member states has been due in part to a lack of responsiveness of prices and wages, which have not adjusted smoothly across products, sectors and regions. This has led to accumulated competitiveness losses and large external imbalances, which in EMU require long periods of adjustment' (European Commission, 2008: 6). Both these fault lines would come to haunt the eurozone when the global financial crisis morphed into an existential crisis for Europe's currency.

In autumn 2008 when the global financial crisis was triggered by the collapse of Lehman Brothers, the giant US investment bank, the European Central Bank (ECB) responded as did other central banks, to ensure that the crisis would not lead to a great depression. Initially, it appeared as if Europe had indeed weathered the storm. There was even a certain amount of hubris because this crisis could be laid at the feet of excessive liberalization in financial services in the Anglo-Saxon world, particularly the USA. The hubris proved short-lived when, in autumn 2009, a newly elected Greek Government discovered a sizeable deficit in their public finances. The Papandreou Government revised the estimate of the 2009 government budget deficit upwards from 6.7 per cent of gross domestic product (GDP) to 12.7 per cent of GDP. In April 2010, Eurostat estimated that the Greek deficit was even higher, at 13.6 per cent of GDP. Both the size of the deficit and the significant upwards revision generated panic in the financial markets and the ability of Greece to borrow to fund itself became ever more precarious. Initially, however, the problem was seen by the other member states as a Greek problem to be solved by Greece. The Maastricht Treaty had a no-bailout clause and the rescue of a member state was not anticipated.

In spring 2010, the Greek problem became a eurozone problem as the risks of contagion became more evident and the position of Greece deteriorated (see Chapter 4). Without intervention, a Greek default was inevitable. By the first week of May 2010, the other eurozone states agreed the first two major interventions in the crisis; these were the bailout of Greece on 3 May and the establishment of the European Financial Stability Facility (EFSF), a temporary crisis resolution mechanism. The rescue of Greece was followed over the subsequent years by the bailout of Ireland, Portugal, Cyprus, and Spain (banks only). The rescues came with a high level of conditionality and a new institutional format, the Troika, which consisted of the Commission, the ECB, and the International Monetary Fund (IMF). The crisis was caused by underlying fault lines in the single currency, which were brought sharply into focus when the global financial crisis triggered market instability. Economic divergences and variations in how the crisis was experienced were the hallmarks of the eurozone's troubles. The crisis translated differently in the diverse economies of the eurozone. The eurozone core weathered the economic storm, whereas the eurozone periphery endured severe economic turmoil. There were also divergences in the framing of the crisis.

What Kind of Crisis?

The fact that the crisis began in Greece, and that one of its core problems was a problem of excessive public spending and public debt, was to have a profound impact on how the crisis was perceived and framed by key political actors and institutions. From the beginning, the crisis was seen as a public finance crisis driven by profligate and uncontrolled spending in a number of EU member states. These states had broken the rules and failed to observe the strictures of the Stability and Growth Pact. Failure of individual countries was identified as the central reason for the crisis. The then President of the ECB, Jean-Claude Trichet, argued that:

> There is no euro crisis. The currency has retained its value very well and is credible and remarkably stable – not just in one country, but in the euro area as a whole. Our problem is that the fiscal policies of some member countries have not been sound and that some countries are also lacking in competitiveness. (ECB, 2011: 1)

Moreover, the designation of the countries in trouble as PIGS or GIIPS added to the contested nature of the crisis.[1] The framing of the crisis fostered a political discourse that pitted feckless southern Europeans against prudent northern Europeans and as the crisis worsened, it opened up a core–periphery divide and a creditor–debtor divide within the eurozone. Framing is a crucial part of crisis management because 'those who are able to define what the crisis is all about also hold the key to defining the appropriate strategies for resolution' (Hart, 1993: 41). Masking may also play an important role in crisis management as political actors seek to downplay the extent of the problems or keep aspects of the crisis off the public agenda (Hart, 1993; Laffan 2014a). The framing of the crisis as a public finance crisis served to mask two important dimensions,

---

[1] PIGS (Portugal, Ireland/Italy, Greece, and Spain), GIIPS (Greece, Ireland, Italy, Portugal, and Spain).

namely the question of the banks and the benefits of the eurozone to countries in surplus.

The global crisis was a financial crisis triggered by the banks and from the outset there was a link between the problems of the eurozone periphery and banks in the core. It took until June 2012 for the European Council, meeting in its eurozone format as the Euro Summit, to acknowledge this when in the first line of the statement it finally said: 'We affirm that it is imperative to break the vicious circle between banks and sovereigns' (Euro Area Statement, 2012: 1). Between 2008 and 2011, €1.6 trillion, the equivalent of 13 per cent of the EU's annual GDP, was committed to saving Europe's banks (European Commission, 2016). The Greek state had borrowed heavily from banks in the core, as did private citizens in Ireland and Spain, and, overall, there were large capital outflows from the eurozone core to the periphery. According to 14 leading economists who sought to establish a consensus narrative on the causes of the crisis: 'When the EZ [eurozone] Crisis started, there was a "sudden stop" in cross-border lending. Investors became reluctant to lend – especially to banks and governments in other nations' (Baldwin et al., 2015: 1). The financial integration of the previous decade unravelled and a number of the peripheral economies were forced out of the financial markets and into Troika programmes of financial support. Public funding from the creditor states replaced funding from the private sector. This, in turn, allowed banks in the core to repair their balance sheets without facing the consequences of a default by the peripheral countries. The peripheral countries, having built up current account deficits and seeing a reduction in competitiveness in the 2000s, found themselves facing internal devaluations which put considerable strain on their political and social fabric.

Divergent Economic Fortunes

The asymmetric impact of the eurozone crisis on its different members and the experiences of the troubled economies introduced a deep fissure into the single currency area. The seeds of that fissure were, however, lurking under the surface during the currency's first decade. One of the most significant impacts of the creation of the single currency was the manner in which it reduced the cost of borrowing for those countries that used to have to pay a premium because of risks identified by the market. In the first decade of the single currency, Greece, for example, was able to borrow at or just above Germany's cost of borrowing. This meant that there was a massive increase in the flow of credit from capital-rich countries to the periphery and the cost of borrowing was low for both governments and private individuals. The main channel though which the lending occurred was private sector banks. The ease of borrowing and reasonable growth masked underlying vulnerabilities in the eurozone which were to come to the fore once the crisis became a perfect storm for Europe's southern periphery and Ireland. The most telling indicator of the problems that had been masked was the presence of current account deficits for all of the countries that ended up in trouble. According to the consensus view of economists:

> The real culprits were the large intra-EZ capital flows that occurred in the decade before the crisis. These imbalances baked problems into the EZ 'cake' that would spill over in the 2010s. All the nations stricken by the crisis were running current account deficits. None of those running current account surpluses were hit. (Baldwin and Gros, 2015: 3)

Six countries entered the crisis with current account deficits. These were Portugal, Greece, Spain, Ireland, Italy, and Cyprus (see Figure 7.1). All of these countries, because of their reliance on foreign borrowing, experienced contagion as the spread between their cost of borrowing and that of Germany rose to unsustainable levels. They were effectively out of the financial markets. Five of these states had to enter either full or partial bailout programmes, while Italy, because of its size, was 'too big to bail' but also 'too big to fail'. Keeping Italy in the markets was a key objective and systemic challenge to the eurozone in 2011/12. Tables showing the spread between the cost of borrowing for an individual eurozone state and the German benchmark became the key graphic signifier of the crisis. In one country after another these tables were

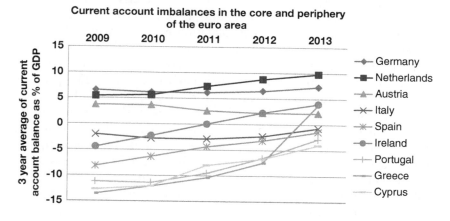

Figure 7.1   *Current account imbalances*
Source: AMECO data base (2016)

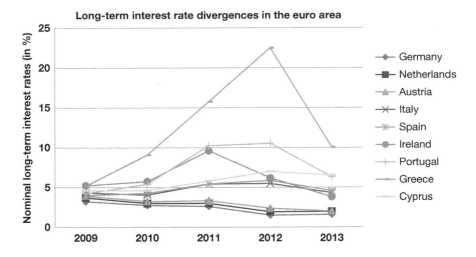

Figure 7.2   *Long-term interest rate spread*
Source: AMECO data base (2016)

the staple diet of daily news spreading alarm though society. The size of the gap and the speed of increase were a good benchmark of which country was in trouble and which had lost credibility with the markets (see Figure 7.2). Spreads and downgrades by the rating agencies were the market's way of signalling the crisis. The financial markets, having failed to price the risk in the first decade of the euro, began to do so in a sustained manner from autumn 2009 onwards.

As the crisis deepened and spread to encompass additional states, the financial crisis morphed into a serious economic crisis in a number of countries. The high level of conditionality associated with the bailout programmes required large fiscal consolidation measures which dampened further economic activity at a time of acute crisis. Public spending was cut back and public services curtailed. The loss in real GDP between 2008 and 2012/13 was extremely large, particularly in Greece (–23.3 per cent) but was also sizeable in Portugal (–7.9 per cent), Italy (–7.1 per cent), and Spain (–6.4 per cent). These figures are in marked contrast to the –2 per cent loss for the eurozone as a whole. The decline in real GDP translated into lower domestic demand, lower household consumption, and reduced public investment. The crisis became a Great Recession for those countries and led to a pronounced rise in unemployment (Figure 7.3). Young people in Europe's periphery bore the brunt of rising unemployment, leading to concern for a lost generation. In January 2016, the rate of youth unemployment was highest in Greece (48.0 per cent in November 2015), Spain (45.0 per cent), and Italy (39.3 per cent). This is

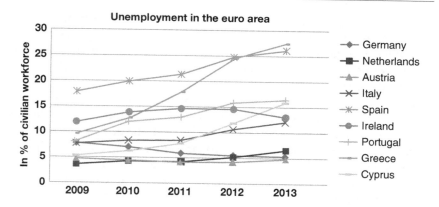

Figure 7.3 *Unemployment in the euro area*
Source: AMECO data base (2016)

in stark contrast to the lowest rates, which were in Germany (7.1 per cent) and the Netherlands (11.2 per cent) at the same time (Eurostat, 2016).

The crisis exposed deep fault lines within the eurozone between creditor and debtor states. The latter had run or developed current account deficits in the decade leading up to the crisis. This was the prime indicator of underlying economic vulnerability which was brought sharply into focus as the crisis developed. The eurozone's peripheral states had to pay the cost of adjustment for the public and private borrowing that the state or citizens had engaged in. The crisis affected tens of millions of people who experienced it in the form of higher unemployment, lower salaries, lower consumption, and poorer public services. Inevitably this led to public protests, which were more pronounced and sustained in some countries than in others. It also led to sharp divergence across the eurozone that manifested itself as stereotyping and caricature. It was most sharply felt in relations between Greece and Germany. A Greek magazine portrayed Chancellor Merkel in Nazi uniform and the Italian newspaper *Il Giornale* spoke of the 'Quarto Reich'. The German mass-circulation newspaper *Bild,* just before one of the Bundestag (national parliament) votes on a Greek bailout, had a large 'NEIN' on its front page followed by 'No More Billions For Greedy Greeks'. The crisis had frayed relations between the member states but had also put major pressure on democratic politics in the member states, particularly in the hardest hit countries.

Crisis Politics

Economic divergence was accompanied by fractious politics as governments came under increasing pressure from their own electorates and parliaments. Governments carried the strain of the crisis at both a European and domestic level. At an EU level, the European Council and the Euro Summit form the arenas for high-level emergency politics, providing a capacity to create a state of exception and thus insulate big decisions from public debate (White, 2015). It was in this arena that heads of state and government struggled to get on top of the crisis and regain market credibility. Because of the nature of the crisis and Germany's well-established preferences concerning Europe's single currency regime, Germany emerged as the pivotal player in crisis management and in developing measures to prevent a future crisis. This, in turn, made Merkel the most important political actor in Europe. From the outset, she was committed to maintaining the euro as she defined it as central to the future of the EU itself. Speaking in September 2011, Merkel argued that 'the euro is the guarantee of a united Europe. If the euro fails, then Europe fails' (Merkel, 2011).

Merkel had to navigate between domestic politics which required her to deliver a majority in favour of every bailout in parliament and ensure that if challenged the crisis mechanisms would survive a challenge in the German Constitutional Court. Domestic politics in Germany militated against policy solutions that would have reduced the debt, particularly for Greece, or mutualized debt at an early stage of the crisis. At various stages, other political leaders attempted to assemble a counter coalition to the creditor coalition led by Merkel, but failed. Italian Prime Minister Mario Monti attempted to push the agenda beyond a politics of austerity to one focusing on growth and had some limited success. François Hollande campaigned on an anti-austerity platform but failed to translate this into practical policy and politics when he was elected President of France in 2012. Germany was simply too central to crisis management to be outflanked by any group of other states. Merkel used the domestic institutional constraints that she faced as leverage in intergovernmental bargaining. Germany's veto power was very effective in ruling out potential policy instruments, notably a mutualization of bonds or other instruments that implied redistribution across the member states. Fear of a 'Transfer Union' was a constant in German calculations.

Crisis management at the EU level, which was difficult, contentious, and lengthy – and best described as a strategy of 'muddling through' – interacted with heightened tensions within the member states. Democratic politics and governance came under extraordinary strain as governments faced competing external and internal pressures at the same time. The effects were immediate in electoral politics. In the first round of crisis elections, in 2010–12, governments and parties experienced dramatic changes of fortune. Crisis elections were characterized by high levels of voter volatility and incumbency losses, with widespread punishment of those in power (Bosco and Verney, 2012). In three of the bailout countries – Greece, Ireland, and Portugal – governments fell (Fernandes, 2011; Little, 2011; Magalhães, 2012). In the case of Greece, a technocratic government took over before elections in May 2012. Once dominant political parties, such as Fianna Fáil in Ireland and Pasok in Greece, suffered historically unprecedented losses of votes and seats. In Spain and Portugal, the Socialist incumbents lost to the opposition centre-right parties (Fernandes, 2011; Martin and Urquizu-Sancho, 2012). In Italy, sustained pressure from the financial markets and the ECB led to the resignation of Prime Minister Silvio Berlusconi in November 2011 and his replacement by the short-lived technocratic government of Mario Monti. Italian elections in February 2013 produced an inconclusive result with no party commanding a majority in both chambers. The Five Star Movement, an anti-politics party, under Beppe Grillo emerged as the third largest party with over 25 per cent of the popular vote, while Monti's Civic Choice mustered only 10.5 per cent of the vote.

Given the length of the crisis, its impact on electoral politics endured. Developments in Greece were the most dramatic as a far-left challenger party, Syriza, assumed power (Katsanidou and Otjes, 2015). The year 2015 was a tumultuous one in Greek politics, with two national elections (January and September) and a referendum (June) on the bailout. In January 2015, Syriza won 36.3 per cent of the popular vote and 149 seats in parliament. Running on an anti-austerity and anti-bailout conditionality platform, its leader, Alexis Tsipras, became Prime Minister and governed with the support of the Independent Greeks party (Stavrakakis, 2015). Lacking in experience, the new government sought to drastically alter the terms of the bailout programme in the first half of 2015 while remaining in the eurozone. It began by seeking to create an anti-austerity coalition at the EU level against Germany, which it failed to achieve. It then tried to get the other eurozone states to loosen the level of conditionality attached to the third bailout offer. Negotiations with the Troika, Ecofin (the Council of Finance Ministers), and the other member states were fraught, which was exemplified by the hostility expressed towards Greek Finance Minister Yanis Varoufakis at an informal Eurogroup meeting (of Finance Ministers of eurozone countries) in April 2015. The other member states refused to release funding to Greece without agreement on a reform package, which the new Syriza government was unable to accept. As time was running out and Greek banks were forced to shut and limit withdrawals, the end game of the negotiations came in June/July 2015. The Greek Prime Minister put the issue to the people in a hastily called referendum in June; a majority of 61 per cent of the Greek voters rejected the bailout package on offer. Those who voted 'no' were convinced that this would strengthen the position of the government in the negotiations, whereas those voting 'yes' were convinced that 'no' might lead to an exit from the euro.

Armed with a strong 'no' from the Greek people, the Prime Minister went to Brussels for a final summit with his counterparts on the memorandum. By this stage, the German Finance Minister, Wolfgang Schäuble, was prepared to let Greece exit the eurozone and argued that any contagion from a Grexit could be contained. This was thus a high-stakes game between Greece, whose economy had weakened even further in 2015, and the other member states. The Prime Minister and the Greek people learnt that their level of dependency on the other member states and the prospect of Grexit, which Greek public opinion did not want, left them in an extremely vulnerable position with little or no bargaining power. The agreement that emerged from marathon negotiations on 12 July 2015 differed little from what was on offer six months earlier. Running through the eventual agreement was an emphasis on the need 'to rebuild trust with the Greek authorities' and the importance of Greek ownership of the agreement (Euro Summit Statement, 2015). If Greece wanted to remain in the eurozone, it was faced with little choice but to accept the package on offer. The memorandum gave rise to another election in Greece as a hard core of Syriza deputies was unwilling to accept the terms on offer. Following a bruising election in September 2015, Syriza was returned to power with 35.5 per cent of the popular vote and 145 seats, having lost 24 far-left deputies who defected. Following the September 2015 election, all of the key parties in the Greek parliament supported the third bailout as the price of staying in the eurozone.

Politics and national elections in the other bailout states – Portugal (October 2015), Spain (December 2015), and Ireland (February 2016) – were less dramatic than in Greece but also brought the political impact of a lengthy crisis sharply into focus. In Portugal, the governing party won the largest proportion of the vote, 36.8 per cent, and 99 seats but the outgoing Prime Minister, Pedro Passos Coelho, was unable to put a sustainable governing coalition together; his government collapsed after 11 days. It fell to the second largest party, the Socialists with 32.4 per cent of the vote and 85 seats, to fashion a left-wing coalition with Communist, Green, and Left bloc parties under Antonio Costa as Prime Minister. The Socialist Prime Minister gave assurances to the Portuguese President that his government would not seek to leave the euro or to restructure the debt but in order to fashion a governing coalition, he had to make concessions to the far-left. Just how long this disparate coalition would govern was an open question. The result in Spain was not dissimilar in that the governing party, Partido Popular (PP), under Prime Minister Mariano Rajoy, won the largest number of votes and seats, but without a governing majority. Unlike in Portugal, the Spanish party system was also significantly changed: the arrival of two new parties, Ciudadanos (Citizens) and the anti-austerity Podemos, broke the two-party system that had governed Spain since the return of democracy in the mid-1970s. Post-election negotiations failed to produce a government and a second election was called for June 2016. The outcome of that election was also inconclusive, but the PP gained seats and the Left, particularly Podemus, did not break through. Ireland's February 2016 election returned the largest governing party with the highest number of seats (50) but far short of a governing majority of 89. Negotiations concluded with an opposition-backed minority government consisting of the 50 Fine Gael deputies and eight independent deputies. The difficulty in all three countries of government formation and the fragmentation of political space underlines the impact of the eurozone crisis on domestic politics in the member states.

Politics in the creditor countries was also affected, with the crisis accelerating and accentuating trends that were evident in politics before the outbreak of the crisis. The most pronounced effect was the further rise of populist right-wing parties that shared an anti-immigration and anti-EU profile. In Finland, the anti-bailout and anti-EU 'True Finns' won over 19 per cent of the vote in the 2011 election, an increase of 15 per cent over its vote in 2007. The Centre Party experienced the largest loss (–7.3 per cent) of any party in Finnish electoral history (Arter, 2011). In the Dutch 2010 election, two established parties suffered significant losses. The Christian Democratic vote was reduced by 12.9 per cent and 20 seats, making it the third largest party in parliament. The anti-EU Freedom Party was a big winner, increasing its vote by 9.6 per cent and its seats by 15 (van Holsteyn, 2011). The collapse of the Dutch government in 2012 was followed by elections in September 2012 that saw pro-European parties, the economically liberal Volkspartij voor Vrijheid en Democratie (VVD), and Labour parties increase their seats by ten each. The populist Freedom party lost heavily, as did the Christian Democrats. The performance of the VVD under Dutch Prime Minister Mark Rutte bucked the trend of the last several years whereby incumbents did badly. Incumbents also survived in Estonia, which only joined the eurozone in January 2011, in Austria (2013), and in Germany (2013). These were all creditor states, but anti-system parties still gained some traction with electorates. The anti-euro Team Stronach entered the Austrian parliament with 11 seats and its German equivalent, the Alternative for Germany, polled just under the 5 per cent threshold to win parliamentary representation and has gone on to win seats in regional elections. In France, Nicolas Sarkozy was only the second French President in the Fifth Republic not to win a second term of office, while his successor, François Hollande, quickly became the Fifth Republic's most unpopular president; the far-right, under Marine Le Pen, continued to make electoral inroads.

Across Europe a number of established parties have suffered unprecedented losses and populist 'challenger parties' have benefited from voter dissatisfaction. By and large, in most euro states voters opted for the available opposition of either the centre-left or -right rather than putting challenger parties in power in the first round of crisis elections between 2010 and 2012. The second round of crisis elections, from 2015 onwards, suggests, however, that the impact of the crisis may go well beyond a rotation of parties in power to further fragmentation of party systems, substantial losses for established governing parties, and further electoral success for populist parties. Only in Greece did Syriza, a challenger party, take power in 2015. Greater voter volatility and the success of populist parties were evident in Europe's party and electoral systems before the crisis but have been greatly accentuated by it (Bardi et al., 2014). The manifest difficulty of government formation in Portugal, Spain, and Ireland following the second round of crisis elections points to the cost of governing in Europe through hard times. Fractured and fractious politics are increasingly evident. The trends are different in the eurozone's core and periphery. In the core, the radical right tended to gain, whereas in the periphery it was the radical left.

Conclusions: What Does the Eurozone Crisis Tell Us About the EU?

The cleavage between creditors and debtors, which has been at the heart of the eurozone crisis, has manifested itself in a deep divergence of economic performance and of political fallout in different parts of the eurozone. The design of the eurozone and the significant increase in capital mobility allowed a divergence of performance between the core and periphery of the eurozone to go unchecked until deep vulnerabilities emerged in the periphery. Those countries that found themselves in bailout programmes, on the periphery, were transformed from member states into programme states, with all that this implied for domestic autonomy and authority. These countries were, together with Italy, most affected by the economic fallout of the crisis. Their governments had to govern in hard times, and at the same time handle the creditors (institutionalized as the Troika) and their own populations who were facing the effects of higher unemployment, poorer public services, and wage cuts. Governments in the debtor countries absorbed the pressures both internally and externally. Governments in the creditor countries were also faced with challenges as they had to persuade their parliaments and electorates to risk public funds in loans to other countries. The initial framing of the crisis as a public finance problem following profligate spending made this much more difficult; it generated a 'them' and 'us' dynamic. In reality, creditor states replaced private funds (much of which had come from their own banks) with public funds. This bought time for the northern banks to take their money out and ensure that the euro did not collapse. The asymmetric interdependence created by the existence of the euro was not addressed in the domestic narratives of the creditor states. Nor was it addressed in the policy toolkit developed to stave off collapse. The crisis led to a significant decline in trust among the member states, which was most evident in relations with Greece. A shared currency and a high level of mutual dependence will need more than a low-trust regime in the longer term.

The politics of crisis management has been entwined with a strategy for crisis prevention. This has amounted to a raft of new legal measures designed to embed member state economic, budgetary, and financial policies in a stronger European regulatory framework. This has been a key demand of the core states, led by Germany. The resulting measures – most notably in the form of the Six-Pack, Two-Pack and the Fiscal Compact (see Chapter 4) – have represented a step change in economic governance within the EU but most particularly within the eurozone. The new framework has implied a ratcheting up of monitoring, surveillance, and possible sanctioning of member states if they violate the new rules. The member states have agreed to bind themselves internally by the rules they have agreed to and externally by significantly enhanced Commission oversight. The new framework alters the balance between what Mair defined as the two key roles of political parties, especially governing parties: responsibility and responsiveness (Laffan, 2014b; Mair, 2009). Governments in democratic systems have always had to balance the need to be responsive to their electorates, but also responsible in the conduct of government. The eurozone crisis has altered this trade-off in a fundamental manner. Member states of the eurozone have to confront their responsibilities to partners and coresponsibility for the common currency area, which has been elevated to a core norm, with responsiveness to their electorates. Are we witnessing a step change in the commitment to responsible government, to the detriment of responsive government? The rise and success of challenger parties in most member states feed off the feeling among a large segment of the population that they are disenfranchised and faced with the politics of 'TINA' – 'there is no alternative'. For governing parties, the challenge is acute, as they have to balance responsiveness and responsibility, whereas challenger parties not wishing to enter government face no such constraints. The fragmentation of politics and party systems has greatly strengthened the pressure on mainstream traditional parties. How this works its way through domestic and EU-level politics will have a profound impact on the future of democratic politics in Europe.

The degree of contestation among the member states and at the EU level sharply underlines the difficulty the EU faces when it attempts to go beyond a regulatory state. The EU has developed a public finance capacity to support market integration but this has remained extremely limited. The EU budget is under 1 per cent of Europe's GDP and all efforts to increase it have failed. Both the eurozone crisis and the migration crisis demonstrate that the EU polity very much struggles with burden-sharing and redistribution. The ties that bind are not strong enough to significantly break through the boundaries of statehood and domestic politics. And the structure of the polity, given the primacy of domestic politics, makes it difficult to generate the resources and agree a strategy for a major development of EU-level capacity and competence. Yet the Five Presidents' Report of 2015 on the future of the single currency acknowledged that in the longer term the eurozone would be stronger and more resilient with a fiscal stabilization function (European Union, 2015). This, however, is only envisaged following further convergence among the member states and greater sharing of budgetary authority which, in turn, exacerbates the trade-off between responsibility and responsiveness at the domestic level.

The challenge for the eurozone is to create the conditions in which Europe's peripheral economies can return to growth and repair the legacy of 'the Great Recession'. This, in turn, would alleviate pressures on governments as they struggle to meet their external obligations and respond to the needs of their electorates. The legacy of the crisis for the EU is a weakening of trust among the member states and in EU institutions, and a growing contestation over Europe in every member state. Political forces that fundamentally oppose the European project have grown in strength, which makes it more difficult for the Union to agree to a set of policy instruments that would add to its core strength as a regulatory and market state. Although it involves a different cast of states, the migration crisis has also triggered divergent core–periphery dynamics, but in this case driven by divergence between the eastern and western parts of the continent (see Chapter 6).

References

Ameco database (the annual macroeconomic database of DG ECFIN) (2016) https://ec.europa.eu/info/business-economy-euro/indicators-statistics/ economic-data bases/macro-economic -database-ameco_en.

Arter, D, (2011) 'Taking the Gilt Off the Conservatives' Gingerbread: The April 2011 Finnish General Election', *West European Politics*, Vol. 34, No. 6, pp. 1284–95.

Baldwin, R., Beck, T., Bénassy-Quéré, A., Blanchard, O., Corsetti, G., de Grauwe, P., den Haan, W., Giavazzi, F., Gros, D., Kalemli-Ozcan, S.,

Micossi, S., Papaioannou, E., Pesenti, P., Pissarides, C., Tabellini, G., and Weder di Mauro, B. (2015) 'Rebooting the Eurozone: Step 1 – Agreeing a Crisis Narrative', VOX, CEPR, http://voxeu.org/article/ez-crisis-consensus-narrative.

Baldwin, R. and Gros, D. (2015) 'What Caused the Eurozone Crisis?', *CEPS Commentary*, 27 November.

Bardi, L., Bartolini, S., and Trechsel, A. (2014) 'Party Adaptation and Change and the Crisis of Democracy', *Party Politics*, Vol. 20. No. 2, pp. 151–59.

Bosco, A. and Verney, S. (2012) 'Electoral Epidemic: The Political Cost of Economic Crisis in Southern Europe, 2010–11', *South European Society and Politics*, Vol. 17, No. 2, pp. 129–54.

Deutsch, K. W., Burrell, S. A., Kann, R. A., Lee, M. Jr, Lichterman, M., Lindgren, R. E., Loewenheim, F. L., and Van Wagenen, R. W. (1957) *Political Community and the North Atlantic Area: International Organization in the Light of Historical Experience*. Princeton: Princeton University Press.

ECB (2011) 'Interview between Die Zeit and Jean-Claude Trichet, President of the European Central Bank, conducted by Mark Schieritz and Uwe Jean Heuser', 16 February, https://www.ecb.europa.eu/press/inter/date/2011/html/sp110216.en.html, date accessed 12 December 2016.

Eichengreen, B. (1996) 'Saving Europe's Automatic Stabilizers', *Center for International and Development Economics Research*. UC Berkeley: Center for International and Development Economics Research. Retrieved from: http://escholarship.org/uc/item/9zb6q3ms, date accessed 12 December 2016.

Euro Area Summit Statement (2012), 29 June, http://www.consilium.europa.eu/uedocs/cms_Data/docs/pressdata/en/ec/131359.pdf, date accessed 12 December 2016.

Euro Summit Statement (2015) 12 July, file:///C:/Users/blaffan/Downloads/20150712-eurosummit-statement-greece.pdf, date accessed 12 December 2016.

European Commission (1993) 'Stable Money and Sound Finances', No. 53, European Commission, http://ec.europa.eu/economy_finance/publications/publication7524_en.pdf, date accessed 12 December 2016.

European Commission (2008) 'EMU@10: Successes and Challenges after 10 Years of Economic and Monetary Union', *European Economy* 2, European Commission, http://ec.europa.eu/economy_finance/publications/publication12682_en.pdf, date accessed 12 December 2016.

European Commission (2016) *Responding to the Financial Crisis*, European Commission, http://ec.europa.eu/economy_finance/explained/the_financial_and_economic_crisis/responding_to_the_financial_crisis/index_en.htm, date accessed 12 December 2016.

European Union (1989) *Report on Economic and Monetary Union in the European Community* (Delors Report), April 17, http://aei.pitt.edu/1007/1/monetary_delors.pdf, date accessed 12 December 2016.

European Union (2015) *Completing Europe's Economic and Monetary Union, Report of the Five Presidents*, https://ec.europa.eu/priorities/sites/beta-political/files/5-presidents-report_en.pdf.

Eurostat (2016) http://ec.europa.eu/eurostat/statistics-explained/index.php/ Unemployment_statistics, date accessed 12 December 2016.

Fernandes, J. M. (2011) 'The 2011 Portuguese Election: Looking for a Way Out', *West European Politics*, Vol. 34, No. 6, pp. 1296–303.

Hart, Paul 't. (1993) 'Symbols, Rituals and Power: The Lost Dimensions of Crisis Management', *Journal of Contingencies and Crisis Management*, Vol. 1, No. 1, pp. 36–50.

Katsanidou, A. and Otjes, S. (2016) 'How the European debt crisis reshaped national political space: The case of Greece', *European Union Politics*, Vol. 17, No. 2, pp. 262–84.

Laffan, B. (2014a) 'Framing the Crisis: Defining the Problems: Decoding the Euro Area Crisis', *Perspectives On European Politics And Society*, Vol. 15, No. 3, pp. 266–80.

Laffan, B. (2014b) 'Testing Times: The Growing Primacy of Responsibility in the Euro Area', *West European Politics*, Vol. 37, No. 2, pp. 270–87.

Lipset, S. M. and Rokkan, S. (1967) 'Cleavage Structures, Party Systems, and Voter Alignments: An Introduction.' In S. M. Lipset and S. Rokkan (eds), *Party Systems and Voter Aignments: Cross-National Perspectives*. New York: Free Press, pp. 1–64.

Little, C. (2011) 'The General Election of 2011 in the Republic of Ireland: All Changed Utterly?', *West European Politics*, Vol. 34, No. 6, pp. 1304–13.

Magalhães, P. C. (2012) 'After the Bailout: Responsibility, Policy, and Valence in the Portuguese Legislative Election of June 2011', *South European Society and Politics*, Vol. 17, No. 2, pp. 309–27.

Mair, P. (2009) 'Representative Versus Responsible Government', MPLfG Working Paper, No. 09/8.

Martín, I. and Urquizu-Sancho, I. (2012) 'The 2011 General Election in Spain: The Collapse of the Socialist Party', *South European Society and Politics*, Vol. 17, No. 2, pp. 347–63.

Merkel, A. (2011) 'If the Euro Fails, Europe Fails', *Der Spiegel*, 11 September, http://www.spiegel.de/international/germany/if-the-euro-fails-europe-fails-merkel-says-eu-must-be-bound-closer-together-a-784953.html.

Rokkan, S. and Urwin, D. W. (1983) *Economy, Territory, Identity: Politics of West European Peripheries*. London: Sage.

Stavrakakis, Y. (2015) 'Populism in Power: Syriza's Challenge to Europe', *Juncture*, Vol. 21, No. 4, pp. 273–80.

Tsoukalis, L. (2003) *What Kind of Europe?* Oxford: Oxford University Press.

Van Holsteyn, J. J. (2011) 'The Dutch Parliamentary Election of 2010', *West European Politics*, Vol. 34, No. 2, pp. 412–19.

Werner Report (1970) 'Report on Economic and Monetary Union', http://aei.pitt.edu/1002/1/monetary_werner_final.pdf.

White, J. (2015) 'Emergency Europe', *Political Studies*, Vol. 63, No. 2, pp. 300–18.

Chapter 8

The Aftermath of the Eurozone Crisis: Towards Fiscal Federalism?

CAROLINE DE LA PORTE AND ELKE HEINS

Introduction

The eurozone crisis, which followed in the wake of the global financial crisis, affected eurozone economies asymmetrically.[1] The seeds of the asymmetric impact were inherent in the structure of Economic and Monetary Union (EMU), which called for a single monetary policy for all members of the club, despite wide-ranging macroeconomic divergence among them. The single monetary policy embodied a very low real interest rate for the peripheral economies in the years preceding the crisis, while the interest rate was de facto high for the northern economies. The challenges of developing a *genuine* single currency area – an 'optimal currency area' in the language of economists – were accentuated further by the absence of (direct) fiscal policy coordination and only minimal financial regulation (Copelovitch et al., 2016). Thus, the persistently low real interest rates set by the European Central Bank (ECB) in the years preceding the crisis had encouraged lax fiscal discipline in the periphery economies, a key reason for the explosion of budget deficit and public debt (Maddaloni and Peydro, 2011). The policy responses to high deficits and debt were determined by the EMU structure, leading to domestic or EU driven austerity policy, accompanied by internal devaluation. With prolonged and drastic austerity in these economies, growth stalled, while unemployment rates and poverty soared (see chapters in de la Porte and Heins, 2016; Copelovitch et al., 2016). The political response to austerity in the south has seen the strengthening of far-left parties, while the north has seen a strong shift to populist-nationalist movements. The former are (implicitly) favourable to redistribution,

---

[1] We would like to thank the participants of the work-in-progress seminar on 4 March 2016 at the Department of Business and Politics, Copenhagen Business School for useful comments on an early draft of this chapter. The chapter builds on our article 'A new era of European Integration? Governance of labour market and social policy since the sovereign debt crisis', *Comparative European Politics*, Vol. 13, No. 1 (2015), pp. 8–28.

while the latter vehemently and openly oppose any prospect of transfer to the south. The polarized geographical socio-economic conditions and political party positions reflect the difficulty of designing a genuine fiscal union in the EU.

This chapter examines how the governance of EMU and of social policy has been altered following the eurozone crisis. The first section, 'Governance of EMU and Social Policy Before the Eurozone Crisis', presents the institutional architecture of EMU and of employment and social policy governance, and then discusses the nature of EU intervention in welfare and fiscal policy before the crisis. The second section, 'Framework for Analyzing Alterations in EU Integration', presents a typology for assessing the degree and type of EU integration associated with governance instruments in terms of objectives, enforcement, and surveillance. The third section, 'EMU and Social Policy Governance Following the Eurozone Crisis', does exactly as its title indicates. The fourth section 'Altering the Governance of the European Social Dimension' focuses on initiatives related to social policy *per se*, such as social investment. The chapter concludes by discussing the significance of the new and altered EMU and social policy governance instruments for member states from the perspective of fiscal federalism.

Governance of EMU and Social Policy before the Eurozone Crisis

EMU embodies multiple structural asymmetries, which explain the divergent effects of the eurozone crisis (see Chapter 4). First, it includes national economies with different growth models and rates of growth, without a common economic policy. Second, the financial sector, and banking in particular, was weakly regulated for a long time, leading to lax lending practices in the years preceding the crisis (Maddaloni and Peyrdro, 2011). Third – and this is our concern here – monetary policy is pooled at the EU level, while fiscal policy remains uncomfortably caught between the EU and national level, with the EU encouraging national governments to curb excessive public spending, but without having formal competency in this area (McNamara, 2005; Scharpf, 2002). The Stability and Growth Pact (SGP) was introduced in 1997 to coordinate economic and fiscal policy of member states, aiming to ensure compatibility with the monetary policy regime that is central in EMU. The SGP is a treaty-based policy coordination process based on quantitative benchmarks (a maximum public debt of 60 per cent of GDP and a maximum budget deficit of 3 per cent of GDP), national reporting, and EU surveillance, with corrective mechanisms, but only in the case of deviation from the 3 per cent budget deficit limit. As social spending typically makes up the biggest share of public expenditure in member states, the SGP exerted considerable indirect pressure on national welfare systems. Despite this, in the run-up to the third stage of EMU – the launch of the single currency in 1999 – the extent of reforms actually undertaken in member states owing to EMU was not as comprehensive as feared, or hoped (Bolukbasi, 2009).

Preceding the global financial crisis, the SGP lacked de facto power to enforce reforms in member states both in the preventive stage, partly because member states were not held accountable to their own 'medium-term objectives' of macroeconomic policy, and in the corrective stage, since the excessive deficit procedure (EDP) was not strong enough to commit member states to make specific reforms to correct deficits (de Haan et al., 2004; McNamara, 2005). Furthermore, the EU benchmarking exercise through the SGP focuses on public expenditure, and only the budget deficit criterion was enforceable. A fully functioning EMU should have had additional instruments, such as regulation of the financial sector, but also fiscal policy, to be able to address structural inequalities between different economies and to prevent and counter asymmetric shocks effectively (Copelovitch et al., 2016; Hinarejos, 2013).

However, this was not politically feasible at the time because social policy is organized, financed, and delivered within the boundaries of EU member states, while there is an EU-wide coordination of social security systems to ensure free movement of people. EMU was a game-changer since it led to greater interdependence among member state economies owing to the centralization of monetary policy, and alongside it, the limitations for eurozone economies to use Keynesian-type stimulus measures in cases of crisis. Since redistributive social policies are at the core of national welfare states, the social dimension of EMU is governed by voluntary policy coordination. Through an open method of coordination (OMC), the EU has agreed to aims such as increasing employment rates to 75 per cent by 2020 and strengthening 'social inclusion', measured by the concrete target to lift at least 20 million people out of poverty and social exclusion by 2020. Contrary to the SGP, there are only non-binding country-specific recommendations (CSRs) in the OMC relating to employment and social policy and no corrective measures in case of non-compliance. National governments remain fully responsible for formulating and implementing their respective policies to meet targets agreed through the OMC. The EU has a small pool of funding – cohesion, structural, and regional development funds – to support employment and social policy initiatives. However, it is of marginal importance compared with the core redistributive function undertaken in EU member states and cannot be characterized as supranational fiscal redistribution on a par with the centralization of monetary policy.

The asymmetry – core–periphery as well as centralized monetary policy vs. national fiscal policy – within EMU surfaced when the global financial crisis hit the eurozone economies. The crisis led to social unrest, high unemployment, and poverty, as well as EU-induced austerity and welfare state reform in the periphery countries (Heins and de la Porte, 2015). At the EU level, this led to great uncertainty about the viability of the eurozone, which was conducive to a rapid succession of decisions that altered instruments and policies in EMU, building on its initial institutional architecture. In social and labour market policy, the main concern has been fiscal consolidation, complemented by a renewed emphasis on social policies designed to invest in individuals throughout their lifetime.

Framework for Analyzing Alterations in EU Integration

This section proposes a typology of European integration that can be used to analyse the instruments that have emerged since the eurozone crisis, and to assess their significance for labour market and social policy along three dimensions: objectives (policy aims), surveillance process, and enforcement mechanisms. For each, there are four possible degrees of EU involvement, ranging from low to very high (see Table 8.1).

Complementing this analysis is an assessment of the type of 'fiscal federalism' associated with changes introduced since the crisis, looking at the capacity to: first, impose fiscal discipline; second, ensure that economies are not too disparate from each other, thereby preventing asymmetric shocks; and, third, counter asymmetric shocks, should they occur. These functions of the federal governance model can take the shape of 'classical' fiscal federalism, whereby the EU would have authority and power in a multi-level system, including the real possibility of developing a common economic policy and a transfer union. The alternative is the 'surveillance model', whereby the EU has a multitude of tools to enforce fiscal discipline indirectly (Hinarejos, 2013).

The *first dimension* of EU integration has to do with objectives (policy aims), which refer to how precisely and to what degree policy change is suggested. Adapting from Hall's conceptualizations (1993) of first, second, and third order change, EU involvement can be considered low if no change or only minor changes to existing policies are suggested. EU involvement would be medium if the EU suggested more wide-ranging alterations to the existing arrangements, but without changing the institutional set-up. High (and very high) levels of involvement would be represented by EU demands that could undermine the existing institutional structure and fundamental principles governing a policy area. For

Table 8.1 *Typology of EU integration of labour market and social policy*

Dimension of integration	Degree of involvement			
	Low	*Medium*	*High*	*Very high*
Objectives (policy aims) *This may differ according to welfare state type (and policy area)*	Uncontroversial objectives, not challenging existing institutional arrangements, merely suggesting some minor adjustments in a particular policy area.	Objectives challenging some existing policies, but not the underlying institutional structure of a policy area.	Objectives requiring comprehensive policy reform with the potential for undermining the existing institutional structure and fundamental principles of a policy area.	Objectives requiring far-reaching structural reform with a high potential for undermining the existing institutional structure and changing the fundamental principles of a policy area.
Surveillance	Infrequent ex post surveillance of national policy reports.	Frequent ex post surveillance of national reports that stipulate country-specific policy which should meet common benchmarks and/or own national targets.	Regular ex ante and ex post surveillance of national policy reports. Member states accountable to EU benchmarks or national targets and required to specify action plan to meet these.	Frequent ex ante and ex post surveillance of national policy reports. Member states accountable for their own policies (which must aim to meet European targets and/or policy).
Enforcement	'Naming and shaming' and/or soft recommendations, with a weak treaty base.	Treaty-based recommendations, and possibility for sanctions in the case of non-compliance.	Treaty-based recommendations *and* quasi-automatic financial sanctions in the case of non-compliance.	Conditionality (specified structural reforms) in order to receive financial assistance.

example, a policy aim such as enhancing social sustainability of pension systems would imply low involvement, unless it was accompanied by specific measures (such as increasing the replacement rate). Conversely, a policy aim requiring a new organizational principle in a pension system, such as a change from a defined benefit to a defined contribution scheme, would signify high or very high EU involvement.

As we know from research on Europeanization of welfare policies (Graziano and Vink, 2008), any policy objective would have a differentiated impact of EU involvement in member states. For example, in states where the family is a main provider of welfare, but without significant state support for this role (Guillén and León, 2011), the promotion of formal childcare policies, with defined targets for the number of children in early childhood education, would be seen as high EU involvement because it challenges the existing male breadwinner/female carer model and demands a significant change in ideas and principles governing this area. In the Nordic welfare states, by contrast, such a policy merely reinforces the existing policy paradigm that supports the reconciliation of work with family life. EU involvement would therefore be low.

The *second dimension* of EU integration is the surveillance of national policy by EU actors, that is, the mechanisms available to EU actors to monitor whether member states are implementing the agreed policies and moving towards EU benchmarks. The strength of surveillance is indicated by the *frequency* of policy monitoring and depends on the legal basis of surveillance (ranging from soft to hard law). Following on from this, some EU actors, such as economic and financial actors, operate in areas where the EU has strong jurisdiction, while the employment and social affairs actors operate where the EU has only weak legislative competence. It is clear that it is 'surveillance fiscal federalism' which defined EU-level activity in this area before the crisis.

The *third dimension* of EU integration is enforcement, referring to the type of measures EU actors have to ensure implementation and/or corrective action in the case of non-compliance with or deviation from EU policy. The most coercive form consists of financial sanctions. Other enforcement mechanisms are an EDP or a CSR that delineates a reform path and timetable to be followed in order to achieve an EU aim. An EDP is treaty-based and designed to ensure that a country effectively corrects a deficit, while a CSR under the OMC is merely a suggestion for reform, with no consequences in the case of non-compliance. In assessing enforcement, it is important to take account of the power balance between European institutions and member states. In particular, the requirement for qualified majority voting (QMV) increases the leverage of a recalcitrant country, as a super-majority of member states must agree to impose an enforcement mechanism, such as a sanction. By contrast, reverse qualified majority voting (RQMV) gives more power to the

European Commission, because a qualified majority of member states would have to agree *not* to enact an enforcement mechanism. A very high level of enforcement, combined with very strict surveillance, occurs in countries that are in an EU financial assistance programme (bailout) and thereby are subject to conditionality in order to receive financial disbursements, as stipulated in Memorandums of Understanding. In such cases, very specific policy objectives and a very high degree of surveillance, as well as enforcement, lead to EU intrusion into domestic settings (Theodoropoulou, 2015). This particular type of EU involvement is captured by the last column of our typology (Table 8.1).

In contrast to this scenario, which has seen the light following the effects of the crisis in the periphery of the eurozone, it would be possible theoretically to conceive of 'very high' involvement of the EU if an EU welfare state were developed for all eurozone member states. A concrete proposal has been made to introduce a European unemployment insurance scheme that would act as a eurozone-wide automatic stabilizer and support countries with high levels of unemployment (Claeys et al., 2014). This would have the potential of providing a foundation for a strengthened political union, as it might make the benefits of the EU more tangible and thus strengthen democratic legitimacy. However, the convergence of labour market institutions would imply meddling with domestic institutions, as well as tripartite or bipartite decision-making in member states. These options are currently not politically feasible, especially since the accentuation of cleavages in the EU following the eurozone crisis (Clegg, forthcoming; Chapter 7 in this volume).

EMU and Social Policy Governance Following the Eurozone Crisis

Since 2011, macroeconomic and social policy coordination mechanisms have been combined in a common annual policy cycle called the 'European Semester'. The instruments to coordinate macroeconomic policies are based on a much stronger regulatory framework than those designed to coordinate employment and social policy, which are based on soft governance.

The main measures to strengthen policy coordination under EMU are the Six-Pack, the Two-Pack, and the fiscal policy part of the Treaty on Stability, Coordination and Governance, known as the Fiscal Compact. The Six-Pack of legislative acts makes a more explicit framework for stronger surveillance of macroeconomic and budgetary policies, beyond the focus of the 60 per cent public debt and 3 per cent budget deficit benchmarks. The Fiscal Compact focuses on strengthening fiscal discipline and was agreed by all EU members except the UK and the Czech

Republic. The Two-Pack of legislative acts enhances EU involvement in member states' budgetary planning and decision-making (European Commission, 2013a). Together, these regulatory initiatives introduce several novelties, which enhance European integration regarding fiscal and macroeconomic policy in terms of precision and breadth of objectives, a higher degree of surveillance, and stricter enforcement. These initiatives are built into the underlying monetarist paradigm and follow the 'surveillance fiscal federalism' model.

Europe 2020, which replaced the Lisbon Strategy in 2010 as the main public policy coordination instrument among member states (European Commission, 2010), specifies core aims to address the social and other non-monetary aspects of EMU. In 2013, the Social Investment Package and Youth Guarantee were added onto Europe 2020 to address social challenges in the EU. The effect of these initiatives is marginal, given the scope of challenges that have appeared following the crisis, especially in the periphery economies. Table 8.2 summarizes the dimensions and degree of EU governance in the instruments of economic and public policy governance before and after the crisis, which are discussed below.

Surveillance fiscal federalism strengthened: Macroeconomic surveillance extended and specified

The legally binding instruments strengthening a 'surveillance' type of fiscal federalism embedded in the EMU are the Six-Pack and the Fiscal

Table 8.2   *EU involvement in economic and public policy before and after the crisis*

	Objectives	Surveillance	Enforcement
SGP (pre-crisis)	High	Medium	Medium
Six-Pack (2011)	High	High	Medium
Fiscal Compact (2012)	High	High	High
Two-Pack (2013)	High	High	High
Council Recommendation on economic policy of the euro area (2015)	Medium	Medium	Low
Europe 2020, Social Investment and Youth Guarantee	Medium	Medium	Low/Medium if co-funded

Source: adapted from de la Porte and Heins, 2015

Compact. Through these instruments, member state economies are more closely monitored in a number of ways, concerning scope and depth of surveillance, as well as tightened enforcement mechanisms.

First, the Commission more broadly monitors member state economies via a Macroeconomic Imbalance Procedure (MIP), comprising key indicators, accompanied by thresholds, to detect potentially 'harmful' imbalances at an early stage. The MIP scoreboard combines indicators to capture short-term rapid deteriorations with those looking at long-term gradual accumulation of imbalances. It is an important addition, compared with the narrow focus on public debt and deficits that were central in the SGP. The wider MIP sensibly takes account of indicators such as private sector debt and private sector credit flow, since private debt was a key reason for the crisis in the periphery. In 2011, the MIP comprised ten headline indicators, which have since been extended to 14 key indicators, complemented by 25 auxiliary indicators.

There has been growing concern about increasing inequality within the EU, partly owing to the very strong focus on fiscal consolidation. Thus, the MIP now includes key labour market indicators such as activity rates, long-term unemployment rates, and youth unemployment rates (European Commission, 2016). The inclusion of labour market and social policy indicators in the MIP is an improvement. The European Parliament, also supported by various EU-level civil society organizations, urges poverty and inequality, but also pensions, health, education, and training to be taken even more into account in the MIP (European Parliament and DG for Internal Policies, 2016).

The underlying assumption of the scoreboard is that all indicators are on an equal footing in terms of their significance for the health of an economy and that each 'imbalance' can be rectified rapidly via a clearly devised government strategy. However, a high long-term unemployment rate may be more difficult to resolve than, for example, a lower activity rate. Many important factors come into play in trying to decrease unemployment rates that also heavily depend on sustainable growth, as well as appropriate labour market policy, with sufficient flexibility, and social policy, such as childcare institutions, to enable the reconciliation of work and family life. More critically, many of the MIP indicators refer to phenomena that are not under the direct control of national governments. As noted by Scharpf (2011: 33): 'Because government capacity to exercise indirect influence over such variables as nominal wages, private saving and spending, consumer credit, may either be non-existent or widely varying among member states, compliance with the "recommendations" issued by the Commission may well be impossible.'

The scoreboard represents a tool for the EU to compare (and therefore rank) national economies. More specifically, the macroeconomic imbalance procedure has enhanced the surveillance capability of the

Directorate-General for Economic and Financial Affairs within the Commission. In addition to the monitoring of debt via the macroeconomic scoreboard, member states must report on their national debt issuance to the Commission and the Council. This entails the expectation to discuss ex ante 'all major policy reforms' and constitutes EU involvement, although indirect, in redistributive areas such as pensions, labour market policy, and social security.

Concerning enforcement, a deviation from a threshold of the headline indicators on the macroeconomic imbalance scoreboard leads to an automatic 'alert' in an alert mechanism report (AMR) for the member state. For example, consolidated private sector debt cannot exceed the defined threshold of 133 per cent of GDP, otherwise an 'alert' is sent to the member state concerned, together with a path to correct this imbalance. In addition to AMRs, the Commission has another tool to support enforcement. It can request in-depth reviews (IDRs) of selected macroeconomic policies of individual member states in order to obtain details about an imbalance and thereby be able to make a targeted and informed recommendation for correcting the imbalance. The AMRs and IDRs are used extensively by the Commission, and some countries have been under pressure to alter their policies accordingly. EU leaders would like this tool to be even stronger: 'It should be used not just to detect imbalances but also to encourage structural reforms through the European Semester' (Juncker et al., 2015: 8). The risk is that the MIP, although sensibly seeking to prevent crises in the eurozone, may have, in contrast to the European Employment Strategy (EES), which has been characterized as 'toothless' (Copeland and ter Haar, 2013), the 'bite' to intervene in decisions on national public budgets and regulation of financial markets. The MIP process of 'governing by the rules' and 'ruling by numbers' may bypass democratic procedure in member states (Schmidt, 2015).

Second, national budgets that are the basis for public policy can be affected via the quantitatively defined 'significant deviation' from country-specific medium-term budgetary objectives (MTOs) or the adjustment path towards it. The enforcement of MTOs is high: the Commission can issue a 'warning' to a member state in case of significant deviation from its own adjustment path. An expenditure benchmark, which is a rule that contains the growth rate of government spending at or below a country's medium-term potential economic growth rate, was introduced and country-specific 'structural' budget deficits are specified, which can range from a structural budget deficit of 1 per cent of GDP to a budget in surplus. The structural deficit, together with the 3 per cent budget deficit, is seen as more accurate than the budget deficit criterion alone, as it aims to filter out temporary fiscal measures and evolutions that are due to cyclical changes in the economy (Hughes Hallett and Hougaard-Jensen, 2012). Furthermore, eurozone countries are required to include the country-specific MTOs in national binding law, preferably in their constitutions. The structural deficit targets, enshrined in both the Six-Pack and the Fiscal Compact, imply a high degree of enforcement and represent a further step in European integration through the 'surveillance' model of fiscal federalism by imposing eurozone-wide fiscal discipline. This preventative approach, combined with more surveillance, aims to keep member state economies healthy in good times. This limits possibilities for expansive fiscal policy.

Finally, the Six-Pack and the Fiscal Compact increase enforcement of the SGP in case of non-compliance, since an EDP can be launched if a member state has breached either the deficit *or* the debt criterion, compared with only the deficit criterion previously. The Fiscal Compact strengthens the enforcement mechanism of the SGP even further, as all stages of the EDP must be implemented within a clearly defined time frame. Furthermore, when the Commission considers that an excessive deficit exists, an EDP is launched almost automatically (unless a majority of member states in the Council is against it). The Fiscal Compact thus strengthens the decision-making capacity of the Commission and reduces the political discretion of member states in the Council. The measures for exiting an EDP and the timetable are negotiated between the Commission and the member state, as was the case in the original SGP.

In contrast to the situation before the crisis, the punitive aspect of enforcing an EDP has been enhanced. If no effective action is taken to correct a deficit or debt when a country is under EDP, quasi-automatic sanctions (of up to 0.2 per cent GDP) can be applied. They can only be blocked by RQMV in the Council. A sanction also involves a high degree of surveillance to verify that agreed measures to correct an imbalance are implemented.

However, while rules on sanctioning in the case of non-compliance de jure strengthen the power of the European Commission, it has not been the case de facto. In early July 2016, the Council unanimously agreed, for the first time ever, that two eurozone members had not taken sufficient action to correct their deficits. Spain and Portugal, already affected by the crisis, economically, socially, and politically, were held responsible for not taking steps to correct their excessive deficits, as specified in their EDPs. Both countries then submitted, in line with the legal possibility to do so, reasoned requests, asking the Commission to reduce sanctions on the grounds of exceptional economic circumstances. The reaction to these requests split the Commissioners, with one group supporting a 'symbolic' fine for Spain and Portugal (representing 0.01 per cent GDP) in order to counter increased populism and euroscepticism in countries such as Austria, Finland, and Germany and to signal de facto political legitimacy of the new legal framework, which had been adapted to rectify the weak legitimacy of the pre-crisis SGP. Another group, led by Commission President Jean-Claude Juncker, and, perhaps surprisingly, supported by Wolfgang Schäuble, the German Finance Minister, favoured a zero penalty, owing to the high social and economic burdens already endured by these countries. In the aftermath of the Brexit referendum, and increased euroscepticism that has led to social unrest and the success of populist parties across the EU, the Commission decided in late July 2016 to opt for a zero penalty (Euractiv, 2016). This shows, on the one hand, that the Commission is acutely aware of political circumstances in the EU and of the high socio-economic costs already seen in these economies, following drastic austerity. On the other hand, it reflects the inherent weakness of EU surveillance fiscal federalism, in that the real capability of the Commission to impose fines is weak, partly because the Commission is not democratically elected and is therefore not perceived as legitimate, and partly because a pecuniary sanction seems to be the wrong instrument to use to correct a deficit or debt. However, even if the punitive aspect of enforcement has been weak, the strength of the altered instrument may be in its preventative rather than its corrective phase.

Overall, it is clear that the alterations made to the procedures governing EMU have enhanced 'surveillance fiscal federalism'. First, it has re-enforced the existing logic with a sharp focus on fiscal consolidation with not only the budget deficit, but also the structural budget deficit and more focus on public debt. Second, the EU now has a much broader focus on the health of member state economies, through the MIP, which is designed to locate macroeconomic imbalances in member states, and thus to decrease strong differentiation in the health of member state economies. The MIP is the basis on which the EU proposes reform paths, implying broader and deeper EU involvement in national economies, compared with before the crisis. However, the biggest issue with the MIP concerns the weaker capability of government to be able to quickly rectify an imbalance, as other factors, such as financial vulnerability of an economy, may come more strongly into play in many of the indicators of the MIP. In addition, as noted by Fritz Scharpf (2011: 33): 'EMU member states cannot expect any help from the European level in the case of macroeconomic imbalances.' Finally, the EU has an instrument of last resort, the European Stability Mechanism, introduced in 2012, which can respond swiftly to a crisis in eurozone countries by issuing debt instruments in order to finance loans and other forms of financial assistance to eurozone countries (see Chapter 4).

Small steps towards classical fiscal federalism

Parallel to the strengthening of 'surveillance fiscal federalism', some new initiatives represent a move in the direction of 'classical fiscal federalism', with the EU having some (albeit limited) authority to decide on fiscal expenditure. The Two-Pack, which came into force in May 2013, specifies objectives in budgetary policy, together with high enforcement and surveillance mechanisms. It introduces a common budgetary timeline and rules for all eurozone countries. The Two-Pack has a significant impact on 'sovereign' budgets – the basis for policy-making – as it requires member states to send their draft budgetary plans (DBPs) for approval to the Commission and the Eurogroup (the finance ministers of countries in the eurozone) *before* discussion and adoption in national parliaments. The fact that national budgets, and thus details of policy reforms, are subject to EU scrutiny implies that eurozone countries develop budgets in the shadow of EU surveillance. It is only in the case of 'particularly serious non-compliance' that the Commission may request a revision of the draft budgetary plan. However, if the Commission assesses that a DBP represents a 'risk of non-compliance', it can request (but not require) member states to alter their DBPs. At the end of 2014, the Commission made such a request to countries that were at risk, but could only ask them to be compliant with the SGP – or correct their EDP – not lean on them in respect of specific macroeconomic indicators (European Commission, 2014b). The member states identified included Portugal and Spain, which subsequently received a symbolic zero fine for failing to rectify their EDP.

It remains to be seen how effective enforcement will be, and how precisely the Commission could require alterations in national budgets. Still, it represents much more interference in member state annual budgetary plans (and their associated budgetary processes) than before the crisis. This is a step towards classical federalism, as it implies that the EU level has the power to alter annual national budgets before they are submitted to national parliaments for scrutiny. It is a clear illustration of the EU potentially affecting fiscal policy through the back door.

To address the challenges of democratic legitimacy that have arisen with the new EMU architecture (Schmidt, 2015) and especially the Two-Pack, EU leaders propose that a representative from the Commission should be involved in the discussion on the national 'draft budgetary proposals' so that it can explain its 'opinion' to national parliaments. This possibility exists in the current regulatory framework, but has thus far not been used. EU leaders also argue that national parliaments should be more involved in the adoption of the national reform and stability programmes that are prepared for the EU (Juncker et al., 2015: 17). This would ensure more communication between the EU bureaucracy and elected politicians, but could solve challenges of democratic legitimacy only if there is a genuine negotiation and dialogue about member state public policy as planned in DBPs.

Thus far, classical fiscal federalism appears through the back door with the EU able to request or require rectification of DBPs should they be out of step with the deficit and debt requirements of the SGP. However, the Commission is not elected and in the aftermath of the Brexit referendum it increasingly faces problems of public and political legitimacy. This implies that its real leverage to redirect national budgetary proposals prior to discussions and decision in parliaments may not be as strong as feared, or as expected. Nevertheless, the annual analysis of DBPs represents more EU involvement in national budgetary processes, which are at the core of national decision-making. This could lead to more prudent planning of the yearly national budgets, in the long run. Yet another repercussion is that what emerges is an increasingly differentiated Europe, with stronger, broader, and more binding EU collaboration and coordination among EMU countries compared with non-EMU countries.

Altering the Governance of the European Social Dimension

This section focuses on initiatives in the European social dimension, especially Europe 2020 which replaced the Lisbon Strategy in 2010 as the main social policy coordination instrument (European Commission, 2010). Like the new instruments governing EMU, Europe 2020 first insists on fiscal consolidation in the crisis context. Beyond that, it is designed to deliver growth – if possible, socially and environmentally sustainable growth. 'Social investment' is the broad policy paradigm within which economic, labour market, and social policy is framed under Europe 2020. It is a comprehensive approach that emphasizes the need to invest in individuals and their skills throughout the life cycle, so that they can participate in the labour market and combine this with other priorities, such as care responsibilities (European Commission, 2013b). It involves investing in institutions for early childhood, schools, vocational training, upper tertiary education, activation, and lifelong learning (Morel et al., 2012). Member states can receive country-specific recommendations (CSRs) in social investment through Europe 2020 (European Commission, 2013b). Policy objectives are defined to a medium degree, while enforcement and surveillance are both weak, although they are medium if EU co-funding is included in pursuing an aim under the Social Investment policy package.

EU surveillance of Europe 2020 is medium, as it takes place ex post as part of an iterative policy cycle, coordinated in the European Semester. CSRs are made to member states on the basis of national reports and suggest policies to be adopted for reaching the policy aims specified in

Europe 2020. Enforcement of the CSRs is low, as the adoption of the suggested measures is voluntary, although in some cases they have been sources of inspiration for reform (de la Porte and Jacobsson, 2012). The European Social Fund and the Youth Guarantee are intended to be well integrated with Social Investment and Europe 2020, offering possibilities for co-funding the aims of social investment, especially concerning youth (European Commission, 2014a). Co-funding can enhance the enforcement of objectives related to public policy and social investment.

Another measure to strengthen EMU is a Council recommendation for a common economic policy for the eurozone (European Commission, 2015), indicating that there has been a stronger shift towards coordination among EMU countries compared with other EU countries. The recommendation is a clear step towards a 'variable-geometry Europe', which has been adopted for the first time for the period 2016–17. The first aim is to focus on macroeconomic imbalances. Accordingly, member states with high debt as well as current account surpluses should take steps to correct these. In labour market policy, the reforms recommended are in line with those prompted in Europe 2020, including flexible and reliable labour contracts that promote labour market transitions and avoid a two-tier labour market, lifelong learning, policies to help the unemployed re-enter the labour market, and social protection systems that support those in need. It seems that identical policies are recommended through various instruments. The added value of this last instrument is thus far not clear, as the same messages are repeated through the EMU governance instruments pertaining to fiscal consolidation, and to Europe 2020 in labour market and social policy.

Conclusions

In the aftermath of the eurozone crisis existing instruments were strengthened and multiple new instruments were added to improve EMU governance and to prevent future crises. The fiscal consolidation objectives are highly specified, they are repeated in multiple instruments, and they are accompanied by strong surveillance mechanisms, de jure strengthening surveillance fiscal federalism. Sensibly, there is a broader array of national macroeconomic policies followed by the EU level through the MIP, but the ability of governments to respond to macroeconomic imbalances may be weak, as governments may not have the necessary instruments. With regard to enforcement, many steps have been taken to ensure that budgets are balanced, preventively, via more indicators, such as the structural budget deficit, and more focus on public debt. In the corrective stage, sanctions are quasi-automatic. However, the decision in July 2016 not to fine Portugal and Spain following prolonged non-action in their EDPs implies that pecuniary sanctions are not de facto applicable.

Parallel to the enhancement of 'surveillance fiscal federalism', steps towards 'classical fiscal federalism', particularly through the Two-Pack, have enabled the EU to encourage or require changes in DBPs before they are approved in national parliaments. This is also introduced through the back door via EU rules giving the Commission a say in the yearly process of deciding on national budgets.

Initiatives for social and labour market policy were added later, partially to reaffirm that the main policy focused on 'social investment' and partly to focus on the challenges arising from the crisis, especially youth unemployment. However, aside from small pools of co-funding, the necessary resources to facilitate investment in human capabilities, let alone to strengthen social protection systems, are not being prioritized. It is up to governments to ensure such investments are realized, which is particularly difficult for countries that are still struggling with the crisis and that do not have the necessary institutions in place already. The addition of employment and social indicators in the macroeconomic imbalance scoreboard suggests that social concerns are now more integrated into EU policy via the European Semester, although not in line with a full-fledged social investment agenda.

Comparative studies are needed to see how greater Europeanization within EMU, compared with the weaker emphasis on social policy, plays out across member states. Thus far, we know that even in the context of the more constraining EMU surveillance and enforcement mechanisms, countries have wide leverage, and may comply differently, depending on the vulnerability of their economies, as well as domestic policies, politics, and institutions.

References

Bolukbasi, T. (2009) 'On Consensus, Constraint and Choice: Economic and Monetary Integration and Europe's Welfare States', *Journal of European Public Policy*, Vol. 16, No. 4, pp. 527–44.

Claeys, G., Darvas, Z., and Wolff, G. B. (2014) 'Benefits and Drawbacks of European Unemployment Insurance', Bruegel Policy Brief 2014/06.

Clegg, D. (forthcoming) 'Labour Market Policies in Europe.' In P. Kennett and N. Lendvai (eds), *A Handbook of European Social Policy*. Cheltenham: Edward Elgar.

Copeland, P. and ter Haar, B. (2013) 'A Toothless Bite? The Effectiveness of the European Employment Strategy as a Governance Tool', *Journal of European Social Policy*, Vol. 23, No. 1, pp. 21–36.

Copelovitch, M., Frieden, J., and Walter, S. (2016) 'The Political Economy of the Euro Crisis', *Comparative Political Studies*, Vol. 49, No. 7, pp. 811–40.

De Haan, J., Berger, H., and Jansen, D. (2004) 'Why has the Stability and Growth Pact Failed?', *International Finance*, Vol. 7, No. 2, pp. 235–60.

de la Porte, C. and Heins, E. (2015) 'A New Era of European Integration? Governance of Labour Market and Social Policy since the Sovereign Debt Crisis', *Comparative European Politics*, Vol. 13, No. 1, pp. 8–28.

de la Porte, C. and Heins, E. (2016) *The Sovereign Debt Crisis, the EU and Welfare Reform*. London: Palgrave Macmillan.

de la Porte, C. and Jacobsson, K. (2012) 'Social Investment or Recommodification? Assessing the Employment Policies of the EU Member States.' In N. Morel, B. Palier, and J. Palme (eds), *Towards a Social Investment Welfare State? Ideas, Policies and Challenges*. Bristol: Policy Press, pp. 117–52.

de la Porte, C. and Natali, D. (2014) 'Altered Europeanisation of Pension Reform in the Context of the Great Recession: Denmark and Italy Compared', *West European Politics*, Vol. 37, No. 4, pp. 732–49.

Euractiv (2016) 'Commission Split on Credibility of Rules as Spain and Portugal Get "Pardon"', Euractiv, 28 July, https://www.euractiv.com/section/euro-finance/news/commission-split-on-credibility-of-rules-as-spain-and-portugal-get-pardon.

European Commission (2010) 'Europe 2020: A strategy for smart, sustainable and inclusive growth'. Brussels: European Commission.

European Commission (2013a) 'The EU's Economic Governance Explained.' Brussels: European Commission, http://europa.eu/rapid/press-release_MEMO-13-318_en.htm.

European Commission (2013b) 'Towards Social Investment for Growth and Cohesion – Including Implementing the European Social Fund 2014–2020', *COM(2013) 083 final*.

European Commission (2014a) 'Policy Roadmap for the 2014 Implementation of the Social Investment Package.' Brussels: European Commission.

European Commission (2014b) 'Communication from the Commission. 2015 Draft Budgetary Plans: Overall Assessment', *COM(2014) 907 final*.

European Commission (2015) 'Recommendation for a Council Recommendation on the Economic Policy of the Euro Area', 26 November, http://ec.europa.eu/europe2020/pdf/2016/ags2016_euro_area_recommendations.pdf.

European Commission (2016) 'Report from the Commission to the European Parliament, the Council, The European Central Bank and the European Economic and Social Committee, Alert Mechanism Report 2016', *COM(2015) 691 final*.

European Parliament and DG for Internal Policies (2016) 'Mainstreaming Employment and Social Indicators into Macroeconomic Surveillance', http://www.europarl.europa.eu/RegData/etudes/STUD/2016/569985/IPOL_STU(2016)569985_EN.pdf.

Graziano, P. and Vink, M. (eds) (2008) *Europeanization: New Research Agendas*. Basingstoke: Palgrave Macmillan.

Guillén, A. M. and León, M. (eds) (2011) *The Spanish Welfare State in European Context*. London and New York: Routledge.

Hall, P. (1993) 'Policy Paradigms, Social Learning, and the State: The Case of Economic Policymaking in Britain', *Comparative Politics*, Vol. 25, No. 3, pp. 275–96.

Hassenteufel, P. and Palier, B. (2015), 'Still the Sound of Silence? Towards a New Phase in the Europeanisation of Welfare Policies in France', *Comparative European Politics*, Vol. 13, No. 1, pp. 112–30.

Heins, E. and de la Porte, C. (2015) 'The Sovereign Debt Crisis, the EU and Welfare State Reform', *Comparative European Politics*, Vol. 13, No. 1, pp. 1–7.

Hinarejos, A. (2013) 'Fiscal Federalism in the European Union: Evolution and Future Choices for EMU', *Common Market Law Review*, Vol. 50, No. 6, pp. 1621–42.

Hughes Hallett, A. and Hougaard-Jensen, S. E. (2012) 'Fiscal Governance in the Euro Area: Institutions vs. Rules', *Journal of European Public Policy*, Vol. 19, No. 5, pp. 646–66.

Juncker, J.-C., Tusk, D., Dijsselbloem, J., Draghi, M., and Schulz, M. (2015) 'Completing Europe's Economic and Monetary Union', http://ec.europa.eu/priorities/economic-monetary-union/docs/5-presidents-report_en.pdf.

McNamara, K. R. (2005) 'Economic and Monetary Union: Innovation and challenges for the euro.' In H. Wallace, W. Wallace, and M. A. Pollack (eds), *Policy-making in the European Union*, 5th edition. Oxford: Oxford University Press, pp. 141–60.

Maddaloni, A. and Peydro, J.-L. (2011) 'Bank Risk-taking, Securitization, Supervision, and Low Interest Rates: Evidence from the Euro-area and the U.S. Lending Standards', *Review of Financial Studies*, Vol. 24, No. 6, pp. 2121–65.

Morel, N., Palier, B., and Palme, J. (eds) (2012) *Towards a Social Investment Welfare State? Ideas, Policies and Challenges.* Bristol: Policy Press.

Pavolini, E., León, M., Guillén, A. M., and Ascoli, U. (2015) 'From Austerity to Permanent Strain? The EU and Welfare State Reform in Italy and Spain', *Comparative European Politics*, Vol. 13, No. 1, pp. 56–76.

Scharpf, F. (2002) 'The European Social Model', *Journal of Common Market Studies*, Vol. 40, No. 4, pp. 645–70.

Scharpf, F. (2011) 'Monetary Union, Fiscal Crisis and the Preemption of Democracy', MPIfG Discussion Paper 11/11.

Schmidt, V. (2015) 'The Forgotten Problem of Democratic Legitimacy: "Governing by the Rules" and "Ruling by the Numbers".' In M. Matthis and M. Blyth (eds), *The Future of the Euro*. Oxford: Oxford University Press, pp. 90–116.

Theodoropoulou, S. (2015) 'National Social and Labour Market Policy Reforms in the Shadow of EU Bail-Out Conditionality: The Cases of Greece and Portugal', *Comparative European Politics*, Vol. 13, No. 1, pp. 29–55.

Chapter 9

The Crisis and the EU's Institutions, Political Actors, and Processes

NEILL NUGENT

Introduction

This chapter examines how the different dimensions of the crisis have impacted on the EU's main political actors and policy processes. It shows that there that have been three main effects. First, the powers of and the influence exercised by the EU's institutional actors have been partially re-shaped during the crisis. They have been so in such ways as to intensify both the extent to which the EU is in some respects intergovernmental in character and in other respects is supranational. Second, the crisis has brought out and exacerbated deep-lying differences between the EU's main non-institutional actors – the member states — on key policy issues. Such has been the depth of some of the differences between member states that policy- and decision-making processes in some spheres have increasingly not involved all member states, while in others they have sometimes been extremely slow and protracted. Third, the crisis has shown how the EU still has a major leadership problem. One of the main concerns of the so-called 'constitutional decade' (the years leading up to the application in 2009 of the Lisbon Treaty) – unsatisfactory EU leadership – has remained, with it often not being clear during the crisis who or what should be providing leadership, and when it has been provided it has often been contested. Further to these aspects of the leadership problem, as the EU has become increasingly differentiated during the crisis such leadership as has been offered has often been so only to parts of the EU. It is thus not going too far to say that one of the dimensions of the crisis the EU has been experiencing in recent years is a leadership crisis.

The chapter shows that after almost a decade of deliberations and negotiations on the contents of the EU's treaties, most of which were focused on trying (once again) to balance institutional and policy process efficiency with preservation of national sovereignty, when the new arrangements were finally 'installed' in 2009, the crisis revealed them (still) to be wanting.

The Crisis, the EU's Institutions, and the Evolving Balance Between Supranationalism and Intergovernmentalism

The Lisbon Treaty advanced both the supranational and the inter-governmental features of the EU. Supranationalism was strengthened most notably by: extended applications to new policy spheres of the Community Method (where the Commission's powers are strong and the jurisdiction of the Court of Justice of the European Union [CJEU] applies); increased legislative powers for the EP, with significant extensions of the policy spheres in which it is a co-legislator with the Council; and increases in the availability of qualified majority voting (QMV) in the Council, which resulted in it now becoming available for over 90 per cent of legislation. Intergovernmentalism was strengthened, or in some areas of activity at least preserved, by: an increase in the capacity of the European Council – by giving it the status of being a separate EU institution and also giving it a full-time President (that is, a President elected for a 2½-year term which can be renewed once, as opposed to the previous system in which the European Council Presidency rotated between the member states alongside the six-month rotating Council Presidency); and the retention of the unanimity requirement in the Council for some very important policy areas, because of the political sensitivities associated with them – including most aspects of foreign, defence, and taxation policies. (For a detailed explanation of the roles and powers of the EU institutions, and of how they were affected by the Lisbon Treaty, see Nugent, 2017.)

This section of the chapter examines how, in the context of the post-Lisbon arrangements, the powers of the EU's institutions have continued to evolve in response to the crisis. The examination is undertaken with particular regard to the ever-changing balance between supranationalism and intergovernmentalism in the EU.

The increasing prominence of the European Council

Since its creation in the mid-1970s, the European Council has been an important EU institutional actor, especially in respect of the taking of major political decisions – so called 'history-making' decisions – in areas such as enlargements, multi-annual financial frameworks, and treaty reforms. It is also the institution that has most embodied the intergov-ernmental nature of the EU, because its principal members are Heads of

Government (or Heads of State if the two positions are concurrent) and its decisions are almost invariably taken by consensus.

The above-noted Lisbon Treaty reforms that strengthened the institutional position and capacity of the European Council were politically agreed in December 2007 and entered into force in December 2009: that is, before the eurozone crisis erupted in 2010. This timing is significant because the eurozone crisis in particular is widely seen as embodying a clear shift towards intergovernmentalism – most noticeably by enhancing the position and role of the European Council. But, in fact, this shift was already under way before the crisis. What the crisis did was to signal and underpin the shift.

To the background of the institutional strengthening they were given by the Lisbon Treaty, the standing and potential capacity of the European Council in the EU system have unquestionably been further increased by the high political salience and stakes involved in a number of dimensions of the crisis. Since 2010 the EU has been subject to an 'emergency politics', which has brought the European Council to the centre of the decision-making stage on crisis-related issues. As part of this, in addition to the four regular meetings that must be held each year, many extra European Council meetings have also been convened. In the particular context of the eurozone crisis, some of these meetings have been restricted to eurozone members, with these Euro Summits being institutionalized by the 2012 Treaty on Stability, Coordination and Governance (the Fiscal Compact). At European Council and/or Euro Summit meetings, a number of high-profile and important decisions have (sometimes) been taken – on such matters as the size and conditions of financial bailouts, sanctions against Russia (in retaliation for the occupation of Crimea and intervention in the Ukrainian civil war), and the renegotiated terms of the UK's membership conditions. (For a more detailed listing of European Council crisis decisions, see European Parliament Research Service, 2016.)

But though the standing and perceived position of the European Council have been elevated by the crisis, whether its increased activity really amounts to an advance in its independent policy role and impact is open to question. Advocates of the 'new intergovernmentalism' perspective on EU politics – which sees European integration since the Maastricht Treaty as being based on an increasingly deliberative and consensual approach to decision-making by representatives of national governments, coupled with a decline in the roles and powers of the Commission and the Court – believe that such an advance most certainly has occurred (see, for example, Bickerton et al., 2015a and b). They note that the suddenness and seriousness of the crisis coupled with the multiple, extremely important and high-profile issues that have had to be addressed by EU decision-makers have inevitably meant that the European Council has had to become much more directly involved and in so doing has had to act differently, both procedurally and substantively.

However, though the European Council has been highly active from the early days of the crisis – especially in respect of the eurozone and migration crises – it is questionable whether at any stage it has exercised greater independent powers than previously. Certainly it has been more involved in the taking of final political decisions on important and contested issues, not least because some of these issues have had implications for the electoral fortunes and prospects of national leaders and their governments. But, as has long been the case, the European Council has remained highly dependent on preparatory work – of both a policy shaping and policy formulation kind – undertaken by the Commission, various Council formations, the Council Secretariat, plus since 2009 the *cabinet* of the European Council President.

To this list of preparers, the crisis has increasingly seen key actors and their private offices getting together and liaising before European Council and Euro Summit meetings so as to try and work together, and perhaps in some cases foist agreements on full meetings. In the early stages of the eurozone crisis, pre-meetings were especially common between President Sarkozy and Chancellor Merkel and later became common, in varying combinations, between Herman Van Rompuy/ Donald Tusk (the European Council Presidents), Mario Draghi (the European Central Bank President from 2011), President Hollande (who succeeded Sarkozy in 2012), and Chancellor Merkel. But though this list of characters may have changed, it is questionable whether the nature of such preparatory processes is really so different from the (often successful) pre-summit agreements reached in the 1980s and 1990s between Chancellor Kohl and President Mitterrand.

The supposed decline of the Commission

In broad terms the prevailing view in the academic literature is that the Commission has been in decline in recent years (see, for example, Bickerton et al., 2015a and b; Kassim et al., 2013; Majone, 2014; Rasmussen et al., 2013). The decline is seen as being accounted for primarily by the growing powers of the European Council and European Parliament (EP), the increasing use of non-legislative policy instruments (where the Commission's formal powers are weaker than they are with legislation) in 'difficult' policy areas, and the growing tendency of the EU's decision-takers to assign implementation and executive tasks away from the Commission to new agencies and bodies outside the Commission.

However, this picture of Commission decline is too often exaggerated, for the Commission continues to have access to many key resources that place it at the centre of EU policy processes. Some of these resources are formal in nature, such as treaty authorization to initiate policies and (on an almost monopolistic basis) to propose and draft legislation, while others are more informal, such as widespread perceptions of it as the most neutral (and therefore in the eyes of most member states, most trustworthy) of the EU's institutions and also the institution that in most policy areas is expected to take the lead. Access to such resources enables the Commission – and throughout the crisis has continued to enable it – to exercise many key functions, not least those of agenda-setter, policy and legislative proposer, and executive. (For examples of very considerable Commission policy influence during the crisis, see the section below on leadership.)

As such, as the present author has argued elsewhere, the supposed decline of the Commission has arguably been overstated (see Nugent and Rhinard, 2015 and 2016). Indeed, in some respects the Commission's powers and tasks have actually increased during the crisis (see Bauer and Becker, 2014; Savage and Verdun, 2016). Although these increased powers and tasks have been primarily executive in nature, they involve a range of responsibilities that are both highly important and necessitate delicate handling. Most notably, they involve significantly stronger fiscal surveillance powers in respect of the signatories of the Fiscal Compact, including punitive financial powers that can only be overturned by 'reverse' QMV in the Council. The extent and significance of the Commission's new fiscal powers were no more clearly demonstrated than in July 2016 when, on the first occasion it could have imposed financial penalties under its new Fiscal Compact powers, it used its judgement and refused to impose financial penalties on Spain and Portugal because they were thought to be making real efforts to move in the approved direction (see Chapter 8).

This continuing importance of the Commission requires that some tempering be placed on putting too strong an intergovernmental interpretation of the impact of the crisis.

The emergence of the European Central Bank as a key policy actor

Beyond the strengthened powers of the Commission, another institutional development during the crisis has also contained a supranational tilt. The European Central Bank (ECB), which was established with a rather narrow remit to contain inflation and not to engage in any type of 'monetary financing', has been increasingly involved in broad deliberations on eurozone economic and financial policy with EU political decision-makers, from European Council and Euro Summit level downwards. As Chang (2016: 496) has noted, during the crisis the

Bank 'transformed from a largely technocratic body with a very specific function to one of the major political actors in the European Union'. It moved beyond being a central bank focused largely on maintaining price stability to become a key advisor to national governments and EU institutions on economic and financial policy, a quasi-lender of last resort, and the main driver behind and the supervisor of the banking union that was created from 2012 (on the ECB's role in creating the banking union, see De Rynk, 2016).

Much of the enhanced role of the ECB has been due to the appointment in 2011 of a highly activist President, Mario Draghi, who has overseen and pressed for a range of bold policy initiatives – including on new lending schemes for indebted member states, quantitative easing, a tight banking union, and more governmental measures to tackle weak growth and demand. Draghi has been seen by markets as a reassuring presence, no more so than when he declared in July 2012, in what perhaps was the single most important utterance of any policy actor throughout the euro crisis: 'Within (its) mandate, the ECB is ready to do whatever it takes to preserve the euro' (cited in Briançon, 2015: 23). This and follow-up policy proposals – including a plan to buy bonds of governments in financial difficulties in exchange for reform commitments – have been crucial in calming markets.

Draghi's success in strengthening the position of the ECB is a classic example of how crises can bring about significant changes to institutional configurations. However, important though the nature of the economic and financial, and more particularly the eurozone, crises have been in providing a favourable contextual setting for a strengthening of the position of the ECB, they have not in themselves automatically produced it. Also important have been two other factors, both of them related to Draghi. The first of these has been that, unlike his predecessor Jean-Claude Trichet, Draghi has not acted within the ECB's main governing bodies – the Governing Council and the Executive Board – in a conciliatory and consensual manner, but rather in a leading and driving manner. The second has been a working relationship established between Draghi and the German Government, especially Chancellor Merkel. Merkel has been highly sensitive to Bundesbank criticism of her handling of the euro crisis and also to anti-ECB sentiments in public opinion, so has had to be careful not to expose herself politically. But a rapport on the essentials of eurozone policy between Draghi and the political leadership of the eurozone's 'economic powerhouse' has been crucial, not least in enabling resistance within the Bundesbank to the ECB's perceived adventurism to be overcome.

* * *

While the European Council, the Commission, and the ECB have been the EU institutions most directly affected by the crisis, there has also been some impact on the EU's other two main policy-making institutions – the Council and the EP.

The Council of the European Union

The Council has lost some of its standing and influence over the years. This has partly been because of the increasing practice of very important and politically sensitive decisions being taken, or at least being channelled through for approval, by the European Council. It has partly also been because of the EP joining the Council to share with it legislative decision-taking powers in most policy areas. However, the Council remains very important, for in addition to its co-equal legislative decision-taking powers it continues to be a sole decision-taker on many non-legislative decisions (including in the foreign policy and external security spheres) and it is a very important player in the preparation of European Council meetings – normally mainly through the General Affairs Council (GAC), but during the economic and financial crisis a highly active preparatory role has also been exercised by the Economic and Financial Affairs Council (Ecofin).

During the crisis, two long-developing features of the functioning of the Council have been intensified. The first of these has been the use of QMV. Although the Council still prefers to act where possible on the basis of consensus and always strives – by looking for 'accommodations' – to bring potential dissenting member states 'on board', it has during the crisis increasingly sought to use QMV where it is available and has certainly sometimes resorted to its use sooner than it formerly did. Where it is available, votes are now explicitly used in about 20 per cent of the cases where they could be, and in about another 10 per cent of cases they are implicitly used in the sense that states that are known not to be in favour of a proposal choose not to register a dissenting vote – though they may issue a dissenting statement. (There is a considerable academic literature on voting in the Council. See, for example: Golub, 2012; Häge and Naurin, 2013; Hosli et al., 2011.) As for the earlier use of QMV, during the crisis this has become a particular feature of policy areas where there has been a need for decisions to be sometimes taken quickly. In the area of freedom, security, and justice (AFSJ), for example, but increasingly in other policy areas also, it has become the practice for Council Presidencies to be looking from an early stage of working party deliberations to see whether or not a qualified majority exists on a proposal, and before the Committee of Permanent Representatives (COREPER) meets all member states must notify the Presidency of their voting intentions.

The other long-developing feature of the functioning of the Council that has been intensified by the crisis is the varying nature of proceedings when not all member states are participating. This situation of varying proceedings has been necessitated by differentiation – which started with the European Monetary System in the 1970s, proceeded through Schengen and EMU, and in the Lisbon Treaty was advanced through the various opt-in and opt-out arrangements that were provided for in AFSJ. Differentiation has given rise to increasingly complex arrangements governing whether states can attend, and can vote in, Council meetings. The two principal areas affected by differentiation, namely economic and financial policy and AFSJ, have been at the heart of the crisis, which has necessitated an increased number of meetings in these policy areas and increased complexities of organizational arrangements. In broad terms, the main arrangements have evolved in such ways that they are now, in brief, as follows:

- All economic and financial policy matters must be formally channelled through and decided at Ecofin, but matters that only concern the euro area are in practice decided by the Eurogroup, whose membership is restricted to ministers (and, at sub-ministerial levels, to officials) of eurozone governments. At ministerial level, Eurogroup meetings are normally held shortly before (usually the day before) Ecofin meetings. This potentially problematic situation – of non-eurozone members participating in eurozone-related Ecofin decision-making – is dealt with by permitting non-eurozone members of Ecofin to contribute to eurozone discussions and debates, but not to vote when decisions are being made.

  Where some states are excluded from voting and QMV is used, the size of qualified majorities is scaled back, using the same proportions that are used for full Council votes. So, for proposals that are made by the Commission (or the High Representative), qualified majorities are deemed to exist when 55 per cent of member states representing at least 65 per cent of the relevant EU population vote in favour.

- The AFSJ area is more complex because: 22 EU states are members of the Schengen system, while six (Bulgaria, Cyprus, Croatia, Ireland, Romania, and the UK) are not; four non-EU states are also Schengen members (Iceland, Liechtenstein, Norway, and Switzerland); and there are various opt-in and opt-out provisions, mainly available only to the UK and Ireland (necessary for Ireland because it has a common travel area with the UK) covering such fields as asylum, visas, migration, and borders. The participatory and voting arrangements are broadly similar to economic and financial policies in that: all EU members are allowed to contribute to deliberations at all

Council levels on Schengen and other AFSJ matters, but they cannot vote on policy matters where they are not participants; and the same scaled-back voting arrangements apply for calculating the necessary size of qualified majorities. The four Schengen members that are not EU members can attend Council meetings for some agenda items, but they cannot vote.

***

One other aspect of the crisis having consequences for the Council was the Brexit vote in June 2016. The UK Government quickly decided not to take up its scheduled Presidency of the Council from July 2017, which resulted in the following Presidencies being asked to move their Presidencies forward by six months. The Estonians in particular, who would now fill the UK's spot, were thus put on rather short notice (member states normally prepare their Presidencies for at least three years).

The European Parliament

The EP is commonly perceived to have been the main institutional 'winner' of the Lisbon Treaty. This is because the remit of the co-decision (now called 'ordinary') legislative procedure (the procedure under which the Parliament has co-equal powers with the Council) was greatly extended in scope and also because the EP was given new powers to approve or reject EU external trade-based agreements. However, the new powers it was assigned in the Treaty did not extend to the EP being given a seat at the intergovernmental deliberations that were to become so much a part of the EU's attempts to deal with the crisis and did not extend either to it being given formal powers over the various intergovernmental agreements that were contracted in response to the crisis. Moreover, the new treaties that have been agreed (by most member states) during the crisis – the Fiscal Compact and the European Stability Mechanism Treaty – have not required the EP's formal approval and have not accorded any significant new roles to the EP.

Apart from where the community method has been used – because legislation has been required, as with, for example, the Six-Pack and the Two-Pack, and the measures giving effect to the banking union (see Chapter 4) – the EP's influence has thus been limited during the crisis. It has done what it can to exercise influence by, for example, passing numerous – what have amounted to advisory – resolutions on the eurozone, migration, and external affairs crises. For example, on the Syria crisis alone it passed no less than 15 resolutions between 2011 and 2015 (European Parliamentary Research Service, 2016: 24). It has also questioned and pressed views on leading decision-makers – including the European Council President and the President of the ECB, both of whom are obliged to periodically appear before the Parliament. But for the most part – especially on politically charged and primarily non-legislative matters, such as financial bailouts, the Ukraine crisis, the migration crisis, and Brexit – the EP has not been a central policy player. On the migration crisis, for example, it has frequently called for a more ambitious and holistic approach to be taken to asylum and migration policy and for member states to be more proactive in seeing to the relocation and resettlement of refugees, but without much effect. And on Brexit it exercised no influence on the contents of the proposed reformed UK membership terms that European Council President Donald Tusk sent in early February 2016, just before the European Council meeting scheduled to deal with the matter, to David Cameron and the leaders of the other 27 member states.

The EP has thus been dissatisfied with its role during the crisis, especially its exclusion from high-level, intergovernmental deliberations and decision-making. It has done what it can to insert itself and has relentlessly attacked the European Council for being 'unaccountable', but often it has been left largely on the sidelines.

The institutional advancement of *both* supranationalism and intergovernmentalism

Both supranationalism and intergovernmentalism have thus advanced as characteristics of the EU during and as a consequence of the crisis. If attention is focused primarily on the high-profile and at times almost seemingly constant decision-making involvement of the European Council, then intergovernmentalism is seen to have most advanced. But if attention is switched to the Commission and the ECB then supranational institutions have also clearly extended their roles and powers.

This dual advance of both supranationalism and intergovernmentalism does, of course, encapsulate the highly complex, contested, and still developing nature of the EU's institutional structures and processes.

The Crisis and the Member States

As the EU has increased in size as a result of widening and in its policy involvements as a result of deepening, the number of positional differences existing between member states has naturally grown. The differences arise from varying demographics, national needs, ideological perspectives, and cultures and national identities. For example, differences arising from ideological perspectives include differences over the extent to which and the ways in which the EU's internal market should be further liberalized and, correspondingly, the circumstances in which protections – which can take many forms – for areas of economic activity should be permitted.

Member states and EU decision-making processes

So as to try and prevent the growth of policy differences between member states weakening the EU's decision-making capacity, a number of adjustments to decision-making processes have been made over the years, three of which have been especially important as the EU has sought to respond to the crises. The first of these has been the above-noted increased availability and use of QMV in the Council. The second adjustment has been the increased use of non-legislative instruments to make policy progress. Because such instruments are not legally enforceable, states with reservations are more likely to accept them. And the third adjustment has been the increased use of differentiation, which has resulted in not all member states participating, or fully participating, in all of the EU's policy activities. Differentiation is not permissible in all policy areas, and generally does not apply in areas directly related to the operation of the internal market (though there are differences between member states regarding precisely what these areas are), but it does allow 'fast stream' states to develop integration and policies in some areas where there would be little development at all if all member states were to be obliged to participate. (On differentiation, see Leuffen et al., 2013.)

The three adjustments that have just been described have been important in enabling integration to continue to proceed, albeit sometimes only on a partial membership basis. All of them have been used as the EU has sought to handle the crisis, especially the eurozone crisis: the availability and willingness to use QMV has been useful in assisting the passage of legislation covering, for example, the banking union; non-legislative policy instruments have been used to intensify economic and financial coordination between all EU states and not just eurozone states; and the exclusion of voting rights to non-eurozone member states in eurozone-only matters has naturally facilitated decision-making.

But notwithstanding the use of the three forms of adjustment, such have been the depth and the political sensitivities of differences between member states on certain crisis-related matters – especially in the context of the economic and financial and the migration crises – that many decision-making processes have still been extremely difficult, protracted, and unsatisfactory in terms of their outcomes. So, in the context of the economic and financial crisis, there have been differences both between eurozone and non-eurozone members and between eurozone members. Regarding the former, the most notable difference occurred during the making of the 2012 Fiscal Compact, which essentially laid the foundations for tighter economic and financial coordination between all EU member states and for a strengthened Stability and Growth Pact that committed eurozone members to balanced budgets (structural deficits not to exceed 0.5 per cent of GDP and public debt not to exceed 60 per cent). The UK Government, in a high-profile campaign, threatened to veto the Treaty, so the other governments responded by making the Treaty an intergovernmental treaty rather than an EU treaty, which meant that governments could choose whether or not to sign it and no state could veto it. (In the event, only the Czech Government joined the UK in not signing the Treaty.) Regarding the latter, differences between eurozone states were most acute during the 2015 Greek crisis when, broadly speaking, northern and 'donor' states, led by Germany, insisted, against the positions of most southern and indebted states, on the imposition of tough austerity conditions on Greece as the price for another bailout. Inevitably, given that they were the paymasters, the northern states had their way. Indeed, Fabbrini (2016: 1) goes so far as to argue that 'EMU has ended up in creating a highly centralized policy regime, where the creditor member states have come to play a domineering role with regard to debtor member states. Hierarchical relations between national governments have finally substituted consensus with domination.'

In the context of the migration crisis, differences between member states have also been sharp, with the most notable lines of division being between: states that are Schengen members and those that are not (important because Schengen states have open borders with each other); states that are geographically located on the 'front line' for refugee arrivals and those that are not (with Mediterranean states being the main front line states); and states that have taken a liberal and welcoming approach to refugees and those that have not (with the most liberal approaches, until late 2015 at least, being taken by Germany and Sweden). Given the many sensitivities and policy and cost implications of accepting large numbers of migrants, EU-level policy progress has, in practical terms, been only modest and has largely been limited to increased financial support for migration camps in EU states, for tackling problems that encourage migration in non-EU states, and for strengthening the EU's external borders. But, on the 'big issue' of what to do with refugees once they have arrived, states have simply not been able to agree, with the consequence that the Commission has made no headway with its solution of mandatory quotas to be imposed on Schengen states. And on the other 'big issue' of reaching an agreement with Turkey that would discourage would-be migrants from using Turkey as part of a transit route to the EU, a (somewhat fragile) deal was eventually reached, but only amid great reservations and difficulties on the EU side given that the member states are deeply divided in their attitudes to the authoritarian Turkish regime (see Chapter 6).

The influence exercised by individual member states during the crisis

As regards the influence exercised by particular member states during the crisis, this has naturally varied across policy domains. Overall, however, Germany has been by far the most influential and powerful actor (as clearly shown by Bulmer, 2014; Bulmer and Paterson, 2013; and Bulmer and Paterson in Chapter 11 in this volume). In large part this has been because Germany *just is* the EU's strongest member state, by virtue of having a range of key power resources at its disposal – including the largest population size, the biggest and strongest economy, and a stable political system in which there is broad agreement on EU policies. In part, too, it has been because on the eurozone crisis the German Government has taken a strong position, to which it has insisted on sticking: a position in which it has required that the imposition of austerity policies is the price of financial bailouts to debtor states – seen most dramatically over the summer of 2015 when the left-wing Syriza Government in Greece unsuccessfully sought to persuade Germany that economic expansionist policies were the way to enable Greece to escape from its economic problems.

From the earliest days of the crises, Germany sought to work closely with its long-time close working partner, France. But the balance of the relationship between these two countries increasingly tilted towards Germany during the crisis, with the stronger partner asserting itself as relations between the two were strained by policy differences on the most high-profile aspects of the crisis: the eurozone crisis and the migration crisis. On the eurozone crisis, France, with its relatively weak economy, preferred – especially after the Socialist, François Hollande, was elected President in 2012 – a policy response that was more expansionist in character than Germany's austerity-based preference, but in practice it mostly fell in line with Germany's lead. On the migration crisis, electoral pressures – especially from the far-right *Front National* – resulted in the French Government being unable to support in 2015 Chancellor Merkel's welcoming, almost open door, stance on refugees, but it was equally unable to persuade her to moderate her stance.

As for the other of the EU's 'big three' member states, the UK has not been a key player in any of the major aspects of the crisis. This has been partly a consequence of domestic politics: a eurosceptic party – the Conservative Party – dominated what was a coalition government from 2010 to 2015, and then a Conservative-only government that was committed to holding an in-out referendum on EU membership was elected to power in May 2015. Inevitably, this domestic situation made the UK more 'inward'-looking. The UK's somewhat marginal position has also partly been a consequence of the issues that have dominated the crisis. So, not being a member of the eurozone, the UK has been excluded from most eurozone negotiations, while it has also been outside many deliberations on broader economic policies. Similarly, non-membership of the Schengen system and explicit statements by the UK Government that it did not wish to be part of any non-voluntary refugee distribution arrangements resulted in it not being central to migration crisis deliberations and negotiations.

The EU's Continuing Leadership Problem

Political leadership takes many different forms. Here, usage of the concept is restricted to the ability of political actors to identify and propose desirable and/or necessary courses of action and to persuade/oblige/motivate other actors to support the identified courses of action.

The EU has long been seen as having a leadership problem. This is because it has never had a single and undisputed source of leadership, such as customarily exists at national levels with governments (in their various institutional forms). Rather, EU leadership has been dispersed, both between EU institutions and member states. Before the Lisbon Treaty and the crisis, the main institutions involved in the exercise of leadership were the Commission, the Council Presidency, and the High Representative (in respect of foreign and external security policy). France and Germany, usually acting together, were the main member states offering leadership, but others sometimes played an important role on specific matters – such as the UK on foreign policy and the Scandinavian states on environmental policy.

Because of concerns that there was not a sufficiently strong source of intergovernmental-based leadership, the Lisbon Treaty strengthened the institutional base of the European Council. The main way in which it did so was, as was noted above, by making the European Council an official EU institution and giving it a full-time President with responsibility to 'drive forward' (article 15: 6(a) TEU) its work. Another source of leadership was thus added to an already crowded field. However, the addition was not, and is not, a bad thing in all respects. For, in one respect at least, it is highly functional. This respect arises from the internally divided nature of the EU: with so many policy differences between the member states, it could be damaging to the confidence of some member states in the EU system if leadership was seen to be always coming from the same place – especially if that place rested on a majoritarian system in which the same states were often in a minority. To strengthen an intergovernmental source of leadership, in which all states participate and in which the approval of all is often required for major initiatives to be approved, can clearly help to promote confidence in the EU system.

So, the EU's leadership 'surplus' has benefits. But it also has drawbacks, which have been openly displayed during the crisis. The most important of these drawbacks is a lack of clarity as to who is and who should be providing policy leads in particular circumstances: the Commission and/or its President?; the European Council and/or its President?; the ECB and/or its President?; member states, groups of member states, or Germany? Such lack of clarity has led to some jostling for position between potential leaders, especially, since they both assumed office in late 2014, between Commission President Jean-Claude Juncker (who believes a more political Commission should be the main driving force of EU policies and reforms) and European Council President Donald Tusk (who believes the member states should provide the political stimulus of the EU). This has led, consequently, to decision-making uncertainties and even, at times, confusion. However, the surplus of potential policy-leaders has meant the EU has not been short of policy ideas and proposals for actions. Taking just the Commission and the economic and financial crisis, examples of its attempted leadership include:

- Throughout the crisis the Commission has actively sought to encourage other policy actors to focus not just on immediate problems but also on longer-term challenges. In particular, it has advanced and promoted ideas and proposals for tightening economic policy coordination and for deepening and strengthening EMU. So, for example, in the spring of 2010 it issued a communication on enhancing economic policy coordination and tightening fiscal discipline (European Commission, 2010). In 2012 it was an important contributor to the Four Presidents' Report on the future of EMU, which was signed by the Presidents of the European Council, the Commission, the Eurogroup, and the ECB, with the first of these in the lead (European Council President, 2012). And, in 2015, it – and more particularly the Commission's President, Jean-Claude Juncker – took the lead in preparing the Five Presidents' Report (signed by the same four Presidents, plus the President of the EP), which outlined a three-stage process by which the eurozone countries could move to full economic and monetary union by 2025 (European Commission, 2015d).
- On becoming European Commission President-elect in July 2015, Juncker sought to persuade EU decision-makers in the European Council, the Council, and the EP that there was an urgent need to generate a momentum behind increased investment within the eurozone. To this end, he called for the creation of a new investment fund,

capable of generating some €300 billion of 'new money'. Soon after the new College assumed office in November 2014, a Commission Communication was issued detailing the nature and purpose of the fund (European Commission, 2014). It was now labelled the European Fund for Strategic Investments (EFSI), the target figure was set at €315 billion, and it was to be used primarily for investing in infrastructure projects related to transport, energy, information technology, and trading. The fund involved new financial thinking in the EU context as it was to be only marginally based on existing EU financial resources: a €16 billion guarantee from the EU budget and a €5 billion contribution from the European Investment Bank (EIB) were to serve as leverage to raise the rest of the money from member states and on capital markets. The investment plan was approved in principle by the European Council in December 2014, which enabled the Commission to issue in January 2015 a proposal for a regulation to give the EFSI legal effect (European Commission, 2015a).

- From its earliest days, a priority of the Juncker Commission was the creation of a fully functioning Capital Markets Union to be in place by 2019. Further to this, a Commission Green Paper was issued in February 2015 (European Commission, 2015b) and an action plan in September 2015 (European Commission, 2015c).

- Where legislation has been required, the Commission has used its monopolistic initiating and proposing powers under the Community Method to advance a raft of legislative instruments. In the early stages of the crisis these were rather modest in character, but as the eurozone crisis intensified they became increasingly ambitious – such as the range of measures advanced (in close consultation with the ECB) to create the banking union.

The Commission has thus been a lead player in respect of many of the EU's responses to the economic and financial crisis. It has, of course, not been the final decision-taker on key issues, but it has been extremely important in initiating and shaping deliberations and advancing proposals on 'what should be done?' In so doing, it has naturally acted not in a vacuum but within a context of ongoing discussions and expressed views by other EU elites – in the European Council, the Council, the ECB, and the member states – regarding the 'way forward'. As such, the Commission has not acted wholly autonomously, but nonetheless – by so often setting the framework of debates and advancing specific measures – it has been much more than an agent of principals located elsewhere.

* * *

The provision of leadership by the Commission, or indeed of any other policy actor, during the crisis has not, of course, always resulted in strong and effective decisions being taken. Many factors have resulted in identified courses of possible action by recognized leaders often not being sufficiently supported by decision-takers. Economic and financial policy and migration policy provide some similarities in this respect:

- Because of reservations, and in some cases outright opposition, not only between EU member states but also between eurozone states, it has not been possible to put either the EU or the eurozone on the road to the building of the fiscal union that the leaders of the EU institutions and most independent observers think it needs. However, because of a general acceptance among EU member states, and eurozone states in particular, that some things needed to be done at EU level in response to the crisis to improve economic and financial performance and coordination, progress has been possible in this policy sphere, albeit usually slowly and only with great difficulty. A number of important integrationist steps have therefore been taken – including with the establishment of the European Semester system (which provides for a coordinated growth and employment strategy), tighter fiscal policy coordination (especially within the eurozone), and the laying of important foundations of a banking union.

- Migration policy has also been troubled by policy differences both between all EU member states and also between 'inner club' members (in this case Schengen states) over what should be done in response to the crisis. As with the economic and financial crisis, there was no agreement on the most radical proposal, which was made in 2015 when, in response to greatly increased migration flows into Mediterranean member states, especially Greece and Italy, the Commission proposed that all Schengen states, and preferably all EU member states, should accept mandatory quotas of refugees. The Mediterranean member states and some others (especially Germany) supported this proposal, but the UK and most Eastern member states strongly opposed it – for a mixture of reasons associated with national identity, sovereignty, welfare costs, rising domestic euroscepticism, and perhaps also racism. In consequence, policy progress, as was shown above, has been possible only on less contentious aspects of the migration crisis.

The EU thus clearly has a leadership problem. In the view of many observers, this is because it has weak, fragmented, and 'woefully inadequate' (Hansen and Gordon, 2014: 1209) institutional arrangements. Unquestionably there is much in this view. But for the EU to have stronger, more robust, and more successful leadership, it would have to be of a different political nature to what most member states want. It would have to be a more fully developed federal system in which there is a source of leadership with the power and authority to impose 'one size fits all' solutions on all member states. Differences of view between the member states on all sorts of policy matters show that such leadership simply would not work.

Conclusions

The EU's political actors have responded to the crisis and have used policy processes to tackle the many dimensions of the crisis in a number of ways. Because the component elements of the crisis have been so varied in character – witness the very different kinds of problems raised by the eurozone, migration, Ukraine, and Brexit aspects of the crisis – there have been no uniform approaches to addressing and/or tackling them.

However, taking a broad view, it can be said that the general picture of the responses of the EU's political actors and policy process systems to the crisis has been one of adjustment rather than of fundamental reform. As Verdun (2015) notes in applying an historical institutionalist explanation to the institutional responses to the euro area crises, the approach has been, for the most part, to use and/or build on existing arrangements rather than to strike out with the construction of new ones.

The building on and the use of existing arrangements is seen most obviously in the lack of creation of new central governing institutional structures, though it could be argued that the establishment of Euro Summits comes close to being such a creation. Other new institutional creations, though important, have been at secondary levels – such as the constitution of the European Stability Mechanism as the main mechanism for distributing loans to indebted states.

But though the overall structure of EU governing arrangements has remained relatively undisturbed, there have been significant developments in the influence exercised by the EU's main institutions. The most important of these developments has been in relation to the eurozone crisis, with the enhanced decision-making role of the European Council/European Summits, the increased executive powers of the Commission, and the growing political involvement of the ECB in policy processes all being part of a strengthening of EMU's institutional capacities. Indeed, as Chang (2016) has noted, the eurozone crisis has promoted a more hierarchical system of governance within the euro area: originally only monetary policy involved hierarchical governance, but during the crisis important aspects of fiscal and financial supervision policy have become more centralized, while economic policy has become more actively centrally coordinated. Indebted states have been particularly affected by the more hierarchical arrangements, with them being forced to undertake structural reforms and improve public finances as the price of being given EU financial support.

The enhancement of the decision-taking role of the European Council reflects the increasing resolve of national leaders to be directly involved in the making of EU policies and decisions, especially on issues that could affect a government's survival. All major decisions on differing aspects of the crisis – including the size and conditions of financial bailouts, whether or not to impose mandatory quotas on member states for the resettlement of refugees, and what should be the terms of the 'new settlement' offered to the UK before the Brexit referendum – have been channelled through European Council meetings and/or Euro Summits. At these meetings and summits, Germany has consistently been the member state to have exercised the greatest influence on economic and financial policy matters but, significantly, it has not exercised a comparable influence in other policy areas, as its inability to persuade most other member states to follow its liberal line on the migration crisis shows.

Overall, perhaps the greatest impact of the crisis on the EU's institutions, political actors, and processes will prove to be increased differentiation. The eurozone crisis has seen eurozone states increasingly coordinating their national fiscal policies and becoming more distant from non-eurozone states. The migration crisis has seen member states being quite unwilling to feel they must adopt a shared policy response on the distribution of migrants. And the Brexit referendum was preceded by the UK being conceded (additional) special dispensations in an attempt to persuade it to continue its EU membership. This last tactic clearly did not convince British voters, but it could tempt existing member states with eurosceptic inclinations to attempt to seek special treatments for themselves.

References

Bauer, M. W. and Becker, S. (2014) 'The Unexpected Winner of the Crisis: The European Commission's Strengthened Role in Economic Governance', *Journal of European Integration*, Vol. 36, No. 3, pp. 213–29.

Bickerton, C., Hodson, D., and Puetter, U. (2015a) 'The New Intergovernmentalism and the Study of European Integration.' In C. Bickerton, D. Hodson, and U. Puetter (eds), *The New Intergovernmentalism: States and Supranational Actors in the Post-Maastricht Era*. Oxford: Oxford University Press, pp. 1–48.

Bickerton, C., Hodson, D., and Puetter, U. (2015b) 'The New Intergovernmentalism: European Integration in the Post-Maastricht Era', *Journal of Common Market Studies*, Vol. 53, No. 4, pp. 703–22.

Briançon, P. (2015) 'The House That Mario Built', *Politico*, Vol. 1, No. 29, 10–16 December, pp. 1 and 22–3.

Bulmer, S. (2014) 'Germany and the Eurozone Crisis: Between Hegemony and Domestic Politics', *West European Politics*, Vol. 36, No. 6, pp. 1244–63.

Bulmer, S. and Paterson, W. E. (2013) 'Germany as the EU's Reluctant Hegemon: Of Economic Strength and Political Constraints', *Journal of European Public Policy*, Vol. 20, No. 10, pp. 1387–405.

Chang, M. (2016) 'The (Ever) Incomplete Story of Economic and Monetary Union', *Journal of Contemporary European Research*, Vol. 12, No. 1, pp. 486–501.

De Rynk, S. (2016) 'Banking on a Union: The Politics of Changing Eurozone Banking Supervision', *Journal of European Public Policy*, Vol. 23, No. 1, pp. 119–35.

European Commission (2010) 'Communication From the Commission ...: Reinforcing Economic Policy Coordination', *COM(2010)* 250 final.

European Commission (2014) 'Communication From the Commission ... An Investment Plan for Europe', *COM(2014)* 0903 final.

European Commission (2015a) 'Proposal for a Regulation of the European Parliament and of the Council of the European Union on the European Fund for Strategic Investments and Amending Regulations (EU) No 1291/2013 and (EU) No 1316/2013', *COM(2015)* 10 final, 2015/0009.

European Commission (2015b) 'Green Paper: Building a Capital Markets Union', *COM(2015)* 63 final.

European Commission (2015c) 'Communication From the Commission...: Action Plan on Building a Capital Markets Union', *COM(2015)* 468 final.

European Commission (2015d) 'The Five Presidents' Report: Completing Europe's Economic and Monetary Union', Brussels: European Commission, 22 June.

European Council President (2012) 'Towards a Genuine Economic and Monetary Union, Brussels', EUCO 120/12, 26 June.

European Parliamentary Research Service (2016) *The European Council and Crisis Management*. Brussels: European Council Oversight Unit, February.

Fabbrini, S. (2016) 'From Consensus to Domination: The Intergovernmental Union in a Crisis Situation', paper presented at the SUMMIT Conference on Grasping the European Council, Brussels, 28–29 January; also forthcoming in *Journal of European Integration*.

Golub, J. (2012) 'Cheap Dates and the Delusion of Gratification: Are Votes Sold or Traded in the EU Council of Ministers?', *Journal of European Public Policy*, Vol. 19, No. 2, pp. 141–60.

Häge, F. M. and Naurin, D. (2013) 'The Effect of Codecision on Council Decision-Making: Informalization, Politicization and Power', *Journal of European Public Policy*, Vol. 20, No. 7, pp. 953–71.

Hansen, R. and Gordon, J. C. (2014) 'Deficits, Democracy, and Demographics: Europe's Three Crises', *West European Politics*, Vol. 37, No. 6, pp. 1199–222.

Hosli, M. O., Mattila, M., and Uriot, M. (2011) 'Voting in the Council After the 2004 Enlargement: A Comparison of Old and New Member States', *Journal of Common Market Studies*, Vol. 49, No. 6, pp. 1249–70.

Kassim, H., Peterson, J., Bauer, M. W., Connolly, S., Dehousse, R., Hooghe, L., and Thompson, A. (2013) *The European Commission of the Twenty-First Century.* Oxford: Oxford University Press.

Leuffen, D., Rittberger, B., and Schimmelfennig, F. (2013) *Differentiated Integration: Explaining Variation in the European Union.* Basingstoke: Palgrave Macmillan.

Majone, G. (2014) *Rethinking the Union of Europe Post-Crisis: Has Integration Gone Too Far?* Cambridge: Cambridge University Press.

Nugent, N. (2017) *The Government and Politics of the European Union*, 8th edition. London: Palgrave Macmillan.

Nugent, N. and Rhinard, M. (2015) *The European Commission*, 2nd edition. London: Palgrave Macmillan.

Nugent, N. and Rhinard, M. (2016) 'Is the European Commission Really in Decline?', *Journal of Common Market Studies*, Vol. 54, No. 5, pp. 1199–215.

Rasmussen, A., Burns, C., and Reh, C. (eds) (2013) *Twenty Years After Codecision in the European Union.* Special Issue of *Journal of European Public Policy*, Vol. 20, No. 7.

Savage, J. D. and Verdun, A. (2016) 'Strengthening the European Commission's Budgetary and Economic Surveillance Capacity Since Greece and the Euro Area Crisis: A Study of Five Directorates-General', *Journal of European Public Policy*, Vol. 23, No. 1, pp. 101–18.

Verdun, A. S. (2015) 'A Historical Institutionalist Explanation of the EU's Responses to the Euro Area Financial Crisis', *Journal of European Public Policy*, Vol. 22, No. 3, pp. 219–37.

Chapter 10

The Legitimacy Challenge

CHRISTIAN SCHWEIGER

Introduction

The EU has been in permanent crisis mode since the onset of the global financial crisis in 2008. The crisis has accentuated the EU's declining legitimacy, which has increasingly manifested itself since the ratification of the Maastricht Treaty in the early 1990s. The failure of national governments to address the EU's legitimacy problem is increasingly coming to haunt them, with the crisis undermining public trust in the problem-solving capacity of EU decision-makers.

The public call for greater transparency and democratic accountability in the EU is getting louder, with the traditional *permissive consensus* giving way to what is now being described as a *constraining dissensus* in which citizens have started to scrutinize the EU's institutions and policies. Under crisis conditions the EU has shown a distinct lack of collective solidarity and engagement, with national governments pursuing a predominantly reactive and functional governance approach. This approach is to a large extent the continuation of the 'experimentalist' governance the EU has applied for some time in policy areas, such as social policy, where there has been strategic uncertainty and where member states have persistently opposed policy harmonization (Sabel and Zeitlin, 2008). National governments are becoming ever more 'risk-averse' in the face of mounting challenges (Pollack, Wallace, and Young, 2015: 473), which manifests itself in the tendency to defend perceived national interests and to determine red lines against deeper political integration. It has consequently become ever more difficult for the EU to swiftly reach collective decisions on key issues.

Instead, we witness a growing differentiation between member states in terms of vertical policy integration and an overall lack of strategic purpose in the EU's leadership. Leadership in the EU has been patchy and inconsistent as a result of continuous enlargement and the emergence of an ever-greater variety of national interests. EU governance has further been weakened by gradually moving some (mainly emerging) policy areas from the traditional Community method of collective decision-making and integration towards differentiated policy coordination and, most recently, increasingly towards 'intensive transgovernmentalism' (Wallace and Reh, 2015: 109). The latter refers to the tendency of groups of member states to deepen policy cooperation in selected policy areas, which frequently is negotiated and operated through intergovernmental arrangements outside of the EU's institutional framework. The transgovernmental governance mode, which is practised often in secretive backroom deals, has deepened the EU's legitimacy problem, as crucial policy decisions are made without public consultation and sufficient input from both the European Parliament (EP) and national parliaments.

This chapter analyses the different dimensions of the EU's legitimacy problem, which has deepened substantially under post-2008 crisis conditions and risks evolving into an existential credibility crisis.

From *Permissive* to *Constrained Consensus*: The EU's Increasingly Contested Legitimacy

The EU possesses formal legitimacy, which is reflected in the superiority of EU law over the domestic law of the member states. The Union is an international organization, but one with a unique structure in that although its member states maintain their own national legal systems they have agreed to the enforceable principle of the primacy of EU law. In practice this means that the EU's steadily evolving treaty structure represents the legal constitutional basis for the rule of supranational law, which is enforceable by the Court of Justice of the European Union (Edward and Lane, 2013: 7). At the same time, even six decades after the partial pooling of economic and political sovereignty was first initiated, the constituent member states of the EU remain essentially sovereign.

The EU hence ultimately derives its formal legitimacy from the member states' governments, which engage in supranational policy-making on the basis of national electoral mandates. Under the traditional *permissive consensus*, EU citizens were content with delegating the authority to negotiate supranational deals at intergovernmental summits to their national governments. Citizens showed sufficient trust in the problem-solving capacity of the resulting supranational policies and in the capacity of Community institutions to implement them effectively.

The *permissive consensus* under which the European public granted the EU legitimacy was consequently rational and passive in nature and lacked the public emotional affiliation with the integration process that neofunctionalist scholars had predicted would emerge as part of functional spillover from economic integration towards deeper political integration (Chryssochoou, 2009: 30). In practice, most national publics, and also many national political elites, have not been much

'Europeanized' in the sense of increasingly identifying with the EU's institutions, procedures, and policies in the way that neofunctionalists had predicted would occur as part of the political spillover of powers towards the 'new centre' of supranational institutions (Haas, 1968: 16; Schmitter, 1970: 867). The 'self-conscious sense of "European identity"' (Lindberg, 1965: 75), which was supposed to emerge as part of this process, has remained profoundly underdeveloped. The predominantly rational support of the *permissive consensus* for the EU was strongly output-orientated and accepted the neglect of direct input channels. This meant that as long as EU-level cooperation was considered to result in efficient policy output, the general public was content with being only indirectly represented through periodic national elections. There was also little public desire to engage in direct input channels. This allowed the EU to operate until the late 1980s on the basis of Jean Monnet's elite-driven collective bargaining method of integration. The output-orientated legitimacy bias of the EU resulted in a profound neglect of direct input mechanisms on supranational level decision-making, as was reflected in the long delay (until 1979) in making the EP directly elected.

The classic Community method created a governance system devoid of a substantial public discourse, direct participatory mechanisms, and parliamentary scrutiny. In essence, there were 'policies without politics' (Schmidt, 2006: 5). This was relatively unproblematic as long as the supranational institutional level had limited governing powers over the member states. However, with the expansion of the EU's legal acquis and the strengthening of the supervisory powers of supranational institutions over the implementation of EU policies in the member states this became increasingly problematic. The growth of EU governance powers and the transformation of domestic politics in some areas into an arena of 'politics without policies' (by which Schmidt refers to the growing number of policies that are decided at the EU level and are removed from national political arenas) have made it hard for national parliaments and governments to control 'changes in governance practices or policies that may clash with more nationally specific political, social and economic values' (ibid.: 24). For, as noted above, the EU has traditionally displayed weak input legitimacy, with very limited influence for national parliaments and the wider public on decision-making processes. This seemed unproblematic as long as the EU delivered effective governance which was fit for the purpose of helping to resolve domestic policy challenges. But, as the internal complexity of the EU's multi-level governance system grew over time, the EU's output-orientated legitimacy became increasingly constrained by an ever more diverse range of national interests and a growing set of actors.

The EU's multi-level governance system of 'shared and contested competence' (Marks, Hooghe, and Blank, 1996: 359) has made it difficult to react swiftly and decisively to internal and external challenges. The lack of problem-solving capacity in central areas of public concern such as employment, education, housing, immigration, and security has contributed to the gradual erosion of the permissive consensus. As the EU has failed to deliver, citizens have increasingly questioned the legitimacy of national governments to make decisions in intergovernmental bargains on their behalf. The result has been the gradual transition from the permissive consensus towards a *constrained consensus*, under which EU level decision-making has become politicized at the domestic level. Since Maastricht, national political elites can no longer take it for granted that domestic public opinion supports their European policy strategies. Instead they 'must look over their shoulders when negotiating European issues' and expect to be sanctioned at the next election if they fail to meet the expectations of the electorate (Hooghe and Marks, 2009: 5).

The constrained consensus has come with a significant level of euroscepticism, which so far has not generally involved much questioning of the purpose of the EU itself. Instead, the politicization of the EU in the domestic political discourse has occurred in the form of an 'inside' euroscepticism, where voters have increasingly scrutinized concrete EU policy areas, institutions, and decision-making procedures, and increasingly have expected better results from them (Bruter, 2012: 26).

The European Parliament and the Lack of *Social Legitimacy*

The decline in the EU's output-orientated legitimacy has substantially contributed to its overall lack of social legitimacy. Deep-seated value-based public support for the EU's institutions and policies in their post-Maastricht shape has been profoundly lacking (Weiler, 1999: 80). Overall, the majority of the public has either an indifferent or even a negative opinion of the EU. Since the onset of the eurozone crisis, around 40 per cent of the general public in the member states have neither a positive nor a negative opinion of the EU, while around 30 per cent are outright hostile to it. In the latest Eurobarometer figures available at the time of this writing (September 2016), in May 2016, 38 per cent of the public in the EU-28 member states expressed a neutral opinion towards the EU while 27 per cent said that they were 'totally hostile' to the Union. Only 34 per cent expressed a 'totally positive' view of the EU (Figure 10.1).

As for national polling figures, in many member states positive attitudes towards the EU are considerably lower than the EU-28 average. Notable cases of low percentages of positive opinions about the EU are

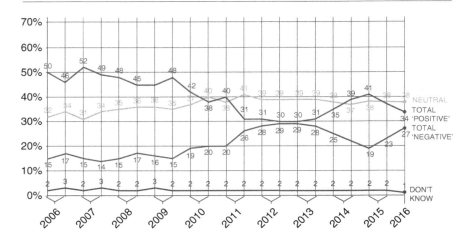

Figure 10.1   *The image of the European Union – trend: 2006–16*
Source: European Commission (2016a: 15)

Greece (16 per cent), Cyprus (27 per cent), Slovakia (30 per cent), the UK (31 per cent), and even Germany (29 per cent). Negative opinion towards the EU is highest in Greece (51 per cent), Cyprus (41 per cent), and the UK (36 per cent), while the strongest levels of indifference towards the Union are found in Latvia (49 per cent), Slovenia (46 per cent), Estonia (47 per cent), Finland (44 per cent), and Spain (44 per cent). The highest percentage of totally positive attitudes towards the EU were recorded in Ireland (58 per cent), Belgium (51 per cent), Poland (47 per cent), and Luxembourg (45 per cent), with the former two being the only countries having a slim majority of the public expressing a positive opinion of the EU. The negative figures in Greece are no surprise given the role the EU has played as an enforcer of austerity in the country. The eurozone crisis and the perception of the EU as a transfer union have also had a significant impact on public opinion in Germany. In Ireland, on the other hand, the initial hostility towards the EU's intervention has subsided. It is also interesting to note that the Polish public stands at odds with the eurosceptic attitude of the Law and Justice government led by Beata Szydło.

Co-decision-maker with limited legitimacy

The EU's lack of social legitimacy makes it problematic for the tendency of political elites to complacently refer to the Union's formal legitimacy. In this respect the steady increase in co-decision powers of the EP is frequently presented as evidence for sufficient input legitimacy in the EU. It is nevertheless obvious that the public does not consider the EP to be a sufficiently efficient operator in scrutinizing and influencing strategic policy-making in the EU and as such an adequate representative of citizens' interests.

The Lisbon Treaty introduced a new provision requiring national governments in the Council 'to take into account the elections to the European Parliament' when proposing the candidate for the position of President of the European Commission. The Treaty did not, however, specify how precisely this should be implemented in practice. The political groups in the EP decided to take advantage of the new Treaty provision by putting forward candidates in the run-up to the May 2014 elections, which acquired the German term *Spitzenkandidaten* (with reference to the nomination of party candidates for the office of German Chancellor). The *Spitzenkandidaten* of the various political groups in the EP for the election were Jean-Claude Juncker (of the centre-right European People's Party), Martin Schultz (of the centre-left Party of European Socialists), Guy Verhofstadt (Alliance of Liberals and Democrats for Europe), Ska Keller and José Bové (European Greens), and Alexis Tspiras (European Left). Ultimately the campaign focused on Juncker and Schulz as the candidates for the two largest groups. The *Spitzenkandidaten* system undoubtedly had a positive short-term effect on the public perception of the EU. This can be seen in the increase in positive attitudes towards the EU in mid-2014 shown in Figure 10.1. As Figure 10.2 shows, the *Spitzenkandidaten* system also temporarily seemed to ease the negative public perception of the EU's democratic deficit. The efforts of the EU to give the public a greater say over the matter of the Commission President by boosting the influence of the Parliament on this important matter made a difference, at least temporarily, in the public view of their input into EU-level decision-making. (On the *Spitzenkandidaten* system, see Corbett et al., 2016.)

The special Eurobarometer conducted in the run-up to the May 2014 elections shows that in each member state a clear majority of 76 per cent of citizens in the EU-28 (from the 64 per cent recorded in Spain to 91 per cent in Malta) considered the role of the EP in running the EU to be 'totally important' (Eurobarometer, 2013: 27). In contrast, only 32 per cent of citizens across the EU considered the EP's role to have been strengthened over the past decade. This explains why the EU was unable to reverse the continuous downward trend in terms of the level of participation in EP elections. The 2014 election continued the steady trend in the decline of voter turnout since the first EP elections in June 1979, when around 61 per cent of voters participated. In 2014 the figure stood at only 42.6 per cent, a further slight drop from 42.9 per cent in 2009 (European Parliament, 2014a). In 14 EU member states turnout did not

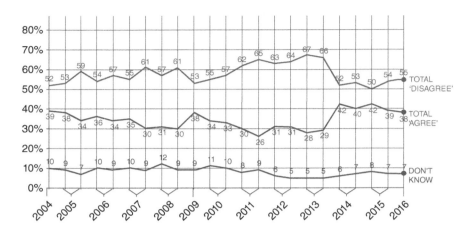

Figure 10.2 *My voice counts in the EU – trend 2004–16*
Source: European Commission (2016a: 17)

even reach the EU average, with the lowest turnout recorded in Slovakia with a staggeringly low 13 per cent (European Parliament, 2014b).

The fact that EP elections tend to still be regarded as second order elections, where many voters either abstain or cast a protest vote against their national government (Hix and Marsh, 2011), stems from voters' overall lack of trust in the EP's capacity to effectively represent their interests. In the Eurobarometer poll conducted immediately after the May 2014 election, a majority of 54 per cent of voters expressed the view that the EP ignores the concerns of the public, which is a marked decline from the post-2009 election survey, where only 41 per cent expressed this view (European Parliament, 2014b: 58).

Crisis Conditions and Germany's Informal EU Presidency

The decline of public trust in the EP can be explained by the fact that the period between 2009 and 2014 was dominated by the management of the eurozone sovereign debt crisis. In these circumstances, the EU operated under Germany's semi-hegemonic leadership (Bulmer and Paterson, 2013; Paterson, 2011). Cautiously, but eventually determinately, driven by German Chancellor Angela Merkel, the EU concentrated on the implementation of functional policy mechanisms which were orientated towards restoring market confidence in the eurozone through the implementation of Germany's ordoliberal economic principles (Bulmer, 2014: 1253; Funk, 2015: 350). The eurozone and internal market governance reforms were conducted in a de-politicized atmosphere where fundamental decisions were frequently taken in intergovernmental backroom deals with only erratic involvement of the EU's institutions (Fabbrini, 2015: 29).

The governance mode applied by Merkel was a form of 'intensive transgovernmentalism'. Under this mode, national governments play a central role in setting the agenda while the Commission and the EP are marginalized. Transgovernmental decision-making, however, does not necessarily take place within the collective framework of the Council, but frequently in informal settings outside of the EU's institutional framework (Wallace and Reh, 2015: 109). To a large extent this is an attempt to circumvent the limitations of the 'joint decision trap' of the traditional Community method, where decision-making is concentrated on achieving unanimous (and over time increasingly qualified majority) consent in the Council, with the Commission acting as the initiator and coordinator of policy decisions (Nugent, 2010: 295; Scarf, 1988: 244; Wallace and Reh, 2015: 99). The circumstances of the eurozone crisis moved Germany into the prime leadership position and allowed Chancellor Merkel to establish selective and informal intensive transgovernmentalism as the new permanent governance mode inside the eurozone and also to some extent in the wider EU. Anthony Giddens has branded this governance mode, which is based on shifting and informal intergovernmental leadership coalitions operating largely behind the scenes, as 'EU2', as opposed to the classic Community method of 'EU1'. 'EU2' has increasingly taken the form of an informal permanent German presidency of the EU, with the German Chancellor determining strategic decisions in a presidential manner with a cabinet of selected fellow national leaders, the European Central Bank (ECB) and also the International Monetary Fund (IMF). Giddens warns of the dangers of this governance mode as it undermines the collective spirit of the EU and deepens the existing divisions between member states (Giddens, 2014: 19).

The informal German presidency of the EU and its selective transgovernmental bargaining, however, has not only undermined solidarity in the EU. As importantly, it has represented a significant retrograde step in terms of democratic accountability and legitimacy, with selective transgovernmental governance having substantially weakened the EP's role as a co-decision-maker. The revised post-crisis policy agenda and the new coordinating mechanisms in the internal market and the eurozone have substantially strengthened the influence of the Commission at the expense of the Parliament which has remained in the role of a cautious backseat driver (Neutel, 2015: 173). The Commission has also been strengthened by the new coordinating annual policy cycle – the European Semester – which was introduced under the 2010 *Europe*

2020 Strategy and puts the Commission in the position of supervisory agent over national budgets and macroeconomic policies such as employment, education and training, and research and development. The annual national economic reform programmes and stability and convergence programmes are determined in direct negotiations between the national governments, the Commission, and the collective representation of member states in the Council. The EP can request feedback from the Commission or the Council at any time during the process, but is not a co-decision-maker with veto powers in the annual cycle of policy coordination (European Commission, 2014).

The strengthening of the role of the Commission and the ECB and the parallel marginalization of the EP is also obvious under the eurozone Six-Pack governance reforms, which are aimed at turning the EU into a stability union, as well as under the emerging banking union. The latter has shown the ability of both the Commission and the ECB to increasingly shape the post-crisis policy agenda (Epstein and Rhodes, 2016). This is mostly noticeable through the activities of the unelected Troika which consists of representatives from the European Commission, the ECB, and the IMF. The Troika, which operates beyond the realm of public scrutiny, effectively tries to implement the German concept of the eurozone as an ordoliberal stability union on the basis of the stricter budgetary rules determined by the Six-Pack, especially the revised Stability and Growth Pact and the 2012 intergovernmental Fiscal Compact (Schweiger, 2015: 41).

Reforming the Governance of the Eurozone and 'the Suspension of Democracy'

The Troika's operation and its exclusive scrutiny by the Council have deepened public scepticism towards how the EU is governed. Its position as an unelected technocratic agent, which was given the mandate to overrule national governments and parliaments in the southern European sovereign-debt crisis countries, has increased a widespread perception of there being a 'suspension of democracy' (Giannone, 2015: 115). So, too, did the efforts in 2010–12 of significant pressure being applied on Greece and Italy by Chancellor Merkel, French President Sarkozy, and Commission President Barroso to accept the installation of unelected technocratic governments with the aim of implementing austerity policies. This was the result of a strategy that promoted the replication at the national level of technocratic governance at the EU level for those countries that suffered from sovereign-debt problems and were expected to seek support from the European Financial Stability Facility (EFSF) and later the European Stability Mechanism (ESM) (Hopkin,

2012). This 'coercive Europeanisation' (Sepos, 2016: 48) resulted in the unprecedented installation of unelected technocratic caretaker governments in Greece under ex-banker Lucas Papademos (2011–12) and in Italy under former European Commissioner Mario Monti (2011–13). In both countries the public responded to the coercive Europeanization approach by subsequently strongly supporting populist eurosceptic parties (Syriza in Greece and the Five Star Movement in Italy) that promised to ease the burden of austerity and to limit the influence of the EU on domestic politics.

Greece and Italy show how the sovereign-debt crisis has split the eurozone between the core of economically stronger northern European creditor countries spearheaded by Germany and the predominantly southern periphery of debtor countries (Hall, 2012: 357). The uneven power balance has allowed the creditor core to determine the post-crisis policy agenda and has pushed the southern periphery into an undesirable dependent and passive policy-taker position (Laffan, 2016: 31–2). This has massively contributed to the growth of 'inside euroscepticism' (citizens increasingly scrutinizing individual policy areas without completely withdrawing their support for further integration – Bruter, 2012) in the affected countries, which explains the extremely low percentage of citizens who consider their voice counts in the EU. Only 16 per cent of the public in Greece and Cyprus thought this in early 2016, 23 per cent in Italy, 31 per cent in Spain, and 34 per cent in Portugal (European Commission, 2016a: 18). This is combined with a distinctive lack of feeling of public ownership of the EU's post-crisis agenda. Figure 10.3 shows that the perception of the economic and welfare reforms that are driven by the EU is far from positive in most of the 28 member states, but is particularly low in the southern periphery eurozone crisis countries (Cyprus, Greece, Italy, Portugal, Spain).

The percentages presented in Figure 10.3 mirror the public hostility across the wider EU towards reforms that are perceived as undermining the traditional European social model with its focus on social cohesion. Since the establishment of the Lisbon reform agenda at the beginning of the twenty-first century, the EU has struggled to convince the public of the *knowledge economy* principle which promotes individual responsibility, labour market flexibility, targeted investment in education and training, and means-tested welfare state spending (Soete, 2006). The core idea of the approach has been increasingly challenged by reality as the notion that employment prevents poverty and through education and training individuals are able to succeed in making a sustainable living in the more competitive environment of globalization has not materialized (Goetschy, 2015). The increase in the number of people who are registered as employed but are classified as being at risk of poverty has especially fundamentally undermined the output legitimacy of the EU's

	Labour market	Reforms in other specific areas	Education systems	Social security system	Taxation	Pension system	Market reforms, as in telecom, gas/electricity (e.g. opening sectors for free competition, privatization)	Reforms in general	Don't know
EURO AREA	17	12	8	5	4	4	4	3	57
BE	15	15	9	8	5	5	5	4	55
DE	29	8	13	8	6	7	4	4	44
EE	4	7	10	4	8	2	5	4	65
IE	18	24	21	6	9	2	5	4	31
EL	2	9	2	8	4	2	3	2	76
ES	8	18	3	4	1	2	2	2	66
FR	10	14	6	7	5	4	4	2	63
IT	22	5	4	1	1	2	4	3	63
CY	6	16	6	1	6	2	3	4	63
LV	5	13	10	6	5	2	6	2	62
LT	17	9	11	7	11	6	11	8	46
LU	19	29	16	11	9	7	9	11	40
MT	26	18	23	10	3	5	10	5	30
NL	16	19	11	7	7	4	9	4	44
AT	10	14	10	6	7	4	4	3	56
PT	4	22	7	8	4	2	1	2	64
SI	13	7	6	7	7	6	5	9	54
SK	30	11	16	12	12	9	4	10	30
FI	10	11	5	4	6	4	6	2	61

Highest percentage per country | Lowest percentage per country

Highest percentage per item | Lowest percentage per item

Figure 10.3   *Evaluation of sectoral reforms*

Source: European Commission (2015a: 75)

economic and social reform agenda under the Lisbon Strategy and its successor Europe 2020 (European Commission, 2016b). This was echoed in a report issued early in the eurozone crisis by the former Internal Market Commissioner and Italian Prime Minister, Mario Monti, on the single market policy framework. The report warned that the lack of national resources to invest in education, training, and welfare risked undermining the social dimension of the single market in favour of free market competition (Monti, 2010: 26).

Muddling Through the Growing Crisis–Legitimacy Gap?

Many of the sentiments expressed in Monti's report capture the wider narrative of public disillusionment with the EU's economic crisis management, which allows eurosceptics on the left and right of the political spectrum to portray the EU as an elitist organization that prioritizes market confidence over ensuring democratic legitimacy and gaining public confidence. The financial crisis has reinforced the EU's tendency to pursue a functional economic governance approach which avoids the active determination of a long-term political vision. Instead, the EU has passively adapted its policies in line with the changing demands of the markets in a frantic, ad hoc, reactive manner. EU policy-making has hence been driven by external events rather than proactively aspiring to shape them – in essence the reactive 'experimentalist governance' that became increasingly the standard governance mode in the EU over the past decade (Sabel and Zeitlin, 2008: 280). The joint decision trap in the Council has frequently resulted in stalemate or at best lowest denominator consensual policy decisions. As the EU has expanded and the variety of national interests has grown, it has become difficult, and in some cases practically impossible, to achieve unanimous decisions. The continuous gradual expansion of qualified majority voting (QMV) by successive rounds of treaty reform was supposed to ensure that the EU would remain functional with a growing set of members. Over time, however, it became obvious that even QMV decisions were difficult to achieve once the EU had reached double-digit membership figures. The change in the Lisbon Treaty from the previous (triple majority) QMV system to the double-majority hurdle – which requires a minimum of 55 per cent of member states in favour, representing at least 65 per cent of the EU population, to achieve qualified majority decisions – attempts to strike a balance between the interests of the smaller and larger member states. In practice, the double-majority requirement has, however, made it harder to reach decisions by QMV (Hix and Hoyland, 2011).

Variable leadership geometry and suboptimal governance

The need for the larger member states to form coalitions to push through or block QMV decisions has also reinforced the tendency for the EU to be led by a *variable leadership geometry*. This set-up usually involves the six largest member states, but also sees them forming leadership coalitions in different configurations depending on the policy area. Germany and France continue to play a central role in this configuration, but they are no longer as able to shape the agenda as they used to be. The joint decision trap of the traditional Community method has become progressively less effective with each enlargement. As the variety of national interests has grown, institutional arrangements and policy outcomes have become increasingly suboptimal. In many cases, they have been neither adequate to tackle the scope of major internal and external challenges nor can they be implemented swiftly enough to prevent the deepening of adverse effects (Goetz, 2009: 208). This is the result of the persistent tendency of national governments to defend the red lines of their national interests and to pursue zero-sum bargains (Scharpf, 2006: 849). Especially under deepening crisis conditions, the European Council has failed to 'provide the Union with the necessary impetus for its development and ... [to] define the general political directions and priorities thereof' (Treaty on European Union, article 15) as envisaged in the Lisbon Treaty. Instead, the European Council has become a theatre for intergovernmental wrangling and delayed decision-making. Overall it has represented progressively less the central decision-making as the EU has increasingly switched towards intensive and selective transgovernmentalist (often backroom) deals.

The EU's declining problem-solving capacity has fundamentally undermined the output-based legitimacy of the formerly permissive consensus and contributed towards the emergence of the inside euroscepticism of what now has to be regarded as an increasingly constrained and potentially declining public consensus. The EU's complex 'fuzzy' institutional architecture and procedures (Schmitter, 2001: 6) and the tendency of governments to collectively *muddle through* internal and external challenges have resulted in profound public scepticism towards the EU's institutional capacity and political ability to protect its citizens from 'negative externalities that result from interdependence' (Innerarity, 2015: 185). In essence, these represent the various challenges that emerge from globalization. The financial crisis and the subsequent eurozone crisis were the first major systemic test for the EU's institutional architecture: a test it has been unable to pass without preventing profound economic, political, and social divisions among the member states (Chang, 2016: 31).

The post-crisis functional economic governance architecture of the EU has failed to consider the necessity to accompany the streamlining of economic governance with democratic scrutiny mechanisms capable of ensuring that decisions remain transparent and can be challenged as part of a process of multi-level interest consultation. The result is the perception of the EU as undemocratic, elite-driven, and orientated towards the interests of big business and finance. This has resulted in a 'crisis–legitimacy' gap where the public fails to detect vision, purpose, and solidarity in the EU. Citizens feel increasingly powerless and unable to change the policy agenda which they consider to 'neither promote nor reflect citizen interests or preferences' (Murray and Longo, 2015:

65, 68). In a climate where trust in politics, especially at the national level, is at an all-time low, this has created a breeding ground for the hard eurosceptic brand of populist politics that is now becoming significant in several EU states.

Rising populism: The UK case

The eurosceptic brand of populist politics just mentioned was witnessed in the most dramatic fashion in the run-up to the June 2016 EU membership referendum in the UK. The referendum emerged against the background of growing domestic British concerns about the future of national and especially parliamentary sovereignty in an EU that seemed to be set on autopilot towards deeper political integration under German leadership. Chancellor Merkel's mantra that the functional policy mechanisms she had pushed through in the eurozone and the internal market areas would be 'without alternative' was met with fundamental scepticism in the UK (Bastasin, 2012: 173). Large sections of the British political elite and the public questioned the need to engage in 'substantial further institutional and policy engineering' in the EU (Usherwood, 2015: 11). Prime Minister Cameron pinpointed these concerns when he vetoed the incorporation of the Fiscal Compact in the EU's treaty structure in 2012. He justified this step with the need to prevent the EU's gradual encroachment on national policy-making autonomy in budgetary and macroeconomic matters (Schweiger, 2016: 67–8).

At the heart of Cameron's demands for the renegotiation of the UK's membership of the EU was therefore the demand to determine safeguards against deeper political integration and to 'strengthen democratic legitimacy' (HM Government, 2013). Cameron, however, still struggled to convince the sceptical British public of his argument that the country would be stronger if it remained inside the EU, even though he had been promised by other EU leaders, as part of the membership renegotiation deal, an opt-out from the principle of *ever closer Union* and the introduction of a red card system for national parliaments. A principal reason for Cameron's lack of success was the dominance of the migration issue in the referendum campaign, which the Vote Leave campaign exploited in a populist manner (see Chapter 5).

By the time the referendum was announced, the EU was experiencing an unprecedented migration crisis during which Germany's semi-hegemonic leadership style again became evident. Merkel put substantial pressure on the rest of the EU to accept a binding refugee distribution quota system which she argued would be a 'moral imperative' (Wagstyl, 2016). This was categorically refused by the UK and also central and eastern European states. Merkel also initiated a bilateral agreement between the EU and Turkey, which remains controversial because it promised, among other things, to accelerate Turkish accession to the EU in return for a refugee exchange between the EU and Turkey (see Chapter 6).

The refugee quotas and the Turkey deal gained significant prominence in the final stages of the British EU referendum campaign, during which the Vote Leave campaign managed to convince a slim majority of the British public that the German strategy would result in substantial uncontrolled immigration and the realistic prospect of swift Turkish EU membership.

Merkelism and weakening output legitimacy

The eurozone crisis and the subsequent migration crisis have shown that the EU remains in the firm grip of 'Merkelism', a governance strategy which fundamentally represents the intensification of the *muddling through* approach which the EU had adopted for some time even before the recent crises emerged. 'Merkelism' feeds itself exclusively from Germany's economic dominance. The German Chancellor's approach is predominantly reactive and often hesitant, but almost always uncompromising and eventually output-orientated (Meiers, 2015: 139). The negative effects of growing internal political and economic disunity and the marginalization of collective governance in the Council have been widely disregarded in the process as the EU concentrates on implementing the means to achieve desired functional policy results. The Merkel strategy has also resulted in the prioritization of immediate crisis management and the neglect of the long-term strategic development of key policy areas, such as foreign affairs, defence, and security. The EU's ability to manage crisis in its near abroad such as in Libya, Ukraine, and Syria has therefore remained disjointed and weak. The dependence on the North Atlantic Treaty Organization (NATO) as the safeguard for the EU's external security is stronger than ever. Even the transatlantic alliance is however increasingly stretched as member states cut defence spending and Washington complains about the persistent lack of military burden-sharing (Schake, 2012: 24). Overall the EU's external profile remains frequently incoherent, even though the institutionalized external representation was strengthened in the Lisbon Treaty through the creation of a reinvigorated High Representative for Foreign Affairs and a supporting External Action Service. As in the area of economic and social affairs, an obvious gap between the expectations of the public and the actual capabilities of the EU has emerged which can no longer be pasted over by official declarations of intent. The weaknesses of the EU in dealing with growing external security challenges – from migration and terrorism to military conflicts in the wider neighbourhood – is only too obvious. Much too often the EU wavers between incoherence and impotence when having to deal with external challenges (Smith, 2011: 190).

This causes a major problem for the EU's output legitimacy, as the public clearly desires greater coherent action in the area of external affairs. Figure 10.4 shows that, in spite of the growth of euroscepticism across the EU, the majority of the public would like to see the deeper political integration of external affairs. These figures are evidence of the 'inside nature' of the euroscepticism that has emerged where (as explained above) citizens pay greater attention to individual policy areas and express their support or opposition to the deepening of these.

Tackling the Legitimacy Deficit

The emergence of new and persistent crises has pushed the EU's legitimacy problem closer towards a dangerous tipping point, which could eventually become a point of no return if national governments continue to try to muddle their way through. The combination of the erosion of public trust in the EU's policy-making authority and the obvious lack of democratic scrutiny of intergovernmental elite-level decisions risks becoming a permanent systemic credibility crisis, where the public begins to question the overall purpose of the EU's existence. If this occurs, the currently widespread euroscepticism will most likely transform from the predominant inside euroscepticism towards a deep-seated and harder-line outside euroscepticism, where citizens no longer just

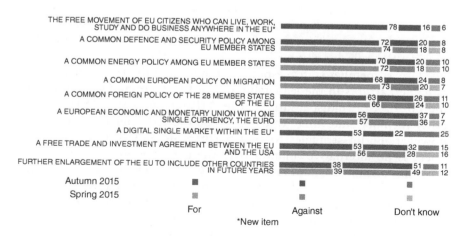

Figure 10.4 *Support for European policies*
Source: European Commission (2015b: 4)

scrutinize individual policy areas but question the integration process as a whole and withdraw their support for membership of the EU (Bruter, 2012; Harrison and Bruter, 2015). Outside euroscepticism is already growing in a number of countries and it has most prominently emerged in the UK, where the result has been the decision of the majority of the British public to leave the EU. Support for political parties that promote a hard-line eurosceptic agenda aimed at destroying the EU, similar to the agenda of the United Kingdom Independence Party (UKIP), has already grown in many member states in response to the uninspiring and technocratic governance of the EU under German semi-hegemony. Fundamental euroscepticism in response to Merkelism is even on the rise in Germany, where the eurosceptic Alternative für Deutschland (AfD) has made substantial gains in regional elections. The AfD originally emerged as an anti-euro party which was focused on opposition to Merkel's eurozone crisis management. More recently, however, it has moved further to the right and now attracts support on the basis of an anti-immigration and anti-Islam agenda, which is closely aligned to the Pegida protest movement. In France, the leader of the far-right Front National, Marine Le Pen, has promised to hold a public referendum on EU membership should her party win national elections. Hard-line euroscepticism is also substantially on the rise in central and eastern Europe, where Merkel's insistence on refugee quotas plays into the hands of anti-immigration parties on the far-right (Magone, 2015).

It will be difficult for the EU to reverse this trend under persistent crisis conditions, which have weakened its internal unity and solidarity. The lingering economic crisis has heightened existing divisions between the member states and resulted in the refocusing of national governments on domestic affairs and national interests.

In addition to its legitimacy crisis, the EU is hence suffering from a noticeable leadership crisis. Germany adopted its current informal presidential role involuntarily as a result of the failure of the other five largest member states, especially France and the UK, to act as sustainable partners in the leadership of the EU. Germany will remain in the position of 'indispensable partner' (Paterson, 2014: 181) for any other member state that wants to shape the EU's agenda. Currently, however, Berlin struggles to find partners in leadership as Merkel's 'there is no alternative' mantra over the eurozone and the migration crisis has alienated traditionally close partners such as France, Poland, and the other central and eastern European member states. Visionary, accountable, and proactive leadership will nevertheless be the essential precondition for the ability of the EU to resolve the growing weakness in its output legitimacy. Germany as the EU's semi-hegemon is clearly too overburdened to manage this unilaterally and is therefore in urgent need of partners in leadership who can steer the EU back from intensive transgovernmentalism towards collective and transparent decision-making, which is more orientated towards strategic policy output than towards ad hoc functional crisis resolution. The EU will also not be able to rely exclusively on its formal legitimacy and will have to find ways to enhance its underdeveloped social legitimacy. This requires a combination of more efficient strategic policy output and improved channels for the general public to influence EU-level decisions.

A further (and, in practice, unlikely) expansion of the EP's powers will not be sufficient to bridge the growing input legitimacy gap in the EU. As the only directly elected institution in the EU, the EP fulfils an important function as a co-decision-maker that holds the Commission and the Council to account. The EP has, however, for a long time been a 'bridge that is almost devoid of traffic' as it has failed to engage civil societies in the EU (Habermas, 2013). The EU will therefore have to find more innovative ways to engage the public. As part of this, it will have to take into account the role of national parliaments, which continue to remain the central focus of national civil societies (Weiler, Haltern, and Mayer, 1995: 13).

In addition to the stronger involvement of national parliaments in the EU's political process, the introduction of direct participatory mechanisms will have to be orientated towards reducing the growing distance between citizens and elite-level decision-making. The Citizens Initiative introduced under Lisbon has in this respect turned out to be of very limited value, as it has not resulted in any substantial civil society input into the EU's policy-making process. Only three civil society legislative initiatives, which require the backing of at least one million signatures collected from across a minimum of seven member states, have actually reached the final stage of being officially considered by the Commission (Anglmayer, 2015). The Citizens Initiative has consequently failed to bridge the gap between civil societies and the EU institutional level, which is reflected in the lack of interest of the general public in the initiative. Across the EU only 27 per cent of the public express interest in using the initiative (European Commission, 2015c). More direct public engagement with EU affairs could potentially be enhanced through the introduction of occasional public referenda on major policy decisions, but these inevitably come with the well-known risks of misinformation and populist manipulation.

The EU seems to have started to grasp the full scale of the legitimacy problem, which essentially boils down to the growing lack of public support for the way it organizes its political process. This is shown in the recommendations made by the 2015 Five Presidents' Report on the eurozone. In their joint report, the Presidents of the Commission, European Council, Parliament, ECB and Eurogroup acknowledged that under crisis conditions the EU had neglected the democratic accountability of its decisions. The Presidents called on the EU to work towards instilling 'more dialogue, greater mutual trust and a stronger capacity to act collectively' by implementing mechanisms which ensure the sustained involvement of the European Parliament and national parliaments in a reformed European Semester annual coordinative policy cycle (European Commission, 2015d: 17). These and other related proposals could offer the basis for a more fundamental reform of the EU's governance process with the integrated consultation of civil society representatives in the European Semester and other policy areas. However, the EU will in the end only be able to resolve its profound legitimacy challenge if it finds the collective resolve to develop its governance towards a genuine system of multi-level interest consultation and representation, which stretches from the elite institutional level down towards the micro-level of grassroots civil society in the member states.

Conclusions

The EU's legitimacy crisis has its roots in the post-Maastricht evolvement of the EU towards a multi-level system of governance, which has weak input legitimacy and declining output legitimacy. Both have, over time, become increasingly intrinsically connected, as under the constrained consensus citizens expect EU policies to reflect their interests (Sternberg, 2015). Interlocked input and output legitimacy has resulted in the public constraining the traditional permissive consensus and scrutinizing the EU's policies in terms of their overall efficiency.

The EU's legitimacy crisis has deepened in recent years as governments have tried to escape the joint decision trap in the Council by engaging in intensive transgovernmental bargaining, which has prioritized swift policy output but substantially neglected public consultation mechanisms. As many recent policy decisions have been substantially controversial, they have resulted in growing overall public scepticism towards the EU. In the future, it will therefore be inevitable for the EU to concentrate on combining effective collective governance with enhanced and sustained public consultation beyond the currently available mechanisms.

References

Anglmayer, I. (2015) 'Implementation of the European Citizens' Initiative: The Experience of the First Three Years', Brussels: European Parliamentary Research Service, available at http://www.europarl.europa.eu/EPRS/EPRS_IDAN_536343_Implementation_of_the_European_Citizens_Initiative.pdf, date accessed 18 August 2016.

Bastasin, C. (2012) *Saving Europe: How National Politics Nearly Destroyed the Euro.* Washington, DC: Brookings Institution Press.

Brunazzo, M. and Della Sala, V. (2016) 'Italy between *transformismo* and transformation.' In J. M. Magone, B. Laffan, and C. Schweiger (eds), *Core–Periphery Relations in the European Union: Power and Conflict in a Dualist Political Economy.* Abingdon: Routledge, pp. 216–28.

Bruter, M. (2012) 'The Difficult Emergence of a European People.' In J. Hayward and R. Wurzel (eds), *European Disunion: Between Sovereignty and Solidarity.* Basingstoke: Palgrave Macmillan, pp. 17–31.

Bulmer, S. (2014) 'Germany and the Eurozone Crisis: Between Hegemony and Domestic Politics', *West European Politics*, Vol. 37, No. 6, pp. 1244–63.

Bulmer, S. and Paterson, W. E. (2013) 'Germany as the EU's reluctant hegemon? Of economic strength and political constraints', *Journal of European Public Policy*, Vol. 20, No. 10, pp. 1387–405.

Chang, M. (2016) *Economic and Monetary Union.* Basingstoke: Palgrave Macmillan.

Chryssochoou, D. N. (2009) *Theorizing European Integration,* 2nd edition. London and New York: Routledge.

Corbett, R., Jacobs, F., and Neville, D. (eds) (2016) *The European Parliament,* 9th edition. London: John Harper.

Edward, D. and Lane, R. (2013) *European Union Law.* Cheltenham: Edward Elgar.

Epstein, R. A. and Rhodes, M. (2016) 'The Political Dynamics behind Europe's New Banking Union', *West European Politics,* Vol. 39, No. 3, pp. 415–37.

Eurobarometer (2013) *One Year to go to the 2014 European Elections: Analytical Overview,* December, http://www.europarl.europa.eu/pdf/eurobarometre/2013/election3/SyntheseEB 795ParlemetreEN.pdf.

European Commission (2014) *European Semester: Who does what – European institutions and bodies,* http://ec.europa.eu/europe2020/who- does-what/eu-institutions/index_en.htm, date accessed 17 August 2016.

European Commission (2015a) *Flash Eurobarometer 429: The euro area,* November, http://ec.europa.eu/economy_finance/articles/pdf/fl_429_en.pdf, date accessed 18 August 2016.

European Commission (2015b) *Standard Eurobarometer 84 Autumn: European's views on the priorities of the European Union,* http://ec.europa.eu/COMMFrontOffice/PublicOpinion/index.cfm/ResultDoc/download/DocumentKy/7244, date accessed 18 August 2016.

European Commission (2015c) *Standard Eurobarometer 83 Spring: European Citizenship,* http://ec.europa.eu/COMMFrontOffice/PublicOpinion/index.cfm/ResultDoc/download/DocumentKy/68530, date accessed 18 August 2016.

European Commission (2015d) '*The Five Presidents' Report: Completing Europe's Economic and Monetary Union*', https://ec.europa.eu/priorities/publications/five-presidents-report-completing-europes-economic-and-monetary-union_en, date accessed 18 August 2016.

European Commission (2016a) *Standard Eurobarometer 85: Spring 2016*, July, http://ec.europa.eu/COMMFrontOffice/PublicOpinion/index.cfm/ResultDoc/download/DocumentKy/74265, date accessed 18 August 2016.

European Commission (2016b) 'In Work at Risk of Poverty Rate', http://ec.europa.eu/eurostat/web/income-and-living-conditions/data/main-tables#, date accessed 18 August 2016.

European Parliament (2014a), *Results of the 2014 European elections: Turnout*, http://www.europarl.europa.eu/elections2014- results/en/turnout.html, date accessed 16 August 2016.

European Parliament (2014b) *2014 post-election survey: European elections 2014 Analytical Overview*, http://www.europarl.europa.eu/pdf/eurobarometre/2014/post/post_2014_survey_analitical_overview_en.pdf, date accessed 16 August 2016.

European Union (2009) *Treaty of Lisbon*, http://eur-lex.europa.eu/legal- content/en/TXT/?uri=CELEX:12007L/TXT, date accessed 16 August 2016.

Fabbrini, S. (2015) 'The Euro Crisis and Its Constitutional Implications.' In S. Champeau, C. Closa, D. Innerarity, and M. Poaires Maduro (eds), *The Future of Europe: Democracy, Legitimacy and Justice after the Euro Crisis*. London and New York: Rowman & Littlefield, pp. 19–36.

Funk, L. (2015) 'The German approach to finance in the European context.' In S. Colvin and M. Taplin (eds), *The Routledge Handbook of German Politics and Culture*. London and New York: Routledge, pp. 349–72.

Giannone, D. (2015) 'Suspending Democracy? The Governance of the EU's Political and Economic Crisis of Neoliberal Restructuring.' In K. Demetriou (ed), *The European Union in Crisis: Explorations in Representation and Democratic Legitimacy*. London: Springer, pp. 101–22.

Giddens, A. (2014) *Turbulent and Mighty Continent: What Future for Europe?* Cambridge: Polity Press.

Goetschy, J. (2015) 'Social Europe.' In N. Witzleb, A. Martinez Arranz, and P. Winand (eds), *The European Union and Global Engagement: Institutions. Policies and Challenges*. Cheltenham: Edward Elgar, pp. 122–37.

Goetz, K. H. (2009) 'How does the EU tick? Five propositions on political time', *Journal of European Public Policy*, Vol. 16, No. 2, pp. 202–20.

Haas, E. B. (1968) *The Uniting of Europe: Political, Social and Economic Forces, 1950–5*, 2nd edition. Stanford: Stanford University Press.

Habermas, J. (2013) 'Germany holds the key to the fate of the European Union', public lecture at University of Leuven, Belgium, http://www.kuleuven.be/english/news/2013/habermas, date accessed 18 August 2016.

Hall, P. A. (2012) 'The Economics and Politics of the Euro Crisis', *German Politics*, Vol. 21, no. 4, pp. 355–71.

Harrison, S. and Bruter, M. (2015) 'Media and Identity – the Paradox of Legitimacy and the Making of European Citizens.' In T. Risse (ed.), *European Public Spheres: Politics is Back*. Cambridge: Cambridge University Press, pp. 165–89.

Hix, S. and Hoyland, B. (2011) *The Political System of the European Union*. Basingstoke: Palgrave MacMillan.

Hix, S. and Marsh, M. (2011) 'Punishment or Protest? Understanding European Parliament Elections', *Electoral Studies*, Vol. 69, No. 2, pp. 495–510.

HM Government (2013) *EU speech at Bloomberg*, 23 January, https://www.gov.uk/government/speeches/eu-speech-at-bloomberg, date accessed 19 August 2016.

Hooghe, L. and Marks, G. (2009) 'A Postfunctionalist Theory of European Integration: From Permissive Consensus to Constraining Dissensus', *British Journal of Political Science*, Vol. 39, No. 1, pp. 1–23.

Hopkin, J. (2012) 'Technocrats Have Taken Over Governments in Southern Europe: This Is a Challenge to Democracy', London School of Economics Blog, 24 April, http://blogs.lse.ac.uk/europpblog/2012/04/24/technocrats-democracy- southern-europe/, date accessed 18 August 2016.

Innerarity, D. (2015) 'What Must Be Democratized? The European Union as a Complex Democracy'. In S. Champeay, C. Closa, D. Innerarity, and M. Meduro (eds), *The Future of Europe: Democracy, Legitimacy and Justice after the Euro Crisis*. London and New York: Rowman and Littlefield, pp. 171–94.

Kundnani, H. (2015) *The Paradox of German Power*. Oxford: Oxford University Press.

Laffan, B. (2016) 'Core–Periphery Relations in the Euro area: From Conflict to Cleavage.' In J. M. Magone, B. Laffan, and C. Schweiger (eds), *Core–Periphery Relations in the European Union: Power and Conflict in a Dualist Political Economy*. Abingdon: Routledge, pp. 19–34.

Lindberg, L. N. (1965) 'Decision Making and Integration in the European Community', *International Organization*, Vol. 19, No. 1, pp. 56–80.

Magone, J. M. (2015) 'Divided Europe? Euroscepticism in Central, Eastern and Southern Europe'. In K. N. Demetriou (ed.), *The European Union in Crisis: Explorations in Representation and Democratic Legitimacy*. London: Springer, pp. 33–58.

Marks, G., Hooghe, L., and Blank, K. (1996) 'European Integration from the 1980s: State-Centric v. Multi-Level Governance', *Journal of Common Market Studies*, Vol. 34, No. 3, pp. 341–78.

Meiers, F.-J. (2015) *Germany's Role in the Euro Crisis: Berlin's Quest for a More Perfect Monetary Union*. London: Springer.

Monti, M. (2010) *A new strategy for the Single Market: At the service of Europe's economy and society – Report to the President of the European Commission José Manuel Barroso*, 9 May, http://ec.europa.eu/internal_market/strategy/docs/monti_report_final_10_05_2 010_en.pdf, date accessed 18 August 2016.

Murray, P. and Longo, M. (2015), 'The Crisis–Legitimacy Nexus in the European Union.' In K. Demetriou (ed.), *The European Union in Crisis: Explorations in Representation and Democratic Legitimacy*, London: Springer, pp. 101–22.

Neutel, F. (2015), 'Pushing the Union forward? The Role of the European Parliament in the Union's Crisis.' In K. Demetriou (ed.), *The European Union in Crisis: Explorations in Representation and Democratic Legitimacy*. London: Springer, pp. 155–80.

Nugent, N. (2010) *The Government and Politics of the European Union*, 7th edition. Basingstoke: Palgrave Macmillan.

Paterson, W. E. (2011) 'The Reluctant Hegemon? Germany moves centre stage in the European Union', *Journal of Common Market Studies*, Vol. 49 (annual review), pp. 57–75.

Paterson W. E. (2014) 'Germany and the European Union.' In S. Padgett, W. E. Paterson, and R. Zohlnhöfer (eds), *Developments in German Politics*. Basingstoke: Palgrave Macmillan, pp. 166–88.

Pollack, M. A., Wallace H., and Young, A. R. (2015) 'Policy-Making in a time of crisis: Trends and challenges'. In H. Wallace, M. A. Pollack, and A. R. Young (eds), *Policy-Making in the European Union*. Oxford: Oxford University Press, pp. 467–88.

Sabel, C. F. and Zeitlin, J. (2008) 'Learning from Difference: The New Architecture of Experimentalist Governance in the EU', *European Law Journal*, Vol. 14, No. 3, pp. 271–327.

Schake, K. (2012) 'US Retrenchment Is Right and Overdue.' In F. Heisbourg, W. Ischinger, G. Robertson, K. Schake, and T. Valasek, *All Alone? What US Retrenchment Means for Europe and NATO*. London: Centre for European Reform, pp. 5–26, https://www.cer.org.uk/sites/default/files/publications/attachments/pdf/2012/rp _089_km-6278.pdf, date accessed 18 August 2016.

Scharpf, F. W. (1988) 'The Joint Decision Trap: Lessons from German Federalism and European Integration', *Public Administration*, Vol. 66 (Autumn), pp. 239–78.

Scharpf, F. W. (2006) 'The Joint-Decision Trap Revisited', *Journal of Common Market Studies*, Vol. 44, No. 4, pp. 845–64.

Schmidt, V. A. (2006) *Democracy in Europe: The EU and National Politics*. Oxford: Oxford University Press.

Schmitter, P. C. (1970) 'A Revised Theory of Regional Integration', *International Organization*, Vol. 24, No. 4, pp. 836–68.

Schmitter, P. C. (2001) 'What Is There to Legitimize in the European Union ... and How Might This Be Accomplished?', IHS Political Science Working Paper Series, No. 75, http://www.eui.eu/Documents/DepartmentsCentres/SPS/Profiles/Schmitter/L egitimizeEU.pdf, date accessed 18 August 2016.

Schweiger, C. (2015) 'The EU-25 *Fiscal Compact*: Differentiated *Spillover Effects* under Crisis Conditions.' In C. Schweiger and J. M. Magone (eds), *The Effects of the Eurozone Sovereign Debt Crisis: Differentiated Integration between the Centre and the New Peripheries of the EU*. Abingdon: Routledge, pp. 35–46.

Schweiger, C. (2016) 'National Interests and Differentiated Integration in the EU under Crisis Conditions: The Cases of Germany, France and Britain.' In J. M. Magone, B. Laffan, and C. Schweiger (eds), *Core–Periphery Relations in the European Union: Power and Conflict in a Dualist Political Economy*. Abingdon: Routledge, pp. 59–71.

Sepos, A. (2016) 'The Centre–Periphery Divide in the Eurocrisis: A Theoretical Approach.' In J. M. Magone, B. Laffan, and C. Schweiger (eds), *Core–Periphery Relations in the European Union: Power and Conflict in a Dualist Political Economy*. Abingdon: Routledge, pp. 35–56.

Smith, M. (2011) 'Implementation: Making the EU's International Relations Work.' In C. Hill and M. Smith (eds), *International Relations and the European Union*. Oxford: Oxford University Press, pp. 171–96.

Soete, L. (2006) 'A Knowledge Economy Paradigm and Its Consequences.' In A. Giddens, P. Diamond, and R. Liddle (eds), *Global Europe, Social Europe*. Cambridge: Polity Press, pp. 193–214.

Sternberg, C. S. (2015) 'Political Legitimacy between Democracy and Effectiveness: Trade-offs, Interdependencies, and Discursive Constructions by the EU Institutions', *European Political Science Review*, Vol. 7, No. 4, pp. 615–38.

Usherwood, S. (2015) 'Britain and Europe: A Model of Permanent Crisis?' In K. N. Demetriou (ed.), *The European Union in Crisis: Explorations in Representation and Democratic Legitimacy*. London: Springer, pp. 3–14.

Visvizi, A. (2016) 'Greece and the Troika in the context of the Eurozone crisis.' In J. M. Magone, B. Laffan, and C. Schweiger (eds), *Core–Periphery Relations in the European Union: Power and Conflict in a Dualist Political Economy*. Abingdon: Routledge, pp. 149–65.

Wagstyl, S. (2016) 'Angela Merkel: Lots of foes, fewer friends', *Financial Times*, http://www.ft.com/cms/s/0/f47edbf8-d401-11e5-829b-8564e7528e54.html, date accessed 18 August 2016.

Wallace, H. and Reh, C. (2015) 'An Institutional Anatomy and Five Policy Modes.' In H. Wallace, M. A. Pollack, and A. R. Young (eds), *Policy-Making in the European Union*. Oxford: Oxford University Press, pp. 72–114.

Weiler, J. H. H. (1999) *The Constitution of Europe: 'Do the new clothes have an emperor?' and other essays on European integration*. Cambridge: Cambridge University Press.

Weiler, J. H. H., Haltern, U. R., and Mayer, F. C. (1995) 'European Democracy and Its Critique', *West European Politics*, Vol. 18, No. 3, pp. 4–39.

Chapter 11

Germany and the Crisis: Asset or Liability?

SIMON BULMER AND WILLIAM E. PATERSON

Introduction

The EU crisis has presented important challenges for Germany. In the early 1990s, Germany's post-unification commitments to deeper integration in the Maastricht Treaty were accompanied by the internal challenges of integrating the former East Germany into the Federal Republic. Later, in the 1990s, the German economy was named the 'sick man of the Euro' (Economist, 1999). However, economic and social reforms in the 2000s under the Red–Green (Social Democrats – Greens) coalition of Gerhard Schröder resulted in a much stronger economic position, prompting Thomas Bagger, the head of policy planning in the German Foreign Office, to write of 'the German moment' (Bagger, 2014: 26). A more apt description may be that Germany has become 'the indispensable power' in the EU. As such, German agreement is a prerequisite for forging EU solutions to most dimensions of the crisis.

Germany may be indispensable, but is it an asset or a liability in helping the EU weather the storms of the 2010s? The traditional view is that it is Germany, 'in the form of … a pro-integrationist regional hegemon that best explains Europe's comparatively very high level of political integration' (Webber, 2014: 355; for wider debate on Germany's role in the EU, see Bulmer and Paterson, 2010). In Webber's view Germany is the EU's major asset and any change would be potentially destabilizing for the EU. The view of Germany as a liability derived from the euro crisis, where Berlin has been criticized for its initial reluctance to play a leadership role, while exporting to debtor states austerity policies that, alongside a beggar-thy-neighbour trade policy, have actually deepened the crisis. Then Germany's lack of consultation on policy, and specifically quotas, for redistributing migrants prompted divisions with central and eastern European states, thus adding east–west divisions to the north–south ones evident in the eurozone crisis. The caution of Germany over the eurozone crisis gave way to a precipitate approach on migration; both resulted in criticism.

The chapter comprises four sections. First, we explore how and why Germany has been thrust into a role of indispensability, with particular reference to whether the necessary domestic consensus holds to play this role. We then turn to three dimensions of the EU crisis, and examine each one in turn: the eurozone crisis, the Ukraine crisis, and the migration crisis. We argue that Berlin's mode of intervention has been shaped by the degree of threat to German interests in each case. In the eurozone crisis, Germany has moved during the sequence of events from 'reluctant hegemon' towards coercive diplomacy, specifically in relation to the third Greek bailout in 2015. In the Ukraine crisis, Germany focused on consensus building and acting as chief facilitator. In the migration crisis, Chancellor Angela Merkel, in office since 2005, exerted early moral leadership, although the Berlin government later came close to coercive diplomacy owing to preferences conflicting with those of east European states. Domestic politics within Germany have played an important contributory role in all three crises. In concluding, we come to a judgement about Germany's leadership capacity in the EU, and whether it represents an asset or a liability.

Leadership and Domestic Politics

Historically Germany has eschewed playing a leadership role in the EU (Bulmer and Paterson, 1996), though it has always been a key supporter of integration. Indeed Franco-German partnership normally served as the vehicle for developing integration policy initiatives. This relationship served as the motor of European integration from the 1970s, and was a stabilizing force during intermittent crises. If France and Germany could agree, then their position usually served as the basis for a common position for the whole EU. Germany's pro-European role was supported domestically by a strongly supportive consensus from its political elite and broad support from across the party spectrum and in public opinion.

The current EU crisis has placed the question of a leadership role for Germany at the heart of EU governance. First, because in each of the three crises examined in this chapter there has been no existing or viable supranational solution in the policy toolkit. For instance, among the several failures in the design of Economic and Monetary Union (EMU), fiscal surveillance mechanisms were too weak to monitor, never mind restrain, the growth of national deficits and debts (see Dyson, Chapter 4 in this volume). In a similar vein the EU's foreign policy worked well in asserting norms, values, and the rule of law internationally but demonstrated persistent difficulties in gaining a consensus between states on the use of military force, often resulting in the North Atlantic Treaty Organization (NATO) or other ad hoc alliances having to act instead. Finally, the EU's refugee policy instrument, namely the Dublin Regulation on the registering and settlement of asylum-seekers, had already come under great strain due to migratory flows to Italy from North Africa before becoming overwhelmed in the autumn of 2015 by flows from the Middle East. In all of these cases either new policy instruments or, in the case of Ukraine, a high-stakes foreign policy position have been needed. The EU's supranational institutions lacked the authority to provide policy solutions in these areas of core state powers. This gap placed the European Council, which brings together the heads of state or government, at the heart of the search for solutions (see Chapter 9).

Second, the crisis has taken place in circumstances of disequilibrium among the leading member states. The Franco-German partnership has been under strain. It had already become less influential owing to the greater diversity of interests in the EU following the enlargements to today's 28 member states. The French rejection of the Constitutional Treaty in 2005 was arguably the first sign of the partnership's decreasing stability. It fell to Germany to affect a salvage operation, in the form of the Lisbon Treaty. The downgrade of French government bonds in 2012 amid the eurozone crisis underlined the growing weakness of the French economy. The British governments led by David Cameron (2010–16) were preoccupied by internal disagreement on European policy. No other state has stepped in to fill the vacuum, resulting in expectations for leadership falling squarely on Germany.

The third factor has been Germany's economic strength once the government had undertaken reforms in the early to mid-2000s. By the 2010s, economic indicators on the trade surplus, labour competitiveness, and public debt placed Germany in the strongest position of the larger EU states. When this is added to Germany's status as the most populous member state and Merkel's position as the pre-eminent political figure in European politics, the expectations placed on Germany were very high, despite it being a 'reluctant hegemon' (Paterson, 2011).

Fourth, there have been increasing signs that Germany is willing to play a more prominent role at both the EU and global levels. This willingness was reflected in Foreign Minister Steinmeier's launch of 'Review 2014' – a fundamental review of German foreign policy – which suggested Germany taking on greater responsibility. Yet Germany's emergence as the EU's indispensable power during the crises has relied more on the absence of alternatives than on a conscious political choice by the Berlin government. Moreover, there are strong domestic reasons – institutional, political, and normative – for German reluctance to play a leadership role.

Institutionally German leadership resources are quite dispersed despite Merkel's strong position. The Berlin government is (since the autumn of 2013) a Christian Democrat–Social Democrat grand coalition. On the migration crisis, the government needs to work with the *Länder* (the states within the federation), which are at the front line of providing facilities to the migrants. In the eurozone crisis there is a competing voice on policy solutions: that of the Bundesbank (Central Bank) in Frankfurt. The Federal Constitutional Court (FCC) also casts a shadow over the federal government, making an increasing number of rulings on EU matters.

The Bundesbank and the FCC have contributed to a politicization of European policy within Germany. On both the eurozone and the migration crises public opinion has become an important consideration for a Chancellor who normally likes to remain in touch with the direction of public sentiment. The party politics of European policy are becoming more contested, albeit from a baseline of widespread pro-EU sentiment. The emergence of the anti-euro *Alternative für Deutschland* (Alternative for Germany) (AfD) party was too recent for a breakthrough in the 2013 federal election. However, the AfD was represented in five state parliaments in late 2015, as well as in the European Parliament. In March 2016, it also secured election to the state parliaments of Baden-Württemberg, Rhineland-Palatinate, and Saxony-Anhalt, polling 15.1, 12.6, and 24.2 per cent, respectively. In September 2016, it achieved a further success in Mecklenburg-West Pomerania, securing 20.7 per cent, forcing Merkel's Christian Democrats into third place.

The normative dimension is reflected in the role of memory in European policy (Markovits and Reich, 1997). Pro-European sentiment has characteristically been seen as normatively embedded in the German policy elite. Resistance to playing a leadership role is linked to that position. In foreign policy, the long-standing commitment to a 'civilian power' approach places limitations on the range of foreign policy interventions Germany will support.

Thus Germany has the assets for indispensability but has a disposition not to deploy them. This is the dichotomy at the heart of the chapter.

The Eurozone Crisis

The eurozone crisis broke in late 2009 when the EU realized the full extent of the Greek budget deficit. It passed through several distinct phases in the following years (see Chapter 4). Germany's role in negotiating the individual financial assistance arrangements (bailouts), the necessary fiscal policy integration to shore up EMU, and in the moves to banking union has been indispensable. In some ways this is unsurprising, as Germany had been particularly influential in the Maastricht design for EMU (Dyson and Featherstone, 1996). The Bundesbank model of price stability and independent central banking had strongly influenced the constitution of the European Central Bank (ECB). The design had included, at German insistence, a 'no-bailout clause' (Article 125 of the Treaty on the Functioning of the European Union, TFEU) and prohibited the ECB from monetary financing of a eurozone state's sovereign debt (Article 123 TFEU). Germany had also pushed for the surveillance of fiscal discipline via the Stability and Growth Pact (SGP). The burden of economic adjustment to the German-inspired model was placed on other member states. Once the eurozone states committed to rescuing the euro, their reform measures had to be consistent with this Maastricht design.

As the eurozone crisis unfolded, it became clear that there was not only a sovereign-debt crisis in certain states (Greece and Portugal) but also a banking crisis in others (Ireland, Spain, and Cyprus) (see Chapter 4). The German government's approach comprised four policy principles. First, debtor states had to 'draw the consequences' and take on board the necessary implications of the stability culture, namely reforms of their public finances and structural reforms of their economies. This principle of conditionality was axiomatic in the government's position. Second, the EMU architecture had to be reformed around a tighter, rules-based order. Third, the link between sovereign debt and the banking system had to be broken, through the creation of a banking union. Finally, bailouts were needed to prevent systemic threat to the euro and to limit contagion effects. The bailouts were dependent on the debtor states accepting strict conditionality. The challenge for Berlin was to secure agreement around these principles by drawing on the assets available, while mitigating the liabilities.

Assets

The German government had several assets in seeking a solution to the crisis. First, Germany would be the biggest contributor to the bailouts, giving it considerable leverage over the terms imposed on debtor states. For instance, Chancellor Merkel insisted on the participation of the International Monetary Fund (IMF) in the rescues because of a wish to have its expertise on such interventions. Second, German ideas were influential. These ideas were based on the distinctive principles of ordoliberalism, which presupposes that markets are inefficient and prescribes an 'economic constitution' to correct these inefficiencies (Dullien and Guérot, 2012). Ordoliberalism entails a strong commitment to monetary stability and fiscal conservatism: to 'sound money' and a 'stability culture' (Howarth and Rommerskirchen, 2013). Intrinsic to the ordo-liberal position is the expectation that states must take responsibility for their own problems so as to avoid moral hazard, that is, a situation in which 'financially prudent' states have to rescue the more profligate. Germany's strong ideational assets entailed setting rules to enforce fiscal self-responsibility rather than offering shared financial responsibility or prioritizing economic growth.

Politically Germany also had a strong hand to play. Chancellor Merkel had established herself as the pre-eminent EU political leader. In the early stage of the crisis (2010–11), the Franco-German relationship, personified by Merkel and President Nicolas Sarkozy (the so-called Merkozy era), served as a vehicle for advancing German-inspired solutions. It shielded Germany somewhat in the period when many of the key fiscal reforms were agreed. The election of François Hollande as President of France in May 2012 reduced this 'cover' for Germany. Hollande, a socialist who was critical of austerity policy, sought more emphasis on economic growth. His election initially strained Franco-German relations.

The final asset that Germany had was its structural power. Germany's economic situation was relatively strong, as demonstrated in 2011 through relatively low unemployment (5.9 per cent) and a large current account surplus (6.3 per cent of GDP). German labour costs had risen less than those in other large EU states in the period since 2005. Germany's budget deficit was only 0.8 per cent of GDP in 2011, while its debt, though high by its own post-war standards at 80.5 per cent of GDP, was under better control than that of France or Italy (see Bulmer, 2014: 1252–3; Eurostat, 2014).

Liabilities

Germany, however, also had a number of liabilities in tackling the eurozone crisis. The political ones are particularly striking. First, as noted earlier, Germany was a 'reluctant hegemon' (Paterson, 2011). Two specific features reinforced Germany's leadership avoidance. Merkel had built her political reputation on a careful consideration of options before adopting clear policy positions. Moreover, the ordoliberal approach implied not intervening too soon for fear of encouraging moral hazard. This reluctance led to criticism in some quarters that Germany's delay had made the crisis worse (Jones, 2010). For Berlin, by contrast, financial intervention had to be a matter of last resort, taken only when systemic stability was at risk. And it had to include a commitment to conditionality.

A second drag upon Germany was the domestic political context. Timothy Garton Ash (Handelsblatt, 2012) has captured this by arguing that Merkel had to be attentive to the 'four big B's': the populism of *Bild Zeitung*, the main tabloid newspaper; dissent in the Bundestag (the German parliament); the reluctance of the Bundesbank; and adverse rulings from the Bundesverfassungsgericht (the FCC). In the early period of the crisis, the print media presented a picture of industrious German workers, who had themselves been contending with cuts to social welfare, rescuing their feckless southern European counterparts. In many ways, it is remarkable that Merkel was gradually able to swing public support behind her government's eurozone diplomacy, assisted by repeated use of the mantra 'if the Euro fails, Europe fails'. Her domestic political reputation emerged intact, and arguably enhanced, enabling her to secure election victory in 2013 (and form a government with different coalition partners).

The FCC served as a further constraint. It became a focus for challenges by eurosceptic politicians and economists. Earlier challenges had been brought before the FCC regarding the compatibility of the Maastricht Treaty and then of the Lisbon Treaty with the Basic Law (German constitution). In each case the FCC had emphasized a rather intergovernmental view of the EU in which the member states are the 'masters of the treaties'. It enhanced the power of the German parliament with each judgement. The shadow of these judgements fell across the Berlin government's eurozone diplomacy. Any threat to the 'no bailout clause' or the prohibition of mutual financing of sovereign debt would be subject to legal challenge. Such challenges came to pass, as well as others based on the government forcing measures through parliament on a very tight schedule. At times the fate of the eurozone seemed to hang on rulings of the FCC, for instance, in January 2014, on the admissibility of the ECB's monetary easing measures.

The FCC's judgement in favour of enhanced parliamentary rights to scrutinize rescue measures added further potential constraints on the federal government's policy. In a number of votes, the 2009–13 Christian Democrat–Free Democrat coalition was reliant on the support of parliamentarians from the opposition Social Democratic Party (SPD) and the Greens to obtain agreement on eurozone measures because of dissent within the coalition parties (Wimmel, 2013).

The resurgence of the Bundesbank under Jens Weidmann, who took office in May 2011, was a further striking background constraint on the Berlin government. Unlike his predecessor, Weidmann was prepared to defend in a very public way the Bundesbank's sound money principles, which he saw as being under threat in the eurozone crisis. Although a member of the ECB Governing Council, Weidmann opposed its monetary easing and even intervened in FCC cases to this effect. The Bundesbank's views served to rally hard-line ordoliberal economists, some of whom were major drivers behind the creation of the AfD.

These liabilities could be 'managed' by the Berlin government, but only through adherence to the ordoliberal policy principles discussed above. However, the resultant austerity policy has itself been regarded as something of a liability for resolving the crisis. It has inhibited eurozone growth, without which it is difficult to reduce deficits and debts as a percentage of GDP. Similarly, the solutions have a northern European bias. The German industrial relations system has permitted wage restraint, increasing its firms' competitiveness, thereby contributing to Germany's huge trade surpluses. Southern European industrial relations systems need major overhaul if they are to arrest declining competitiveness vis-à-vis Germany and other northern European states. In other words, the ordoliberal prescriptions simply do not suit the circumstances of some of the debtor states over the longer term, including even France and Italy.

As the eurozone crisis unfolded, Germany's competitive position strengthened further. Its foreign trade surplus rose to 7.3 per cent of GDP in 2014, close to the 2007 record of 7.5 per cent. This particular imbalance in the European economy has received less attention than debt levels, though it may not be any less pernicious. Moreover, the position of German banks was strengthened. Irresponsible lending by German and French banks to debtor states had been an initial risk (Thompson, 2015), since a default by Greece would have struck at their liquidity. The bailouts had the indirect effect of enabling these banks to reduce their exposure.

Review

Germany has played an indispensable role in the eurozone crisis. Slow to intervene, its involvement then became decisive. Germany insisted on the incorporation of the conditionality principle for the debtor states. It exported important components into the eurozone rescue. For instance, in the Fiscal Compact it required that there be:

> a balanced budget rule; a debt-brake rule to reduce debt ratios of states currently over the 60 per cent threshold; an automatic correction mechanism if these rules are not complied with; and the requirement of the states to accord these rules at least the status of law. (Bulmer, 2014: 1254)

This design came straight out of the ordoliberal toolkit: strict fiscal rules with limited scope for discretionary intervention. Equally, Eurobonds – the idea of mutualizing eurozone debt – were thwarted by Berlin's veto power, thus eliminating a measure that would have been more solidaristic and growth-oriented. Eurobonds were incompatible with Germany's ordoliberal principles and antithetical to German public opinion.

The crisis has continued, most acutely for Greece. In July 2015, German Finance Minister Wolfgang Schäuble proposed that Greece should take a 'timeout' from membership of the eurozone as well as transfer €50 billion of its state assets to a Luxembourg trust in preparation for their privatization. Although this proposal was not pursued, it seemed to symbolize a German willingness to use coercive power. More broadly, austerity has suppressed the eurozone economy, raising questions about the sustainability of German policy prescriptions. Germany had insisted upon the participation of the IMF alongside the Commission and the ECB in the so-called Troika. However, by late 2015 the IMF was noting the need for debt relief for Greece, a policy that was anathema to Berlin. This development hinted at limits to the influence of Berlin's policy prescriptions.

The Ukraine Crisis

As seen in Chapter 14, the Ukraine crisis arose out of the projected expansion of the EU eastwards. A proposed Association Agreement with Ukraine produced a very strong reaction from President Putin who pressured Ukrainian President Yanukovych to reject it in favour of a Russian-led customs union. This triggered a strong popular reaction culminating in massive public demonstrations in Kiev and the flight of Yanukovych to Russia. These events in turn led to Russia's annexation of Crimea and active Russian support for dissident movements in eastern Ukraine. While these escalations represented deliberate steps on the part of the Russian leadership, the crisis entered a new phase following the downing of Malaysian Airlines MH17 in July 2014, allegedly by insurgents using a Russian-built and supplied guided missile. An uneasy ceasefire had been concluded in the Minsk Agreement agreed between Russia, Ukraine, Germany, and France in February 2015. The ceasefire held but Western reaction strengthened.

The Ukraine crisis presented a challenge and a dilemma for Germany. Chancellor Merkel had been a supporter of the Association Agreement and Germany is a strong supporter of the rule of law. Germany had a strategic partnership with Russia based on the premise that engagement with Russia would promote modernization. Germany benefited from trade with Russia and was dependent on Russian energy, and elite and mass opinion in Germany was understandably reluctant to disturb these relations. How to respond represented a major dilemma.

Similar uncertainty was apparent in many of Germany's EU partners. Doing nothing was not an option, however, as some fellow members such as Poland pressed for a hard line and President Obama made it clear that he expected Germany to manage the crisis. Chancellor Merkel 'led from the middle' in her crisis management in three senses. She was at the centre of EU and domestic efforts to coordinate a response and managed to win over both her domestic public and her EU partners to support sanctions against Russia. While coordinating the EU response she kept in constant touch with President Putin and was a central figure in the negotiation of the Minsk Agreement, which established a cease-fire between the contending parties. Finally, she remained the vital link between President Obama, who would have favoured a harder line, and her European partners. Chancellor Merkel's task in keeping these competing priorities in harmony was greatly aided by the shooting down of MH17 which swung domestic and European opinion in her favour.

In the following sections we will look first at the assets favouring German diplomacy and then the liabilities impeding it.

Assets

Germany's key assets included closeness to the two superpowers, the prestige of Chancellor Merkel, Germany's skill in coalition building, and its attachment to international law.

In the crisis following Russia's invasion of Georgia in 2008, France had played a much more prominent role than Germany. With the Ukraine crisis, it was clear from the beginning that Germany would play the leading role. It had lost its traditional 'leadership avoidance reflex' (Paterson, 1993) under the pressures of the eurozone crisis. Crucially the USA, overburdened with domestic and international challenges, sought to outsource management of the crisis. Merkel's Germany was the inevitable choice, cementing its leadership position. Outsourcing the crisis management did not mean that the USA remained uninvolved. Indeed, the USA remained concerned about the security needs of east European states while Germany sought to contain and resolve the crisis. This led to tension in the early part of the crisis when the USA, under pressure from its east European allies, contemplated supplying arms to Ukraine. Such a step would have significantly escalated the crisis and was firmly opposed by Germany. Subsequently Merkel kept in lockstep with the USA, whose support put extra pressure on those European states that were reluctant to take a firm line on sanctions.

Germany had been the dominant interlocutor of the EU with Russia since the achievement of German unity. Merkel's ability to speak fluent Russian and President Putin's knowledge of German from his service with the KGB in Leipzig, enabled communication in a way denied to other leaders. While President Putin often dissembled, such contact helped to prevent the crisis from running out of control, a key goal of German policy.

Chancellor Merkel had unrivalled prestige and experience on the international stage: the undoubted champion of negotiations whether in the European Council or other summitry. Her wide range of contacts, her patience, and her ability to spot where agreement might be possible made her indispensable to achieving agreement both between partners and with Russia. Germany and Merkel showed remarkable skill in coalition building and managing to persuade her reluctant European partners to back sanctions against Russia. The same skill was evident in the multilateral diplomatic negotiations leading to the Minsk Agreement, which brought about a precarious ceasefire in February 2015. This agreement froze rather than resolved the crisis and fighting has continued on a much-reduced scale in eastern Ukraine (Pond and Kundnani, 2015).

Germany's inglorious past has led to the strong enshrinement of the rule of law including attachment to international law. Indeed, this attachment is a key component of the civilian power approach, which has been a fundamental characteristic of German foreign policy (Maull, 2000). The clear breaches of international law in the annexation of Crimea and the downing of MH17 helped convince domestic adversaries of sanctions to change their minds. German legalist discourse was also influential with other member states.

Liabilities

If the assets looked to be formidable, so were the liabilities. They included an elite and public sentiment broadly favourable to Russia, the strong support of German economic interests for Russia, the lack of broad support among European partners, and a weak security stance associated with the civilian power doctrine.

So-called Russlandversteher (Russophiles) played a major role in German public life. This tendency was especially marked in the SPD, with the most prominent examples being former Chancellors Gerhard Schröder, who accepted a post with Russian energy giant Gazprom, and Helmut Schmidt, who based his attitude towards Russia on realist principles. In the early stages of the crisis, Merkel's SPD coalition partner was sceptical about sanctions and pleaded for understanding of the Russian positions. Opinion in the SPD and public opinion generally swung behind the Chancellor in the wake of the downing of MH17.

A minority of member states, including the UK and a range of east European and Baltic states, were in favour of strong sanctions against Russia but the majority were reluctant to impose them, given their strong economic interest in trade with Russia. Merkel was quick to capitalize on the MH17 atrocity to secure the support of other EU members for sanctions and managed to preserve this consensus.

Before the crisis Germany had a very weak ability or willingness to intervene on behalf of her allies, because of the civilian power doctrine. Immediately before the outbreak of the crisis, German policy-makers had started to address the intervention issue in a series of speeches, notably by the Federal President and the Foreign and Defence Ministers at the Munich Security Conference in February 2014. Review 2014, an official German Foreign Ministry analysis of how its foreign policy might be improved, followed these speeches. Germany's security weakness was manifest in a crisis in which it faced a ruthless adversary prepared to use force. The crisis acted as a major external shock and in mid-October 2014 the Federal Government decided to increase military spending, to modernize German combat troops and to streamline its strategic armaments policy. At the NATO Summit in Wales, in September 2014, Germany agreed to an increase in military infrastructure in Poland and the Baltic states and to the establishment of a NATO Response Force. Clearly, Germany had recognized its own limitations under changed international circumstances.

Review

In the management of the Ukraine crisis Germany was able to exploit its assets and reduce its liabilities in a very skilful way and increase its agency. Germany's opposition to the US proposal to deliver lethal defensive weapons to Ukraine in the early days of the crisis prevented a dangerous escalation. Russia's continuing support for insurgency in eastern Ukraine remained a danger point, however, and one over which Germany had little control. In any crisis, much depends on the tactics of the adversary, and the downing of MH17 by a Russian-built guided missile, the insensitive behaviour of the insurgents in picking through the wreckage, and Putin's refusal to take any responsibility handed the initiative to Merkel. She was able to change domestic and elite opinion in Germany and persuade other EU member states to support sanctions. Questions remain about the degree to which President Putin has influence over the insurgents in eastern Ukraine and this uncertainty remains a continual threat to the Minsk Agreement.

In the Ukraine crisis Germany has managed to craft a fragile ceasefire (the Minsk Agreement) and to rally and maintain domestic and external support for Western sanctions against Russia, though doubts persist about how long this can be maintained. This has all been achieved at a cost. Russia will not leave Crimea and will retain significant influence in eastern Ukraine and over the future direction of Ukraine.

The Ukraine crisis was the second contemporaneous crisis that Germany had to deal with and many feared overstretch (Applebaum, 2015). This was all the more so since in dealing with this crisis Germany could not rely on the structural power that was so important in the eurozone crisis and governmental policy was not supported initially by popular or elite opinion. What was needed was skill and persuasion in intergovernmental diplomacy. The MH17 atrocity provided the opportunity for Chancellor Merkel to successfully deploy her diplomatic skills.

The Migration Crisis

In creating the Schengen passport-free travel zone without a common border police force and immigration policy the EU had created a crisis in waiting. For a number of years there was a slow-burning crisis as migrants entered from North Africa largely as a result of turmoil in Libya. At the end of 2014, as the fulcrum of the crisis shifted to south-western Europe, the German government was insistent on the maintenance of the Dublin Regulation, whereby refugees must apply for asylum in the first EU state upon arrival, and remain there while their application is being processed. Italy in particular was seen as not fulfilling its responsibilities. Germany also proposed quotas to distribute refugees across the EU but without success.

The German government's position changed as the influx of Syrian refugees coming through Greece swelled alarmingly. It altered its policy abruptly without consulting its partners apart from the Austrian Chancellor. In taking this approach in September 2015, Germany's hand was arguably forced by the situation in Budapest, where refugees defied the Hungarian authorities and set off by foot for the Austrian border. Merkel responded by bussing the refugees to Germany. Her pronouncement that 'Wir schaffen es' (we can manage) suggested that Germany would act as Europe's default liberal political hegemon (Benner, 2016). This was a very surprising initiative for a Chancellor as careful and cautious as Merkel given that the refugees were coming from 'safe third countries'. She might have been well advised to hedge the welcome to the Syrians with caveats regarding duration and entitlement and to consult her partners. Merkel's lead was accompanied by a welcoming culture and public support.

There were no obvious supranational solutions to the migration crisis and Chancellor Merkel, at what may prove to be the zenith of her power, thought Germany could 'do it'. In addition, amid the turmoil of divergent member state responses in late August 2015, Germany suspended the Dublin Regulation that it had earlier been insisting on.

Assets

In choosing to take the lead in the management of this crisis, Merkel and her government had a number of assets. Unlike other leaders, Merkel was in command of the domestic political landscape and there was no electorally potent political movement against her. Her EU leadership had been reinforced during the euro and Ukraine crises and *Time* magazine had chosen her as its 'Person of the Year' for 2015, reflecting her dominance internally and externally. Within her own party, Merkel had no rivals and looked likely to run in the next federal election, in 2017, while on the Left she had received support on migration from her coalition partners in the SPD and from the Greens and die Linke. There was thus no political space to the left of the Chancellor on this issue, whilst taking a stance to her right would encourage forces such as Pegida (the Patriotic Europeans Against the Islamization of the West), a movement formed in 2014 and quickly condemned by Merkel, and the AfD, which had embraced opposition to the flow of refugees.

Germany's economic muscle lay behind Merkel's attempt in October 2015 to persuade Turkey to attempt to stem the flow of refugees. A bilateral consultation took place in January 2016, where it was agreed that such consultations would be institutionalized. Previously the EU had agreed that Turkish applications for visas to enter the EU would be fast-tracked, and that the EU would contribute €3 billion to Turkey in return for its help in stemming the flow of refugees (Janning, 2016a). EU aid was slow to arrive and Turkish help was scarcely visible in the near term, as the EU wanted Turkish action plans while Ankara sought the financial support first. Agreement was finally reached at a summit in Brussels on 17 March 2016. The key points of the agreement were that refugees crossing from Turkey into Greece would be sent back. For each Syrian returned to Turkey, a Syrian migrant would be resettled in the EU. Turkish nationals were to be granted visa-free entry to the Schengen area after June 2016. The EU agreed to speed up the allocation of €3 billion to Turkey and to 're-energise' Turkey's bid to join the EU. Major issues remained about the practicalities and the compatibility of the agreement with EU and international law but it was the only plan on the table.

The strength of its economy made Germany the only possible candidate to play a leading role in an EU response to the migration crisis. Additionally, large-scale immigration could possibly provide an answer to Germany's growing demographic crisis. Germany has the lowest birth rate in the Western world and its workforce is expected to shrink by 6 million over the next six years. Immigration is vital for Germany to sustain its welfare and industrial base.

Liabilities

While Merkel's Christian Democratic Union (CDU) and parties on its left have been an asset, parties to the right proved to be a growing constraint. The Christian Social Union (CSU), the CDU's Bavarian sister party in the grand coalition, quickly abandoned its initial support as the flood of refugees continued in the latter half of 2015. The CSU is based in one state – Bavaria – where its top priority is to retain its long-standing majority. Accordingly, it is a basic principle of the CSU not to allow any political space to its right. The CSU is very sensitive to any policies that could encourage support for the right-wing AfD and consequently shifted to the right. Moreover, the flow of refugees from Austria was overwhelming the reception capacity of Bavaria.

The CSU therefore demanded secure external EU borders, stronger controls of the German border, and an annual cap of 200,000 refugees (1.1 million had arrived in Germany in 2015). Bavarian Minister President Seehofer sent these demands in a letter to the Chancellor in mid-January 2016, raising the possibility of an appeal to the FCC. Merkel, secure in the support of the SPD, refused to back down (Tagesschau, 2016).

An even greater liability was the surge in support for the AfD that was dramatically demonstrated in the state elections of 13 March 2016 (in Baden Württemberg, Rhineland Palatinate and Saxony Anhalt). While the results were a major reverse for the CDU it is less clear that it was a defeat for the migration policy in the two western states since both Winfried Kretschmann, the Green Minister President in Baden-Württemberg, and Malu Dreyer, the SPD Minister President in the Rhineland Palatinate, openly backed Merkel's refugee policy. Ironically the CDU candidates in both elections had flirted with opposition to Merkel's policy. The AfD surge did not produce an immediate crisis for Chancellor Merkel but has coincided with a noticeable tightening of German policy.

As with the parties on the right, so public opinion became a liability as the flow of refugees showed no sign of slackening. This mood was greatly magnified by the events around Cologne railway station on 31 December 2015, when gangs of young men, allegedly migrants, harassed and sexually assaulted women. A subsequent poll revealed that 81 per cent of the German population thought Merkel had mishandled the refugee crisis (Dempsey, 2016).

Chancellor Merkel had assumed that other states would have little choice in the absence of a supranational solution to support the German position. This proved to be a huge miscalculation. Attempts by the EU Commission with French and German support to impose a mandatory resettlement of 160,000 refugees across the EU provoked a huge backlash from eastern European states and little progress has been made.

The policies of President Putin constituted another liability. His bombing campaign in support of the Assad regime created new waves of refugees (Dempsey, 2016). Russia also stood accused of using black propaganda to whip up anti-refugee feeling in Germany, encouraging the right-wing parties (Gressel, 2016).

Yet one huge liability dwarfed the others, namely the seemingly unstoppable flow of migrants. Merkel drew parallels with the refugees from Bosnia who fled to Germany in the 1990s, about 70 per cent of whom eventually returned. Yet the constellation of international and domestic forces in Syria means that no one believes peace and order is possible. The seemingly never-ending flow of migrants created a diffuse sense of panic and hopelessness throughout the EU until the agreement with Turkey stemmed the flow.

Review

In the summer of 2015, Merkel and Germany appeared to be at the pinnacle of international prestige, with positive perceptions of German leadership. Less than a year later Merkel had conspicuously failed to create a followership among other EU member states for her plans to deal with the migration crisis and was embattled domestically. Germany's attempts to impose a quota system for the redistribution of refugees were fiercely resented, especially by the east European states. Their key objection was that Merkel created a fait accompli by welcoming refugees without consultation and then sought to share the burden with other member states. Germany's leadership credibility was also weakened by its very swift decision in September 2015 to suspend the Dublin Regulation, having been until then its most militant defender.

In her reaction to the eurozone and Ukraine crises, Merkel had handled public opinion very carefully, by never getting ahead of it in the eurozone crisis and not confronting it directly in the Ukraine crisis. After a short honeymoon on the migration crisis she has consistently faced a hostile public opinion. The CSU flirtation with opposition to the Chancellor's policy was one consequence. More fundamentally, public opinion on the migration crisis has strengthened the AfD and raised the real prospect of a sizeable representation of a eurosceptic party in more state parliaments, a development fraught with incalculable consequences. In the 2017 federal elections, the migration issue could become even more politicized, especially if parties to the left sense an opportunity.

Conclusions

Germany's structural power and pro-European position make it 'the indispensable partner' in EU crisis management (Webber, 2014: 354–8). There is recognition of the need to play a stronger role, as Foreign Minister Steinmeier (2016) notes. The issue in the absence of supranational solutions, and with the Franco-German relationship much less effective than in the past, is that there has been no real alternative to German-led solutions. In concluding, we explore whether the crises have changed Germany's European diplomacy and then seek to judge the implications for its contribution to crisis management and the EU's future.

Since unification in 1990, Germany's role in the EU has been subject to a slow shifting of tectonic plates (Jeffery and Paterson, 2004). The EU crisis, by contrast, has resembled volcanic eruptions in close succession that have quickly changed the landscape of German European policy. First, Berlin can now be seen as an intergovernmental actor rather than one predestined to support further steps towards political integration. Salvaging the Lisbon Treaty would appear to have been the last German step along the road to political union. To be sure, integration has occurred amidst the crisis, as evidenced by delegating, especially to the Commission, new central powers in relation to fiscal surveillance and banking union. However, these steps have been borne of necessity rather than of a historic commitment. Second, Germany is prepared to use its power in a relatively uninhibited manner that differs from the past: veto power on Eurobonds; conditionality in relation to eurozone rescues; and the threat of coercive power in the case of the third Greek rescue and in relation to a quota system for EU refugees. Third, European policy has become politicized at home, as manifested in backbench rebellions on the eurozone rescues, the rise of the AfD during the crisis, and a more critical public opinion.

These developments have built upon the slower shifts in both German and EU tectonic plates. Domestically, the intergovernmental character of the rulings of the FCC has been important in the background, creating new constraints and institutional opportunity structures. At the EU level, they have been matched by the shifting terms of the integration cleavage. In the post-Maastricht era, the divide is no longer between integrationists and intergovernmentalists but, rather, is between integration-minded intergovernmentalists on the one hand and 'sovereignists' on the other (Janning, (Merkel, 2010), 2016b). Germany has moved from an integrationist state to an integration-minded intergovernmental state. This shift reflects Chancellor Merkel's call for a new 'union method' which, in a speech at the College of Europe, she defined as 'coordinated action in a spirit of solidarity' (Merkel, 2010).

At the heart of the union method is the European Council (see Chapter 9), the institutional arena in which Germany's political and economic assets are most influential, backed up by Merkel's own negotiating skill. Germany's role has also been enhanced by its ability to exercise discursive leadership. It has considerable 'productive power', owing to 'the attribution of power to Germany by external actors' (Fix, 2015).

Germany's ability to form international coalitions (see Maull, 2008) was most apparent in the Ukraine crisis, where Merkel managed to marshal her reluctant EU partners in favour of sanctions against Russia.

However, in an EU of 'sovereignism' these skills may not always be effective. The power asymmetry between creditors and debtors assisted with the finding of solutions in the eurozone crisis. However, in the migration crisis Germany lacked similar leverage and was only able to secure the reluctant and uncertain support of ten other countries for the application of a quota system for the distribution of migrants among member states. Thus 'sovereignists' have begun to question German leadership in the European Council.

As can be seen, Germany's changed role at EU level is closely connected to the changing domestic context. The contrast between the eurozone and migration crises is striking. Berlin is at its most effective where its policy has domestic support and benefits from power asymmetries at the EU level, as was the case with its diplomacy during the eurozone crisis. In the migration crisis Merkel's policy failed the test of her own description for the union method – a reliance on 'a spirit of solidarity' – and then became embroiled in increasing domestic contestation as a result of the AfD's electoral performance. Germany's influence and productive power declined markedly.

Do these developments herald a failing commitment to the integration project, which would have enormous potential consequences for European politics? Here we enter the realms of speculation. Two scenarios may help envisage the implications.

The positive view anticipates the crisis and the conflicts surrounding them gradually subsiding. The migration crisis, for example, could give way to agreement on a supranational formula that can cope with migration from outside the EU while protecting the Schengen passport-free zone (perhaps for a smaller group of states?). Under these circumstances the issue of German power could become less pressing, allowing the EU institutions to regain responsibility for the EU's diverse policy agenda. This change might also be accompanied by reduced salience of European policy at the domestic level. Clearly, German power is less contentious in the absence of a crisis.

A more negative view is that Germany is going to play more of a hegemonic role in the EU. This scenario is even more likely with the Brexit vote of June 2016 because of the consequent loss of a like-minded state. It could be further exacerbated by deteriorating circumstances in Italy, triggered by banking instability (Economist, 2016). At worst, under this scenario the EU could become more explicitly an extension of the German state: projecting 'what they collectively regard as self-evident, natural and reasonable onto *their* outside world, and ... puzzled that anyone could possibly fail to see things the way they do' (Streeck, 2016: 8). Streeck warns against German 'hegemonic self-righteousness', which during the height of the eurozone crisis was evident in the devotion to ordoliberalism in Berlin and Frankfurt.

This self-righteousness is especially grating when Germany makes an exception for itself (as it did when breaching the SGP in the early 2000s) or drops a principle, such as the Dublin Regulation that had been sedulously invoked early in the migration crisis. If this scenario were compounded in the EU by further euroscepticism in key member states and further sovereignism in the diplomacy of EU states (encouraged by the Brexit vote in the UK), it would not take too much for the kind of EU ineffectiveness over the migration crisis to become systemic.

The increasing politicization of integration within the EU has greatly complicated the efforts of both the supranational institutions and Germany to provide leadership. It could get worse. A Chancellor with declining domestic political authority, due perhaps to the rise of the AfD or indeed a change of power in 2017, could create considerable uncertainty for Berlin's European policy. A Germany with a more constrained or unpredictable European policy could move from asset to liability in the EU.

Given German centrality to the EU, it is worth recalling the observation of Douglas Webber (2014: 359) that the EU has 'never so far had to confront a crisis "made in Germany"'. Germany nonetheless remains the indispensable power. Historically constrained by its leadership-avoidance reflex, Germany has shown greater propensity to lead during the current EU crisis. However, the question raised in this chapter is whether European policy is becoming politicized in such a way that may weaken Germany's future ability to help solve future crises and contribute to the EU's governance more broadly.

References

Applebaum, A. (2015) 'The Risks of Putting Germany Front and Center in Europe's Crises', *Washington Post*, 20 February, https://www.washingtonpost.com/opinions/germanys-central-role/2015/02/20/d1119cd4-b8f8-11e4-aa05-1ce812b3fdd2_story.html, date accessed 16 February 2016.

Bagger, T. (2014) 'The German Moment in a Fragile World', *The Washington Quarterly*, Vol. 37, No. 4, pp. 25–35.

Benner, T. (2016) 'Europe's Lonely Liberal Hegemon', *Politico*, 3 February, http://www.politico.eu/article/merkel-shock-refugee-crisis-germany-policy-europe, date accessed 16 February 2016.

Blyth, M. and Matthijs, M. (2011) 'Why Only Germany Can Fix the Euro: Reading Kindleberger in Berlin', *Foreign Affairs*, Vol. 90, http://www.foreignaffairs.com/articles/136685/matthias-matthijs-and-mark-blyth/why-only-germany-can-fix-the-euro, date accessed 22 February 2016.

Bulmer, S. (2014) 'Germany and the Eurozone Crisis: Between Hegemony and Domestic Politics', *West European Politics*, Vol. 37, No. 6, pp. 1244–63.

Bulmer, S. and Paterson, W. E. (1996) 'Germany in the European Union: Gentle Giant or Emergent Leader?', *International Affairs*, Vol. 72, No. 1, pp. 9–32.

Bulmer, S. and Paterson W. E. (2010) 'Germany and the European Union: from "Tamed Power" to Normalized Power?', *International Affairs*, Vol. 86, No. 5, pp. 1051–73.

Dempsey, J. (2016) 'Putin Uses the Refugee Crisis to Weaken Merkel', *Carnegie Europe*, 8 February, http://carnegieendowment.org/2016/02/08/putin-uses-refugee-crisis-to-weaken-merkel/itmo, date accessed 16 February 2016.

Dullien, S. and Guérot, U. (2012) 'The Long Shadow of Ordoliberalism: Germany's Approach to the Euro Crisis', *European Council on Foreign Relations*, February, http://ecfr.eu/page/-/ECFR49_GERMANY_BRIEF.pdf, accessed 5 February 2016.

Dyson, K. and Featherstone, K. (1996) 'EMU and Economic Governance in Germany', *German Politics*, Vol. 5, No. 3, pp. 325–55.

Economist (1999) 'The Sick Man of the Euro', 3 June, http://www.economist.com/node/209559, date accessed 18 January 2016.

Economist (2016) 'The Italian Job', *Economist*, 9 June, http://www.economist.com/news/leaders/21701756-italys-teetering-banks-will-be-europes-next-crisis-italian-job, date accessed 12 July 2016.

European Commission (2014) Statistical Annex of European Economy, DG Economic and Financial Affairs, Spring, http://ec.europa.eu/economy_finance/publications/european_economy/2014/pdf/2014_05_05_stat_annex_en.pdf, date accessed 22 March 2016.

Fix, L (2015) 'The Different Shades Of German Power – A "Germanification" of EU Foreign Policy during the Ukraine Crisis?', UACES Conference, Bilbao, September.

Gressel, G. (2016) 'Russia's Hybrid Interference in Germany's Refugee Policy: Note from Berlin', *European Council on Foreign Relations*, 4 February, http://www.ecfr.eu/article/commentary_russias_hybrid_interference_in_germanys_refugee_policy5084, date accessed 16 February 2016.

Handelsblatt (2012) 'Wir brauchen eine europäische Geschichte', 16 June, http://www.handelsblatt.com/politik/international/timothy-garton-ash-wir-brauchen-eine-europaeische-geschichte/6755112.html, date accessed 5 February 2016.

Hellmann, G., Jacobi, D., and Urrestarazu, U., eds (2015) *'Früher, entschiedener und substantieller'?: Die neue Debatte über Deutschlands Aussenpolitik*. Wiesbaden: Springer-VS.

Howarth, D. and Rommerskirchen, C. (2013) 'A Panacea for all Times? The German Stability Culture as Strategic Political Resource', *West European Politics*, Vol. 36, No. 4, pp. 750–70.

Janning, J. (2016a) 'Germany's Gambit: Turkey and the Refugee Crisis', *European Council on Foreign Relations*, 28 January, http://www.ecfr.eu/article/commentary_germanys_gambit_turkey_and_the_refugee_crisis5080, date accessed 16 February 2016.

Janning, J. (2016b) 'Germany—Europe's lonely leader', *European Council on Foreign Relations*, 7 January, http://www.ecfr.eu/article/germany_europes_lonely_leader5061, date accessed 23 February 2016.

Jeffery, C. and Paterson, W. E. (2004) 'Germany and European Integration: A Shifting of Tectonic Plates.' In H. Kitschelt and W. Streeck (eds), *Germany: Beyond the Stable State*. London: Frank Cass, pp. 59–75.

Jones, E. (2010) 'Merkel's Folly', *Survival*, Vol. 52, No. 3, pp. 21–38.

Krupa, M. and Ulrich, B. (2016) 'Wird Sie Springen?', *Die Zeit*, 30 January.

Markovits, A. and Reich, S. (1997) *The German Predicament: Memory and Power in the New Europe*. Ithaca, NY: Cornell University Press.

Maull, H. W. (2000) 'Germany and the Use of Force: Still a Civilian Power?', *Survival*, Vol. 42, No. 2, pp. 56–80.

Maull, H. W. (2008) 'Germany and the Art of Coalition Building', *Journal of European Integration*, Vol. 30, No. 1, pp. 131–52.

Merkel, A. (2010) 'Speech by Federal Chancellor Angela Merkel at the Opening Ceremony of the 61st Academic Year of the College of Europe', Bruges, 2 November, https://www.bundeskanzlerin.de/ContentArchiv/EN/Archiv17/Reden/2010/2010-11-02-merkel-bruegge.html, date accessed 11 April 2016.

Paterson, W. E. (1993) 'Muss Europa Angst vor Deutschland haben?' In R. Hrbek (ed.), *Der Vertrag von Maastricht in der wissentschaftlichen Kontroverse*. Baden-Baden: Nomos, pp. 9–18.

Paterson, W. E. (2011) 'The Reluctant Hegemon? Germany Moves Centre Stage in the European Union', *Journal of Common Market Studies*, Vol. 49 (Annual Review), pp. 57–75.

Pond, E. and Kundnani, H. (2015) 'Germany's Real Role in the Ukraine Crisis', *Foreign Affairs*, March/April, https://www.foreignaffairs.com/articles/eastern-europe-caucasus/germany-s-real-role-ukraine-crisis, date accessed 23 February 2016.

Seibel, W. (2015) 'Arduous Learning or New Uncertainties? The Emergence of German Diplomacy in the Ukraine Crisis', *Global Policy*, Vol. 6, No. S1, pp. 56–72.

Spiegel (2012) 'Spiegel Interview with Polish Foreign Minister "We Want To See the Euro Zone Flourish"', 16 May, http://www.spiegel.de/international/europe/poland-s-foreign-minister-explains-why-his-country-wants-to-join-euro-zone-a-833045.html, date accessed 5 February 2016.

Steinmeier, F.-W. (2016) 'Germany's New Global Role', *Foreign Affairs*, Vol. 95, https://www.foreignaffairs.com/articles/europe/2016-06-13/germany-s-new-global-role, date accessed 12 July 2016.

Streeck, W. (2016) 'Scenario for a Wonderful Tomorrow', *London Review of Books*, Vol. 38, No. 7, pp. 7–10, http://www.lrb.co.uk/v38/n07/wolfgang-streeck/scenario-for-a-wonderful-tomorrow, date accessed 31 March 2016.

Tagesschau (2016) 'Kauder ruft zur verbalen "Abrüstung" auf', Tagesschau, 26 January, http://www.tagesschau.de/inland/csu-brief-103.html, date accessed 23 February 2016.

Thompson, H. (2015) 'Germany and the Euro-Zone Crisis: The European Reformation of the German Banking Crisis and the Future of the Euro', *New Political Economy*, Vol. 20, No. 6, pp. 851–70.

Webber, D. (2014) 'How Likely Is It That the European Union Will *Disintegrate*? A Critical Analysis of Competing Theoretical Perspectives', *European Journal of International Relations*, Vol. 20, No. 2, pp. 341–65.

Wimmel, A. (2013) 'Fachliche Expertise und abweichendes Verhalten bei Abstimmungen zur Euro-Krise im Deutschen Bundestag', *Zeitschrift für Politikberatung*, Vol. 6, No. 3–4, pp. 125–36.

Chapter 12

Greece: A Crisis in Two-Level Governance

KEVIN FEATHERSTONE AND DIMITRIS PAPADIMITRIOU

Introduction

The Greek economic crisis dominated the international headlines for much of 2010–16. It was the first and most acute case in the sovereign-debt crisis that emerged in the eurozone during that time. The fact that Greece received three bailouts and is the only eurozone member not to have exited its 'adjustment programme' points to the extreme conditions of the case. More than any other episode in the history of the Economic and Monetary Union (EMU), the Greek crisis encapsulates the vulnerabilities and dilemmas inherent in the two-level governance – European and national – of the single currency. It also highlights the lack of preparedness for the crisis, owing in large part to the inadequate provisions of the Maastricht Treaty; the challenges of creating a mechanism for domestic intervention, especially in light of low-quality national institutions that struggle to deliver reform; the conflicts of interest that arise from loan conditionality; and normative issues that are prompted concerning choice and democratic accountability. The bailouts brought the EU into uncharted territory and raised existential questions about EMU's operation.

For Greece, the strains on its institutional capacity were exacerbated by the onset of a second crisis: that of handling thousands of new migrants, desperate to flee conflicts in Syria and beyond, entering the country from Turkey. In 2015 alone, the United Nations High Commission for Refugees (UNHCR) calculated that 856,723 migrants arrived in Greece by sea. The country already had a poor record in processing asylum-seekers and flows on this scale overwhelmed the public authorities. While highlighting the problems of institutional capacity in Greece, domestically the two crises mostly remained separate in the reactions and narratives they provoked.

This chapter focuses on Greece and the euro crisis and examines it as a case of eurozone crisis management that straddles the European and national levels. In doing so, it seeks to highlight the key issues raised for

EMU's governance. The section titled 'Preparing for the Crisis' considers the preparedness of the eurozone for this crisis. The section 'Two-Level Governance: The Challenges of Institutional Capacity' examines the institutional capabilities for managing the crisis. The section 'Bailout Conditionality as a Lever of Domestic Reform' analyses the strategic interests and interactions of the bailout conditionality. The section 'Normative Europe: Consequences of the Crisis' discusses the normative consequences for the meanings and reputations of Europe. The Conclusions draw out the unresolved issues.

Preparing for the Crisis

Although the Greek crisis exploded onto the EU's agenda in early 2010, the toxic cocktail of policy failures that fanned its flames had been brewing for several years. In June 2000, the European Council agreed that Greece would become the twelfth member of the eurozone in time for the introduction of euro notes and coins, on 1 January 2002. It is now hard to believe that Greece's accession into the eurozone at the time made very few headlines outside Greece and that, by and large, its key macroeconomic indicators were not considered a serious threat to the health of the euro area. Indeed, on some key convergence criteria Greece outperformed many of the other eurozone entrants. In 1999 (the reference year upon which Greece's qualification was agreed), for example, its budget deficit stood at 1.8 per cent, compared with 2.7 per cent for Portugal, Italy, and Germany, and 3.2 per cent for Spain for their reference year of 1997 (Eurostat, 2002: 203). A similarly positive trajectory was also recorded with regards to Greece's inflation rate and long-term interest rates, which were drastically cut in the run-up to eurozone membership (see Table 12.1).

From the outset the one indicator that, above all, exposed the vulnerability of the Greek economy was the accumulated government debt, which in 1999 stood at 103.9 per cent of GDP, the third worst among eurozone members behind Belgium and Italy (see Table 12.1). Yet, of the twelve aspiring eurozone members, only five (Germany not being one of them) came under the 60 per cent threshold set in the Maastricht Treaty. This led European leaders to interpret 'flexibly' the debt criterion, focusing more on its trajectory rather than its actual size. Greece was well placed to benefit from this interpretation. Having reduced its sovereign debt by nearly ten percentage points in the preceding three years and with its economy growing faster than the EU average, the government of Costas Simitis could make a plausible claim that Greece's debt problem was under control.

Table 12.1 *Performance against key EMU convergence criteria*

	1999				2009			
	Budget Deficit/ % GDP	Gross Debt/ % GDP	Inflation rate (HICP)[1], %	Yield of 10-year bond, %	Budget Deficit/ % GDP	Gross Debt/ % GDP	Inflation rate (HICP), %	Yield of 10-year bond, %
Greece	-1.8	103.9	2.1	6.3	-15.6	129.4	1.3	5.17
Spain	-1.1	63.4	2.2	4.7	-11.2	53.9	-0.2	3.98
Portugal	-2.1	54.5	2.2	4.8	-10.2	83.1	-0.9	4.21
Italy	-1.8	114.6	1.7	4.7	-5.4	116	0.8	4.31
EZ	-1.3	72.1	1.1	4.7	-6.4	79.9	0.3	3.82

[1] Harmonised Index of Consumer Prices

Source: Eurostat (2002, 2012)

In the immediate aftermath of Greece's entry into the eurozone, the Greek economy experienced an explosive growth fuelled primarily by a drastic reduction in the cost of borrowing (both private and sovereign) and significant levels of foreign investment in the run-up to the 2004 Olympic games. Yet, at the same time, the first evidence of reform fatigue began to emerge. The escalating budget for the 2004 Olympics and persistent demands for greater government spending put significant strain on public finances during the later stages of the government. Key Simitis government initiatives aimed at improving the competitiveness of the Greek economy, such as pension and labour market reform in 2000–01, were either watered down or abandoned altogether in the face of severe domestic opposition (Featherstone and Papadimitriou, 2008).

The arrival of a new centre-right government in Greece in March 2004, under Costas Karamanlis, recast much of the debate over the merits of Greece's eurozone qualification. Responding to a reservation expressed by Eurostat over the precise level of the deficit of social security funds for 2004, the incoming Finance Minister, George Alogoskoufis, announced that the government was to perform a 'fiscal audit' of the figures that its predecessors had used in the run-up to (and the aftermath of) Greece's membership of the eurozone (Featherstone, 2008). The audit concluded that the Greek government had misreported data to Eurostat on 11 different counts, leading to a considerable revision (upwards) of the figures on the budget deficit and government debt by up to three and seven percentage points respectively (Eurostat, 2004). At the heart of the controversy was whether Greece's considerable military expenditure should have been recorded in the budget at the time of the delivery of the equipment ('delivery method') or at each point that payments were made for these orders ('cash method'). Contravening Eurostat's own practice, which championed the 'delivery method' (Eurostat, 2004: 13), the new Greek government opted for the 'cash method', arguing that the delivery dates of Greece's defence orders could not be estimated with sufficient accuracy.

The political ramifications of this apparent technicality were soon to be felt not only in Athens, but also across the EU. Former Prime Minister Simitis and his close associates vehemently denied the accusation that they had manipulated Greece's accounts, accusing Karamanlis of sabotaging the country's reputation for party political gains, namely the 'shifting' of forthcoming defence spending into the past, so that his own government could enjoy greater fiscal autonomy (Christodoulakis, 2015; Simitis, 2014). Karamanlis and Alogoskoufis, on the other hand, insisted that their sole objective was to set the record straight and inaugurate a period of greater openness regarding Greece's national accounts. Beyond the political introversion in Athens, however, the onset of the 'Greek statistics' drama was to inflict long-term damage to both Greece's economic credibility and the European Commission as the 'guardian' of member states' compliance with the EU treaties. Both issues would later resurface with a vengeance as the health of Greece's economy came under increased scrutiny towards the end of the decade.

The Commission's response to the Greek fiscal audit involved a twin strategy. With regards to the reliability of data produced by the Greek Statistical Agency, the Commission opened an infringement procedure against Greece and made a series of recommendations on how to improve the quality of statistical data on national accounts across the EU (European Commission, 2005). Yet, by the Commission's own admission, the monitoring system put in place was not robust enough (not least because of resistance within the Ecofin Council of eurozone finance ministers against further Commission intrusion in this field) and was largely confined to the principle of self-regulation (European Commission, 2010: 9). In a parallel development, in June 2004, the Commission initiated an excessive deficit procedure (EDP) against the Greek government under the terms of the Stability and Growth Pact (SGP), as the revised data put the budget deficit for 2003 at 3.2 per cent of GDP – just above the Maastricht reference point of 3 per cent (European Commission, 2004). In September 2004 the figure was further revised to 4.6 per cent of GDP, along with Greece's debt which was re-estimated at 109.9 per cent of GDP (Eurostat, 2004: 61–2).

Over the course of the next 30 months the government in Athens attempted to quell doubts about its reformist zeal by pointing to the continuing high levels of economic growth and the apparent improvement of the country's budgetary position. Indeed, in May 2007 the Commission proposed the abrogation of the EDP for Greece, alongside that of Germany and Malta, having concluded that 'the deficit has been brought below the Treaty reference value in a credible and sustainable manner' (European Commission, 2007). Five months earlier the infringement procedure on the operation of Greece's Statistical Agency was also dropped, despite continuous doubts over its professionalism and independence from political interference (European Commission, 2010: 13).

The exit from the EDP in 2007, however, was far from the onset of a virtuous circle for the Greek economy. In the run-up to a snap election later that year, the profligacy of the government in Athens went unchecked. By the time the global financial crisis struck in 2008, the Greek economy was heading for a recession for the first time in 15 years, exposed to a 'perfect storm' of growing budget and current account deficits and increasing levels of indebtedness. Despite reassurances that Greece was 'insulated' from the unfolding global crisis (Dokas, 2008), the credibility of the Karamanlis government to manage the situation had all but evaporated, accelerating the calling of a snap election in November 2009. Over the same period, concerns about the reliability of the government's data on the Greek economy intensified, both within Greece and across Brussels (European Commission, 2010: 18).

By the time that George Papandreou took office as the new Greek Prime Minister, the true scale of Greece's economic predicament became apparent. In the Ecofin meeting of December 2009, the Finance Minister, George Papakonstantinou, revealed that the country's budget deficit was around 13 per cent of GDP rather than 6 per cent as previously reported. Subsequently, the figure was further revised to 15.9 per cent of GDP. With the cost of refinancing Greece's debt skyrocketing, European leaders were soon forced to accept the inevitable: the eurozone would have to be heavily implicated in a bailout package for Greece (Hawley, 2010). The May 2010 Memorandum of Understanding (MoU) between the Greek government and the Troika of creditors – the Commission, the European Central Bank (ECB), and the International Monetary Fund (IMF) – came to epitomize multiple failures of economic governance within the eurozone. At one level the agreement was a response to a policy problem of unprecedented scale and urgency: at €110 billion Greece's was the largest ever bailout programme of its type. It was also put together against the backdrop of extreme volatility in global financial markets and a near institutional 'void' at the European level, given the 'no-bailout' clause contained in the Maastricht Treaty.

On a different level, the fact that Greece's problems were not detected earlier dealt a damaging blow to the Commission, whose own credibility had already been eroded by the Franco-German non-compliance with the terms of the SGP in 2005 (Little, 2012). In 2007, the Commission had given the Greek authorities a clean bill of health, on both the operation of statistical services and the EDP. Two years later, the saga of the Greek statistics and the derailment of public finances had returned to the EU agenda with a vengeance, this time threatening the stability of the entire eurozone. Caught right in the middle of the changeover from the first to the second administrations of José Manuel Barroso, the Commission watched the early stages of the crisis with a mix of complacency and bewilderment. As late as February 2010, the outgoing Commissioner for Economic and Monetary Affairs insisted that the eurozone had 'instruments enough [sic] to deal with this issue and solve this problem [Greece]' (Euractiv, 2010). In reality, however, Germany (in particular) had lost faith that the scale and type of reforms necessary for the rebalancing of the Greek economy could be overseen by purely European means.

The institutional set-up of the Troika and the governance mode surrounding the Greek bailout were clear manifestations of Germany's concern. The crisis, in that sense, heralded a departure from the EU's established ways of doing things (see Chapter 4). The involvement of the IMF in the Greek programme might have caused considerable reputational damage to the eurozone, but at the same time brought additional funding and know-how of external monitoring that the Commission alone lacked. During the early stages of the crisis, the EU's response seemed to be shaped exclusively by France and Germany. Subsequently, the frequent activation of the European Council as the main platform of the EU's policy response perpetuated a sense of crisis and consolidated the impression that EU leaders were falling behind the curve. The EU's bailout fund (initially the European Financial Stabilization Mechanism, subsequently the European Stability Mechanism) was also a purely intergovernmental arrangement outside the EU's institutional framework and completely detached from the EU's own budget. As a result, all bailout programmes escaped systematic scrutiny by the European Parliament, thereby depriving them of the EU-level democratic legitimacy that such an involvement would entail. Such a heavily technocratic, executive-driven response might have initially been justified in the name of 'crisis management', but was ill-equipped in the long term to maintain an adequate level of popular support for the scale of domestic change it necessitated. Nowhere else would this predicament become more apparent than in the case of Greece.

Two-Level Governance: The Challenges of Institutional Capacity

The Greek debt crisis placed the EU in a new institutional position. For the first time, the EU was required to monitor the conditionality of loans to a eurozone member. This confronted the EU with a wider and enduring reality: that the quality of public administrations in some member states raised major impediments to the effective delivery of reform. More than any other bailout state, Greece exposed the challenges of two-level governance in an acute form and became an extreme case that highlighted core issues and risks.

Faced with the challenge of domestic intervention in Greece, the EU fell back on its recent experiences in central Europe. More particularly, the EU had provided major financial support to three non-eurozone countries (Romania, Hungary, and Latvia) under Article 119 of the Treaty Establishing the European Community, a provision for non-EMU states. In each case, the EU had operated in parallel to an aid programme from the IMF. At this stage, the EU did not have the financial resources and the technical experience to rescue Greece by itself. Involving the IMF in a joint operation for Greece also provided political advantages. Several governments, led by Germany, saw IMF involvement as lending credibility and assurance to the operation, and a way to assuage rest-less voters at home. As with its innovation in the case of Latvia, the EU would conduct joint review missions with the IMF to monitor Greece's compliance with the conditions elaborated in the MoU. Far more than in the other cases with which the EU had dealt, Troika review missions were soon embroiled in domestic political controversy. Yet, at different stages of the Greek saga, it was the IMF that showed a softer stance – far from its enduring 'Washington consensus' image of unrelenting austerity – and the EU that 'very actively promoted orthodox measures in return for loans' (Lütz and Kranke, 2010: 2). Repeatedly, the IMF questioned whether Greece's debt would be sustainable after the bailout(s) and even admitted in 2013 that the Greek programmes had underestimated the multiplier effects of austerity (International Monetary Fund, 2013). By contrast, the Commission and the ECB were heavily influenced by the policy paradigm of German ordoliberalism.

The successive Greek bailouts (2010, 2012, and 2015) prioritized adjustments to the government's fiscal position – reducing its debt levels via tax increases and expenditure cuts – suggesting that responsibility for the crisis rested with the mistakes of previous Greek governments. In that sense, the austerity measures carried with them retrospective pen-alties for mistakes of budget indiscipline, to be corrected according to basic ordoliberal principles to create financial stability at home. Athens had broken the rules and 'moral hazard' had to be corrected. There was no acknowledgement that eurozone policies themselves might have con-tributed to the crisis. More particularly, there was little recognition that Greece's continuing lack of adjustment to the eurozone was the result of an institutional incapacity to deliver the required reforms (Boerzel and Risse, 2010; Featherstone, forthcoming).

In reality, the quality of domestic government institutions varies greatly across the EU. Greece is exceptional, but not unique in this regard. The World Bank has developed a composite scale to measure institutional quality, the Worldwide Governance Index (WGI), and, using four of its components ('government effectiveness'; 'regulatory quality'; mainte-nance of the 'rule of law'; and 'control of corruption'), differentiates EU member states over the period 1996–2013 (Featherstone, forthcoming). The rankings of member states remain relatively stable over the 17 years and Greece is not the lowest. Significantly, nine of the current eurozone member states score low on the WGI scale. Among the five eurozone member states requiring financial support, only Ireland ranks high in terms of its quality of governance and it was the first to exit its loan programme. Moreover, its debt problem emanated from the private, not the public, sector. More generally, EU member states with low-quality government institutions are far more likely to have poor records in complying with EU laws, transposing EU legislation, and absorbing

EU funding; while they are also found to have inefficient tax collection systems, low economic competitiveness, and higher levels of public debt. In short, administrative capacity matters for member state performance.

The problems of public administration in Greece are well established. It has a deeply embedded administrative culture that displays the historic influence of the Napoleonic model (hierarchical and centralized), with a stress on legal formalism (the regulation of procedures) rather than problem-solving or innovation (Spanou, 2008). It has suffered from being low skilled and low tech, while appointments and operations have been subject to clientelism (jobs and contracts via patronage) and corruption, further undermining its efficiency. Low levels of trust create something of a 'social trap', stultifying reform of and by the state machine (Rothstein, 2005).

In the Greek case, the Troika resembled 'a state machine deficient in its ability to deliver targeted measures on a set of priorities and according to an agreed schedule, solutions were (thus) found in horizontal cuts in public expenditure (salaries, pensions, jobs, etc.) that further recalibrated the pay-offs for political actors' involved in the reform process (Featherstone, 2015: 15). Institutional weakness intensified the pain of the adjustment process. After an initial optimism, successive monitoring visits to Athens by the Troika reported failures to reach agreed targets, placing Greece well behind the other bailout states.

Undoubtedly, the greater depth of the Greek recession weakened the political will to comply with the tough austerity measures that were a condition of the loans. Indeed, with strong political conflict over the measures, ministers charged with reform have had incentives to protect their own positions by thwarting implementation (Zahariades, 2013), a process partly facilitated by the silo-like fragmentation of central government and the weaknesses of the Prime Minister's institutional position for control and coordination (Featherstone and Papadimitriou, 2015). But institutional weakness is also a significant factor in the ability to deliver the required reforms and this poses a systemic challenge for the EU.

The more immediate institutional lessons for the EU centred on its own involvement in the Troika and the performance of the Commission's Taskforce for Greece, an ad hoc body established in 2011 to provide technical assistance to Greece. In February 2014, the European Parliament's Committee on Economic and Monetary Affairs released a lengthy report on the 'Role and Operations of the Troika with Regard to the Euro Area Programme Countries' (Greece, Ireland, Portugal, and Cyprus), which criticized the potential for a conflict of interest on the part of the Commission stemming from a confusion of its conventional role and its part within the Troika (European Parliament, 2014: 17). The report also noted that 'the Troika is made up of three independent institutions with an uneven distribution of responsibility between them, coupled with differing mandates, as well as negotiation and decision-making structures with different levels of accountability, [and this] has resulted in a lack of appropriate scrutiny and democratic accountability of the Troika as a whole' (European Parliament, 2014: 17–18). The transition to four institutions (the Troika plus representatives of the European Stability Mechanism) in the 2015 bailout did not erase such concerns.

In 2015, the European Court of Auditors similarly highlighted the shortcomings of the Commission's Taskforce for Greece (European Court of Auditors, 2015), pointing out that it had been set up very rapidly, without a full analysis of other options, and without a dedicated budget. The Taskforce had no single comprehensive strategic document for the delivery of technical assistance (TA) or for deciding between competing priorities, despite its mandate to identify and coordinate the TA. In the absence of such a document, the Taskforce worked with the Greek authorities 'on demand' and based on the programmes' conditionality. Moreover, it did not systematically monitor either the way the Greek authorities followed up recommendations or the broader impacts of TA, although it would be useful for TA planning (2015: 7, 8). There was also a wider process problem: the Taskforce spent a lot of its time coordinating with a large number of member states, international organizations, and EU bodies.

Overall, the interaction between the external agents (the Troika and the Taskforce) and Greek public administration raised a number of institutional issues. The operational effectiveness of EU-level bodies amid a complex and disparate leadership was juxtaposed with an often-dysfunctional government machine in Athens, struggling to deliver results. These suggested a need to draw lessons – particularly the recognition that Greece was not alone among EU member states in sustaining low-quality government machines – in order to enhance capabilities and effective performance. The situation also raised normative issues of political accountability and legitimacy.

Bailout Conditionality as a Lever of Domestic Reform

The rescue packages implemented in bailed-out countries brought a degree of intrusion into national policy-making never before seen in the context of EU membership or the EU's enlargement process. The conditions attached to these programmes were extensive in coverage (particularly in Greece) and detailed in the degree of their specificity. Previously, Schimmelfennig and Sedelmeier (2004) have sought to conceptualize the conditions under which EU-prescribed rules were transferred to central and eastern European countries (CEECs) in the context of enlargement.

Their 'external incentives model' identified four key factors that determine the extent to which domestic elites would be able to withstand the adaptational costs of such policy change: (1) the determinacy of conditions set by the EU; (2) the size and speed of rewards associated with successful compliance; (3) the credibility of threats and promises deployed by the EU in case of (non-) compliance; and (4) the size of adoption costs, defined in both political and economic terms (2004: 664).

It is somewhat surprising that the bourgeoning literature on the eurozone bailouts has so far neglected to draw parallels with the conditions attached to the enlargement process. Although a systematic comparative perspective is beyond the scope of this chapter, the application of the 'external incentives model' in the Greek case reveals some interesting insights. Much like EU accession of the CEECs, the size of the reward associated with the successful implementation of the Greek MoU was immense: ultimately, it was about the country's European vocation. The power asymmetry between Greece and its creditors also paralleled the one observed between the EU and the CEECs in the context of enlargement negotiations. So did the determinacy of conditions contained in the Greek MoU (particularly in the second and third bailouts), which prescribed in detail the list of 'prior actions' to be undertaken by the Greek authorities and the time frame for their implementation. Similar to the process of opening/closing of 'chapters' in enlargement negotiations, the gradual release of funds (upon successful fulfilment of Troika conditions) in the Greek bailout reflected the strategy of 'reward by instalments' which has also been standard practice in IMF programmes around the world. Monitoring and reporting also bore similarities: the periodic reviews of the Greek programme mirrored the Commission's Regular Reports on accession candidates, although the intensity and intrusion of Troika monitoring in the Greek programme was arguably greater, particularly as trust between the Greek government and its creditors was depleted as a result of poor implementation.

Yet enlargement and bailout conditions were framed by very different logics. If the EU's eastwards enlargement was enveloped in the optimism of the 'return to Europe' narrative, the Greek bailout was couched in a discourse of 'sinners' and 'moral hazard', which had biblical connotations (Papadimitriou and Zartaloudis, 2015). The surrounding 'noise' mattered. As the first bailout of its type, the example set in Greece was significant not only for other eurozone members which could potentially find themselves in the same situation, but also for the global markets at large, which nervously tried to grapple with the eventuality of a European 'Lehman Brothers' moment, reminiscent of the US financial crash in 2008. The need to reassure and innovate under extreme time contingencies did not suit the EU's institutional operation, where consensus builds slowly. This was reflected in both the dysfunctionalities of the Troika and the unrealistic assumptions behind the design of the Greek programme itself.

Inevitably, the biblical-like discourse of the Greek bailout had a very different effect on domestic empowerment than had EU enlargement. In the process leading up to EU accession, reformist coalitions in central and eastern Europe were empowered and encouraged, although the reformist momentum was not always maintained post-accession. In Greece, the two mainstream parties (PASOK and New Democracy), which had dominated political life since the country's transition to democracy in 1974, came under severe external criticism given the severity of Greece's economic problems and the manner in which they were exposed. Yet it was the same two parties (in different governing constellations) to which Greece's creditors turned in order to implement the most ambitious programme of fiscal adjustment ever seen in peacetime Europe. An already fragile and underperforming political system was put under extreme pressure: externally discredited as corrupt and inept and domestically accused of looting Greece and selling out to its creditors. A rise of populism and extremism since the 2012 election has been the outcome of this process (Vasilopoulou, Halikiopoulou, and Exadaktylos, 2014).

There were also differences elsewhere. One of the main observations of Schimmelfennig and Sedelmeier (2004) for accession applicants was the relative weakness of veto players restricting government policy in eastern Europe (2004: 667). Greece's experience was very different. The idea of TINA ('there is no alternative') never took hold with respect to the MoU, particularly as New Democracy (up to 2012) and the emerging challengers of the political mainstream – notably Syriza – refused to acknowledge its legitimacy and/or inevitability. Nor did Schimmelfennig and Sedelmeier fully acknowledge the importance of administrative weaknesses as effective 'veto points' for the transposition of externally prescribed policy change. In the case of Greece this was a very significant factor, particularly given the ambitious targets set by the programme.

The scale of macroeconomic adjustment required as a condition of the Greek bailout also set its associated adoption costs apart from those observed in the context of EU enlargement. The adoption of the voluminous *acquis communautaire* (body of EU law and regulations) in the CEECs might have involved significant policy change at the domestic level, but the overall fiscal burden was modest. In addition, as candidate countries edged closer to EU membership, the domestic economic climate improved markedly, with most countries registering high growth rates and significant levels of inwards investment. The Greek programme, on the other hand, was a front-loaded austerity package, pursued against the backdrop of severe international turbulence and financial drought. Between 2010 and 2015 Greece's GDP shrank by a quarter, bringing with it massive cuts in wages, pensions, and public services. The breadth and depth of these cuts made it very difficult for reformist coalitions to take ownership of the programme, leaving successive governments in Athens desperately short of friends.

If the costs of Greece's bailout soon became apparent to all, its benefits were much harder to identify and communicate. In the context of its enlargement policy to the CEECs, the EU had made explicit commitments for the opening and closing of accession negotiations and set specific dates for these to be achieved (Laeken 2001; Madrid 1995). The time frame between the opening of negotiations and EU accession was also relatively short at six years (1998–2004). This reinforced the credibility of enlargement-led conditionality, leaving accession candidates under no doubt that successful compliance with its conditions would lead to the reward of EU membership. In the Greek case, the reward was less clearly defined. The first bailout programme was built on the assumption that the Greek economy would contract by 5.5 per cent, but return to growth within two years. By the end of 2012, however, the depth of the recession had reached 17 per cent and modest growth did not return until the second quarter of 2015. Similarly, the Troika estimated unemployment levels would peak at 15 per cent but, in practice, the figure reached 25 per cent, the highest in the eurozone (International Monetary Fund, 2013: 12).

The apparent failure of the first programme to deliver on its objectives pushed Greece's 'reward' further down the line and cast doubt over the ability of the Troika to restore confidence in the Greek economy. The second bailout programme (€109 billion in 2012) contained a promise to reduce Greece's debt burden once primary surpluses were achieved. However, while Greece met this target in 2014, discussions over debt reduction did not materialize. Against this background, the credibility of bailout conditionality was damaged as the nature of the 'reward' became harder to define, as did the time frame of its delivery. Greece's creditors were right to argue that their intervention in 2010 had rescued Greece from the Armageddon of a disorderly default and the economic hardship that this would have entailed. Yet, as the effects of a prolonged and deepening recession hit hard, neither the Troika nor its allies in Athens were able to construct a convincing discourse for legitimizing the bailout programme to an increasingly hostile public opinion in Greece.

Much like its difficulty in producing credible rewards, the Troika's ability to deploy convincing threats against non-compliance was also limited. The issue of 'Grexit' was critical in this respect, particularly since there was no legal base in the EU treaties for the eviction of a eurozone member. In the early stages of the crisis, the deployment of such a threat on behalf of Greece's creditors would have been counterproductive given the potential implications of a Greek default for the European banking sector and particularly French and German banks that were overexposed to Greek debt. The threat of Grexit first appeared on the agenda in the context of Papandreou's ill-fated call for a referendum on the second Greek bailout in November 2011, although at that stage the idea was primarily advocated by the German Finance Minister, Wolfgang Schäuble, rather than making it into official European policy (Sokou, 2014).

The spectre of Grexit returned with a vengeance in the context of the stand-off between the anti-austerity Syriza-led government and Greece's creditors in 2015. By that time the fear of contagion to other eurozone members from a possible Grexit had subsided. The increasing dependence of the Greek banking sector on emergency financing by the ECB made Greece vulnerable to the threat of Frankfurt 'pulling the plug' if the new government of Alexis Tsipras did not comply with the creditors' demands. ECB President Mario Draghi's decision in September 2012 to intervene in the bond markets in order to support Spain and Italy was widely regarded as the ECB's most decisive gesture to save the euro. Nearly three years later, the might of the ECB was directed to the disciplining of the government in Athens. By that time, the Greek Prime Minister was totally isolated. At the Euro Summit (of leaders of countries in the eurozone) on 12 July 2015, he was confronted with the Commission's blueprint detailing the sequence of Greece's exit from the eurozone. For the first time since the crisis began, the nuclear button of Grexit seemed about to be pressed. Later that night, the Greek government agreed the terms of a third bailout package worth €86 billion (Traynor, 2016).

Normative Europe: Consequences of the Crisis

When Jyrki Katainen, EU Commission Vice President, responded to the election of the Syriza government in Athens and the challenge to Greece's bailout terms with a much-quoted remark that 'We don't change our policy according to elections' (Pop, 2015), he was highlighting the intrinsic tension between common EU-level agreements and the scope for democratic choice and accountability within national political systems. During 2015, Greece voted in two parliamentary elections (25 January and 20 September) and one national referendum (5 July). Each returned decisive victories for the anti-austerity parties. Yet none of them led to an abandonment of austerity – indeed, the subsequent course reaffirmed the application of such policies. The normative challenge for the EU polity was, therefore: what can elections decide in bailout states? The impression was of the EU riding roughshod over popular mandates.

In reality, the crisis provoked contending claims. Do debtor states have the right to determine the terms of their rescue? What of the rights of voters in donor states to have their finances protected? Under what conditions can a state justify breaking international agreements and default on its debts? There are conflicting moralities here: between the obligations of a Union to show solidarity and the responsibility of individual states not to 'free-ride' and to avoid moral hazard.

Critics of the eurozone's stance could advance one or more of the following propositions: (1) a Keynesian-type reflation would boost economic growth, overcoming the pain of the recession and easing the debt burden; (2) the accumulated high debt in Greece was not created by the people, who therefore bore no responsibility for settling it; (3) the severity of the austerity measures infringes on the human rights of the Greek people. The first proposition is a matter of technical debate between economists. Keynesians were more likely to diagnose the crisis as being related to structural flaws in a very heterogeneous eurozone – with implications for joint responsibility at the EU level. By contrast, in view of the Maastricht Treaty's provisions for the single currency, the eurozone has been 'locked-in' to the policy paradigm of ordoliberalism (Featherstone, 2012). This stressed 'sound money, sound finances' (European Council, 1997: 236 C): it is the responsibility of governments themselves to create stability policies and, in this environment, growth becomes more sustainable (Dyson and Featherstone, 1999; Seims and Schnyder, 2014).

Successive reforms of eurozone governance since the debt crisis began have reinforced these precepts. The EU's Fiscal Compact (formally the Treaty on Stability, Coordination and Governance in the Economic and Monetary Union), signed in 2012, entrenched the existing rules on deficits and debt more deeply: Article 3(ii) committed member states to put into their national laws or constitutions that such provisions be an obligation and that a 'correction mechanism' for deviations be established. Article 4 made it a requirement that national debt be kept within 60 per cent of GDP. Article 8(ii) allowed for one government to challenge the fiscal position of another before the EU Court, which could impose a lump sum payment or fine (Featherstone, 2012). This represented the near-constitutionalization at the European level of supply-side economics and of ordoliberalism (Bellamy and Weale, 2015). Certainly, the 'policy agenda [of EMU] confronted political cultures in continental Europe that placed a high valuation on full employment policies and solidarity' (Dyson and Featherstone, 1999: 796). Normatively, the euro has been given an increasingly narrow base, which focuses the blame for the crisis on the debt-stricken states themselves.

The Syriza party in Greece campaigned against the first two bailouts on the grounds that they inflicted punitive measures on a people that bore no responsibility for the high levels of public debt. Critics saw this as a populist turn, absolving 'the people' and castigating as a kleptocracy the political class that had alternated in government since 1974. When PASOK's Theodoros Pangalos, the then Deputy Prime Minister, commented that *'mazi ta fagame'* ('everyone had their snouts in the trough'), he was castigated as these were the sins of the elite, not 'the people'. The election victory of Syriza in January 2015 carried hopes that it would cleanse Greek politics, though its opponents were soon quick to highlight its seeming contradictions. The allocation of blame for the debt crisis creates a logic for political change, but a culture of clientelism and corruption tends to be enveloping and systemic – not an easy cleavage for guilt and virtue.

As part of its campaign in government, Syriza created 'The Truth Committee on Public Debt' in April 2015, seemingly emulating Archbishop Desmond Tutu's Truth and Reconciliation Commission in post-apartheid South Africa. This was the initiative of the President of the Parliament, Zoe Konstantopoulou, and critics saw it as rather preposterous – a vanity project for its instigator – but its deliberations made a distinct normative case. Its task was to investigate 'the creation and the increase of public debt, the way and reasons for which debt was contracted, and the impact that the conditionalities attached to the loans have had on the economy and the population' (Hellenic Parliament, 2015: 1). Lest there be any doubt about its role in justice, its mandate was 'to formulate arguments and options concerning the cancellation of the debt' (2015: 1). For the bailout conditions 'have directly affected living conditions of the people and violated human rights, which Greece and its partners are obliged to respect, protect and promote under domestic, regional and international law' (2015: 2). Indeed, '[t]he drastic adjustments, imposed on the Greek economy and society as a whole, have brought about a rapid deterioration of living standards, and remain incompatible with social justice, social cohesion, democracy and human rights' (2015: 2). Greece had a right to the unilateral repudiation of the debt owing to: the absence of good faith; the violation of domestic laws; the precedence of human rights over other contractual obligations; the coercion in the debt restructuring; debt suspension on grounds of state necessity; and, ultimately, the right to unilateral sovereign insolvency (2015: 58–62). Sympathetic academics gave further justification for these arguments (Salomon, 2015). The work of the Committee was brought to a halt when the government called for elections in September 2015, and Konstantopoulou resigned from Syriza. In a follow-up move, Prime Minister Tsipras announced in March 2016 a fresh parliamentary investigation into the debts owed by Greek political parties as well as media groups. His focus was New Democracy and PASOK, which had dominated previous governments, and the cosy financial links with banks and media tycoons, a relationship known as *diaploki* (collusion).

No allowance had been made in the Truth Committee's report for the social and economic rights being claimed for the Greek people being dependent on economic conditions. Rather, these rights were portrayed as having been established under various laws; their contravention was actionable. The discourse served the clear political purpose of overturning austerity, but it was far from the assumptions of Greece's eurozone bailouts: that socio-economic benefits were conditional and the scope for them had to be improved by supply-side reforms and greater flexibility in regulation. Indeed, Greece seemingly had to pay for its past indulgences.

The Greek debt crisis had, thus, exposed a number of normative conflicts: of democratic choice and accountability; of ideological and policy content; and of rights and legitimacy. That a crisis produces political conflict is almost a truism; the challenge for the EU is that the process of European integration has grown in a largely depoliticized climate, facilitated by a permissive public opinion. The Greek crisis shattered such normative assumptions.

Conclusions

The creation of the single currency represents, perhaps, the most ambitious and far-reaching project of European integration to date. The diversity of its membership, the challenges of governance across two levels, and the specific shocks of the global financial crisis have combined to bring its very credibility into question (see Chapter 4). No case highlighted these more than Greece. The eurozone was ill-prepared for the debt crisis: it lacked the policing mechanisms to properly monitor national actions (preventing 'moral hazard') and the instruments to manage a correction. Subsequent reforms of eurozone governance, including the Fiscal Compact and other measures, reinforce the original ordoliberal precepts of the Maastricht design (Featherstone, 2012), placing responsibility firmly at the national level rather than providing stronger systemic management (for example, of a Keynesian kind). Institutionally, the EU's crisis response in the form of the Troika and the Taskforce was marked by a complexity of arrangements, but also limitations of strategy; while it met in Greek public institutions a dysfunctionality that delayed and skewed its efforts. The dilemma is how to overcome the problems of low-quality institutions and of lack of social trust in order to deliver reform with a degree of consensus. Given the severity of the Greek recession, the lessons of the conditionality strategy were the uncertainty of reward and the early ambiguity of threat. Together, the Greek rescue – with its pain and doubtful outcome – challenged the normative basis of the EU with respect to choice, accountability, and legitimacy. In short, the eurozone was ill-prepared, incapacitated, armed with uncertain threats and promises, and lacking in popular engagement.

Systemically, the Greek crisis reveals the Achilles' heel of EMU – the incompleteness of its provisions for governance across two levels, especially when the domestic dimension is so problematic. The significance of a critical case like Greece is that it can highlight dilemmas and vulnerabilities within the system that may occur in some other form elsewhere. If so, as yet, there is little to suggest that these challenges have been properly met.

References

Bellamy, R. and Weale, A. (2015) 'Political Legitimacy and European Monetary Union: Contracts, Constitutionalism and the Normative Logic of Two-Level Games', *Journal of European Public Policy*, Vol. 22, No. 2, pp. 257–74.

Boerzel, T. and Risse, T. (2010) 'Governance without a State: Can it Work?', *Regulation and Governance*, Vol. 4, No. 2, pp. 113–34.

Christodoulakis, N. (2015) *Greek Endgame: From Austerity to Growth or Grexit*. London and New York: Rowman and Littlefield.

Dokas, A. (2008) 'Conspiracy Theories from the Ministry of Finance about the Spread Rise', Kathimerini, 4 December, http://www.kathimerini. gr/342252/article/oikonomia/epixeirhseis/anadiata3eis-stoys-omiloys-loylh-kai-katselh, date accessed 11 December 2016.

Dyson, K. and Featherstone, K. (1999) *The Road to Maastricht: Negotiating Economic and Monetary Union*. Oxford: Oxford University Press.

Euractiv (2010) 'Brussels vows to hold Greece to austerity', Euractiv, 4 February, http://www.euractiv.com/euro/brussels-vows-to-hold-greece-to-austerity, date accessed 11 December 2016.

European Commission (2004) 'Recommendation for a Council Decision on the Existence of an Excessive Deficit in Greece', *SEC(2004)* 815, 24 June.

European Commission (2005) 'Recommendation for a Council Decision Giving Notice to Greece, in Accordance with Article 104(9) of the EC Treaty, to Take Measures for the Deficit Reduction Judged Necessary in order to Remedy the Situation of Excessive Deficit', *COM(2005)* 71, 2 February.

European Commission (2007) 'Commission Recommends Abrogation of Excessive Deficit Procedure for Germany, Greece and Malta', Press Release IP/07/672, Brussels, 16 May, http://europa.eu/rapid/press-release_IP-07-672_en.htm, date accessed 11 December 2016.

European Commission (2010) 'Report on the Greek Government Deficit and Debt Statistics', *COM(2010)* 1, 8 January.

European Council (1997) 'Resolution of the European Council on the Stability and Growth Pact, Official Journal C 236, Brussels, 17 June, http://eur-lex.europa.eu/legal-content/EN/TXT/?qid=1412156825485&uri=URISERV:l25021, date accessed 11 December 2016.

European Court of Auditors (2015) 'Special Report No. 19: More Attention to Results Needed to Improve Technical Assistance to Greece', Luxembourg, 1 September, http://www.eca.europa.eu/Lists/ECADocuments/SR15_19/SR_TFGR_EN.pdf, date accessed 11 December 2016.

European Parliament (2014) 'Report on the Enquiry on the Role and Operations of the Troika (ECB, Commission and IMF) with regard to the Euro Area Programme Countries', Brussels, 28 February, http://www.europarl.europa.eu/sides/getDoc.do?pubRef=-//EP//TEXT+REPORT+A7-2014-0149+0+DOC+XML+V0//EN, date accessed 11 December 2016.

Eurostat (2002) *Yearbook 2002: The Statistical Guide to Europe*. Luxembourg: Office for Official Publication of the European Communities.

Eurostat (2004) 'Report by Eurostat on the Revision of the Greek Government Deficit and Debt Figures', Brussels, 22 November, http://ec.europa.eu/eurostat/documents/4187653/5765001/GREECE-EN.PDF/2da4e4f6-f9f2-4848-b1a9-cb229fcabae3?version=1.0, date accessed 11 December 2016.

Eurostat (2012) *Europe in Figures: Eurostat Yearbook 2012*. Luxembourg: Office for Official Publication of the European Communities.

Featherstone, K. (2008) 'Greece and EMU: A Suitable Accommodation?' In K. Dyson (eds), *The Euro at Ten: Europeanization, Power and Convergence*. New Haven, CT: Yale University.

Featherstone, K. (2012) 'Le Choc de la Nouvelle? Maastricht, Déjà vu and EMU Reform', LSE Europe in Question Series Paper, No. 52, London School of Economics and Political Science.

Featherstone, K. (2015) 'External Conditionality and the Debt Crisis: The "Troika" and Public Administration Reform in Greece', *Journal of European Public Policy*, Vol. 22, No. 3, pp. 295–314.

Featherstone, K. (forthcoming) 'Europe's Soft Underbelly: The EU's Shared Governance and the Variation in Fulfillment of Key Obligations by Member States.'

Featherstone, K. and Papadimitriou, D. (2008) *The Limits of Europeanisation: Reform Capacity and Policy Conflict in Greece*. Basingstoke: Palgrave.

Featherstone, K. and Papadimitriou, D. (2015), *Prime Ministers in Greece: The Paradox of Power*. Oxford: Oxford University Press.

Hawley, C. (2010) 'The World from Berlin: "Lies, Damned Lies and Greek Statistics"', *Der Spiegel*, 16 February, http://www.spiegel.de/international/europe/the-world-from-berlin-lies-damned-lies-and-greek-statistics-a-678205.html, date accessed 11 December 2016.

Hellenic Parliament (2015) 'Truth Committee on Public Debt: Preliminary Report', Athens: Hellenic Parliament.

International Monetary Fund (2013) 'Greece: Ex Post Evaluation of Exceptional Access under the 2010 Stand-By Arrangement', International Monetary Fund (IMF) Country Report No. 13/156, June.

Little, A. (2012) 'Did Germany Sow the Seeds of the Eurozone Debt Crisis?', *BBC News*, 29 January, http://www.bbc.co.uk/news/world-europe-16761087, date accessed 11 December 2016.

Lütz, S. and Kranke, M. (2010) 'The European Rescue of the Washington Consensus? EU and IMF Lending to Central and Eastern European

Countries', LSE Europe in Question Series Paper, No. 22, London School of Economics and Political Science.

Papadimitriou, D. and Zartaloudis, S. (2015) 'European Discourses on Managing the Greek Crisis: Denial, Distancing and the Politics of Blame'. In Karyotis, G. and Gerodimos, R. (eds), *The Politics of Extreme Austerity: Greece beyond the Crisis*. Basingstoke: Palgrave.

Pop, V. (2015) 'EU to Greece: No Debt Relief, Stick to Your Promises', *EU Observer*, 29 January, https://euobserver.com/economic/127406, date accessed 11 December 2016.

Rothstein, B. (2005) *Social Traps and the Problem of Trust*. Cambridge: Cambridge University Press.

Salomon, M. (2015) 'Of Austerity, Human Rights and International Institutions', *European Law Journal*, Vol. 21, No. 4, pp. 521–45.

Schimmelfennig, F. and Sedelmeier, U. (2004) 'Governance by Conditionality: EU Rule Transfer to the Candidate Countries of Central and Eastern Europe', *Journal of European Public Policy*, Vol. 11, No. 4, pp. 661–79.

Siems, M. and Schnyder, G. (2014) 'Ordoliberal Lessons for Economic Stability: Different Kinds of Regulation, Not More Regulation', *Governance*, Vol. 27, No. 3, pp. 377–96.

Simitis, C. (2014) *The European Debt Crisis: The Greek Case*. Manchester: Manchester University Press.

Sokou, K. (2014) 'Geithner reveals "frightening" plans for Grexit in 2012 meeting with Schaeuble', *ekathimerini*, 15 May, http://www.ekathimerini.com/159951/article/ekathimerini/comment/geithner-reveals-frightening-plans-for-grexit-in-2012-meeting-with-schaeuble, date accessed 11 December 2016.

Spanou, C. (2008) 'State Reform in Greece: Responding to Old and New Challenges', *International Journal of Public Sector Management*, Vol. 21, No. 2, pp. 150–73.

Traynor, I. (2015) 'Three Days that Saved the Euro', *The Guardian*, 22 October, http://www.theguardian.com/world/2015/oct/22/three-days-to-save-the-euro-greece, date accessed 11 December 2016.

Vasilopoulou, S., Halikiopoulou, D., and Exadaktylos, T. (2014) 'Greece in Crisis: Austerity, Populism and the Politics of Blame', *Journal of Common Market Studies*, Vol. 52, No. 2, pp. 388–402.

Zahariades, N. (2013) 'Leading Reform amidst Transboundary Crises: Lessons from Greece', *Public Administration*, Vol. 91, No. 3, pp. 648–62.

Chapter 13

Central and Eastern Europe: The Sacrifices of Solidarity, the Discomforts of Diversity, and the Vexations of Vulnerabilities

TIM HAUGHTON

Introduction

In the wake of its multi-faceted crisis, the EU appears 'battered and bruised', with the states of central and eastern Europe (CEE) having taken their fair share of the blows (Phinnemore, 2015). Even before the crisis began, it had been quite a ride for CEE. Over the preceding two decades, the region had experienced the collapse of the communist regimes, democratization, marketization, state-building, and the time-consuming and often demanding process of meeting the onerous entry criteria for the EU. A brief respite for the 2004 entrants was followed by the global economic downturn, which not only hit the economies of CEE hard, especially in the Baltic states, but also put the eurozone – of which an increasing number of CEE states were becoming members – under severe strain, provoking bailouts and austerity measures. A sense of crisis engendered by pressure on the purses of states and citizens was soon compounded by Russian aggression in Ukraine, by the migration crisis, and by concerns over Brexit.

This chapter examines not only how the EU crisis has manifested itself in, and impacted on, the countries of CEE, but also how these states have contributed to the search for (common) resolutions. In particular, it focuses on four dimensions of the crisis: the woes afflicting the eurozone, the migration crisis, Russian aggression in Ukraine, and Brexit. All of these highlight different aspects of the three underlying drivers of the region's interaction with the EU and stances taken in respect of further integration: evolving notions of solidarity; national identity in the twenty-first century; and the deep underlying vulnerabilities that propelled the CEE states towards EU membership in the first place.

For the CEE states, the initial drive for EU membership was inextricably linked to concerns about well-being, security, and place – the last of these being tied to questions of where and with whom they belonged (which was, broadly speaking, with the western states of Europe). In the first years after accession, the EU was successful in helping to supply solutions to these concerns. But the multiple crises facing the Union from 2008 onwards have underlined the burdens as well as the benefits of being in a club that requires the CEE states to contribute to the supply of solutions.

CEE is, of course, a region that is characterized by considerable diversity, with even just a casual glance at its features showing many variations of culture, religion, geography, size, political actors, economic models, currencies, and levels of prosperity. The various dimensions of the EU's crisis have, moreover, arguably highlighted and exacerbated this diversity across and within the states that are commonly grouped under the CEE umbrella. Nonetheless, the common historical experiences of communism and post-communist transformation and the entry of most of the states into the EU during the big bang enlargement of 2004–07 mean that it makes sense to treat the countries as a group, while being cognizant that for every common claim it is easy to find an exception.

Motivations, Expectations, and Realities of Membership

Membership of organizations entails costs and benefits, but it was not so much the costs as the benefits of EU membership that came to the fore during the early days of the accession process. Entry into the EU offered not just access to markets and increased trade and an ability to milk the EU 'cash cow' (Haughton and Rybář, 2009: 550), but also the chance to escape from the past and – in the case of the Baltic states in particular – from the clutches of the big neighbour to the east. Accession, however, was not just about money and security: it was also about the countries' 'rightful' place encapsulated in the slogan 'Return to Europe' – combined with a lack of any alternatives (Nugent, 2004; Schimmelfennig, 2003).

These motivations for membership have been reflected in the process of national preference formation following accession to the club (Copsey, 2013; Ehin, 2013; Haughton, 2010; Mišík, 2015; Papadimitriou and Phinnemore, 2013). The CEE states are on the whole small, trade dependent, and net beneficiaries of the EU budget whose process of national preference formation – as with all member states – is linked to vulnerabilities and perceived weakness. Recognizing the limitations of what can be achieved domestically, integration is therefore advocated as a means of compensating for domestic weakness. The preferences these states hold on EU issues, therefore, is not just rooted in economic statistics such as the openness of the economy or trade dependency; external and geopolitical vulnerabilities are also significant in preference formation.

Vulnerabilities can be addressed by solidarity. In its broadest sense, solidarity can be seen as a 'willingness to participate' (Jones, 2012: 57), but two meanings are central to understanding the motivations of CEE states. The first stems from the notion of deserving poor: we were behind the Iron Curtain for four decades and are significantly poorer. Solidarity in this understanding is the flow of funds from west to east (Galpin, 2017). But this notion of solidarity has been challenged in more recent times initially by the eurozone crisis and the bailouts which required that the poorer CEE states help longer-standing fellow member states in the interests of maintaining the single currency, but more significantly in the demands for burden-sharing in the light of the migration crisis.

Of all the CEE states, only Poland had any expectation of influencing decision-making in a significant way, especially in the early years of membership, when the states were coming to terms with the reality of being a subject and not just an object of EU policy-making. Indeed, some CEE states such as Bulgaria and Romania generally adopted a low profile (Bechev, 2009; Papadimitriou and Phinnemore, 2013). The rotating EU Council Presidency, even with the limitations under Lisbon Treaty arrangements, however, offers small states a moment in the sun and a chance to play a more significant role. During their six months at the helm the Czechs, Poles, Hungarians, Lithuanians, Latvians, and Slovenes pushed priorities driven by their national interests in terms of enlargement, neighbourhood, and energy, but they also contributed to the making of crisis-management policies (Ágh, 2012; Auers and Rostoks, 2016; Beneš and Karlas, 2010; Kajnč, 2009; Pomorska and Vanhoonacker, 2012; Vilpišauskas, 2014).

During their presidency in 2014, for instance, Lithuania played an important role in brokering deals on the multi-annual financial framework (the EU budget) and banking union. Although the negotiations around the banking union highlighted the powers of the big three (France, Germany, and the UK) the Lithuanian Presidency proved to be effective partly because it had 'no particular pre-defined national interest in terms of the substance of the agreement, but rather acted as a broker' and aimed at 'forging a consensus' (Vilpišauskas, 2014: 105). In other cases, though the CEE states did not remain neutral, rather they advocated certain solutions and particular directions. The Czechs, for example, helped the resistance against French President Nicolas Sarkozy's push for protectionism in the early stages of the crisis. Sarkozy's offer of €6.5 billion in aid to French car manufacturers in January 2009 and his suggestion for them to repatriate their activities from CEE provoked an 'open war of words' between Paris and Prague and a declaration against protectionism at the February European Council (Beneš and Karlas, 2010: 74).

Before embarking on a closer analysis of particular crises, two broader contextual points need to be made about politicization and the direction of domestic politics. The crisis fuelled an increased politicization of European issues across the EU. With the important exception of the migration crisis discussed below, in terms of domestic politics at least, European issues were far less politicized in CEE than in southern Europe (Haughton, 2014; Kriesi, 2016). Nonetheless, while during accession almost all mainstream political actors across CEE engaged in pro-European rhetoric, albeit occasionally tinged with a hint of euroscepticism (Szczerbiak and Taggart, 2008), the crisis made it more acceptable to articulate eurosceptic sentiments. The conservative right had long expressed reservations about the (perceived) social liberalism of the European project (Haughton, 2010; Szczerbiak, 2011), but it was those who once claimed to be liberal who became some of the most trenchant critics of the EU. Richard Sulík in Slovakia, for example, whose newly formed party proclaiming its commitment to both economic and cultural liberalism had won parliamentary representation in 2010 (Deegan-Krause and Haughton, 2012), brought down the ruling coalition in 2011 by refusing to support the Greek bailout.Hungarian Prime Minister, Viktor Orbán, whose party, Fidesz, had begun as a federation of liberal youth, compared the empire of Brussels to the Soviet Union.

Orbán's increasingly trenchant criticism of the EU owed much to his domestic political agenda. A new media law and a new constitution which, along with a raft of cardinal (or super-majority) laws, made many constitutional institutions and rights in Hungary less secure, were rushed through after his 2010 election victory. These changes combined with a further turn of the screw after Fidesz romped to another election victory (aided by changes to the electoral law) in 2014 (Scheppele, 2014), which led prominent observers to suggest Hungary was developing into a defective Potemkin democracy (Ágh, 2016). Equally, Law and Justice in Poland, which had gained a reputation for awkwardness when they held the reins of power from 2005 to 2007 (Szczerbiak, 2011), triumphed in the parliamentary and presidential elections in 2015 and began enacting a series of measures which to many observers echoed Orbán's illiberalism (Kelemen and Orenstein, 2016; Ost, 2016). These changes in domestic politics in the two CEE states with arguably the greatest potential influence on EU politics mattered for the development of the Union. Hungary under Orbán and the Law and Justice government in Poland were more interested in keeping the EU from meddling in their internal politics than in finding solutions to the challenges facing the EU. Moreover, the actions of the Hungarian and Polish governments posed a deeper challenge to European liberalism. As Krastev (2015) has noted: '[w]hile the south challenges Berlin's financial policies and rules, Central Europeans are challenging [the EU's] model of the open society'.

The Eurozone: Bailouts and Burdens

The response and actions of the CEE states to the eurozone crisis underscore the salience of solidarity and underlying vulnerabilities. It is worth recalling that only one CEE state, Slovenia, was a member of the eurozone when Lehman Brothers collapsed in September 2008 or even in August 2007 when the 'global financial turmoil' began with the European Central Bank (ECB) and the US Federal Reserve injecting $90 billion into jittery financial markets (Trichet, 2010: 8). Two more CEE states, Slovakia and Estonia, had joined by the time Mario Draghi announced in July 2012 that he would do 'whatever it takes' to defend the euro. By the time quantitative easing began in March 2015, another couple of CEE countries, Latvia and Lithuania, had adopted the single currency (Hodson, 2013, 2016).

The decision to join the eurozone in the face of the crisis, while the Czechs, Hungarians, and Poles stubbornly remained outside, owes much to the sense of economic vulnerabilities, intimately linked to a sense of size and clout at the international level. The Baltic states, in particular, were hit hard by the global credit crunch, experiencing some of the most severe contractions in the world (Connolly, 2012). With their greater dependence on Germany's economic motor, the central Europeans' fall was less bruising thanks to the 'German cushion' (Handl and Paterson, 2013; Učeň, 2015).

Much of the attention surrounding the crisis has focused on Greece, Spain, Italy, and Portugal, but as Jacoby (2014: 60) has argued, 'it is easy to forget that in the autumn of 2008 some of the gravest fears for Europe were concentrated in CEE'. Latvia's slowdown between 2008 and 2010 was 'particularly dramatic', with unemployment soaring from 5.7 per cent to over 20 per cent and GDP dropping 18 per cent in 2009. The country was granted €7.5 billion in bailout funds through a combination of the International Monetary Fund (IMF), European Commission, and individual European states, but 'it only utilized 4.5 billion of this loan facility and even repaid the loan early, at the end of 2012' (Auers, 2015: 177). Although treaty-bound to adopt the euro, joining the single currency appeared to offer shelter and strength in numbers against the harsh winds of the global credit crunch, even if there were fears that countries like Estonia were 'about to board a sinking ship' (Ehin, 2013:

220). For some CEE countries, such as Lithuania, however, the step into the eurozone was not as great given the fact their national currencies had been pegged to the euro for some time, in the case of Lithuania since 2002 (Vilpišauskas et al., 2014: 43). Nonetheless, the very fact that the crisis was seen as an argument in favour of eurozone membership in the Baltic states, but a reason to hold back in Poland, highlights the differential impact of the crisis across CEE.

Once inside the eurozone, the CEE states have been among the least sympathetic to the woes faced by the southern Europeans and the least accommodating to their pleas. Their hard stance owes something to their own experiences. They had endured stormy economic weather several times since the exit from communism and had developed much more of what could be dubbed a 'culture of patience' (Vilpišauskas et al., 2014) or perhaps just a resignation to the fact that life in modern market economies involves enduring occasional tough economic times. Latvia's willingness to take on the chin the acute austerity measures post-2008 was compared unfavourably with the squealing (louder in some cases than others) of the so-called PIIGS (Portugal, Ireland, Italy, Greece, and Spain).

Nonetheless, the tough line and harsh rhetoric directed at the Greeks in particular owed much to notions of solidarity. For many in CEE, solidarity in the post-communist era meant the flow of money from the rich west to the poorer east, but the realities of the eurozone crisis challenged that simple equation. The fact that CEE states were required to contribute to bailouts to countries where wages were higher and pension entitlements more generous provoked howls of discontent. In the eurozone's call for solidarity with Greece, ironically it was the leader of a party called Freedom and Solidarity in Slovakia, Richard Sulík, who refused to back the country's involvement in the Greek bailout, provoking the downfall of the government led by Iveta Radičová in 2011. But it was not just the market liberal right in Slovakia who lambasted the Greeks. Peter Kažimír, Finance Minister of the left-leaning Smer-Social Democracy, was among the harshest critics of the demands of the Syriza government and its flamboyant Finance Minister, Yanis Varoufakis, during 2015 (Featherstone, 2016; Hodson, 2016).

Solidarity with the ordoliberal orthodoxies of northern Europe aside, the CEE states have been limited in their ability to influence outcomes in part owing to their light economic weight (Copeland, 2014). In the early days of the eurozone crisis only Slovenia and Slovakia were present at key meetings of the Eurogroup of finance ministers whose countries had adopted the euro. Yet it was striking that the British Prime Minister Gordon Brown was invited to a special meeting of the Eurogroup in October 2008, despite the UK's non-membership of the eurozone. This suggests that the size of EU member states' economies was probably more important than whether the states were in the eurozone or not. Indeed, west European medium-sized states also had only limited influence both within the Eurogroup and larger global fora such as the G20.

Nonetheless, despite austerity and the travails of the eurozone, the attitudes of ordinary citizens towards the EU did not shift significantly after 2008. Indeed, Slovakia's economic dependency on the EU single market and its people's sense of Slovakia's vulnerability outside the EU, 'all but silence[d] any voices for exit' (Malová and Dolný, 2016). That attitude of permissive consensus, however, changed once large numbers of refugees escaping the Syrian conflict landed on Europe's shores in 2015, provoking debates about European solutions.

The Migration Crisis: Numbers and Nationalism

While the consequences of the global credit crunch and woes of the eurozone were palpable across CEE, the migration crisis posed a more significant challenge to both the states of CEE and the wider EU because it touched on security, identity, and deeper senses of vulnerability. Ironically, it was an aspect of the EU which had most appealed to the CEE states which was central to the way the crisis unfolded: Schengen.

The Schengen zone has particular resonance for the CEE states and their citizens over a certain age. Travel restrictions were one of the great frustrations of the communist era. Joining the Schengen zone, with the associated chances to travel without having to show documents or be questioned by border officials, was not only practical, but also symbolic. Indeed, in symbolic terms 2007, when many of the CEE states joined the Schengen zone, was close in significance to their joining the EU in 2004. But the problem with border-free travel is that the right is extended to all, not just one's own citizens and rich Westerners. Through a mixture of fences (to keep people out) and special buses and trains to transport the migrants across the countries' territory as quickly as possible, many CEE states wanted to pass the buck. Politicians in Hungary, Slovakia, Slovenia, and elsewhere on the route justified their actions by blaming German Chancellor Angela Merkel and her promise to offer help to the refugees, pointing out that few of the Syrians in particular wanted to stay in CEE; rather, they expressed a strong desire to go to Germany.

The burden-sharing and a willingness to participate – at the heart of solidarity mentioned above – were in short supply from CEE as the crisis escalated over the summer and persisted into the autumn of 2015. At an extraordinary Justice and Home Affairs (JHA) Council convened by the Luxembourg Presidency in September, a Commission proposal to increase the number of refugees to be relocated 'according to a complex mathematical formula', was met in particular by 'staunch resistance' from the Visegrad Four (the Czech Republic, Hungary, Poland, and Slovakia), which were keen to focus on border protection measures (Monar, 2016). Another JHA Council later in the month adopted the proposal, but only after Poland lifted its objections and by foregoing consensus and passing the measure by qualified majority. The Czech Republic, Hungary, Romania, and Slovakia voted against (Council of the European Union, 2015; Monar, 2016).

As Monar (2016) has argued, for the first time since the 2004 enlargement an 'East–West' split emerged on JHA. The opposition of the CEE states was further enhanced by the announcement of newly elected Polish Prime Minister Beata Szydło in November, that Poland would stop accepting refugees because of security concerns following the Paris terrorist attacks. In December, the Slovak and Hungarian governments filed an action for annulment against the Council Decision on relocation, helping to make that Council decision 'the most Member State contested JHA measure ever' (Monar, 2016).

The flow of refugees fuelled protests across CEE. The focus of much ire and concern was the cultural and religious background of many of those fleeing the Middle East. In early 2016, for example, a Rally Against Islam took place in Prague, with similar rallies railing against the Islamization of Poland taking place in Warsaw. In his Christmas address to the nation, Czech President Miloš Zeman (2015) warned that Europe faced an organized invasion, not a spontaneous movement, musing that the young male migrants should stay in their countries to fight ISIS instead. Zeman's speech followed just a month after the Paris terrorist attacks which, in the minds of many politicians in CEE, helped to reinforce a perception that the integration of Muslim immigrants into Western societies had failed, a feeling reinforced by the Brussels terrorist attacks in March 2016.

The anti-refugee rhetoric was directed at a domestic audience. Orbán's government put up posters all over the country imploring refugees not to take jobs away from Hungarians and demanding they should respect law and order in Hungary. Given that they were written in Hungarian, a language even the most linguistically talented refugee was unlikely to understand, underlines that the posters were clearly directed at reassuring the domestic audience that the government was 'protecting' Hungary (Ágh, 2016).

The migration crisis tapped into a deeper sense of vulnerabilities. A quick glance comparing the map of Europe in 1988 and 2016 reminds us that for many of the states of CEE, statehood was a relatively recent phenomenon, albeit in a number of cases concerned with *re-creation* rather than *creation* of statehood. The insecurities of statehood had manifested themselves before the crisis: Slovenia, for instance, had delayed Croatia's EU accession in December 2008. Slovenes' sense of vulnerability and their willingness to rock the boat owed much to the country's sense of insecurity linked to fishing rights, access to the sea, and the 'fear' of a large neighbour. Moreover, the thorny issue of the Beneš decrees, which expelled ethnic Germans from the Czech lands after World War II, and the associated fears of demands for the restitution of property if they were to be revoked, had been raised during accession and was invoked by the then Czech President, Václav Klaus, in 2009 when he was mulling over whether to sign the Lisbon Treaty (Haughton, 2010; Novotná, 2015).

States like Slovakia had been defined controversially in the post-communist period as belonging to the titular ethnic group rather than the citizens who lived within the borders of the state. 'Others' pose a potential threat. While in the post-communist period the 'others' have been other Europeans, the refugee crisis brought the prospects of very different others into a region which had not witnessed systematic waves of external migration. As Petsinis (2016) remarked, '[t]he latest refugee influx from Greece to Central Europe, via the former Yugoslavia, is a unique experience that has drastically impacted upon these societies' perceptions as well as actual management of *otherness*.'

On the Edge: Russian Aggression in Ukraine

The migration crisis and the Greek eurozone drama may have dominated the headlines in 2015 and early 2016, but Russian aggression in Ukraine underscored the deeper vulnerabilities which pushed states towards pooling sovereignty in Western clubs such as the North Atlantic Treaty Organization (NATO) and the EU in the first place. It was symbolic that the trigger for the Maidan demonstrations in the heart of the Ukrainian capital Kiev was the refusal of the Yanukovych government under pressure from Moscow to sign the Deep and Comprehensive Free Trade Agreement with the EU at a summit in the former Soviet city of Vilnius, now a capital city of an EU member state (Dragneva-Lewers and Wolczuk, 2015). For the Baltic states in particular, the reaction to the Maidan demonstrations and the fall of Yanukovych in February 2014, which resulted in Russia's annexation of Crimea and destabilization of eastern Ukraine, reinforced fears that many in Moscow had not fully reconciled themselves to the end of the Soviet Union. Given that claims of discrimination had provided pretexts for Russian intervention in Georgia in 2008 and Ukraine in 2014–15, the presence in some CEE states of large numbers of Russian-speaking minorities who had been discriminated against during the post-communist period (Auers, 2015) only heightened fears that Russian President Vladimir Putin's territorial ambitions and geographical meddling went further.

Fearful of a resurgent Russia, countries such as Poland and Lithuania had long been at the forefront of developing the EU's eastern policy and seeking to exert pressure in Washington (Copsey and Pomorska, 2014), even if their impact and effectiveness has been exaggerated (Lightfoot et al., 2016). Poland's influence, however, became increasingly marginal. Indeed, the Poles felt aggrieved to be left out of the Normandy format, made up of representatives of Germany, France, Russia, and Ukraine, designed to resolve the conflict in eastern Ukraine. Poland was fearful that the Germans in particular, with one eye on the German-Russian Nord Stream gas pipeline, would sacrifice Poland's neighbour in the interests of long-term stability.

What was more striking, however, was less the expected fear of the Russian bear, but rather the distinctly pro-Russian sentiments articulated by some leading central European politicians. Perhaps with one eye on their countries' heavy dependence on Russian energy, Bulgarian and Slovak politicians criticized sanctions against Russia imposed in the wake of Russia's annexation of Crimea. Russian influence also appeared central to Orbán's stance. The Russians offered a loan of €12 million for Hungary's Paks II nuclear reactor project to be built by the Russian company Rossatom. Moreover, opponents of the Hungarian Prime Minister were quick to quip that Orbán's frequent trips to Moscow before European summits were visits to his bank manager. Divisions over the stance towards Russia across the EU also appeared to be shaped by Russia's influence over far-right forces in particular member states (Orenstein, 2014). Not all states, however, responded to energy dependence by cosying up to Moscow, and driven by deeper existential vulnerabilities, the Baltic states sought to diversify and reduce dependence on Russian energy.

Brexit and Its Consequences

David Cameron's referendum gamble put the prospect of Brexit on the EU agenda (Copsey and Haughton, 2014). The UK had long been a strong advocate of EU enlargement to the east and most CEE states shared the UK's pro-market, liberal, and Atlanticist positions (Nugent, 2004; Schimmelfennig, 2003). In the run-up to the referendum, CEE states worried that the prospect of Britain's departure might provoke some of the remaining 27 member states to leave. The pro-European Czech Prime Minister Bohuslav Sobotka, for example, feared Brexit might be used as a springboard to Czechxit, especially given the long-standing streak of euroscepticism in Czech politics (Hloušek and Pšeja, 2009). Moreover, Baltic politicians feared Brexit might have implications for security.

For CEE as for the EU as a whole, three of the four baskets of Cameron's proposed 'new settlement' – greater competitiveness, an opt-out from ever closer union, and safeguards for non-eurozone countries were broadly unproblematic; indeed, this last demand had benefits – for Bulgaria, Hungary, Poland, Romania, and the Czech Republic which remained outside the single currency. The sticky issue was welfare benefit entitlement (Oliver, 2015). Thanks to Britain's decision not to impose transitional arrangements, plentiful job opportunities, and the chance for migrants to use and achieve command of the English language, the 2004 enlargement has led to significant migratory flows from CEE to the UK. Indeed, it was the numbers of CEE migrants and their impact on public services and the character of English towns which helped fuel the rise of the United Kingdom Independence Party (Ford and Goodwin, 2014). Driven in part by their desire for a deal and the contributory nature of their own welfare systems, the CEE states accepted the principle that EU migrants should not be entitled to welfare benefits from day one, but with their own citizens living in Britain very much in mind, they helped forge the concession that any deal to restrict child benefit should be phased in.

The result of the June 2016 referendum and the UK's decision to exit will have profound implications for the EU (see Chapter 5). How profound and significant will depend on the complex process of negotiations over the coming years. In terms of CEE, early indications highlight that the responses were much as one would have expected. Eurosceptics, such as Hungary's Orbán, used the British vote to leave as ammunition in their call for the EU to be reformed. Moreover, as 'Brexit means Brexit' became the mantra of Theresa May's new government, concerns about security and the UK's departure from the EU setting a potential precedent for other member states heightened. Nonetheless, in the Baltic states in particular, there was a notable difference between public discussion, which tended to focus on the future status of their citizens living in the UK, and discussions among policy elites who were more concerned about the security implications and the impact of Brexit on policy towards Russia.

The UK's decision to leave also created a headache for two CEE states due to hold the rotating EU Presidency. Slovakia held off presenting the priorities for its presidency in the second half of 2016, but more significantly Estonia, originally scheduled to take up the role in the first half of 2018 after the UK, was forced to bring forward its presidency by six months, thereby forcing the country to speed up and prioritize its preparations – much to the chagrin of officials in Tallinn and the Estonian Permanent Representation in Brussels.

Conclusions

CEE countries had sought membership in the EU in order to address some of their deep underlying vulnerabilities, linked to economic dependency, security, and a sense of where they rightfully belong. Membership had broadly delivered these goals. Nonetheless, the crisis exposed the burdens as well as the benefits of being in the EU. Solidarity meant not just the flow of money from west to east, but also contributing to common solutions. There was much reluctance to the idea of bailing out richer member states, with more generous welfare systems, which had not experienced the economic rollercoaster of post-communism and had eschewed the type of tough structural reforms implemented by the CEE states since 1989. Nonetheless, despite their reservations, the CEE eurozone members understood the need to protect the single currency and implement the sacrifices necessary to do so, thereby allowing them to accept the solutions preferred by the northern European countries. They knew something greater than the sum of its parts would be lost if the single currency failed.

But it was the migration crisis that posed a far greater challenge to the CEE states and appeared to mark a retreat in the process of European integration. Nothing illustrated this dynamic better than the erection of fences and border controls which had been dismantled over the previous two decades. Although this did not amount to the recreation of the Iron Curtain, the undermining of Schengen and the use of anti-refugee rhetoric underlined that the values of openness and tolerance were perhaps not as deeply rooted in CEE as many had previously thought. Progress in European integration masked a lack of progress on integration of a more fundamental kind.

Politicians from across the region made anti-migrant appeals for political ends. With one eye on the impending elections in March 2016, Slovakia's Prime Minister, Robert Fico, for instance, 'mercilessly exploited the Syrian refugee crisis to whip [up] nationalism' (Henderson, 2016). Not only did his party's main election slogan shift from 'we will work for the people' to 'we protect Slovakia', but also the government announced it would only accept Christian refugees after repeated comments by Fico that Muslim communities 'could not be integrated' and that Muslims needed to be monitored. In his party's last election rally, his call to reject all Muslim refugees was received with thunderous applause (Haughton et al., 2016).

More than any other issue, migration exposes the strengths and weaknesses, the advantages and drawbacks, of European integration to the CEE states. Entry into the EU and the resultant right to live and work anywhere within its borders was a major attraction of accession. Many CEE citizens took the opportunity, gaining valuable experiences and skills and sending remittances to their homeland. Yet the outward migration of young, educated, and motivated citizens has been a major problem faced by the CEE states, which has only compounded the deeper demographic crisis of an ageing population. The potential supply of young, motivated refugees from Syria who could help address this crisis was lost on most CEE politicians. The migration crisis highlighted that whatever progress had been made in European integration in political, economic, and social terms, attachments to national identity, particularly those seen in ethnic rather than civic terms, and the fears associated with challenges to that identity, have stubbornly remained.

References

Ágh, A. (2012) 'The Hungarian Rhapsodies: The Conflict of Adventurism and Professionalism in the European Union Presidency', *Journal of Common Market Studies*, Vol. 50, No. 2, pp. 68–75.

Ágh, A. (2016) 'The Decline of Democracy in East-Central Europe', *Problems of Post-Communism*, Vol. 63, Nos. 5–6, pp. 277–87.

Auers, D. (2015) *Comparative Politics and Government of the Baltic States: Estonia, Latvia and Lithuania in the 21st Century*. Basingstoke: Palgrave Macmillan.

Auers, D. and Rostoks, T. (2016) 'The 2015 Latvian Presidency of the Council of the European Union', *The JCMS Annual Review of the European Union in 2015*, Vol. 54, pp. 83–90.

Bechev, D. (2009) 'From Policy-Takers to Policy-Makers? Observations on Bulgarian and Romanian Foreign Policy Before and After EU Accession', *Perspectives on European Politics and Society*, Vol. 10, No. 2, pp. 210–24.

Beneš, V. and Karlas, J. (2010) 'The Czech Presidency', *The JCMS Annual Review of the European Union in 2009*, Vol. 48, pp. 69–80.

Connolly, R. (2012) 'The Determinants of the Economic Crisis in Post-Socialist Europe', *Europe-Asia Studies*, Vol. 64, No. 1, pp. 35–67.

Copeland, P. (2014) 'Central and Eastern Europe: Negotiating Influence in an Enlarged European Union', *Europe-Asia Studies*, Vol. 66, No. 3, pp. 467–87.

Copsey, N. (2013) 'Poland: An Awkward Partner Redeemed.' In Bulmer, S. and Lequesne, C. (eds), *The Member States of the European Union*, 2nd edition. Oxford and New York: Oxford University Press, pp. 186–212.

Copsey, N. and Haughton, T. (2014) 'Farewell Britannia? "Issue Capture" and the Politics of Cameron's EU Referendum Pledge', *The JCMS Annual Review of the European Union in 2013*, Vol. 52, pp. 74–89.

Copsey, N. and Pomorska, K. (2014) 'The Influence of Newer Member States in the European Union: The Case of Poland the Eastern Partnership', *Europe-Asia Studies*, Vol. 66, No. 3, pp. 421–43.

Council of the European Union (2015) 'Council Decision (EU) 2015/1601 of 22 September 2015 establishing provisional measures in the area of international protection for the benefit of Italy and Greece', OJ L 248, 24 September.

Deegan-Krause, K. and Haughton, T. (2012) 'The 2010 Parliamentary Elections in Slovakia', *Electoral Studies*, Vol. 31, No. 1, pp. 222–5.

Dragneva-Lewers, R. and Wolczuk, K. (2015) *Ukraine Between the EU and Russia: the Integration Challenge*. Basingstoke: Palgrave Macmillan.

Ehin, P. (2013) 'Estonia: Excelling at Self-Exertion.' In S. Bulmer and C. Lequesne (eds), *The Member States of the European Union*, 2nd edition. Oxford and New York: Oxford University Press, pp. 213–35.

Featherstone, K. (2016) 'Conditionality, Democracy and Institutional Weakness: the Euro-crisis Trilemma', *Journal of Common Market Studies*, Vol. 54, No. 1, pp. 48–64.

Ford, R. and Goodwin, M. (2014) *Revolt on the Right: Explaining Support for the Radical Right in Britain*. London: Routledge.

Galpin, C. (2017) *The Euro Crisis and European Identities: Political and Media Discourse in Germany, Ireland and Poland*. Basingstoke: Palgrave Macmillan.

Handl, V. and Paterson, W. E. (2013) 'The Continuing Relevance of Germany's Engine for CEE and the EU', *Communist and Post-Communist Studies*, Vol. 63, No. 3, pp. 327–37.

Haughton, T. (2010) 'Zranitelnost, povstupní kocovina a role předsednictví: Formováni národních preferencí nových členských států EU', *Mezinárodní vztahy*, Vol. 45, No. 4, pp. 11–28.

Haughton, T. (2014) 'Money, Margins and the Motors of Politics: the EU and the Development of Party Politics in Central and Eastern Europe', *Journal of Common Market Studies*, Vol. 52, No. 1, pp. 71–87.

Haughton, T., Malova, D., and Deegan-Krause, K. (2016) 'Slovakia's Newly Elected Parliament Is Dramatically Different and Pretty Much the Same: Here's How', *Washington Post*, 9 March, https://www.washingtonpost.com/news/monkey-cage/wp/2016/03/09/slovakias-newly-elected-parliament-is-dramatically-different-and-pretty-much-the-same-heres-how/, date accessed 8 April 2016.

Haughton, T. and Rybář, M. (2009) 'A Tool in the Toolbox: Assessing the Impact of EU Membership on Party Politics in Slovakia', *Journal of Communist Studies and Transition Politics*, Vol. 25, No. 4, pp. 540–63.

Henderson, K. (2016) 'Slovakia's Surprise Election Result: A New Attitude to the EU?', https://epern.wordpress.com/2016/03/10/slovakias-surprise-election-result-a-new-attitude-to-the-eu/, date accessed 8 April 2016.

Hloušek, V. and Pšeja, P. (2009) 'Europeanization of Political Parties and the Party System in the Czech Republic', *Journal of Communist Studies and Transition Politics*, Vol. 25, No. 4, pp. 513–39.

Hodson, D. (2013) 'The Eurozone in 2012: "Whatever It Takes to Preserve the Euro"', *The JCMS Annual Review of the European Union in 2012*, Vol. 51, pp. 183–200.

Hodson, D. (2016) 'Eurozone Governance: From the Greek Drama of 2015 to the Five Presidents' Report', *The JCMS Annual Review of the European Union in 2015*, Vol. 54, pp. 150–66.

Hokovský, R. (2016) 'How migrants brought Central Europe together', *Politico*, 17 February.

Hooghe, L. and Marks, G. (2009) 'A Postfunctionalist Theory of European Integration: From Permissive Consensus to Constraining Dissensus', *British Journal of Political Science*, Vol. 39, No. 1, pp. 1–23.

Jacoby, W. (2014) 'The EU Factor in Fat Times and in Lean: Did the EU Amplify the Boom and Soften the Bust', *Journal of Common Market Studies*, Vol. 52, No. 1, pp. 52–70.

Jacoby, W. (2015) 'Europe's New German Problem: The Timing of Politics and the Politics of Timing.' In M. Matthijs and M. Blyth (eds), *The Future of the Euro*. Oxford and New York: Oxford University Press, pp. 187–209.

Jones, E. (2012) 'The JCMS Annual Review Lecture: European Crisis, European Solidarity', *The JCMS Annual Review of the European Union in 2011*, Vol. 50, pp. 53–67.

Kajnč, S. (2009) 'The Slovenian Presidency: Meeting Symbolic and Substantive Challenges', *The JCMS Annual Review of the European Union in 2008*, Vol. 47, pp. 89–98.

Kelemen, R. D. and Orenstein, M. (2016) 'Europe's Autocracy Problem', *Foreign Affairs*, 7 January.

Krastev, I. (2015) 'Will Germany Give Up on Integration?', *New York Times*, 8 February.

Kriesi, H. (2016) 'The politicization of European integration', *The JCMS Annual Review of the European Union in 2015*, Vol. 54, pp. 32–47.

Lightfoot, S., Szent-Iványi, B., and Wolczuk, K. (2016) 'Mesmerized by Enlargement: The EU's Eastern Neighbourhood Policy and New Member State Transition', *East European Politics and Societies and Cultures*, Vol. 30, No. 3, pp. 664–84.

Malová, D. and Dolný, B. (2016) 'Economy and Democracy in Slovakia during the Crises: From a Laggard to the EU Core?', *Problems of Post-Communism*, Vol. 63, Nos. 5–6, pp. 300–12.

Mišík, M. (2015) 'The influence of perception on the preferences of the new member states of the European Union: The case of energy policy', *Comparative European Politics*, Vol. 13, No. 2, pp. 198–221.

Monar, J. (2016) 'Justice and Home Affairs', *The JCMS Annual Review of the European Union in 2015*, Vol. 54, pp. 134–49.

Newman, A. (2015) 'Germany's Euro Experience and the Long Shadow of Reunification.' In M. Matthijs and M. Blyth (eds), *The Future of the Euro*. Oxford and New York: Oxford University Press, pp. 117–35.

Novotná, T. (2015) *How Germany Unified and the EU Enlarged: Negotiating the Accession through Transplantation and Adaptation*. London: Palgrave Macmillan.

Nugent, N. (ed.) (2004) *European Union Enlargement*. Basingstoke: Palgrave Macmillan.

Oliver, T. (ed.) (2015) 'Cameron's letter: European views on the UK's renegotiation', http://blogs.lse.ac.uk/europpblog/2015/11/10/camerons-letter-european-views-on-the-uks-renegotiation/, date accessed 24 June 2016.

Orenstein, M. (2014) 'Putin's Western Allies: Why Europe's Far Right Is on the Kremlin's Side', *Foreign Affairs*, 29 March, http://www.freerepublic.com/focus/news/3138720/posts/, date accessed 8 April 2016.

Ost, D. (2016) 'Regime Change in Poland, Carried Out From Within', *The Nation*, 8 January.

Papadimitriou, D. and Phinnemore, D. (2013) 'Romania – Uneven Europeanization.' In S. Bulmer and C. Lequesne (eds), *The Member States of the*

European Union, 2nd edition. Oxford and New York: Oxford University Press, pp. 236–58.

Paterson, W. E. (2011) 'The Reluctant Hegemon? Germany Moves Centre Stage in the European Union', *The JCMS Annual Review of the European Union in 2010*, Vol. 49, pp. 57–75.

Petsinis, V. (2016) 'The refugee question in Europe: "south" vs "east"', *open-Democracy*, 7 January, https://www.opendemocracy.net/can-europe-make-it/vassilis-petsinis/refugee-question-in-europe-south-vs-east/, date accessed 8 April 2016.

Phinnemore, D. (2015) 'Crisis-Ridden, Battered and Bruised: Time to Give Up on the EU?', *The JCMS Annual Review of the European Union in 2014*, Vol. 53, pp. 61–74.

Pomorska, K. and Vanhoonacker, S., (2012) 'Poland in the Driving Seat: A Mature Presidency in Turbulent Times', *The JCMS Annual Review of the European Union in 2011*, Vol. 50, pp. 76–84.

Scheppele, K. L. (2014) 'Hungary and the End of Politics: How Viktor Orbán launched a constitutional coup and created a one-party state', *The Nation*, 6 May.

Schimmelfennig, F. (2003) *The EU, NATO and the Integration of Europe: Rules and Rhetoric.* Cambridge: Cambridge University Press.

Szczerbiak, A. (2011) *Poland within the European Union: New Awkward Partner or New Heart of Europe?* London: Routledge.

Szczerbiak, A. and Taggart, P. (eds) (2008) *Opposing Europe? The Comparative Party Politics of Euroscepticism.* Volume 1: *Case Studies and Country Surveys.* Oxford: Oxford University Press.

Trichet, J.-C. (2010) 'State of the Union: The Financial Crisis and the ECB's Response 2007–2009', *The JCMS Annual Review of the European Union in 2009*, Vol. 48, pp. 7–19.

Učeň, P. (2015) 'The Delayed Crisis and the Continuous Ebb of Populism in Slovakia's Party System.' In H. Kriesi and T. Pappas (eds), *European Populism in the Shadow of the Great Recession.* Colchester: ECPR Press, pp. 217–34.

Vilpišauskas, R. (2014) 'Lithuania's EU Council Presidency: Negotiating Finances, Dealing with Geopolitics', *The JCMS Annual Review of the European Union in 2013*, Vol. 52, pp. 99–108.

Vilpišauskas, R., Nakrošis, V., and Kuokštis, V. (2014) 'The Politics of Reacting to the Crisis in Lithuania from 2008–2013: Exiting the Crisis, Entering Politics as Usual?' In K. Bukovskis (ed.), *The Politics of Economic Sustainability: Baltic and Visegrad Responses to the European Economic Crisis.* Riga: Latvian Institute of International Affairs, pp. 38–63.

Webber, D. (2014) 'How Likely is it That the European Union Will Disintegrate? A Critical Analysis of Competing Theoretical Perspectives', *European Journal of International Relations*, Vol. 20, No. 2, pp. 341–65.

Zeman, M. (2015) 'Vánoční poselství prezidenta republiky Miloše Zemana 2015', http://www.ceskatelevize.cz/ivysilani/10997921071-vanocni-poselstvi-prezidenta-republiky-milose-zemana/215411033221226/, date accessed 26 December 2015.

Chapter 14

The European Union, Ukraine, and the Unstable East

WOLFGANG SEIBEL

Introduction

Developments in Ukraine in 2013–14 and a new, aggressive Russian foreign policy represent the most pressing challenge the EU has faced to its Common Foreign and Security Policy (CFSP). What is at stake is both the integrative capacity of the EU vis-à-vis its east European member states and a coherent response to the threat of destabilization resulting from 'a Russia that has made unpredictability a signature element of its strategy' (Bagger, 2015: 31). The Ukrainian crisis thus 'undermines key elements of the post-World War II political and security arrangements in Europe' (Menon and Rumer, 2015: 157). This chapter describes the failure of the EU to achieve the ambitious goals of its European Security Strategy and Eastern Partnership and it analyses the perceptions, responses, and learning patterns that shaped EU policy towards Russia and Ukraine before and during the crisis. The crucial argument is that a mixture of misperceptions and successful learning explain the EU's actions and that future effectiveness hinges on the commitment and diplomatic skill with which the EU implements what eventually emerged as a relatively coherent position in response to Russian aggression against Ukraine.

For the EU, from the early 2000s the idea of building a *cordon sanitaire* along its southern and eastern flanks and combining it with a new tool known as the European Neighbourhood Policy (ENP) was pragmatic and unrealistic at the same time. Like the USA, the EU identified democracy and good governance, built on freedom and prosperity, as the main pillars of international stability. Unlike the USA, the EU rejected the use of military force or possible regime change. Yet the EU lacked a concept, let alone a realistic idea, of how to build democratic institutions embedded in lively civil societies in countries that lacked such essential features. The EU also entirely ignored or merely paid lip service to the perspective of its most important regional rival, Russia, for whom geopolitics alone mattered.

269

This one-sidedness of EU and Russian mindsets and strategies has to be understood in order to make sense of the Ukraine crisis, which broke out in November 2013 when Ukrainian President Viktor Yanukovych suspended negotiations with the EU on an Association Agreement and declared Ukraine's readiness to join the Russian-led Eurasian Union. This triggered a wave of civil unrest known as the Euromaidan movement, named after the square in Kiev where the demonstrations began, which resulted in Yanukovych's ousting.

Yanukovych's accusations of a Euromaidan coup d'état gave Russia the rhetorical ammunition to justify what it portrayed as measures to protect the ethnic-Russian minority in the Donbass region of eastern Ukraine, but in reality was barely concealed military aggression against its neighbour. The first and most significant step was Russia's annexation of Crimea in early March 2014. The second was the establishment and provision of military support for separatist forces in the Donbass region. The Russian-backed insurgency in Ukraine has produced a 'frozen conflict' that threatens the eastern flank of the EU and the stability of eastern Europe as a whole.

Writings on the Wall, Misread

In April 2005, Vladimir Putin famously described the collapse of the Soviet Union as 'a major geopolitical disaster of the century', which, 'for the Russian nation ... became a genuine drama. Tens of millions of our co-citizens and compatriots found themselves outside Russian territory' (Putin, 2005). Two years later, at the annual Munich Security Conference, Putin turned his analysis of the collapse of the former Soviet empire into aggressive accusations against the USA, the North Atlantic Treaty Organization (NATO), and the West in general (Stent, 2014: 135–58). In doing so, he laid the groundwork for what became the dominant Russian narrative of its relations with the West. NATO, according to Putin, had expanded beyond what the former World War II allies and guarantors of German reunification had agreed to in 1990, thereby undermining mutual trust (Putin, 2007). The EU was not a target of Putin's accusations, but it was clear from the overlap between NATO and EU membership for most eastern European countries that Putin saw NATO and EU expansion as essentially the same process.

The EU soon became caught up in the consequences of Russia's understanding of NATO expansion. The key development was the Russian–Georgian war of 2008 (George, 2009; Saparov, 2014; Van Herpen, 2014). With the USA in the middle of a presidential election campaign, by default the EU for the first time became the manager of a serious international crisis. Unlike its indecisiveness during the Yugoslav wars of the 1990s, in August 2008 the EU reacted quickly and decisively in an effort to quell the military confrontation in Georgia and reach a binding agreement to safeguard the territorial integrity of the country against what was clearly Russian military aggression under the pretext of protecting Russian nationals in two separatist provinces. French President Nicolas Sarkozy, then in the European Council Presidency, brokered a peace plan with his Russian counterpart, Dmitry Medvedev, entailing a ceasefire and a withdrawal of military forces, but leaving the final status of the disputed provinces and the general security regime for Georgia to be settled in a broader international framework. At the end of August, Russia unilaterally recognized the two provinces as independent states, thus undermining the very agreement that Sarkozy and Medvedev had brokered less than two weeks earlier.

The Russian–Georgian war and the fate of the Sarkozy–Medvedev agreement became a defining moment for EU–Russian relations. On the one hand, it was clear that Russia was determined to make unscrupulous use of a wide array of formal and informal, legal and illegal, overt and clandestine, and military and non-military means to check what it saw as additional advances by its NATO/EU rival. Alarm bells should have rung in Brussels when, later in 2008, word spread that Russian consular agents in Crimea had started to issue passports to ethnic Russians, regardless of their Ukrainian citizenship (Artman, 2014; Blomfield, 2008) while, at the same time, Russia declared that the protection of ethnic Russians in Georgia was the main reason for its military intervention there. Russia thereby established a model of reaction combined with a narrative of justification that would repeat itself when Russia sought to regain control in Ukraine.

On the other hand, the EU tolerated the open breach of the Sarkozy–Medvedev agreement and, by implication, Russia's violation of Georgia's territorial integrity. This signalled that the EU was neither willing nor able to maintain a credible commitment to its own purposes and pledges. In all likelihood, Russia interpreted the EU's passivity as a sign of encouragement to pursue a course of limited military aggression in what it saw as its legitimate sphere of influence.

Most EU member states were unwilling to abandon a pragmatic and, if possible, constructive partnership with Russia. This held especially for Germany, whose politico-economic linkages with Russia were particularly broad and tight and whose foreign policy elites were strongly committed to the notion of a Russian–German 'partnership in modernization'. Chancellor Angela Merkel's visit to Tbilisi in August 2008 (Deutsche Welle, 2008) and her support – in principle – for Georgia's NATO membership bid could not alter the fact that Germany wanted to return to the status quo of business as usual with Russia. The determination of newly elected President Barack Obama to 'reset' relations with Russia contributed greatly to the 'business as usual' mentality of Germany and other leading EU member states (Stent, 2014: 211–34).

Run-up to the Crisis

It was in this 'business as usual' manner that the EU approached its relations with Ukraine. After all, the EU was cooperating with both Russia and Ukraine within the framework of well-established and more or less successful institutional settings. These included the Partnership and Cooperation Agreement (PCA) with Russia, inaugurated in 1994, under which annual summits took place. The PCA was meant to create, step by step, the conditions under which Russia could join a free trade zone with the EU. Attached to the PCA was a Cooperation Programme through which Russia received €2.7 billion in support of economic and infrastructural development. A major step ahead was agreement, at the St Petersburg summit of May 2003, to create 'Common Spaces' covering such areas as the environment; rule of law; external security; and research, education, and culture (House of Lords, 2015: 15–16).

At the EU–Russia summit in June 2008, shortly before Russia's invasion of Georgia, both sides agreed to begin negotiating an entirely new agreement to succeed the PCA, and intended to include deeper and legally binding commitments across the entire spectrum of the existing partnership (House of Lords, 2015: 16). As a step in the same direction, the 2010 EU–Russia summit launched the Partnership for Modernization, the most explicit and comprehensive cooperation agreement between the EU and Russia, and very much in accordance with the German approach to productive relations with Russia, despite serious disaccord in core areas such as human rights and the rule of law in general.

Negotiations for a new EU–Russia agreement continued through January 2014 (House of Lords, 2015: 16). There could not have been a clearer sign that the EU was willing to ignore the turn of the tide triggered by the Russian invasion of Georgia and was following the path of 'Partnership for Modernization', despite Russia's role in the suspension of the EU–Ukrainian Association Agreement. In the meantime, substantial parts of the 'Common Spaces' programme had become obsolete owing to Putin's openly repressive domestic policy, which featured the intimidation of the judiciary, the dismantling of a free press, and the denunciation of civil society organizations, all of which had no effect on the tactical disposition – let alone the strategy – of the EU towards Russia. 'Business as usual' not only characterized the EU's policy towards Russia but also determined the EU's approach to the Ukraine issue in the framework of the ENP. Just as the EU had not learned from Russia's new assertiveness, the EU now treated Ukraine as just another country in the EU enlargement queue.

Whereas the ENP had existed since 2004, the EU launched the Eastern Partnership only in 2009. Organized in the spirit of, and in accordance with, the European Security Strategy, the Eastern Partnership sought to promote democracy, good governance, energy security, economic and social development, and general political stability. Its main tools were Association Agreements. It was the prospect of such an agreement that triggered the Ukraine crisis in November 2013 (Menon and Rumer, 2015: 107–44).

What distinguished Ukraine was that it was the largest and by far the most important country of the 'Shared Neighbourhood' of the EU and Russia, which included the countries participating in the Eastern Partnership, all of which had been part of the Soviet Union. These countries form a zone of particular sensitivity for both Russia and the EU. Already in the 1990s, Russia made it clear that these countries in its 'close neighbourhood' formed a special area as far as Russian security interests were concerned.

For the EU, the idea of spheres of interest, let alone hegemony, was incompatible with the principles and basic ideas of a European order based on the freedom and self-determination of sovereign states. Clearly, the Russian notion of 'Shared Neighbourhood' was incompatible with the EU's position, an incompatibility that culminated in what Jervis has characterized as the risk of mutual misperception and instability (Jervis, 1978a; 1978b), whereby, for the EU, closer association with Georgia, Moldova, and Ukraine was simply the consequence of self-determination under the auspices of promoting prosperity and security, but for Russia such association became the proof and symbol of encirclement and military threat.

The EU and Russia were fully aware of this security dilemma and tried to limit its likely consequences. This may explain the EU's mild reaction to Russia's aggression against Georgia and Russia's initially limited attempt to prevent Ukraine from signing the Association Agreement with the EU. Just as the EU did not take measures against Russia after the war in Georgia, Russia did not directly intervene against Ukraine's early initiatives ultimately to join the EU. However, whereas the EU eventually accepted the post-2008 status quo in Georgia, Russia increasingly resorted to what may be called clandestine diplomacy to thwart the EU–Ukraine Agreement. At any rate, both sides tried to avoid open confrontation over what was clearly the most contentious issue in EU–Russia relations, namely the future of Georgia and Ukraine as key states of the 'Shared Neighbourhood'.

The decisive difference between the cases of Georgia and Ukraine was that in Ukraine civil society emerged as a powerful player. The very notion of civil society is alien to the Russian political elite, a legacy of its Soviet-style thinking. That a secret Russian deal with Yanukovych could be stifled by civic unrest without foreign initiative or interference was beyond the grasp of Russia's leaders. Yet this is precisely what happened between November 2013 and February 2014.

The Fate of the Association Agreement

Negotiations between the EU and Ukraine for the Association Agreement started in 2007. It took Russia some time to understand fully the actual nature of the planned agreement and its immediate consequences for economic relations between Ukraine and Russia (House of Lords, 2015: 53–5). Apparently, it was only with the preparation of its own free trade initiative, the Eurasian Union, that Russia became concerned about the likely impact of an EU–Ukraine Agreement, thereby prompting Russia to exert serious pressure on Ukraine to suspend negotiations with the EU altogether (ibid.: 44–5).

In August 2013, Russia started to restrict Ukrainian imports, which the Ukrainian opposition immediately described as 'a trade war to pressure the country against signing a cooperation pact with the European Union' (Danilova, 2014; see also Pepescu, 2013). In September 2013, the first signs appeared that Yanukovych might give in to the Russian pressure and possibly reject the Association Agreement (House of Lords, 2015: 54–5).

What made Yanukovych ultimately do so was allegedly the mismatch between the $15 billion loan to be granted by the International Monetary Fund (IMF), with EU support but also with EU conditions attached, versus a $15 billion loan offered by Russia unconditionally (ibid.: 55). The Russian loan was part of a 'Ukrainian-Russian Action Plan', based on a bilateral treaty signed by Yanukovych and Putin in December 2013 (Euronews, 2013). The prospect of this agreement led Yanukovych to abandon the Association Agreement with the EU, which was to have been signed at the European Partnership summit in Vilnius, in November 2013. Yanukovych's change of heart at the Vilnius summit was the proverbial wake-up call for the EU.

The protests triggered by this sudden anti-EU move quickly gained momentum and culminated in a domestic crisis whose international ramifications were clear from the very outset. The EU responded rapidly to the crisis, initially in an ad hoc way on the basis of the Franco-German-Polish 'Weimar Triangle'. In February 2014, the foreign ministers of France, Poland, and Germany, together with a senior Russian diplomat, brokered an agreement between Yanukovych and representatives of the

Maidan. The main elements of the agreement were the restoration of the constitutional rights abolished by the Yanukovych regime since 2010, further constitutional reforms, presidential elections later in 2014, and an independent investigation into the violence during the protests. The agreement faltered almost immediately. Yanukovych disappeared the following night and resurfaced a couple of days later in southern Russia, where he was given refuge.

Russia's Annexation of Crimea and EU Crisis Management

What followed was Russia's annexation of the Crimean peninsula in early March 2014, a clear breach of the Budapest Memorandum on Security Assurances of 1994, in which, in exchange for Ukraine's accession to the Treaty on the Non-Proliferation of Nuclear Weapons, the UK, the USA, and Russia had pledged to 'respect the independence and sovereignty and the existing borders of Ukraine' (United Nations, 1994). In response, the European Council agreed in March 2014 that phased sanctions would be implemented in accordance with Russia's compliance or non-compliance with EU efforts to reach a diplomatic solution to the conflict (for a full 'timeline of the restrictive measures of the EU in response to the crisis in Ukraine' and an overview of their subsequent implementation, see European Council, 2015 and 2016; de Galbert, 2015). At the same time, the EU ended its long-standing efforts to expand and deepen its relations with Russia. The renewal of the PCA, based on the EU 'Common Spaces' programme, was suspended.

The European Council's decision established a mechanism that was flexible enough to accommodate the divergent interests of all 28 EU member states as far as their respective bilateral relationship with Russia was concerned, but bold enough to signal EU determination not to return to 'business as usual' unless Russia ended its aggression against Ukraine and reversed the annexation of Crimea. Moreover, it was in the period between the European Council meeting in March and the Wales NATO summit in September that Germany became the key player of the EU crisis management (House of Lords, 2016: 21–3; Seibel, 2015; see also Chapter 11 in this volume).

Germany's role was particularly delicate. Owing to geographic proximity, economic interdependence, and overlapping zones of regional interests, Germany and Russia share a common history of rivalry and partnership (for a comprehensive account, see Szabo, 2015). Germany had been the most ardent torchbearer of the 'Partnership for Modernization'. Accordingly, Germany had much to lose, economically and politically, from a dramatic change of course in relations between the EU and Russia. By the same token, however, a coherent and determined German policy vis-à-vis Russia became the capstone of a coherent and determined response by the EU in general.

What emerged was a double pattern of delegation and fragmented responsibility within the EU that differed substantially from the governance structure of the concurrent eurozone and migration crises. Both the eurozone crisis and the migration crisis required continuous mutual adjustment of operational details among a considerable number of directly affected EU member states (see Chapters 4 and 6). Crisis management was, therefore, intense and highly visible in terms of media coverage and public attention. By contrast, operational management of the Ukraine crisis was soon delegated to an effective but relatively low-profile ad hoc group that, from early June 2014, became known as the 'Normandy Format', an allusion to the group's first meeting in Normandy on the occasion of the 70th anniversary of the Allied landings there. The Normandy Format replaced the Weimar Triangle that had been instrumental in forging the agreement with Yanukovych in February 2014. The two brokers on the EU side were now France and Germany. By implication, the other member states had essentially delegated their responsibility for a solution to the Ukraine crisis to those two countries.

The overall situation that EU crisis management was facing after the Russian annexation of Crimea was similar to what it faced after Russia's invasion of Georgia, though on a much larger scale. As in Georgia, Russia initiated and supported separatist militias, this time in the Ukrainian provinces of Donetsk and Luhansk, also known as the Donbass. Russia's aggression triggered an outright civil war in April and May 2014, when the Ukrainian government mobilized its insufficiently equipped and poorly trained army in defence of the Donbass region.

On 17 April 2014, the USA, Russia, Ukraine, and the EU reached an agreement in Geneva in which the conflicting parties affirmed their willingness to refrain from 'violence, intimidation or provocative actions', and pledged that all 'illegal armed groups will be disarmed' (Washington Post, 2014). It soon became apparent, however, that Russia had no intention of implementing the accord. On the contrary, Russia continued to arm and equip the pro-Russian insurgents in the Donbass, in an effort to destabilize Ukraine to a degree that would make unfeasible the presidential elections scheduled for 25 May. In response, the G7 (Group of the seven major advanced economies) announced on 26 April that 'the continued efforts by separatists backed by Russia to destabilize Eastern Ukraine', and the absence of any 'concrete actions [of Russia] in support of the Geneva Accord' required its members to 'move swiftly to impose an additional sanction on Russia' (G7, 2014). Neither France nor Germany advocated sanctions, but instead pushed for the stabilization of the Ukrainian government and renewed talks with Russia. The former happened as a result of the presidential elections, which indeed took place and resulted in Petro Poroshenko becoming the new President of Ukraine.

In the run-up to the meeting of the European Council in June 2014, it was evident that Russia had done nothing to honour a unilateral ceasefire pronounced by Ukraine, a fact that should have triggered new sanctions in accordance with the European Council's decision in March. Following its June meeting, the European Council gave Russia three more days 'to actively use its influence over the illegally armed groups [in eastern Ukraine] and to stop the flow of weapons and militants across the border [between Russia and Ukraine], in order to achieve rapid and tangible results in de-escalation'. Otherwise, 'further significant restrictive measures' – sanctions – would be imposed (European Council, 2014a).

No such measures were taken, however, as Merkel and French President François Hollande, in a telephone conversation with Poroshenko and Putin on 29 June, agreed to support Putin's demand to extend the ceasefire, unilaterally declared by Ukraine and constantly violated by Russian-supported insurgents (Deutsche Welle, 2014). Although Merkel and Hollande once again asked for the implementation of Poroshenko's peace plan, the immediate effect of their agreement with Putin was to suspend the decision of the June European Council. This could only undermine the credibility of the EU's commitment to the sanctions regime. Not surprisingly, a subsequent meeting of the foreign ministers of Germany, France, Russia, and Ukraine, held in Berlin in July 2014, produced little of value, resulting only in a joint declaration' through which the foreign ministers 'strongly reconfirm[ed] their commitment to sustainable peace and stability in Ukraine' and to 'the necessity of a sustainable ceasefire' (German Federal Foreign Office, 2014). Nothing of the sort materialized.

From Minsk I to Minsk II

The downing of Malaysian Airways flight MH17 on 17 July 2014 and the death of all on board, on Ukrainian territory controlled by pro-Russian insurgents, became the proverbial game-changer in EU crisis management. Given that the passengers included 196 Dutch citizens, the incident generated a strong sense of EU solidarity. The following month, the pro-Russian insurgents, reinforced by Russian military personnel and heavy weaponry, launched an offensive against Ukrainian regular forces and soon made substantial territorial gains. These developments made the period of July–September 2014 a crucial time of active diplomacy for the EU and NATO, which had three main results.

First, the Presidents of the European Council and of the European Commission issued a joint statement in July 2014 announcing 'a package of significant additional restrictive measures [by the EU] targeting sectoral cooperation and exchanges with the Russian Federation'. Among other things, this would limit access to EU capital markets for Russian state-owned financial institutions; embargo trade in arms; ban exports of dual-use goods; and curtail Russian access to sensitive technologies, particularly in the oil sector (European Council, 2014b). It was the first time that so-called sectoral sanctions were imposed on Russia, according to the plan of phased sanctions agreed to by the European Council in March.

Second, it was due to Merkel's efforts that a balance was struck at the Wales NATO summit between, on the one hand, the claims of Poland, Lithuania, Latvia, and Estonia for a deployment of substantially more NATO ground forces in these countries and, on the other, the German goal of not suspending NATO–Russia links altogether and preserving the NATO–Russian founding act of 1997. This was reached through an agreement on the substantial enhancement of military infrastructure in the aforementioned countries and the creation of a special unit within the NATO Response Force (NATO, 2014).

Third, bilateral contact between Putin and Poroshenko began in late August 2014. Given that, for several months, Russia had simply ignored the existence of a legitimate Ukrainian government and had even tried to obstruct the recent presidential elections, this amounted to a sign of diplomatic progress. A meeting between Putin and Poroshenko in the Belarus capital, Minsk, on 26 August, and a follow-up phone call on 3 September, paved the way to a truce between Ukraine and separatist forces. The agreement, known as the Minsk Protocol (and later as Minsk I), was based on a series of mutual assurances of the conflicting parties, the most relevant of which were an immediate ceasefire; a monitoring and verification mission under the auspices of the Organization for Security and Cooperation in Europe (OSCE), including the permanent monitoring of the Ukrainian–Russian border as well as the creation of security zones on both sides of that border; the release of hostages and illegally detained persons; and the organization of local elections in accordance with Ukrainian law in the Donetsk und Luhansk districts (OSCE, 2014).

The Minsk Protocol was the closest so far to a comprehensive diplomatic accord designed to overcome the Ukrainian crisis. Still, it hinged on the willingness of Russia to honour its own pledges. No such sign of goodwill was in sight. Instead, the UN Human Rights Monitoring

Mission in Ukraine (HRMMU) reported that, in the period between 6 September and 18 November alone, 957 persons had been killed in eastern Ukraine and 'the number of internally displaced people (IDPs) has also sharply increased'. The report noted 'the continuing presence ... [in] the territories under the control of the [self-proclaimed] "Luhansk Peoples Republic" ... of a large amount of sophisticated weaponry, as well as foreign fighters that include serviceman from the Russian federation' (HRMMU, 2014).

By January 2015, the ceasefire in eastern Ukraine had totally collapsed in heavy fighting that culminated in the battle of Debaltseve, in which some 6,000 Ukrainian troops were entrapped by separatist military units supported by regular Russian forces numbering up to 17,000 troops (Kyiv Post, 2015; New York Times, 2015).

It was under these conditions – a failed ceasefire due to continued Russian aggression and a substantially weakened Ukrainian military position – that Germany and France undertook the most serious diplomatic initiative at the highest levels. Merkel and Hollande presented a new peace plan in February 2015 (BBC News, 2015). This was seen as an alternative to initiatives by the US government to directly support the Ukrainian army with sophisticated weaponry. It was precisely the prospect of a decisive escalation through direct military intervention to which Hollande alluded when he said that the Franco-German proposal was the 'last chance' for peace in Ukraine. The stakes were extremely high in terms of the double risk of a serious military escalation and the loss of political capital and prestige. Merkel and Hollande simply could not afford *not* to reach an agreement.

On 11 February, Merkel and Hollande met with Poroshenko and Putin in Minsk. The leaders of the self-proclaimed 'People's Republic' of Donetsk and Luhansk were also present. The outcome of the meeting, which lasted 16 hours, was that, under the auspices of the OSCE, an immediate and full ceasefire in the Donbass was to take place by midnight on 14 February. Beyond that, the crucial components of the agreement were successive steps for the demilitarization in the disputed region; a full-scale exchange of hostages and illegally held persons; and, above all, a package of measures designed to restore a new constitutional order in eastern Ukraine, the rule of law, and the territorial integrity of Ukraine, including full control of the Ukrainian–Russian border by Ukrainian authorities. The key element of the constitutional reform was described as 'decentralization', pertaining to the districts of Donetsk and Luhansk. This was due to take place by the end of 2015 and was to be complemented by local elections based on Ukrainian law and monitored by the OSCE and its Office for Democratic Institutions and Human Rights (ODIHR) (OSCE, 2015).

If there was any progress connected to 'Minsk II', as the agreement soon became known, it was the establishment of a firm framework or 'road map' guaranteed by four national leaders, including Merkel and Hollande. This was the first time that the authority and prestige of the two most influential national leaders in the EU had been invested in a comprehensive peace plan for Ukraine.

Inherent Asymmetry

The fundamental weakness of Minsk II was the imbalance in leverage that the agreement entailed for the signatories. In the absence of any military option, the EU and its main representatives, Germany and France, were obliged to rely on the sanctions regime established by the European Council. By contrast, Russia and its puppet regimes in Donetsk and Luhansk could escalate and de-escalate tensions at will. The immediate effect of that imbalance was Russia's indirect control over domestic political stability in Ukraine. As Minsk II was heavily contested on the right-wing of the political spectrum in Ukraine, even minor military moves by Russian-supported separatist militias in eastern Ukraine reduced the leeway of the Ukrainian government to honour its own obligations resulting from the agreement.

Minsk II was therefore characterized by a series of inconsistencies and asymmetries. The representatives of the EU and Ukraine had committed themselves to maintaining a situation that was beyond their control. The EU and Ukraine had finally established the kind of close ties previously obstructed by Yanukovych, when they concluded the Association Agreement in June 2014. Together with Minsk II, this implied that further EU crisis management was tied to domestic conditions in Ukraine in two ways. One was the usual logic of conditionality that comes with an Association Agreement in the framework of the ENP. The other resulted from Ukraine's obligations within the framework of Minsk II. Whereas the Association Agreement called for serious domestic reforms, primarily in terms of good governance and anti-corruption measures, Minsk II required domestic political consensus on a constitutional reform designed to grant substantial autonomy to the Donbass region controlled by pro-Russian separatists.

One year after Minsk II it was evident that the Ukrainian government had met neither of these requirements. In early February 2016, Ukraine's Economy Minister resigned over what he described as a deeply rooted unwillingness of the politico-economic elite in Ukraine to pursue an effective anti-corruption policy (BBC News, 2016). This greatly alarmed EU officials and member states alike. IMF President Christine Lagarde joined the EU in sharply criticizing Ukraine's inability to honour its obligations to both the EU and the IMF. Lagarde made it clear that the domestic reforms in Ukraine were a binding prerequisite for continued financial support, amounting to a total of $40 billion, to which the IMF was contributing $17.5 billion and the EU $12.5 billion, the rest coming from various other sources. Moreover, officials from EU member states directly linked Ukraine's failure to meet IMF and EU requirements in terms of good governance and corruption to the difficulty of maintaining EU sanctions against Russia. Thus, Denmark's Foreign Minister warned that further stalling of domestic reforms in Ukraine would make it 'very difficult for Europe to remain united in support for sanctions against Russia', and Lithuania's Foreign Minister remarked that current developments in Ukraine 'played into the hands of Russia' (Emmott, 2016). In April 2016, the domestic situation in Ukraine was partly re-stabilized when Prime Minister Arseniy Yatsenyuk, whose dissent with President Poroshenko had become obvious, resigned as well and was succeeded by one of Poroshenko's closest associates, Volodymyr Groysman.

Yet the sanctions regime, based on the united commitment of the EU's member states, was the only bargaining chip available to the EU to exert some leverage over Russia. Throughout 2015 and 2016, Merkel continued to insist on strict linkage between full implementation of Minsk II and the possible suspension of EU sanctions against Russia. The Chancellor reiterated the point on the occasion of Poroshenko's visit to Berlin in February 2016, and again in a joint appearance with Hollande the following month (Ukrinform, 2016). By that time, it was obvious that none of the crucial arrangements of Minsk II had been implemented as envisaged. Poroshenko accused Russia of continuously delivering weaponry and ammunition to the pro-Russian separatists. Skirmishes were frequent and the OSCE's Special Monitoring Mission (SMM) in Ukraine was denied freedom of movement in the separatist-controlled Donbass region. Ukraine's control of the border with Russia remained tenuous at best. In its status report of 23 March 2016, the SMM noted 'a high level of violence' in the Donetsk area, that 'proscribed weapons' were present within what was supposed to be weapon-free security zones, and that 'more than 90 percent of [cease-fire] violations are carried out on the territories outside the control of the Ukrainian government' (SMM, 2016; see also Spiegel-online, 2016).

When the foreign ministers of Russia, France, Germany, and Ukraine met in Paris in March 2016 in the Normandy Format, they were unable to find a viable solution to the conflicting demands of Russia and Ukraine, with Russia insisting on the relevant constitutional reform in Ukraine and, above all, local elections in the Donbass region, and Ukraine insisting on the restoration of Ukrainian law and overall security in the Donbass as a prerequisite for local elections (German Federal Foreign Office, 2016a). In a joint article in the influential German newspaper

Frankfurter Allgemeine Zeitung, in February 2016, just before a visit to Kiev, the French and German foreign ministers had urged Ukraine to return to the pledged domestic reform agenda (Ayrault and Steinmeier, 2016), without explicitly addressing any message to Moscow. That said, Germany's Foreign Minister expressed concern about a new deterioration in the Donbass, immediately after the meeting in the Normandy Format, to the Russian and Ukrainian side alike (Frankfurter Allgemeine Zeitung, 2016a).

In effect, the French and German statements treated Ukraine and Russia as being equally responsible for the stalemate that blocked implementation of Minsk II (Frankfurter Allgemeine Zeitung, 2016b). The even-handedness displayed by the French and German ministers vis-à-vis Ukraine and Russia inevitably reduced even more the EU's ability to achieve full implementation of Minsk II. After all, Russia constantly denied that its military forces were involved in the Ukrainian conflict at all and that it should assume any responsibility for the behaviour of the separatists in the Donbass. Not to challenge what clearly was a Russian attempt to conceal the obvious violation of Ukraine's territorial integrity, while at the same time admonishing Ukraine to fulfil its pledges within the framework of Minsk II, reduced the likelihood of Russian compliance with its international commitments.

German Uncertainties

Alleviating the pressure on Russia and increasing the pressure on Ukraine inevitably weakened the bedrock of EU crisis diplomacy, namely a credible link between the sanctions regime and implementation of Minsk II, the only peace plan at hand. This, in turn, suggested the emergence of another 'frozen conflict', this time in the middle of Europe, and acceptance for the foreseeable future of a constant threat by Russia to the political and economic stability to the east of the EU. This was exactly the opposite of what had been the core objective of the European Security Strategy of 2003.

The ambivalence of German foreign policy contributed to this unsatisfactory situation. Germany had become the key player in EU crisis management, and had to accommodate serious ambiguities as far as Russia and EU–Russia relations were concerned. The main reasons for this were Germany's broad and dense economic ties to Russia, complemented by a thick web of consultation and cooperation mechanisms, of which regular meetings between the two governments, held once a year, were the crucial elements until 2013. The flip side was Germany's considerable dependence on supplies of Russian oil and gas. Within Germany, there was an implicit, albeit unlikely alliance between the conservative, business proponents of economic cooperation with Russia and the political heirs of the *détente* policy of the Cold War era on the political Left. Thus, behind the facade of Merkel's determination to use the EU sanctions regime to make Russia comply with its obligations according to Minsk II, considerable fault lines remained.

Consequently, Berlin sent mixed messages, exposing serious incoherence in terms of strategic communication. Lack of commitment to the EU sanctions regime and, accordingly, to implementation of Minsk II was widespread in Social Democrat and business circles. The business-sponsored Committee on eastern Europe Economic Relations was particularly outspoken against EU sanctions from the very beginning (Frankfurter Allgemeine Zeitung, 2014), and continued to insist that sanctions be lifted unconditionally (n-tv news, 2016). Even more remarkable was that Sigmar Gabriel, the Vice-Chancellor and Economics Minister, who was also the leader of the Social Democratic Party, challenged the notion of full implementation of Minsk II as a prerequisite for lifting the sanctions against Russia (Zeit-online, 2015).

Gabriel made another move that inevitably weakened the coherence and the bargaining position of the EU while indirectly strengthening Russia when he publicly declared the Federal Government's support for a second route for Nord Stream, the gas pipeline through the Baltic Sea connecting the ports of Wyborg in Russia and Greifswald in Germany. The pipeline is operated by a consortium of Russian, German, Austrian, Dutch, and French energy companies, with the Russian state-owned Gazprom as the majority shareholder. The chairman of the shareholders' committee is none other than former German Chancellor Gerhard Schröder, who also happens to be Gabriel's mentor. The current Federal Chancellery confined itself to the comment that a second Nord Stream route (Nord Stream 2) would be considered a private business – a remarkable statement given the obvious political implications of the project.

Nord Stream 2 directly affects the political and economic interests of Ukraine as it would make superfluous the transit pipeline on Ukrainian territory through which a major share of Russian gas is being delivered to central and western Europe, while yielding some $2 billion in fees to the state-owned Ukrainian Naftogaz corporation. At the same time, Nord Stream 2 would increase western Europe's dependence on Russian gas supply. For a substantial minority of EU member states, notably in central and eastern Europe, concerns about a German–Russian agreement were so grave that they addressed a common letter to the European Commission in November 2015, criticizing Nord Stream 2 as being incompatible with the EU's Third Energy Package and with the overall security interests of the EU (Gotev, 2015; Lewis, 2015).

The EU Third Energy Package stipulates that the supply and transportation of energy has to be separated in order to 'unbundle', or deconcentrate, energy consortiums and to prevent powerful corporate trusts from emerging in the energy sector (European Commission, 2015). The aim is not just 'to promote competition and create a liberalized energy market throughout the EU' (Dempsey, 2016), but to counter or prevent abuse of the energy market for geopolitical purposes, that is, political blackmailing by Russia.

Russia can neither meet the requirement of 'unbundling' the supply and transportation of natural gas nor abandon the notion of using energy policy for geopolitical purposes. Consequently, Russia cancelled Gazprom's so-called South Stream Project, which was the south-east European counterpart to Nord Stream. Italy would have been a key beneficiary of South Stream. Indeed, it was Italian Prime Minister Matteo Renzi who, in December 2015, openly complained about German economic selfishness at the expense of the credibility and effectiveness of the EU sanctions regime vis-à-vis Russia (Financial Times, 2015). According to the *Financial Times*, the existing Nord Stream pipeline at that time only operated 'at 50 percent capacity because it violates EU competition regulations', which obviously made obsolete 'any commercial need for doubling its size'. The *Financial Times* quoted experts who claimed that 'the project is part of a Russian strategy to build pipelines that bypass Ukraine, which would diminish the war-torn country's strategic importance' (ibid.).

German experts and politicians alike made considerable efforts to circumvent the stipulations of the Third Energy Package, stating that EU regulation would not be applicable to Nord Stream 2 because the pipeline would be built through international waters (Die Zeit, 2016), while the EU Energy Commissioner, by contrast, stated bluntly that Nord Stream 2 'could undermine EU policies aimed at diversifying energy supplies away from Russia' (Financial Times, 2015).

Vice-Chancellor Gabriel, instead of insisting on the political and economic substance of the EU Third Energy Package, reacted as if the EU was threatening mutual German–Russian interests. He was quoted as telling Putin that Nord Stream 2 would remain 'under the competence of the German authorities …[so that] opportunities for external meddling will be limited' (Oliver and Wagstyl, 2015). By 'external meddling', Gabriel did not mean Russia, whose use of energy policy for political blackmailing had precipitated the EU's Third Energy Package in the first place. Rather, he meant the EU itself. When criticized by his European partners, Gabriel countered that Russia would be willing to agree not to de-couple Ukraine from the existing gas transit pipeline system (Die Zeit, 2016). He seemed not to understand that EU policy in the form of the Third Energy Package was designed to achieve exactly the opposite objective, namely to make EU member states less dependent on Russian 'guarantees', whose lack of trustworthiness was what had brought the

Third Energy Package into being. Together with the unconcealed scepticism displayed by a strange alliance of Social Democrats and business leaders as far as the EU sanctions regime was concerned, the Nord Stream 2 episode made apparent a rift within the German Federal Government. Germany's commitment to the spirit and the mechanisms of the EU sanctions regime and, thus, the implementation of Minsk II, looked extremely doubtful.

This was accentuated by the visit of German Foreign Minister Steinmeier to Moscow in March 2016, where he pointed out that German–Russian relations 'draw their lifeblood from a wealth of contacts in the social and cultural spheres, in business and politics. It is my conviction ... that it is precisely in difficult times like these that we have to give these contacts plenty of space.' It was obvious that Steinmeier was using the language of the EU Common Spaces, which had been suspended in response to the annexation of Crimea. In a demonstrative act, Steinmeier and Russian Foreign Minister Sergeij Lavrov sponsored the signing of an agreement between the Association of Leading Universities of Russia and the German Academic Exchange Service (DAAD), the first of its kind after the annexation of Crimea (German Federal Foreign Office, 2016b). Steinmeier's Moscow visit thus signalled a clear will to return to 'business as usual' with Russia and, once again, Germany's flagging commitment to the sanctions regime. Steinmeier had a record of making unilateral concessions to a Russia unwilling to honour them (Seibel, 2015). In May 2016, there were speculations that he was advocating a partial lifting of EU sanctions against Russia even before complete fulfilment of Russia's obligations according to the Minsk II agreement (Frankfurter Allgemeine Zeitung, 2016c).

Germany's approach inevitably undermined both the strength and the credibility of the entire EU policy vis-à-vis Russia. By the same token, it encouraged Russia to exploit tensions and rifts within the EU while maintaining the very destabilization in Ukraine that the sanctions were supposed to end. What came to bear in the German uncertainties were the contradictions of the country's new role as an unexpected hegemon within the EU (see Chapter 11). On the one hand, Germany took the lead in EU crisis management as far as Russia's aggression and the conflict over Ukraine were concerned, in cooperation with France. The Normandy Format, embedded in a series of similar initiatives primarily in the framework of the OSCE, was a well-adapted setting to make Germany's role compatible with both intra-EU consensus building and the requirements of coherent diplomacy vis-à-vis Russia. On the other hand, Germany's economic position made the country's foreign policy vis-à-vis Russia seem incoherent. Moreover, Merkel had used up much of her political capital within the EU while dealing with the eurozone and migration crises in 2015.

Insisting on a coherent sanctions regime towards Russia against latent and open resistance within both the EU (concerning Hungary, Bulgaria, Italy, and a reluctant France) and her own government (concerning the Social Democrats) became an increasingly unmanageable task. What resulted was the inability of the German foreign policy-making elite to conceptualize a counter-strategy in response to the new threat of enduring instability in the east of the EU which contributed to the erosion of an initially robust crisis management.

Conclusions

The Ukraine crisis originated in the determination of a foreign power, Russia, not to tolerate an EU foreign policy initiative. However, what shaped both the origin and the management of the crisis was a deep-seated incompatibility of mindsets and political spirit that, on the one hand, made the EU's approach to further enlargement naive and short-sighted and, on the other hand, made the Russian reaction both break-neck and aggressive. At the same time, the EU's other crises inevitably reduced the EU's capacity to handle the situation in Ukraine.

The post-war European project was envisioned as a fundamental alternative to what for centuries had been the logic of international order on the European continent: hegemony and balance of power. The notion of a supranational order with strong institutions at the European level, to which national competences were delegated, was a response to the recent, disastrous attempt to establish a hegemonic order, which had left Europe in ruins.

The impulse behind the European project was implicitly geopolitical in nature, but was necessarily based on a worldview that denied geopolitics altogether. West European integration was designed to create stability through economic prosperity and political freedom. At the same time, it was part of a bipolar hegemonic order dividing the continent during the Cold War. Yet the very hegemonic stability that characterized the European condition between 1945 and 1989 was entirely alien to the supranational institutional order in western Europe. Geopolitics and regional hegemony were unacknowledged dimensions of the political and intellectual space in which EC took root.

Even when the linkage between geography and power became more than obvious in the course of EU enlargement into central and eastern Europe, coinciding with the creation of the Common Security and Defence Policy, the problems of geopolitics and regional hegemony remained unaddressed. Geopolitics simply had no point of reference within the institutional setting of the EU and the related perception patterns. Misperceptions and ignorance caused major problems of orientation when the EU had to confront serious consequences of geo-political reality.

That reality was shaped by the end of the Cold War, which caught the EC, then in the process of implementing the single market programme, completely off guard. During the 1990s, the nascent EU proved unable to respond to the Yugoslav wars and the ensuing humanitarian disasters. Enlargement was a plausible concept for regaining stability in eastern Europe while remaining perfectly compatible with the normative mindsets and the institutional routines of the EU so far (for a contemporary assessment of exemplary optimism, see Baldwin, 1995). According to the perceptions and practices of the EU, eastern enlargement was entirely in line with previous waves of enlargement, notably in the 1970s and 1980s (Schimmelfennig, 2003).

So serious and, for EU elites, so self-evident was the project of European stability through enlargement that Russia, in essence, became part and parcel of a related political effort. Russian membership in the EU was not an issue. But integrating Russia into a network that combined mutual dependency and mutual benefits according to the model that had worked so effectively between Germany and France after 1945 was more or less what characterized the general approach of the EU in the framework of eastern enlargement and the Eastern Partnership. Out of this emerged the PCA with Russia, followed by the 'Common Spaces' and the 'Partnership for Modernization'.

At the same time, the EU accepted the Eurasian Union as a structure of regional integration compatible with its overall policy goals. This was quite a leap of faith, given that all of the Eurasian Union's member states are former Soviet republics and that Russia's overwhelming dominance was more than evident. Once again, the EU acted as if the shadow of geopolitics and regional hegemony would disappear if they simply were not acknowledged. This was evident when, in the middle of the Ukraine crisis, Merkel reiterated that negotiations between Russia and the EU on 'possibilities of cooperation in a joint trade area', including the Eurasian Union, should be launched as soon as 'a comprehensive resolution' of the conflict in Ukraine could be reached (Deutsche Welle, 2015). Such geopolitical naivety underlined the inescapable fact that the EU, and Germany in particular, continued to treat Russia as an indispensable partner, both politically and economically. For its part, Russia was single-mindedly focused on geopolitics alone, thereby misreading the actual philosophy and intentions of the EU and ignoring the prospects of a true partnership for modernization so energetically heralded by Germany.

What best explains Russia's perceptions of the EU is the coincidence of a misguided narrative about the loss of power and status in the wake of the collapse of the Soviet Union and an inability to modernize the Russian economy in an attempt to overcome extreme dependence on the energy sector. Putin's State of the Union address of April 2005 demonstrated self-denial of the demise of Russian imperialism, in which the free will of nations in the Russian periphery and the dynamics of their respective civil societies remained unacknowledged and misinterpreted.

As a result, mutual ignorance made the EU and Russia enter a political space that for both was suboptimal. Neither side developed an appropriate sense of their interaction. Just as the institutionalized patterns of actions and perceptions within the EU were not designed to reflect the geopolitical consequences of eastern enlargement, the Russian mindset and narratives were not able to understand the inherent dynamics of EU enlargement as a process driven by the will of central and eastern European nations to join a political community representing the promise of freedom and economic prosperity (Tolstrup, 2014: 193–236). The Ukraine crisis thus became for the EU and Russia a culminating episode in which the consequences of their mutual ignorance and the opportunity for learning clashed.

Three years into the Ukraine crisis, it is unlikely that the limitations of learning on both sides – the EU and Russia – will soon be overcome. As a result, Russia, while enjoying the short-term success of again being taken seriously as a powerful player on the international stage, is ultimately losing out. It will not be able to re-establish a trusting and productive relationship with the EU in the foreseeable future and will find it much more difficult to modernize economically in the face of falling energy prices and an ageing population. While there is no recognizable Russian grand strategy to complement the country's efforts to modernize economically, the EU remains unable to define its own geopolitical role as a benevolent hegemon in eastern Europe. The result is a mutual lack of strategic direction. Russia's foreign policy, for the foreseeable future, will be confined to creating and exploiting instability in Ukraine as a lever of containment towards EU and NATO. The EU has no remedy to counter such obstructionism. Much will depend, therefore, on second-best solutions based on available political and diplomatic skills and on returning the EU to a level of stability prevalent before the outbreak of the multiple crises examined in this book.

References

Artman, V. M. (2014) 'Annexation by Passport: For Russian Interests in Ukraine, the Humble Passport Can Be as Mighty as the Sword', *Al Jazeera America*, 14 March, http://america.aljazeera.com/opinions/2014/3/ukraine-russia-crimeapassportizationcitizenship.html, date accessed 1 April 2016.

Ayrault, J.-M. and Steinmeier, F.-W. (2016) 'Kiew muss handeln,' *Frankfurter Allgemeine Zeitung*, 22 February. http://www.faz.net/aktuell/politik/ausland/europa/gastbeitrag-kiew-muss-handeln-14083020.html, date accessed 6 April 2016.

Bagger, T. (2015) 'The German Moment in a Fragile World', *The Washington Quarterly*, Vol. 37, No. 4, pp. 25–35. [The author is head of policy planning in Germany's Foreign Ministry.]

Baldwin, R. E. (1995) 'The Eastern Enlargement of the European Union', *European Economic Review*, Vol. 39, No. 3–4, pp. 474–81.

BBC News (2015) 'Ukraine Crisis: "Last Chance" for Peace Says Hollande', *BBC News*, 7 February, http://www.bbc.com/news/world-europe-31185027, date accessed 6 April 2016.

BBC News (2016) 'Ukraine Minister Abromavicius Quits Over Corruption', *BBC News*, 3 February, http://www.bbc.com/news/world-europe-35481699, date accessed 6 April 2016.

Blomfield, A. (2008) 'Russia "distributing passports in the Crimea"', *The Telegraph*, 17 August, http://www.telegraph.co.uk/news/worldnews/europe/ukraine/2575421/Russia-distributing-passports-in-the-Crimea.html, date accessed 1 April 2016.

Danilova, M. (2014) 'Russia Accused of Trade War against Ukraine', Associated Press, 15 August, https://www.yahoo.com/news/russia-accused-trade-war-against-ukraine-094801685.html, date accessed 6 April 2016.

De Galbert, S. (2015) 'A Year of Sanctions against Russia – Now What? A European Assessment of the Outcome and Future of Russia Sanctions', Center for Strategic and International Studies (CSIS), October. Lanham: Rowan & Littlefield.

Dempsey, J. (2016) 'Germany, Dump Nord Stream 2', Carnegie Europe, 16 February, http://carnegieeurope.eu/strategiceurope/?fa=62567, date accessed 6 April 2016.

Deutsche Welle (2008) 'Merkel Signals Support for Georgia's NATO Membership Bid', *Deutsche Welle*, 17 August, http://www.dw.com/en/merkel-signals-support-for-georgias-nato-membership-bid/a-3570539, date accessed 7 April 2016.

Deutsche Welle (2014) 'Merkel, Hollande join Ukraine-Russia talks in bid for peace', *Deutsche Welle*, 29 June, http://news.ge/en/news/story/95507-merkel-hollande-join-ukraine-russia-talks-in-bid-for-peace, date accessed 6 April 2016.

Deutsche Welle (2015) 'Merkel and Gabriel offer Russia free-trade agreement', *Deutsche Welle*, 23 January, http://www.dw.com/en/merkel-and-gabriel-offer-russia-free-trade-agreement/a-18211951, date accessed 7 April 2016.

Die Zeit (2016) 'Die Rohrbombe Nord Stream 2: Deutschland hält an der umstrittenen Gaspipeline mit Russland fest – und verärgert damit den Rest Europas', *Die Zeit*, 5 February, http://www.zeit.de/2016/06/nord-stream-2-deutschland-russland-pipeline, date accessed 6 April 2016.

Emmott, R. (2016) 'EU Sanctions on Russia at risk without Ukraine reforms', Reuters, 5 February, http://uk.reuters.com/article/uk-ukraine-crisis-eu-idUKKCN0VE22Q, date accessed 6 April 2016.

Euronews (2013) 'Anti-government Protesters in Kiev Reject Ukrainian-Russian Pact', Euronews, 18 December, http://www.euronews.com/2013/12/18/anti-government-protesters-in-kyiv-reject-ukrainian-russian-pact/, date accessed 6 April 2016.

European Commission (2015) 'Questions and Answers on the third legislative package for an internal EU gas and electricity market' [Press Release Database], 22 October, http://europa.eu/rapid/press-release_MEMO-11-125_de.htm?locale=en, date accessed 25 March 2016.

European Council (2014a) 'European Council Conclusions – Ukraine', 27 June, http://www.consilium.europa.eu/uedocs/cms_Data/docs/pressdata/en/ec/143419.pdf, date accessed 13 May 2016.

European Council (2014b), Statement by the President of the European Council Herman Van Rompuy and the President of the European Commission in the name of the European Union on the agreed additional restrictive measures against Russia, Brussels, 29 July 2014, http://www.consilium.europa.eu/uedocs/cms_data/docs/pressdata/en/ec/144158.pdf, accessed 31 March 2016.

European Council (2015) 'List of Persons and Entities under EU Restrictive Measures over the Territorial Integrity of Ukraine', 16 February, http://www.consilium.europa.eu/en/press/press-releases/2015/02/pdf/17022015-russia-sanctions-table---persons--and-entities_pdf, date accessed 6 April 2016.

European Council (2016) 'Timeline – EU Restrictive Measures in Response to the Crisis in Ukraine', http://www.consilium.europa.eu/en/policies/sanctions/ukraine-crisis/history-ukraine-crisis/, date accessed 31 March 2016.

Financial Times (2015) 'Italy's Renzi Joins Opposition to Nord Stream 2 Pipeline Deal', *Financial Times*, 15 December, http://www.ft.com/intl/cms/s/0/cebd679c-a281-11e5-8d70-42b68cfae6e4.html#axzz452JmY3aB, accessed 6 April 2016.

Frankfurter Allgemeine Zeitung (2014) 'Die Wirtschaft und die Ukraine-Krise, Versuch einer Vereinnahmung', *Frankfurter Allgemeine Zeitung*, 10 April, http://www.faz.net/aktuell/politik/die-wirtschaft-und-die-ukraine-krise-versuch-einer-vereinnahmung-12889824.html, date accessed 6 April 2016.

Frankfurter Allgemeine Zeitung (2016a) 'Steinmeier warnt vor neuer Eskalation in der Ukraine', *Frankfurter Allgemeine Zeitung*, 4 March, http://www.faz.net/aktuell/politik/ausland/europa/verhandlungen-in-paris-steinmeier-warnt-vor-neuer-eskalation-in-der-ukraine-14104869.html, date accessed 6 April 2016.

Frankfurter Allgemeine Zeitung (2016b) 'Steinmeier appelliert an Moskau und Kiew', *Frankfurter Allgemeine Zeitung*, 11 May.

Frankfurter Allgemeine Zeitung (2016c) 'Nichts Neues im Osten. Beim Krisentreffen zur Ukraine bemüht Außenminister Steinmeier sich um gute Stimmung – auch aus parteitaktischen Erwägungen heraus', *Frankfurter Allgemeine Zeitung*, 12 May.

G7 (2014) 'G7 Leader's Statement on Ukraine', 26 April, https://www.g7germany.de/Content/DE/_Anlagen/G8_G20/G7-leaders_statement-ukr-2014-04-26-eng.pdf?__blob=publicationFile&v=6, date accessed 6 April 2016.

George, J. (2009) *The Politics of Ethnic Separatism in Russia and Georgia*. Basingstoke: Palgrave Macmillan.

German Federal Foreign Office (2014) 'Joint Declaration by the Foreign Ministers of Ukraine, Russia, France and Germany' [Press Release], 2 July, http://www.auswaertiges-amt.de/DE/Infoservice/Presse/Meldun-gen/2014/140702_Statement.html, date accessed 6 April 2016.

German Federal Foreign Office (2016a) 'Normandy Format Meeting on Ukraine in Paris: Toddling Little Steps Aren't Enough Any More' [Press Release], 3 March, https://www.auswaertiges-amt.de/EN/Aussenpolitik/Laender/Aktuelle_Artikel/Ukraine/160303_Normandietreffen.html, accessed 28 March 2016.

German Federal Foreign Office (2016b) 'German Russian Contacts Need Space', http://www.auswaertiges-amt.de/EN/Aussenpolitik/Laender/Aktuelle_Artikel/RussischeFoerderation/160323-BM-Moskau.html, date accessed 13 May 2016.

Gotev, G. (2015) 'EU Leaders to Clash Over North Stream 2 at Summit', Euractiv, December, https://www.euractiv.com/section/europe-s-east/news/eu-leaders-to-clash-over-nord-stream-2-at-summit/, date accessed 6 April 2016.

House of Lords (2015) 'The EU and Russia: Before and Beyond the Crisis in Ukraine', European Union Committee, 6th report of session 2014–15, HL Paper No. 115, 20 February, London: The Stationery Office, http://www.publications.parliament.uk/pa/ld201415/ldselect/ldeucom/115/115.pdf, date accessed 6 April 2016.

House of Lords (2016) 'Europe in the World: Towards a More Effective EU Foreign and Security Strategy', European Union Committee, 8th report of session 2015–16, HL Paper No. 97, 16 February, London: The Stationery Office, http://www.publications.parliament.uk/pa/ld201516/ldselect/ldeucom/97/97.pdf, date accessed 6 April 2016.

HRMMU (2014) 'Serious Humans Right Violations Persist in Eastern Ukraine Despite Tenuous Ceasefire – UN Report', UN Human Rights Monitoring Mission in Ukraine (HRMMU), Geneva, 20 November, http://www.ohchr.org/en/NewsEvents/Pages/DisplayNews.aspx?NewsID=15316&LangID=E, date accessed 6 April 2016.

Jervis, R. (1978a) 'Cooperation Under the Security Dilemma', *World Politics*, Vol. 30, No. 2, pp. 186–214.

Jervis, R. (1978b) *Perception and Misperception in International Politics*, Princeton: Princeton University Press.

Kyiv Post (2015) 'Russian Media Admits That Regular Russian Troops Took Debaltseve', *Kyiv Post*, 25 February, http://www.kyivpost.com/article/content/ukraine-abroad/examiner-russian-media-admits-that-regular-russian-troops-took-debaltseve-381468.html, date accessed 6 April 2016.

Lewis, B. (2015) 'Ten EU nations say North Stream gas extension not in EU interests', Reuters, 27 November, http://www.reuters.com/article/ukraine-crisis-nordstream-idUSL8N13L4MG20151127, date accessed 6 April 2016.

Menon, R. and Rumer, E. (2015) *Conflict in Ukraine: The Unwinding of the Post-Cold War Order.* Cambridge, MA: MIT Press.

NATO (2014) 'NATO Leaders Take Decisions to Ensure Robust Alliance' [Press Release], 5 September, http://www.nato.int/cps/pl/natohq/news_112460.htm, date accessed 28 March 2016.

New York Times (2015) 'U.S. Faults Russia as Combat Spikes in East Ukraine', *New York Times*, 13 February, http://www.nytimes.

com/2015/02/14/world/europe/ukraine-fighting-escalates-ahead-of-truce. html?_r=0, date accessed 6 April 2016.

n-tv news (2016) 'Exporte nach Russland schrumpfen. Deutsche Wirtschaft fordert Signal an Moskau', 17 March, http://www.n-tv.de/wirtschaft/ Deutsche-Wirtschaft-fordert-Signal-an-Moskau-article17035701.html, date accessed 6 April 2016.

Oliver, C. and Wagstyl, S. (2015) 'Tusk Joins Italian Premier in Attacking Berlin over Gas Pipeline: Germany Accused of Hypocrisy for Protecting Its Own Interests in Nord Stream 2 Project', *Financial Times*, 18 December, http://www.ft.com/intl/cms/s/0/4dc4f66c-a5a3-11e5-97e1-a754d5d9538c. html#axzz48Sw4zC9P, date accessed 13 May 2016.

OSCE (2014) 'Protocol on the Results of Consultations of the Trilateral Contact Group, Signed in Minsk, 5 September 2014' [In Russian], Organization for Security and Cooperation in Europe, 5 September, http://www. osce.org/home/123257, date accessed 6 April 2016.

OSCE (2015) 'Package of Measures for the Implementation of the Minsk Agreements', Organization for Security and Cooperation in Europe, 12 February, http://www.osce.org/cio/140156, date accessed 28 March 2016.

Pepescu, N. (2013) 'The Russia–Ukraine Trade Spat', EU Institute for Security Studies, August, http://www.iss.europa.eu/uploads/media/Alert_Ukraine_ trade.pdf, date accessed 6 April 2016.

Putin, V. (2005) President of Russia, Annual Address to the Federal Assembly of the Russian Federation, 25 April, Kremlin, Moscow, http://en.kremlin. ru/events/president/transcripts/22931, date accessed 1 April 2016.

Putin, V. (2007) President of Russia, Diplomacy and External Affairs, Speech and the Following Discussion at the Munich Conference on Security Policy, Munich, 10 February, http://en.kremlin.ru/events/president/tran- scripts/24034, date accessed 1 April 2016.

Saparov, A. (2014) *From Conflict to Autonomy in the Caucasus: The Soviet Union and the Making of Abkhazia, South Ossetia and Nagorno Kara- bakh*. London: Routledge.

Schimmelfennig, F. (2003) *The EU, NATO, and the Integration of Europe: Rules and Rhetoric*. Cambridge: Cambridge University Press.

Seibel, W. (2015) 'Arduous Learning or New Uncertainties? The Emergence of German Diplomacy in the Ukrainian Crisis', *Global Policy,* Vol. 6, No. 1, pp. 56–72.

SMM (2016) 'Status report', OSCE Special Monitoring Mission to Ukraine, 23 March, http://www.osce.org/ukraine-smm/229756, date accessed 28 March 2016.

Spiegel-online (2016) 'Ukraine-Krise: Europas vergessener Krieg,' *Spiegel- online*, 19 March, http://www.spiegel.de/politik/ausland/ukraine-es-geht- weiter-mit-raketenwerfern-und-haubitzen-a-1082662.html, date accessed 25 March 2016.

Stent, A. E. (2014) *The Limits of Partnership*. Princeton: Princeton University Press.

Szabo, S. F. (2015) *Germany, Russia, and the Rise of Geo-Economics*. London and New York: Bloomsbury Academic.

Tolstrup, J. (2014) *Russia vs. the EU. The Competition for Influence in Post-Soviet States*. London: First Forum Press.

Ukrinform (2016) 'Merkel, Hollande Say Sanctions against Russia Stay until Minsk Deal Fulfilled', Ukrinform, 17 March, http://www.ukrinform.net/rubric-politics/1984107-merkel-hollande-say-sanctions-against-russia-stay-until-minsk-deal-fulfilled.html, date accessed 6 April 2016.

United Nations (1994) 'Letter dated 7 December 1994 from the Permanent Representatives of the Russian Federation, Ukraine, the United Kingdom of Great Britain and Northern Ireland and the United States of America to the United Nations addressed to the Secretary', United Nations Journal Assembly/Security Council, A/49/765 and S/1994/1399, 19 December, http://www.un.org/en/ga/search/view_doc.asp?symbol=A/49/765, date accessed 6 April 2016.

Van Herpen, M. H. (2014) *Putin's Wars: The Rise of Russia's New Imperialism*. Lanham: Rowman & Littlefield.

Washington Post (2014) 'Joint Geneva Statement on Ukraine: The full text', *Washington Post*, 17 April, https://www.washingtonpost.com/world/joint-geneva-statement-on-ukraine-from-april-17-the-full-text/2014/04/17/89bd0ac2-c654-11e3-9f37-7ce307c56815_story.html, date accessed 6 April 2016.

Zeit-online (2015) 'Gabriel schlägt Ende der Sanktionen gegen Russland vor', *Zeit-online*, 25 September, http://www.zeit.de/politik/ausland/2015-09/sigmar-gabriel-russland-sanktionen-syrien, date accessed 6 April 2016.

Chapter 15

The EU's Global Image

AMELIA HADFIELD

Introduction

The multi-dimensional EU crisis explored in this book has generated negative and positive images of the Union. Critics argue that the crisis has resulted in the EU losing credibility both as an international economic player and as a 'soft power' foreign policy actor and that its lack of decisive responses to key international events has critically impaired both its institutional integrity and its overall presence. Defenders of the EU, in contrast, contend that, despite setbacks, the EU's global image remains intact, based on its many and varying worldwide initiatives that range from promoting peace and stability in its neighbourhood to development policy, humanitarian assistance, and climate change mitigation.

Critical matters examined in this book are the various *impacts* the crisis has had on the EU and the overall *consequences* for the EU in the short and long term. This chapter takes an outside-in approach by examining the challenges to the EU in terms of the abiding identity that it currently holds in the eyes of a range of external others, the reputational damage done to this identity as a result of the EU's responses to the crisis, and the subsequent impact this has had on the EU's strategic relationships with Russia, the USA, and China.

Drawing upon a rich interdisciplinary background, both *role theory* (perceptions of decision-makers) and *image theory* (externally held views of a given entity) have proved helpful in deconstructing and categorizing the myriad perceptions and subsequent behavioural practices – both domestic and international – of states and actors in the international system. Simply put, the EU's self-perception, and the roles envisioned for it by others, 'are linked as the EU's external image influences its self-image and thus the EU's behaviour as a global and regional actor' (Chaban and Holland, 2014: 1). As Chaban and Holland illustrate, 'external images of the EU operate as a "reality check" for the EU's own vision of its role as an international leader and its status as a recognized power in an increasingly multipolar world' (2014: 1).

Perceptions are key, because they denote both the meaning invested *by* the EU in its own institutional construction, and the perceived capability *of* the EU as an international actor by others. Perceptions are also vital to the EU's ability to gauge its positioning vis-à-vis strategic partners like Russia, the USA, and China, particularly after the onslaught of the various dimensions of the crisis. In sum, global perceptions of the EU, whether homogenous or heterogeneous, play a key role in providing observers with a substantive and testable repertoire of externally generated views on the EU and constitute much of the international ecosystem of which the EU is fundamentally composed and in which it is invested.

After briefly exploring the role and impact of the largely soft power-based external images of the EU, the chapter proceeds with a non-exhaustive overview of perceptions derived from three of the EU's chief strategic partners: Russia, the USA, and China. Inevitably, a range of viewpoints emerge, some confirming positive images of the EU's soft and normative power base in terms of promoting peace and stability and others indicating that various dimensions of the crisis have seriously dented the EU's ability to project global or even regional influence.

EU External Perceptions: Raw Material or Raw Power?

Images and perceptions held by third parties provide an increasingly helpful corpus of data with which to analyse external understandings of the EU as an actor, as well as the nature and efficacy of its foreign policies. Scholars are presented with positive, neutral, and negative images of the EU flowing from a variety of sources: primary documents from and beyond the EU; policy analysis by academics, think tanks, and consultants; media coverage that is generally 'quick to report on the economic troubles and social unrest' which contextualize crises; and official and unofficial member state outputs, which of late have 'merely intensified the already existing external images of internal EU divisions' (Chaban and Holland, 2014: 4).

The challenge is to mine such data in a meaningful and useful way. Until recently, much image, role, and perception-based data have contributed less than they might to relevant academic and analytical disciplines, including International Relations (IR) theory, foreign policy analysis, and EU studies. Observations by leading scholars (such as Barnett, 1993; Boulding, 1959; Dagestan, 2006; Holsti, 1970; Jervis, 1976; Mišík, 2013; and Mohavedi, 1985) have, however, gradually moved from the determinative connections between Self-referential images and Other-based perceptions, to more useful examinations of the behavioural frameworks by which such images are actively deployed in pursuit of foreign policy goals. Within EU studies, image and perception analyses have become better positioned, although their ultimate efficacy in producing workable analyses remains uneven. Models attempting to capture the nature, impact, and perceptions of the EU, from Duchêne (1972) to Manners (2006) and from Hill's capabilities–expectations gap (1993) to the impact of EU norms (Lucarelli and Manners, 2006), all integrate implicitly the soft power role played by external images and perceptions but rarely explain explicitly the precise connections between the EU's *planned* and *perceived* impact. In other words, while studies old and new cite the cardinal role of socio-political identities in structuring the actorness of the EU and its foreign policy choices, little has been done to incorporate the counterpart processes of image-building *of* the EU by a range of external Others.

To redress this imbalance, a nexus is needed to connect current EU foreign policy analysis and earlier image and perception studies where, as Jervis (1976: 28) first argued, 'it is often impossible to explain crucial decisions and policies without reference to the decision makers' beliefs about the world and their *images of others* … these cognitions are part of the proximate cause of the relevant behaviour'. Given the enormous range of variables that go into identifying perceptions and demonstrating them as integral to foreign policy behaviour, categories are key, because perceptions themselves operate as modes of classification by which we organize the world and negotiate our way through it, both collectively and individually. A taxonomy is therefore helpful in structuring the EU Self and the nature of its actorness, and indeed Otherness imparted by third parties into perceptions of the EU and its perceived ability to respond to crises. Building on work by Beller and Leerssen (2007) and Horstkotte and Peeren (2007), Chaban and Holland (2014) suggest a four-staged basis for a taxonomy of perceptions of actorness, which has been further extended for the purposes of this chapter:

1   *positive expectations* of, and attitudes towards, the EU (appreciation and respect);
2   *alterations* in the identity of third parties, and their expectations of the EU in response to the EU itself, and as a result of their positive expectations of the EU (for example, normative and structural transformations);
3   *negative attitudes* and a 'negation of the EU's international persona or actions' stemming from the perceived inadequacy of current policies or historical prejudices against the EU; and
4   *'an active rejection* and consolidation of the Self-views against the EU' in which the EU represents the ultimate 'Other', taking the form of competition at best and hostility at worst (2014: 12–13, emphasis added).

These dynamics, and the positive–negative spectrum along which they range, are key to the contemporary views of the EU afforded by a review of its strategic partners that follows, as well as to contextualizing their understanding of EU responses to aspects of the crisis. The methodology for this overview is both qualitative – single actor and comparative studies, making use of perceptions from key groups (including decision-makers, the media, and public opinion) – and quantitative – mainly data derived from Rasch modelling (a psychometric model for analyzing categorical data). Other information and observations are drawn from public opinion tracking surveys, think tank assessments, official government statements, and EU-funded research projects.

The case studies that follow focus on the three most important countries with which the EU conducts external relations. It sheds light on country-specific reasons for shifts in these relations, as well as incorporating recent developments pertaining to the crisis, especially the eurozone and migration crises.

Russian Perceptions: Between a Rock and a Hard Place

As was noted in Chapter 14, Russia and the EU share a long and complicated history. The seismic geopolitical shifts of the late twentieth century are key to this, notably the collapse of the Soviet bloc as the 'main competing structural power' and the erosion of Russia's global clout, forcing Russia into the position of 'economically and politically weak junior partner' (Keukeleire and Delreux, 2014: 279). With the loss of the Soviet Union's satellite states in central and eastern Europe, ten of which joined the EU between 2004 and 2007, and the persistence of serious differences between the EU and Russia in terms of common objectives and practicable bilateral frameworks, the years since the EU–Russia Partnership and Cooperation Agreement of 1997 have been largely characterized by 'quite separate visions' (ibid.: 280). Clashes owing to normative differences, including integrationist vs. interventionist approaches towards states in the shared neighbourhood (Russia's 'Near Abroad'), and the appropriateness of military action, have revolved around a quartet of issues and initiatives: EU enlargement, North Atlantic Treaty Organization (NATO) enlargement, the EU's European Neighbourhood Policy (ENP), and EU–Russia engagement over various 'Common Spaces'.

Russian revanchism – a quest to regain great power status – is arguably driven by Russia's own sense of Self and perceptions of EU aggrandizement. The result is that Russia is the only one of the EU's strategic partners that has shifted visibly and radically from one end to the other of the attitudinal spectrum: moving since 2000 from positive and change-based perspectives of the EU to increasingly entrenched negative perceptions entailing an active rejection and 'Othering' of virtually every aspect of the EU. Relations have shifted from positive in the mid-1990s, which produced structural and even normative shifts encompassing stages 1 and 2 above, to a series of increasingly abrupt volte-faces in which Russian perceptions of disappointment, disillusionment, and even betrayal by the West stemming from its post-Cold War treatment have replaced former positive engagement (House of Lords, 2015: 20). Views from the Russian elite appear divided into political and cultural areas, with the EU being seen as politically 'disappointing' and culturally 'decadent'. Paradoxically, however, while Russian views of the EU include an image of it as a dictatorial bureaucracy, relentless in its drive for standardization of Russian rules and regulations based on an EU template, and institutionally weak in the face of concurrent crises, Europe itself is viewed as prosperous, largely benign, and the natural destination of Russian trade and private capital. Indeed, Europe's 'wealthy countries with high standards of living' operate as 'a goal for Russia in raising standards of living" (House of Lords, 2015: 22).

In deconstructing these seemingly contradictory attitudes, one finds that the first major shift in Russia's stance towards the EU arose from a growing dissonance between Russia and macro-level EU attributes, based largely on the nature of the key strategic partnerships between the EU and Russia, Japan, China, India, and the USA during the 2000s. The nature of the EU's strategic partnership with Russia is complex, but the parts that have proved particularly problematic for Russia have been the normative nature of the EU's actorness, the geographic scope and ambition of the ENP, and the integrationist dynamic associated with enlargement. Taken together, agreements constructed for Russia and its neighbours seemed to indicate an EU keen on the multipolar 'retrieval' of key aspects of its eastern frontier, using a combination of normative instruments and trade tools to spread its paradigm of prosperous good governance. Unsurprisingly, both the combination on offer and the type of actorness proved unpalatable to Russia.

An image of the EU as a new Western hegemon with continental designs, operating on the basis of norm diffusion and trade clout, reduced Russia's willingness to cooperate, and indeed simply to understand key facets of EU actorness. This, in turn, diminished Russia's sense of *visibility/awareness* of the EU as a key foreign policy actor, reduced acceptance of the legitimacy of the EU's *actorness*, heightened mistrust in the *effectiveness* of the EU–Russia relationship, and ultimately resulted in the wholesale rejection of the EU as a *norm setter*. These regressions have had a deleterious effect on key policy areas involving the two sides, specifically trade, energy, security, commerce, and civil society. The result is a hardening of identities within the Self/Other dyad, leaving the EU with diminished areas of engagement with Russia on the one side, and Russian perceptions of the EU as a 'geopolitical and ideological competitor' on the other (House of Lords, 2015: 22). The outcome has been a *reification* in terms of identity sets, with oppositional ontologies, which in practical terms has seen the two sides squaring off over a range of policies, chiefly focused on the appropriate treatment of key states in their shared neighbourhood. Russia's attempt to carve out its own Eurasian Economic Area was a hurried response to the EU's own Neighbourhood Policy, in which both sides presented a range of robust free trade 'plus' agreements to key states, the most crucial being Ukraine. As seen in Chapter 14, the downward spiral of defensive stand-offs following Russia's annexation of Crimea and interference in eastern Ukraine has gradually produced offensive foreign policy stances towards the EU by Russia on a wide range of issues, including trade, energy, and security policies, as well as ongoing disputes about the treatment of the states inhabiting the intra EU–Russia neighbourhood.

In terms of public attitudes, while Russians historically have had a positive view of the EU, the politics of crisis have had a visible effect on opinion, with the Russian public increasingly viewing the EU in a negative, even hostile light. Fifty-nine per cent of respondents to the 2015 Levada-Center (2015a) survey stated that 'Russia has never been the aggressor or initiator of a conflict with other countries', while 26 per cent argued that in the majority of cases 'Russia has been the victim and innocent party in conflicts'. An impressive 62 per cent of respondents stoutly defended the rightness of ignoring Western criticism of Russia, largely because – in their view – the EU now sees itself as a competitor with Russia rather than an ally, with policies designed to weaken rather than support bilateral relations (2015a). The West, in other words, initiated and perpetuated the EU–Russia conflict, which, in turn, prompted Russia to take defensive actions.

The data of even the most objective surveys in Russia should be appraised judiciously, given the lack of public and media freedom in Russia since 2000. Russian civil society opinion is not an entirely robust variable in this sense. Nonetheless, Russian perspectives suggest that regional crises are entirely of the EU's own making. Thus, the triple threat of EU enlargement, NATO enlargement, and the ENP are seen as constituting direct and deliberate aggrandizement on the part of the EU. Russian responses, ranging from incursions into Georgia in 2008 to ongoing trade embargoes against the Baltic states, to the annexation of Crimea and intervention in eastern Ukraine in 2014, are seen as not only 'entirely legitimate but appropriate to the perceived threat' (Romanova, 2015). The growing tensions in the neighbourhood since the early 2000s have changed Russian perceptions of the EU from stable partner, even ally, to ambiguous neighbour, to political and geostrategic threat. However, as the previously cited House of Lords report (2015) argued, the 'Euromaidan' protests and the ousting of the pro-Russian President Viktor Yanukovych 'radically altered Russian threat perceptions', suggesting to Russian elite and popular opinion that the sum total of these past events equated to 'a deliberate plot against Russia', effected by the USA and the EU, with the aim of implementing a government in Kiev permanently 'hostile to Russian interests' (2015: 57).

Remoter challenges are less direct but equally key, and are premised on perceptions of the EU's identity as a single market and a single currency area, and on its integrationist power. The Russian response has been the gradual cultivation, within and beyond the shared neighbourhood, of a Eurasian Economic Union, operating as a rudimentary customs and monetary union, possibly resulting in a rival entity for Russia to promote its regional geopolitical interests. EU energy dependence provides Russia with vital national revenues; yet its lack of a clear external energy policy sends signals to Russia of the EU's overall inability to act coherently, making it – in the form of its member state energy markets – a ready target for strategies of divide and rule. Likewise, the EU's inability to construct a viable neighbourhood policy that could benefit both sides is perceived as naive at best and threatening at worst. Thus, even where there are perceived economic advantages in working with the EU, 'there is little or no clear confidence in the EU's ability to take a role as a leading international actor' (Lucarelli, in Chaban and Holland, 2014: 56). Nevertheless, the pull of the EU's economic power is so great that imitation in the form of a rival Union has been the latest development in EU–Russia relations.

Perceptions are key here. A Rasch analysis conducted across ten Eurasian states, including Russia, used by Chaban and Beltyukova (in Chaban and Holland, 2014: 157–8), indicates that the EU is viewed by Russians as being 'modern' and 'united'. However, in terms of 'current and future importance', the EU is seen as being less important than the USA and China. Most important for the politics of crisis are the paradoxical results that show public perceptions of 'which partner was closer to their country in terms of cooperation'. Here, the EU was seen to be closest to China, then the USA and Japan, and lastly to Russia (ibid.: 159) – indicating problematic estrangement between the two blocs in the eyes of Russia and others. And yet, simultaneously, the EU and Germany 'both at present and in the future, were significantly more important to the respondents from Russia' (ibid.: 159) – indicating an ongoing reliance between the two. The combination is 'quite a peculiar one, with the shadow of the past still looming over the current relationship' (Keukeleire and Delreux, 2014: 279).

The result is something of a stalemate that is consolidated by the EU's creation of the post-Ukraine crisis economic sanctions on Russia and is worsened by perceptions from both sides that the Other is the sole architect of the current crisis. Russian President Vladimir Putin articulated as much at the September 2015 Eastern Economic Forum in Vladivostok, when he referred to the migration crisis as being due to 'misguided' foreign policy carried out by the EU and its allies in the regions of the Muslim world, the Middle East, and North Africa (President of Russia, 2015). From Putin's perspective, the EU is guilty of neo-imperialism via the ENP, with its imposition of 'standards without taking into consideration the history, religion, culture and national characteristics of these regions', and of 'blindly following American orders' (Russian Times, 2015). The ENP remains totemic of the fundamental divide between the two sides, producing deep anger in terms of EU relations with Russia, disappointment in the EU's Eastern Partners, and resentment in the EU's Middle East and North African partners. The latter – along with volatilities within and beyond key ENP states – is viewed as the prime explanation in Russian eyes for the home-grown terrorist attacks sweeping the EU in 2015 and 2016. The 2015 Levada-Center survey (2015b) suggests as much, with the majority of Russian respondents identifying the *Charlie Hebdo* attacks in Paris in January 2015 as stemming primarily from provocative cartoons, and secondarily from 'the weakness of French authorities in effectively fighting terrorism', 'the spread of Islamic fanaticism and the growth of Islamist groups who oppose democratic values and freedoms', and 'the consequences of France's immigration policy, which is designed to allow immigrants into the country without significant adaptation' (2015b).

* * *

A decade of increased EU–Russia mistrust is a poor foundation on which to respond intelligently to challenges, and inevitably has produced a range of responses in which misinterpretations, misperceptions, and threats have featured prominently. The challenges have been both proximate and remote in nature and have been instigated by both sides, with proximate challenges within the shared neighbourhood of eastern Europe particularly entailing activities perceived as being politically expansionist, which has produced visions of the Other as being aggressive and antagonistic.

The deterioration in EU–Russia relations has been exacerbated by the virtual collapse of Germany's relations with Russia following the 2014 Ukraine crisis. Berlin had long conducted a 'business as usual' approach to Russia, which was usually translated into political pragmatism and attitudes of empathy based on the shared Soviet past. As such, during the immediate post-Cold War era, until the end of Gerhard Schröder's Chancellorship in 2005, Germany enjoyed the position of privileged

Russian partner and until 2014 was the chief EU–Russia interlocutor. However, as Adomeit (2015) argues, the 2014 events resulted in a 'precipitous' decline in relations, occasioned by the 'Kremlin's support for separatism and thinly concealed military intervention in eastern Ukraine' (2015: 4). While the sanctions remain in place, 'business as usual' remains on pause. The question is whether perceptions by Germany of Russia have changed so substantially that a post-sanctions relationship would constitute an entirely new paradigm, or whether they would merely be reset along earlier lines of established pragmatism.

American Debates: Brave Old World

Support for European integration has long been a keystone 'of a US structural foreign policy', grounded in the Marshall Plan of the immediate post-World War II period (Keukeleire and Delreux, 2014: 275). The relationship between the USA and the EU rests on interdependent economies, shared norms, and 'co-ownership' of such global institutions as the International Monetary Fund, the World Bank, and the World Trade Organization. This suggests not only a high degree of like-mindedness, but a relationship that has become institutionalized both in time and substance, and that has produced an oft-challenging, but ultimately durable, partnership. The US public and its elite decision-makers thus inhabit the upper end of the aforementioned scale, operating on the basis of positive expectations regarding the EU on points of high policy and grand strategy, tempered by short-term disturbances when aspects of policies go awry but with only limited scope for entrenched negative attitudes fuelled by deep-seated prejudices.

However, unlike Russia and China, both of which have strong and coherent views (both official and in civil society) regarding their perception of the EU, the USA offers a more diverse range of views. Various scholars have attempted to cohere the critical mass of broad viewpoints regarding the relative nature of power exemplified by the EU and the USA (for example, Kagan's [2002] Mars-like America vs. Venus-style Europe). The hard/soft power dualities of political and military power are accompanied by protectionist/neoliberal divisions traversing the Atlantic, and the fallout from events such as the invasion of Iraq (2003) and the US sub-prime crisis (2007–08) have on occasions strained transatlantic verities. Unlike EU–Russia relations, however, discord between the EU and the USA has been a question neither of raw power nor proximity, but rather a high-stakes game involving trade, investment, and competition which both sides can afford to play with little risk of significant material costs or of high-profile diplomatic contretemps.

Differences of perceptions of global governance – notably on such issues as the desirable extent of multilateralism and the role of international treaties – do, however, exist and should not be underestimated. Both sides operate with widely divergent systems of government, use contrasting fiscal, economic, and monetary methods, and have radically different perspectives of federalism and integration, as well as contrasting modes of foreign policy. As witnessed in recent years, transatlantic tensions go well beyond trade spats and can range in nature from 'a profound sense of disproportion in terms of security-based burden-sharing in the European neighbourhood' to disputes and litigation on competition, state aid, software, aviation, media access, and data privacy (American Chamber of Commerce interviews, 2016).

Set against this are the long-standing assessments within scholarly and political circles that traditionally view EU–US relations as 'an interplay between competition and convergence', in which 'competitive interdependence' foregrounds EU and US 'common understandings about many issues' (McGuire and Smith, 2008: 3). From this perspective, mutual transatlantic perceptions enable each side to regard the other as a stable regional power and a reliable trade and investment partner whose relations are deepened by a shared social and political proximity of historic and cultural overlaps. Data indicates that citizens on both sides largely support the transatlantic relationship, although antagonisms over the contents and negotiations of the Transatlantic Trade and Investment Partnership (TTIP) have resulted in some deterioration. In terms of perceptions, TTIP came to operate as something of a trope for the regional identities of its two protagonists, with Americans portrayed as purely commercially driven, anti-regulation profiteers pitted against overly bureaucratic, laborious Europeans requiring reams of regulations to guarantee supposedly superior European standards against the might of corporate America. Ultimately TTIP fell victim to popular resistance in key EU states and to ideological opposition in the Trump administration.

Impact of the crisis

Thanks to a considerable improvement in transatlantic relations during the Obama administration, US officials have indulged in relatively little *Schadenfreude* regarding the various aspects of the EU's crisis. Nevertheless, as is shown below in respect of four aspects of the crisis, US officials have expressed concern about certain developments, with the consequence that the crisis has had a noticeable impact on EU–US relations.

The eurozone crisis

From its outset, the eurozone crisis was seen as directly connected to the global financial and banking crisis, with 'contagion' triggered by the USA in 2008. Both sides suffered from the fallout, implemented local solutions via budgetary overhauls and improved governance, and were generally careful not to be judgemental. When various national economies (notably those of Ireland, Spain, Portugal, and Italy) teetered, the USA largely kept to the side. But the Greek situation left Americans baffled because of the apparent haplessness of EU institutions and leaders. By 2015, while US opinion towards changes to Europe's fiscal governance remained largely positive, attitudes towards the EU's handling of the Greek debt crisis were generally negative. A number of prominent US economists criticized the tough conditions placed upon Greece by eurozone leaders, believing them to be counterproductive with regards to the situation in Greece and impracticable in restoring the credibility of Economic and Monetary Union (EMU) (Dempsey, 2015). US opinion was particularly critical of EU institutional culpability for permitting the debt issue to snowball into a full-scale political crisis that risked the integrity of the entire eurozone. US officials perceived their European counterparts as simultaneously 'responsible and irresponsible': guilty of both failing to intervene and then of intervening in a cumbersome way (American Chamber of Commerce interviews, 2016). The Obama administration itself generally viewed the crisis from a strategic perspective in terms of overall EU–US relations (Dempsey, 2015), attempting to persuade EU leaders and the European Central Bank (ECB) to strengthen the eurozone's institutional framework (including advocating the seemingly impossible equation of balancing growth alongside fiscal belt-tightening), while making clear that the prospect of Grexit remained a problem for European leaders to manage (Lee, 2015).

The Ukraine crisis

As noted above, the Ukraine crisis produced attitudes of solidarity and sympathy for the EU, tempered with impatience and ultimately diplomatic tedium. In US eyes, the EU moved from being a well-meaning actor with budding regional ambitions to being an amateur hybrid, swiftly out of its depth when confronted with the strategic implications of Ukraine's pro-Brussels fervour, and the consequent ire of Russia. There was an understandable, though overstated, reaction on the part of some US officials that the USA alone was capable of managing European geopolitical stability. The EU meanwhile appeared to have compromised its own values and undermined the few geopolitical stripes that it had earned in the region. However, EU defiance of Russian behaviour, including the imposition of sanctions, as well as its continued support for Ukraine within the Eastern Partnership, slowly turned the tide. The EU still lacks strategic depth in much of its eastern neighbourhood, but has a normative embeddedness that has garnered US approval and alongside which much US policy now runs.

Both the USA and EU face the same diplomatic impasse vis-à-vis relations with Russia. Whether they operate separately, concurrently, or cooperatively remains to be seen.

The migration crisis

The US – like many in the EU itself – viewed EU responses to the migration crisis as tardy and generally symptom-based. The lack of strategic thinking, the perceived slow responsiveness, and the only limited collaboration between EU actors quickly became a source of anxiety in American quarters. The main complaints were of: introverted thinking about the remote causes of migration (rather than the EU's main focus which was on the proximate impact on key member states), including 'the threat posed by the Islamic State organization' (Archick, 2015: 12–13); and ungenerous attitudes to the treatment, distribution, and duty of care to both refugees and economic migrants.

US responses to the migration crisis have been clearly geared towards maintaining a stable Europe in light of growing regional threats, balanced against growing concern about the political fallout caused by home-grown fundamentalism in key European capitals, including Paris and Brussels. The worry is that the EU's perceived weak response to the migration crisis is fuelling concerns among US policy-makers that the EU is lacklustre at best and ineffective at worst in handling major challenges. Such a perceived weakening of a key ally could, in turn, be thought to diminish the ability of the EU and the US to address 'strategic challenges such as the rise of China and historic instability in the Middle East' (Archick, 2015: 12–13).

The Brexit crisis

The USA paid close attention to the 2016 Brexit referendum, while Europeans were captivated by the US presidential election. Unedifying comments by the then Republican presidential candidate Donald Trump that 'migration has been a horrible thing for Europe, a lot of that was pushed by the EU', may have coalesced US opinions regarding EU ineptitude in some quarters (Sandhu, 2016: 14). However, Obama's long-standing support for European integration, climate policy, and UK membership of the EU suggested that both elite decision-makers and informed civil society in America were aware of the magnitude of the schisms within the EU and were willing to advocate a strong response in order to guarantee the stability and integrity of the EU itself, and a sustained relationship with it. Obama made clear in an interview with the BBC that in terms of grand strategy 'Washington had much greater confidence in the transatlantic union with the UK as part of the EU' (Wintour and Sparrow, 2015). However, the passion of Obama's anti-Brexit intervention, in April 2016, took many by surprise, with his core message revolving around the magnifying role played by the EU for the UK, as well as Britain's inherent safety and security within the Union. Yet Obama tempered positive cues with a negative image of Britain being relegated to 'the back of the queue' when it came to negotiating a UK–USA bilateral trade deal. Obama made it clear not only that bloc-to-bloc relations made sense in trade terms, but also that the UK's future with the USA very much rested upon its decision to remain within the EU. Given the outcome of the referendum, the seismic shifts it has caused across the EU, and the unexpected victory of Donald Trump in the November 2016 presidential election, a variety of new relationships between the USA, the EU, and the UK may well be forged in the coming years.

Persistent concerns

The result of recent crises for US–EU relations is a combination of strategic concerns tempered with broader reassurances. Domenech (2015: 6), for example, has argued that 'the EU is paralyzed and ineffective, unable to sort out the multiple crises besieging it – while nation-states ravaged by recession and fiscal crises struggle to offer effective policies to escape the recession, reduce poverty and inequality, or help regions left behind'. NBC blogs from April 2016 suggest that while transatlantic relations were healthy and that the 'United States advocates a strong, stable Europe', the UK's Brexit vote has raised the spectre of a 'rump EU [which] could begin to unravel', weakening America's allies and bringing instability' (Bishop and Jamieson, 2016). In the short term, foreign and security policy may be a key casualty. For many in Europe, Obama's foreign policy has been confusing (including Asian pivots and post-pivots) and ambivalent, particularly regarding Libya and Syria. There has been little strategic interaction on either side in solving neighbourhood issues, migration challenges, or any of the specific crises occurring across the Middle East and North Africa region, the Sahel, and Afghanistan and Iraq. While the Obama administration's perception of the EU as a strategic partner remained generally positive, despite the uneven responses of EU institutions and member states in managing the slew of crises they faced, there is little evidence that either side was ever fully aware of, or indeed invested in, the strategic requirements of the other. Arguing that the EU needs to become a 'global security provider', and should develop genuine 'strategic autonomy' in doing so, the 2016 EU Global Strategy provides no explanation as to its relationship with the USA beyond that of a key partner. US Department of State references to the EU remained under Obama equally broad and non-committal.

Serious threats to European integration, whether for economic reasons or owing to growing political disenchantment, have for many years been a matter of concern for US governments. This has been because self-interest in maintaining the world's most prosperous international trade and investment relationship has been a key factor in shaping US policy. However, this policy now appears to be at risk, given President Trump's hostility to multilateral structures and preference for bilateral relationships. This risk to EU–US relations may be multiplied by a divide and rule policy in which the UK is favoured and the standing of Germany, previously seen in Washington as the main guarantor of transatlantic stability, is downgraded.

Chinese Perceptions: A Bridge Too Far?

China and the EU have had a relationship since the 1980s, which was formally established in 2003 under the aegis of 'A Maturing Partnership – Shared Interests and Challenges in EU–China Relations'. The ties connecting the two entities and the differences in terms of their mutual perceptions remain riddled with tension, and yet have proved surprisingly durable. Each represents 'the ultimate in otherness' (EEAS interview, 2016). Yet these oppositional categories have also proved cooperative, if not necessarily progressive.

Discerning public and elite perceptions in China is a challenge in terms of not only sourcing key material but also the general fluidity of such perceptions overall. Much of this challenge stems from distinct divisions between educated elites and ordinary citizens in China regarding basic knowledge of the EU, with 77.6 per cent of the former correctly identifying Brussels as the headquarters of the EU as against 28.3 per cent of the latter (Dong, 2014: 762). However, China is second to Australia in its overall ranking of ten Asian nations in terms of its general knowledge of the EU (Chaban and Beltyukova, in Chaban and Holland, 2014: 158).

Following well-established studies by Holland and Chaban (2007) and Chaban and Holland (2013, 2014), the two overarching categories by which to discern Chinese attitudes towards the EU have traditionally been political and economic. Initial studies on Chinese attitudes from 2006 to 2007 suggest that in Chinese perceptions the euro was seen as 'the strongest symbol of European identity' and that most Chinese attention was focused heavily on the potential of EU–China trade relations and the scope of foreign direct investment (FDI). By contrast, the political focus was concentrated on what separated and integrated the EU's member states, and the emerging attributes by which the EU was attaining a global identity (Holland and Chaban, 2007: 28). These same studies indicated a low level of EU coverage by Asian media sources, yielding only general understandings of the EU and perpetuating a high degree of Self/Other variation, which, in turn, explains the difficulty – then and now – of framing the EU's hybrid actorness within China's own strategic and cultural framework.

However, by 2016 some shifts had taken place. While Chinese perceptions of EU values have remained challenging to identify and generalize, they suggest that the multi-level relationship between the EU and China is 'more than just a trade in goods alone' (Chaban and Holland, 2013: 26) and contains a deepened awareness of the norms-based quality of EU actorness, as well as a strategic appreciation of the EU's ability to bestow a degree of legitimacy on aspects of China's global standing.

Economic perceptions – including of trade, finance, commerce, and investment – continue to operate as 'the main area of recognition' for China vis-à-vis the EU. The imperatives of trade itself are particularly compelling, with EU exports to China in 2014 worth €164 billion, making China the EU's second-largest trading partner after the USA. EU market access remains a highly desired goal for China, not only because of the size of the European market but also because China perceives the EU as more open and inviting towards Chinese imports than the USA, Canada, and India.

Chinese views of the EU as regards trade, business, and finance opportunities are thus generally positive, though market access problems tend to partly blur this perspective. Moreover, there are areas that have recently seen bilateral tensions (of a somewhat similar nature to EU–US tensions), including in respect of competition, state aid and subsidy rules, FDI regulation and taxation, and the EU's internal energy market. Perceptions of the EU as being in economic crisis as a result of developments in the eurozone 'have proved deeply worrying to the Party leadership, business elites and the media' (EEAS interview, 2016). However, positive Chinese perceptions of European science and technological expertise offer something of a counterbalance and help to keep the EU as a prime trade partner and a prospective equal for China's globalizing ambitions. At the heart of these ambitions is China's Silk Road project, which is designed to connect Asia and Europe at key points via the construction of substantial infrastructure, including roads, railways, and ports, with the goal of merging the Chinese economy with that of its European and global counterparts. Cautiously supported by the EU in recent summits and strategy papers, the Silk Road is viewed rather more cynically by US sources, such as Bloomberg, as 'a favorite subject of top leaders [including President Xi Jinping], who sell it as an international initiative to foster peace and prosperity' (Schuman, 2015).

Such ambitious projects intimate a serious long-term bid at global leadership by China. China's immediate requirements, however, are to cultivate more progressive political ties with the EU, despite the profound normative differences between the two. The problem is that knowledge of the EU itself is not only rare, but very basic. Chinese awareness of the EU was initially divided into two broad categories: its trade/economic clout and its social/ environmental policies (Holland and Chaban, 2007). These have gradually been supplemented with a more recent awareness of the 'EU's international political character' (Holland and Chaban, 2007: 233), including in respect of the Iran nuclear issue, the ENP, and Strategic Partnerships with perceived rivals, including Japan, India, and the USA. Here the divisions between elite and public perceptions are sharpest. Elite Chinese views are driven by attempts to reconcile incommensurate values with complementary bilateral strategies: efforts to be seen as each other's 'number one' without limiting their diplomatic latitude to deal with other major players, while endeavouring to remain a trustworthy, and favoured, partner. Diplomatic tensions over the so-called 'Three Ts' – Taiwan, Tibet, and Tiananmen Square (the military crackdown in 1989 against anti-government protesters) – as well as repressive political, social, and media freedoms in China continue, however, to be extremely difficult for the EU to raise because Chinese elites view them as deeply, even deliberatively, provocative.

Both the EU and China are architects of contemporary actorness: the EU in regional, normative, and trade terms; China in regional, trade, and possibly strategic terms. Much of this is bound up with Chinese perceptions that the EU and its member states have a negative appreciation of the Chinese Communist Party leadership. The current Chinese approach is therefore one of diplomatic rehabilitation, using key instruments such as trade agreements, FDI, and EU–China summits to soften the European perceptions of dealing with a one-party state. Perhaps for this reason, there is strong Chinese governmental support for the EU's non-trade relations, which are perceived as part of the broader weaponry of rehabilitation and which include aid programmes benefiting Chinese civil society, improved people-to-people contacts, and enhanced business and education exchanges.

Between economic and political relations, there are complex perceptions entailed in climate change policy. As a touchstone of EU–China relations, and based on the four-point stages outlined above, climate policy has undergone a visible shift from defiant forms of anti-EU 'otherness' and antagonistic stances to more positive attitudes and expectations. On the basis of policies including the 2010 EU–China Environmental Governance Programme (involving increased public participation and improved corporate responsibility), and the 2015 EU–China Joint Statement on Climate Change, the two sides have increasingly fallen into step. At the COP21 summit in Paris in November–December 2015, the EU relied on active Chinese support to guarantee targeted reductions of 1.5 and 2 degrees in each state's Intended Nationally Determined Contribution (INDC). Chinese agreement rested largely on its perceptions of the overall correctness of the EU's approach and the reliability of its own climate change policies. In so acting, China has moved from an active differentiation of itself against the EU to a balancer in which Otherness operates relationally, rather than oppositionally. At best (as exemplified in COP21), Chinese perceptions of EU climate change and governance now generally operate on the basis of positive expectations.

What remains opaque at this point is Chinese interest in and attitudes towards the EU's ability to effectively tackle its current crisis. Issues such as fiscal governance, neighbourhood policy, and even migration are at present not proximate enough to register as major concerns for Chinese elites, suggesting that the EU has an obligation to sort out its own problems (EEAS interviews, 2016). Fault lines may nonetheless arise. Significant norm-based disputes continue to divide the two with, for example, China being enormously effective in pushing its 'emerging power' identity on the basis of 'West vs. the Rest' perceptions, which provides at least domestic assurances as to the correctness of its political and economic approaches.

The foreign policy lessons to be learned are compelling and uncomfortable. Chinese perceptions indicate an abiding interest in the EU and the innovations of integration, but China will brook no criticism from the EU of China's own policy. This means emphasizing economic relations at the expense of social, political, and cultural openness, even honesty. This is evident in bilateral and multilateral relations in which Chinese 'Other' perceptions remain so fundamentally mismatched as to enable both sides to skirt major issues of import. Despite its acceptance of regulatory standards in economic terms, China remains defensive over its fear of absorbing European norms in political and cultural terms, and frequently makes this clear. So, for example China insists that EU–China relations must be guided entirely by the 'One-China Principle', which effectively quashes any mention (or indeed visit to) Taiwan by EU officials. Human rights dialogue with the EU is directed by the principle of non-interference in internal affairs, with the EU being warned 'to stop using individual cases to interfere in China's judicial sovereignty and internal affairs' (Ministry of Foreign Affairs, 2014).

Perceptions and misperceptions thus need to be carefully handled. The EU's criticism of China's handling of human rights, of minorities, and of regions seeking greater independence has proven uncomfortable for the Communist Party, yet the EU is itself perceived as inefficient in exerting precisely this pressure. The long-standing arms embargo, instituted after the crackdown in Tiananmen Square, remains in place. Critics argue it has little material effect, with EU member states still exporting dual-use goods capable of being used in advanced systems, such as submarines and fighter planes. China likely perceives a feebly applied sanctions regime as a sign of EU weakness and as an irritation. Yet cultivating a positive view of itself in EU eyes will remain a key part of China's approach, not least because of its desire to be granted full market economy status by both the EU and the USA. Divisions here are deep. The USA is adamantly opposed to granting this status, while the EU is ambivalent, torn between the economic advantage of trading with China and the undoubtedly restricted market access provided by China to European companies. Like the USA, China has a strong interest in a unified Europe, and reductions in current EU economic and political uncertainty rank highly in Chinese bilateral objectives at the elite level (Holslag, 2006). But Chinese perceptions of the EU's overall responsiveness as an actor count for much, particularly where they touch on trade and investment. If it appears to be failing as a multilateral trading operative, the EU may gradually be relegated in terms of China's perception of it in the global pecking order. The EU, in turn, is likely to remain torn between norms and interests, between value-based actorness in which the perceptions of others like China feature heavily and pragmatic external policies that can afford to be less watchful.

Conclusions

External perceptions of the EU do much to shape the nature of the Union's external relations, with positive perceptions being vital if key bilateral relations are to be managed successfully and possibly improved. The four-point scale outlined on p. 296 suggests that the EU is capable of generating both positive and negative perceptions. Positive perceptions, which can be translated into diplomatic advantage, tend to exist primarily with those international actors with whom the EU already has political and cultural affinities, while negative perceptions are usually based on some combination of the EU's ethos, complex institutional make-up, and normative foreign policy.

Both positive and negative external perceptions of the EU have seen changes in recent years, partly, but by no means exclusively or indeed even primarily, as a result of the EU's crisis. The main reason for the changes has been perceptions of the nature of the EU as a soft power, and particularly its ability to manage its way out of severe crises, such as those that have been so challenging in recent years. Accordingly, the soft power identity of the EU is central to the transatlantic axioms of the USA in regarding their European ally as a political counterpart, economic equivalent, and normatively like-minded thinker. However, a colleague in conflict, such as Europe has been during the crisis, does not breed confidence and makes for future uncertainties about the nature of the relationship.

For Russia, the EU has made deliberate and perverse use of its soft power. It purports to operate as a normative actor via a level playing field of values, but has favoured some states over others, as seen in the ENP. It has used its trade clout to extend its geopolitical ambitions, as with enlargement. And it has masked its civilian identity in US-backed NATO expansion. The crisis in EU–Russian relations is thus seen by Russia as being entirely a result of the EU's overweening regional ambition. Russian responses have been calibrated accordingly.

China has an increasingly clear sense of the EU as a regional power in political terms. While unwilling to compromise on the values that lie at the normative heart of the EU's soft power, China is perfectly willing to invest in, and trade with, the strong economy that underwrites EU soft power. The crisis-driven volatilities of the EU may offer a degree of potential opportunism for China in terms of long-term pan-Eurasian expansion, but its present requirements – however politically agnostic – are for an EU that can swiftly re-establish a functioning eurozone, an operable migration policy that keeps labour markets intact, and, according to the *South China Morning Post*, can prevent the 'economic and political fallout from a [UK] withdrawal' from the bloc, which it argues is 'needed like a hole in the head' (Spiro, 2016).

The challenge for the EU, therefore, is to take a leaf out of its own, least well-known, foreign policy success stories: those of crisis management. The EU's soft power credentials are in large part founded upon its ability to maintain a low profile while achieving quality results by the strategic use of preventive strategies, post-crisis rehabilitation, and reconstruction. The first two approaches are eminently suitable for rebuilding key aspects of the EU's geostrategic, political, economic, and social governance, while the third can be drawn upon – to rebuild fractured, failing, or feeble relations with key third parties – to ensure that the EU remains as positively viewed an actor as possible.

References

Adomeit, H. (2015) 'German-Russian Relations: Change of Paradigm versus "Business as Usual"', *Note du Cerfa 120*, IFRI, February, http://www.ifri. org/sites/default/files/atoms/files/ndc_120_ad bilateral relationships omeit_ en_0.pdf, date accessed 1 April 2016.

Aggestam, L. (2006) 'Role Theory and European Foreign Policy: A Framework of Analysis.' In O. Elgstrom and M. Smith (eds), *The European Union's Roles in International Politics: Concepts and Analysis*. London: Routledge.

American Chamber of Commerce (2016) interviews conducted on condition of anonymity, Brussels, May.

Archick, K. (2015) 'The European Union (EU): Current Challenges and Future Prospects in Brief', *Congressional Research Service*, 27 October, https://www.fas.org/sgp/crs/row/R44249.pdf, date accessed 22 January 2016.

Barnett, M. (1993) 'Institutions, Roles, and Disorder: The Case of the Arab States System', *International Studies Quarterly*, Vol. 37, No. 3, pp. 271–96.

Beller, M. and Leerssen, J. T. (2007) *Imagology: The Cultural Construction and Literary Representation of National Characters: A Critical Survey*. Amsterdam: Rodopi.

Bishop, M. and Jamieson, A. (2016) '"Brexit" Vote: Why Britain Could Quit E.U. and Why America Cares', *NBCNews*, http://www.nbcnews.com/news/world/brexit-vote-why-britain-could-quit-e-u-why-america-n526386.

Boulding, K. E. (1959) 'National Images and International Systems', *The Journal of Conflict Resolution*, Vol. 3, No. 2, pp. 120–31.

Bretherton, C. and Vogler, J. (2006) *The European Union as a Global Actor*. London: Routledge.

Chaban, N. and Holland, M. (2013) Special Issue. 'Lisbon and the Changing External Perceptions of the EU: Visions from the Asia-Pacific', *Baltic Journal of European Studies*, Vol. 3, No. 3.

Chaban, N. and Holland, M. (2014) *Communicating Europe in Times of Crisis: External Perceptions of the European Union*. Basingstoke: Palgrave Macmillan.

Christie, R. (2015) 'EU Rebuffs U.S. Criticism of Asset-Backed Debt Revival Drive', *BloombergBusiness*, 16 December, http://www.bloomberg.com/news/articles/2015-12-16/eu-rebuffs-u-s-criticism-of-asset-backed-debt-revival-drive, date accessed 22 January 2016.

Cornish, P. and Edwards, G. (2005) 'The Strategic Culture of the European Union: A Progress Report', *International Affairs*, Vol. 81, No. 4, pp. 801–20.

Dempsey, J. (2015) 'Why the United States and Germany Differ Over Fixing Greece', *Carnegie Europe*, 13 July, http://carnegieeurope.eu/strategiceurope/?fa=60679, date accessed 22 January 2016.

Domenench, J. (2015) 'Editor's Note', *Perspectives on Europe*, Council for European Studies, Autumn, http://councilforeuropeanstudies.org/publications/perspectives-on-europe, date accessed 10 January 2016.

Dong, L. (2014) 'Chinese Perceptions of the European Union', *Journal of Contemporary China*, Vol. 23, No. 88, pp. 756–79.

Duchêne, F. (1972) 'Europe's Role in World Peace.' In R. Mayne, *Europe Tomorrow*. London: Fontana.

Engdahl, W. (2014) 'US, EU meddling in Ukraine battle', RT.com, 30 January, https://www.rt.com/op-edge/us-eu-interference-in-ukraine-402/, date accessed 24 February 2016.

European Commission (2015) 'Proposal for a regulation of the European Parliament and of the Council laying down common rules on securitisation and creating a European framework for simple, transparent and standardised securitisation and amending', http://eur-lex.europa.eu/legal-content/EN/TXT/PDF/?uri=CELEX:52015PC0472&from=EN, date accessed 22 January 2016.

European External Action Service (2016), anonymised interview with EU–China Delegation Official, Brussels, 15 January.

Goldgeier, J. and Kupchan, C. A. (2008) 'Crisis Brings Some Clarity to EU Policymaking', *Expert Brief*, Council on Foreign Relations, http://www.cfr.org/world/crisis-brings-some-clarity-eu-policymaking/p17760, date accessed 15 March 2016.

Hill, C. (1993) 'The Capability–Expectations Gap, or Conceptualizing Europe's Role', *Journal of Common Market Studies*, Vol. 31, No. 3, pp. 305–28.

Holland, M. and Chaban, N. (2007) 'The EU Through the Eyes of Asia: Media Public and Elite Perceptions in China, Japan, Korea, Singapore and Thailand', Asia-Europe Foundation (ASEF), http://www.asef.org/pubs/asef-publications/1892-the-eu-through-the-eyes-of-asia, date accessed 22 January 2016.

Holslag, J. (2006), 'The European Union and China: The Great Disillusion', *European Foreign Affairs Journal*, Vol. 11, No. 4, pp. 555–80.

Holsti, K. (1970) 'National Role Conceptions in the Study of Foreign Policy', *International Studies Quarterly*, Vol. 14, No. 3, pp. 233–309.

Horstkotte, S. and Peeren, E. (2007) *The Shock of the Other: Situating Alterities*. Amsterdam: Rodopi.

House of Lords (2015) 'The EU and Russia: Before and Beyond the Crisis in Ukraine', European Union Committee, 6th report of session 2014–15, HL paper No. 115, 20 February, London: The Stationary Office, http://www.publications.parliament.uk/pa/ld201415/ldselect/ldeucom/115/115.pdf, date accessed 22 January 2016.

Jervis, R. (1976) *Perception and Misperception in International Politics*. Princeton: Princeton University Press.

Kagan, R. (2002) 'Power and Weakness', *Policy Review*, Vol. 113, June/July, http://faculty.maxwell.syr.edu/rdenever/PPA-730-27/Kagan.pdf, date accessed 10 February 2016.

Keukeleire, S. and Delreux, T. (2014) *The Foreign Policy of the European Union*. Basingstoke: Palgrave Macmillan.

Lee, D. (2015) 'How Does the Greek Debt Crisis Impact the United States?', *Los Angeles Times*, 7 July, http://www.latimes.com/business/la-fg-greece-us-impact-qa-20150707-story.html, date accessed 22 January 2016.

Levada-Center (2015a) *Russia-West Relations*, http://www.levada.ru/eng/russia-west-relations, date accessed 22 January 2016.

Levada-Center (2015b) *Charlie Hebdo and Muslims*, http://www.levada.ru/eng/charlie-hebdo-and-muslims, date accessed 22 January 2016.

Lucarelli, S. and Manners, I. (2006) *Values and Principles in European Union Foreign Policy*. London: Taylor and Francis.

McGuire, S. and Smith, M. (2008) *The European Union and the United States*. Basingstoke: Palgrave Macmillan.

Manners, I. (2006) 'Normative Power Europe Reconsidered: Beyond the Crossroads', *Journal of European Public Policy*, Vol. 13, No. 2, pp. 182–99.

Ministry of Foreign Affairs (2014), 'China's Policy Paper on the EU: Deepen the China–EU Comprehensive Strategic Partnership for Mutual Benefit and Win–win Cooperation', Ministry of Foreign Affairs, The People's Republic

of China, 2 April, http://www.fmprc.gov.cn/mfa_eng/wjdt_665385/wjzcs/
t1143406.shtml, date accessed 24 January 2016.

Mišík, M. (2013) 'How can perception help us to understand the dynamic
between EU member states? The state of the art', *Asia Europe Journal*, Vol.
11, No. 4, pp. 445–63.

Mohavedi, S. (1985) 'The social psychology of foreign policy and the politics
of international images', *Human Affairs*, Vol. 8, No. 19, http://www.faculty.
umb.edu/siamak_movahedi/Library/social_psychology_of_foreign_policy.
pdf, date accessed 24 January 2016.

Pew Global Attitudes (2016) Pew Research Centre, 'Publications', http://www.
pewglobal.org//search/?query=EU, date accessed 22 January 2016.

President of Russia (2015) 'Vladimir Putin Answered Russian Journalists'
Questions', http://en.kremlin.ru/events/president/news/50234, date accessed
30 January 2016.

Romanova, T. (2015) 'EU-Russia-Ukraine Geopolitical Shifts', Skype-based
Conference, University of St Petersburg and Canterbury Christ Church
University Energy and Governance Group, Canterbury, UK.

Russia Today (2015) 'EU Refugee Crisis "Absolutely Expected" – Putin',
4 September, https://www.rt.com/news/314318-putin-vladivostok-eu-
migrants/, date accessed 22 January 2016.

Sandhu, S. (2016) 'Good news for the Remain camp? Trump's backing Brexit',
Weekend I, 7 May.

Schuman, M. (2015) 'China's New Silk Road Dream', *Bloomberg Business-
week*, 25 November, http://www.bloomberg.com/news/articles/2015-11-25/
china-s-new-silk-road-dream.

Spiro, N. (2016) '"Brexit" is the Last Thing Europe Needs Right Now',
South China Morning Post, 28 April, http://www.scmp.com/business/
article/1939437/brexit-last-thing-europe-needs-right-now, date accessed
12 January.

Tolksdorf, D. (2014), 'The European Union to Ukraine's Rescue', *Poli-
tique étrangèr*, Vol. 3, Autumn, http://www.cairn-int.info/article-E_
PE_143_0109--the-european-union-to-ukraine-s.htm, date accessed 20
October 2016.

Wintour, P. and Sparrow, A. (2015) 'Obama's Remarks on UK Remaining in EU Get Hostile Eurosceptic Reaction', *The Guardian*, 24 July,
http://www.theguardian.com/politics/2015/jul/24/barack-obama-uk-eu-
european-union-hostile-eurosceptic-reaction, date accessed 22 January
2016.

Zabarowski, M. (2005) 'How the US views the European crisis', *Analysis*,
European Union Institute for Security Studies, http://www.iss.europa.eu/
publications/detail/article/how-the-us-views-the-european-crisis/, date
accessed 1 February 2016.

Chapter 16

Theorising Crisis in European Integration

FRANK SCHIMMELFENNIG

Introduction

The manifold crises of the EU have not only put pressures on policy-makers but also present a challenge to theories of European integration, which explain the dynamics of integration and suggest how and under what conditions integration progresses, stagnates, or recedes. Such theories should therefore be able to tell us about the causes and effects of crises in integration, on the basis of general, abstract conditions and mechanisms of integration.

For the purpose of this chapter, a crisis in European integration means a decision-making situation with a manifest threat and a perceived significant probability of disintegration (see Chapter 17). Disintegration means a reduction in the existing level, scope, and membership of integration (Leuffen et al., 2013: 8). In other words, a crisis in integration threatens to reduce the extent of pooling and delegation, repatriate EU policy competences, or lead to the exit of states from the EU or one of its integrated policies. This definition fits many aspects of the current EU crisis, including the eurozone crisis, the Ukraine crisis, the Brexit crisis, and the migration crisis. Whereas the eurozone and the migration crises are multi-dimensional (potentially impacting on the level, scope, and membership of integration), the Ukraine and Brexit crises primarily just affect the (differentiated) territorial borders of European integration. All of the crises are open-ended: they may result in disintegration but also lead to a reassertion of the status quo or to more integration. This conceptualization is similar to Philippe Schmitter's 'revised theory of regional integration', with its rich typology of possible outcomes of 'crisis-provoked decisional cycles', including 'spillback', 'encapsulation', and 'spillover' – which refer to different combinations of positive and negative changes or stability in integration level and scope (Schmitter, 1970: 842, 845).

The chapter has two parts. The first part focuses on the main schools of theorising European integration: intergovernmentalism, neofunctionalism, and postfunctionalism. None is specifically a theory of crisis, but all see crises as 'an integral part of the process of European integration' (Lefkofridi and Schmitter, 2015: 4) and formulate general propositions on European integration which can serve as hypothetical expectations on the emergence of and reactions to crises. The second part of the chapter focuses specifically on the eurozone crisis, which has been the deepest crisis of integration so far. This part applies the assumptions and propositions of the three integration theories to the eurozone crisis and suggests that intergovernmentalism provides a plausible explanation of the negotiations and outcomes of the eurozone crisis based on state preferences and power. For a full explanation, however, the intergovernmentalist account needs to be embedded in a neofunctionalist analysis of the context and the dynamics of European integration. By contrast, postfunctionalism highlights the role of politicization during the crisis but cannot explain the crisis outcomes.

Integration Theories and Explanations of Crisis

Integration theories differ with regard to the most important origins and causes of crises, the mechanisms that shape the course of a crisis, and the conditions that determine the integration or disintegration outcome. These expectations derive from their general assumptions and hypotheses about the driving forces and conditions of European integration (see Table 16.1).

Whereas intergovernmentalism regards crises in integration as mainly exogenous to the integration process and contingently generated by crises in the international environment of the EU or domestic change in the member states, neofunctionalism and postfunctionalism assume that crises result from prior steps of integration. Whereas neofunctionalism highlights spillover processes at the international level, postfunctionalism emphasizes eurosceptic reactions to integration at the domestic level.

According to intergovernmentalism, crisis interactions are characterized by intergovernmental bargaining and the crisis outcome depends on the intergovernmental constellation of integration preferences and bargaining power. According to neofunctionalism, integration crises are shaped by path-dependency. If transnational interdependence and the autonomy and capacity of supranational organizations are high, crises are likely to strengthen integration. By contrast, postfunctionalism generates more negative expectations. Integration crises are characterized

Table 16.1   *Integration theories and explanations of crisis*

	Intergovernmentalism	Neofunctionalism	Postfunctionalism
Crisis origins	Exogenous: international challenges, domestic change	Endogenous and international: spillover	Endogenous and domestic: euroscepticism
Crisis mechanism	Bargaining	Path-dependency	Politicization
Conditions of crisis outcome	Intergovernmental preference and power constellation	Interdependence, supranational autonomy and capacity	Insulation
Typical crisis outcome	—	Positive feedback: resilience, integration	Negative feedback: stagnation, disintegration

by eurosceptic politicization. Unless European crisis management can be insulated, this politicization is likely to constrain integration or even lead to disintegration. The following sections discuss intergovernmentalism, neofunctionalism, and postfunctionalism in more detail.

Intergovernmentalism

Intergovernmentalists have linked both the emergence of European integration and its limits to crises. The post-World War II crisis of European reconstruction was at the origin of European integration (see Chapter 2). According to Milward (1984, 1994), European integration was designed to rescue the nation state from deep economic and social crisis and, according to Rosato (2011), to balance the Soviet threat. In turn, the 'empty chair crisis' of 1965–66 exemplifies the early limits of European integration. Against the background of French President Charles de Gaulle's veto of British membership and his opposition against the further supranationalization of the European Economic Community (EEC), Stanley Hoffmann published his seminal 'Obstinate or Obsolete?' article on the resilience of the nation state in European integration (Hoffmann, 1966). Hoffmann formulated the basic tenets of traditional intergovernmentalism: states are the major actors of European integration and shape it according to their national interest;

European integration is limited by the states' interest in self-preservation and autonomy and the persistence of national identities and diversities; states resist the autonomy of supranational organizations, especially in areas of 'high politics'. By contrast, Andrew Moravcsik's liberal-intergovernmentalist account is much less tied to the idea of crisis but regards European integration as a response to increases in exogenous, predominantly economic, interdependence, mediated by domestic interest constellations and intergovernmental bargaining power (Moravcsik, 1998).

In the intergovernmentalist perspective, the sources of change in integration are predominantly exogenous to the integration process itself. The same can be assumed for crisis. For one, integration crises may be the result of security and economic threats and challenges in the wider international environment. This is largely true for the EU crises with the exception of the Brexit crisis: the financial, migration, and Ukraine crises originated outside the EU. International challenges may change the intergovernmental interest and power constellation of the member states and undermine the rationale for regional integration. Alternatively, if individual states are unable to deal with the international challenge effectively and efficiently on their own, and if more integration promises to enhance their de facto autonomy in comparison with unilateral responses, they are willing to delegate and pool additional national competences.

In addition, state preferences may change as a result of domestic changes owing to developments such as elections, referendums, and economic shifts, which may call into question the original intergovernmental preference constellation. As a consequence, member states may become less integration-friendly and seek to repatriate integrated competences or even exit the EU altogether. This is the Brexit scenario. Alternatively, member states may become more integration-friendly and push for further steps of integration that others are unwilling to follow.

Both internationally and domestically induced crises can lead to threats of disintegration. According to intergovernmentalism, the outcome is due – as always – to hard intergovernmental bargaining and the intergovernmental constellation of preferences and power, understood as asymmetrical interdependence. Those states that are hardest hit by a crisis – and stand to gain most from (more) integration, or stand to lose most from disintegration – find themselves in a weak bargaining position and are most willing to compromise (Moravcsik, 1998: 3). By contrast, the states that are least affected by the crisis and most content with the status quo are able to attain a bargaining outcome that is close to their preference and extract concessions. According to the logic of the 'two-level game' (Moravcsik, 1993; Putnam, 1988), domestic politics influences bargaining power and bargaining outcomes. Governments that negotiate under severe domestic constraints can credibly reject compromises and threaten non-ratification unless their preferences (or the preferences of the domestic veto players) are accommodated.

Intergovernmentalist assumptions do not lend themselves to a generally positive or negative outlook on the integration outcomes of crises, which depend on the kind of challenges and the intergovernmental preferences and power constellations at hand. For instance, domestic changes and challenges in major member states are more likely to have a positive or negative impact on integration than those in small member states. In principle, when faced with international security or economic threats, states are willing to delegate or pool sovereignty to the extent necessary to provide for an effective welfare- and security-enhancing crisis response. If the crisis demonstrates that existing institutions are incomplete or insufficient, states are willing to reform them in line with their original policy goals. The weaker the states' capacities are in dealing with the crisis, and the higher the incentives are for states to defect from an agreement, the more willing they are to centralize policy-making and to invest supranational organizations with monitoring and sanctioning powers (Moravcsik, 1998: 9, 486–7). Intergovernmentalists assume, however, that the integration process and the supranational organizations created in its course remain instruments under the control of the member states. It is this assumption that differs most clearly from neofunctionalism.

Neofunctionalism

Whereas intergovernmentalism claims that European integration is shaped by the preferences and power of states, and remains under their control, neofunctionalism argues that transnational society and supranational organizations are relevant actors, too, and that the initial steps of European integration build sufficient momentum to push its functional scope, level of centralization, and territorial extension beyond what governments had originally intended. Neofunctionalism stresses the transformative potential of European integration as a gradual, incremental process 'whereby political actors in several distinct national settings are persuaded to shift their loyalties, expectations, and political activities towards a new and larger centre, whose institutions possess or demand jurisdiction over pre-existing national states' (Haas, 1961: 366–7). Successive crises are part of this process (Schmitter, 1970).

In contrast to intergovernmentalism, neofunctionalism focuses on endogenous crises: 'It presumes that the crises that emerge are produced by the very functioning of the integration process' (Lefkofridi and Schmitter, 2015: 10). In the neofunctionalist perspective, integration is a highly complex, unpredictable, and dynamic process. States may shape the initial integration deals according to their preferences, interdependencies, and power constellation but are unable to anticipate or fully control their further development. A key reason for this is that initial steps of integration create or empower new actors: transnational actors such as multinational corporations and interest groups and supranational organizations such as the Commission or the Court. These actors develop preferences and capacities of their own, which might run against member state interest. Moreover, the initial intergovernmental integration decisions are not shaped exclusively by functional necessity and efficiency but are constrained by state interests in maintaining autonomy and by interstate power constellations. As a consequence, they are prone to incomplete contracting, negative externalities, and dysfunctions.

Neofunctionalist theorising subsumes these (generally unintended) effects of integration under the concept of 'spillover'. Functional spillover refers to the negative externalities between policy areas and countries at different levels of integration; political spillover captures changes in the preferences and power of firms, interest groups, and political parties as a result of integration; and institutional spillover encompasses agency drift and socialization effects at the level of supranational organizations (Niemann, 2006; Tranholm-Mikkelsen, 1991). Spillover does not necessarily trigger crises (manifest threats of disintegration) but may result in gradual, incremental change. If crises occur, however, neofunctionalism assumes that they are typically driven by massive spillover.

How do the actors of European integration react to such crises? Neofunctionalists generally assume that integration proves resilient due to institutionalization (Stone Sweet and Sandholtz, 1997) and path-dependency (Pierson, 1996). Spillovers create demand for further integration: externalities will be internalized, dysfunctions repaired, integration contracts updated, and transnational and supranational actors accommodated (Lefkofridi and Schmitter, 2015: 4–5; Stone Sweet and Sandholtz, 1997). For path-dependence to work reliably in favour of integration stability and progress, disintegration must become increasingly unattractive – even if integration develops in unintended ways, becomes inefficient due to changing circumstances, or contradicts the preferences of the major member states. Several factors contribute to path-dependence: sunk costs, that is, the irredeemable investments states and other actors had to make to adapt their institutions and strategies to an integrated policy; endogenous interdependence, that is, the further deepening of interdependence produced by previous integration steps; exit costs, that is, the relative losses that countries incur when leaving the EU or an integrated policy area; the autonomy of supranational institutions such as the Court or the European Central Bank (ECB), which act to preserve and expand integration; and decision-making procedures such as unanimity or qualified majority voting that make it hard to muster support for disintegration (Pierson, 1996). As long as integrated policies are at low levels of supranational autonomy, institutional capacity, membership, transnational exchange, and interdependence, they run a high risk of disintegration under conditions of crisis (Lefkofridi and Schmitter, 2015: 7). The more they are entrenched and institutionalized, however, the more difficult and unlikely it becomes to leave the path of integration.

Postfunctionalism

Just as the rise of intergovernmentalism is closely connected to the 'empty chair crisis' of the mid-1960s and related developments, the rise of what came to be known as postfunctionalism is intimately linked to a decade of (temporary) defeats of European integration projects due to referendum results spanning the negative Danish referendum on the Maastricht Treaty in 1992 and the rejection of the Constitutional Treaty in France and the Netherlands in 2005. These events signalled the coming of a new force in European integration: mass politics.

In a path-breaking article bringing together various strands of research on the mass politics of European integration, Liesbet Hooghe and Gary Marks (2008) claim that neofunctionalism and intergovernmentalism, united by a common focus on the functional, efficiency-based rationale for regional integration, economic preferences, and bargaining between interest groups, 'have become less useful guides for research on the European Union' (2008: 3). Under the changed circumstances characterized by politicization engaging mass publics and extending into the domain of domestic politics, European integration has become, according to postfunctionalists, more salient and contested in public opinion and party competition. As European integration has moved into core areas of state sovereignty and national identity and has produced effects reaching deeply into national economic, financial, and welfare policies, public opinion has turned against the EU. Eurosceptic parties have exploited this sentiment during national elections and in an increasing number of referendums. As a result, EU-friendly elites now regularly face a 'constraining dissensus' when making decisions on European integration, which supersedes the 'permissive consensus' of the earlier integration period (Hooghe and Marks, 2008).

In contrast to neofunctionalism, postfunctionalism considers the sources of crisis in the EU to be profoundly domestic. The relevant actors are citizens and parties rather than firms, interest groups, and supranational bureaucrats, and they are not so much motivated by gains in profit, efficiency, and institutional autonomy as they are concerned by losses in national identity and welfare. In contrast to intergovernmentalism, postfunctionalism considers domestic change to be endogenous. It is the progress in integration – the deepening of economic integration, the expansion of integration into areas of core state powers, and the massive enlargement of the 2000s – that increases the salience of European integration; raises concerns about competitiveness, redistribution, sovereignty, and immigration; and helps eurosceptic parties mobilize voters.

Integration crises are characterized by politicization, the growing salience of European politics, the proliferation of actors and audiences, and the polarization of their attitudes and opinions on European integration (De Wilde, 2011). As such, an increase in politicization does not imply either integration or disintegration effects. Neofunctionalists such as Schmitter (1969) hypothesized a politicization effect of progressive integration but expected it to work in favour of transcending the nation state and promoting political integration. By contrast, postfunctionalism expects politicization to mobilize eurosceptic citizens, empower eurosceptic parties, and undermine support for European integration. Hooghe and Marks (2008) 'expect to see downward pressure on the level and scope of integration', a limitation of governments' room to manoeuvre, and a mismatch of functionally efficient and politically feasible solutions (2008: 21–3). Both neofunctionalism and postfunctionalism regard crises as feedback mechanisms of integration, but whereas neofunctionalists think of crises as positive and integration-reinforcing feedback, postfunctionalists expect negative feedback undermining integration and possibly producing disintegration.

Whether and to what extent this happens depends on two sets of conditions, however: the degree to which tensions and crises in integration actually affect the welfare and identity of citizens; and how well governments and EU institutions are able to insulate EU policy-making from the impact of domestic politics, for instance by forming government coalitions of EU-friendly mainstream parties, shifting decisions to regulatory agencies, or circumventing controversial referendums (Hooghe and Marks, 2008: 22; Schimmelfennig 2014a: 11–16).

In sum, whereas all major integration theories agree that crises are important catalysts of both theoretical and real-world change in European integration, they disagree on the relevant sources, processes, and effects of crises in integration. The next section examines the eurozone crisis based on the propositions derived from the three integration theories in this section.

Integration Theories and the Eurozone Crisis

The eurozone crisis is particularly relevant for a theoretical assessment of the broader integration crisis. It is arguably the deepest and longest crisis in the history of European integration and it has affected the most ambitious and most defining project of the EU and its most centralized policy: monetary union. Disintegration in the core of the EU has been a potential crisis outcome and has been a manifest and imminent threat, especially in the case of possible Greek exit from the eurozone (Grexit). The eurozone crisis has featured a record high in both crisis diplomacy at the EU level and street-level politicization and anti-EU protest. It has been a key reason why support for the EU and national governments has tumbled. More than other crises in European integration, the eurozone crisis has been a systemic crisis affecting all levels of the EU's multi-level governance system and a centrepiece of the European order. In this respect, it differs clearly from the Ukraine crisis and Brexit. Only the migration crisis has had a similar scope. Second, and in contrast to the migration crisis, the eurozone crisis has been with us for many years and has produced outcomes that we can assess against the propositions of the integration theories.

This part of the chapter makes the following three arguments, which are developed more fully elsewhere (Schimmelfennig, 2014a, 2015). First, intergovernmentalism offers a plausible account of the member states' positions, their negotiations, and the integration outcomes of the eurozone crisis. Second, this account needs to be embedded in a larger neofunctionalist explanation of the dynamics of European integration. Third, whereas postfunctionalism is corroborated by the unprecedented politicization of integration during the eurozone crisis, the effects of politicization on the integration outcomes of the crisis have been weak.

Intergovernmentalism and the eurozone crisis: mixed preferences, chicken-game negotiations, and institutional commitments

The eurozone crisis broke out at the end of a chain reaction starting with the sub-prime mortgage crisis in the USA, which triggered a global financial and banking crisis, and spilled over into a balance-of-payment and debt crisis of several euro area countries, which put in question their ability to retain the euro as their currency (see Chapter 4). The eurozone crisis thus corresponds to a typical intergovernmental crisis scenario: an exogenous economic shock threatening the welfare and autonomy of the member states and dramatically increasing their interdependence. The euro area's responses to the crisis can be explained plausibly as a result of intergovernmental bargaining based on partly converging and partly diverging member state interests that were designed to strengthen the credibility of member state commitments to the common currency.

National preferences in the eurozone crisis resulted from the typical mix of a common interdependence-induced interest in integration, on the one hand, and conflicting preferences on the terms of integration, on the other. Since the beginning of the crisis, governments had been united in their commitment to the survival and defence of the eurozone, a position underpinned by a strong sense of negative interdependence and prohibitive costs. At the height of the crisis, even Grexit was considered too high a risk of market panic and contagion (Spiegel, 2014).

At the same time, the euro area countries held conflicting views on the means to achieve the common goal of preserving and consolidating the euro. In line with their fundamentally different fiscal and economic positions, they proposed vastly different schemes for the distribution of the adjustment costs. The 'northern' coalition of Germany, Austria, Finland, and the Netherlands sought to minimize their liabilities and financial assistance. Rather than mutualizing the debt through eurobonds or other instruments, these countries demanded that crisis countries adjust through internal devaluation by means of austerity. What united these northern countries was their favourable balance-of-payments and fiscal position: high solvency and strong credit ratings. By contrast, the southern coalition of Greece, Portugal, and Spain was in a worse economic and fiscal position: less wealthy, more highly indebted, and under pressure from the financial market. Accordingly, it pushed for the 'Europeanization' of sovereign debt and soft adjustment policies.

These mixed motives constituted a 'chicken game' characterized by dynamics of hard bargaining and brinkmanship. Whereas all actors had a strong joint preference for avoiding an extremely costly outcome – the end of the euro – they also sought to avoid the costs of backing down and taking over the burden of adjustment. Brinkmanship in the eurozone crisis was apparent in that the solvent northern countries repeatedly rejected and delayed (additional) support to the indebted southern countries and pushed them to make fiscal cuts up to the point at which sovereign default was imminent. The southern countries, in turn, sought to postpone painful adjustment measures and demonstrate their incapacity to counter financial market pressure until the northern countries came to the conclusion that rescue was inevitable.

Yet interdependence in the eurozone crisis was asymmetrical. Whereas the stakes were high for all eurozone countries, the immediate consequences of the crisis and potential disintegration were significantly more severe for the highly indebted countries. As a result, the northern countries, and Germany in particular, were in a better position to realize their preferences than the southern countries. At each stage of crisis decision-making, Germany was able to shape the terms of integration in return for giving up its opposition to bailing out insolvent eurozone members. Germany prevented the introduction of eurobonds or any other formally mutualized sovereign debt. In addition, Germany was able to link financial assistance to strict austerity conditionality, the strengthening of the EU's monitoring and sanctioning of national budgets, and the adoption of the Treaty on Stability, Coordination and Governance (Fiscal Compact), including a balanced budget rule to be enshrined 'preferably' in domestic constitutional law. Whereas the citizens of the southern countries have, in consequence, suffered huge losses in wages, subsidies, and social security benefits, and increases in taxation, the northern states have successfully opposed any write-off of their rescue money (so far). Even though Germany and the other northern countries cooperated by providing financial assistance to help the debtor countries avoid sovereign default, they were able to shape the terms of the assistance programmes in line with their adjustment preferences.

Again in line with intergovernmentalism, governments were the dominant actors of crisis management. Proponents of the so-called 'new intergovernmentalism' claim that governments did not limit themselves to negotiating and deciding on the rules of policy in the euro crisis. Rather, intergovernmental institutions such as the European Council, the Euro Summit (the leaders of the eurozone members), the Euro Group (the finance ministers of the eurozone countries), and the Ecofin Council (the finance ministers of all the EU countries) coordinated and implemented the rescue programmes and macroeconomic policy themselves – thereby circumventing the classical community method, in which supranational actors exercise considerable influence. In addition, many of the institutional reforms during the eurozone crisis, ranging from the European Stability Mechanism (ESM) to the Fiscal Compact, bear the hallmarks of intergovernmentalism. 'New intergovernmentalists' generally emphasize that 'more integration' is not tantamount to more supranational delegation, especially in the area of core state powers (Bickerton et al., 2015; Genschel and Jachtenfuchs, 2016; Chapter 9 in this volume).

As expected by liberal intergovernmentalism, institutional reform generally conveys a concern for a more credible commitment to the stability of the eurozone area. The eurozone crisis exposed several enforcement problems in Economic and Monetary Union (EMU). First, the Stability and Growth Pact (SGP), established in 1997 to commit countries to fiscal discipline, had already proven malleable and ultimately toothless ahead of the financial crisis. Second, the eurozone crisis demonstrated that even countries without excessive budget deficits – such as Ireland and Spain – could be hit by exogenous shocks, sudden stops, and balance of payment difficulties. In this case, the enforcement problem was how to commit other member states credibly to providing a fiscal backstop or coming to their rescue. Third, EMU was accompanied by financial market integration based on mutual recognition of national banking regulation. The eurozone crisis highlighted the inadequacies of national banking supervision and resolution: lax supervision, regulatory arbitrage across member states, and burden-sharing as well as blame-shifting among national regulators when transnationally operating banks ran into trouble.

The three major blocks of institutional reform undertaken since the beginning of the eurozone crisis (see Chapter 4) are clearly linked to the three major problems that together made the eurozone crisis possible: the financial crisis, the sovereign debt crisis, and the lack of instruments to counter loss of financial market confidence and sudden stops. The Fiscal Compact and the legislation on the surveillance of member states' fiscal and economic policies are intended to overcome the enforcement problems of the SGP; the legislation on banking union tackles the sovereign-bank nexus and the enforcement problems of national regulation in an integrated financial market; and the ESM is meant to overcome the problem of committing solvent countries to the rescue of insolvent ones.

More specifically, however, the design of the common institutions largely follows the preferences of the northern countries, and especially Germany – the countries with the strongest bargaining power. Their institutional preferences have been strongly linked to their material preferences: whereas they have sought to strengthen the credibility of the highly indebted countries' commitment to fiscal discipline, they have tried to limit their own financial commitment and exposure. As a consequence, the new and reformed institutions feature intergovernmental financial assistance with a fixed limit on lending capacity, together with supranational fiscal and economic surveillance in the reformed SGP and the Fiscal Compact, and a banking union that combines supranational supervision with more intergovernmental resolution.

In sum, intergovernmentalism provides a plausible explanation of the eurozone crisis from origins to outcomes. The global financial crisis presented the eurozone with a formidable challenge. The asymmetrical exogenous shock produced by the crisis threatened to disintegrate the eurozone, and set off a hard intergovernmental bargaining process in which governments had a common preference for saving and consolidating the euro but tried to shift the burden of adjustment. The euro area countries that were less hard hit by the crisis and less in need of international support used their superior bargaining power to attain their preferred terms of crisis management and integration.

Neofunctionalism and the eurozone crisis: endogenous deficiencies, non-state actors, and path-dependency

Critics of intergovernmentalism have long pointed out that it is best at explaining isolated, individual intergovernmental negotiation processes and treaty outcomes but fails to account for the long-term, dynamic endogeneity of the integration process, that is, how current integration decisions are shaped by the effects of earlier integration decisions. In the words of Paul Pierson, 'Attempts to cut into ongoing social processes at a single point in time produce a "snapshot" view that is distorted in crucial respects' (Pierson, 1996: 127). According to his historical-institutionalist analysis, any integration decision produces unanticipated consequences, adaptations of preferences, and endogenous interdependencies, which shape and constrain the next integration decision and create a path-dependent process over time.

This section argues that, even though the eurozone crisis originated from an exogenous shock, it only became an integration crisis because of endogenous deficiencies resulting from earlier intergovernmental bargains. Moreover, the common preference for the preservation and con-solidation of the eurozone was not an exogenous, fundamental national interest but an endogenous consequence of the prior decision to create monetary union and the path-dependencies that this decision created. Finally, intergovernmental negotiations and decisions were strongly driven and flanked by transnational and supranational actors: financial markets and the ECB.

On the first of these points, whereas the eurozone crisis was trig-gered exogenously, the global financial crisis could only turn into an integration crisis because of the inherent economic tensions and institu-tional flaws of EMU. In other words, the exogenous shock exposed the endogenous tensions and deficiencies of the original construction. These tensions and deficiencies consisted of the juxtaposition of supranational monetary integration with intergovernmental fiscal and economic coor-dination, and the creation of monetary union without fiscal union in a non-optimal currency area. The eurozone area lacked a common fiscal backstop or lender of last resort to absorb shocks, a system of social transfers to mitigate adjustment, and a regime of centralized fiscal super-vision or an institutionalized procedure of state insolvency to enforce fiscal discipline.

This construction was the outcome of prior intergovernmental bar-gaining. It reflected a conflict between France and Germany, and essen-tially the same coalitions that emerged in the eurozone crisis, about the design and purpose of monetary union. Due to superior bargaining power, Germany was able to shape monetary union largely according to its preferences for inflation targeting, central bank independence, and fiscal supervision – and against debt financing, bailouts, and transfers (Moravcsik, 1998: ch. 6; Walsh, 2000; Wolf and Zangl, 1996). At the same time, as a result of political compromises, the convergence criteria for joining monetary union and fiscal discipline rules of the SGP were relaxed and weakly enforced; and countries with divergent macroeco-nomic preferences and growth strategies turned monetary union into a non-optimal currency area.

Second, the common interest of eurozone countries in preserving and stabilizing the euro and their preparedness to engage in institutional reforms strengthening the credibility of their commitment to the euro is best explained as endogenous to the previous decision to create a common currency. In Pierson's terms, the euro crisis was a 'heavily discounted or unintended effect' (Pierson, 1996: 149). Counterfactually, however, it is doubtful that the member states would have introduced the single currency in 1999 had they known the situation they would face ten years after. In 2010, however, returning to the status quo was no longer an efficient option. The euro contains considerable 'sunk costs' for states, firms, and citizens. In addition, monetary union strengthened transnational capital movement and interlocking among financial services in the eurozone. EMU thus created additional, endogenous interdependence. The institutional hurdles were also high: there is no orderly exit procedure from the eurozone.

Thus, faced with unanticipated negative consequences of integration and realizing that the earlier decision to join EMU had increased international interdependence and put them in a situation without credible exit options, the member states reluctantly agreed on new rules and institutions that they had rejected in the Maastricht negotiations on EMU and would not have agreed to had the financial crisis occurred in a pre-EMU institutional setting. Even Germany, the most powerful euro area country during the crisis, found itself constrained to give up its previously rigid anti-bailout policy. This counterfactual argument is supported by the observation that EU member states outside the eurozone have in general not committed themselves to the rescue of banks or banking resolution funds, to the stricter sanctioning of excessive deficits, or to supranational banking supervision (Schimmelfennig, 2014b). The decision for more integration in the eurozone crisis was thus dependent on the path that states embarked on 20 years before.

Third, the apparent centrality of intergovernmental politics during the crisis needs to be put in perspective. Though governments took the major bailout decisions and established or upgraded the rescue funds, they were driven by the financial markets. At the very beginning, the exogenous shock was facilitated by the globalization of finance. In the chicken-game bargaining that followed the shock, the northern coalition tried to delay providing financial help and the southern countries sought to avoid painful austerity measures for as long as possible. They were forced to act and compromise, however, when the bond yields of the deficit countries increased sharply and sovereign default appeared imminent. Regarding the acute crisis in Greece, therefore, Germany and France faced the choice of either rescuing Greece from default or exposing their own banks to the risk of Greek insolvency. Later on, creditors were forced to increase their initially limited rescue funds when financial markets continued to test the credibility of the eurozone area's commitment.

Without the help of the ECB, however, governments might not have been able to prevent further contagion from the eurozone crisis. It was only after ECB President Mario Draghi announced in July 2012 that the ECB would do 'whatever it takes' to save the euro that financial market pressure subsided and bond yields started to decrease durably. Generally, markets took ECB signals more seriously than signals from national governments (Bølstad and Elhardt, 2015). Contrary to the intergovernmentalist account of supranational institutions being instruments of states, it needs pointing out that the ECB played this crucial stabilizing role in rescuing the eurozone by stretching its mandate to the limits, if not overstepping them (see Chapter 4). By buying the bonds of deficit countries (quantitative easing), supplying banks with cheap long-term credit, and turning into a de facto lender of last resort, the ECB pursued policies and acquired a role that it was originally not designed to have, and which many leading German officials – within and outside the ECB – opposed. It could do so because governments had accorded it the necessary independence, financial capacity, and decision-making capacity (majority voting based on one member, one vote in the ECB Council before the introduction of a rotation system in 2015).

In sum, the neofunctionalist account qualifies the intergovernmentalist triple tenet of state preferences, state power, and state control. Governments lost control of the original design of monetary union; state preferences were largely endogenous to the initial integration decision and its unintended effects; and state power was severely circumscribed by financial markets and supranational organizations. The eurozone crisis suggests that intergovernmentalism is best embedded as a theory of intergovernmental negotiations and decisions in a neofunctionalist theory of long-term, path-dependent development of integration. Neofunctionalism explains how earlier integration decisions created endogenous interdependence, preference updates, and path-dependent pressures towards more integration. Intergovernmentalism, in turn, captures how governments negotiate and decide in the altered context. It also shows that divergent national preferences, hard intergovernmental bargaining, asymmetrical interdependence, and differential bargaining power remain consequential even in a path-dependent integration process. As a result, the crisis outcomes that states negotiate are typically lowest-common-denominator solutions that are likely to produce further problems down the line. This is what Erik Jones, Daniel Kelemen, and Sophie Meunier (2015) have aptly termed 'failing forward'.

Postfunctionalism and the eurozone crisis: mainstream coalitions, avoidance of referendums, and the dominance of asymmetrical interdependence

From a postfunctionalist perspective, the eurozone crisis presents a major puzzle. On the one hand, it marks the apex of anti-EU politicization in the history of European integration. Never before has EU integration had such a directly attributable, visible, and negative effect on the welfare of member state citizens as in the austerity measures imposed on the highly indebted eurozone countries as part of the rescue packages organized by the EU and the International Monetary Fund (IMF). These measures triggered unprecedented mass protest against the EU, the Commission–ECB–IMF 'Troika', Germany, and the implementing national governments. Public support for and trust in the EU plunged toward historic lows. Attitudes towards the EU have soured most dramatically in the southern European countries hit hardest by the crisis, bringing these traditionally Europhile countries to levels of eurosceptic public opinion formerly reserved for the UK and the Nordic countries (Debomy, 2013; Hobolt, 2014).

Like no other European issue, the eurozone crisis has dominated the foreign and domestic policy agendas of the euro area countries. Almost everywhere in the eurozone, the crisis has produced early elections and the fall of incumbent governments, and reinvigorated populist and eurosceptic parties. In sum, the crisis has produced all the ingredients for a 'postfunctionalist moment' in European integration. According to the postfunctionalist scenario, we should thus have observed strong dissensus constraining governments in EU decision-making, stagnation, and even setbacks in integration, and a further differentiation of integration. And yet, the EU has embarked on a far-reaching reconstruction of EMU, resulting not only in the preservation of the eurozone but also in a major leap of supranational and technocratic integration in fiscal and financial policy. How has this been possible? As pointed out above, politicization requires open gateways to EU-level policy-making to have a constraining effect on European integration: through governmental elections, parliamentary involvement and ratification, and referendums. During most of the crisis, the eurozone has been able to keep these gateways closed thanks to the existence of EU-friendly governments and coalitions and the avoidance of constraining referendums.

Until the end of 2014, all eurozone governments formed during the crisis were mainstream governments, that is, governments composed of parties supporting the euro and further European integration. However, as the eurozone crisis intensified from late 2014, high governmental instability began to set in, with elections often being snap elections and with incumbents generally being voted out of office. But the new governments formed as a result were mostly supportive of eurozone cooperation and deepening. Often, they consisted of formal or informal grand coalitions uniting the mainstream parties against eurosceptics from the left and right. This process mitigated the effect of domestic politicization, even where popular dissatisfaction with crisis-related policies was boosted by eurosceptic parties. It ensured smooth cooperation with EU partners and, in the case of the highly indebted countries, compliance with financial assistance conditionality.

Avoiding referendums (or limiting their impact) has been the second instrument used to shield the rescue and reform of the eurozone from constraints of mass-level dissensus. So, in 2011, the eurozone governments successfully put tremendous pressure on the Greek Prime Minister, George Papandreou, to call off a referendum on whether or not to accept austerity measures being proposed (by the EU, the ECB, and the IMF) for Greece. More generally, eurozone governments have been unwilling to embark upon new treaties and treaty reforms that would risk failed ratifications. When treaties, such as the ESM Treaty and the Fiscal Compact, have been deemed necessary, they have been put in a form that has not required unanimous ratification to enter into force. Thus, the veto power of treaty referendums has been reduced.

In 2015, however, both insulation mechanisms failed in Greece (see Chapter 12). The left-wing populist Syriza party, a fierce critic of the austerity policies administered by the Troika, emerged as the strongest force from the parliamentary elections in January 2015 and formed a government coalition with a right-wing populist party. For the first time during the crisis, a eurozone member state was governed by a coalition that excluded all mainstream parties and brought together parties from opposite ends of the traditional left–right spectrum, whose main commonality was the rejection of EU crisis policies. In July 2015, the Syriza-led government held a successful referendum against the EU's bailout conditions. And yet, only a few days after the referendum, the Greek government accepted a new bailout package with even harsher austerity conditions (pension cuts and tax increases). Even though politicization exacerbated the hard bargaining and brinkmanship in this eurozone crisis chicken game, the outcome reflected Greece's inferior bargaining power and confirmed the bailout-for-austerity compromise established in earlier iterations of the game. International constraints trumped domestic constraints.

To sum up, whereas postfunctionalism rightly points to the mass-level eurosceptic politicization effects of European integration, its negative predictions for EU-level politics have not materialized. Politicization arguably has made intergovernmental negotiations more difficult, but has not prevented the eurozone from progressing on the path towards more integration. The 'constraining dissensus' has proved ultimately not that constraining after all. However, the more far-reaching neofunctionalist expectations of a 'transcending', 'good crisis' supported by EU citizens and increasing the legitimacy and political integration of the EU have not materialized either (Lefkofridi and Schmitter, 2015).

Conclusions

All three integration theories make important contributions to explaining the eurozone crisis and its outcomes. *Intergovernmentalism* provides a plausible but shallow explanation of the exogenous origins, the mixed state preferences, the chicken-game intergovernmental negotiations, and the commitment-enhancing integration outcomes during the crisis. By embedding the intergovernmentalist explanation in its historical, transnational, and supranational contexts, *neofunctionalism* provides depth to the intergovernmentalist explanation. It shows how the exogenous shock exposed the defects of the construction of monetary union, how state preferences were partly endogenous to monetary integration, how intergovernmental negotiations were pushed by financial market actors and were flanked by the ECB, and how the integration outcomes of the crisis were path-dependent on the original decision to create a single currency. By contrast, the crisis failed to mobilize public support and facilitate the transition to political integration expected in early neofunctionalist theorising. *Postfunctionalism* explains this failure based on the elite bias of integration, the economic and identity losses incurred by many citizens as a result of integration, and the rise of eurosceptic parties – but it does not account for the significant progress made in institutional integration during the crisis.

The analysis of the eurozone crisis from the vantage point of integration theory points to three general crisis-related factors that governments need to navigate: exogenous shocks to the integration edifice; spillovers pushing for 'more Europe'; and politicization inhibiting further integration. Beginning with the first of these, the EU is subject to exogenous shocks not only from financial and economic crises in its international environment but also from security crises in its eastern and southern neighbourhood, which produced the recent Ukraine and migration crises. Second, the EU finds itself ill-equipped to deal with such crises owing to its 'half-way' integration, which leaves neither EU institutions nor national governments capable of dealing with crises quickly and effectively – as has been apparent in the Ukraine and migration crises. Whereas the EU has increased its competences in both internal and external security policies since the 1990s, it is nowhere near having an autonomous operational capacity. Third, exogenous crises are reinforced by populist reactions, which capitalize on the capacity problems of both the EU and its member states but hamper the making of common and effective policies at the same time.

In this situation, successful crisis solutions depend on the value that member states attach to having integrated policies and on the relative capacities of member states and supranational organizations. In the eurozone crisis, the risks and costs of a monetary disintegration together with the impotence of the debt-ridden euro countries and the capacity of the ECB propelled the member states towards 'more Europe'. In the Ukraine crisis, the EU has had neither a highly integrated policy to defend nor the capacity to act decisively against Russian intervention. The migration crisis is in-between these constellations. Whereas free movement and the abolition of internal border controls are highly popular and economically beneficial integrated policies, the costs of disintegration are nowhere near the costs of a disruption of the eurozone. National capacities are high, with even weak states being able to effectively counter migration by closing their borders and waving through refugees. And there is no equivalent of the ECB to back up central policies and to circumvent governments that do not want to cooperate.

References

Bickerton, C. J., Hodson, D., and Puetter, U. (2015) 'The New Intergovernmentalism: European Integration in the Post-Maastricht Era', *Journal of Common Market Studies*, Vol. 53, No. 4, pp. 703–22.

Bølstad, J. and Elhardt, C. (2015) 'To Bail Out or Not To Bail Out? Crisis Politics, Credibility, and Default Risks in the Eurozone', *European Union Politics,* Vol. 16, No. 3, pp. 325–46.

De Wilde, P. (2011) 'No Polity for Old Politics? A Framework for Analyzing the Politicization of European Integration', *Journal of European Integration*, Vol. 33, No. 5, pp. 559–75.

Debomy, D. (2013) *EU No, Euro Yes? European Public Opinions Facing the Crisis (2007–2012)*. Paris: Notre Europe.

Genschel, P. and Jachtenfuchs, M. (2016) 'More Integration, Less Federation: the European Integration of Core State Powers', *Journal of European Public Policy*, Vol. 23, No. 1, pp. 42–59.

Haas, E. B. (1961) 'International Integration: the European and the Universal Process', *International Organization,* Vol. 15, No. 3, pp. 366–92.

Hobolt, S. B. (2014) 'Public Attitudes towards the Euro Crisis.' In O. Cramme and S. B. Hobolt (eds), *Democratic Politics in a European Union under Stress*. Oxford: Oxford University Press, pp. 48–66.

Hoffmann, S. (1966) 'Obstinate or Obsolete? The Fate of the Nation State and the Future of Western Europe', *Daedalus*, Vol. 95, No. 4, pp. 861–98.

Hooghe, L. and Marks, G. (2008) 'A Postfunctionalist Theory of European Integration: From Permissive Consensus to Constraining Dissensus', *British Journal of Political Science*, Vol. 39, No. 1, pp. 1–23.

Jones, E., Kelemen, R. D., and Meunier, S. (2015) 'Failing Forward? The Euro Crisis and the Incomplete Nature of European Integration', *Comparative Political Studies,* Vol. 49, No. 7, pp. 1–25.

Lefkofridi, Z. and Schmitter, P. C. (2015) 'Transcending or Descending? European Integration in Time of Crisis', *European Political Science Review*, Vol. 7, No. 1, pp. 3–22.

Leuffen, D., Rittberger, B., and Schimmelfennig, F. (2013) *Differentiated Integration. Explaining Variation in the European Union*. Basingstoke: Palgrave.

Milward, A. S. (1984) *The Reconstruction of Western Europe, 1945–51*. London: Routledge.

Milward, A. S. (1994) *The European Rescue of the Nation-State*. London: Routledge.

Moravcsik, A. (1993) 'Preferences and Power in the European Community: A Liberal Intergovernmentalist Approach', *Journal of Common Market Studies*, Vol. 31, No. 4, pp. 473–524.

Moravcsik, A. (1998) *The Choice for Europe: Social Purpose and State Power from Messina to Maastricht*. Ithaca, NY: Cornell University Press.

Niemann, A. (2006) *Explaining Decisions in the European Union*. Cambridge: Cambridge University Press.

Pierson, P. (1996) 'The Path to European Integration. A Historical Institutionalist Analysis', *Comparative Political Studies*, Vol. 29, No. 2, pp. 123–63.

Putnam, R. D. (1988) 'Diplomacy and Domestic Politics: The Logic of Two-Level Games', *International Organization*, Vol. 42, No. 3, pp. 427–60.

Rosato, S. (2011) *Europe United. Power Politics and the Making of the European Community*. Ithaca, NY: Cornell University Press.

Schimmelfennig, F. (2014a) 'European Integration in the Euro Crisis: The Limits of Postfunctionalism', *Journal of European Integration*, Vol. 36, No. 3, pp. 317–37.

Schimmelfennig, F. (2014b) 'Differentiated Integration Before and After the Crisis.' In O. Cramme and S. B. Hobolt (eds), *Democratic Politics in a European Union under Stress*. Oxford: Oxford University Press, pp. 120–34.

Schimmelfennig, F. (2015) 'Liberal Intergovernmentalism and the Euro Area Crisis', *Journal of European Public Policy*, Vol. 22, No. 2, pp. 177–95.

Schmitter, P. C. (1969) 'Three Neo-Functional Hypotheses about International Integration', *International Organization*, Vol. 23, No. 1, pp. 161–6.

Schmitter, P. C. (1970) 'A Revised Theory of Regional Integration', *International Organization*, Vol. 24, No. 4, pp. 836–68.

Spiegel, P. (2014) 'How the Euro Was Saved', *Financial Times*, 11 May 2014. https://www.ft.com/content/f6f4d6b4-ca2e-11e3-ac05-00144feabdc0.

Stone Sweet, A. and Sandholtz, W. (1997) 'European Integration and Supranational Governance', *Journal of European Public Policy*, Vol. 4, No. 3, pp. 297–317.

Tranholm-Mikkelsen, J. (1991) 'Neo-functionalism: Obstinate or Obsolete? A Reappraisal in the Light of the New Dynamism of the EC', *Millenium: Journal of International Studies*, Vol. 20, No. 1, pp. 1–22.

Walsh, J. I. (2000) *European Monetary Integration and Domestic Politics: Britain, France, and Italy*. Boulder: Lynne Rienner.

Wolf, D. and Zangl, B. (1996) 'The European Economic and Monetary Union: "Two-Level Games" and the Formation of International Institutions', *European Journal of International Relations*, Vol. 2, No. 3, pp. 355–93.

Chapter 17

Can the EU Survive?

DOUGLAS WEBBER

Introduction

It is a measure of the depth of the current crisis that in 2015 and 2016 an increasing number of political leaders and observers publicly expressed fears that the EU was on the verge of collapse. The aim of this chapter is to assess to what extent these fears are justified – that is to say, how likely it is that the EU will survive or *dis*integrate. The notion of political integration (or disintegration) has three distinct dimensions. *Horizontal* (dis)integration refers to the decline/growth in the number of EU member states; *vertical* (dis)integration to the decline/growth in the competence and powers of the EU's supranational organs – the European Commission, the European Parliament, the Court of Justice of the European Union (CJEU), and the European Central Bank (ECB) – vis-à-vis national governments; and *sectoral* (dis)integration to the decline/ growth in the number of issue areas in which common policies have been adopted in Europe.

So far, Europe's political integration has been a quasi-unidirectional process. The number of member states has grown from six to 28, more than doubling since the end of the Cold War. The powers of the Parliament, CJEU, and ECB are at an all-time high. No issue area in which the EU has been empowered to intervene has been 'handed back' for member governments to manage. Even during the present crisis, the EU's intervention capacity has been strengthened rather than weakened, notably in respect of the management of Economic and Monetary Union (EMU) (Schimmelfennig, 2014).

The apparent robustness of European integration provides reassurance for those, like Jean Monnet, one of the founding fathers, who believe that 'Europe will be forged in crises and will be the sum of the solutions adopted for these crises', that it is through crises that Europe has become politically more integrated. Even if this reading of EU history is misplaced (Parsons and Matthijs, 2015; Chapter 2 in this volume), past crises have certainly not durably derailed the integration process.

This chapter argues that the EU's record of survival is nonetheless no guarantee that it will surmount the current crisis, because this one is different from its predecessors. After examining competing theories of international relations, European integration, and comparative politics for clues as to what, if anything, might lead to the disintegration of the EU, the chapter identifies two variables that will be decisive: the evolution of domestic politics in the member states and the evolution of Germany's stance towards the EU. Domestic political trends in most member states heighten the likelihood of European *dis*integration, leaving its fate increasingly dependent on the orientation of Germany, whose capacity and, even more so, willingness to provide benevolent 'pro-European' leadership is increasingly in doubt. Hence it is becoming increasingly unlikely that the EU as we know it will survive the current crisis.

The Historical Perspective: This Crisis Is Different

The EU is no stranger to crisis (see Chapter 2). Indeed, it has been 'in crisis' for much of its history. However, there are grounds for thinking that the current crisis is unique in its intensity and the magnitude of the challenge it poses to the EU's survival. No previous crisis combines all its traits (Webber, forthcoming). First, as noted in Chapter 1, this crisis is *multi-dimensional*; in fact, it is an accumulation of successive crises. On top of the eurozone crisis, which has ebbed and flowed since 2009, have come the post-Arab Spring conflicts (2011) and the Ukraine crisis in the winter of 2013–14, the migration crisis, precipitated by the civil war in Syria, and the unexpected result of the Brexit referendum on UK membership of the EU in 2016. Second, the current crisis is unusual in its *duration,* having so far gripped the EU for almost a decade (since the outbreak of the eurozone crisis). A third trait that sets it apart from earlier crises is the extent of its *mass politicization,* exemplified by the way in which it has been accompanied by the creation and sometimes meteoric growth of 'anti-European' political movements, EU-related popular referendums, and popular protest and demonstrations. The final trait relates to the *cost of inaction* (Parsons and Matthijs, 2015). Not every crisis in the past jeopardized the EU's survival or existing level of integration. In the case of the eurozone crisis in particular, however, there can be little doubt that if no EU agreement had been reached to aid crisis-stricken debtor states, the interest rates they would have had to pay on government bonds would have exploded and the eurozone would have collapsed either partially or completely.

Can the EU Disintegrate? Theoretical Perspectives

It will thus be more difficult for the EU to survive this multi-dimensional, protracted, and dangerous crisis than preceding crises. Just how difficult it will be requires identification of the forces that have hitherto driven the integration process and assessment of whether they will enable it to withstand the powerful centrifugal pressures that have been unleashed by the crisis. A good starting point is the existing theoretical literature, whether it derives from the analysis of European integration as such or from broader contributions to comparative politics, international relations, and international political economy. In this section the various different theoretical angles are summarized, ranging from the most optimistic regarding the EU's capacity to survive to the most pessimistic (see also Chapter 16).

Neofunctionalism, transactionalism, and liberal intergovernmentalism

Neofunctionalist, transactionalist, and liberal intergovernmentalist analyses of European integration differ significantly, notably in respect of the balance of power in the EU between member state governments, which for liberal intergovernmentalists remain the decisive actors, and the supranational organs, which for neofunctionalists and transactionalists have grown increasingly autonomous of member states. But all three theoretical perspectives view political integration as being driven by the same fundamental force: the growth of economic interdependence or 'transnational society'. As long as these processes continue, the three theoretical perspectives regard the threat of political disintegration as negligible. Indeed, over time, according to two transactionalist theorists, a self-sustaining dynamic of institutionalization will increasingly insure the EU against any negative political fallout – by implication, even in the event of a profound economic crisis (Stone Sweet and Sandholtz, 1997, 1999). Similarly, the liberal intergovernmentalist Andrew Moravcsik emphasized the powerful incentives for policy coordination generated by the 'increasing transborder flows of goods, services, factors, or pollutants' (Moravcsik, 1993: 485). For this reason, he was confident that the eurozone crisis would not derail European integration. As Europe was the world's most economically interdependent continent, EU member states had 'no choice but to cooperate' (Moravcsik, 2010: 25). He was no less certain that even if the UK voted – as it subsequently did – to leave the EU, it would not end up actually withdrawing from it. Rather, a new membership deal would be negotiated and put to the British public in a second referendum, which would pass (Moravcsik, 2016).

Historical institutionalism

To a large extent, historical institutionalists share the same fundamentally optimistic assessment of the EU's prospects as neofunctionalists, transactionalists, and liberal intergovernmentalists. For them (as for neofunctionalists and transactionalists) political integration becomes increasingly irreversible as, over time, supranational organs become increasingly autonomous of national governments. Gaps open up in the capacity of member governments to control supranational 'agents' as a result of these organs' partial autonomy, the restricted time horizons of political decision-makers in the member states, unanticipated consequences, and shifts in the preferences of governments that facilitate the adoption of new EU policies which (under existing decision-making rules) cannot be reversed by their successors (Pierson, 1998). 'Massive sunk costs' and the high price of exit made it in practice almost 'unthinkable' that a member state would leave the EU (Pierson, 1998: 319–20).

Some historical institutionalists admit that at critical junctures, 'relatively abrupt institutional change' can occur (Thelen and Steinmo, 1992: 15). According to the (biological-theoretical) notion of punctuated equilibrium, such change occurs when a 'stable structure is stressed beyond its buffering capacity to resist and absorb' (Krasner, 1984: 242–3). This is conceivably the situation in which the EU found itself in 2016, but historical institutionalists fail to provide more concrete pointers that would enable us to determine whether the current crisis will actually produce irresistible disintegrative effects.

International relations institutionalism

Like their sociological counterparts (Olsen, 2009), international relations institutionalists argue that, beyond macro-historical forces and human agency, (in this case, international) institutions can have an independent effect on political outcomes. They may prove resilient and survive by helping states overcome potentially insurmountable collective action problems, inter alia by helping to negotiate agreements, monitor compliance, stabilize expectations, and generally reduce uncertainty (Keohane, 1993; Keohane and Nye, 1993). Such theorists were typically confident that the EU would flourish and remain a 'durable and important entity' after the end of the Cold War (Keohane, 1993: 291).

Compared with neofunctionalists, transactionalists, liberal intergovernmentalists, and historical institutionalists, however, international relations institutionalists are more circumspect about the autonomy and strength of international institutions like the EU, warning that 'without a basis either of hegemonic dominance or common interests, international institutions cannot long survive' (Keohane, 1993: 295). Over

20 years since Keohane suggested this, one might ask whether the now 28 EU member states have sufficiently common interests to maintain or expand their existing level of political integration. In international relations' institutionalist analysis, the importance of a hegemonic power for the durability of international institutions such as the EU underlines the critical role of the stance on European integration taken by the most powerful member states (formerly Germany, France, and the UK) or the single most powerful sate today – Germany (see the section below: European *Dis*integration: Key Determinants).

Traditional intergovernmentalism

Traditional intergovernmentalists (e.g. Hoffmann, 1966) dismissed the notion that international institutions can achieve meaningful autonomy from their member states or survive against their will in the long term. Member states would jealously guard their sovereignty over key issue areas such as security and defence, and regional political integration was therefore bound to remain 'limited, conditional, dependent and reversible' (Hoffmann 1966: 156). From this perspective, as exemplified in the early work of Moravcsik (1991), integration depends on the convergence of the preferences of the most powerful member states, although, in the absence of such convergence, two of three of those states could use the threat of exclusion to coerce the other to acquiesce in closer integration.

With hindsight we can see how, beginning with the single currency, the UK chose to exclude itself from several major integration projects, and that bilateral Franco-German accords, subsequently multi-lateralized, sufficed to sustain (closer) political integration. While this suggests that the conditions of political integration may be less demanding than Moravcsik posited, it implies that the EU's survival is heavily dependent on the capacity of the French and German governments to find common 'pro-European' ground. Unlike what neofunctionalist, transactionalist, liberal intergovernmentalist, or historical-institutionalist analysis suggests, neither is inevitably compelled by 'objective' constraints to promote or uphold European integration.

Actor-centred institutionalism

In contrast with the aforementioned theories, actor-centred institutionalism (ACR) (Scharpf, 2006) is concerned with the policy implications of the EU's institutional structures. On the one hand, the predominant, consensus-oriented decision-making rules of the EU limit the extent and speed with which the EU can react to changing circumstances, raising the probability that policy will become increasingly dysfunctional and tensions more acute. On the other, in the limited areas where democratically less accountable supranational organs such as the ECB can impose hierarchical solutions, it is likely that citizens will perceive these as illegitimate, all the more so given the persistence of strong national identities and the absence of a strong common EU identity. By implication, an EU with 28 diverse member states and powers of intervention in politically salient issue areas (such as fiscal and monetary policy) is likely to be vulnerable to powerful centrifugal forces.

Comparative federalism and polity-formation analysis

In as far as the EU may be regarded as a quasi-federal state or at least as a political system, the literature on the preconditions of survival of political systems may be as useful for elucidating the EU's survival prospects as the more voluminous literature on European integration and international relations. Seen from this perspective, the survival of the EU is anything but self-evident. Not only have most regional organizations collapsed (Mattli, 1999), but so too have many states, including most federations (Lemco, quoted in Kelemen, 2007: 53). The centrifugal tendencies in some EU members – notably the UK and Spain – bear testimony to the potential fragility of some states. If there is a realistic possibility of more than one of its member states breaking apart, why should the EU be immune from this danger?

Recurrent themes in this literature (see, for example, Bartolini, 2005; Kelemen, 2007; McKay, 1999) are the importance for the cohesion of federal polities of pan-systemic political parties and interest organizations, and the existence of an overarching common identity that serves as a counterweight to more parochial ethnic, linguistic, religious, or cultural loyalties. Their absence, or at least weakness, in the EU explains why McKay (2004: 182) feared that the euro could generate acute distributional conflicts, mobilize strong populist movements, and ultimately prove unsustainable. They also explain why Bartolini (2005: 387), who emphasizes the obstacles to the development of these attributes in a relentlessly expanding EU posed by divergent 'economic, coercion and administrative-legal boundaries', posited that the EU could break up in a phase of 'mass mobilization', just as the Ottoman, Habsburg, and Soviet empires did.

Neorealism

Of all theoretical perspectives, neorealism provides the bleakest assessment of the EU's survival prospects. Mearsheimer (1990: 47) argued that once the Cold War and the Soviet threat to west European security ended, the USA would wind up its military presence in Europe, the North Atlantic Treaty Organization (NATO) would perish, and relations between west European states would be fundamentally altered: they would 'begin viewing each other with greater fear and suspicion, as they did for centuries before the onset of the Cold War'. The prospects for major crises and war in Europe would consequently increase markedly.

While the EU has crises aplenty, as Mearsheimer anticipated, these have not been provoked by growing distrust between the (west) European states. (In Mearsheimer's view, this is because the USA has retained a military presence in Europe and NATO has survived.) In as far as the crises have been about security, they have been non-traditional security crises that have been generated by developments beyond the EU. So, the Ukraine crisis, rather than dividing the EU, has fairly closely mirrored old Cold War divisions (see Chapter 14). Neo-realist analysis nonetheless points to a factor that has conceivably made the current crisis more difficult to manage: the decline of the common threat posed to EU member states by the Soviet bloc, which helped to forge a common (anti-communist) European identity.

European *Disintegration*: Key Determinants

The theoretical perspectives reviewed above point explicitly or implicitly to a range of divergent variables that may jeopardize the survival of the EU. For neo-realists it is the disappearance of the Soviet threat, NATO, and the American military presence in Europe. For comparative federalists and polity-formation analysts it is the absence of a common European identity and pan-EU political parties and interest organizations. For traditional intergovernmentalists and international relations institutionalists it is the divergence of the EU-related preferences of the most powerful member states (France and Germany). For neofunctionalists, transactionalists, liberal intergovernmentalists, and historical institutionalists it is primarily a decline of socio-economic interdependence or transnational European society – which they imply is highly unlikely.

Each of these perspectives furnishes 'a piece of the puzzle' in seeking to explain the magnitude of the threat of European disintegration, but none per se suffices. Arguably, the prospect of European disintegration can only be explained by a (longitudinally as well as latitudinally) comparative analysis that incorporates variables from both the EU and member state levels.

What enabled the EU to become politically so closely integrated in the first place ...

If we could assume that the forces that brought about European political integration would resist the current crisis, we could confidently dismiss the prospect of disintegration – in line with liberal intergovernmental-ists, neofunctionalists, transactionalists, and historical institutionalists, who stress the role of socio-economic interdependence and transnational society and the 'high and rising costs of exit' to which these give rise.

The costs of exiting from the EU, or components of it such as EMU, may indeed be intimidatingly high, as the radical-leftist Syriza govern-ment in Greece reluctantly concluded at the height of the Grexit crisis in 2015 (see Chapter 12). This is not to say, however, that disintegration is thereby precluded altogether, not least when member states can be expelled against their will, as nearly occurred with Greece. The con-fidence exuded by those who are dismissive of the prospects of future EU disintegration may not be wholly warranted, and may even be mis-placed. Contrary to what Moravcsik (1998: 494–6) claims, regional political integration does not closely follow levels of intra-regional trade. Such levels are no longer much higher in Europe than in North America or in East Asia – and are actually below those in the Asia-Pacific region (Webber 2014: 355). Nonetheless, the level of political integration among members of the North American Free Trade Agreement (NAFTA), the East Asia Summit, and Asia Pacific Economic Cooperation (APEC) is nowhere near that in the EU, suggesting that intra-regional trade levels, although they may unleash pressures to eradicate trade barriers, have only a limited impact on regional political integration.

Perspectives on the unlikelihood of disintegration also suffer from two other shortcomings. First, they display a truncated conception of domes-tic politics and its significance for regional political integration. For the liberal intergovernmentalist Moravcsik, voters, elections, and political parties are largely irrelevant in determining the European policies of member states (Moravcsik, 1998: 24–50). In his political-economic explanation of national preferences, domestic politics is largely about 'producer groups'. For Stone Sweet and Sandholtz (1997: 299, 309, 315), voters, elections, and parties are no less marginal: the domestic politics of regional political integration is dominated by business, 'the segment' with the most obvious material stake in promoting cross-border transactions. For traditionalist neofunctionalists, the 'spillover' of policy-making competences from the national to the supranational level should generate a comparable transfer of loyalties among domes-tic groups that undergirds and legitimizes closer political integration. However, it is clear that such EU-level loyalty exists only to a very lim-ited extent, leaving the EU exposed in crises to national-populist back-lashes (Fligstein, 2008; Kuhn, 2011).

The second shortcoming relates to the durability of the growth of economic interdependence and transnational society. While cross-bor-der expansion is part of the inherent logic of capitalism, this process is unlikely to be smooth, continuous, and politically uncontested. It is equally part of capitalism's inherent logic to generate periodic crises during which the process is disrupted – witness the recent global financial crisis and the eurozone crisis. International economic exchange generates winners and losers, hence the stability of the process can be ensured only if buttressed by governance structures that facilitate effective crisis management. Such structures were gravely lacking when the eurozone crisis exploded in 2009–10 (see Chapter 4). Those that have since developed may not suffice to prevent the eurozone from disintegrating, at least partially.

Even if the growth of economic interdependence or transnational society did explain Europe's high level of political integration (which it does not), there is no reason to assume that it would continue to grow or that this level would suffice to preclude disintegration in the future. Comparing (western) Europe with North America and East Asia, two other variables appear, especially in the period up to the 1990s, as having contributed more decisively to the exceptionally high level of regional political integration reached in Europe.

Pro-integrationist political parties
The first variable concerns domestic political constellation(s), specifically the dominance of 'pro-European' – that is, 'pro-integrationist' – political parties in the EU member states. Following the outbreak of the Cold War, in most of the EU's founding states the political party landscape was dominated by 'pro-European', internationalist forces that ranged from the moderate-left (social democracy) across the centre (liberalism) to the moderate-right (christian democracy). World War II, the Third Reich, and the Holocaust had discredited the extreme-right; anti-communist sentiment in response to the military threat posed by the Soviet bloc likewise marginalized the radical-left. European integration was largely motivated by the simultaneous goals of strengthening western Europe's capacity to resist communism and suppress any resurgence of (extreme right-wing) German nationalism.

The dominance of the broad pro-European centre varied from one member state to another. France, for example, with its strong nationalist and communist movements, was the furthest outlier in that it displayed the greatest ambivalence about European integration in the 1950s and 1960s. Over time, however, the Gaullists (nationalist supporters of General Charles de Gaulle) mutated into a largely pro-European party while the communists shrank into political insignificance, leaving a void filled in part by the Front National. Italy initially also had a strong communist party, but it abandoned its opposition to European integration by the mid-1970s and became a conventional party of the centre-left.

It was only following the EU's enlargement from the 1970s onwards and the adoption of more contested policy areas from the 1980s that opposition to European integration came to be more forcefully expressed in the party systems of the member states. Before the Cold War ended, the only widespread change in the party system – beginning in the 1980s – was the growth of environmental parties, which, while representing a new current in west European politics, nonetheless resembled the established parties in being broadly 'pro-European'.

Until at least the 1990s, pro-integrationist positions thus generally enjoyed strong support in the mainstream political parties of west European states. It was not a support that existed among counterparts in other regions (in as far as states in the latter were liberal democracies in which parties could freely organize). Most countries in non-communist Asia, for example, became independent only after World War II and were dominated by nationalist movements committed above all to maintaining their new-found national independence, a goal antithetical to the pooling of sovereignty in powerful regional organizations. Smaller non-communist states rejected any regional integration projects that might have exposed them to the perceived risk of being dominated by Japan (Webber, 2001). The doctrine of non-interference in member states' domestic affairs remained (and remains) central to the norms of the Association of South-East Asian Nations (ASEAN) and other regional bodies in whose creation it played a role. And the NAFTA project, which from its launch in the early 1990s was much more limited in scope than European integration, provoked from its outset intense political conflict: so much so that in the USA no major new trade liberalization projects were adopted in the following decades.

Pro-integrationist hegemonic leadership

The second variable that helps to account for Europe's specificity in respect of regional integration is the existence for most of its history of a 'pro-integrationist' hegemonic power or coalition. Comparative historical analysis of systems of regional cooperation and regional monetary unions tends – with qualification – to confirm hegemonic stability theory (Cohen, 1998; Mattli, 1999), which holds that only hegemons have an incentive to supply the critical public goods indispensable to the maintenance of an international (in the current context, regional) system of cooperation rather than to 'free-ride' on the system at other members' expense. For hegemonic stability theorists, the 'overwhelming dominance of one country' is necessary to underpin a stable and open world (regional) order (Milner, 1998: 113). Hegemonic power is not, however, a sufficient condition for regional political integration; the hegemon must not only be capable but also *willing* to play such a role. Kindleberger (1973) thus found that in the 1930s, at the time of the Great Depression, the UK was no longer able and the USA was not yet willing to supply stabilizing international monetary leadership.

Other regions have or have had (actual or putative) hegemonic powers – be it the USA in North America, Japan in former non-Communist East Asia, China in contemporary East Asia, and Russia in the former Soviet Union or the Commonwealth of Independent States – but none has aimed at forging a level of regional political integration comparable to that in Europe. In this respect the European experience is unique. Contrary to what Kindleberger (1973: 307–8) regarded as possible, the EU has long been guided not so much by a single hegemon as by 'cooperative hegemonic' leadership (Pedersen, 1998). Under successive political leaders, France and Germany developed a uniquely intensive bilateral relationship which has no equivalent among major powers elsewhere (Krotz and Schild, 2013; Webber, 1999). Their prominent role in negotiating the 'grand bargains' that marked the history of the EU earned the relationship the label of 'engine', 'motor', or 'locomotive' of European integration.

In Mattli's view (1999: 42), benevolent regional hegemons provide a 'focal point in the coordination of rules, regulations and policies' and, as regional paymasters, mediate conflicts over the distribution of the costs and benefits of integration. With the largest economy in the EU even before reunification, Germany was from the outset the biggest contributor to the budget – and thus to the Common Agricultural Policy, without which France would not have agreed to (further) European integration in the 1960s, and to the EU's regional development policies, which for poorer member states were a condition of their acceptance of internal market liberalization and closer monetary integration (Moravcsik, 1991: 43; Lange, 1992).

In respect of other EU policies and the EU treaties, Germany's influence was arguably more limited. Burdened by its responsibility for two world wars and the Holocaust, and fearing that other EU states would form coalitions to balance German power if it became too dominant, successive German leaders tended to defer to French leadership. The creation of the European Monetary System (EMS) in the late 1970s was 'arguably the first major act of German leadership' in the EU's history (Ludlow, 1982: 290). Even after that, French policy leadership was more the norm on issues of high politics. In this regard, the Maastricht Treaty, the momentum for which came primarily from France, was more typical than the EMS. In earlier decades, a Franco-German agreement, once reached, frequently provided the template for an overall accord, given that within the EU the two states represented 'to a certain extent opposed poles' (Couve de Murville, 1971: 262). This facilitated the exercise of broad-based, fairly consensual Franco-German leadership. If it seemed for a time in the 1980s that trilateral leadership (with the UK) was developing (Moravcsik, 1991), the UK's subsequent decisions to opt out of several major integration projects (notably the eurozone and the Schengen Accord on the free movement of people) led to its growing (self-) marginalization.

... And why now there is a very significant threat of European disintegration

The dominance of pro-European political parties in most member states and the leadership provided by the Franco-German coalition thus help to account for Europe's exceptionalism in respect of regional political integration. If the prospect of European disintegration is looming today, it is not per se because the EU is managing several simultaneous crises, but because its capacity to survive has been undermined by the erosion of these two pillars on which regional political integration has largely been built.

Decreased support for, and increased contestation of, European integration

The erosion of support for pro-integration political parties is part of a broader process in which European integration itself has come to be increasingly contested. The origins of this erosion date back to the 1990s when, in the wake of the Maastricht Treaty, austerity policies were adopted by some member states to meet the criteria for admission to the future eurozone. Since the 1990s, and more especially since the onset of the crisis in the EU, there has been a major decline in support for 'pro-European' parties occupying the political middle ground, and an equally strong increase in support for 'anti-European' movements of both the extreme-left and right, some 'softer' and others 'harder' in the degree of their opposition to European integration.

The magnitude of, and the cross-country variations in, the trend of declining support for pro-European political parties are depicted in Table 17.1. While the pro-European centre is still holding to the extent that in most of the larger member states most voters still prefer moderate left-wing, centrist, or moderate right-wing parties that support European integration, in Greece, Hungary, Poland, and Italy anti- or deeply sceptical EU parties have won support from over half the electorate. Moreover, in the majority of the 20 most populous member states, anti-EU parties are rising fast, be it on the left (especially in eurozone states that have been forced to adopt austerity policies since 2010) or the right (especially in Central Europe and the 'creditor states' in the eurozone). In winter 2015–16, opinion polls indicated that deeply sceptical or anti-European parties were the largest in terms of popular support in Austria, France, Greece, Hungary, the Netherlands, Poland, and the UK (where the Conservative Party even increased its popularity after the Brexit referendum). They were also growing fast in Germany,

Table 17.1 The decline of the 'pro-European' parties in the EU since 2010 (20 selected member states; percentages of the vote)

Member	Last pre-2010 elections			Most recent elections			Latest surveys (December 2015; January 2016)			2010/ last elections	2010/ last surveys
	AEL	PE	AER	AEL	PE	AER	AEL	PE	AER	PE	PE
Austria	1	68	28	1	68	30	–	62	34	0	–6
Belgium	2	84	8	2	85	4	n/a	n/a	n/a	+1	n/a
Czech Rep.	13	48	36	15	68	17	14	63	11	+20	+15
Denmark	15	67	14	12	67	21	13	59	20	0	–8
Finland	9	79	4	7	69	18	7	78	9	–10	–1
France	7	79	10	13	67	18	12	57	30	–12	–22
Germany	12	83	2	9	80	5	9	71	13	–3	–12
Greece	13	80	6	46	41	11	39	45	9	–39	–35
Hungary	–	49	49	1	31	65	–	24	70	–18	–25
Ireland	2	87	–	18	62	–	n/a	n/a	n/a	–28	n/a
Italy	5	81	11	3	61	32	3	47	49	–20	–34
Netherlands	17	73	6	10	73	10	11	51	24	0	–22
Poland	–	64	33	4	45	52	n/a	n/a	n/a	–19	n/a

Portugal	18	77	–	20	70	–	15	75	–	–7	–2
Spain	4	85	–	22	65	–	23	66	–	–20	–19
Sweden	6	88	3	6	77	13	8	67	22	–11	–21
UK	–	58	35	–	42	50	–	39	56	–16	–19
Romania	–	74	5	–	59	15	–	85	4	–15	+11
Bulgaria	–	82	13	–	76	18	n/a	n/a	n/a	–6	n/a
Slovakia	4	79	12	1	50	47	n/a	n/a	n/a	–29	n/a

AEL = anti-European (Communist and far) left.

PE = pro-European (Green, Social Democratic, Liberal, Christian Democratic, and non-eurosceptic Conservative) parties.

AER = anti-European (extreme, nationalist, national-populist, and eurosceptic Conservative) right.

Parties have been classified primarily according to their group affiliations in the European Parliament.

Numbers set in bold indicate the decline in the share of the vote of pro-European parties.

Percentages are for the presidential elections in France and for parliamentary elections in the other 19 states.

The table excludes eight EU member states with populations below 4.5 million (Estonia, Latvia, Lithuania, Slovenia, Croatia, Cyprus, Luxembourg, and Malta).

No nationwide opinion polls were available for December 2015 or January 2016 for Poland, Bulgaria, and Belgium. No polls are given for Ireland and Slovakia, where elections took place in March 2016.

Sources: Wikipedia; electograph.com

Italy, Spain, and Sweden. Such parties were: the main governing parties in the UK, Greece, Poland, and Hungary; minority governing parties in Finland and Portugal; and supporters of the government in Denmark.

In an optimistic analysis (from the viewpoint of supporters of European integration), this growth of party political opposition to the integration process would be no more than a manifestation of an emerging European political system, as these parties would in time be integrated into a new European polity. If the eurozone, migration, and other crises were resolved, these parties would recede. A more pessimistic view would be that these crises will not be resolved and that, as eurosceptic parties continue to grow, they will oblige 'established' pro-European parties to themselves become more eurosceptic in order to stave off a loss of popular support – the implication being that the young EU polity will eventually collapse, as did many young democratic polities in interwar Europe, notably in Germany and Italy. Given the evolution of the eurozone crisis, the optimistic analysis appears credible, but the pessimistic analysis is perhaps more persuasive in view of the way that most pro-European governments and parties have reacted to the migration crisis and in view also of the staging and then the result of the Brexit referendum.

In either case, the rise of deeply sceptical and anti-European parties is but one of several dimensions of a broader, post-Maastricht phenomenon of mass politicization and political contestation of European integration (see de Wilde, Leupold, and Schmidtke, 2015).

A second dimension of this phenomenon is the increasing recourse to popular referendums to ratify and legitimize EU projects and the relatively low levels of support for European integration that have been displayed in some of them. Along with elections, popular referendums are the most pristine manifestations of the mobilization of public opinion, whether they are driven by legal requirements or, as in the UK case (Laws, 2016: 241; Chapter 5 of this volume), the exigencies of domestic politics. Excluding accession referendums for candidate states, some 22 referendums relating to the EU treaties have been staged in the member states since the Maastricht Treaty. Eleven produced 'anti-European' and 11 'pro-European' results – three of the latter being re-runs of prior 'lost' referendums, held after the governments involved (Ireland and Denmark) had negotiated new agreements that were designed to assuage objections to the original terms. Since the turn of the century, more popular referendums have rejected than approved EU projects.

And a third dimension of the increased politicization and declining support for integration is the growth since the onset of the eurozone crisis of anti-European protests and strikes, notably in the member states hit hardest by the crisis and subjected to the toughest austerity policies. According to one estimate, no less than 30 per cent of the Greek population participated in some way in anti-austerity actions between 2010 and 2013 (Rüdig and Karyotis, 2013). These actions included 27 general strikes, large-scale demonstrations, sit-ins, arson attacks on public buildings, widespread destruction of private property, and attacks against the Parliament and parliamentarians. Some 11 per cent of Spaniards took part, according to another estimate, in the protest movement organized by the Indignados (those most affected by austerity policies) (Kriesi, 2016). Austerity measures in Portugal likewise provoked 'huge demonstrations' (Kriesi, 2016). Other protest movements such as the anti-Muslim German Pegida were galvanized by the migration crisis.

The mass politicization of the last 25 years largely mirrors the growth of mass political opposition to the EU and operates primarily at the level of the member states. While not necessarily heralding the collapse of the EU, the political polarization that is embodied (as reflected in the Council of the EU, in which national governments are represented) constrains the EU's collective capacity to mediate conflicts, at least in a way that preserves the existing level of political integration. The old 'permissive consensus' has gone and a new 'constraining dissensus' has taken its place (Hooghe and Marks, 2008).

A less effective EU leadership?

The centrifugal forces generated by changing domestic political constellations make the EU's survival increasingly dependent on the kind of leadership provided by the strongest member states. As noted earlier, long before the 2016 Brexit referendum the UK had relegated itself to the sidelines in major issue areas, thereby obviating any notion of an EU leadership triumvirate emerging. Indeed, with its very decision to stage the referendum, the UK exacerbated existing crises and became a destabilizing force in the EU. In contrast, the Franco-German relationship has shown formidable resilience in as far as the two governments still prefer to reach common positions on significant issues (Krotz and Maher, 2016; Krotz and Schild, 2013). However, the balance of power between them has shifted, with France's pre-eminence in the early decades increasingly giving way to parity from the 1970s. With the end of the Cold War, German reunification, and the outbreak of the eurozone crisis, parity has been superseded by unequivocal German pre-eminence. As the former European Commission President and Italian Prime Minister Romano Prodi has put it, 'The Germans decide, and the French get to announce it during their joint press conference' (as quoted in Matthijs and Blyth, 2015: 258). Compared with post-reunification Germany, France is less populous and has a smaller economy, a comparatively higher government deficit (notwithstanding the 'bill for reunification' that Germany paid), and a weaker foothold in the EU's supranational organs (see Le Monde, 2014). Unlike Germany, its economic model no longer works, diminishing its ability to persuade other members.

Thus, while the crises in the EU have multiplied and become more acute, the (potential or actual) base for the provision of stabilizing leadership has narrowed. The periphery has expanded, but the core has shrunk. The key question is whether Germany has the capacity and the will to supply this kind of leadership (see Chapter 11).

It is necessary in this context to differentiate not only between hegemonic leadership capacity and willingness, but also between the financial, institutional, and diplomatic dimensions of this capacity and between different issue areas. 'Capacity' here means the ability to: define a collective project that mediates conflicts of interest between member states (if necessary by persuading or coercing them to make concessions); to bear a burden commensurate with if not larger than that borne by other member states relative to their respective resources; and, in case of crisis, to provide the last line of defence to forestall European disintegration.

Germany has been closely involved in managing almost all of the EU's current crises, helped by the fact that as long as the EU budget has remained small and European integration has been relatively cheap there have been no question marks over Germany's financial capacity to keep the EU on the rails. Hitherto, the cost of managing the eurozone has hardly exhausted Germany's financial capacity, as the greater part of the financial aid provided to the debtor states has been loans rather than grants. The crisis has lowered the borrowing costs of the German government and some aid has flowed back to German banks that had made loans to indebted states. Throughout the crisis, Germany has managed to maintain a roughly balanced budget, although this might change if a eurozone country should declare bankruptcy and/or be unable to repay loans – especially if the country needing to be rescued was the size of Italy or Spain, which have substantially larger economies than Greece, Cyprus, Portugal, or Ireland (Streeck and Elsässer, 2016).

However, institutional limits have increasingly been placed on Germany's capacity to manage the eurozone crisis. The German system of government was designed after World War II to prevent a concentration of power and strong executive leadership, but the eurozone crisis has led to tighter constraints being imposed on the capacity of the federal government to bail out other eurozone members. Changes have been made to the jurisprudence of the Federal Constitutional Court which limit the government's manoeuvrability, and a change has also been made to the Basic Law (Germany's constitution) under which the major political parties have agreed to tie their own hands and oblige the federal government to maintain a balanced budget.

Domestic politics have also restricted the German government's options. During the crisis, Germany's willingness to prevent the eurozone falling apart has waned as electoral difficulties and political pressures have supplemented widely shared ordoliberal predispositions hostile to deficit spending. From the outset of the eurozone crisis, public opinion on proposed bailouts has been predominantly negative. The number of bailout opponents in the Christian Democratic Union/Christian Social Union (CDU/CSU) parliamentary group of Chancellor Merkel has grown from four (in 2010) to 63 (in 2015). Overall, German policy on the provision of financial aid during the eurozone crisis can be summed up as: as little as possible, as late as possible, and under the strictest possible conditions. Arguably, it was the ECB, once it decided in 2012 'to do whatever it takes' to keep the eurozone intact, that did the most to avert European monetary disintegration (see Chapter 4).

As illustrated by Merkel's decision to open Germany's borders to over a million migrants in 2015, the capacity of the federal government to act in the migration crisis was less constrained than in the eurozone crisis. Institutionally, neither German constitutional law, nor the Constitutional Court, nor any obligation to submit the decision to a parliamentary vote prevented the Chancellor from an atypically bold act of leadership. Financially, although the immediate cost of absorbing such a large number of immigrants promised to be considerable, it amounted to a 'small stimulus package for the economy' (Deutsche Welle, 2016). To the extent that the immigrants were employed, the financial burden would be offset in the longer term by the tax and social insurance revenues they generated – in a country whose economy was increasingly dependent on immigration.

Diplomatically, however, Germany's writ did not extend as far as it had in the eurozone crisis. Once Germany had agreed to provide further financial aid during the eurozone crisis, there was no doubt that the smaller, equally reluctant 'creditor states', such as the Netherlands and Finland, would follow suit. But Germany could not persuade many other EU member states to share the burden of managing the migration challenge, either by accepting a significant number of the migrants already in Germany or by contributing to the costs of assisting them. No 'carrots' or 'sticks' that Germany could wield seemed to impress other EU governments as much as the fear that if they acquiesced they would antagonize their own citizens and lose the next elections. Germany tried to lead, but others would not follow (The Economist, 2016: 22). Instead, a growing number of member states suspended the application of the Schengen Accord at least temporarily, including even Germany itself.

In the face of the wave of immigration and its repercussions, the *Willkommenskultur* ('welcome culture') that many Germans had initially exhibited waned rapidly. The most striking indicator of a declining willingness to accept large numbers of refugees and migrants was the rapid growth in voter support for the nationalist right-wing party, the Alternative for Germany (AfD). The AfD had been founded as an 'anti-euro' party rather than as an anti-EU party as such, but did not manage to clear the 5 per cent threshold to obtain parliamentary representation at the 2013 federal elections. The sudden sharp increase in immigration to Germany coincided with a shift by the party further to the right and a strengthening of its cultural-nationalist and anti-European profile. Riding a burgeoning wave of anti-immigrant sentiment, the AfD's voter support was reaching as high as approaching 20 per cent in national opinion polls in the autumn of 2016.

All previous attempts to establish a viable electoral-political force to the right of the CDU/CSU had failed. Germany had long remained exceptional among the older, larger EU member states in having no mass political movement of the nationalist, anti-European right. The domination by pro-European parties for several decades had enabled successive federal governments to play an instrumental role in forging closer European political integration. If, during a period of unprecedented crisis, the key member state in the EU were to become the home of a durable, strong right-wing nationalist movement – as has happened in several other member states – the prospects for European disintegration would increase significantly.

Conclusions

In principle at least, it is possible to envisage a wide range of outcomes to the current crisis in the EU and European political integration. At one end of the spectrum would be a sudden, qualitative leap into a federal state in which the authority of the EU's central organs are strengthened, its policy-making competences are extended, and the EU retains all its existing member states. At the other, following a series of events that had initiated a downward spiral over which the EU and key members lost control, would be the EU's sudden collapse and dissolution. In this scenario, the EU could be likened to the cartoon strip character Wile E. Coyote, who, having run over the edge of a high cliff, is suspended momentarily in mid-air before crashing to the ground. Neither of these is as plausible as some other, less extreme, scenarios.

Among these, the preservation of the status quo in terms of the degree of centralization of power, the range of the EU's policy-making competences, and the existing make-up of member states may be the least likely outcome. If, as seems quite possible, the present policy mix of limited financial aid, austerity, and 'structural reforms' should fail irreparably, it is unlikely that the eurozone could survive in its present composition without higher levels of fiscal redistribution and a stronger EU control of national fiscal policies. Equally, the migration crisis could be aggravated if more effective measures are not taken to control the influx of refugees and migrants from third countries into countries in the Schengen area. In both of these cases, the maintenance of the status quo would exacerbate already acute centrifugal tensions and sooner or later lead to the (lasting) dissolution of the Schengen area in the one case and the collapse of the existing eurozone in the other.

Until 2016, the EU survived the crisis largely by 'muddling through', arguably the only crisis strategy that its institutional structures permitted. In respect of the eurozone, centripetal pressures for more supranational or at least intergovernmental policy and institutional solutions prevailed – only just, it seemed – over centrifugal political dynamics. In the migration crisis, the latter dynamics proved even more difficult to contain. In the Brexit crisis, they triumphed.

The Brexit crisis in fact highlighted the two critical trends, examined in this chapter, that have been gnawing away at the underlying foundations on which the EU is built: the accelerating erosion of the dominance of 'pro-European' parties in the political landscape of the member states, and the increasingly uncertain capacity and willingness of its most central member state, Germany, to bear the costs of sustaining the EU that we know today. Under the Conservative government of David Cameron, the UK's European policy was more than ever tailored to meet the requirements of domestic politics, while the referendum itself showed clearly that anti-Europeanism had become the dominant force in the British political landscape (see Chapter 5). For its part, the German government did not make very strenuous efforts to secure new terms of British membership that would have given the 'remain' camp a better chance of winning the referendum (Webber, 2017). There was less German leadership in this than in the EU's other crises.

Given these two trends, it seems increasingly unlikely that the EU will be able to carry on 'muddling through' as well as it has so far. The UK will more than likely leave the EU within the next few years and, sooner or later, Greece may well be forced out of the eurozone. As for Schengen, the question is not whether it will collapse – at the end of 2015, Commission President Jean-Claude Juncker opined that it was 'comatose' (Le Monde, 2015b) – but rather whether, when, and how it can be resurrected. Certainly, the Commission's self-confessed impotence to enforce EU decisions on the member states relating to the migration crisis does not augur well for Schengen's future (Juncker, 2016). The EU may thus well come to exhibit a stronger 'variably-geometric' pattern than hitherto.

But this will likely be less the product of the process of differentiated *integration* that characterized the post-Cold War period than one of differentiated *disintegration*, whereby: individual member states leave the EU entirely, or withdraw, or are expelled from specific EU institutions; or some issue areas are – de jure or de facto – renationalized and/ or the authority of supranational organs vis-à-vis national ones grows weaker.

In this scenario, two vital questions arise. The first is whether and at what point such a process, once triggered, would stop. Would the end of Schengen mean the end of the eurozone, as Juncker (quoted in Le Monde, 2015a) has feared? Would the end of the eurozone be the end of the EU, as Merkel has warned? Will Brexit, assuming it is indeed executed, become contagious among other member states? The answer to the latter question may depend heavily on how well the UK is perceived by citizens in other member states to manage any post-referendum crises compared with how well the EU manages its other crises.

The second vital question is in what kind of reconfiguration the EU might survive or re-emerge, given that, especially among the most interdependent member states, the objective economic constraints pushing them towards cross-border cooperation would remain very strong. If the EU looked like it was beginning to disintegrate, one might expect a renewed debate about the development of a 'hard-core' Europe organized around France and Germany to fill any emerging void. However, in both Paris and Berlin the domestic political obstacles confronting such a project are even higher now than in the past, when it was already stillborn (Webber, 2012). Certainly, the Brexit referendum result failed to provoke any resolute collective attempt to 'relaunch' the EU.

Following the terrorist attacks in Paris in 2015, the city's motto, *Fluctuat nec mergitur* ('It is tossed about by the waves, but does not sink'), was evoked to underline the city's capacity to survive major challenges. As the character Rick Blaine (Humphrey Bogart) said famously in the film *Casablanca* (with a different meaning and in a different context), 'We will always have Paris.' It is much less certain that we will always have a Europe as closely integrated politically as it is today.

Acknowledgements

The author would like to thank Stefan Auer, Simon Bulmer, Fraser Cameron, Yves Mény, William E. Paterson, Martin Rhodes, Stefan Schepers, Magnus Schoeller, and Jonathan Story for their useful comments on an earlier version of this chapter. The author alone remains responsible for all its shortcomings.

References

Bartolini, S. (2005) *Restructuring Europe: Centre Formation, System Building and Political Structuring between the Nation State and the European Union.* Oxford: Oxford University Press.

Cohen, B. (1998) *The Geography of Money.* Ithaca, NY: Cornell University Press.

Couve de Murville, M. (1971) *Une politique étrangère.* Paris: Plon.

De Wilde, P., Leupold, A., and Schmidtke, H. (2015) 'Introduction: The Differentiated Politicisation of European Governance', *West European Politics*, Vol. 39, No. 2, pp. 3–22.

Deutsche Welle (2016) 'The Costs of the Refugee Crisis', Deutsche Welle, 1 February, http://www.dw.com/en/the-costs-of-the refugee crisis/a-19016394), date accessed 8 February 2016.

The Economist (2016) 'Charlemagne: An Ill Wind', *The Economist*, 23 January.

Fligstein, N. (2008) *Euro Clash: The EU, European Identity, and the Future of Europe.* Oxford: Oxford University Press.

Hoffmann, S. (1966) 'Obstinate or Obsolete? The Fate of the Nation State.' In M. Eilstrup-Sangiovanni (ed.), *Debates on European Integration: A Reader.* Basingstoke: Palgrave Macmillan, pp. 134–59.

Hooghe, L. and Marks, G. (2008) 'A Postfunctionalist Theory of European Integration: From Permissive Consensus to Constraining Dissensus', *British Journal of Political Science*, Vol. 39, No. 1, pp. 1–23.

Juncker, J.-C. (2016) 'European Solidarity in a World of Crises', Project Syndicate, 8 January, https://www.project-syndicate.org/european-solidarity-greek-crisis-refugees, date accessed 11 January 2016.

Kelemen, D. (2007) 'Built to Last? The Durability of EU Federalism.' In S. Meunier and K. McNamara (eds), *Making History: The State of the European Union*, Vol. 8. Oxford: Oxford University Press, pp. 51–66.

Keohane, R. (1993) 'Institutional Theory and the Realist Challenge after the Cold War.' In D. Baldwin (ed.), *Neorealism and Neoliberalism: The Contemporary Debate.* New York: Columbia University Press, pp. 269–300.

Keohane, R. and Nye, J. (1993) 'Introduction: The End of the Cold War in Europe.' In R. Keohane, J. Nye, and S. Hoffmann (eds), *After the Cold War: International Institutions and State Strategies in Europe, 1989–1991.* Cambridge, MA: Harvard University Press, pp. 1–19.

Kindleberger, C. (1973) *The World in Depression, 1929–1939.* Berkeley: University of California Press.

Krasner, S. (1984) 'Approaches to the State: Alternative Conceptions and Historical Dynamics', *Comparative Politics*, Vol. 16, No. 2, pp. 223–46.

Kriesi, H. (2016) 'Mobilization of Protest in the Age of Austerity.' In M. Ancelovici, P. Dufour, and H. Nez (eds), *Street Politics in the Age of Austerity: From the Indignados to Occupy.* Amsterdam: University of Amsterdam Press, pp. 73–96.

Krotz, U. and Maher, R. (2016) 'Europe's Crises and the EU's "Big Three"', *West European Politics*, Vol. 39, No. 5, 1053–72.

Krotz, U. and Schild, J. (2013) *Shaping Europe: France, Germany, and Embedded Bilateralism from the Elysée Treaty to Twenty-First Century Politics.* Cambridge: Cambridge University Press.

Kuhn, T. (2011) 'Individual Transnationalism, Globalisation and Euroscepticism: An Empirical Test of Deutsch's Transactionalist Theory', *European Journal of Political Research*, Vol. 50, No. 6, pp. 811–37.

Lange, P. (1992) 'Maastricht and the Social Protocol: Why Did They Do It?' University of California Berkeley Center for German and European Studies, Working Paper, No. 1.5.

Laws, D. (2016) *Coalition: The Inside Story of the Conservative–Liberal Democrat Coalition Government.* London: Biteback.

Le Monde (2014) 'La perte d'influence de la France à Bruxelles', *Le Monde*, 23–24 November.

Le Monde (2015a) 'Réfugiés: le retour de l'Europe forteresse', *Le Monde*, 26 November.

Le Monde (2015b) 'Migrants: l'Europe menace d'exclure la Grèce de l'espace Schengen', *Le Monde*, 2 December.

Ludlow, P. (1982) *The Making of the European Monetary System.* London: Butterworth Scientific.

McKay, D. (1999) 'The Political Sustainability of European Monetary Union', *British Journal of Political Science*, Vol. 29, No. 3, pp. 463–85.

McKay, W. (2004) 'William Riker on Federalism: Sometimes Wrong But More Right than Anyone Else?', *Regional and Federal Studies*, Vol. 14, No. 2, 167–86.

Matthijs, M. and Blyth, M. (2015) 'Conclusion: The Future of the Euro: Possible Futures, Risks, and Uncertainties.' In M. Matthijs and M. Blyth (eds), *The Future of the Euro.* New York: Oxford University Press, pp. 249–69.

Mattli, W. (1999) *The Logic of Regional Integration: Europe and Beyond.* Cambridge: Cambridge University Press.

Mearsheimer, J. (1990) 'Back to the Future: Instability in Europe after the Cold War', *International Security*, Vol. 15, No. 4, pp. 5–56.

Milner, H. (1998) 'International Political Economy: Beyond Hegemonic Stability', *Foreign Policy*, No. 110, pp. 112–23.

Moravcsik, A. (1991) 'Negotiating the Single European Act: National Interests and Conventional Statecraft in the European Community', *International Organization*, Vol. 45, No. 1, pp. 19–56.

Moravcsik, A. (1993) 'Preferences and Power in the European Community: A Liberal Intergovernmentalist Approach', *Journal of Common Market Studies*, Vol. 31, No. 4, pp. 473–524.

Moravcsik, A. (1998) *The Choice for Europe: Social Purpose and State Power from Messina to Maastricht.* Ithaca, NY: Cornell University Press.

Moravcsik, A. (2010) 'In Defense of Europe', *Newsweek*, 7 June.

Moravcsik, A. (2016) 'The Great Brexit Kabuki – A Masterclass in Political Theatre', *Financial Times*, 8 April.

Olsen, J. (2009) 'Change and Continuity: An Institutional Approach to Democratic Dovernment', *European Political Science Review*, Vol. 1, No. 1, pp. 3–32.

Parsons, C. and Matthijs, M. (2015) 'European Integration Past, Present, and Future: Moving Forward Through Crisis?' In M. Matthijs and M. Blyth (eds), *The Future of the Euro*. New York: Oxford University Press, pp. 210–32.

Pedersen, T. (1998) *Germany, France and the Integration of Europe: A Realist Interpretation*. London and New York: Pinter.

Pierson, P. (1998) 'The Path to European Integration: A Historical Institutionalist Analysis.' In M. Eilstrup-Sangiovanni (ed.), *Debates on European Integration: A Reader*. Basingstoke: Palgrave Macmillan, pp. 304–24.

Rüdig, W. and Karyotis, G. (2013) 'Beyond the Usual Suspects? New Participants in Anti-austerity Protests in Greece', *Mobilization*, Vol. 18, No. 3, pp. 313–30.

Scharpf, F. (2006) 'The Joint Decision Trap Revisited', *Journal of Common Market Studies*, Vol. 44, No. 4, pp. 845–64.

Schimmelfennig, F. (2014) 'European Integration in the Euro Crisis: The Limits of Postfunctionalism', *Journal of European Integration*, Vol. 36, No. 3, pp. 321–37.

Stone Sweet, A. and Sandholtz, W. (1997) 'European Integration and Supranational Governance', *Journal of European Public Policy*, Vol. 4, No. 1, pp. 297–317.

Stone Sweet, A. and Sandholtz, W. (1999) 'European Integration and Supranational Governance Revisited: Rejoinder to Branch and Øhrgaard', *Journal of European Public Policy*, Vol. 6, No. 1, pp. 144–54.

Streeck, W. and Elsässer, L. (2016) 'Monetary Disunion: The Domestic Politics of Euroland', *Journal of European Public Policy*, Vol. 23, No. 1, pp. 1–24.

Thelen, K. and Steinmo, S. (1992) 'Historical Institutionalism in Comparative Politics.' In S. Steinmo, K. Thelen, and F. Longstreth (eds), *Structuring Politics: Historical Institutionalism in Comparative Analysis*. Cambridge: Cambridge University Press, pp. 1–32.

Webber, D. (ed.) (1999) *The Franco-German Relationship in the European Union*. London: Routledge.

Webber, D. (2001) 'Two Funerals and a Wedding? The Ups and Downs of Regionalism in East Asia and Asia-Pacific after the Asian Crisis', *Pacific Review*, Vol. 14, No. 3, pp. 339–72.

Webber, D. (2012) 'The Politics of Differentiated Integration in the European Union: Origins, Decision Making and Outcomes', Monash University European and EU Centre, Working Paper Series 2012/1.

Webber, D. (2014) 'How likely is it that the European Union will *disintegrate*? A Critical Analysis of Competing Theoretical Perspectives', *European Journal of International Relations*, Vol. 20, No. 2, pp. 341–65.

Webber, D. (forthcoming) *European Disintegration? The European Union in Crisis*. London: Palgrave.

Chapter 18

Conclusions: Crisis Without End?

DESMOND DINAN, NEILL NUGENT, AND
WILLIAM E. PATERSON

The Unprecedented Nature of the Crisis

At the beginning of this book – in the Introduction and in the
editors' opening chapter – much was made of the large number of
specific crises that have simultaneously existed within the general crisis
that has affected the EU in recent years. The headline crises revolving
around the eurozone, migration, and Brexit have been accompanied by
deep concerns about a number of related issues, including the diminu-
tion of popular support for the EU, legitimacy and identity issues, strains
in the EU's system of governance, divisions between North and South
and East and West, and the role of Germany – the last of which has been
a common factor to most of the crises.

As was shown by Desmond Dinan in Chapter 2, the EU has faced
crises before, but not on such a scale. Past crises in the EU's history have
typically been about one set of issues, such as the disputes over the size
and distribution of the budget in the 1980s and the problems with treaty
ratifications in the 1990s and 2000s. But the crisis of recent years has
been multi-dimensional and, consequently, quite unprecedented.

The crisis has been unprecedented not only in the large number of
specific crises it has contained but also in the severities of these crises.
This combination of large numbers and severities has posed a perfect
storm of challenges for the EU, with the consequence that a demand–
supply disconnect has been created. In this disconnect, the demand side
has greatly exceeded the supply side of effective and acceptable solutions. The Franco-German relationship, the principal source of solutions
to crises in the past, has lost traction as economic decline has rendered
France unable to uphold adequately its end of the relationship. The
capacity of the Commission to solve crises has also declined, though
it remains a potent force in policy initiation and implementation. And
the attempts in the Lisbon Treaty and during the crisis to strengthen the
crisis-solving capacity of the EU by increasing the role of the European
Council has had only a limited effect.

The various dimensions of the crisis have been of a kind that are sometimes referred to as 'wicked crises', where any attempts to mitigate a particular crisis causes further crises: a sort of reverse 'spillover'. For example, the EU's approach to the Greek, and the broader eurozone, crisis and the consequent negative impact on the already weak Greek economy, have made mitigation of the Greek part of the migration crisis much more intractable. This wicked character of the crisis arises largely from the EU's increasingly inter-linked nature. The linked nature of the issues involved in the crisis has also meant that the crisis is constantly mutating.

Another way in which the crisis has been unprecedented is that it has fundamentally disturbed the very nature and functioning of EU governance. Resolution mechanisms for dealing with EU problems have been underdeveloped, which is a key reason why, during the crisis, some problems have been intractable and the EU has been seen to lack leadership. Since member states have often been deeply divided on crisis-related issues, meetings of national representatives, from the European Council downwards, have often been unable to be wholly decisive or authoritative. This lack of leadership is one of the reasons why public support for the integration process has receded during the crisis and why, as Christian Schweiger shows in Chapter 10, the perceived decline of EU legitimacy has itself become an important component of the crisis.

Finally, the crisis has been unprecedented in that possible EU disintegration has arisen more seriously than ever before. This has occurred most obviously in two respects. First, in mid-to-late 2015, during the height of negotiations on the third Greek bailout and as the migration crisis intensified, there were (separate) suggestions from leading EU figures that Greece's membership of the eurozone and of the Schengen system should perhaps be suspended. In other words, consideration was given to whether a member state, against its wishes, should be excluded from participating in important spheres of EU activities, though in neither case was the possibility of suspension followed through. Second, Brexit resulted, for the first time, in the exit of a member state from the EU being put firmly on the table, as Lee McGowan and David Phinnemore show in Chapter 5. Moreover, the Brexit referendum result, occurring alongside the other crises in the EU, prompted much discussion of possible widespread EU fracturing and disintegration contagion, as Douglas Webber shows in Chapter 17.

A Tale of Three Crises

When she visited the London School of Economics in November 2008, Queen Elizabeth asked the assembled economists why they had not seen the global economic recession coming. This was a question they appeared to find very difficult to deal with. By contrast, a question economists (and national leaders) have had no great difficulty in dealing with was why the global recession was followed by a eurozone crisis. For the eurozone system was known to contain original design faults, which it had long been recognized might not be sufficiently robust should the system ever be put under severe strain.

The failure to prepare for the eurozone crisis, and later the migration crisis, and the fact that responses to both crises were delayed, gives the crisis in the EU some of the characteristics of sleepwalking – a term applied by the historian Christopher Clark to describe the actions of World War I leaders, where disastrous outcomes were less the result of deliberate strategies and more the product of individual miscalculations (Clark, 2015). The use of the term sleepwalking applies especially to the eurozone crisis, as the design faults of the absence of political and economic union were recognized at the point of creation but could not be tackled at Maastricht or in the following years. In the absence of firmer foundations, decision-makers put their trust in convergence among members of the eurozone. Sleepwalking applies also to design weaknesses that contributed to the migration crisis and the difficulties in developing solutions to it, but here no one could have reasonably anticipated the implosion of North African and Middle Eastern states which have been key drivers of the crisis.

The temper of the EU has generally been optimistic and has generally assumed best-case scenarios. This reflects the fact that the EU has largely existed in economic fair weather and, before the crisis, it did not have, unlike national governments, the longer institutional memory of managing in troubled times. Nowhere was this optimism more strongly displayed than in relation to the establishment of the eurozone, where it was decided to press ahead despite the EU not being an optimal currency area and despite also the failure to agree on a fiscal union and a political union at the Maastricht European Council – both hitherto regarded as essential components of a successful monetary union. This failure to put on the barn roof while the sun was shining built a basic design fault into the eurozone construction. The same insouciance was again apparent in the construction of the Schengen system, where internal freedom of movement was not flanked by robust external frontiers.

There are thus, as was shown in some detail by Kenneth Dyson in Chapter 4 on the eurozone crisis and by Laurie Buonanno in Chapter 6 on the migration crisis, strong similarities in the backgrounds of two of the EU's three headline crises – that is, the crises that have most dominated both elite and public attention. The third headline crisis – Brexit – was, as Lee McGowan and David Phinnemore show in Chapter 5, mainly a consequence of rising, party political-driven, euroscepticism in the UK.

The eurozone crisis

The creation of Economic and Monetary Union (EMU) in the 1990s represents a high-water mark of European integration. However, EMU was always based on narrow foundations in that while its provisions for monetary policies were strong there was relatively little in the way of accompanying fiscal policies or central political authority. These absences were to be at the heart of the eurozone crisis and attempts to tackle it.

The EU does not exist in a vacuum and the onset of the global recession and credit contraction, occasioned initially by the collapse of the sub-prime mortgage market in the USA, put huge pressures on banks and financial institutions worldwide. EMU had not planned for an external shock and the contraction of credit led swiftly to a sovereign-debt crisis in some of its 'peripheral' member states (including Greece, Ireland, and Portugal). The sovereign-debt crisis was quickly joined by a banking crisis, in which there were great uncertainties about whether debts could be paid.

The EU found it very difficult to generate agreement about collective action at a European level. Divergences of national preferences – which had caused the original eurozone design faults – persisted and a weakened European Commission was less able and empowered than formerly to broker solutions. In the absence of a strong supranational input, the enabling role was largely passed to Germany, the overwhelmingly strongest member state. Germany, of course, had its own preferences and interests, which both aided and impeded the search for collective agreement. At the heart of the problem for Germany was that while the nature of the EU as essentially a regulatory state played to German strengths, the crisis raised major redistributive issues with which the EU has always struggled to deal and which German governments, with their emphasis on fiscal consolidation and austerity, have found especially challenging.

EMU was intended to reduce the power differentials within the EU in that it had been preceded by a system whereby, in effect, monetary policy was set by the Bundesbank, but would now be set by the European Central Bank (ECB), a supranational institution providing access to relatively low interest rates which were expected to benefit periphery states and reduce the core–periphery divide in the EU. The onset of the crisis confounded these expectations and shone a harsh spotlight on power relations in the eurozone, as Brigid Laffan shows in Chapter 7. Neither the Commission nor the Franco-German couple were able to deal with the situations of debtor countries. The strength of the German economy and its creditor status meant that Germany quickly emerged as the key player, though it was a very 'reluctant hegemon' (Paterson, 2011) and was determined to avoid a 'benign hegemon' role. Nevertheless, Germany was now in a very powerful position and sought to impose its key policy precepts of the promotion of austerity and strong conditionality for any support mechanisms. Germany's leadership helped stabilize the EMU system, but its austerity preferences deepened the crisis in Greece, increased the divergence between the core and the periphery, and resulted in distrust between eurozone states (Streeck, 2016).

A key feature of the eurozone crisis has been the expanding role of the ECB, which has to some extent acted as a counterforce to the austerity policies favoured by the German government. The ECB's strengthening position encapsulates a key reason why the eurozone crisis has been, if not solved, at least contained: the euro has a lot of stakeholders and institutional actors (notably the Eurogroup of Finance Ministers, the Euro Summits of national leaders, and the ECB itself) that want to see the currency succeed. So, in 2012, when the German-led austerity policy appeared to be deepening the crisis, the ECB made large amounts of money available to European banks in a form of quantitative easing and in July Mario Draghi, the President of the Bank, did much to pacify restive markets by famously declaring that the ECB would do 'whatever it takes to preserve the eurozone'.

As Kevin Featherstone and Dimitris Papadimitriou show in Chapter 12, Greece has been at the centre of the eurozone crisis. It is deeply indebted and, with Greek public debt standing in late 2016 at 180 per cent of GDP, has little prospect of being able to repay the sums owing on its various bailouts. Germany has taken the lead in insisting on visible progress in the reform of the dysfunctional Greek economy, including requiring steep reductions in public spending to achieve a primary budget surplus of 3.5 per cent. Various attempts by Greek governments to invoke popular sovereignty to resist these demands have ended in failure, but in 2016 their case came to be supported by the International Monetary Fund, which made further support contingent on significant debt relief. By presaging a 'transfer union' and by implying that Greece was no longer solvent and therefore not eligible to be a member of the eurozone, this was seen as being unacceptable in Germany. However, the prospect of Brexit and Greece's key role in tackling the refugee crisis was always likely to mean that Germany would be forced to give ground on the debt relief issue. This proved to be the case at a key meeting of Finance Ministers in May 2016, when further sums were made available to Greece and debt relief was envisaged for 2018.

The firefighting of the eurozone crisis has necessarily been accompanied by attempts to craft measures to prevent a future crisis. This has been a key demand of the creditor states, led by Germany. Agreed measures have created a far higher degree of regulatory surveillance, but this has stirred anti-European sentiments and weakened feelings of solidarity. Progress towards creating a fiscal stabilization function, as recommended by the 2015 Five Presidents' Report on EMU, appears as distant as ever (European Commission, 2015).

The migration crisis and Schengen

The EU's regime for controlling external borders under the Schengen system was built for normal times when the Union, as one of the richest areas of the world, faced a constant but containable migratory pressure – especially from sub-Saharan Africa. Schengen's external borders were, when the migration crisis erupted in 2015, consequently under-resourced and under-powered, but Schengen states continued resisting the need to create common and powerful frontier protection instruments, preferring to rely mainly on traditional national controls. Their motives were partially budgetary and also stemmed from a fear of reinforcing a state-like appearance of the EU.

The trigger points for the migration crisis that hit the EU in 2015 were, as Laurie Buonanno shows in Chapter 6, the failure of an authoritative government to emerge in Libya following the ousting in 2011 of the regime of Colonel Gaddafi and the descent of Syria into civil war chaos from 2011. The latter in particular led to an apparently unstoppable wave of refugees, in their case across the Aegean Sea from Turkey into Greece. In default of an obvious supranational solution, Chancellor Merkel announced in September 2015 that Germany would extend a welcome to migrants. Her optimistic pronouncement that *Wir schaffen es* (we can manage it) put the Schengen system under huge pressure as the crisis unfolded.

One partial solution to the crisis, proposed by the Commission and strongly supported by Germany, was that Schengen states should be obliged to accept the internal redistribution of migrants, via proportionate quotas. As in other EU policy areas, this question of obligatory sharing and redistribution showed itself to be too great a challenge for the EU. It provoked a fierce backlash, especially in eastern Europe where, as Tim Haughton shows in Chapter 13, states exhibited an unwillingness to accept any refugees, pleading that Merkel had not consulted them in advance and was seeking retrospectively to share the burden with them. While there was some merit in this argument, another argument against sharing that was advanced by east European leaders – that their people could not accept diversity – aroused little sympathy in western Europe.

This resistance to quotas coalesced with increasingly right-wing and populist governments in eastern Europe, notably in Hungary and Poland. Intra-European solidarity, which was already in short supply across the continent, thus declined further as a new east–west cleavage opened up alongside the pre-existing north–south cleavage. Populist resentment about the flood of immigrants was, however, not restricted to eastern Europe but fuelled the growth of right-wing populist parties throughout western Europe and played a crucial role in the victory of the pro-Brexit forces in the UK referendum.

Another, and perhaps even more fateful, aspect of the crisis for the course of European integration was the decision of the EU in early 2016 to seek the support of an outside power, Turkey, to play a key role in solving the migration crisis. The balance of power between Turkey and the EU on this issue is asymmetric in that the EU is the *demandeur*, which creates for itself a huge vulnerability. Turkey has strong leverage in this situation in that it can afford to wait, whereas the EU cannot. This has already resulted in Turkey exacting a high price for its cooperation – including insisting on visa-free entry to the Schengen area for its citizens, progress in Turkish EU accession negotiations, and financial payments – all of which are viewed with caution by EU member states, and in some cases are politically unacceptable. Nonetheless, Turkey is firmly in the driving seat, and any suspicion of backsliding on the deal by the EU could possibly halt Turkish cooperation. The degree to which the EU is dependent on Turkey is illustrated by the decision to carry on with the agreement despite massive internal repression after the failed coup in Turkey in July 2016.

The migration crisis highlights a number of EU failures. These include the absence of supranational migration policy instruments, the weakness of EU foreign policy in the Middle East, the failed European Neighbourhood Policy, the massive solidarity deficit, and the EU's leadership shortcomings. None of these will be resolved quickly, not least because, unlike the eurozone system, migration does not have influential stakeholders or institutional actors. Merkel initially believed that Germany could make up for these deficits as a 'benign hegemon' until a European consensus emerged, but developments have largely gone in the opposite direction.

Whereas the eurozone crisis is largely played out within the EU, the migration crisis reflects the external environment and is thus less susceptible to management. There is little prospect that migratory pressures from Syria and sub-Saharan Africa will lessen, while the damage limitation exercise of relying on Turkey is both inherently risky and fraught with moral hazard given the character of the Turkish regime.

While the eurozone crisis looks like a chronic condition, the migration crisis contains many more flashpoints, including security emergencies and threats to political stability – such as are apparent in the increased electoral support for non-mainstream political parties such as the Front National in France. At the core of the EU's Schengen regime is the concept of free movement of people, but the lack of influential stakeholders in the migration crisis and the absence of a supranational institution capable of playing a stabilizing role equivalent to that of the ECB in the eurozone crisis have resulted in fences being erected along the Austrian–Slovenian border, around Hungary and Croatia, and temporary checks being imposed on internal EU borders in many member states. These developments represent an existential threat to peace and prosperity, to fundamental EU values, and suggest that the migration crisis is a greater challenge to the EU than even the eurozone crisis.

The Brexit crisis

The decision by the British people to vote by a narrow majority in the referendum of 23 June 2016 in favour of withdrawal from the EU came as a massive shock to UK political elites. Continued membership had been supported by a large majority in the House of Commons and by all the major political parties. In this sense, the UK had conformed to the general rule that governments found EU membership to be, on balance, advantageous. However, for a complex mixture of reasons, which are explained by Lee McGowan and David Phinnemore in Chapter 5, the UK Government was unable to convince the British people of this view.

In the aftermath of the referendum, Theresa May replaced David Cameron as Prime Minister. Her mantra quickly became 'Brexit means Brexit', which came to be used as the main device for avoiding unwanted (and at the time unanswerable) questions of 'what happens next' and 'what are to be the UK's aims in the upcoming Brexit negotiations with the EU 27?' Domestic attention became focused on a number of matters, of which four were widely seen as being especially important. First, what would be the economic consequences of Brexit? All sorts of views and assumptions were advanced on this, but the fact is that only time can provide hard answers. Second, what would be the future of the UK's relations with the EU? The prevailing inclination was to give priority to remaining in the single market, in the interests of both the crucial UK financial sector and the manufacturing sector which would otherwise be confronted with possible tariff and non-tariff barriers. However, continued access to the single market without accepting freedom of movement (opposition to which was one of the main planks of the 'Leave' campaign) was recognized as being difficult to achieve, not least because concessions to the UK on this would run up against deep-rooted objections in eastern Europe and would raise the danger that it would be followed by comparable demands from other member states. Third, would there be a threat to the cohesion of the UK as a result of the majorities who voted to remain in the EU in Scotland and Northern Ireland and the majorities who voted to exit in England and Wales? Particular attention was focused on the boost that could be given to the already existing pressures for a second referendum in Scotland on independence. Fourth, would there be the prospect of a hard border being established between Northern Ireland and the Republic of Ireland post-Brexit, with this putting a possible strain on the peace process?

Attention in other EU states was also centred on a variety of considerations. One was the way in which the latter part of the referendum campaign was dominated by the migration issue. With anti-immigration feelings running strongly in many member states and with, as always, several national elections looming, including in France and Germany in 2017, the threat to political stability was obvious. A second focus of attention in EU circles was anxieties about contagion and the possible encouragement to anti-EU sentiments that the referendum outcome might give to 'exiteers' elsewhere. In the immediate aftermath of the referendum, it seemed that no other country would follow the UK example, though euroscepticism was certainly significantly on the advance in some EU states and Brexit offered considerable temptations to political parties and electorates elsewhere. And a third focus of attention was, of course, the consequences of Brexit for the image, confidence, and future direction of the EU. Losing the UK, with its considerable market, trading, financial, diplomatic, and security resources, naturally added to the impression of crisis in the EU, so there was a need to display confidence and firmness of purpose about the future. But, when the leaders of the EU-27 (that is, minus the UK Prime Minister) met in the Slovak capital, Bratislava, in September 2016 to discuss the future of the EU, nothing bold or definitive could be agreed and after the meeting several leaders tarnished the intended purpose of exuding unity by expressing their dissatisfaction with the meeting's outcome. For example, Italian Prime Minister Matteo Renzi declared: 'If things go on like this, instead of the spirit of Bratislava [to which Angela Merkel had referred] we'll be talking about the ghost of Europe' (Reuters, 2016).

The Challenges of Legitimacy

The Brexit referendum result dramatically showed the distance between the views of the governing elite and the public in the UK. But this was part of a more European-wide distance between elites and publics, as was dramatically demonstrated in December 2016 when internal reform proposals put forward by Matteo Renzi were decisively rejected in a referendum, thereby prompting his resignation.

These referendum defeats in two of the EU's larger member states have contributed to a legitimacy challenge to the EU, stoked as it has been by a strongly flavoured euroscepticism that has attracted support across much of the Union. The challenge has involved a fracturing of traditional values, which at European level has seen a weakening in support for solidarity and burden-sharing.

As part of this legitimacy challenge, public support for European integration has been on the decline since Maastricht (Eichenberg and Dalton, 2007) and 'the permissive consensus' that characterized mass–elite relations for so long has, as Christian Schweiger shows in Chapter 10, been replaced by a 'constraining dissensus' (Hooghe and Marks, 2008). This weakening of public support for European integration was masked for a long period by the continued support of established political parties, even though the public disenchantment with integration was not salient enough to change the preferences of these parties.

However, the austerity policies of the majority of European governments during the crisis has led to a perceptible change in the position of political parties. As Douglas Webber shows in Chapter 17, there has been a major decline in support for moderate 'pro-European' centrist parties and a growth in support for anti-European parties of both left and right. In Chapter 3, Ben Rosamond points to the importance of these developments when he states that the delivery of EU-level solutions by governing elites results in them being caught in a vicious circle in which euroscepticism may thereby be further engendered.

Perhaps even more important than these changes has been the overall hollowing-out of parties as instruments of mediation. Peter Mair (2009) sees this as a product of the tension between responsibility and responsiveness. Political parties owe a responsibility to their European partners and the maintenance of the EU, which makes their responsiveness to eurosceptic discontent very difficult. This may turn out to be impossible in the case of the EU where obligations among member states, especially if set out in treaty form, trump voter discontent. It was, for example, very clear for a number of years that immigration on a large scale was unacceptable to a majority of UK voters, which resulted in concessions on free movement being at the centre of Prime Minister Cameron's pre-referendum attempts to be given manoeuvrability on the issue. But, his European partners felt unable to compromise on free movement, which contributed significantly to the outcome of the Brexit vote.

The inability of the political system to respond to popular demands that run counter to EU rules thus undermines the legitimacy of the political system for many in the mass public. They consequently turn to supporting protest parties. The decline in trust is not, moreover, confined to political parties but also applies to interest groups. A very striking example of this is the massive popular rejection of the Transatlantic Trade and Investment Partnership (TTIP) in Germany, despite it being endorsed by the main German economic interest groups.

Increasing Integration

Crises can have a deepening (or centralizing) impact on political and economic systems that contain a considerable measure of decentralization, as the experience of most federations testifies. This deepening impact is because central authorities have greater geographical scope and normally also potentially greater resources to bring to bear on system-wide problems. It might, therefore, be expected that deepening would duly have occurred during the EU crisis.

However, in practice, such deepening as has occurred has been relatively modest in nature given the scale of the problems the EU has been facing. A number of inter-linked reasons explain this, including the dispersed (and sometimes competing) nature of EU leadership, the reluctance of member states to give much financial autonomy to EU-level decision-makers, and low levels of Union-wide solidarity on the one hand, coupled with attachments to national identity and autonomy on the other.

Three forms of deepening have occurred:

- In terms of *institutional deepening*, the European Council, the Commission, and the ECB have been the institutions to have had their powers and influence most affected by the crisis, as Neill Nugent shows in Chapter 9. The European Council, most notably, has assumed a greatly increased leadership position, with many special summits being held to deal with crisis-related issues – notably those associated with the eurozone, Ukraine, and migration crises – and with most major EU political decisions either being taken by, or being approved at, meetings of national leaders. The scale and gravity of the issues dealt with, along with their implications for legitimacy, have required that they be considered by national chief executives. However, given that the European Council is an intergovernmental institution, its greater powers hardly amount to a significant institutional deepening of the EU.

  The supranational Commission, which has been widely portrayed as an institution in decline since the 1990s, has shown itself during the crisis to be often a proactive policy initiator but, as its calls for tighter fiscal integration and for stronger central powers to deal with migration issues have demonstrated, it has remained ultimately dependent on the member states for decisions to be made. That said, the Commission has gained new powers of fiscal oversight and implementation during the crisis. The ECB, another supranational actor, has also enhanced its institutional position, by establishing itself as an important policy actor in respect of eurozone policy.

- Regarding *policy process deepening*, although the Lisbon Treaty, which entered into force at a relatively early stage of the crisis (December 2009), made it possible and/or easier for legislation to be passed in some crisis and crisis-related areas, a marked feature of the crisis has been for policy solutions often to be sought not by legislative means but rather by intergovernmental agreements and by soft policy approaches.

- As for *policy content deepening*, the crisis certainly stimulated significant new additions to the EU's policy portfolio – as with, for example, the (still being constructed) banking union and credit union. But there has not been agreement on 'big and lasting' solutions to major problems. This has not been so much because of a lack of supply of solutions – witness, for example, the Four Presidents' and Five Presidents' reports on avoiding the eurozone crisis from recurring by making deep-rooted reforms so as to pave the way for a fiscal union – as an inability/unwillingness of national governments to agree on what the solutions should be.

Accordingly, integration has not advanced as much as might normally be expected in a crisis. Moreover, there is little likelihood of any further significant deepening occurring in the immediate future, given the continuing existence of the explanatory factors mentioned above and the continuing robustness of euroscepticism.

Two other points about the nature and extent of integration deepening during the EU crisis merit attention. The first is that, to the extent that it has occurred, deepening has been almost covert in nature in that it quite deliberately has not been incorporated into the EU's treaties. Bickerton and colleagues (2015) argue that this reflects an 'integration paradox', whereby European political elites continue to support integration in the face of increasing public scepticism. In this situation, EU leaders have not wished to risk treaty-based deepening, as this would have resulted in highly politicized and protracted processes and also because treaty revisions would have risked being rejected in the national referendums that some member states would have felt obliged to hold. The second point is that much of the increased integration that has occurred has not occurred in all member states. The crisis has made the EU even more differentiated then previously.

Increasing Differentiation, Leading to Disintegration?

The European integration process is based on member states working together in ways that enhance collective benefits. However, there are constant differences between states regarding how closely and in what policy areas they wish to work together. These differences stem from varying policy needs and preferences, which are mixed in with distinctive historical traditions and feelings of self-identity.

In consequence, integration has always proceeded in a somewhat hesitant and disputed manner, with states in the 'fast track' – both generally and on specific issues – usually being at least partly reined in by states that are more reluctant to advance. As the EU has enlarged over the years, this has increasingly created a situation in which it is no longer possible, as it was in the past, for all states to 'swim abreast' on all issues.

Four main mechanisms have been used to deal with this situation. First, there has been an increased willingness of governments to take decisions by majority vote (or qualified majority vote in the Council). This, of course, means that governments lose out on some issues. Second, a few key issues – such as most of those touching on domestic taxation and foreign and defence policy – have been signalled as being so important as to require unanimous decisions. In such situations, states retain a veto. Third, in some sensitive, mainly socio-economic, policy areas, policy decisions rest on intensive transgovernmental cooperation rather than binding EU legislation. And fourth, it has become increasingly common in policy areas that are judged not to be part of the EU's internal market core, for not all member states to be full participants. This can be either because they are thought by other members to be unsuitable or unprepared, or because states themselves choose not to participate.

Differentiation, as this fourth mechanism is called, was first used in the late 1970s for the purpose of establishing the European Monetary System (EMS), and it has become increasingly common since. Significantly, its most frequent user by far has been the UK, most notably with its opt-outs from monetary integration, the Schengen System, and aspects of the area of freedom, security, and justice (AFSJ). The significance of the opt-outs from monetary integration and Schengen were clearly seen during the eurozone and migration crises, when the UK did not directly participate in the eurozone decisions to tighten fiscal coordination and when it refused to become involved in the Commission's (ultimately unsuccessful) plans for the forcible distribution of migrants between the EU's member states.

This frequent use of differentiation by the UK appeared to lull its leaders into believing, before the Brexit referendum, that all issues were susceptible to the differentiation/opt-out formula. Prime Minister Cameron thought that he could obtain a differentiation solution in the area of freedom of movement and unwisely made it the focus of his pre-referendum 'renegotiations' with the EU which were designed to win over domestic opinion. He found, to his cost, that some issues are too central to EU concerns to be bargained away. Differentiation is not a panacea for the EU to accommodate all national differences, and comes with restrictions.

* * *

The question arises, at what point does differentiated integration, which allows integration that otherwise would not be possible to proceed, become differentiated *dis*integration? Clearly since the launch of the

EMS, and more particularly since the Maastricht Treaty, there have been two parallel developments in the EU. A core group of member states has proceeded with further integration (sometimes covertly) while others (most often the UK) have made increasing use of opt-outs. At first glance this looks like a 'win–win' situation, with all member states achieving their preferences. However, this holds true only as long as differentiation is used sparingly. When it becomes the norm for a sizeable number of members not to participate in policy activities, there is the risk of excessive fragmentation.

The dangers of promiscuous differentiation for the EU are greatly increased by the lack of strong leadership. The stronger the leadership at the centre, the more the EU is likely to be able to tolerate some measure of differentiation without the system itself becoming endangered. But a marked feature of the EU crisis has been a general failure of leadership. France and Germany would formerly have been prominent in providing this, but they no longer have a common project (except to save the EU!) or a shared leadership role. The two national leaders have cooperated closely during the crisis, but they can hardly be said to have driven through reforms. Germany did seek to provide leadership during the eurozone crisis, but this was largely confined to eurozone-related issues and was normally the result of the disposition of structural power rather than the compelling vision of the era of German Chancellor Helmut Kohl and French President François Mitterrand. Where structural power could not easily be deployed, as in the migration crisis, Germany struggled to make its preferences effective. Moreover, German leadership was divisive, creating a north–south cleavage on eurozone issues and an east–west split on migration.

Crisis Without End?

If differentiation fails, then, as noted above, disintegration becomes a possibility. This would likely be initially apparent in regime disintegration, which has already been floated as a possibility by EU decision-makers in the context of Greece's continued membership of the eurozone and Schengen systems. Italy's ability to sustain eurozone membership has also been questioned, especially in the wake of the government's defeat in the December 2016 referendum. The EU could thus move from differentiated integration to differentiated disintegration. A crucial question here is at what point differentiated disintegration becomes irreversible.

In their surveys of integrationist theories in this volume, Frank Schimmelfennig (Chapter 16) and Douglas Webber (Chapter 17) find little anticipation of disintegration beyond the spillback literature that arose in reaction to the empty chair crisis of the mid-1960s. The spillback literature was generated by the neofunctionalists, who had anticipated a more or less automatic spillover process in integration until they met the political challenge of French President Charles de Gaulle, which engendered a spillback (Lindberg and Scheingold, 1970). This finding illustrates a key failing of many integration theories in their neglect of the role of domestic politics. As seen throughout this book, domestic politics now plays an immeasurably greater role in European integration, and if disintegration were to occur it would likely be triggered by domestic demands to which governments felt they must yield. Brexit is the classic example of this.

Total EU disintegration is highly unlikely, but a collapse, followed perhaps by a re-modelling of, parts of the system is possible, with Schengen and even conceivably the eurozone as the most likely policy areas in which it could occur. Reflecting on the troubles in Northern Ireland after yet another imminent disaster had been avoided, a British minister noted the capacity of the participants to move the abyss. As has been shown in several chapters of this book, movable abysses are characteristic of the EU – with the worst seemingly always being averted. One of the key ways in which they have been averted in recent years has been through differentiation, which may be thought of as a possible precursor of, or soft alternative to, disintegration.

However, despite all the forces that seem to point in the direction of disintegration, the elemental value of the EU to member governments is likely to triumph over all other factors. This point was famously made by Alan Milward (1992) when he noted that delegating certain functions to multilateral organizations strengthened, rather than weakened, states and governments.

The most likely possibility for the future is thus some form of muddling-through rather than a dramatic re-invigoration or collapse of the integration process. However, prediction is more hazardous than at any point in the past given the advent of President Trump, the first 'anti-EU' American President. His assumption to office is full of incalculable consequences, with immediate effects including amplification of the prospects of a 'hard' Brexit and the placing of pressures on EU leaders, especially Chancellor Merkel, to defend the liberal world order, of which the EU is a central pillar. Given their view of the unquestionable value of European integration, governments in the era of the 'permissive consensus' possessed both the will and the ability to make muddling-through tolerable. But, in being able to settle for this they were backed by political parties and interest groups which were able to mediate with mass publics. This mediation function has now been weakened, which means that, in the era of increased populism that is so clearly demonstrated by the Brexit vote and Trump's election, muddling-through is likely to become akin to riding the rapids.

Yet even surviving the crisis may not be enough. If the epithet 'sleep-walking', with its suggestion of ill-preparedness and inability to find solutions, is to be avoided in the future, something more than emergency patching and muddling-through will be needed. The failure to anticipate the crisis and to then find long-lasting solutions to its various challenges has been hugely damaging. The opportunity must be taken to address basic design weaknesses and faults.

Of course, national systems also exhibit failings of the kind exhibited by the EU, but national systems are more resilient because citizens have much deeper and stable loyalties to nation states, even if not to individual governments. Given the damage already done, a way will have to be found to restore trust between EU mass publics and elites. This is likely to be a long and arduous road.

References

Bickerton, C. J., Hodson, D., and Puetter, U. (2015) *The New Intergovernmentalism: States and Supranational Actors in the Post-Maastricht Era*. Oxford: Oxford University Press.

Clark, C. (2013) *The Sleepwalkers: How Europe Went to War*. London: Penguin.

Eichenberg, R. and Dalton, R. (2007) 'Post Maastricht Blues: The Transformation of Citizen Support for European Integration, 1973–2004', *Acta Politica*, Vol. 42, No. 2–3, pp. 128–52.

Euractiv (2016) 'Frustrated Renzi Attacks EU After "Boat Trip" Bratislava Summit', 19 September.

European Commission (2015) 'The Five Presidents' Report: Completing Europe's Economic and Monetary Union'. Brussels: European Commission, 22 June.

Hooghe, L. and Marks, G. (2008) 'A Postfunctionalist Theory of European Integration: From Permissive Consensus to Constraining Dissensus', *British Journal of Political Science*, Vol. 39, No. 1, pp. 1–23.

Lindberg, L. and Scheingold, S. (1970) *Europe's Would-Be Polity: Patterns of Change in the European Community*. Cambridge, MA: Harvard University Press.

Mair, P. (2013) *Ruling the Void: The Hollowing Out of Western Democracy*. London: Verso.

Milward, A. S. (1992) *The European Rescue of the Nation State*. London: Routledge.

Paterson, W. E. (2011) 'The Reluctant Hegemon? Germany Moves Centre Stage in the European Union', *The JCMS Annual Review of the European Union in 2010*, Vol. 49, pp. 57–75.

Reuters (2016) 'Italy's Renzi Steps Up Attack on EU, Merkel', Reuters, http://www.Reuters.com.article/us-eurozone-italy-Renzi-IDUSKCN1100)H7.

Streeck, W. (2016) 'Scenario for a Wonderful Tomorrow', *London Review of Books*, Vol. 38, No. 7, pp. 7–10.

Index

A

accession negotiations, 242–5
actor-centered institutionalism (ACR), 340–1
Africa, migration from, 123. *See also* migration crisis
alert mechanism report (AMR) for member states, 158
Ali, Zine el-Abidine Ben, 104
Alogoskoufis, George, 236
Alternative for Germany (AfD) party, 143, 204, 215, 226, 353–4
AMR (alert mechanism report), 158
Amri, Anis, 121
Amsterdam Treaty of 1997, 26–27
Anelay, Joyce, 114
anti-austerity coalition, in EU, 141
APEC (Asia Pacific Economic Cooperation), 343
Arab Spring of 2011, 6, 104, 337
area of freedom, security, and justice (AFSJ) policies, 81, 106–10, 173–5, 372
ASEAN (Association of South-East Asian Nations), 345
Ash, Timothy Garton, 217
Asia Pacific Economic Cooperation (APEC), 343
Assad regime, in Syria, 226
Association Agreement with Ukraine, 220, 270, 274–5, 280
Association of Leading Universities of Russia, 285
Association of South-East Asian Nations (ASEAN), 345
asylum law and immigration policy in EU, 105, 110–11, 118–19
asymmetric economic shocks, 69
austerity policies
    enforcing, 44–5
    from growth to permanent, 40–3
    as recession response, 2–3, 11
welfare state *versus,* 41–2
    See also Greece
Austria, 27

B

Bagger, Thomas, 212
bailouts
    of Cyprus, 134
    German opposition to, 328, 353
    of Greece, 134, 242–6
    of Ireland, 134, 142
    no-bailout clause in Maastricht Treaty of 1992, 72, 134
    of Portugal, 134, 142
    of Spain, 134, 142
Balance of Competences review of 2012 (UK), 83, 85
Bank for International Settlements (BIS), 57
banking union, 6, 60–2. *See also* European Central Bank (ECB)
Bank Recovery and Resolution Directive of 2013, 60–1
bargaining power, domestic politics and, 319–20, 327
Barroso, José Manuel, 11, 238
Bastille Day Islamist cargo truck attack in Nice, 2016, 110
Belgium, as creditor state in 1950s, 70
Beneš decrees, 260
Berlin Wall, fall of (1989), 25
Berlusconi, Silvio, 141
Best of Both Worlds, The: The United Kingdom's Special Status in a Reformed European Union (UK White Paper, 2016), 88
BIS (Bank for International Settlements), 57
Bloomberg, 308
Bové, José, 193
bovine spongiform encephalopathy (BSE), 27

Breedlove, Philip M., 107
Bretton Woods system, 18, 23, 35–6, 40, 69
Brexit. *See* United Kingdom (UK)
'Britain Stronger in Europe' group, 89
Brittan, Samuel, 44
Brown, Gordon, 258
Budapest Memorandum on Security Assurances of 1994, 275
Bundesbank (German central bank)
  as constraint in eurozone crisis, 218
  on ECB intervention in bond markets, 67
  European Central Bank modeled after, 215–6
  Helmut Kohl pressure on, 61
  Merkel sensitive to criticism from, 172
  monetary policy set by, 363
  monetary stability in Europe, 72
burden sharing
  in migration crisis, 115–16
  military, 202
  in monetary unions, 69–73
  security-based, for Europe, 303
  weakening support for, 368

C
Cameron, David
  Brexit referendum promise of, 8, 77
  doctrine of state multiculturalism, 109
  Fiscal Compact vetoed by, 201
  "new settlement" from EU negotiated by, 85–7
  OMN opposed by, 114
  Parliamentary pressure for referendum and, 83–5
  referendum gamble of, 262
  referendum results and, 88–90
  UK European policy under, 81, 355
capabilities–expectations gap (Hill), 296
capitalist-democratic compact, 34–8
Capital Markets Union, 182

Cecchini Report, 41–2
central and eastern European countries (CEECs), 253–68 *passim*
  accession negotiations with, 242–4
  Brexit consequences and, 262–3
  conclusions about, 263–4
  eurozone bailouts and burdens, 257–9
  migration crisis and, 259–61
  motivations and expectations of EU membership, 254–7
  overview, 253–4
  Russian aggression in Ukraine and, 261–2
centralization, from multi-dimensional crisis, 9–10
Centre party (Finland), 143
CFSP (Common Foreign and Security Policy), 26, 269
Charlie Hebdo attacks (Paris, 2015), 301
Charter of Fundamental Rights, Article 18, 105
chicken-game negotiations, in intergovernmentalism, 324–7
China
  perceptions of EU of, 307–11
  trade interest in EU, 312
christian democratic political parties, 27, 38, 45, 143. *See also* Merkel, Angela
Christmas market attack (Berlin, 2016), 121
Churchill, Winston, 81
Citizens Initiative, 205
Ciudadanos (Citizens) party (Spain), 142
Civil Liberties, Justice and Home Affairs Committee of European Parliament, 111
CJEU (Court of Justice of the European Union), 111, 168, 189
Clark, Christopher, 362
classical fiscal federalism, 160–2, 164
Coelho, Pedro Passos, 142
co-funding social investment, 163
College of Europe, 228

Commissioner for Economic and
    Monetary Affairs, 238
Commission's Taskforce for Greece,
    241–2
Committee of Permanent Representa-
    tives (COREPER), 173
Committee on eastern Europe
    Economic Relations, 283
Common Agricultural Policy, 346
Common European Asylum System
    (CEAS), 101, 104–5, 110–11
Common Foreign and Security Policy
    (CFSP), 26, 269
Common Security and Defence
    Policy, 286
Common Spaces programme, 297
Community Charter of Fundamental
    Social Rights for Workers
    (1988), 81
Community Method, 168, 182, 188
comparative federalism, 341
consensus, permissive to constrained,
    189–91
Conservative Party (UK), 77–9, 81–2.
    See also Cameron, David;
    United Kingdom (UK)
Constitutional Treaty of 2005, 17, 28
constrained consensus, from permis-
    sive, 189–91
Convention for the Protection of
    Human Rights and Fundamen-
    tal Freedoms (1950), 105
convergence criteria of EMU, 234–5
"cooperative hegemonic" leadership
    in EU, 346
COP21 summit of 2015, 309
Corbyn, Jeremy, 89
COREPER (Committee of Permanent
    Representatives), 173
Costa, Antonio, 142
Cotonou Agreement, 121
Council of the European Union, 173–5
country-specific recommendations
    (CSRs), in OMC, 151, 154,
    162–3
Court of Justice of the European
    Union (CJEU), 111, 168, 189

Creutzfeldt-Jakob disease, 27
Crimea annexation by Russia, 275–7
crisis-legitimacy gap, 200
"crisis-provoked decisional cycles"
    (Schmitter), 316
crisis without end, 360–75
    Brexit crisis, 367–8
    differentiation increases, 371–3
    disintegration possibility, 373–5
    eurozone crisis, 363–5
    integration increases, 369–71
    legitimacy challenges, 368–9
    migration crisis, 365–7
    unprecedented nature of, 360–1
crises in EU history, 16–32
CSRs (country-specific recommen-
    dations), in OMC, 151, 154,
    162–3
Cyprus, bailout of, 134

D
DAAD (German Academic Exchange
    Service), 285
Davis, David, 91
DBPs (draft budgetary plans) of
    member states, 161–2
debt. *See* sovereign debt
debt sustainability crisis, 71
decision-making procedures, 167–87
    passim
    cleavages in EU and, 155–6
    community method, 168, 182, 188
    on crisis-related issues, 169
    decentralized on fiscal policy, 12
    differentiation and, 167
    elite-level *versus* citizen-level, 205
    empty chair crisis and, 21–3
    euroscepticism reducing transfer
        of, 13
    in eurozone crisis, 325–6
    Fiscal Compact impact on, 159
    informal, 195
    institutionalized, 35
    insufficient, 2, 200
    intensive transgovernmental
        cooperation in, 372
    leadership issues and, 181, 184

member states and, 177–9
in national budgetary processes,
    162
non-eurozone members in Ecofin,
    174
output-orientated legitimacy bias
    and, 190–1
public view of, 193
SEA impact on, 24
in Single Resolution Board, 60–1
Deep and Comprehensive Free Trade
    Agreement (Ukraine and EU),
    261
de Gaulle, Charles, 20–2, 318, 344,
    373
de Larosière Group, 57
Delors, Jacques, 24
Delors Report on Economic and
    Monetary Union of 1988, 132
democracy 196–8
    democratic deficit, 63
    dynamics of European capitalist,
        33–8
    eurozone governance and, 196–8
    government overload from, 44
    "hollowing" of, 45–8
    leadership factors and, 4
    market association with, 45–7
    national sovereignty and economic
        integration and, 42
demographic trends, in migration
    crisis, 114–15
differentiation
    core-periphery, 10
    in European Council meeting
        attendance, 174, 177
    increasing, 371–3
    politics and processes affected by,
        185, 188
    surveillance fiscal federalism to
        reduce, 160
    in UK territories, 92
    by Worldwide Governance Index
        (WGI), 240–1
Directorate-General for Economic
    and Financial Affairs, 157–8
disintegration of EU

decreased support for integration,
    347–51
differentiated, 372–3
eurozone crisis and, 55, 73
horizontal, vertical, and sectoral,
    336
integration factors *versus,* 338–42
in intergovernmentalism theory,
    319
leadership ineffectiveness impact,
    351–4
in neofunctionalism theory, 322
possibility of, 373–5
risk of, 14, 30
theoretical perspectives on, 338–42
divide and rule policy, 307
Domenech, J., 306
domestic credit expansion, 57
draft budgetary plans (DBPs) of
    member states, 161–2
Draghi, Mario
    activism of, 172
    bond market intervention by, 246
    crisis management by, 62–3
    euro protected by, 68, 257, 330,
        364
    pre-meetings of, 170
Dreyer, Malu, 226
Dublin IV proposal, 118
Dublin Regulation for processing
    asylum-seekers, 7, 104–5,
    110–11

E
EAA (European Agency for Asylum),
    118–20
EASO (European Asylum Support
    Office), 105, 119
East Asia Summit, 343
eastern European countries. *See*
    central and eastern European
    countries (CEECs)
Eastern Partnership, 273
EBCG (Regulation for a European
    Border and Coastguard), 117
EBCGA (European Border and
    Coastguard Agency), 117–18

ECHR (European Court of Human Rights), 111
Ecofin (Council of Finance Ministers), 141, 173–4, 238
Economic and Monetary Union (EMU) 3–6, 54–76 *passim*, 131–66 *passim*, 263–5
common eurozone economic policy proposal for, 163
credibility of, 304
endogenous interdependence created by, 329
enforcement problems exposed by eurozone crisis, 326
EU crisis threat to, 1
failures in design of, 213
Germany and, 215–20
Germany on fiscal responsibility in, 133
governance after eurozone crisis
classical fiscal federalism, 160–2
macroeconomic surveillance extended, 156–60
overview, 155–6
governance before eurozone crisis, 150–2
Greek crisis and, 233–52
See also eurozone crisis
economic issues
centralization of policy on, 184–5
divergent fortunes in eurozone, 136–9
in EU history, 23–24
migration crisis impact on growth, 122
security concerns in, 62–3
underperformance, 2–3
See also Greece; political economy context
EDC (European Defence Community), 19–20
EDP (excessive deficit procedure), 151, 159, 161, 237
EES (European Employment Strategy), 158
EFSF (European Financial Stability Facility), 73, 134

EFSI (European Fund for Strategic Investments), 182
EFTA (European Free Trade Association), 38, 110, 131
Eichengreen, Barry, 38, 133
Elizabeth II, Queen of United Kingdom, 361
"embedded liberalism," 36
EMF (European Monetary Fund), 62
EMN (European Migration Network), 105
empty chair crisis, of EEC, 21–2, 318, 373
EMS (European Monetary System), 24, 69, 346, 372
endogenous deficiencies, in eurozone crisis, 327–30
England. *See* United Kingdom (UK)
ENP (European Neighbourhood Policy), 269, 297–9, 366
EPP (European People's Party), 81
EPU (European Payments Union), 38, 69–70
Erdogan, Tayyip, 102
ESDP (European Security and Defence Policy), of 1999, 26
ESM (European Stability Mechanism), 60, 160, 184, 196, 326–7
ESRB (European Systemic Risk Board), 57
EU–China Environmental Governance Programme of 2010, 309
EU–China Joint Statement on Climate Change of 2015, 309
EU Global Strategy of 2016, 306–7
Eurasian Economic Area, 299–300
Eurasian Union, 270, 274
EU Regional Trust Fund in response to the Syrian Crisis (Madad Fund), 119
Eurobarometer polls, 193–4
EURODAC Regulation of 2013, 105, 111, 119
Euromaidan protests, 261, 270, 275, 300

Europe 2020 strategy, 156, 162–3, 195–6
European Agency for Asylum (EAA), 118–20
European Agenda on Migration (2015), 117
European Asylum Support Office (EASO), 105, 119
European Border and Coastguard Agency (EBCGA), 117–18
European Border and Coast Guard Agency (Frontex), 121
European Border Surveillance System (Eurosur), 104
European capitalist-democratic compact, 34–8
European Central Bank (ECB)
    in balancing supranationalism and intergovernmentalism, 171–3
    Bundesbank influence on, 215–6
    eurozone policy set by, 370
    as fiscal rule enforcer, 45
    Greek banks dependent on financing from, 246
    injection of money into financial markets by, 257
    low interest rates of, 149
    monetary policy set by, 363–4
    monetary union from, 54
    Outright Monetary Transactions (OMT) programme of, 67
    overview, 12
    quantitative easing approach of, 63–4
    and recession of 2008, 134
    Single Supervisory Mechanism located in, 60
    southern debtor state treatment by, 40
    in transgovernmentalism governance of EU, 195
    US perceptions of, 304
    See also Troika arrangement (EC, ECB, and IMF)
European Coal and Steel Community (ECSC), 16–17, 19
European Commission
    decline of, 170–1
    fiscal oversight power increasing, 370
    overview, 11
    southern debtor state treatment by, 40
    See also Troika arrangement (EC, ECB, and IMF)
European Convention on Human Rights (1950), 105
European Council
    in balancing supranationalism and intergovernmentalism, 168–70
    decision-making difficulties in, 11–13
    increased leadership of, 370
European Court of Auditors, 242
European Court of Human Rights (ECHR), 111
European Defence Community (EDC), 19–20
European Economic Community, 19–20
European Employment Strategy (EES), 158
European Financial Stability Facility (EFSF), 73, 134, 196
European Free Trade Association (EFTA), 38, 110, 131
European Fund for Strategic Investments (EFSI), 182
European integration. *See* theorising crisis in European integration
European Migration Network (EMN), 105
European Monetary Fund (EMF), 62
European Monetary System (EMS), 24, 69, 346, 372
European Neighbourhood Policy (ENP), 269, 297–9, 366
European Parliament (EP)
    in balancing supranationalism and intergovernmentalism, 175–6
    Civil Liberties, Justice and Home Affairs Committee of, 111
    Committee on Economic and Monetary Affairs of, 241

in eurozone crisis, 65
limited influence of, 11
Spitzenkandidaten system elections
   to, 193
United Kingdom in, 80
vote of censure against
   Commission by (1999), 27
European Payments Union (EPU), 38,
   69–70
European People's Party (EPP) group,
   81
European Recovery Program
   (Marshall Plan), 35
European Regional Development
   Fund, 80
European Security and Defence
   Policy (ESDP) of 1999, 26
European Semester system, 57, 183,
   195
European Social Fund, 163
European Stability Mechanism
   (ESM), 60, 160, 184, 196,
   326–7
European Stability Mechanism
   Treaty, 175
European Systemic Risk Board
   (ESRB), 57
European System of Financial
   Supervisors, 57
*European Travel Document for the
   Return of Illegally Staying
   Third-Country Nationals,* 118
Europol AFSJ agency, 107
euroscepticism
   in Czech politics, 262
   decision-making transfer reduced
      by, 13
   inside, 197
   integration crises characterized by,
      318–9
   outside, 203–4
   overview, 8, 10
   in political parties, 347–50
   in postfunctionalist theory of
      integration, 323
   in United Kingdom, 77–8, 82, 84,
      362

Eurostat, 134
Eurosur (European Border
   Surveillance System), 104
eurozone crisis, 54–76 *passim,*
   131–66 passim
   burden-sharing in monetary
      unions, 69–73
   CEECs low sympathy for southern
      Europeans in, 258
   crisis type in, 135–6
   divergent economic fortunes in,
      136–9
   EU and, 144–6
   existential threat of, 65–8
   fiscal and financial supervision
      centralization in, 184–5
   fiscal rules tightening across, 40
   "genuine" EMU, need for, 12
   Germany in, 215–20
   governance reform in, 196–8
   integration theories and
      intergovernmentalism, 324–7
      neofunctionalism, 327–30
      overview, 323–4
      postfunctionalism, 331–3
   multi-dimensional and mutating
      as attribution phenomenon, 56
   banking union creation and,
      60–2
   EU identity crisis overriding, 63–4
   excessive domestic credit
      expansion, 57
   individual countries and, 55–6
   migration crisis impact on, 65
   overriding economic security
      issues and, 62–3
   overview, 1, 4–6
   Troika arrangement to rescue
      member states, 64–5
   Union Method as solution,
      57–60
   ordoliberal stability union in, 196
   politics of, 139–44
   single currency as "holy grail" of
      European integration, 132–5
   UK refusal to adopt single
      currency, 80–1

US perceptions of, 304
See also fiscal federalism
EU–Russia Partnership and Cooperation Agreement of 1997, 297
EU survival, 336–59
current crises differences, 337
disintegration factors
decreased support for integration,
347–51
leadership ineffectiveness, 351–4
theoretical perspectives on,
338–42
political integration factors, 342–7
EU–Turkey Joint Action Plan and
Turkey Facilitation, 119–21
exceptionalism approach of UK to
EU, 80–2
excessive deficit procedure (EDP),
151, 159, 161, 237
exchange rates
breakdown of stability in 1960s,
23
desirability of fixed, 5
floating, in 1970s, 41
1990s turmoil in, 25–6
symmetrically functioning
exchange-rate mechanism
(ERM), 70
external incentives model of transferring EU-prescribed rules, 243

F
Farage, Nigel, 84
Federal Constitutional Court (FCC)
of Germany, 67, 215, 218,
228, 352
federalism, 341. *See also* fiscal
federalism and comparative
federalism
Federal Security Service (Russia), 107
Fianna Fáil party (Ireland), 141
Fico, Robert, 264
Fidesz party (Hungary), 256
financial crises in EU history, 23–4.
See also economic issues;
eurozone
Fine Gael party (Ireland), 143

Fiscal Compact (Treaty on Stability,
Coordination and Gover-
nance) of 2012, 12, 59, 66, 83,
85, 155–7, 159, 169, 201, 247,
326–7
fiscal federalism, 149–64 *passim*
alterations in EU integration,
analysis of, 152–5
EMU governance after eurozone
crisis
classical fiscal federalism, 160–2
macroeconomic surveillance
extended, 156–60
EMU governance before
eurozone crisis, 150–2
governance of European social
dimension, 162–3
See also eurozone
fiscal union, lack of, 6. *See also* Five
Presidents' Report and Four
Presidents' Report
Five Presidents' Report of 2015,
12, 146, 181, 365
Five Star Movement party (Italy),
141
foreign direct investment (FDI), 307,
309
four freedoms of EU, 91, 124. *See
also* free movement of people
in EU.
Four Presidents' Report of 2012, 12,
59, 63, 181
Fox, Liam, 91
France
Constitutional Treaty of 2005
rejected by, 28
economic model failure in, 351–2
German partnership with, 10,
213–14, 217, 227, 340, 346–7,
351, 360
German preferences *versus*, 179
France Stratégie research, 122
Freedom party (Netherlands), 143
free movement of people in EU, 1,
88, 366, 369, 372. *See also*
migration crisis and Schengen
system

Frontex (European Border and Coast Guard Agency), 104, 121
Frontier's Operation Triton, 114
Front National party (France), 204
functional spillover concept, 321

G
Gabriel, Sigmar, 283–4
Gaddafi, Muammar, 104
German Academic Exchange Service (DAAD), 285
German-Russian Nord Stream gas pipeline, 262, 283
Germany, 212–232 *passim*
    Alternative for Germany party, 143, 204, 215, 226, 353–4
    anti-Muslim Pegida in, 351
    austerity preferences of, 363–4
    divisive leadership of, 373
    domestic politics of, 213–15
    early deferment to French leadership in EU, 346
    EU burden-sharing scheme for refugees and, 65
    European Financial Stability Facility (EFSF) and, 73
    eurozone crisis, 54–76, 215–20, 325–6
    EU sustaining costs and, 355
    on fiscal responsibility, 133
    France partnership with, 10, 213–14, 217, 227, 340, 346–7, 351, 360
    Greek bailout concerns of, 238–9
    influence of, 10–11, 55–6, 179, 351–3
    influence on common institution design of, 327–8
    informal EU presidency of, 194–6, 204–5
    migration crisis,114–16, 224–7, 353–4
    politico-economic links with Russia, 271
    in Ukraine crisis, 220–4, 275–6, 282–6
    unification of, 25, 212
    US perceptions of, 307
    See also Merkel, Angela

Gibraltar, EU "remain" majority in, 79, 90, 92
Giddens, Anthony, 195
global image of EU, 294–315, *passim*
    American perceptions, 302–7
    Chinese perceptions, 307–11
    external perceptions, 295–7
    Russian perceptions, 297–302
Golden Dawn party (Greece), 116
Good Friday Agreement (Northern Ireland and Republic of Ireland), 93
Gove, Michael, 89, 91
Governance 167–87 *passim*
    of EMU after eurozone crisis
    classical fiscal federalism, 160–2
    macroeconomic surveillance extended, 156–60
    of EMU before eurozone crisis, 150–2
    of European social dimension, 162–3
    issues of, 2
    reform of eurozone, 196–8
    "share and contested competence" in EU, 191–2
    suboptimal, 199–201
    transgovernmental mode of, 189, 195
    US *versus* EU perceptions of, 303
Great Britain. *See* United Kingdom (UK)
Great Depression of 1930s, 69
Great Recession, 138. *See also* eurozone crisis
Greece, 233–52 *passim*
    anti-austerity actions in, 350–1
    bailout conditionality to influence domestic reform, 242–6
    bailout of, 134
    burden-sharing of refugees and, 65
    capital flows dropped to, 6
    choices regarding crisis in, 329–30
    German austerity policies and, 179
    in migration crisis, 7–8, 116, 361
    negative public opinion on EU, 192
    Papademos government of, 197

Papandreou government of, 134
populism in, 332
sovereignty arguments to resist
   austerity, 364
Syriza government of, 247–9
two-level governance problems in
   EU and, 239–42
US perceptions of crisis in, 304
warning of problems in, 234–9
Greek Statistical Agency, reliability of
   data from, 237
Grexit (Greece exit from EU),
   likelihood of, 245–6
Grillo, Beppe, 141
Groysman, Volodymyr, 281
G7 advanced economies group,
   276
G20 economies group, 56–7

H

Habermasian pan-European
   democratic governance, 42
hegemonic stability theory, 345
High Representative for Foreign
   Affairs, 202
historical institutionalism, as
   integration theory, 339
Hoffmann, Stanley, 318–19
Hollande, François, 140, 143, 170,
   179, 217, 277, 279–80
Hooghe, Liesbet, 322–3
horizontal disintegration, 336
Hotspot approach to asylum, 118
HRMMU (UN Human Rights
   Monitoring Mission in
   Ukraine), 278–9
humanitarian obligations in
   migration crisis, 113–14
Hungary, migration crisis and, 116
Hungary's Paks II nuclear reactor
   project, 262

I

identity of EU peoples
   as crisis dimension, 3
   eurosceptic forces impact on, 95
   eurozone crisis intensifying
      problems of, 62–3, 74

in migration crisis, 109, 117, 121,
   124, 183
UK distinct from, 80
underdevelopment of, 190
See also member state relations
IDRs (in-depth reviews) of
   macroeconomic policies, 158
Il Giornale newspaper (Italy), 139
image of EU. *See* global image of EU
image theory, 294
Immigrants. *See* migration crisis
Independent Greeks party, 141
in-depth reviews (IDRs) of
   macroeconomic policies, 158
industrial relations systems, EU
   member state variations in,
   219
inflation targeting, 328
institutional deepening, 370
institutionalism, as integration
   theory, 339–41
integration. *See* crisis without end;
   EU survival; theorising crisis in
   European integration
Intended Nationally Determined
   Contribution (INDC), in
   climate change negotiations,
   309–10
intensive transgovernmental cooperation, in decision making, 372
intensive transgovernmentalism, 189,
   195
interest rates, divergences in
   eurozone, 137–8
intergovernmentalism
   in eurozone crisis, 324–7
   as integration theory, 317–20, 333,
      338, 340
   See also supranationalism and
      intergovernmentalism balance
International Monetary Fund (IMF)
   austerity measures in rescue
      packages of, 331
   eurozone crisis and, 56
   EU-US "co-ownership" of, 302
   Merkel interest in eurozone crisis
      involvement of, 216

southern debtor state treatment
by, 40
in transgovernmentalism governance of EU, 195
in Ukraine crisis, 280–1
Ukraine to receive loan from
(2013), 274
See also Troika arrangement
(EC, ECB, and IMF)
international non-governmental organizations (INGOs) on refugee
relief, 103, 112–13
international relations institutionalism, as integration theory,
339–40
International Relations (IR) theory, 295
Ireland
bailout impact on elections in, 142
bailout of, 134
capital flows dropped to, 6
exogenous shock impact on, 326
Nice Treaty of 1992 rejected by,
27–8
Northern Ireland border with, 367
Islamic extremism
CEECs concerns about, 260
Charlie Hebdo attacks, Paris 2015,
301
as root of migration crisis, 6
uncertainty increase from, 4
Islamic State organization, 305
Islamization of Poland, rally against
(Warsaw, 2016), 260
Italy
banking instability in, 229
burden-sharing of refugees and, 65
Monti government of, 197
Operation Mare Nostrum (OMN)
of, 114

J
Jenkins, Roy, 24
JHA (Justice and Home Affairs)
Council, 259–60
Johnson, Boris, 89, 91
Juncker, Jean-Claude, 11, 85, 116,
160, 181–2, 193, 355–6

Justice and Home Affairs (JHA)
Council, 259–60

K
Karamanlis, Costas, 236–8
Katainen, Jyrki, 246
Kažimír, Peter, 258
Keller, Ska, 193
Keynesian Welfare State, 36–7, 41, 43
Kindleberger, C., 345–6
Klaus, Václav, 261
knowledge economy principle, 197
Kohl, Helmut, 25, 61, 65–6, 170,
373
Konstantopoulou, Zoe, 248
Kretschmann, Winfried, 226

L
Labour Party (Netherlands), 143
Labour Party (UK), 89, 117
Lagarde, Christine, 280–1
Lavrov, Sergeij, 285
leadership 167–87 *passim*
continuing problems in, 180–4
"cooperative hegemonic," 346–7
crisis in, 204
differentiation dangers without
strong, 373
disintegration of EU from
ineffective, 351–4
European Council assuming, 370
German, 213–15, 373
issues of, 2
lack of accountable, 4–5
underdeveloped resolution mechanisms and, 361
variable leadership geometry from
coalition, 199–201
legitimacy, 188–211 *passim*
crisis without end and issues of,
368–9
eurozone governance reform,
196–8
lack of social, 191–4
muddling through gap in, 199–203
perceived decline of, 361
permissive to constrained
consensus, 189–91

public trust decline, 194–6
tackling deficit in, 203–6
Lehman Brothers bankruptcy, 5,
  55–6, 134
Le Pen, Marine, 143, 204
Levada-Center survey of 2015, 299,
  301
liberal intergovernmentalism,
  318–20, 338
Lisbon Treaty of 2007
  crises after Maastricht Treaty, 25–8
  on European Commission President
    candidates, 193
  European Council strengthened by,
    169
  limited impact of, 360
  overview, 11
  ratification of, 28
  supranational and the intergovern-
    mental features advanced in,
    168
  UK interests accommodated in, 81
Luxembourg Compromise, 22, 30

M
Maastricht European Council of
  1991, 65, 362
Maastricht Treaty of 1992
  crises until Lisbon Treaty, 25–8
  Delors Report influence on,
    132–3
  economic integration spurt from,
    42
  German influence EMU design in,
    215–6
  monetary union design in, 71
  no bailout clause in, 72, 134
  overview, 2, 5
MacDougall Report of 1977, 132
macroeconomic Imbalance Procedure
  (MIP) scoreboard, 157–8, 160
macroeconomic surveillance, 156–60
Madad Fund (EU Regional Trust
  Fund in response to the Syrian
  Crisis), 119
mad cow disease (bovine spongiform
  encephalopathy), 27

Maidan demonstrations, 261, 270,
  275, 300
Mair, Peter, 46–7, 145, 369
Major, John, 27, 92
Malaysian Airlines MH17, 2014
  downing of, 220–2, 224, 277
market society prioritization, 34,
  43–5
Marks, Gary, 322–3
Marlière, Philippe, 45–6
Marshall Plan, 18, 35
mass politics, 322, 337, 351
Maturing Partnership – Shared Inter-
  ests and Challenges in
  EU–China Relations, A, 307
May, Theresa, 79, 91, 114, 263, 367
Mearsheimer, J., 341–2
medium-term budgetary objectives
  (MTOs), enforcement of,
  158–9
Medvedev, Dmitry, 271
member state relations
  migration crisis and, 111–17
    administrative problems, 113
    demographic trends, 114–15
    disparate burdens on, 115–16
    historical experiences, 112–13
    humanitarian obligations,
      113–14
    immigrants in total population,
      115
    public opinion and, 116–17
  multi-dimensional crisis and, 2, 10
  political issues in crises, 176–80
  See also Germany; United
    Kingdom (UK)
Merkel, Angela
  British scepticism about policies
    of, 201
  CEECs blaming for migration
    crisis, 259
  Draghi working relationship with,
    172
  and eurozone crisis, 140, 217–8
  and free movement of workers
    principle, 88
  Germany influence in EU, 11

on IMF involvement in eurozone
crisis, 216
and leadership avoidance of, 217–8
media coverage of, 56
and migration crisis, 1, 7, 115, 123,
213, 224–7, 365
monetary union importance to, 65
ordoliberal economic principles of,
194–5
politico-economic links with
Russia, 271
as pre-eminent EU political leader,
217
Troika arrangement backed by, 64
and Ukraine crisis, 3, 220–4,
277–81, 285–7
uncompromising and output-
orientated approaches of, 202
"union method" defined by, 228–9
See also Germany
Middelaar, Luuk van, 22–3
migration crisis, 6–8, 100–30 passim,
224–7, 265–7
anti-Muslim German Pegida
motivated by, 351
area of freedom, security, and
justice (AFSJ) policies, 106–10
asylum law and immigration policy
in EU, 110–11
EC agenda implementation on,
117–21
EU burden-sharing scheme and, 65
eurozone crisis affected by, 65
exploited to win elections, 264–5
Germany and, 215, 224–7
Greek institutional capacity
strained by, 233
high volume seeking European
entry, 101–3
implications of, 121–5
Islamic extremism and, 4
member state differences on, 178
member states and, 111–17
administrative problems, 113
demographic trends, 114–15
disparate burdens on, 115–16
historical experiences, 112–13

humanitarian obligations,
113–14
immigrants in total population,
115
public opinion and, 116–17
in multi-dimensional EU crisis, 1,
6–8
as never-ending, 365–7
populist political parties and,
353–4
trends in, 103–106
UK anti-immigrant rhetoric, 84–5
US perceptions of, 305
Miller, David, 123
Milward, A. S., 18, 34–5, 318, 374
Minsk Agreement of 2015, 3,
220–3
Minsk Protocol, in Ukraine crisis,
277–80
MIP (Macroeconomic Imbalance
Procedure) scoreboard, 157–8,
160
Mitterrand, François, 170, 373
Mollet, Guy, 20
Monnet, Jean, 17–19, 29, 190, 336
Monti, Mario, 140–1, 197–9
Moravcsik, Andrew, 319, 338, 343
MTOs (medium-term budgetary
objectives), enforcement of,
158–9
Multiannual Financial Framework
(EU, 2014–20), 83
multi-dimensional nature of the EU
crisis, 1–15 *passim*, 360–74
passim
Munich Security Conference of 2014,
223, 270

N
Nasser, Abdel, 20
NBC blogs, 306
neofunctionalism
on EU legitimacy, 189–90
in eurozone crisis, 327–30
as integration theory, 317–8, 320–2,
333, 338
neoliberalism, 43–5

neorealism, as integration theory, 341–2

Netherlands, Constitutional Treaty of 2005 rejected by, 28

"new intergovernmentalism," 326

"new settlement" demands, of UK (2015), 86–7

Nice Treaty of 1992, 27–8

Nixon, Richard M., 40

no bailout clause, in Maastricht Treaty, 72

non-state actors, in eurozone crisis, 327–30

Normandy Format, to deal with Ukraine crisis, 276, 281–2, 285

North American Free Trade Agreement (NAFTA), 343, 345

North Atlantic Treaty Organization (NATO)
  enlargement of, 297, 299
  EU dependence on, 202, 213
  on migration impact, 107
  NATO Response Force establishment, 223
  neorealistic view of, 341–2
  Putin against expansion in, 270–1
  Russian aggression in Ukraine and, 261, 278

Northern Ireland
  EU "remain" majority in, 79, 90, 92–3
  Republic of Ireland border with, 367

O

Obama, Barack, 89, 220, 271–2, 303–6

Obstfeld, Maurice, 61

Obstinate or Obsolete? (Hoffmann), 318–19

OECD (Organisation for Economic Co-operation and Development), 62

Office for Democratic Institutions and Human Rights (ODIHR), of OSCE, 279, 281

old-age dependency ratio, 115

OMT (Outright Monetary Transactions) programme, of ECB, 67

One-China Principle, 310

open method of coordination (OMC), 151

Operation Mare Nostrum (OMN, Italy), 114

optimal currency areas (OCA), 132

Orbán, Viktor, 116, 256, 260, 262–3

ordoliberalism, 194, 216–9, 247

Organisation for Economic Co-operation and Development (OECD), 62

Organization for Security and Cooperation in Europe (OSCE), 278–9, 285

Osborne, George, 84

Outright Monetary Transactions (OMT) programme, of ECB, 67

P

Pangalos, Theodoros, 248

Papademos, Lucas, 197

Papakonstantinou, George, 238

Papandreou, George, 238, 332

Papandreou Government of Greece, 134

Partido Popular party (Spain), 142–3

Partnership and Cooperation Agreement (PCA, EU with Russia), 272

Pasok party (Greece), 141

path-dependency, in integration theory, 317–18, 321, 327–30

Pegida protest movement, 204

perceptions of EU. *See* global image of EU

permanent austerity, 40–3

permissive to constrained consensus, 189–91

Pierson, Paul, 41, 328–9

Podemos party (Spain), 142–3

Poland, 192, 255, 260, 262

policy content deepening, 371

policy process deepening, 370

political economy context, 33–53
  compact unraveling
    from growth to permanent
      austerity, 40–3
    market society prioritization,
      43–5
    overview, 39–40
    political parties impact, 45–7
  European capitalist-democratic
    compact, 34–8
  overview, 33–4
  See also economic issues
political issues, 167–87
  in European integration, 322–3
  of eurozone crisis, 139–44
  in Germany, 213–15
  Greek austerity measures, 332
  Greek economic problems and,
    244
  leadership problems, 180–4
  member states and crisis, 176–80
  overview, 167–8
  political integration affected by,
    343–4
  See also EU survival
political parties 41 45–7, 139–44,
  345–54
polity-formation analysis, 341
populations, immigrants as
  proportion of, 115. *See also*
  migration crisis
populism
  in CEECs, 365–6
  in Greece, 244, 247–8, 332
  rise of, 46, 62, 201–2
  Trump election (US) based on,
    374
  in United Kingdom, 366
Poroshenko, Petro, 277–9, 281
Portugal
  anti-austerity actions in, 351
  bailout impact on elections in, 142
  bailout of, 134
  capital flows dropped to, 6
  EDPs of, 159, 163
postfunctionalism
  in eurozone crisis, 331–3

  as integration theory, 317–8,
    322–3, 333
Prodi, Romano, 351
proportionate quotas, for migrant
  redistribution, 365
protectionism, declaration against
  (2009), 255–6
public debt crisis. *See* sovereign debt
  crisis. public opinion
  decreasing for integration,
    188–212 *passim*, 322, 347–51,
    361
  German, on eurozone and migra-
    tion crises, 215, 226
  of migration crisis, 116–17
  referendums to motivate, 350
public trust, decline in, 194–6
punctuated equilibrium concept, 339
Putin, Vladimir
  Assad regime supported by, 226
  denial of demise of Russian imperi-
    alism, 288
  desire to restore Russia's global
    standing of, 3
  at Eastern Economic Forum of
    2015, 301
  Malaysia Airlines MH 17 downing
    and, 223
  at Munich Security Conference of
    2007, 270
  territorial ambitions of, 261
  Ukraine insurgents supported by,
    277–9
  Yanukovych pressured to reject EU
    by, 220–1
  See also Russia

Q

Quadro Group (Cyprus, Greece,
    Italy, and Malta), 104
Qualification Directive of 2011, 105
Qualification regulation proposal of
    2016, 118
qualified majority voting (QMV), in
    EU, 154, 168, 173–4, 177, 199
quantitative easing approach of ECB,
    63–4, 257

R

Radičová, Iveta, 258
Rajoy, Mariano, 142
Rally Against Islam (Prague, 2016), 260
Rasch analysis, 297, 300
Reception conditions directive proposal of 2016, 119
Receptions Conditions Directive of 2013, 105
recession, 2–4, 6. *See also* eurozone crisis
referendums
  avoiding, 332
  on Greek bailout of 2011, 246
  on Greek bailout of 2015, 246
  Italian 2016, 373
  low support for integration in, 350
  for Scotland independence, pressure for, 367
  See also United Kingdom (UK)
reflation, Keynesian-type, 247
refugee quota system, 201–2
Regulation for a European Border and Coastguard (EBCG), 117
Renzi, Matteo, 284, 367
Resettlement Framework proposal of 2016, 119
reverse qualified majority voting (RQMV), 154–5, 159, 170
Rodrik, Dani, 42
role theory, 294
Rome Treaty, 20–1, 29
Rompuy, Herman Van, 103, 105, 122, 170
RQMV (reverse qualified majority voting), 154–5, 159, 170
Ruggie, J. G., 35–6
Russia
  CEECs concerns about, 261–2
  Crimea annexed by, 275–7
  energy policy in geopolitics by, 284
  EU's use of "soft power" with, 312
  Federal Security Service of, 107
  German public sentiment toward, 222
  Partnership and Cooperation
    Agreement (PCA) with EU, 272
  perceptions of EU in, 287–8, 297–302
  in Ukraine crisis, 3–4, 65, 220–3
  US and EU diplomatic impasse with, 305
  See also Putin, Vladimir
Russian–Georgian war of 2008, 270–1
Rutte, Mark, 143

S

Saarland protectorate, status of, 20
Safe Country of Origin List, 118
Sarkozy, Nicholas, 143, 170, 217, 255, 271
Save the Children, 114
Schäuble, Wolfgang, 62, 64, 142, 160, 219, 246
Schengen system
  AFSJ area complexity and, 174–5
  burden-sharing of refugees and, 65
  CEECs interest in, 259
  as crisis in waiting, 224
  Dublin Regulation companion to, 110
  as EU policy achievement, 1
  external frontier weaknesses in, 362
  future of, 355–6
  member state differences and, 178
  migration crisis and, 365–7
  UK refusal to be part of, 80–81, 372
  unraveling of, 9, 122
  weak foundations of, 4, 7
Schmidt, Helmut, 222
Schröder, Gerhard, 212, 222, 283, 301
Schultz, Martin, 193
Schuman Declaration of May 1950, 17–18, 29, 34
Scotland
  EU "remain" majority in, 79, 90, 92–3
  referendum for independence, pressure for, 367

sectoral disintegration of EU, 336
Simitis, Costas, 234, 236
Single European Act (SEA) of 1986, 17, 23–4, 42
single market programme, 24
Single Resolution Board (SRB), 60
Single Resolution Fund (SRF), 60
Single Supervisory Mechanism, in European Central Bank (ECB), 60
Sinn Féin party (Northern Ireland), 93
Six-Pack of legislative acts, 155–7, 159, 196
Smer-Social Democracy party (Slovakia), 258
Sobotka, Bohuslav, 262
social democratic political parties, 38, 45–6
social investment, co-funding, 163
social legitimacy, lack of, 191–4
social market economy, German model of, 56
"soft power" of EU, 311–12
solidarity
    deficit in, 366, 368, 370
    of US for EU in Ukraine crisis, 304–5
    as welfare nationalism, 42
    See also central and eastern European countries (CEECs)
South Stream Project pipeline, 284
sovereign debt crisis
    ECB prohibited from financing member states, 216
    euozone split from, 197
    "Europeanization" of, 325
    in eurozone crisis, 6, 55, 57, 131–40
    of Greece, 30, 234, 236
    public trust decline and, 194
    See also Economic and Monetary Union
sovereignty
    as "big picture" issue avoided by EU, 12–14
    conceding, 5, 54, 68

defence of, 42, 183
    Greek use of to resist austerity, 364
    in traditional intergovernmentalism theory, 340
Spain
    bailout impact on elections in, 142
    bailout of, 134
    capital flows reduced to, 6
    EDPs of, 159, 163
    exogenous shock impact on, 326
spillover concept, 321, 343, 374
Spitzenkandidaten system, in EP elections, 193
SRB (Single Resolution Board), 60
SRF (Single Resolution Fund), 60
Stability and Growth Pact (SGP), 57, 133, 135, 150–1, 161, 216, 326–7
Stable Money–Sound Finances (European Commission), 133
stagflation in 1970s, 40–1
Stark, Jürgen, 67
Steinmeier, Frank-Walter, 214, 285
Stockholm Programme Action Plan, 2010–14, 111
Streeck, Wolfgang, 37, 229
Suez Canal, nationalization of, 20
Sulík, Richard, 256, 258
Sunday Telegraph (UK), 85
supply-side economics, 247
supranationalism and intergovern-mentalism balance, 168–76
    Commission decline, 170–1
    Council of the European Union decline, 173–5
    European Central Bank emergence, 171–3
    European Council prominence, 168–70
    European Parliament strength, 175–6
    institutional advancement of, 176
survival of EU. *See* EU survival
"suspension of democracy," percep-tion of EU as, 196–8
Syria, asylum-seekers from. *See* migration crisis

Syriza party (Greece), 141–2, 144, 179, 244, 246–8, 332
Szydło, Beata, 192, 260

T
Taiwan, diplomatic tensions over, 309
Team Stronach party (Austria), 143
terrorist attacks in EU crisis, 4
TEU (Treaty on European Union), 132–3
Thatcher, Margaret, 24
theorising crisis in European integration, 316–35 *passim,* 338–43
  conclusions on, 333–4
  eurozone crisis and
    intergovernmentalism, 324–7
    neofunctionalism, 327–30
    overview, 323–4
    postfunctionalism, 331–3
  overview, 316–17
  theories and explanations of
    intergovernmentalism, 318–20
    neofunctionalism, 320–2
    overview, 317–18
    postfunctionalism, 322–3
Third Energy Package, of EU, 283–5
Tiananmen Square, diplomatic tensions over, 309–10
Tibet, diplomatic tensions over, 309
"time inconsistency thesis" (Kydland and Prescott), 44
trade, migration crisis impact on, 122
traditional intergovernmentalism, as integration theory, 340
transactionalism, as integration theory, 338
Transatlantic Trade and Investment Partnership (TTIP), 303, 369
transgovernmentalism, 189, 195
Treaty Establishing the European Community, 239
Treaty of Amsterdam (1997), 81
Treaty on European Union (TEU), 79, 81, 132–3
Treaty on Stability, Coordination and Governance (Fiscal Compact)

of 2012, 12, 59, 66, 83, 85, 155–7, 159, 169, 201, 247, 326–7
Treaty on the Non-Proliferation of Nuclear Weapons of 1994, 275
Trichet, Jean-Claude, 62, 71, 135, 172
Troika arrangement (Commission, ECB, and IMF)
  Greek negotiations with, 141, 238–42
  inability to restore confidence in Greek economy, 245
  lack of public scrutiny of, 196
  overview, 40
  to rescue member states, 63–5, 134–6
True Finns party (Finland), 143
Trump, Donald, 62, 303, 305–7, 374
Trust Fund for Africa, 119
Tsipras, Alexis, 72, 141, 193, 246, 248
TTIP (Transatlantic Trade and Investment Partnership), 303, 369
Turkey
  EU–Turkey Joint Action Plan and Turkey Facilitation, 119–21
  and migration crisis, 12, 102, 366
Tusk, Donald, 86–7, 122, 170, 176, 181
Tutu, Desmond, 248
Two-Pack of legislative acts, 155–6, 161, 164

U
Ukraine crisis, 269–93 *passim*
  Association Agreement, fate of, 274–5
  CEECs concerns about, 261–2
  Crimea annexation by Russia, 275–7
  economic sanctions against Russia, 65
  EU collision with Russia in, 3
  Germany and, 220–4, 282–6
  leverage imbalance in, 280–2

Minsk Protocol, 277–80
run-up to, 272–4
Russian perceptions of EU from,
    299
US perceptions of, 304–5
warnings of, 270–2
Ukrainian-Russian Action Plan of
    2013, 274
unemployment
    in Great Recession, 138–9
    in Greece at 25 percent, 245
    rise of in 1970s, 41
UNHCR (United Nations High
    Commissioner for Refugees),
    103, 111, 113, 121, 233
UN Human Rights Monitoring
    Mission in Ukraine
    (HRMMU), 278–9
Union Method, 57–60, 228
United Kingdom (UK), 77–99 *passim*
    beef exports banned from (1996),
        27
    Brexit
        CEECs concerns about, 262–3
        as disintegrative impulse in EU,
            40
        erosion of pro-European politi-
            cal parties and, 355
        as EU crisis, 8, 43, 94–5, 361,
            367–8
        European Council presidency
            affected by, 175
        euroscepticism as factor in, 362
        German role resulting from, 229
        migration crisis impact on, 117
        other member states and, 356
        populism as factor in, 366
        referendum on, 82–90
        US perceptions of, 305–6
    "British budget question" of 1980s,
        24
    crisis point in EU membership,
        78–9
    differentiation of territories mak-
        ing up, 92
    on EU sidelines before Brexit, 351
    exceptionalism approach of, 80–2

inward-looking domestic situation
    of, 179–80
joining EEC in 1960s, 20–1
overview, 77–8
populism politics in, 201–2
renegotiation on EU membership
    of, 85–90
United Kingdom Independence Party
    (UKIP), 8, 78, 82, 84–5, 204,
    263
United Nations Convention against
    Torture and Other Cruel,
    Inhuman or Degrading Treat-
    ment or Punishment (1984),
    105
United Nations Convention Relat-
    ing to the Status of Refugees
    (1951), 105
United Nations High Commissioner
    for Refugees (UNHCR), 103,
    111, 113, 121, 233
United States
    China perceived by, 308
    financial crisis impact on eurozone,
        6
    perceptions of EU from, 302–7
    Ukraine crisis and, 221
US Department of State, 307
US Federal Reserve, 257

V
Van Rompuy Task Force on EU
    economic governance, 57
Varoufakis, Yanis, 141, 258
Verhofstadt, Guy, 193
vertical disintegration, 336
Visegrad Four (Czech Republic,
    Hungary, Poland, and Slova-
    kia), 260
Volkspartij voor Vrijheid en
    Democratie (VVD) party
    (Netherlands), 143

W
weaponizing migration, 107
Weber, Axel, 67
Weidmann, Jens, 218
welfare nationalism, 42

Werner Plan of 1970, 23, 132
White Paper on UK membership in
EU (2016), 77
World Bank, 240, 302
World Trade Organization, 302
Worldwide Governance Index (WGI),
240–1

X
Xi Jinping, 308

Y
Yanukovych, Viktor, 220, 261, 270,
274, 300
Yatsenyuk, Arseniy, 281
Yom Kippur War, in Israel, 1973, 23
Youth Guarantee, 163
Yugoslavia, break-up of, 26

Z
Zeman, Miloš, 260